WITHDRAWN

FOREVER CHINA

FOREVER CHINA

by ROBERT PAYNE

DODD, MEAD and COMPANY, NEW YORK

PUBLISHED SEPTEMBER 1945
SECOND PRINTING OCTOBER 1945
THIRD PRINTING DECEMBER 1945

★   ★   ★   ★

PRINTED IN THE UNITED STATES OF AMERICA
AMERICAN BOOK—STRATFORD PRESS, INC., NEW YORK

To ALAN

TO ALAN

PREFACE

THIS is an account of one man's experiences in China during the years when she was cut off from the world. Like all diaries it is incomplete—it is too personal to offer more than a cross-section of the kind of experiences that might have been encountered, and men with different experiences might have recorded a different story. It is inevitably one-sided. I lived with professors and students and farmers, and after the first few weeks saw little of the soldiers. At the battle of Changsha I saw the Chinese soldier in his glory, and long months in the Universities taught me to respect the professors and students. If this book does nothing else, it will have served its purpose if it turns men's minds to the achievements of the Chinese Universities, whose obscure sufferings during seven years are so far unrecorded. One day a Chinese novelist will write a novel about their epic journeys across the width of China, and like those other books which are being written in Europe and the South Seas now, it will show man's pride and greatness reaching to the stars. Today the Chinese Universities, which once occupied the palaces of princes, are living in poverty. They were too proud to ask help from abroad. At the mercy of a continually changing battle-front, without security of tenure, with bombardment and hunger facing them at every turn, they continue quietly and unobtrusively to fulfil their allotted tasks. From the small mud-houses of the Universities, from the damp unheated cubicles where the professors and students shiver like Diogenes in his tub, while the paper windows flap in the wind, a revolution is sweeping over China. Unlike other revolutions, it has its source in the spirit, in rigorous scholarship and in an understanding of the passions let loose by the War. China, the first to be invaded, may yet be the first to achieve a just peace. From the earliest times this country of continual wars has produced prophets of peace. Today the prophets of peace are gathering their strength for the final battle which will prove whether their philosophers are justified by their fruits.

When I came to China, the islands of the Indies were already being invaded by the Japanese; Burma and the Philippines were at the mercy of the Japanese; Hongkong was being bitterly contested, but there was no doubt of the end. I arrived in Kunming on the day after the "Flying Tigers" had landed. This journal ends on Easter Day, 1944. In these two and a half years I have seen more miracles accomplished than at any other time of my life. China changed beyong recognition. With the fall of the Far Eastern Empires, the Chinese did not panic: they had other things to do, and went on quietly doing their job. It was the first time for fourteen hundred years that they had been cut off from the outside world. Later historians will relate that this was a blessing in disguise, for having no assistance from outside, they were forced to find refuge in themselves, and having found it, to make out of expediency a weapon of steel. They had little arms; the best food-bearing lands were in the occupation of the enemy; prices were mounting at the rate of a thousand per cent a year. Yet the scholars, the farmers and the soldiers carried on, proving that "faith can move mountains and lakes across ten thousand *li*".

China was once a country in mythology: it is now an arsenal. At the Naval Base in Singapore I watched virgin earth assume the colours of an industrial city. There is enough virgin earth to make China in the next fifty years one of the greatest industrial powers on earth. And there is an essential purity in the minds of the young Chinese which will make her formidable only to the enemies of good will. The old China has gone for ever, and the *taipans* and the legation officials who came to China before the war had better not return, for they will be hopelessly lost in this new, vigorous world of young China. There are evils in China—officials and merchants whom the Government would willingly grind to dust—but the heart of China lies in her youth, and her youth is clean-limbed and handsome, determined to do away with the past. Those who are concerned with the future of the peace of the world would do well to read the Chinese philosophers and take a glance at her vigorous youth. One day, at the castle of Fontainebleau, Napoleon turned to a globe of the earth and pointing to the yellow square of China, which stretches like a golden fleece nailed to the furthest extremities of Asia, remarked: "China is a vast slumbering lion which will astound the world when it awakes." The lion is awake now. In all the vigour of his untrammelled youth, he goes in pursuit of his inheritance.

In this diary I have been concerned with the small details which make up the whole. There is nothing of politics here, or so little that it may pass unobserved. I have used initials rather than names only because a page filled with Chinese names is confusing to the reader. The story of Bergery is true; but here again the names and a few dates including the date of his death have been changed. This is a rough sketch of a landscape, and how it seemed in the lonely years when only a few aeroplanes and camels brought evidence of the existence of an outside world. But here and there you will hear the authoritative voices of the Chinese.

ROBERT PAYNE.

FOREVER CHINA

1941

December 16th . . . It was dark when we crossed the airfield at Lashio, but suddenly the searchlights went on, and we saw a ring of machine-guns trained on us, moving and following us as we moved across the silver field. In the darkness of the journey from the railway station to the airfield we had seen nothing except clumps of trees and houses, but in the sudden brilliant light of the searchlights we saw one another more clearly than we ever shall again, shining with a kind of metallic sheen which poured out of our dark overcoats. Blinded, we walked in the direction of the D.C.3, and Bergery kept on whispering: "In Germany, when you are about to be shot, they have the kindness to blind you with searchlights." But the machine-guns were as silent as the dark aeroplane on the edge of the field, and here and there were guards with fixed bayonets.

We are high above Burma, but one half of my mind is still on the landing-ground at Lashio. I remember we crossed the field very slowly. The searchlights went off, there was a faint spluttering as of a fire being damped down with water, and then there was only the blue light of the aeroplane to guide us across the frozen ground. The moment of glory, when we saw each other as figures of heraldry, was extinguished so quickly that it seemed to have been a dream. Meanwhile the propellers were slowly revolving, shining with thin silver rings of light, and a comforting blue light from the cabin shone in the faint snow.

All over Europe, Africa, America and Asia men are walking across dark fields to waiting aeroplanes. The rustle of grass, the frost melting on trees, the whistle of unseen leaves and the sudden apparitions of silver moonlight—coming from the sky or from

3

the earth or from a secret river—are taking possession of men's minds, and perhaps there is a new reverence for the silence of the night . . .

As we climbed into the aeroplane, Bergery said something to this effect, but I was too drowsy and cold to understand what he was saying. He stood there, on the folded steps, his great cape billowing in the wind, looking out over the darkness of Asia with eyes which were dusted with snow. The blue light shone on one half of his face, and the silver light from the propellers shone on the other; and he smiled grimly, like a man stepping up to the scaffold. "A journey into the interminable darkness," he murmured and was silent, for some birds flying low had disturbed the machine-gunners, who thought they were enemy planes. In the shadow of the aeroplane the snow melted from our coats, but inside the cabin we could still hear the wind blowing. I am writing in the dark. They have turned out the lights. A few moments ago, while I was writing this, the engine began purring and two immensely powerful searchlights from the wings illuminated the propellers still more brilliantly, so that they resembled two immense stars revolving close to our eyes. A few moments later the searchlights were switched off again, the aeroplane left the earth, the bumpy field died away and we were moving suddenly into something smoother and softer than silk. It is a dark night, murderously cold, with a howling wind shaking the wings, and now that the propellers no longer shine like immense stars, the faint white towers of the clouds rush purposefully towards us and we seem to be imprisoned in their grasp. We flew low over the fields three times, catching glimpses of the customs shed and the trees bending in the wind, but the clouds are low and it is difficult to see clearly—a few stars, a ghostly mist, the earth rushing below and a few dark trees. We are travelling on a dark ribbon of air, high above the uplands of northern Burma, and it is strange to think that only a few hours ago we were flying over the Irrawaddy delta, looking down at golden rice-fields and the spires of gilt temples. The blinding light of the searchlight at Lashio has cut us off from the past.

I can hear the soft purring of the motors, and very faintly the whistle of the wind. The night is so thick that even the few stars disappearing in the haze of mist comfort us. Outside the blue windows snow is falling silently, and there is no comfort in the

4

ice-cold world beneath. Snow everywhere, and on the wings are faint layers of ice.

Bergery has just turned the little bell-shaped ventilator, and the wind begins to ruffle his grey hairs. He looks old and worn in this light, which softens all outlines but changes the colour of flesh until it resembles those curiously veined bluish rocks which are found in deserts.

"What is so extraordinary is that we haven't seen Lashio," he said. "It might have been anywhere—some European houses, taxis, a station courtyard, dark trees, a few faint lights burning behind shuttered doors. It's exactly like all the cities in Europe. From Berlin to Lashio—everywhere black-out!" A little while later he said: "In the future the historians will say that we were afraid of the light, and they will be wrong. What we are afraid of is the blinding light of an explosion, and the still more blinding light of truth." He was silent then, gazing out of the blue window. It was very warm in the aeroplane—too warm. He smiled, settled himself comfortably in the arm-chair with *The Statesman* and went to sleep.

He is asleep now, but even in sleep he looks weary—the weariness which comes to all war correspondents in time, for travelling is the most rigorous occupation in the world and leaves its stigmata, as the years leave rings on trees. I met him first in Munich, in the summer of 1938. Nine months later we were together in Austria, taking part in some absurd scheme to kill Hitler. I met him again in Spain. I had not expected to meet him on the windswept aerodrome in Lashio on his way to Kunming. He is sleeping lightly, his ears keened to the vibrations of the aeroplane, and I remember his saying in Austria that he had seen too much of war ever to sleep perfectly again. "When I am sleeping, I think I can always see what is happening all round me, and I am sure I can hear everything. I sleep deeply—with one eye open. It is not a question of nerves. It is a question of being eternally vigilant." Sometimes he smiles in his sleep, and sometimes he seems to be about to cry; and it is always curious to watch him as he sleeps, his head bent a little to one side—that immense head with the iron-grey hair—his silk scarf fluttering in the wind from the bell-shaped ventilator. Bergery was one of the greatest of the American war correspondents during the Great War. Retired, he lived in a small flat in Florence or in a grey stone building in Pekin, entirely absorbed by the world but completely remote

5

from it, until the Greater War caught him up in its folds, and once more he began to fly across continents in aeroplanes at night.

I am quite sure I have not slept. The starlight has come out, thick waves of clouds appear from the direction of China and the small moon, curving and diving among the clouds, is so beautiful that I cannot take my eyes from the window. Gradually the moon grows brighter, and a thick white light falls on his sleeping head.

"Where are we?" he awoke suddenly. "Oh yes, I remember. We are on our way to Kunming. Perhaps Kunming has already fallen, perhaps at this very moment the Japanese are entering the North Gate. The trouble about being a war correspondent is the remorseless uncertainty. We can never know if we can get there in time. The situation is terrible. The Japanese can come in at any time they please. I remember Kunming in 1917, when poppies were growing in all the fields, and the mountains were purple and red with poppy-flowers. The local warlord had just sent a punitive expedition against Szechuan and returned with so many dancing girls that he had no idea what to do with them. He offered some of them to me. I remember how beautiful the place was—the lakes and the sunlight and the mountains and the blue heavens. There is no more beautiful place in the world." He began to talk about the eagle which alighted on a milestone at Maymyo just as the train was leaving the station. "The eagle—it was red and blue, with great streaks of violet on the breast. And a bronze beak. And quite timeless. It did not fall out of the sky, it came through the sky, through the spaces in the sky. And there was blood on the bronze beak." It was as though now he were suffering from a passion of the past. Stage by stage he went over the journey from Rangoon. He had come down from Calcutta in a small tramp steamer, which churned up all the mud of the Indian Ocean. Calcutta, where he had stayed a week, was dark, vicious, and somehow disappointing. "The black-out—that was terrible! Not because it was dark, or because of the heat, or because of the presence of the thieves at night, but because for the first time I experienced a black-out in tropical weather. In the heat darkness is worse. It must have been terrible in Singapore." I nodded, though it was no more terrible in Singapore than in Barcelona. "In the beginning the earth was dark and without form and void . . ."

He is not sleeping, but whenever he talks he seems to be talking from a great distance away. There is a story that during a rail-

6

crash in Germany he walked among the survivors all night, in the rain, with a smoking lantern, while jets of boiling steam made the scene resemble a phantasmagoria of Hell, and simply by his presence he made people conscious of their human dignity. They did not scream when he had passed by. And perhaps they were terrified, for that enormous head and those square shoulders comfort people with their strength, and sometimes they terrify for the same reason. He gazes out of the window like someone obsessed with the immense depths below. It is difficult to believe that people are dying and giving birth in the darkness and immensity of this night. The wind is coming up, the aeroplane is shivering and gliding in gusts of snow, a wing dips and the ice is brushed away with invisible finger-tips. We are flying high. A small lake shines in the moonlight, and since half the lake is in shadow it resembles a reflection of the young moon in the old moon's arms. Yet the moon is nearly at the full. We can see the faint courses of rivers below, the shadows of clouds. The aeroplane, buffeted by the wind, drops a hundred feet, regains height, slews sideways, and still the engine purrs gently and solemnly. We do not hear the wind, for we are enclosed in a hollow tube, but we feel it lapping the ailerons and the wings, as a fisherman sitting in the bottom of a boat will hear the waves on the strakes.

I must have fallen asleep. It is broad daylight. Green fields, red hills, small thatched houses with yellow roofs and long purple shadows—and the blue sky, this above all. The blue of a thrush's egg, but deeper, an immensity of sky, falling or sweeping to the earth like a blue coat or curtain, and like a curtain rippling as it falls. I do not think that this is an inaccurate description. Imagine an immense blue silk tent and the wind rippling the surface, its coolness and the faint ripples on the surface. It glitters with silver while in Malaya the sky glitters with bronze. Perhaps the colour of the sky is due to the reflected colour of the earth—a deep red, with here and there a few patches of green rice. We are already flying over Kunming. The walls of the city throw long purple shadows, and over the airfield there are small white objects glittering in the sun. Are they pebbles?

Bergery says quietly: "There is smoke over the city. She is burning." He looks pale, his face pressed against the window-glass.

A moment later: "There are nearly a hundred aeroplanes on the airfield. Where have they come from?"

7

In the dazzling blue sunlight aeroplanes lie on the aerodrome to the north-east of the city. The city is blood-red and biscuit-yellow, the walls very high. And beside the city, stretching towards the bronze hills in the distance, lies an almost circular lake the colour of emeralds dipped in milk. They have asked us to pull the curtains over the windows. Why? No one knows. Or perhaps the pebbles are really aeroplanes?

There are hundreds of aeroplanes on the field, painted dead white, the fuselages inscribed with the teeth of tigers. As we step out of the aeroplane someone says: "Haven't you heard? We were bombed yesterday. Four hundred were killed. There are no shelters. You have to run into the country, outside the walls. Twenty-seven aeroplanes—always twenty-seven in three groups of nine —came over in the morning. The 'Flying Tigers' came in the afternoon." He pointed to the aeroplanes lined up on the tarmac, the young Chinese mechanics in blue overalls, the armourers with their immense serpentine belts of silver-and-bronze machine-gun bullets. He said slowly: "Waal, I guess the tiger is growing wings."

The air is so pure that we can see the faintest incisions in the distant mountains. We are a mile above sea-level. My heart is thumping. There is a lane of poplars leading from the airfield to the city. In the mist-laden morning, the roads and the poplars and the small wooden carts driving down the shadowy road remind me of France. We have spent a few minutes in the *estaminet*, where there is a girl who is obviously French, though her features are Chinese and she wears a pair of dark blue slacks. Drinking hot coffee out of enamel mugs, we envy the American airmen in their heavy furs. They call themselves "Flying Tigers", as though they were acrobats taking part in an aerial tournament. Stamping the blood back into our legs and breathing the cold frosted air, we dare hardly go out into the frozen field. And when at last we return to the waiting aeroplane, we watch the milk-white mist rising about the long rows of planes. The mist is like silk; you can touch it and it flows in your hands. Suddenly, out of this mist, a silvery-white aeroplane begins gliding over the field. I have taken up a handful of Chinese earth. It is red like blood, the same colour as the earth in Catalonia, Cornwall and Malaya.

We are flying again. The blue lake mysteriously turns red. Small fishing vessels glide over the lake, their orange sails turning an even deeper red than the lake. Sunlight is coming over the
8

hills, and behind us Kunming sparkles like orange juice. Everything red—bare foothills, faint tracks curving over the summits, small houses, gardens, peasants working in the misty fields; and then for some reason the earth's redness disappears and everything is blue. It is like looking through a stereoscope—the patterns in the bright liquid colours of China. Blue everywhere—the blue lake, the blue city, the long stretches of blue fields the colour of the sea. We have been seeing the earth through the shadow of the aeroplane's wing, which cuts out the sun, but even now, with the sun ahead of us, the colours are so clear they appear to have been painted. On the horizon a great white cloud like a sea of milk is slowly moving towards us.

We are still in the cloud. According to Bergery we shall be in the cloud until we reach Chungking. It is pure white, and here and there faint rainbows springing from the wing-tip and following us relentlessly colour the cliffs of the cloud. For though the cloud is shapeless, there are occasional immense cliffs, vertical darknesses, and we look down through the cliffs at the misty green world beneath. In this whiteness we travel the road to Chungking.

When I was a child, I was always dreaming of China, but I never dreamt of anything so beautiful as Kunming. And yet the moment I saw it, I knew I had been perfectly familiar with it since the earliest days. The high biscuit-coloured walls were the fortresses I played with; the temples and the lakes accompanied my dreams. Somewhere, perhaps in *Grimm's Fairy Tales*, I read of an old man who kept a princess of China in a bottle at the bottom of a deep well, and I would think of her late at night when my mother brought the night-lamp into my room. She was small and perfectly formed, with waxen features and oiled black hair, dressed in a gown of some delicate silk material, and there were glass slippers on her feet and roses in her hair. Later I discovered that there were no longer any princesses in China, and the highest aim of the Chinese poet or scholar was to marry the daughter of a Prime Minister, and particularly his youngest daughter. Then, surrounded by courtiers in silk, with jade bracelets on their wrists and jade necklaces hanging over their shoulders, writing delicately with an ivory brush while one of the courtiers laid a chrysanthemum on the table in order that his handwriting should imitate the softness and strength of the petals,

9

he would write a few lines of greeting to the bride he had never seen.

I have been thinking of this legendary China as we ride through the white cloud, wondering whether it still exists and whether I shall ever again see it in my lifetime. In the ancient dynasties of China there existed an ordered beauty of gesture and benevolence which has disappeared from the rest of the world, and may have disappeared still more completely in China herself. I remember an old man in Singapore, who would talk at length of the last days of the Ch'ing Dynasty, for he had taken part in the political manœuvres of the time, financing Sun Yat-sen's revolutions, devoting himself to the care of the dispossessed and the exiled. A few days ago I saw him for the last time, and as we walked along the muddy beach at Tanglin, he asked me what I thought I would do in China. I told him I wanted to see everything there was to be seen, because I wanted to exorcise the demons and fairies who tormented and delighted my youth.

"But China has changed—changed—changed——" He repeated the words perhaps twenty times. "There is no longer grace in my country. The reverence and love for things has gone from the earth. It has disappeared even from China. This war has made us all soldiers."

"Do you regret the change?"

He said nothing, though there was pain in his eyes. He asked me about the future of Singapore.

"I am quite sure it will hold out," I replied. "The best roads are in the south. We have the communications, and we have learnt a lot from the loss of Penang. In a week or so we shall drive them out again."

"It is like the wars in China," he smiled, and nodded his head in agreement. "A village is captured, the people flee to the mountains, a week later it is recaptured and then the village is forgotten. Perhaps it is mentioned in a military communiqué, but more likely it is wholly forgotten—it is always so!"

We walked back to the small white house on Amber road. The fishing-smacks were still riding among the islands, and they shone for a moment like those jewels of the sea, for which an early Chinese Emperor sacrificed his kingdom, since so much wealth was expended on these expeditions. In the Mongol dynasty Malaya paid tribute to the Emperor in Pekin, and the Chinese who work in the rubber fields of Malaya are only returning to a country

10

over which they once possessed sovereignty. Singapore was so peaceful that it was easy to understand the Chinese philosopher who said he could recapture the atmosphere of the T'ang dynasty more easily in Malaya than in Pekin, for it was easier to contemplate under a living palm-tree than in the decaying dust of the Chinese capital.

"I refused to return to Pekin when Feng Yu-hsiang deprived the last Emperor of his rights. He abdicated. The revolutionaries promised him dignity and freedom. This is a promise we have failed to keep." A little later he said: "A new China is being born here. Have you noticed the influence of the overseas Chinese? It is growing every year, every month, every hour. It was the overseas Chinese who made the revolution of 1911 possible. You cannot understand the new China in China, for there is still corruption which we thought had ended with the Ch'ing dynasty. China must be tested against all the other nations of the earth, not against her rapacious officials. And so you will see the new China in Singapore and Java and the Philippines, and you will see it better here than anywhere else."

A few days before I left Singapore, I went to see Dr. George Yeh of the Chinese Ministry of Information. He lived in the immense white building called the Cathay, for it was built by an enormously wealthy Chinese merchant. At the beginning of the war it was taken over by the Singapore Government, and down one of the long white corridors, where you feel as lost as I feel in this white cloud, I found him in a small bare room—a table, two chairs, a few books and little else. He was once head of the Foreign Languages Department of Tsinghua University, which has moved from Pekin to Kunming. He has been editor of a newspaper in Shanghai and the trusted adviser of many high officials within the Kuomintang party.

"There is a new China," he said. "You will not find it in the pages of Lin Yutang or in the ancient classics. The new China is vigorous and strong. She has turned her back on the past and is making an effort to grasp the future. We do not call the war a war against the Japanese only. It is also a war of reconstruction —an implacable war fought against the earth and ourselves, against the shoddiness of our ancient customs, and their inadequacy. *China is tough!* If you understand this, you will understand China better. Think of our coolies, stripped to the waist,

11

hacking roads out of mountains. Do not think of our philosophers."

He complained that even in China too few people realised the vigour of the peasants. There were many intellectuals in the capital who were disposed to see the old order continued indefinitely.

"Go near the front line," he repeated. "You will find that the air is cleaner and purer than in many other places. We have a slogan: 'Those who are poor give strength; those who are wealthy give money.' The poor have given their strength, but not all the wealthy have given their money."

I do not know which I believe, and perhaps both Dr. Yeh and the old philosopher are right. On the night before I went by seaplane from Singapore to Rangoon, I telephoned to a friend who has spent many years in Chungking. He refused to talk about the Chinese in China—national characteristics are the invention of the sinister and the half-baked. "It's damp and cold and miserable," he said. "There is no sun half the year, and when the sun comes, it boils you until you are the colour of a beetroot. Yes, the river is beautiful, and the mountains. Take a torch, because in winter there are three million muddy steps and it is better to be sure where you are putting your feet." He went on to speak of the lights shining on the Yangtse, the river boats and the terrific energy of the people in the government offices, but he seemed glad to be remaining in Malaya. "You'll wish you were back again within a week." And looking at this white cloud, with its purple precipices and the faint flicker of blue lightning on the wings, I am already wondering whether it is possible to go back.

A few hours ago, in a cold blizzard, the aeroplane dropped out of the clouds flying low over the river, flashing past the white rocks on which Chungking is built. For the last two hours we were travelling by beam. The cloud thickened and seemed to turn black, and occasionally there were blue tongues of flame on the wings, and sometimes the cloud was so thick that it was impossible to see the wing-tips. Sitting there, drowsy with the heat of the aeroplane, looking at our pale blue faces reflected in the blue window-glass, at the swift-flowing river and the white cliffs and towers of Chungking, we felt like strangers about to enter an undiscovered country as visionary as any we had ever seen in our childhood dreams.

The aeroplane flew low over Chungking, and we caught a

12

glimpse of white house-tops, burnt-out buildings, small black paddle steamers riding the broad river and far away in the west a yellow sandspit in midstream. We flew low over the sandspit and then roared up into the windy sky. A few minutes later we turned back, wings dipping, the silk on the wings rippling in the wind and rain, slowly circling over Chungking and gaining height. It was then that I noticed for the first time the immense height of the rocky cliffs upon which Chungking is built, for when we descended and skimmed over the river, Chungking towered above us, gleaming-white in the faint sun. The grey towers of a cathedral, the blackened ruins near the water's edge, wattle and bamboo huts perched on cliffs, steps carved out of rock and leading down to the grey smoky water. We were gliding lower and lower, until the wheels were touching the wave-caps and a white spume was flung over the wings and over the windows. When the spume had been washed clean from the windows, we were following the chalk-line on the sandspit to the end. Near some bamboo huts, the aeroplane came to a halt and we were surprised by the engines' silence, for it seemed as though the aeroplane would go on for ever, as elemental a thing as a bird, fuelless, perfectly proportioned to the air.

In the air everything was white and peaceful, but on the sandspit a storm was raging. White spray was flung on the sand, and the small ships on the river looked as though they would be dashed to pieces on the rocks. It began to rain in torrents. We shivered. We wished we were back in Malaya, where the rain is warm and does not wound with sharp points of frost. At the far end of the sandspit we found a small boat to take us over the river. The river was in spate, black and oily, the rain streaking whiteness on the black troughs of waves. The rain lashed everything within sight. Cowering in the small boat, the luggage piled in the bow, with the blinding rain cutting us like knives, we looked at Chungking through a mist of rain and grey descending clouds and saw only a grey smoky rock and a few lights burning. Bergery sat hunched up on the sternsheets. It was midday, the river a mile wide and we were rowing against the current for fear of being swept downstream. It grew darker. In the sternsheets Bergery was repeating in bewilderment: "Is this Chungking?"

December 21st . . . WE HAVE been wandering in the city all morning. At seven o'clock we left the south bank, wandering

13

down a muddy road carved out of rock and filled with horse droppings, slippery with ice and in places almost vertical. There was a white mist over the river, but the mist cleared when we were half-way across and suddenly Chungking rose in splendour on the north bank, resembling once again a white ship, superb in her mourning bands of dead streets and blackened chimneys. At the top of the Wang Lung Men steps the enormous broken stumps of blackened chimneys pointing heavenward have a kind of prophetic menace, and we hurried past them in the direction of the centre of the city, escaping by the skin of our teeth the green motor-buses crowded with five times as many passengers as they were meant to hold and throwing up black poisonous clouds of wood-oil smoke.

In the winter rain the city is desolate beyond words. At Mora de Ebro and Tarragona, the bombardments did not altogether destroy the character of the Spanish earth; at Barcelona the bombardments of the docks made them more beautiful than they were before; but here a whole city has been wiped clean off the slate, and the small stucco façades which have been built up at intervals during the past two years have no character. Nothing of the old Chungking is left, and she is glorious only when the mist lifts from the river, or at night perhaps——

Sunk in his great overcoat, Bergery walked down the long road which runs along the river bank complaining bitterly of the ugliness:

"Nearly all Chinese cities are beautiful, and only this one is ugly, but you must remember that nearly all Chinese cities are built for the night and for the full blaze of sunlight. There are towns where no one should go except in a winter darkness, and other towns where no one should go except at noonday. The Chinese countryside, of course, loves the mist, but the towns love only the extremes of darkness and light."

It was not light and it was not dark. There was no sun. The buildings were the colour of old water, and the nightmare was made worse by the presence of Chinese characters written over the doorways in every imaginable form of degraded calligraphy. Again and again Bergery returned to the subject of these Chinese letters painted over the doorways or modelled in plaster.

"If you want to understand the greatness of a nation, look first at its lettering. Do you remember the tombstones of the Dutch conquerors in Malacca? And the Trajan column? There has never
14

been a great period in a nation's history when there was not great lettering. The characters of the Chinese language are the most beautiful in the world; but modern industrialisation has allowed the inefficient and the insane the privilege of writing the letters in the streets of Chungking."

He was as angry as I have ever seen him, raging at the miserable letters as though he expected them to burst into powder under his vituperation. It became comic. He would look up at the gold characters written over a bank, shaking his fist. "Look at it! The fat swollen body of 'chung'—no character, a fat pig of a character. No Chinese will learn anything by looking at pigs. Pigs have no structure—no lines! If you make a character look like a horse or a fly or a tiger, that's something, there's grace in it. But the man who painted that character knows nothing except pigs."

"It looks all right to me."

"It looks all right to you! You're myopic, you're insensitive, you're beyond hope. Some of the greatest art in the world comes from Chinese characters—and look what they do to it. Calligraphy is the key to China. You can read a man's character from his Chinese handwriting, and you can read the progress of a civilisation in China by the handwriting of the people. I thought the war would produce a calligraphy as firm and moulded as the calligraphy of the Han dynasty. Look at that sign for 'chia'. It's a flea dipped in ink. And that sign for 'ying'. It's like a sickly girl, dying of an incurable disease. This is impossible. I beg you not to lift your head—the pavements at least have no characters written on them."

He had taken an immediate dislike to Chungking, but shortly afterwards it became clear that he was like a lover who finds more faults in the beloved as his ardour increases. It was damp and misty, the grey sky almost within arm's reach. Motor-buses groaned past, and inside the motor-buses men, women and children were crowded together in black confusion. The postmen in green, the policemen in black, the soldiers in every conceivable shade of blue and brown were lost in the immense crowds—colourless like water. Colour was so rare that even the bleached white sackcloth of the mourners fell pleasantly on our eyes, but a single mourner with white head-band, white apron and white belt would have passed unnoticed, so colourless is the air and so dark are the skies. There are no red cheeks in these crowds. Many are diseased, and in one street which we passed through we saw a dead child lying in the mud of the roadside, the body of a man covered over with a tarpaulin and seven people suffering from deformities—a woman without a nose, a child with only one arm, a man who hobbled on crutches, waving in front of him a naked and paralysed foot. But suddenly in this same street, at the moment when we thought we had entered a nightmare from which there was no return, we saw a bride in red silks coming from her home. Crackers were lit, and a flaming torch was waved backwards and forwards in front of her path and before her eyes. Her face was painted dead-white, but her lips were pomegranate-red and her eyebrows were thickly arched. She was pretending to struggle, but she was smiling, and when at last she was locked in her red and gilded bridal chair, the long carrying-poles wound in green silk and green ribbons descending from the crown of the chair, it was as though our eyes were flooded with colour. Her appearance in these grey streets produced an effect like that of a rippling stream that springs over sand, over pebble, through sunlight and shadow.

And so we wandered down the colourless damp lanes overlooking the river, remembering the sudden glory of red and green. We were hungry for colour. The smallest spark of red, even a cigarette glowing in the distance, quickens our heart-beats. Occasionally there passes us a young student, in his blue Sun Yat-sen uniform, and on his cheeks there are the two red circles of a consumptive. A green motor-car slid past. We paused for five minutes before a shop-window filled with crumpled silver and gold paper, a Christmas tree and three or four coloured dolls. By midday it was raining, but the rain did not absorb the mist, for the mist remained. In this darkness and in this misery we wandered back to the swollen river.

Bergery disappeared in the afternoon. He came back in the evening covering with mud, saying that in the whole of Chungking he had found only one thing beautiful—a courtyard and a bridge on the south bank, and a dead plum-tree standing against a high wall.

"You must come," he insisted.

It was nearly dark. The rain was still falling, and Chungking on the north bank is almost invisible in the mist, though the lights are shining down the Wang Lung Men steps. We scampered along muddy roads in the half-darkness, listening to the

16

scurry of rats and the bark of the night-dogs. The narrow streets on the south bank are covered with granite stones, but sometimes the stones are missing and you plunge into a morass of treacle. Here, in the darkness, yellow light coming from the paper windows of houses and a faint white illumination coming from the sky, you are conscious of a darkness greater than any imaginable blindness. Shapes of the night come from the dark walls. In the silence your footsteps are echoed by footsteps in a parallel road, and it is impossible to tell whether they are your own footsteps or another's. We climbed up a slag-heap. It was black; and neither of us knew whether the slag-heap was solid. Crouched against the walls black beggars threw out pale white hands.

Bergery was more excited than at any moment since we left Kunming. He walked with quick steps, continually talking about China.

"You understand . . . China at night . . . This is something that is alive, terribly alive. Can you hear it?"

We stood still. From far away, or from the earth, we heard a dull roar like the roar of the blood in your ears when you have been running hard. I have heard the same kind of sound once in Spain when, walking over a deserted field at night, I heard through the earth the engines of an underground armament factory.

"What can you hear?"

"Nothing—a kind of dull roar."

"You'll hear it nowhere else—it is particularly Chinese, and no one has been able to explain it."

We were crossing a small bridge. At the bottom of an immense ditch there was a faint trickle of silvery water passing under the bridge. Bergery turned round, and there it was—the plum-tree, the wall, the small bridge all white in the pale moonlight.

"Is this what you want me to see?"

"Yes, for God's sake look at it! Look at the proportions! Look at the height of the wall and the shape of the dead plum-tree and the curving arches of the bridge, and ask yourself whether they are not made for one another. A Chinese must have spent hours working out these proportions. Don't tell me it is an accident. The bridge was built first, then the wall, then the plum-tree was planted. There can be no doubt about it. Look how splendidly the plum-tree reflects the curve of the bridge and how the height of the wall——"

17

He stood there very silently, and it must have seemed to him that all the squalor of Chungking had disappeared. The black branches were gnarled and rimed with silver, and this silver was reflected upwards from the bottom of the foul-smelling ditch; and we heard the tinkle of water over rough stones. He stood there for perhaps five minutes, completely absorbed in the beauty of proportions and these reflections of silver in which he must have seen, as by a miracle of accomplishment performed by a Chinese scholar who once inhabited a garden in Chungking, the answers to innumerable questions long since forgotten by the Chinese who inhabit these desolate lanes.

"There was perhaps a garden," he said, as we made our way over slag-heaps to the house where we were living. "I imagine a merchant from Szechuan who retired from business early. He devoted himself to art. He built this wall and this tree—and this is Chinese civilisation."

When we returned the moon had disappeared completely from behind the clouds. It was the dusk of night, when a faint illumination shines from the sky, but it is impossible to tell where it comes from. Muffled in our coats we sat on the verandah, gazing at the lights of Chungking twinkling on the opposite bank. Some sampans, black against black water, passed in the direction of Ichang. It was very silent. Suddenly, on the opposite bank, a forked tongue of red flame leapt into the still sky, as though an immense match had been struck on the rough surface of the city. The flames were deep red, the colour of blood. They grew violently and changed into other things—the faces of golden cats, falling pillars, ceremonies of revolving cherubs. There were so many flames, each leaping from a different source, that we instinctively stepped back. The glow of the flames shone on the black waters.

We watched the flames for a long time. We heard the fire-engine, and we saw, like faint silver ropes of rain, the jets of water scurrying sky-high above the flames. But the flames continued. Chungking is built on rock, but the houses are paper, matchwood and plaster. There was something terrible and revengeful in the sudden reddening of the rock on the other side of the river. The flames continued all night. We heard the crash of dynamite, a long silky yellow flame poured out of the house on the west side of the house which was burning, and slowly—very slowly—like the drooping wave of a waterfall, this house perished.

18

Occasionally we heard screams, and once we saw a river-boat two hundred feet below the houses attempting to spray the cliff-edge of the rock with its white jets. There was nothing that could be done. We went back to bed, but all night the red flames flickered on the bedroom wall.

December 23rd . . . AT NIGHT columns of soldiers are marching through the streets. They are Kwangsi troops, wearing heavy greatcoats which reach to the feet, grey packs on their backs, straw sandals on their feet. They look healthy, and in the glow of the street-lamps their faces are deep red like apples. I have seen them because I have been wandering at night with Bergery. At night Chungking is beautiful; by day it is depressing beyond words. We have seen nothing to compare with the dead plum-tree against the grey wall; but there are moments, walking down the great canyons of streets near the river's edge, when the height of the buildings and the sudden apparition of a curving roof in the moonlight, in the vague whiteness which shines overhead, seems to presage a sudden awakening into beauty; but though we wait, nothing beautiful arrives. But last night, hearing the distant tramp of feet at three o'clock in the morning, the city awakened into life.

I do not know why it is, but the sight of soldiers moving through dusk or darkness, even when they are moving silently, fills me with sudden excitement. The gleam of bayonets, the officer riding at the end of the procession with his sword swinging over the pony's rump, the fixed gaze of the soldiers and the *relentlessness* of their marching steps fill me with amazed delight.

As we were crossing the river this morning, a Chinese officer came up to us and saluted smartly. He wore the usual yellow uniform and leather belt; on his collar were the three-barred gold triangles which denote a colonel. He looked very young, and later when we learnt that he was twenty-three and had taken part in the battle for Chapei ten years ago, it was astounding to think that a man so young could be so experienced. We talked of many things, and as the paddle-boat reached the opposite side, he asked us to lunch the next day. He gave us an address near the British Consulate. At least once in every half-hour Bergery returns to the subject of the boy:

"The youth of these people! In the old days, if you had a beard, you were on the way to become Prime Minister. None of the

19

great soldiers were young. Think of Tseng Kuo-fan and Yuan Shih-kai who were brought back into the army to win their greatest victories after their retirements." We passed some soldiers near Liang Lou K'o. They carried paper umbrellas, and many of them were walking barefoot, their feet bleeding. "They are so young— they are only children!" he exclaimed, like someone thunderstruck. "The most extraordinary thing is that they are all peasants —perhaps fourteen years old. In Szechuan, of course, a boy who looks fourteen may be eighteen—the people are small. But surely these boys——" Then he would look again, looking for the signs which reveal their character; and finding none, for it was dusk and the rain was coming out of low cotton-wool clouds, he stamped his feet in impatience. "How do they expect to fight the Japanese with boys?"

The rain came down, soaking them, but they laughed cheerily. We watched them as they marched down the road until they disappeared in the mist.

Later . . . THE Chungking Club on the south bank reminds me of one of those extraordinary aquariums you could see in Berlin before the war. The most extraordinary fish appear in it; you rub your eyes at the spectacle of a pink monster, wearing horn-rimmed spectacles, little white fins and a spotted breast with horns protruding where one had imagined a throat, and you say: "It is extraordinary that this is a fish! How did God make these things?"

There is a Swedish doctor who has flown from Stockholm. In the ballroom he spits out blood all night, and he is extremely sick. He is small and partly paralysed and talks in a thick German voice, and every now and then he will glance over his shoulder as though he expected to surprise the listening spies. But there are no spies. There is a Dutchman who growls irritably whenever a Chinese passes through the room: "You understand, sir, this is a European Club. What the devil have the Chinese to do here?" And yet he is a perfectly sympathetic person, speaks several Chinese dialects admirably and has a passion for everything Chinese. Once a week he goes out in search of a prostitute, and when he returns he is still more irritable, his face turns dark red when he is seen climbing the club staircase, and he whispers malevolently: "The country is going to the dogs. Two hundred dollars. Outrageous!"

Sitting among the black leather arm-chairs, uncomfortably manœuvring among the broken springs, you can watch the foreign population off their guard. There are the fanatical bridge-players, two young Jews whispering in a corner, the wife of an insurance agent, three or four customs officials, the soldiers and the sailors. There are the young who have fallen in love with China. There are the old who are disillusioned and continually complaining. There are the malevolent and the stupid, missionaries who have taken to business, armament vendors, dope smugglers, the failures and the bitterly afraid. It is more surprising when you come upon a man who is white-haired and holds himself stiffly as he drinks his last glass of the extremely potent drink which is known as "Chungking Gin". He has been in China for forty years. He has known everyone and seen everything. As he goes upstairs he says: "Young man, this is the best country in the world if you understand the Chinese, but God help you if you misunderstand them." He was saying this to Bergery, who is almost his own age; and he smiled, flicked an imaginary speck of dust from his sleeve and passed out of sight. Bergery explained that he was one of Sir Robert Hart's men, one of the few men from the remote past who have kept their heads in the present.

The derelicts were afraid; during the day they are lost among the Chinese; at night they drink down their sorrows in the bar. There is no mercy for them—and endless repetition of dull cloudy days, a few games of billiards, smoke-room stories, the drudgery of crossing the river every morning, the drudgery of waiting for the steamer, the drudgery of climbing the Wang Lung Men steps. They are accustomed to the luxury of the treaty ports, and finding none in Chungking they are apt to explode in sudden fits of violent temper or bouts of morose silence. Many of them came to China because they could find no other place where they could go —remittance-men, men who had failed completely and who believed that in China they could find the satisfactions which were denied to them abroad. There are others who have come with a sense of dedication. The insurance agent, who loves birds; the missionary who has made a study of the primitive languages in the southwest; the naval captain who reads in a corner all day long; the young American who sits nervously in a corner, fumbling with his tie and reading one of the ancient Chinese classics. They are dedicate, because China represents for them something which is eternal and at the same time comprehensible. In this

21

aquarium they are queer fish swimming silently beside the still queerer fish who play bridge and talk loudly about the decadence of the world.

There is something sinister in these old European houses built on the south bank. The ghosts of the dead are everywhere. In the billiard room there are lists of breaks going back to 1909, the names painted in gold paint on a brown board. Few of the old billiard-players are alive. The old merchants who came here when Chungking was opened as a treaty port have not entirely disappeared. Their names appear on walls, and sometimes in remote valleys behind the hills their widows remain in possession of ancient houses. There is so much sadness in the place that Bergery has decided to live elsewhere, even in one of the new stucco buildings which are being erected in the north of Chungking. "It will be safer there," he said. "The dead are not so present."

December 24th . . . CHRISTMAS EVE dinner with the young colonel. He lives in a small white brick house high up on the cliffs. You reach it through many archways, climbing innumerable stone steps. There is no sign of the sun, but the clouds are whiter than yesterday and the misery of the unbroken cloud is relieved by the presence of a faint glow in the sky.

The rooms are terribly bare. The leaves have fallen from the high trees outside, and only the spears of yellow bamboos remain. There is the soldier, his mother and his wife, who will soon have a child. In all the three rooms the only splash of colour comes from the heavily embroidered quilt on the large double-bed. Through the house three black kittens wander like dissolute eighteenth-century emperors.

"It is an honour, it is an honour," the young colonel keeps on saying. Although he spoke English perfectly yesterday, the presence of his wife and his mother has made him tongue-tied.

Bergery is almost angry. We notice that a fortune has been spent on food. There is a whole chicken, a great cask of rice, seven or eight courses. We mumble apologies over our lack of finesse in eating with chopsticks. He is ashamed of his mother's hobbled feet and her lack of English, and when we laugh at frail jokes, we are conscious that his mother is laughing out of politeness. The colonel works at military headquarters.

"In Shanghai I was captured by the Japanese. I escaped. I decided I would make it my mission in life to kill Japanese. I have
22

not killed very many yet, and so I am dissatisfied. I have been ordered to teach in the Staff College." He shrugs his shoulders. He is trying to convey that he can teach nothing, he is too ignorant. He asks Bergery endless questions about the war in Europe and in the Far East. He begins to talk about the Generalissimo who preaches to the staff college every Monday morning. He speaks of the Generalissimo in hushed voices—many voices. He is not one person, but three or four people. He is the young soldier who escaped miraculously from the dark lanes of Chapei; he is the young husband; he is the soldier who stands for three or four hours every morning while the Generalissimo makes a speech; he is the old man, ten thousand years old, who has seen invasion after invasion of conquerors in China.

He admired the Generalissimo above all men, living or dead, yet he could say that the speeches were too long, they were all the same, there were times when he was a little bored with them. When the Generalissimo makes a speech, he writes down the headings on a sheet of paper—perhaps three or four words; but the speech is endless. The same words are heard every morning. Loyalty, Death, the Japanese, the Spirit of the New Life Movement. The soldier said that the Generalissimo was probably quite conscious of the length of his speeches; he was repeating deliberately and endlessly in the hope that a few simple ideas would be understood by the officers and those who served under him. His voice dropped in reverence and regret. "But recently he has been getting old. He looks tired after his long speeches. Physically he is as active as ever, and mentally perhaps he is more understanding and compassionate, less like a priest. But we fear for him. The loneliness, and the terrible responsibilities. And what will happen when the Generalissimo dies?"

I have already heard this question many times in China. The king-pin is inviolate. Even Chou En-lai, the Communist member of the Supreme Military Defence Council, believes that he is completely necessary for the future of China. "And what will happen when the Generalissimo dies?" The words are spoken not in haste, but in anguish. What will happen? In England, Russia and America men know that the death of the elected leader will cause barely a ripple on the surface of the country. In China it is different. There is heart-ache in the question; for though not all the men around the Generalissimo are universally beloved, and he

23

himself is reverenced rather than loved, there is no one else to take his place.

We spoke of many things in the bare rooms, where the wind came through the open windows. Here darkness came early, and we watched the small Tibetan ponies on the rocks beneath. They are a little larger than Kansu ponies, and they have a curious resemblance to the ponies shown on Han dynasty reliefs. They are sure-footed, sturdy, with heavy manes and long tails. As they fly across the rocks, the bells ring and they seem to be shaking their heads from side to side to produce a continuous ringing-sound. In the morning I had said to Bergery: "I would like to see a boy riding one of these horses at night and carrying in his hand a bamboo flare." These bamboo flares are offered to passengers from the ferry on dark nights, when it is impossible to see the steps carved out of the rock. They shine with a blood-red smoky light, which turns the rocks into crimson pools and the faces of passengers into ripe apples. And now, looking down from the house perched on the cliffs, we saw a small white pony ridden by a boy carrying a red smoking light.

It was late. We had an appointment with a famous philosopher on the other side of the river. The soldier pressed something into our hands. We did not know what it was, and we did not look until we had reached the ferry, for the rocks were dark and the boy with the twisted bamboo flare had already disappeared. At the ferry we looked in our hands. Neatly folded lay a sheet of silk the size of a handkerchief. On the silk there was embroidered in large red letters the character for "good-luck".

Climbing the steps. Climbing the steps. Climbing the steps. There are ten million steps in Chungking. There are steps from the ferry, there are steps in the main roads, there are steps in houses. One imagines there are invisible steps leading up through the clouds into the sunlight.

But tonight we did not cross the river by ferry. The ferry is out of action, and we crossed by sampan. The river was high, and we measured the current by the sampans which passed by so quickly that they seemed to be instantaneous photographs—appearing suddenly and disappearing still more suddenly.

The river was angry, and the passengers crouching in the bottom of the sampan were muttering prayers. I don't think anyone trusted the boatman. When we were alone in the middle of the

24

river, looking up at the high black rocks, it was such a loneliness that one might almost go mad. The swirling current, the river's darkness, the depth of the river and the masts of three or four sampans standing above the water in midstream did not inspire confidence, and Bergery whispered pleasantly: "No one has ever come out of the Yangtse alive." Three boats were wrecked in the morning. More would be wrecked tomorrow, and many more in the days that followed. We lay in the bottom of the boat, wondering whether we were already sinking, lost in the dark river among the groans of the passengers, the curses of the boatmen and the silvery gleams on the river like knives. The tide was so swift that we passed the landing-stage, a rickety affair of wooden planks laid out over the shallow water; but in the darkness we did not know that the water was shallow, and we were impatient to land. It was already eight o'clock. The philosopher had been waiting for us since seven. Climbing up the lanes of steps, we began to wonder whether the philosopher had already gone to bed.

In the centre of the city, not far from the British Embassy, the Street of the Seven Stars curves northward and at the same time climbs steeply. Between the high stucco frontals of the shops occasional small alleyways lead towards the river. We went down one of these small dark alleyways, noisome with the smell of dead rats and refuse, and came to an unexpectedly well-lit courtyard where a few clumps of bamboos and small pines rustled in the evening wind. One side of the square courtyard was open to the Chialing river, which joins the Yangtse at Chungking; and looking down at the lights twinkling in the distance and the black serpentine flow of the river beneath we felt dizzy and at the same time surprised by the immense height we had climbed. The philosopher lived in a small room, hardly larger than a cupboard, and occupied almost entirely by an enormous bed.

He wore a blue gown embroidered with flower-patterns of a darker blue. His long forked beard was grey, nearly white. On his wrists he carried ivory bracelets.

"You have come a long way," he said. "I should have sent a car for you, but unfortunately it was too late."

We wondered whether he possessed a car, for cars are rarities outside official circles.

We began to talk about India and Singapore. The Chinese are beginning to believe the rumours which have been spreading fast during the past few days. The Japanese have command of the air.

Singapore was defended from the coast, but there were no defences in the land. The Burmese are preparing to co-operate with the Japanese. The Chinese had offered to send expeditionary forces overseas, but these were refused. A note of bitterness crept into his voice until we turned the subject of conversation to China.

"You mustn't judge us by our failures, you must judge us by our victories. In economics our victories are greater than foreigners believe. The industries of China have been removed from the coast to the south-western provinces, and if you think of our appalling lack of transport, then you will say that it is a miracle. We are like one of those old Chinese houses. The rafters are falling in, the walls are breaking open, and we have decided to live in the courtyard. The Chinese race is nomadic. We can live in the courtyard for many years, but the time will come when we want to return to the house. And then——" He paused for a while, handed us handleless bowls of sweet flowered tea and then plucked three notes in quick succession on his Chinese lute, a beautiful instrument which once belonged to the Imperial Court. "I do not believe in revolution," he concluded, and it was some time before we realised that the last statement was indissolubly connected with the ominous phrase "and then——"

Down below, the bowl of the night was indistinguishable from the bowl of the earth. Scattered lights glittered, and the earth and the sky seemed to be uniformly starred from top to bottom. Only the faint glimmering line of the Chialing river, cutting its way through the mountains, broke the scattering of these heavenly stars.

Bergery began to speak as though the revolution were already upon us. The philosopher smiled.

"It is said in the *Book of Changes*: 'The symbol of the earth and that of brightness entering into the midst of it give the idea of "wounded brightness". There will be advantage in crossing the great stream.' I do not know how you translate these old hexagrams into European languages. They were invented, they say, by the Duke of Ch'u. It may be true. But the symbol of 'wounded brightness' is very much in my mind. The Revolution has not yet succeeded. Sun Yat-sen made his fatal journey to the north in the hope of discovering a method through which the popular will can be determined, and still we have not discovered the method. Perhaps it is because the country is so large, perhaps it is because
26

we are not yet politically mature—though we are four thousand years old!—perhaps it is because we have lost contact with the heavenly principle. We are still young. What is four thousand years in the history of the world?"

He spoke of the decay of manners since his childhood. "The pure reverence and love for things have gone from the world. We are all materialists. There was a time when filial respect meant something deeper than you can imagine. It meant that the father was burdened with immense and terrible responsibilities. Now no one loves responsibility."

He possessed in this small bedroom in the hotel all those things that characterised the old philosophers. There was a fly-whisk, an incense burner, paintings and scrolls on the wall, a small bamboo bookcase containing paper-backed Chinese books neatly arranged in rows. With the fly-whisk he would occasionally flick entirely imaginary flies from Bergery's coat.

"Do not think that I am against the Government. I welcome almost everything they have done, and praise their courage. The New Life Movement has shocked me to the core, but——" he waved his hands in a gesture which sent the jade bracelets revolving wildly on his thin wrists. "It will pass, like all the other curious importations we have brought from abroad. But the other things——" his face became grave. "The lack of reverence and understanding for the past, the breaking of the city walls, the lack of respect paid to scholars, the knowledge even of our past already forgotten, the Americanisation and Britishisation of all our old and most respected customs—this is what is terrible, and it is still more terrible when you remember that it has been brought about by the wars. I who am speaking to you have one foot in the grave. It is necessary that I should protest. If I could alter the course of Chinese history by hanging myself on a tree— in the old days one could commit suicide and thereby rebuke the Emperor—I would do so. But whom shall I rebuke? Certainly not the Generalissimo. Certainly not the Chinese people. I rebuke history, and history pays no attention to suicides."

As he spoke we grew accustomed to the small room and began to look at the beautiful carvings and oriental scrolls on the wall. The room was full of priceless objects, moon stones, jade ink-stands, stone rubbings. There were paintings of valleys in the mist, not unlike the valleys of the Chialing river. On these paintings blue and green mountains were placed, not according to the

27

conventions of perspective, one behind the other, but as though each were suspended in airy vapour, independent of one another and yet somehow touching one another by their proximity. The black jaw of the window was wide-open. Occasionally the scrolls would move in the wind, and the sound of the wooden roller which hangs at the bottom of the scroll, as it continually taps the wall, had a nightmarish quality, reminding us that the words spoken by the old man in the flowered blue gown were words spoken from the grave of his cherished illusions.

"I believe that China has no future if she surrenders her soul to the West."

"The birthplace of the Revolution was Honolulu, but we must not be expected to believe that the culture of Honolulu has anything to offer us."

"It is time the West learnt from us the arts of calligraphy. The writing of Westerners is shocking beyond words."

"The image of China in the future is something I cannot discern; but that we must go back to our old virtues, and revive the nobility of scholars—of this I am convinced."

He said many other things, some bitter and trenchant, some lukewarm, as though he were already tired of the problems which a rejuvenated China imposed upon him. He wrote scrolls for us. He presented us with small jade rings, and refused to let us go. Bergery delighted him with his knowledge of international politics, and his sudden suavity of manner. In Bergery's understanding glance the old philosopher saw evidence of a pupil.

"Would you say that if China retains her reverence for things, she will still be able to compete with the West? Can you have reverence for battleships?"

The old philosopher thought for a while. "Yes, certainly," he said at last; "but what is more difficult to understand is whether we can have reverence for bureaucracy. Perhaps bureaucracy is as old as China, but my heart bleeds when I go into some of our government offices and see the young boys and girls doing nothing—nothing whatsoever. They look up at the clock with their arms folded over their desks. No task has been given to them. They are there because their fathers or mothers were related to the manager of the office. I would have all the youths in the banks and government offices in the war. If they were learning something, I could forgive them, but they are learning nothing at all."

28

He was bitterly disturbed by the fate of the young generation. The students in the Universities, the soldiers and even the social workers possessed no traditions. They were too young to have learnt anything from the traditional authority of the dynasties. The New Life Movement, though admirable in many ways, failed as a substitute for the ancient traditions. They were purposeless. They lived in a world where there were no accepted customs and everything was being invented for the first time. And yet there was no freshness, they had not leapt into a new culture, they were hag-ridden by the old and incapable of seeing the new.

"I have been asked by the Generalissimo to write on the new culture. What can I do? Am I to invent a culture out of my head? We must wait patiently for the light, and I fear it will be a long time coming."

Just before we left Bergery reminded him that the same problem was being faced in the West and no solution was in sight. The generation which returned from the last war was helpless in the face of historical necessity. In this small room overlooking the river, the wind knocking the scrolls against the wall, he recited the lines of *The Waste Land* which moved him above all others:

> *"What is the sound high in the air*
> *Murmur of maternal lamentation*
> *Who are those hooded hordes swarming*
> *Over endless plains, stumbling in cracked earth*
> *Ringed by the flat horizon only*
> *What is the city over the mountains*
> *Cracks and reforms and bursts in the violet air*
> *Falling towers*
> *Jerusalem, Athens, Alexandria,*
> *Vienna, London . . ."*

As we left, the Chinese philosopher said: "The plains do not go on for ever, sometimes we find the city over the mountains. After this war you must come and help us to find these ancient cities."

We were sorry to leave the old philosopher, with his books, his small collection of scrolls, his delightful view over the river. In the dark night the tremendous city was humming still, though it was nearly midnight. A few green motor-buses were still climbing the Street of the Seven Stars, throwing up immense black

29

pillars of wood-oil vapour. The red banners over the streets were blowing gustily and the silvered paper characters sewn on the banners still announced the coming of Christmas. Bergery repeated under his breath: "Falling towers—Paris, Singapore, Rangoon—Moscow, London . . ."

December 25th . . . I HAVE been up with Bergery in the hills. We had two small white ponies with bushy tails and stragling manes. There were no blinkers and only an apology of a saddle. From the south bank we climbed over the wet rocks towards Huang-k'o-ya, where a slender white pagoda commemorates an ancient Empress of China who was born on the hills. The road winds through narrow villages, under the shadow of the old German Embassy, until it comes out in a pine forest. The road is granite stone winding and weaving up the mountain slope, and so well graded that the ponies can trot up the steps without growing tired. Under the coldish white of the pale sky, under the dark bulk of the grey mountains, the ponies scattered the sedan-chairs and the peasants who came down from the heights. They rolled their necks from side to side, so that the sound of the bells could be heard in the farthest valleys, down in the green slopes and canyons full of broken and stripped pines, up among the yellow villas on the mountain-tops, far away across the river. Already we could see the river above the green foothills. The river was like a silver spoon, the thin handle facing Chungking and the broad estuary glinting silver amid sandbanks in the west. We rode single-file, Bergery on his sleek white pony the colour of ivory, I on a grey mare who frisked and ferreted, and disliked her rider from the first.

As we climbed higher, the mist which had been hovering over Chungking all morning turned grey-blue. Ever since childhood I have had a passion for walled cities, and from the narrow stone road leading to Huang-k'o-ya it was possible to see traces of the ancient walls of Chungking on the north bank. A walled city has an unmistakable quality of pride. Impenetrable, throwing down gaunt brown shadows, the Chinese walled city in a plain stands isolated as an island, self-sufficient as a ship, unassailable in its own fortresses. On the spur white rock, shining in the blue misty morning, Chungking resembled more than ever a ship inclining in a storm. The whiteness of the walls and towers under a white cloud, the faint greys and blues of the open roads, the mountains
30

beyond and the wide-flowing river beneath added to the illusion, and there may be some significance in the fact that the ship points towards the east and the Japanese. In the west among shelving sandbanks and wide estuaries, the Yangtse flows into the River of Golden Sands; but in the slanting light of morning, the sun not yet risen high above the mountains, the western river shone silver like floods, and we caught our breaths at the sweep of the encircling river and the purple mountains rising in the distance.

The road narrowed and became rocky. Huang-k'o-ya stretches a quarter of the way down the hill-side, winding in blue shadow among the silvery barks of pine-trees. Already we could hear the "wave" of the pines on the summit and the tramp of soldiers in the muddy streets. The shops were crowding in on every side. We rode in single file, while children ran for shelter and old women remained motionless on the stones, so that we brushed our shoulders against the stucco houses and wondered whether any of the houses we had touched had fallen into the valley below. Here, on the heights, enormous banyan trees and oak-scrub litter the narrow cobbled streets, where the foundation walls of the houses are old tombstones. But the village is dull, and nearly everyone is suffering from a disease of the eyes which swells the eyeball and turns it violet. At a turning in the road we paused and looked at the river away below, the horses struggling up the rock-face, the foothills and the silence of the bare trees. The plum-trees were black. There were no flowers. We rode down the street like men who have hoped in these altitudes to find an answer to all their problems, and find only a more complete disillusionment.

But once past the village, there is an extraordinary light on the hills. Behind these hills are more valleys and more mountains, and the light spreads out, no longer hemmed in as in Chungking. The main road was blocked by a landslide. We took a smaller road, the horses scrambled down slippery red mud hills, splashed across a stream between rice-fields, frightened the coloured ducks in the yellow ponds and the blue magpies, slithered on the edge of fields where neither rice nor winter barley was growing, across grey-green lakes and meres. They plunged onward in silence. They were accustomed to us and no longer shook their heads from side to side, but moved with a slow effortless tinkling of bells. We felt that we had come out of prison. There was an immense area of sky above. High up, away in heaven, larks were

31

singing. The resinous sap of the pines filled our nostrils. "Do you see the bird——" An eagle swept out of the sky, pricked a field rat with its talons and swept into the sky again, bearing the rat gently in its curved and sharpened cornelian claws, flying against the yellow-green mountains and the white chalk road, flying horizontally—away, away into the silence of the morning light. We watched the eagle as though there were some magic in its solitary flight. Like memory it disappeared into a small space of sky, pale turquoise blue, the first pale stretch of blue sky we had seen in Chungking. We prayed that the sun would move swiftly from its place in the clouded east to this small square of pale blue in the west. But the clouds hung above us still, and sometimes we watched wisps of clouds above the rice-fields rising to meet the white sheet above our heads.

We were fairly high at last, having crossed the chalk road which leads to Kweichow. There was little traffic on the road, though here as everywhere innumerable lorries lurk under pine-branches. There is a motor-road leading from these high cliffs to a motor-ferry across the Yangtse, and we have promised that we shall find the best motor-car in Chungking and drive recklessly round thirteen hairpin bends. But there is quietness in the hills and misty mornings dropping dew.

In the evening, when it was quite dark in the streets except for candles—for the lights have gone out—we wandered through the streets. A few red and gold scrolls, with pictures of Father Christmas, hang across the roads, and there are small fir branches in the shop of my favourite pastry-cook. But on the whole Christmas is dark and solemn, and the grey river flowing between the high rocks is still rising.

But just as we were about to descend the interminable steps to the ferry, we noticed an old coolie selling lanterns. They were not like ordinary lanterns. They were made of wood and green paper and small porcelain bowls of rape-seed oil were suspended on wires inside them; and also suspended on wires were curious shapes cut out of cardboard which revolved and threw their shadows on the green paper frame. There were two shapes of cardboard—one representing an army on the march, bearing a flag on which the Chinese character for the Han dynasty had been inscribed, and on the other there was depicted a peaceful scene in a country village—a goose-girl followed by a long line of

32

waddling geese, a marriage cart with ribbons hanging from the posts, an old farmer with his scythe and his buffalo. These two shapes revolved in opposite directions and at different speeds. "This is so Chinese," Bergery exclaimed. "No one else would have thought of the world as two revolving rings of peace and war." We lit the oil lamp, and carried the lantern tenderly down the steps, afraid that the wind might blow out the light or break through the thin paper screen. And at the bottom of the steps there was no paddle-steamer, and we were compelled to search among the broken rocks and the sand for a small boat which would take us across. The current was strong. We waited for over half an hour, shielding the lantern with our bodies. And when at last we were rowed across the river, the shapes on the lantern continued to revolve and young children and old men craned forward and peered at it, their faces illuminated by the pale green light. Even the river shone with the faint reflected green light; and though we were often lost in midstream, and though nothing of the shore was visible except the distant glow of candles, we watched the revolving shapes with extraordinary exhilaration, and the Chinese shouted out: *"Hao jee-la,"* delighted at the continual progress of the shapes.

I shall remember this Christmas for the faint green light of spring which shone on the waters, and the faces of the children as they craned forward, for they, too, were like the faces of idols painted green to announce the coming of spring.

December 27th . . . "We have come to the end of one civilisation and we are beginning another. Perhaps today, or perhaps yesterday, a whole civilisation was destroyed. But civilisations do not entirely disappear—they revive, as the dead mummy-seeds in Egyptian tombs revive, and new splendours may come out of what has been destroyed."

He looked ill and dazed as he looked down on the river. Hong-kong had fallen; he had a cold and a feverish temperature, but he insisted on gazing at the river. The lights shone, and in the distance we could hear the throbbing of invisible dynamos, dogs barking and the song of a sing-song girl who lived in a house high up on the hills.

"I now have little hope for Malaya or the Philippines," he said a little later. "It is not that we have committed faults, or that you have committed faults; but we did not understand the people we

33

ruled. We must learn to understand." And a little later he said: "In the *Analects* it is related that Confucius stood by a stream and wept because everything passes away."

"Yes, this civilisation will perish, as perhaps it deserves to perish. We have had sympathy for the races we have ruled, we have learnt their languages, we have sent ethnologists and anthropologists to partake in their rituals; but we have failed to love them, and therefore they did not trust us. But if we learn to love——"

He did not go on. Small black boats, like beetles, were creeping into moonlight. A faint red glare shone from a distant furnace; and as we stood there, on a piece of rock jutting out over the Yangtse, it seemed that we were standing on the bridge of an immense ocean liner, which at any moment would escape from its moorings. Bergery looked exactly like the captain of a ship, and we could almost hear the creaking of the wheel as it turned to and fro, and we could see the blue mast-lamp and the helmsman nodding over the charts. "Well, we're sailing now—there's nothing to stop us. But the charts won't be any use, and the reefs are dangerous, and we have more valuable cargo on board than we have ever had before." A mist came floating up the river. There was nothing to be seen; for even when the eyes had grown accustomed to the darkness, we saw only the candles, the dark, starless sky and a darker river, and two pale wakes where the prow of some river-boat or other pried the water apart and sped it backwards.

And then, after a long silence: "I hope *they* realise that it is a dangerous moment in the most complete sense. Europe is threatened by the attack on the East as she has never been threatened before. We preserved the spirit of Europe against the Huns, the Mohammedans, the Turks and the Goths. We preserved it against the Northmen, and absorbed them, and in absorbing them we lost nothing except some of our graces. But this time we are faced with greater problems than ever simply because the Japanese are a more authentic foe than the Germans. The Germans can be fought and the issue of the battle can be decided without destroying the spirit of Europe, for the Germans are inevitably Europeans and cannot stay for long outside the fold. The Japanese can stay *for ever* outside the fold. They are not built like us, they do not think like us, they possess nothing in common with us; and therefore we must destroy them or they must destroy us. Not a

34

single value in their civilisation is cherished by us, and not a single value of European civilisation is cherished by them. We cannot agree; and yet we must learn to love them."

I asked him what he meant by love.

"Surely the love we have for beautiful people and for beautiful objects is the same as the love we have for beautiful civilisations. In the *Symposium* Socrates describes the nature of love. 'He is not delicate and lovely as most of us believe, but he is a hardy youth, barefoot and homeless, sleeping on the naked earth, in doorways or in the very streets beneath the stars of heaven, and always partaking of his mother's poverty.' So we must love nations as though we were beggars, holding out our alms-bowls and hoping that out of the charity of their hearts they will sometimes offer us food and nourishment; sleeping naked on their earth and looking at their stars throughout the night; in tempest and storm; and fearing their animals and taking part in their sacrifices. We have not learned to love. The Americans and the British in China have lived in houses apart. They have not learned the language. They have not been equals. They have always ordered. Like the Japanese, we filled the estuary of the Yangtse with our warships, and like the wild tribes on the frontiers we plundered their goods. And this is our reward—that at a time when we are allies, they no longer trust us."

It was very late. Down below, great waves shot up from the rocks viciously, exhausting their energies in furious hissing sprays. But now there were almost no boats creeping beetle-like along the faint silvery river; and though a faint moon shone, and the slender black plum-tree waved in the breeze, Chungking seemed to be a desert, black and remote, where a few candles like fireflies shone beneath a cold black wintry sky.

"It is not too late," Bergery kept saying. "But nations must know that it is not enough to send ambassadors—we must send the best spirits of our age. How many of the best spirits of England and America have come to China? We have sent tradesmen, not philosophers. We have sent pirates, not legislators. We have sent the dregs of our public schools, and we have never sent our sons to be educated in Chinese Universities, though they have sent the best brains of China to Oxford and Harvard. We have only a few years left in which we can repair this wrong, and perhaps already it is too late." It may be true. Sitting here by the light of candles, I remember everything he said, and more than

35

anything else I remember the desperate notes of his voice when he said: "What on earth is the good of a Grand Alliance if it is only a piece of paper? We must save it even if necessary at the expense of the politicians."

December 29th . . . WE HAVE been invited to lunch with the British Ambassador. In the grey morning we set out on a small black launch, waving the Union Jack—the only dash of colour in this remote whiteness of fog. We hear bells and cries, but the sounds come from a long way away. The *remoteness* of morning in China—nearly all night Bergery has been attempting to conjure up his memories of mornings in China. "It is then that she is magnificent beyond every country on earth. The hot sun rising across the lake at Hangchow, the sudden illumination of a pagoda, which resembles a figure of white frost rather than something solid which you can see with your eyes, and then the sunlight slowly descending the whole length of the pagoda, and the green reeds, and the long level lines of pine-trees planted by Su T'ung-po nearly a thousand years ago. Remoteness, as of something ancient and permanent, and yet impermanent, for every moment it changes . . ." But in this damp fog, the oily water of fog trickling through our upturned coats, I saw no beauty and understood nothing of what he said. Besides, it was nearly twelve o'clock and the morning had turned stale and colourless, the wind had died down and still the thick vapour hung over the streets and the river.

Once, as the car which fetched us from the river travelled along the long winding muddy road to the Ambassador's house perched on a cliff-edge, we saw the river below. There was a magic circle where no fog entered. And there, in that small circle, like a blue eye radiantly blue, we saw small ships like grasshoppers moving silently down-river. There was a ghostliness about the scene which shocked us, for we had not expected it and there were moments as we gazed down at the blue eye of the river that we seemed to be gazing at a mirage. And slowly the eyelid of mist folded over the blue eye, and still more slowly the car wound up the muddy road, where even the stucco buildings exuded moisture and the trees resembled green fountains continually dripping.

But once inside the Ambassador's house we were in another world. In a small room, which was once the pavilion of a Chinese general, a great log fire was blazing. There were photographs, enormous bookcases, a collie dog, comfortable arm-chairs—a sense of security and good taste, of quiet contemplation and infinite common sense. In Singapore George Yeh told me: "Please be careful of him. He comes into your room, rolls up his shirtsleeves, takes out his pipe and says quietly, 'Let's get down to the root of the matter', and before you know where you are you agree upon everything, there are no clouds in the sky and you wonder what all the fuss was about." It was, I felt, a good description. The pipes on the mantelpiece, the collie dog sprawled out before the fire, the table in the ante-room set for dinner in Chinese style, with small blue bowls and ivory chopsticks, the books and the candles and the mahogany radio were carefully chosen and belonged to a man "who rolled up his sleeves and got down to the root of the matter".

Sir Archibald Clark Kerr came in five minutes later. He had been walking along the cliffs, and he brought with him the tang of winter on the Scottish moors. He wore a check coat and grey flannel trousers; the long aquiline nose, the sunburn and the bushy eyebrows were those of a Scottish laird, and his enormous hands were like the hands of an artist. But what was so extraordinary was that from a man so tall there should come a voice so quiet and gentle, and even hesitant, and when he went into another room to order the dinner, Bergery whispered: "It is not the voice of a Scottish laird, or even of an artist, but of a musician." We waited. A clock was ticking sonorously on the mantelpiece—an English clock, even to the little whirring sound before the chimes. And once more he returned, and the room was flooded with the scent of heather and pines, and in our imagination we were travelling through some distant landscape of Scotland, where the mist was the same as the mist of Chungking and even the sampans and the people in the crowded streets were the same.

"And later on," the Ambassador was saying, "it becomes even more like Scotland. In spring the mountains on the south bank remind me of the mountains of Scotland, very grey and green, and the air has the same quality of mist and light as in Scotland."

He said he was happy there; he liked the Chinese and spoke of their tolerance and magnificent staying power. The Chinese love informality with a kind of passion, and it was clear that he shared their passion and would have been even more informal if circumstances had allowed. He read omnivorously. Joyce's *Finne-*

37

gans Wake stood proudly on his shelves in its blazing orange
cover, and before long the Ambassador and Bergery were deep in
an argument about Joyce. Bergery opened the book and began
to read in his deep, heavy voice the passage about Anna Livia
Plurabelle, until it seemed that not only the mountains of Scotland but the rivers of Ireland were also wandering through
Chungking, till at last, wearying of argument, the Ambassador
began to read a passage towards the end of the book on night and
death, a passage so heavily laden with the shadows of elms and
yews that it resembled the birth of the night and of all nights;
and reading it in that quiet voice, peering through horn-rimmed
spectacles, his face coloured by the yellow flames of the log-fire,
he had surrendered so much to the charm of Joyce's prose that he
forgot the sound of the dinner-bell and the new guest who had
just been announced, he forgot his secretary's quiet reminder of
the passing of time, and absent-mindedly taking a perfectly white
feather-pen from the table, he began to wave it up and down in
tune with the majestic sonority of the prose. The sunlight was
beginning to creep into the room, a faint yellow sunrise which
would disperse in a moment or two. The collie dog uncurled at
his feet and walked solemnly across the room; and when at last
he had finished the passage and placed the book silently on the
shelves, he smiled with a smile of such beauty that Bergery was
immediately conquered. And like someone in a dream I watched
them going into the dining-room with their arms on each other's
shoulders.

The sunlight flooded the green windows in the dining-room; it
flooded the blue porcelain bowls and spilled over the dead white
table-cloth. White-robed servants entered silently with great
bronze tureens. The conversation changed from the state of the
defences of Singapore to *Alice in Wonderland,* from the second
battle of Changsha to Chinese novels. The Ambassador had cultivated Chinese novelists. He invited them to his house and discussed the technique of novel-writing with them. He was proud
that a recent novel had been dedicated to him, and prouder still
of his connections with the Sackville-Wests and Virginia Woolf.
He had a deep love for Chinese paintings and porcelain, and
spoke regretfully of the difficulty of transporting them from Pekin.
A black dispatch-box came in. In white letters there was printed
the inscription: "The British Embassy, Pekin," but there was no
British Embassy left in the old capital of China, and he gazed at
38

the letters tenderly, opened the box with his key, glanced for a moment at the papers inside and then resumed his conversation with Bergery on the merits of Japanese painting. On the glass door separating the dining-room from the circular drawing-room the firelight flourished and gleamed, and sometimes the collie dog would nestle at his feet and he would throw a bone in the air and watch the dog with an extraordinary affection.

All through the still, quiet afternoon the conversation continued. There was no one present except his secretary, a Chinese professor, Bergery and myself. The Chinese professor taught English in a University near Chungking. He was quiet and handsome, and I found it difficult to take my eyes away from his long thin fingers. Where did the fingers end and the chopsticks begin? He talked so softly, without any inflection of accent, in a voice that was neither American nor English, but of such perfect control that it seemed to achieve the excellences of both. He discussed the problems which faced the modern novelist in China—the rise in the cost of living, the censorship, the lack of traditions and the extraordinary virility of the new writers who wrote without quite understanding what they were writing, for they resembled lost sheep in a desert. The collapse of the Ch'ing dynasty had ended a tradition, and nothing had come to replace it. So they wrote only of what they saw and could not relate what they had seen to anything more permanent. The Ambassador suggested that the present war and the revolutions of the last twenty years would provide a tradition in time. The young professor thought otherwise. He thought that there could be no traditions in the present, for there was no tranquillity and too much suffering. They were still arguing gently when we left at four o'clock.

All the way down to the river Bergery continued to talk about the Ambassador. He had watched the Ambassador like a cat watching a mouse, or like an opponent waiting to find a chink in his armour. He had the usual American distaste for British diplomacy and he had spoken at great length of the impression left upon him by Sir Nevile Henderson's book—an impression of distaste and at the same time complete incomprehension that a man so placed should wilfully throw off his disguises and reveal himself so incompetent—but he was completely won over by the Ambassador, comparing him with ambassadors he had known in other quarters of the world.

39

December 31st, The End of the Year . . . I DO not know
how many years are left to me, or whether I shall stay for long
in China, or whether I shall ever see the sun again. At the beginning of the year I was helping to design a new form of depth-
charge, and a little later I was making some mysterious flights by
aeroplane over Malaya. A chance conversation with George Yeh
in a hotel in Singapore brought me to China, and still I have no
idea what I shall do or what is expected of me.

I remember what happened perfectly. I had taken an English
lieutenant to the Japanese Gardens in Singapore, and we wandered there among the lotus lakes, the pines and the cedars, talking of the Japanese in Thailand, and the Australian soldiers he
would lead into combat if ever the Japanese crossed the frontier.
It was a heavy, cloudy day with thunder in the air. Some Malays
passed, walking in single file silently among the green paths; and
we agreed that we had never seen anything more beautiful than
a Malay girl who walked at the end of the small procession in her
flowered silk sarong and with a small baby tied to her back. She
walked like a goddess with a curiously firm tread, swinging her
hips a little but remaining completely upright. "She walks, and
at the same time she seems to be perfectly still." And then a little
later, as we passed the attap huts, he said: "I shall remember
when I get to the north." He was leaving the next day for an
army encampment in the north and if the Japanese came over the
frontier his would be the first battalion to be attacked. He had
little hope that the Thais would fight, and he was filled with a
kind of purposeless resentment against those who allowed the
Thais to enter Malayan territory by the Bangkok railway at the
same time as they continued their negotiations with the Japanese.
He spoke of spies and sudden explosions in ammunition dumps.
He was weary of the Malayan heat and yet he loved the Malayan
people with a curious candour. I left him in my car, for he was
sleepy and I had a headache. It was sunset. I walked down to the
shore with my Chinese friend and we began to talk of Chungking, not as something that one might one day go to see but as
something which even here it might be possible to understand.
When we returned the English lieutenant had gone, a storm was
coming up and I decided to return to the Naval Base. It was one
of those electric evenings when the sky thunders with distant
cloudbursts, and faint streaks of silver lightning colour the sky.
There is a heaviness in the air, like the heaviness which precedes
40

a great explosion, and though no rain fell and the streets were still full of people, and though Singapore resembled with its flame of the forest trees and ancient Georgian architecture the same city which I had known for nearly three years, there was a depressing feeling in the air, as though this cloudburst might be followed by others even more severe. The rain began to fall in heavy warm drops. The Chinese dancing-girls were beginning to flock to the Great World, in tight-fitting silk costumes which gave them the appearance of china statues; and slowly the umbrellas were coming out. The air was blue, as always in the Malayan evenings. I was thinking of the novel I was writing about Malaya, of the extraordinary beauty and charm of these people who come from all the corners of the earth to live in tranquillity on this island on the Equator, and suddenly the young Chinese, who was one of the leaders of the Kuomintang party in Singapore and therefore a friend of all the Chinese in the place, said: "You have only seen George Yeh for three or four minutes. You should go and see him in his hotel." I was very tired. The thunderstorm was coming nearer. Almost without knowing what I was doing, I nodded to my Chinese *syce* and said: "Turn left." If I had said: "Turn right," I would never have come to China.

I went to the hotel. George Yeh was staying there with a tall English historian called Barger, a lecturer at Bristol University and an authority on the ancient cities of central Asia. My Chinese friend disappeared. We discussed the approaching Japanese invasion of Yunnan. If Kunming were cut off, and the Chinese armies were driven back towards Kweichow, no one knew what would happen. The Chinese Press was talking about the approaching invasion of the South Seas by the Imperial Japanese Army. We drew maps on the table-cloth. The salt-cellar was Chungking, the Chinese armies drawn up along the frontiers of Burma were represented by a knife, the Japanese were forks and the British armies in Burma were enormous spoons.

"And what happens?"

"If Burma holds out, we drive down here. We cut through Indo-China, and the British and American fleets prevent them from returning to their bases by making a landing on the south coast of China, and perhaps the war will be over in a week, and perhaps it will not be over."

I knew then with fixed certainty that the opportunity for the Japanese had come. A few days later under a white moonlit sky I saw two British battleships firing their anti-aircraft guns at six Japanese aeroplanes which remained above their line of fire. Singapore was bombed. Late one evening, rushing ammunition to some destroyers, I watched the survivors of the *Prince of Wales* and the *Repulse* come dripping to shore, and heard the Admiral in the War Room saying: "We have taken worse knocks than this. The time will come when we shall beat them." And wondering at the quiet certainty of his voice and the complete silence which reigned over the powerful Naval Base, I came back to the white house on the hills, threw the revolver and the tin hat on the table and made arrangements to go to Chungking. I thought Chungking would be more exciting than Singapore. I no longer think so. And now in these long dark misty evenings, I think I can hear, as though I were present in the forests, the thunder of guns over Malaya.

I have never known any place so peaceful as the islands of the South Seas. The calm green waters, the scent of the casuarina trees, the red flowers of the flame of the forest, the Malays walking through their huddled rice-fields or squatting cross-legged under the green shade of the palms belong to a civilisation so distant from ours that they are almost incomprehensible. The landscape is incomprehensible, the people and even their least movements, their dances and their sacrifices are incomprehensible. We can approach closely towards comprehension, but we are always in fear of some sudden revelation which may reduce our hastily acquired comprehension to nothing. We can love them—certainly, but unlike Bergery I do not believe that love is enough.

As the year ends with dust and ashes, I think of Malaya. I think of the small beehive temple of Buddha at Chandi Mendut near Soerakarta, a Buddha of brown sandstone perfectly preserved in the forests where Sir Stamford Raffles found it more than a hundred years ago. There was so much majesty in the face of the enormous Buddha, so much peace and charity in the great open palms and so much blessedness in the expression, in the weary eyes and the still-smiling lips, that we felt so awed before its perfect beauty, and for the first time since I left the city of Chartres I recognised the authentic crystallisation of a whole culture. Everything was here. All of India and Malaya lay prostrate before the knees of the god, whose bare feet had been kissed by so many pilgrims that they shone like silver. The smell of frangipani flowers and butterlamps on the pedestal reinforced but did

42

not increase the sense of overwhelming beauty conveyed by the naked god sitting on his throne. I have seen the same expression and the same beauty in a Balinese boy walking across the corn-fields in Bali, where the level fields lay like mirrors under the sun. There were days when I knew that all that was best in the East had come to the islands of the South Seas, and there were other days when I knew that I knew nothing, and would never pene-trate through those dusky masks. A young prince dancing in a silver robe under the moonlit trees of Den Pasar, a Malay girl calling to her lover at night on the edge of a forest in Malaya, the workmen in the Naval Base and the small Chinese boys riding on the buffaloes in the padi-fields of Johore—I had seen them, and perhaps loved them to despair, but I wondered then whether I understood them, tortured by the difference between their cus-toms and ours. And now I know that the torture will go on, there is no escape from it and it will be many years before I come closer to the masks I love.

I know now, and must have known it before, that civilisations are mortal. In every forest in every island of the South Seas there are vestiges of great civilisations, our own among them. I know that scattered in various parts of the world, in Kathmandu in Nepal, in Uranda-Urundi in Central Africa, in the island of Bali and perhaps also in some long-forgotten valleys of China there remain ancient civilisations which the West would do well to study with complete humility. We are not perfect, and we are so mortal in spite of steel and concrete that perhaps no other civilisa-tion has reached such a state of mortality, and certainly no other civilisation has devised such lethal weapons. In ten thousand years' time there will be only one civilisation and only one people; and in the years of terrible decision which lie ahead, the nature of this future people and this future civilisation is being forged. We are deciding now the nature of a possible world, and every mistake, every conquest is fraught with dangers. The nature of this world is in our hands, and for the next ten thousand years we must remember that we have only one duty—the duty of mak-ing this future civilisation as authentic and tolerable as our dreams. We know that this future civilisation will conserve many of the characteristics of the three great civilisations which sur-vive; we can calculate within wide margins the characteristics of our inheritors. And in this calculation we are not lost. We can work on mathematical probabilities, we can even describe the

43

features of our inheritors and we may even prophesy something
of their culture. And if, indeed, this is the last of the great wars,
and if we are victorious, and if also we cherish the best spirits of
the civilisations already formed, we need have no fear of the
future.

The immediate future is dark for all men, but the long shadows
we have thrown down point to the sunrise. We, who are the inheritors of a great past and the ancestors of a still greater future,
live in blind darkness, from which perhaps even now we may
emerge. But on one condition: that from now on we cherish all
that is best in the civilisations of India, China and the West.

It is midnight. The mist is rising on the river, and the smoke of
the mist floats over the faint white lights of Chungking. Bergery
is sleeping over his book, the candles are going out and the small
Buddha on the window-sill shines fitfully in the misty light. Let
us drink to this future race and preserve our traditions.

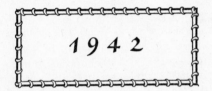

1942

On January 2nd the author was sent as "Times" correspondent to the battle of Changsha, which had broken out on the night of December 23 when the Japanese crossed the Milo river. No heavy engagements took place until the last day of the year, when the Japanese attempted to rush the gates of the city. A short critical battle took place, lasting three days, but on the fourth day the Japanese, harassed by guerrillas and the main forces of Lieutenant-General Hsueh Yueh's forces, retreated in the direction of Yochow.

January 4th . . . THE river has been covered with a faint mist ever since we left Hsiangtan early this morning, before daybreak. There was a wet cold in the air, and we shivered on the sweeping edge of land, so cold that our fingers were like icicles, and the dawn coming over the mountains was even colder than the night. The curlews cry on the great granite steps which lead down to the river. In the small town, everything was dark, and the beggars sleeping in doorways paid no attention as we passed. And then suddenly, just as we stepped on to the small launch, the bamboos began to quiver, the blue jays or magpies burst out cawing and all the trees began to shake. It had rained during the night, and the trees on the foreshore seemed to be ornamented with small pieces of jade, which touched one another and separated with the passing of the wind, leaving in the air the sound of distant bells and the sudden sparkle of water. And the river lay before us, dark green, the colour of malachite, and the greyish-red hills took light from the ascending sun, till at last our fingers thawed and we climbed down into the small dark cabin, with the broken windows shuttered over with pine boards, and made ourselves comfortable round the small table, where an empty flowerpot and a samovar surprisingly accompanied us down the Hsiang river.

The thumping of the petrol engine prevented us from sleeping; and gradually as we watched the low green hills giving place to copper-red mountains, we took heart and escaped from the over-heated cabin into the cold wind of the deck. We swept between the white columns of an immense bridge which has never been completed, and watched with a sensation of awe the great white-sailed sampans sweeping down-river. They are bigger than the sampans in the Yangtse—bigger and cleaner; and they glide softly like sea-birds, silent and leaving no wake, and with no sign of life except the small coke fires burning redly on the foredeck. A few fishermen, with black cormorants, were fishing near the high banks. It is the height of the banks which astounds us—the river flows deep below the surface of the land, and on this green pool with white wave-caps, nosing our way against a blustering north wind, our faces like ice, our hands frozen to our sides, we make our way to Changsha under a cloudless sky the colour of the brightest steel.

The sampans came down-river like immense swans, gliding gently and noiselessly, the wind creeping along the sails but never altering their shape. The ships were painted all colours, but the sails were white; and still there was no life on them. They were like ghost-ships swiftly coming down the green river.

Afternoon came. The voices downstairs are becoming softer and drowsier. We are throwing up great mountains of spray, and sometimes the water-fowl which hangs obstinately over our bows is blinded by the spray and slides towards the centre of the river, screaming. We are gliding near the bank, perhaps because we want to avoid the attentions of Japanese aeroplanes, and all the ships are gliding near the bank, so that it seems as though the centre of the river possessed some magical quality. We could see the ploughmen on the banks ploughing through the frost, and as night came and we were still chugging slowly close to the banks, bridges began to pass more frequently, we passed small islands and sandbanks and it was clear that we were drawing towards the capital. And all night we chugged still more slowly along the bank by the light of a faint circle of moon, and in the morning the air was colder. We went out on deck to see the landscape

46

unchanged—the same green-and-red cliffs, the same small temples, and the same fishermen were throwing out their lines with wide-winged black cormorants into the blue river.

I have no idea how far we have travelled. Wet and dripping in the misty cabin, the oil-lamp continually flickering out, the grey-blue discoloured windows and the boards seem to have been accomplices since the beginning of time. The river is in spate, very blue and sweetly cold. The wind rushes up the river, billowing out the white sails which are beginning to drift upstream—strange transformation!—and we no longer ride close to the bank. And suddenly out of the mist and the white morning, low on the horizon, behind the red cliffs and the islands, Changsha shines in the sunlight, all white in the frosted air, flanked by the white sails of sampans, luminous and clear, a rock of white marble amid the red hills.

And so we come ashore. We have flown from Chungking to Kweilin; from there we have taken the Blue Express to Henyang and Hsiangtan; and from there, since the railway has been cut by the Japanese, we have taken the motor-launch to Changsha. It stands there gleaming, "the city of the sands". We climb ashore, make our way slowly through the knee-deep sand, while gusts of wind blow in our faces, and at the moment when the Japanese aeroplane appears we are already walking along a road, between the sunken fields white with broken ice, while the magpies crawk on the branches.

Later . . . WE ARE living in a small country house painted green. There are plank beds which smell strongly of pine resin, very sweet in this frosty air. It is four years since I have seen frost or snow, and all afternoon as we lazed under the pines I have been dreaming of the whirlwind of snows in the Boulevard Montparnasse, and dreaming of Spain. I left Europe from Spain and France. In the winter of 1938 the whole of Europe was like a whirlwind of snow, in which sometimes you would see the faces of the suffering and the insane. But here the cold wind drives insanity away, and I have been dreaming of the promise made with a Spaniard—a promise that we would both go to China. He was still young, this Spanish general, and he had led the Republican Air Force against the Moors, the Germans and the Italians; but though he was embittered, he had not lost his power to understand the world. "There is only one place left where they

47

are fighting honestly—above all, fighting honestly. I should like to fight there. I should like to pit some of my Spanish pilots against the Japanese." Then he sighed, and quoted the old Spanish proverb: *"Mi venga la muerte de Spagna."* "But let my death come from Spain."

Within half a mile from here lie the ruins of the University of Hunan, and all that is left of one of the greatest libraries of central China are two stone doric columns. I have walked up among the small green hills, where Chinese officers have made small models of cities out of coloured clay—cities which they will capture later—but more impressive even than the green pine-clad slopes of Yulosan or the distant spires of Changsha are these solitary columns on the plain. The Japanese came two years ago. They destroyed the whole University without warning; they burnt and plundered. We sit along benches beside the great table downstairs. A Chinese military officer is recounting the story of the battle for Changsha, which ended two days ago; and his voice goes on, droning mysteriously in the candlelit darkness, and his fingers move across the map, a map which is still to us imaginary, for we have been in Hunan only a short time and cannot translate the names of cities into the walled fortresses we shall perhaps see later. And at night strange lights flicker in the gardens, soldiers stand at sentry-go and in the distance we hear the explosions of bombs.

January 6th . . . IN THE darkness we were given breakfast. Wrapped in furs or padded cotton, we walked down the bare wooden steps and marched out into the morning. And then suddenly the sun rose over the red hills and threw down long spears on the broken squares of ice in the fields. Already the peasants were ploughing up the soil, and the blackbirds (which are really blue) were cawing in that harsh, ungainly tongue which mirrors perfectly the austerity of these fields in the early morning.

We climbed through the thick sand to the waiting launch, drove out into the middle of the wind and watched the yellowish-red hills slide past. Changsha suddenly appeared behind an island, whiter than ever, the foreshore littered with the stumps of broken buildings, but the factory chimneys still pointing to the sky. Better than yesterday, for as we come closer it shows its scars, and somehow those scars only add to the impression of beauty. When the current drove us close to the banks and we saw

48

the body of a Chinese soldier in sky-blue uniform spread-eagled on the red earth close to the waterline, it became more beautiful still, for he was the only soldier we saw there—killed perhaps by an unlucky shot from a low-flying aeroplane, or by the small group of Japanese who are known to have reached the river in an effort to encircle the town. The white city, the dead boy on the red cliff and the gulls swooping low over the blue river—till at last we came to leeward of the wind, hiding in the island's shadow from the aeroplane overhead, and salt-spray flew up over the bow and stern—"There's a lot of salt in the river," said the captain, "and if ever you see the river in flood, you'll know it's a sea, and the Tungting lakes are salt and when they flood over the valleys——" but I forget the rest, for we were already coming close to the white city in the miraculous morning air, and I remembered reading about the Tungting lake in a children's geography book and wondered whether it was the same.

We saw the shell-holes and the bomb-craters gaping red in the moist earth; the broken ships at anchor with holes in their bows like sharks' mouths; the smouldering debris of a house blackened by bombs; the blue-clad soldiers following a coffin swung on yellow ropes across the shore. Details—a curving chimney stack, blown out of shape by an explosion, a red stain high up on the wall of a house, a body floating in the glacier-green river, and yet not moving, for the bare legs were caught in barbed wire; and then the city, whose name was inscribed on the front pages of newspapers all over the world, towering high above us, brooding in the morning silence among wraiths of smoke. Someone had inscribed, in yellow paint which glistened in the sunshine, the words "Changsha will not fall". The Chinese characters were vigorous with action. "Chang" means "long", and "sha" means "sands", and there is a line like a descending spear-head in the character for "sands" which looked for all the world like a vigorous incitement to battle. But on the left bank of the river there are no sands at all, and as the motor-boat bobbed in the swift transparent water, we could see high above us the slowly descending rubble of the city—a few trickles of stones, a few bricks, a few pillars, which tumbled in clouds of black dust towards the river's edge.

We marched ashore, picking our way carefully through rubble. Bergery took photographs, and forgot that the lens was covered with spray from the river. As he marched ashore, he hummed:

"Sie werden lachen,
Ich liebe
Meine eigene Frau . . ."

"What makes you sing this kind of nonsense?" I asked.

He laughed gently and turned towards the city. "I am so used to bombed cities," he said sadly, "and now it is almost as though I am married to them. When I go into a city which isn't bombed, it seems that something is wrong. In Lisbon, I felt that nothing was so necessary as a bomb, I couldn't find my bearings, I felt completely lost. To be comfortable my legs must be searching for a foothold among debris. *Sie werden lachen . . ."*

We didn't laugh. At that moment, making our way through broken walls, we saw the first white coffins of the defenders. There were no flowers, and no cock was tied to the coffin-lid. Swinging on the bamboo poles so heavily that you could hear the movement of the body inside, it passed along the ruined road in front of us in the direction of the burial mound at the East Gate.

And now from everywhere there appeared blue helmeted soldiers in light blue padded cotton uniforms. They were all young. They walked in the sunlight out of the shelter of bomb-holes with an unexpected swagger, their bayonets gleaming. We photographed them. They smiled. They were very eager to talk about the battle, and they mentioned Colonel Li, who had defended the city from within, with extraordinary respect and affection. A general or an officer who obtains the respect of his soldiers in China can work miracles, someone said, and it was easy to believe him, for these youths, fingering their bayonets and gazing dreamily at the passing coffins, are soldiers of whom any country could be proud. They were nearly all Hunanese, fighting for their homes—farmers' lads, mostly, with faces like ripe apples and a gay swing in their movements. All winter they had been waiting. To while the time away, they had planted vegetables on their block-houses, and it was curious to turn into a side street and see, through a curtain of bayonets, lettuces sprouting above corrugated iron houses.

We followed the soldiers along a broken street, where the charred buildings were still smoking. Occasionally only a single wooden post would remain standing. A tree-stump or a lamp-post with bullet-holes was like a wound still bleeding, but those bullet-marks on wooden posts were so fresh that they seemed to have

50

been made only a few moments before. Here the nakedness of war appeared in all its violence, for bodies still lay in the houses and the sound of pick-axes echoed in the still wintry morning. It was strangely quiet. The magpies, with their white collars, sang on the branches, and the footsteps of the soldiers echoed against stone walls. High above the city aeroplanes flew and fought in the cold winter sun. Sentries blew their whistles, and we were told to seek shelter near the river edge; but no one took notice and shortly afterwards the aeroplanes disappeared. When they had gone, the city was more silent than ever, until suddenly we heard the sound of squealing pigs and turning a corner we watched three Hunanese peasants wheeling their barrows—with immense centre wheels and curved flanks, which were so delicately carved that they would grace a museum of modern industrial art. The barrows contained children in bright red leggings and woollen mufflers, and their expressions were oddly at variance with the expressions of the peasants, who looked grimed and sat with too much wandering. Behind the peasants came the squealing pigs. The peasants told us that they were going back to their homes on the west bank of the river, and their faces under their black turbans lit with relief when the soldiers gave them a right of way. And still we wandered through the burnt-out debris, and we well understood the number of bodies lying there. But the sun shone on the walls and in the yellow puddles, and steam rose from the coffins lying beside the road, and slowly the film of water disappeared from the smooth surface of pine, leaving the fresh scented wood golden in the burst of sunlight.

There may be some beauty in cities when they are bombed, but the outskirts of Changsha were bleak with an agony of black rubble, and at the Eastern Gate the bleakness became intensified by the presence of Japanese dead. They lay in the mangled earth where they had been shot down with rifle-fire and hand-grenades, their faces swollen and broken, naked, the flesh turning green. They were not pleasant. They had, as the dead often have, supercilious expressions, and their bared teeth did not commend them to our souls. Their toes were turned outward—our first lesson in recognising the Japanese and some of them possessed beards. They lay there in a small enclosure behind an armament store, and the grass was already curling around their bodies. The photographers knelt down and took the inevitable close-ups, and

51

occasionally it was necessary to change the position of an arm or a leg.

The hill was steep and overlooked the river; here and there the green turf was stained with blood. The day was warm and a cool breeze came up the Hsiang river. We walked up the hill towards the grey tombstones on the summit, conscious only of the clear beauty of the day and the white puffs of transparent cloud in the sky until suddenly, stumbling over the first of the naked bodies in the grass, seeing the print of the machine-gun legs in the mud —prints like black claws—and down below the red roof of the arms factory white with pigeons, we knew at once that the rest of the day would revolve about this dead soldier in the grass, as a universe revolves about its suns.

There are days when some small irrelevant thing assumes tremendous proportions; and perhaps this soldier was no smaller than the least of these things. He had died; he had been stripped of his clothes; his face was turned to the city which refused to accept him. He was young; he smoked cigarettes; he saw the sun shining, and became sentimental when he watched the moon through the cherry-trees; he was lonely like all Japanese in China; and hopeless like all Japanese in China; and underfed and bullied and made stupid with pnuishment, and this too like all Japanese in China. Was it his fault that he lay dead? He himself, alone, could he have prevented his death? And in community with his brothers, could he have prevented his death? The sadness of the field of battle, paper lying in every tombstone, burnt-out cigarettes in the hands of the dead—and then, in the silence, the singing of a bird. It is unnecessary to be compassionate, but even the photographer crouching over the dead face in order to show the splintering wound which broke the red teeth must know that this death is at the same time sudden and expected, and perhaps welcomed. The battle took place over thirty-six hours ago. Five times the burial mound at the East Gate changed hands. The young Chinese soldiers in blue, the Japanese in brown, with steel helmets, which few of the Chinese possessed. The Japanese wore leather sandals, the Chinese wore sandals of bark or rice-straw. The Japanese were far from their homes, the Chinese were fighting outside the walls of their homes.

There are other bodies. A man does not die alone on the battle-field. Always there were small indentations in the mud where rifles or machine-guns had been; always pieces of paper—why

52

are battlefields crowded with pieces of paper?—always there are photographs. I have picked up the photograph of a Japanese girl sitting against a painted backcloth showing cherry-trees in full bloom, and there is in her gaze so much tenderness and expectation that she seems to be about to walk out of the photograph and stand by my side. One must fight.

—To live in peace is terrible.

—If we could preserve the virtues which come from war, would war be necessary? Even in peace there are dangers. Boats sink, houses burn, there are always cries of suffering.

—War demonstrates the greatest heroism in comradeship, and death sanctifies everything. There is nothing in peace, no imaginable adventure, so beautiful as the adventure of war. We must die in order to live. That our women shall live, we must die. Death sanctifies all.

I do not know why I should have remembered this conversation in a railway carriage in Germany three years. Here there is only a lesson in military strategy. The Japanese had attempted to gain possession of the burial mound which overlooked the city. From there, with their heavy guns, they could dominate the fortress. And everything in their plans they achieved except that they had failed to bring up any heavy guns at all, for the roads were cut by the partisans. They had obeyed the pure theory, and failed to make it a reality. They fought a battle of the imagination, and inevitably they failed.

Bergery said: "They are young, but the Chinese were younger. This is what I find extraordinary in the fighting here. The older and more experienced must have been sent down to fight against Malaya and the Philippines. They were superbly confident that they could capture Changsha without trained men."

All the bodies were young, and many of them showed no signs of wounds. In the cold air, among the columns of the tombs, their flesh as white as paper, they embraced the grass and smiled in death like men who have found their home, though they were surprised at finding it so quickly. And this is what has always seemed to me so strange about war; the noise, the shouting and the anger are followed inevitably by the silence. No birds called. In the white haze the white sands of Changsha were shining, and already peasants in blue smocks, old women mostly, were burying the bodies which were as yet untouched by Chinese earth.

We walked back through the charred black roads of the city

53

and through wide thoroughfares where no bombs had fallen. The city was immense. Burnt down in 1927 and again in 1938, it had been rebuilt in plaster. There were shops where the plaster was still fresh, with window decorations smiling under plate-glass. Less than ten days ago, the governor of the province ordered the evacuation of the civilians; the houses were to be left exactly as they were, and he promised that everything would be returned intact. In the streets there were notices calling upon the people to evacuate. There were also small red squares of paper which had been dropped by Japanese aeroplanes calling upon the people to surrender:

The Great Pacific War has started—Abandon your fight and tell your soldiers to abandon this senseless war. Our imperial army is once again entering Hunan. We have killed no Hunanese people. We are opposed to killing. We fervently hope your war of resistance will cease. Lay down your arms if you wish to preserve the land and restore peace to the people. This is our advice.

The pamphlet was signed by the Commander-in-Chief of the Japanese Armies in China.

In the centre of the city, in a small building in a courtyard flanked by stone lions, General Li who had been in command of the defence of the city was waiting for us. In a small upstairs room, filled with magazines, small handleless cups of greyish-brown tea, scrolls and comfortable sofas, we listened to his report of the progress of the battle from the moment when, on the evening of the 31st, less than a week ago, the Japanese attacked the suburbs from the south, east and north-east to the moment three days later when they were in full flight to the north. He had received orders from General Hsueh Yueh that the city must not be abandoned. He had fought well. He had made three sorties from the West Gate, eight sorties from the East Gate, he had cleaned up the small Japanese column who penetrated into the city, and he had done all this without a single reconnaissance aeroplane. There were guns on Yulosan manned by Russian and Chinese artillerymen, but they alone could not have put the Japanese to flight. There were many dead Chinese, and they were still being buried. There were many buildings destroyed, but the centre of the town had been preserved . . .

I cannot follow military discussions. I can understand battles

54

better without maps, for what is important is not the names of places but "the tree", "the house", "the ridge between the rice-fields" where the defenders took cover, and "the river" which they cross at night and defend till daybreak. These are things which the ordinary mind appreciates, while the maps, even when they are faithfully inscribed on great sheets of paper in thirteen coloured inks, are nearly meaningless. It was better to look at the face of the young general, a face tanned almost grey by the sun and full of mysterious spiders' webs of wrinkles. He looked—his dumpy arms sprawled over the map—like someone who has been afraid and is no longer afraid; who has given orders— defend that tree, that wall, that house—and who has known the enjoyment which comes when orders are actually obeyed; and as he continued speaking, in a gaunt, clipped Hunanese voice, it was easy to imagine the concentration of power in the small ugly hand on the table. It was not well-formed. It was a soldier's hand, scarred not by wounds but by continual knocking against solid objects, and the thick green jade ring seemed somehow out of place. He smiled: "So the defenders became the attackers—yes?" It was the only English he spoke, and it was like a sudden revelation of how victories are accomplished in China.

In a courtyard three miles away blood-soaked Japanese flags, machine-guns, rifles, diaries, poison-gas bombs were littered in confusion against the wall. Only the bullets were carefully stacked in neat little piles. The sun shone on the thick dried blood; it shone on the broken helmets and the fur-lined gloves, the green tent-cloths and the photographs which had escaped from some pocket-book. A white horse, also captured from the Japanese, neighed and sometimes it would start to run round the courtyard, and then stop dead; a magnificent horse, no longer cared for, but once belonging to a young officer who took a special pride in its appearance. Shell-shocked, whinneying, it continued to make these sudden furious little spurts round the bare sunlit courtyard until we had left.

And so we returned through the deserted streets of Changsha. A few guards stand at the cross-roads. A few peasants make their way through the burnt-out charred houses on the eastern corner of the streets. A pill-box covered with mud, and green lettuces growing from the roof—and always the scent of gunpowder and danger. The city has been burnt down to the ground so many times that no one cares to remember how many times it has had

55

to be rebuilt; but very little has been destroyed, the shops are still standing and the bullet-marks leave curious little vertical traces, showing that they have come from aeroplanes. It was not always like this. Ten years ago there would have been no vertical traces, the shops would have been pillaged and there would be no foreign correspondents riding through the walled city.

Towards evening we came to the ruins of Yale-in-China. The great roofless walls of the immense buildings are charred and blackened; the floorboards have fallen in; the radio-therapy installations and the X-ray equipment are black wires and molten metal. There is nothing left—nothing at all; even the beds are twisted strips of iron still hot to the touch.

Dr. Petit, who left for the south ten days ago and returned this morning, surveys the buildings without resentment, without bitterness and without realising exactly what has happened. "The damage is about two million dollars gold." He is still dazed, and those enormous black eyes as they survey the scene reflect every detail so brightly that I have watched a small drift of smoke rising from a corner of the building without taking my eyes from his.

We have been trying to reconstruct exactly what happened. All round Yale-in-China there are small buildings built on the European model, with gabled roofs and rose gardens. They are untouched; the grass is still green in their gardens. On January 1st the Chinese had almost decided to bombard Yale-in-China, knowing that the Japanese could turn the immense hospital into a fortress. When the Chinese made their sorties from the North Gate on the 2nd and 3rd there was serious fighting in the neighbourhood of the hospital, but except for a few bullets fired from the windows the Japanese found little use for it. On the night of the third, when they were finally driven away, they set fire to it coldly and methodically. They emptied tins of kerosene on the floors and on the beds, and set fire to them with hand-grenades; and the walls blazed all night and long into the next day. Into this funeral pyre they threw some of their own dead—and they must have warmed their hands by the flames, for it was bitterly cold that night, according to the Chinese officer who accompanied us. Afterwards, having abducted and murdered two or three of the Chinese nurses who were caught between the two fires and having killed all the patients who could not be removed, they retreated northwards.

Bergery wandered through the debris and came back, looking more pale than I have ever seen him, for he discovered only afterwards that he had been walking through the ashes of the dead.

We came home slowly in·the gathering dusk, the long clouds drifting over the Hsiang river. We passed old rock-gardens, small country houses on the edge of the city which seemed to have heard no sound of bombardment or fighting. Still the soldiers marched down the empty streets; and in this great darkness of dusk the gleam of bayonets was brighter than starlight. We were footsore, and besides had seen so much of destruction that each unharmed house was like an affront. The Chinese colonel, who had stayed in the city throughout the bombardment and the furious counter-attacks, kept murmuring to himself: "Not long, not long——" but whether he was referring to our passage across the river or the rumoured defeat of the Japanese in a pitched battle on the north bank of the Milo river, we could not tell. We crossed the river in starlight, but when we had reached the other side and we were walking in sand nearly to our knees, the stars went out; and we travelled down the long dark road between the pines seeing only the small guttering candles which the Chinese soldiers lit for us.

And we were grateful for the darkness and the light.

January 7th . . . AGAIN we set out early in the morning, again we crossed the river at the point of silence, wondering at the redness of the cliffs, the whiteness of the town and the green trees standing at the foot of the burial mound. The town is becoming familiar to us. We know—or think we know—every street and ruin; we are friends of the water-fowl who dive low over the hills; and at the same time we know that we are passengers, who will depart for the south-west, leaving the blue-clad soldiers alone in possession of the green hills.

But this morning we are provided with donkeys. They are round-barrelled, well-fed, and very sleek. At the place where we crossed the river, the donkeys were waiting for us—twenty or thirty of every imaginable colour. They frisked their long silky ears and pretended to be the most docile donkeys in the world, but as soon as we mounted them, they showed an extraordinary reluctance to keep still.

The long road led north, through every imaginable painting of Chinese scenery. The sun came out, and shone on the small

57

earth-temples; it shone on the dead Japanese horse red and swollen which lay in a deserted farmyard; it shone on the dead Japanese and Chinese lying by the roadside, among the broken, twisted telegraph wires and the small lakes with ducks floating on them. The atmosphere was cooler when we came out of the city. Its taste was the taste of an air which has been blown over leagues of rice-fields, a taste like cool milk in summer. Here and there the dead lay in small companionable groups, like lovers. Nearly all the Japanese were naked, stripped of their clothes by the Chinese soldiers who knew the coldness of the long nights. And so, as we rode in single file through the stone-thatched villages, where everything was silent as the grave, the doors padlocked, the villagers gone, only the fireflies and the neighing donkeys seemed to be truly living. Oh—and the ducks. There were a thousand small green ponds strung like necklaces between these small villages, and there the ducks roamed at will, giving an impression of life to the austere landscape, where frost still glittered and the descending clouds were the same colour as the fields.

In the distance we heard guns. We heard them rarely, when the villages acted as sounding-boards or when the wind was favourable, a sound which the small green mountains must have deflected into our ears. So we wandered through the tapestry, the hooves of the small donkeys treading delicately and deliberately along the broken road, now less than a foot across, a road which once could have taken a carriage and pair. It was a road raised above the level of the rice-fields, but the earth and stones at each side had been removed until there was no more than a thin wall between the reddish-grey fields, and it might have been easier to ride on the plains. Once or twice we saw people, and spoke to them. They had hidden in wells, or in the small fortress-like crests of the hills. And once, when we were completely lost in the tapestry, we saw a man driving a buffalo over the hard flinty earth, making a little dark solid picture in the corner of the landscape—the ploughman, the brown buffalo and the white steam rising like plumes from their bodies.

On a field near the edge of a small green lake, under the lowering clouds, a heap of charred black bodies lay in confusion. The area of the funeral pyre was about the size of a tennis-court, and the bodies lay thickly together. They were black as cinders, shrunken like old charred wood, small sticks of bluish-black charcoal lying in confusion. And beside them, a little way away and

58

nearer the pool, lay two Chinese peasants—father and son. The old man grey and grizzled, the young handsome still in spite of the crust of blood on his forehead. The funeral pyre had been lit at night; and it seemed certain that the old peasant and his son, who lived in a house nearby, had been found spying on them; then they were shot, their bodies were thrown in the pool and the Buddhist priests in their yellow robes flung dismembered limbs in the flames. The rain had fallen towards the end of the ceremony, for in one corner of the field a few bodies remained half-burnt, very yellow and black, teeth gaping, heads split open, hands flung out.

It was growing late when we came to the Liuyang river, the air already blue with dusk; and in the darkness of the huddled streets, crowded with peasants and soldiers, our small donkeys allowing no one else to pass, we wandered in a kind of daze. It was warm in the village. Behind a small church the headquarters of the Chinese advance forces resembled headquarters everywhere else. Bare tables, maps, uniforms, impossibly young soldiers standing guard with blue bayonets. But though we had left our donkeys in the yard, we could still feel the thumping motion of their barrel bodies as they rode across the stone paths; and it was difficult at first to realise that we were among stone houses, and friendly people. Food was set out for us. We ate ravenously; but we were not sure that we were not dreaming. Throughout the whole journey we had not thought there were towns.

The commander of the Chinese forces made a speech. He was a small wiry man with six days' growth of beard; and as he spoke, rapidly and almost silently, occasionally pointing to the maps on the wall, it was as though the army itself were speaking, so solemnly and so quietly did he announce the totals of the dead Japanese and Chinese, the number of captives, the lists of captured machine-guns, bullets, Samurai swords. He reviewed the merits of the Japanese and Chinese forces, and when I look at the statement which I scribbled down at the time, it looks curiously simple and misleading, and yet it was in this way that Modesto would list the virtues and vices of his Republican Army in Spain:

Our merits: (1) Determination on the part of officers and men, (2) advantages fully made use of, (3) secret dispositions, (4) mobility of our troops, (5) capacity to hold out at strategic points.

Our weaknesses: (1) lack of telegraphic communications and liaison, (2) lack of guns and tanks.

Their merits: (1) Better equipment, co-operation between guns and air-force, (2) courage and refusal to surrender, (3) understanding of terrain.

Their weaknesses: (1) tendency to advance without heed to menace at sides and rear, (2) failure to hold strategic points, (3) ineffective intelligence and reconnaissance, (4) neglect of defence.

But when the speeches were over, and the young commander was walking with us down the steep slope to the river, the battle became again a part of our lives. It was no longer a thing of statistics, but of the air we breathed; and the willows on the banks of the green river, and the great sail-less junks which floated us over the sandy beaches, showed bullet-holes at the stern; and there were more bullet-holes on the stone steps.

It was a raw afternoon, the wind coming down from the north-east and the clouds very high. A few starlings rose from a bamboo coppice. Small boys who had taken part in the fighting were swinging their legs from the gunwales, smiling now that the enemy was out of earshot; and the water-fowl rose screaming high in the air. There was nothing in this village on the Liuyang river to distinguish it from a thousand other villages in Hunan—grey walls, white stone steps, a few old junks berthed under the green edge of the river. In silence we crossed the river. In silence we walked through the first white strips of evening mist which lay over the banks; and still there was no sign of the war. It was half an hour later when we came to a turn in the river that we saw for the first time in China the effect of enfilading fire. The rice-fields were unsown, the earth hard and brittle underfoot; but from the rise of the rice-fields down to the sloping sandy beach the dead lay in confusion. They were naked, their bodies very white in the frost, and often they showed no signs of wounds. They lay there in the wintry stillness underneath the mist, perhaps two hundred of them, and we passed in silence, while an immense water-wheel continued to revolve and sometimes the white water-fowl would perch on the buckets of the wheel, cawing loudly.

The dead were everywhere. A young Chinese sergeant, in a sky-blue uniform, explained how the Japanese had crossed in the evening, when there was a thick mist and how he had posted guards along the river bank. Suddenly one of the soldiers came running towards him, shouting that the Japanese were coming, and he had ordered him to return and wondered what would happen to him. The telegraph system had broken down. He kept on shouting "The Japanese are coming", until at last reinforcements arrived in time to stop the steady flow of Japanese from the island, but already many of them had crossed in rubber barges. Throughout the night there was fighting, and for the greater part of the next day. They fought between the high earth-ridges between the rice-fields; and it was there, below the ridges and along the bank, that the dead lay with their faces turned to heaven, so quiet and harmless now that they were stripped of their uniforms.

Near the river we could hear the tock-tock of mattocks as the peasants built shallow graves. The river flowed silently at our feet, the watermill continually revolving. Empty cartridge cases, blood-stained handkerchiefs, cigarette cartons, little pieces of paper which had been torn and scattered by the wind, a rifle buried in the high grass at the edge of the fields—this was the landscape where they lay. There are moments when the Chinese are proud of their adversaries, and I was surprised when a soldier who cannot have been more than twelve years old came and led me to the body of a Japanese officer whose fingers had been broken and whose teeth were still clenched tightly over five bullets. "He fought to the end," the soldier said. "Look at the bullets in his teeth. We had to cut off his fingers to get at his revolver, so tightly did he hold it." He smiled. It seemed then that the Japanese were an enemy worth fighting; until the memory of the charred funeral pyres and the dead Chinese peasants near the green pool obliterated all sense of pity. But those who were young were still beautiful, and those white bodies lying among the green tufts of grass like swimmers sleeping after their bathe, tormented us throughout the rest of the journey.

The Chinese counter-attacked. They forced the Japanese back across the island, where the saplings gave no shelter and the earth was so hard that it resembled brown ice. We walked in silence, hardly daring to think of the blackbirds and the wild dogs who gorged themselves on this unnatural feast; but already many of the bodies had been buried, and there was sadness on the faces of the peasants who leaned on their spades. Even here the dead appeared to be sleeping. At any moment they would rise and plunge into the river; and while the mist hung round them, it was easy to imagine that the white breath rose from their lips. They were young soldiers mostly. They had come down from the north without knowing that the Chinese were waiting for them, and so often on their dead faces there was an expression of surprise, the brows uplifted and the mouth parted.

The island had been occupied by the Japanese for a week, yet they left little sign of their occupation except scraps of torn paper which one of the Chinese cavalry officers was attempting to piece together. When three-quarters of the letter had been dove-tailed, he read it quietly and then blew the pieces away, complaining that he had no time to read love-letters in Japanese; and yet he was strangely moved. As you left the main track through the saplings, wandering among dead mules and spent cartridge cases, you found everywhere the small evidences of a soldier's intimate life—a blue leather diary, three or four sheets of notepaper covered over with a thin black scrawl which was now illegible, for the heavy dew had run the letters together, a notebook which contained Japanese banknotes, a gold-studded saddle, even a short Japanese sword. And yet, though these things were real, they were less real than the terrible sound of the mattocks and the spades, and the expressionless faces of the peasants who had buried more bodies than they could count, and the terrible watermill which continued to revolve in the half-darkness of the winter afternoon.

We rode over the red hills of Hunan, along the broken pathways, and as night fell the small shuttered homesteads became smaller, little pools of blackness in the starlight. I have often wondered why farmhouses seem to contract at the approach of night, but it was easier to understand near the battlefield. Here and there we noticed small glittering objects in the grass and on the muddy fields—spent bullets, a Japanese cap, the spectacles of some Japanese officer crushed underfoot and shining like a small heap of diamonds.

I have forgotten how long it took to bring us from the Liuyang river to Changsha. It seemed an eternity. Occasionally we noticed the glitter of spurs or a Chinese belt, but everything else was muffled for a while in the thick night. But soon the stars came out, the air was pure and clean, washed by the starlight and the soft transparency of recent rains.

Bergery was saying something by my side, but at first I could not hear him. I was listening to the roar of distant waves, or perhaps it was only the vast soughing of the distant trees. Bergery was riding a little in front of me, one hand resting on the bridle and the other swinging clear.

"Do you know, this is almost the heart of Chinese civilisation," he said, pointing in the direction of the great walls of Changsha. "The greatest Chinese poet drowned himself in the river which the Japanese are now crossing. He was Chu Yuen, and he wrote two poems to the mistresses of the Chiang River.

> 'The Lady comes not; she stays her steps.
> How slow! Who detains her on the island,
> She who is so beautiful and so adorned?
> I would fetch her in a boat of scented sandalwood,
> Let the Hsiang and the Yuan rivers be without waves,
> Make the waters of the river flow gently . . .'

I have forgotten the rest, there are many verses and Chu Yuen mentions all the flowers he ever saw, and besides it is too late to talk of poetry. You remember the island opposite Changsha. It is perhaps the same island where he waited for the Lady of Hsiang and sighed because the Emperor no longer paid him the courtesies he expected. But the river still flows and you can still hear the waves."

He drew up his pony and gazed into the distance, but Changsha was still far away in the south. I asked him to tell me more about the mysterious poet who sang the praises of the river, but he was silent until he noticed the evening star rising above Yulosan; and then he began to talk quickly and nervously, and when he quoted the Chinese verses he would speak them first in Chinese, lisping a little, enjoying their flavour, before translating them into his own tongue.

"He was a great poet, perhaps the greatest poet the Chinese have ever possessed. For a long while he served Prince Huai of the Ch'u State, but he was so zealous in his duties that the other ministers of state did everything to discredit him. I think he must have known he would drown, just as Shelley in his poetry seems to be quite certain that he will one day return to the sea whence he was born. The great Chinese poet Li T'ai Po wrote much the same thing, and Keats too ordered, you remember, that they

63

should write on his tombstone, 'His name was writ in water'. There is a curious identity between the greatest poets and the element of water—you will see it again in the last plays of Shakespeare and in the last poems of the German poet Friedrich Hœlderlin. But more than any other poet Chu Yuen was in love with water:

> 'I will build my house in the water,
> Covering it with lotus leaves,
> The walls of iris, the court of purple shells,
> The hall carpeted with narcissi,
> The roof-beams of cassia, the rafters of orchids.
> I will make my curtains of saffron leaves,
> And all about the house there will be magnolia . . .

And so he goes on, making of flowers the wreaths which he will wear when he is dead. He wrote a book called nine songs, which characteristically—for the Chinese are not very accurate about numbers—contains eleven, and a long poem on his own grief, which he must have written in the week before he died. The Chinese Dragon Festival commemorates his memory, but no one knows exactly when he lived or why he died, whether it was because he was grief-stricken because the Emperor no longer trusted him or because some girl had thrown him over for a younger man."

In the starlight Bergery's enormous head shone like silver. As we rode on a little way, we saw the grey walls of Changsha appearing in the distance, and behind us lay the Liuyang river, the dead Japanese and the advancing soldiers. The night shone, the snaffles of the ponies glittered like bayonets and the long cavalcade of riders turned out of the shadows of trees and faced the sudden apparition of the moonlight. And thinking of the dead, he murmured:

"In these things we are always at a loss. Death is never something we can understand. Death is easy and simple, and at the same time difficult and dangerous. What do we know—we who have seen the dead bodies of the Japanese lying on the sands? They were naked, and that at least was a blessing, for it made them similar to the rest of us, and perhaps it is easier to understand death when it is naked."

There was no answer. My pony reared at a shadow; the moon-

64

light disappeared under a heavy curtain of clouds; and once more the riders rode in single file along the road. From the lakes and meres, from the distant hills and from the white sky itself the evening mist seemed to be about to leap upon us, and now at last our loneliness became intolerable, and the memories of battle and the distant sounds of gunfire demanded an explanation. Bergery must have read my thoughts, for out of the darkness I heard him speaking softly: "In the West we lay flowers on the tombs of the heroes. In Szechuan have you noticed that they tie a cock to the coffin? We must think of the living!"

"And then?"

"Always we must think of the living. Everything that lives is holy. This was said by your greatest English poet, but it is true, nevertheless, in China and elsewhere. There are many Japanese dead—but we must think of the living."

I remembered then how in one of the suburbs of Changsha, near the old burial ground and the paulownia trees, the Japanese lay in ranks like paper lanterns after rain; they were colourless, expressionless, grey like lead, miserable like imprisonment. And I remembered too how years ago I would visit an old Chinese carpenter in Singapore, and watch the logs which came in the huge-masted sampans along Singapore river, and how he would unleash them and drop them into the mud and silt of the river. Years later they would be dredged up, finer and tougher than they had ever been before they were immersed in the grey, oily water. But these Japanese would never arise from the multitudinous rivers of death. They were dead, and the living had no time to remember them.

Already we were approaching the walls of Changsha. The long winter afternoon was over. A few black-turbaned Chinese peasants were wheeling their delicate hand-barrows along the muddy roads. Once a rape-seed oil-lamp swung across a field, then the lovely glimmer vanished, and we galloped right up to the crenellated walls of Changsha, where sentries stood on guard and the barricaded streets echoed our hoof-beats.

"Listen, can you hear the blue-bird?" Bergery asked suddenly, reining in his pony. "They say it is a sign of good luck. I have forgotten the Chinese name, but it means, I think, the bird of good omen. Shall we drink a toast to the blue-bird?" and I saw him lifting an imaginary glass to his lips and I am sure he was smiling.

Now at last we entered the deserted town, where the shops were shuttered and the houses were sounding-boards for our ponies' hoof-beats. Somehow or other we had become detached from the rest of the party, and there was only the Chinese colonel, Bergery and myself. We rode by the stars. Changsha at night is so vast that it would have been easy to get lost. Bergery had picked up a Japanese helmet on the battlefield; now it glinted in the faint starlight—this helmet with the two bullet-holes and the Japanese star and the blood congealed on the crown.

The Chinese colonel rode ahead, upright on his white Tibetan pony. Once the snaffles gleamed, and he swung round on the saddle to tell us to go more quickly. Soldiers were marching down a side-street parallel to ours, and their ghostly tread mingled with the hoof-beats and formed another kind of music altogether. We rode hard, but it was half an hour before we reached the river.

"If we are not careful, we shall meet the Lady of the Hsiang River," Bergery said as we watched the swift-flowing river in the moonlight. The river shone with a blinding intensity, and very faintly in the sky I thought I saw its silver reflection; but the Milky Way, with its weaving clusters of spindrift silk, was motionless in the heavens, while the river roared tumultuously at our feet.

Bergery was still thinking of the Japanese, though he had long ago promised to put them out of his mind.

"It is good that they are dead," he said after a while. "I counted four hundred in the cremation yards and in the fields. Once I left you and walked through the ice over the fields where the Japanese were lying. The ice formed after the fighting, and under the ice I saw blades of grass still red with blood or white with brains. Oh, why did they come south? They were underfed, they were young, they were conscripts. They cut off the arms of the dead, they built great funeral pyres and sometimes they employed poison gas. They are mad! That's why they must be shot down like mad dogs!"

The Chinese colonel stood up in the stirrups and pointed to the waiting barge moored in mid-stream. As we rode slowly along the shore, our shadows floating black against the silver river, Bergery continued: "Certainly we must shoot them down like mad dogs, but every time we kill them we must remember the living. They are less mad than dead. Yes, they are dead—without love, without life, without wisdom. I have seen them in a hun-

66

dred wars and now, thank God, these wars are coming to an end. I have seen them in Spain, in Germany, in Hungary, in Poland, in Finland—and now here! They are the same everywhere. We are fighting for life, for the sake of the life we see in young children and lovers. This is all I have learnt from twenty years of war."

Our three ponies plunged into the river, drinking up great fountains of water, the moonlight shining on their glossy flanks. Somewhere on the other bank lay the headquarters of General Hsueh Yueh who, like General Yo Fei in the time of the Tartars, gave the famous order: "We must get back the rivers and the hills."

"Let us remember this night," said Bergery. "I have seen many victories, but never a night like this. This is China! This is what I have come to see, so that I can remember it always and speak about it to my friends abroad. Wireless is a strange thing, but useful. I shall speak about this on the wireless, so that millions of people will know what the Chinese Army is suffering, and then I shall speak of this silence and the brilliant white lane of the river like a searchlight carved through the darkness." Bergery was silent for a while, then he said: "This silence, this light."

The barge in mid-stream was slowly moving to the shore. Along the bank, curvetting among the ruins, more ponies were coming to meet us. Once more Bergery turned to me and said: "We must remember the living. We must fight for the young, the lovers, all those who have not got this madness in their souls. This is what we have in common among the democracies—a love for life and the flowering of life. This is why we shall win, for everything that is alive is holy." And as we crossed the river later, I heard him chanting the song of the Chinese fishermen of the Hsiang river, and the Japanese helmet gleamed in his hand and he looked straight ahead like a seaman.

Afterwards we ploughed knee-deep through the thick sands on the opposite shore, while a gale came up and the sand whistled like a lament for the dead. We could see only a few yards in front of us, but I remember Bergery striding by my side and shouting into the teeth of the gale: "Everything that lives is holy!"

January 8th . . . WE HEARD the rain all night, but when we awoke the sky was clear, pale blue, with here and there a few patches of deeper blue. I noticed the same phenomenon when we

67

were coming up the Hsiang river—in China there are deep blue clouds which hover over the heavens.

This morning a Japanese prisoner, captured near the East Gate, was brought to the house. He sat in the open courtyard in the sunlight, his face very grey and tired, and there was about him an extraordinary air of sorrow, as though he no longer cared to live; but he was happy to see the sunlight. His name is Kyoshi Kowahara, a twenty-five-year-old insurance agent from Nagoya. He has a wife and three children; his father owns a small mill employing eight employees. His chief was Colonel Madono, who appears to have escaped. We clustered round him, while Colonel Liu acted as interpreter, and occasionally Bergery would say a few words in Japanese, and the young Japanese would look up, thinking by the tone of his voice that Bergery was a friend.

Of all the Japanese I have met, he was the only one who impressed me. His sorrow was so deep that he seemed to have much in common with Bergery. He sat there in his brown coat, his head bowed, the black hair shaven to the skull and so dark that it resembled a smear of black paint, his hands folded between his knees, never looking up.

"What regiment do you belong to?" Colonel Liu asked.

"The Sixty-eighth of the Fifth Brigade."

"How much do they pay you?"

"Twelve *yen* a month."

He explained that everything was food—food, transport, uniform. There was a faint smile on his face. The winter sunlight shone through the bare plum-trees, and in a broken voice, the voice of someone who no longer believes even in his own words, he explained that twelve *yen* was sufficient at the base camp for one woman a week or two hundred packets of military cigarettes.

"Women must be cheap in Japan?" Colonel Liu asked, smiling a little; but the soldier said nothing. A cold wind shook the plum-trees, and from time to time he would nod his head quickly, as though anxious to finish the conversation.

"Will you shoot me?" he asked.

No one said anything.

After a while he spoke in quick nervous tones about his food, for he had been asked to give a complete list of the food supplied to the Japanese Army. He said that his food consisted of rice, compressed beef and a kind of powdered sauce; he complained that since the Chinese soldiers had only two meals a day, while the

Japanese soldiers had three, he had felt hungry ever since his captivity five days before; and shortly afterwards, when someone brought sugared rice from the house, he smiled gratefully, took the food on his lap and gazed at it without interest. He was courteous and gentle, and in the end when Colonel Liu gave him the freedom of the garden, he smiled to himself, made the faintest inclination to the correspondents who had crowded round him until it seemed that they were all peering within an inch of his face and sat cross-legged on the grass facing the red cliffs of Changsha. All afternoon he sat there, so quiet and impassive that it was difficult to believe that in the confused fighting at the East Gate less than a week before, he had attempted to blow himself up with a hand-grenade; and when the grenade failed to explode, he quietly surrendered, expecting no mercy and receiving only kindness.

Later . . . THIS evening there was a storm. The rain came down, and the small river which we jumped across this morning is now a torrential stream. The house shakes, there is lightning and as we wait in the cold, uncomfortable bedrooms, for the storm to cease, it is difficult not to think of the soldiers in the rain north of the Milo river. There are winds in Hunan which can break a man's back; there is a fierceness in this earth and a still greater fierceness in the sky, and perhaps this is why the Hunanese are famous for their ferocity.

But when the storm cleared a little we made our way through the muddy roads to a small timber-stacked farm-shed near the river, and there among small hand printing-presses we toasted the Chinese Press at the front line.

Wherever there is an army in China, there is a small printing-press. Young soldiers, perhaps twelve years old, lift the lead characters from the boxes where they are arranged in order, and insert them carefully in slots on the printing-machine. The characters are so small that they become blinding when you read them; and the ink is so bad that the letters run. Yet the press functions perfectly, the characters are always replaced in their proper order and three or four hours after the newspaper has been printed, a fast motor-car takes them to the front line. There are wireless sets on which the news is received, and here and there you will find small portable electric motors. And while the small red-cheeked typesetters worked in the half-darkness, the

69

tables were lit in another side of the room under immense flaring acetylene lamps. Bergery sat next to the Russian correspondent, the *Times* correspondent sat next to the *Ta Kung Pao*, the best and the least official of all Chinese newspapers. A tremendous feast was set out for us. No one knew where the food had come from. There was white sweet rice, pigeon, duck, innumerable dishes of pork with sweet and sour sauce. There were four kinds of wine and six kinds of fruit—and it was winter, and there was a battle raging less than thirty miles away. The Chinese Press kept repeating that they were delighted to have us; and since we had burnt our throats with their white wine, and since we had nothing but admiration for them, we were not even amused when the *Daily Express* correspondent began to make a speech which continued to our amazement for over an hour in which he repeated his love for the Chinese and his displeasure at all those who did not love the Chinese people. The Chinese had won a great victory. The evidence of the victory which we had seen was already splashed across the front pages of the leading newspapers of the world, and we were in no mood for what the Chinese call "small speeches". We congratulated him, and carried him home through the storm, while the great winds howled through the pine forest and only the faintest glimmer of lights shone from the house buried in a nest of leaves.

January 9th . . . ALL day we have done nothing except stare at the leaden sky. There were plans for further excursions—even as far as the Milo river, but as the day wore on, it became clear that no permission would be given us. The air has become colder than ever, the wind breaks up the small pieces of ice on the frosted fields; and the blue magpies still shriek from the black branches. A day of desolate and streaming winds, grey clouds which would be slimy if you could touch them with your fingers, and always waiting.

I am beginning to understand the life of a journalist. Bergery's patience is something which he has learnt by years of partial failure. "And all journalism is failure," he said later this afternoon, before the banquet. "We prepare ourselves to tell the truth, we go into journalism with the one object of telling the truth, as though we were dedicated to the task, and afterwards when we look back on the life of constant travel and terrible vicissitudes, it amounts to so little." When we are doing nothing, he lies in

70

bed with his eyes closed. The eyes are heavily lidded, and a single blue vein can be seen throbbing on each lid. He smiles sometimes to himself while he sleeps, but more often his lips are pursed, and seem to be suggesting the eternal nightmare of the journalist who sees so much and can explain so little.

"Perhaps Hitler is right," he murmured this evening. "The journalist has a great responsibility for the present war. A single misplaced emphasis, a single statement that was not true——" But he knows that there are others who have a greater responsibility. "In the old days the statesmen were frightened by nobody. Now, at least, they are frightened by the good journalist. And how good it is that the statesmen and ambassadors should know that their opinions will be scrutinised, and how much better that these opinions should.be passed on, whether they will or not, to the great majority of the people.

The more I see of Bergery the more I come to the conclusion that in spite of his ancestry, which includes great-grandfathers from three different countries in Europe, he is predominantly the product of New England. Alone of the correspondents he attended the banquet this evening in a formal dress-suit.

We had seen General Hsueh Yueh before when, on the verandah of his house some miles away, he showed us the secret papers which had been found on the body of the Japanese Colonel Kato. Three months before the Pacific War broke out documents from Japanese sources had passed into the possession of the Chinese High Command, and according to General Hsueh Yueh the information had been passed on to the American and British Governments. Neither the Americans nor the British had apparently paid very much attention to the documents. He smiled, rubbed his hands and seemed to be saying: "We are an old race and these young races have still so much to learn." He looked remarkably young, the face of a fourteen-year-old boy, very slim, reddish, with hair turning grey. He smiled frequently. The tables were set for dinner, and he talked to me of Singapore, where he had been in the years before the Kuomintang Party assumed power in China. "I was arrested three times in Indo-China by the French authorities for the small part I played in helping the Chinese revolutionaries to obtain arms, but I could always find a refuge in Singapore." About the war in Malaya he refused to be drawn at first, but afterwards he said: "If they carry out the scorched

71

earth policy, the Allies will be victorious." It looked a simple phrase, and we would have dismissed it as a polite irrelevancy if he had not continued: "We have won the war in China, or rather we have prevented the Japanese from assuming complete political power over China, and we have done this simply by employing the scorched earth policy. This has been our major strategy. We have destroyed China—removed every stone, burnt down every farm, torn up every railway track upon which we could lay our hands, and we have done this so successfully that the Japanese have already repented of their invasion. They are tired and weary of their invasion." As he said this, we remembered the face of young Kyoshi Kowahara, and his statement that the Japanese Army in Yochow had greeted the opening of the Pacific War without enthusiasm. "We knew that it would be a much longer time now before we would see our homes."

General Hsueh Yueh was born in 1893. He was therefore nearly thirty years younger than Dr. Sun Yat-sen, whom he adored with the kind of devotion which is reserved only for the great. In 1918 he graduated with the rank of major from the Kwantung Military Academy, and he fought under Chen Chi-mei, the father of the present Minister of Education, in the revolutionary battles of the south which made Canton in summer a place of desolation and hopelessness. He was perfectly sure of himself, and his long thin hands would drum on the table with pleasure whenever anyone made a remark which particularly pleased him. Someone mentioned Genji Doihara. His face lit up, he smiled broadly and without the slightest trace of self-satisfaction, but as though he had taken the measure of his opponent and succeeded in beating him away, he said: "Doihara is my particular enemy. We have fought and are still fighting a duel together, but I flatter myself that my weapon—the Chinese Army—will outlast his."

In a neighbouring room a telephone bell rang. An aide came to announce that the Generalissimo was on the telephone. He excused himself and returned two minutes later, smiling: "The Generalissimo has asked me for the assurance that the foreign war correspondents here are being well treated." We assented gratefully. Throughout the rest of the meal the General ate nothing, but insisted on handing to us on his chopsticks the more savoury morsels which he had detected on the immense shining plates lying before us.

72

January 10th . . . THERE should have been ice-floes. It was bitterly cold, and we envied the Chinese soldiers in their green-grey caps, for these caps contain two strips of heavy cloth kept in position by a blue-and-white Kuomintang button, and these strips of cloth can be folded down over their ears. Bergery wore his heavy fur-lined coat, but the rest of us shivered. The grey road, the grey sky lit by occasional streaks of a heavenly blue, the immense stretches of level sand by the river, the small boat plunging in the heavy waves, and slowly Changsha fades away in the distance.

I have been watching it with Bergery from the stern as we roll in the enormous swell. It is still white and ghostly, with river-fowl screaming above us. The dead soldier who lay at the foot of the red cliffs is still there, but now there are thin grey puffs of smoke rising from the chimneys. Thousands are returning. We can see them lining up the bank, a black mass of people on the water-line waiting for the sampans to take them across. The green island, which stands like a sentinel between Changsha and the opposite shore, is greener than ever under the lowering clouds. We watched the city until it was out of sight, and at last Bergery drew his fur collar higher and whispered: "They will talk about it in all the newspapers of the world, but they will not understand. They will not understand that the Chinese have fought victoriously, while the rest of us have fought only to our shame."

Later . . . TOWARDS evening we were still running desperately against the current. The engine had broken down, and for a while we drifted northward till a Chinese engineer stripped the engine and put it right. While a thick mist lies outside, and the last cormorants have gone to sleep in the boats, we glide down the mysterious river. Bergery sits with his eyes glued on the window, and suddenly he turns to me and says:

"No other river in the world has had such great poetry written about it. I used to wonder why, since it is not more magnificent than the Yangtse and less terrible than the Yellow river. But its proportions are so good—exactly the right width—and how mysteriously the villages appear to rise above its banks. Chu Yuen is perhaps the greatest Chinese poet, and therefore the greatest poet who has ever lived——" and he began to recite, in the same low-pitched voice which accompanied his recitations as we rode

73

back from the Liuyang river, the song which Chu Yuen addressed to the Lord of the Hsiang River:

> "With you I wander the Nine Rivers,
> The whirlwind and the wave rises.
> Floating in a water chariot
> With its roof of lotus leaves,
> I climb above the K'un Lun mountains
> And search eagerly in the four directions.
> My spirits wander over the face of the deep.
> The day is waning; bemused, I forget my home.
> And dream of the furthest reaches of the river.
> In an abode of fish-scales, in a hall of dragons
> Under a purple-shell gateway, in a palace of pearl,
> O Spirit, why do you dwell in the waters?
> Riding the white tortoise and chasing the spotted fishes
> I wander with you among the small islets,
> The melting ice comes swirling down river.
> With a gentle bow you turn towards the East
> And I accompany you to the south anchorage.
> Wave after wave comes to welcome me.
> Multitudes of fishes come to bid me farewell."

January 11th . . . WE HAVE slept again at Hsiang-tang, in the same hotel, in the same terrible bedrooms overlooking the courtyard—everything dark and damp. Rice cauldrons boiling under the black eaves, the red candles and their redder flames. A girl singing in some distant street, and the muted notes of violins. The dust and the dirt and the tremendous swirling shadows which move across the courtyard walls—someone gambling—the tuck-tuck of mahjong tablets—and those momentary quietnesses when the sounds of the night seem to be gathering themselves for the furor ahead.

There is no silence in these small villages. Hsiang-tang was at one time the centre of the trade in fireworks, but the noise comes from the refugees who have come down to swell this small town from the north. Perhaps I shall never see this town in daylight. We came in the darkness of a late afternoon, and disappeared before sunrise. We are to leave at five o'clock tomorrow morning.

We slept fitfully. There were rats and the continual tramp of feet on the loose floor-boards outside; there were sudden squeals

74

like the squeal a rat makes at the moment when the wire trap closes over its neck; and perturbing menacing silences. On his pallet bed of straw and boards near the window Bergery has been reading by candle-flame. Of all the correspondents he alone is enjoying himself. "Three thousand years ago life in China was like this," he said happily. "Nothing has changed—straw, wood, broken pieces of porcelain, a cracked mirror. They possessed all these things. And perhaps here, two thousand years ago, in the same room, holding a candle to the same words, another scholar was reading the *Analects* of Confucius."

"And this pleases you?"

"Yes, of course. Why do you look surprised? Everything that suggests the continuity of the past and the present pleases me, for in these ages we are doing everything in our power to destroy the dominance of the past. We believe we are new. Not only in China, but all over the world people believe that they are born into a new world. And yet the world is so old, so old—and they have so little reverence for its old age. Think of this room! There must have been a village here three thousand years ago, perhaps five thousand years ago, for the Hsiang river has been navigable since the earliest records of Chinese history. There must have been a hotel here—perhaps it was very little different from this hotel with its square courtyard and overhanging eaves. Think of the people who have slept in this room—scholars, merchants, murderers, prostitutes, courtesans. Emperors have fled in disguise down this river. Kingdoms have been proclaimed from Changsha, and great armies have fled in barges to the north and the south. And perhaps the straw in the bed you are lying on has not been changed for three thousand years, and generations upon generations of people have been born there, and the murderer——"

I fell asleep, dreaming of the eiderdown blanket and the fur cap and the thick underwear I bought this evening. Hsiang-tang is cheaper than Chungking, and its narrow black streets are more Chinese than anything I have yet seen in China.

January 12th . . . WE TRAVELLED from Chungking by air to Kweilin and then by the Blue Express to Hsiang-tang. There was a time when the Blue Express travelled between Pekin and Shanghai, and romances were written about the train which the Chinese Government preserved from the Japanese only by the greatest use of dexterity. It is a train-de-luxe, with sleeping berths and soft cushions, excellent lavatories and immense windows from which we can look upon the countryside. Painted naval blue, streamlined and efficient, it comprises the only well-built set of carriages left in Chinese hands.

We have been travelling all morning through a bleak countryside. The grey fields are being ploughed, but only rarely do we see the peasants. A damp mist, dripping from the clouds, covers everything; and there are few trees. A short while ago we passed one of the famous five sacred mountains of China. It was not impressive—a small purple mound on the sky-line. And no one knows why this mountain should be chosen as one of the five sacred mountains except that it is in the dead centre of China.

And so the Chinese countryside flows on, grey and misty, with sedges and small brakes where pheasants are flying, and a few greyish-yellow stone-walled cottages near the winter skyline. There are no soldiers. The land is not dead but sleeping in its winter agony. The river, which gave life to the villages, is far away, and Bergery speaks of the monotony of the small villages in China where there are often no rivers or streams within fifty miles. "They live in a perpetual seclusion and have only their ceremonies to keep them together. Or rather, this is their chief glory. When I first came to China, I would ride across the country-side for miles, and suddenly I would alight on a deserted village. The villagers would be kind to me. They would entertain me, knowing that I was unarmed and friendly and possessed a passionate interest in their customs, and so they would arrange an archery contest or perhaps a boxing match or some sword-play for my benefit. It was only twenty years ago, in the intervals between the civil wars, yet they still kept up the old customs which gave them strength and self-pride. The most handsome youths of the village would be chosen for the archery costumes. They would be dressed in their long loose silken robes, and with those splendid bows made of the muscles of bears or heavy-horned cattle, they would perform the contest to music. Then, indeed, I believed I was living in the age of Confucius. Near the green fields and the stone temples these handsome boys would throw out their chests, smile at their bearded fathers and shoot the plumed arrows. But now——" He gazed out of the window, expecting perhaps to see the sun shining on a green meadow and to hear the cracking of bear-sinews as the bows were stretched by the boys. But there
76

was nothing—only the grey mist and a skylark spiralling into the sky.

At Henyang we noticed a hospital train. The sun was shining faintly, and the great doors of the cattle-wagons had been thrown open; and there, lying in small heaps on the straw, lay the wounded who had returned from the battle. They were bandaged well, though here and there we noticed a bandage which should have been removed, for there were often yellow stains seeping through the grey bandages. They looked pale and weary; and we wondered how long they had been there, shunted down this small side-track on the edge of the railway station.

Henyang is not beautiful, though there are wide roads and a river flows at the bottom of the city. The railway station resembles a provincial railway station in France, all grey stucco and brocade uniforms. But immediately you leave the railway station you are among broad thoroughfares, small white houses, and then the city no longer reminds you of France but of some delightful village in the south of Poland. There are duck-ponds and small lakes. There are promenades beside the river, where in the broiling sunlight which appeared shortly after we arrived, girls were walking in light dresses and old men were sleeping in the shade of chestnut trees. Scattered over the red hills, the city branches out in all directions and seems to resemble nothing so much as a delightful spider's web. The centre of the web consists of four streets crowded with shops and beggars and wailing infants who walk about quite naked. Beggars followed us from the moment we left the railway station. They were harmless and said nothing, but continually stretched out their bony arms; and if we refused them, they would go away for a little while only to return a little later, chastened perhaps but still hopeful.

I shall remember Henyang for the dust and the green hills, and the Japanese aeroplanes which came over five minutes after we left for Kweilin. At first the driver had not heard that there were aeroplanes. The train went on, while the aeroplanes flew low over the town; but a little later we came to a siding, the train roared into silence, shuddered and stopped dead on its tracks, while we staggered out among the low green grave-mounds and wondered how we should return if the train was hit by a bomb. But the warmth was glorious. The sun shone on a small farm of bamboos, on the white-lettered graves and on the peasants who worked still in the fields, oblivious of the distant thunder of anti-aircraft guns.

77

S ring comes early in Henyang. The bright ploughshares flashed in the sun, the peasants called to one another, a small boy brought them porcelain cups containing food. An hour later we went on with the memory of a small grave-mound surrounded by fields so deeply impressed on our minds that we knew it would be many years before these things were forgotten.

Bergery looks puzzled. He gazes at the disappearing landscape and murmurs: "But what is so extraordinary is that for a moment I thought I was in England. I smelt the hay, and heard the cricketers on the fields——" He is still gazing out of the window, his brow furrowed, dreaming of another country on the other side of the earth. "It was like a dream—no, it was not like a dream. The sound of the ploughshares in the earth, a child calling, the old mare lumbering under the shade of the coppices, I must have seen something like that many years ago in England. I had forgotten it, and now this small corner of China will remain in my memory as long as I live."

Later . . . THE countryside turned grey and then blue, streaked with blackish lines, and then at last even the trees were immersed in the landscape. Then the mist rose and the moon, and the countryside turned white, as though veiled in transparent white cloth. And still the train throws out bright red sparks the size and shape and colour of oranges; and the tunnels roar; and the wheels click on the rails at the exact measure of our heartbeats.

We are living in the greatest comfort we have known since we reached China. The mattresses and all the bedclothes are new; the carriages have been recently painted; we walk down the corridors for the pure pleasure of walking on the green carpets. In the uncurtained windows our faces are blue, for a small blue light shines in the ceiling; and this blue light reminds Bergery of his travels in Europe. "There was a time when I hated it, when the thought of the long journeys at night would terrify me into taking an aeroplane or a steamer—to get from Havre to Rome, I would prefer to wait a week and take the steamer through the Straits of Gibraltar—and then again there were years when it seemed to be possible that the blue light was a friend, a kind spirit which never went out, burning continually." Occasionally the blue light flickered. Faintly through the darkness we could see the bamboo roofs of Chinese houses, but no lights shone and only the pale moonlight glowed high above the clouds.

This evening I finished the poem I began on the battlefield:

THE CHINESE SOLDIER SPEAKS OF DEATH

The grain is ripening in the seed.
We who have seen the cities fall
Take from our harvest all we need,
And leave on earth no death at all.
When all the birds are singing wild
And death lies caged within their tread,
To die is greenness for the child
And comfort for the lonely head.

Lest others climb the bitter tree
I drove my knife within the soil:
Killing the world's last enemy,
I ended all this human toil.
In shielding light or summer storm
The waving branches of the dead proclaim
Historic images reform
Into the style and semblance of my name.

This country nourished me and fed
Upon my wealth of blood and shame.
May others carve around my head
Heraldic emblems of my fame.
I was once proud to choose my fate.
The green earth takes me to its side.
The yellow wheat grows soon or late,
The yellow earth shall be my bride.

I have given it to Bergery. He reads it in the faint blue light, smiling gently and perhaps mercifully. For a long while he read it, reading it so many times that I lost patience and asked him why he was so capricious in returning it. At last he said: "There are two good lines which could only have been written on the battlefield," but he refuses to tell me which they are.

In the slow night, while the train moved across central China, her lights shining in small yellow squares on the interminable rows of bushes and spidery trees beside the railroad, a solitary green lamp swinging across the country suddenly became two lamps and once more became single.

"It is a farmer who has gone out to tend his buffaloes, and in going out he was forced to cross a stream."

Then for the first time I recognised that Bergery should never have left China.

January 13th . . . THERE was mist and rain when we came to Kweilin. There was mist and rain before, when we arrived from Chungking on our journey to Changsha, but this time the whole town has changed out of recognition. Ten days ago it was still a small provincial town in France, the broad streets lined with dusty plane trees, and even the houses and shops were so French that we expected to see French signboards hanging from iron chains. But the signboards are in Chinese, and there are few Frenchmen left in the city. Once Yunnan and Kwangsi were provinces within the French sphere of interest. There were French reading-rooms, and returned students from these provinces brought back with them some of the graces and many of the evil habits of France; and at meetings of the provincial pro-governments it was not unusual to hear French spoken across the council chambers. But they have all disappeared to a small lake in the north-east of the city, and there the French community awaits the end of the war, visited occasionally by the provincial Chamber of Commerce, the provincial police, and the old aristocrats who have found in Kweilin safety from the more eager prejudices of the Central Government.

Even in the rain, there is an atmosphere of leisurely progress in this city. The streets are broad and flat. There are no rocky hills to climb as in Chungking; and the people are calmer and hurry less often than their relatives in the capital. Here on the pavements you will see the most exquisite lace and silverware; four or five cinemas; so many good bookshops that we have lost count. Things are cheaper here than in Chungking. You can buy, for example, an enormous thermos flask, brightly painted and guaranteed to last little short of a lifetime, for seventy dollars. It would cost more than two hundred in Chungking. You can buy innumerable French books, innumerable translations of Chinese stories into English. Until the Pacific War broke out, there was continuous communication between Kweilin and Hongkong, but now the communication has broken and the old city, once the capital of

China, seems to be stupefied by the absence of contact with the south. It is not self-sufficient like Chungking. It has none of Chungking's overwhelming majesty. It is simple and a little childish, and perhaps a little afraid of itself, and its old history. And so, as you walk down the avenues of limes or plane-trees, or wander through the damp roads leading to the river, where for the first time you notice the poverty that has spread like a sore over China since the beginning of ages, the city no longer bewitches you; and the first enchantment passes as it passes always when, after meeting a pretty girl, you discover that she is interested only in the artifices of her beauty.

For Kweilin is beautiful, and she knows she is beautiful. For fifteen hundred years artists have travelled down the great trunk roads to paint those incredible cliffs. Standing by the bank of the green swirling river, you see the pointed limestone mountains like immense candles raised to heaven. There, in the grey afternoon, you gaze out at a fantastic landscape of cloud and slender grey pillars, like petrified trees, four or five hundred feet high, with a few trees growing on the summits. The earth is flat like a draught-board, and these mountains rise out of the earth like enormous chessmen, separated from one another by five or six hundred feet of intervening fields, so tall that their summits are sometimes buried in the clouds. I have seen these mountains in Chinese paintings, and did not believe that they could exist. But there they are; and in the shadow of the immense, towering cliffs black-sailed sampans move steadily down the green stream.

Later . . . THE airfield lies under the shadow of the great cliffs. There is a small shed, a weighing machine, innumerable red-painted barrels of petrol—and no aeroplane. We wait for an hour, surrounded by the impedimenta we have brought from the battlefield. Nearly everyone has a Japanese helmet; the lucky ones have Samurai swords; a bloodstained Japanese banner is draped over someone's luggage. And as the afternoon lengthens, and a cold wind comes from the direction of the river, we begin to wonder whether the aeroplane will ever arrive. At last it came, very suddenly, dropping out of the low clouds and almost touching the mountain.

It was an old Junkers aeroplane built for the South American service, so that all the inscriptions were in Spanish and German; but the young pilot, a fair-haired American, possessed an extraordinary affection for the old machine and spoke about it as though it were more than human. He was a little afraid of its lifting power, and there were long discussions before we were allowed to pile all our baggage in the wings; and then immediately we soared up into white cloud and looked down on the small straggling green-and-white city with its enormous white cliffs thinly veiled by floating bubbles of cloud.

Sunlight came through a gap in the clouds, and down below we could still see people farming small squared acres of green land, and the gaunt reflections of the cliffs in the shadowy waters. Our wings were almost brushing the pinnacles. We were flying above the cloud in a clear sunlight, in a frozen world of glass and white snow, and this perfectly white cloud, shining with the light of the sun and with some interior light, was spread out to infinity in every direction. The sky was a very deep blue, the sun a violent orange and the white cloud was whiter than anything I have seen, dazzlingly brilliant and unbelievable. The wireless operator was tapping on the Morse dial. We were flying by beam. Occasionally small feathers of cloud would wrap themselves round the wings, and sometimes we saw vast cliffs of clouds riding below, immense chasms in which the aeroplane might be swallowed up for ever. And so it went on—mile upon mile of dazzling white cloud, never changing, stretching from Kweilin to the south-westernest point of China.

Bergery slept, a Japanese helmet with its bronze star and the lips of a bullet wound on his knees. From time to time he turned a little, and seemed to be gazing out of the window with his eyes closed. The sun became smaller, and brighter, a great orange glow, which seemed to throw no light upon the incandescent clouds, which burned with their own flame.

It was dark when we came into Chungking. It was raining, and there were thick damp clouds over the moon. The small yellow spit of yellow sand in the Yangtse had turned black, and only a faint light came from the cliffs of the city. There were no chairbearers. In the rain, without lights, stumbling blindly and carrying our luggage, we walked up the stone steps which wind along the cliff-side. The city was plunged in darkness—only a few yellow candles glowing.

January 14th . . . BERGERY is ill. He caught a cold when we left the warm aeroplane and walked through the streaming cold rain. There were no ricksha drivers; the road to the ferry from the airport was long and steep, and the rain came uninterruptedly out of a dead black sky. He looked like the ghost of a bear in his fur coat, and his lips curled with a kind of sickening grief whenever he looked down at the battered Japanese helmet. "The rain, the helmet——" I do not know what connection he saw between the two things, but he was almost delirious and he kept talking about the South Seas as we crossed the ferry. The lights were watery on the coast and he stood for a long time gazing at them, with the fur cap he had bought at Hsiang-tang perched precariously on his head. But when we reached the south bank, and the small bamboo twists were handed to us by small boys drenched to the skin, he nearly fainted, and I half carried him up the stone steps.

Today he is better, but he is coughing. He is forty-seven. He has lived at least eighteen lives, and he talks a little about the prospect of death. And what is worse—far worse—is that he is continually talking about the past, his life at Heidelberg and Cape Ann and Paris, the villa in France, Florence, the Himalayas and the Andes. He talks mostly about mountains. He insists on having the Japanese helmet and the bloodstained Japanese flag near the bed. And this evening the lights went out again on the south bank, though they glittered brilliantly in the rain on the north bank. He still looks like a bear. "In five days I shall be up again —it always takes five days to get over these spells." Afterwards, while I read to him by the bedside, I wondered what he meant by spells.

January 15th . . . HE IS no better. The cough, in fact, has become worse. A telephone message this morning said that the films taken in Changsha were being developed, and in a few days we would be invited to see the war-correspondents on donkeys charging across the green plains of Changsha. For some reason this angered him. At first he pretended not to have heard. Afterwards he burst out in furious denunciations. "Why do they take these stupid films? We were correspondents—we were nothing. They should take films of the Chinese soldiers fighting, while the water-mill silently revolves, and the hard frost shines on the ground." More than once he referred to the extraordinary beauty of the dead white bodies in the green grass. "The frost preserves, the heat kills."

But in the evening he took supper. As the sun set, throwing a red glow over low clouds, Chungking resembled a nest of burnt-out shells on the high rocks, and when at last the sun set, the rock retained its light, as the clouds from Kweilin retained their light, and Chungking stood out proudly on her soaring rock-ledge; and it seemed then, among these crowns of clouds, as visionary a city as Toledo.

He is still unwell. Sweat streams down his high forehead and over his cheek-bones; he coughs a little, and sometimes, like a visionary speaking in riddles, he proclaims curious ideas about the war:

"This is what the politicians forget—the dead will arise, they always arise. They will arise to take terrible vengeance if we refuse to make a sincere peace after the war. The dead will arise in our own blood, their voice is unmistakable, the dead of each country and kingdom speaking in the voice it has inherited from the past."

And again:

"I have been dreaming of the dead soldier lying on the bank of the Liuyang river. He was handsome, perhaps more handsome in death than in life; and in death he was smiling. I could not imagine how he was killed, for there were no signs of wounds. Yes, he was brave—there was no doubt that he was brave, for of all the Japanese soldiers in that part of the field he was the nearest to the place where the Chinese were fighting. One must reconstruct the battlefield, do you understand? Everything there has meaning, and it necessary that we should understand the battlefield, and the tragedy of the battlefield, in order that we should prevent war. This is the task of my generation and yours—to reconstruct. And that is why the Chinese above other races are so right when they talk of Reconstruction and of *Hsin Min*—the new people. Everything must be changed and everything must be new."

And once more:

"The water-wheel continued to turn during the battle; the blackbirds and magpies continued to sing; the dogs continued to run about in the fields. In battle, when you are fighting, everything seems to have changed, the earth is a different colour and I do not know why it is but the sky seems to be nearer, and every blade of grass and ripple of the water is more clearly seen. These are the common experiences of all battlefields, but only the Chinese philosophers of the fourth century have understood the relation between the unchanging background and the changing forms of life as they appear to our eyes. Study the relation between the man and the mountains in a Chinese painting. What do you see? The man is not dwarfed by the immense hills; he is not dwarfed by the dragons coiling in the thunderstorm—he is in another world, separate and apart. To the Chinese the water-wheel is real and abiding, and men themselves have no part in its revolutions. No Chinese can understand the idea of a hidden God—it is men themselves who are hidden in their dreams, and you find them only with the greatest difficulty, hidden in some secluded pastureland, rowing on a winter lake, lost in the immense and terrible silences of the visible world. But then—the white frosted youths in the green grass, and the water-wheel . . ."

And finally, when it was very late and the book of Chinese philosophy had slipped from his hand:

"Descartes said: 'I think, therefore I am.' The Chinese are perhaps more correct in saying: 'The mountain thinks, and therefore I am born.' Did you notice how in the afternoon, when we returned from Changsha, riding in single file along the edge of the river, the landscape absorbed us? We were a part of the landscape, and perhaps the landscape had no desire to let us free of her embrace, and perhaps the earth loves us, and we fear her for her love. When we are dead we are buried in the earth, and our greatest happiness in the West is to soar high above the earth and to leave her. But the Chinese understand that the earth must be loved in return. This is the commandment . . ."

I do not know how long he kept talking about Chinese philosophy. It consoled him to think of the great priest kings of the past, King Wen and the Duke of Chou, of whom Confucius said that no one else inspired so great a love. Chu Yuan, the poet, who wandered hither and thither over the mountains and rivers of Hunan, belonged to the same order of kings from whom he was prepared to take advice, and he quoted many of those extraordinary poems, half passionate, half wise, in which Chu Yuan announced his extraordinary mythology. It seemed, then, that the room grew full of dragons and spirits, and the Ladies of Hsiang, and the various gods of the river, walked untrammelled through the small bedroom.

There are not many things one can do in company with an impatient invalid. He slept a little, while I read carefully and slowly,

85

looking up nearly each word in the great blue-covered dictionary, the words of the great Chinese philosopher Chuan-tzu. They were strange words, and the artifices of metaphor were still stranger, but they possessed an almost insane power of conviction. The Taoists, in the beginnings of their religion, reduced everything, it seemed, to pure form; and they were triumphantly successful in convincing themselves that they had found the answer to the universe. And what was so terrifying, while the Yangtse poured ceaselessly between its rocky banks and a small moon quivered in the grey murk of sky, was that every phrase resembled a window opening on an intensity of daylight until, as phrase succeeded phrase, the illumination became blinding, as sometimes one is blinded by lightning. There was a passage towards the end of the book which Bergery had underlined carefully in red ink. When someone asked Chuan-tzu how he desired to be buried, he answered—"With Heaven and Earth for my coffin and shell; with the sun, moon and stars as my burial regalia; and with all creation to escort me to the grave, what more do I need for my funeral regalia?" But already, on the small bed, the patient was awakening into life again. He looked better and the colour was flooding his cheeks.

January 16th . . . THE river is still high, a great turbulent white sheet flowing under a thick mist. It is impossible to see the sky or the clouds, and in this whiteness everything dissolves in patches of mist. This morning, as we crossed the river in the motor-boat, we saw a small sampan gliding past us, caught up in the current, and three or four small brown figures cowering at the bottom of the boat. There was no expression on their faces; they looked neither backwards nor forwards. As sometimes happens in a dream, when the figures suddenly lose colour and great black spiders' webs begin to dissolve the picture, I had the impression that at any moment a black hand would descend from the clouds and carry them away. Our small motor-boat chugged in circles. There was the occasional sound of rocks grating against the iron bottom of the boat; and in the mist the small yellowish-grey sampan was still gliding past us, so slowly that I felt certain that this was a dream. When the sampan was about to disappear from our field of vision, it suddenly stopped and began to sway backwards and forwards, caught against the rocks, swinging like scissors, until suddenly the roar of the river came to our ears and at that
86

moment the sampan broke in two, spilling the occupants into the white river. For two or three seconds—certainly not more than five seconds—we watched three or four small black heads bobbing up and down against the smooth rock; then they disappeared, following the boat which was already disappearing downstream.

I am told that this happens always in time of floods. The rocks are treacherous, and the current so deceptive that the most skilled boatmen have been known to lose their lives in the Yangtse. The river is quite merciless; and though in some places rocks have been dynamited, and though the masts of sampans can be seen protruding above the river at all seasons, every year the river claims its victims. I am beginning to believe that the Yangtse is a living and breathing thing, a smooth turbulent dragon who never relinquishes her claim on the lives of the Chinese who live on her banks. This morning, after we had watched the sampan breaking in two, we were lost in midstream. The mist was as thick as a waterfall. Somewhere a boy was beating a drum on the high rocks, and we heard the continual hooting of motor-cars high up on the rocky cliffs of Chungking. We were continually turning in circles, and once we hit a rock with such a sickening crash of plates that we instinctively made ready to dive overboard; but if we had dived, we would have lived for ten seconds—no more. It was half an hour before we reached the other side of the river, we were drenched with mist and our cigarettes wouldn't light— they were so wet. And as we began to climb the immense reach of steps which leads to the Dragon Gate of Chungking, I looked back and watched the river through a break in the clouds. The river was white and full, swirling along, hurrying, talking to itself, in absorbed intent tones. And the suspicion that it was a dragon, a real dragon, with scales and fins and great golden eyes, with an immense lashing tail and huge hairy arms, with which it could climb on the shore and engulf everything within sight, became so overpowering that I began to understand why at times of high flood there are more suicides in the river than at any other time.

But at night the river is beautiful beyond words. The little black paddle-steamer, with its ghostly oil-lamps, lies reflected in the torrent. Armies of cloud march in rank across the sky, obscuring the mountains with their ragged banners, and through the mist you can see the faint silver lights shining on the south bank and the great red puffs of smoke coming from the bamboo flares on the landing-stage. Sometimes it may take an hour to cross the river, even in the paddle-boat. But once you have arrived on the rocky shore of the south bank, small boys run forward with plaited yellow bamboo flares, and the smoky red flares shining on the granite steps and on the faces of the passengers are so vivid and so consoling that you forget the tedium of the journey and the loneliness in mid-river, when the paddle-boat mills round in a whirlpool or fights against the sheer weight of the current.

January 17th . . . THE city is still covered with mist, but a faint yellow sun pierced the clouds this afternoon. I have never been so overjoyed at seeing the sunlight. There was something in the air of Chungking, something beyond analysis, a tremor in the air, a quickening of the roots, which told us that the sun would appear perhaps for no more than a moment or two, but during that moment we would be bathed in its faint glory. On days when the sun does not appear the streets seem to be full of cripples, people with one eye, people without noses, and people with sores. But even on the most terrible days, when a grey ghostly fog settles on the city and the mud-walls exude moisture like pus, the knowledge that the sun will appear sends everyone out of their houses in their gayest costumes. This afternoon, walking through the canyons of high buildings near the banking quarter, I saw three children marching in procession. They wore red silk clothes and carried wooden swords painted silver. Their faces were painted; even the little boy had a great splash of red paint on his cheeks. And so they marched quietly down the street towards the dragon-river, keeping step, singing some tune or other, stepping with jaunty steps through the grey blanket of fog which engulfed them, it was as though an army with banners had taken the white city captive and made us all their liege-men.

It is at night that the city wakes into life. The electric lamps in the street are fainter than the stars in Malaya, but the roads are so wet that the light seems to come, not from the electric-light standard, but from the million puddles in the street. We have been in search of Rewi Alley. We found him at last in a small bedroom in the north-east of the city, one of those barren rooms which you reach across interminable rabbit-warren court-yards. There was the usual low Chinese bed, the usual distempered wall, the usual bare naked lamp throwing down a faint whiteness on the unpolished wooden floor. Rewi Alley looks extraordinarily like T. E. Lawrence, deeply sunburnt, stocky, with

88

immense brown hands, a continual amused expression on his lips. He is short and powerful round the shoulders, with the build of a wrestler.

"I'm going back to the north-west as soon as the papers come through," he said, shivering at the thought of the cold weather which lay before him. "It's so cold in Sian in winter that if you spit at somebody, you can kill him with your spittle—it turns to ice."

We went out into the cold streets, where the shadows revolved on the high walls. Chungking at night is eerie with invisible ghosts, whose pattern of behaviour is to darken all exits. Shadows climb out of gutters, stretch black and silver arms from half-open windows. They breed shadows, and you feel as you walk down the deserted streets that they are palpable and malevolent, and covered with sticky gum-like spiders' webs.

He began to talk of the north-west, the million blankets which had been ordered by the Chinese Army, the extraordinary sense of co-operation among the peasants. Into the dark night he brought an unsuspected glow of sunlight and physical strength.

"We invented the co-operatives, but the Chinese peasants have made them their own. I've never come across people so willing to work at a trade. They are in love with their tools—they make them with a kind of instinctive love and understanding. Give a Chinese boy the roof of a motor-car, and he will make a lathe. Give him a lathe, and he will not stop until he has made a factory. The million blankets are ready three months before they are due. We started the second million a week ago. But if the Burma Road closes, and we have no petrol, how are we going to transport them?" He told us about some of the methods of transport which were now being used. "Drums of oil are floated down rivers in Kansu on inflated pigs' skins. Whole armies of coolies are being employed to carry drills to the northern oil-fields. These are people living in the Stone Age who carry on their shoulders the whole weight of modern transport.

"Don't forget that this is the fourth year of the war, and they are undernourished and weary beyond endurance. In the old days disease would have swept them away, but they seem to live longer now—perhaps because they have something to fight for. This is a popular war. You realise that the nearer you get to the front line. Hatred for the Japanese has bitten deep in their souls." He spoke of farmers who would plough their lands by day and make blankets on their looms at night. He was full of a fierce kind of admiration for the people in the north, and it is clear that they love him. He has T. E. Lawrence's trick of being abstracted from the scene, while remaining at the centre around which everything revolved. In the dark streets, clinging to the walls, he hurled defiance at the dark shadows.

January 18th . . . A DARK day, no sun. The news from Malaya bad. I have given a lecture on the strategical situation in Malaya—the main lines of communication are in our hands, Singapore an impregnable fortress, etc. A week ago I would have been sure we could hold out, but if the main pipe-line from Johore is cut, I shall know it is the end.

This evening Rewi Alley came. He was furious about something and looked magnificent in his wrath—a sunburnt Achilles brooding in his tent. But in a few days he will leave for the north, taking his tent with him. He told us that his salary is only $600 a month; with the depleted rate of exchange this cannot carry him far. He doesn't worry. "In New Zealand I have lived on less." I imagined him staying on desolate farmsteads, sleeping on straw mattresses among the rats, weaving out of three cigarette tins and four lengths of copper wire a loom which could be worked by electricity. He laughed. "We are making things out of nothing —really out of nothing." As I watched him going down the steps, remembering the rats of Lanchow and the desolate winter plains, it was as though a young god were disappearing into the mist.

January 19th . . . THE clouds low, the day grey and the rocks along the road were spitting out dew. I have never known a day which so much resembled the end of the world. Sometimes the smoky mist cleared over the Chialing river, and you saw far down a glassy pool of bluish-green light with a sampan riding at anchor. Fog-horns, boys beating drums on high rocks, the soft slurring sound of the river and the distant roar of motor-cars high up on the rock behind us. Ragnarok—the end of the world.

But the mist cleared later in the morning, and though the sky was low, colours began to appear again—a girl's red dress, the green uniform of the postmen, black street-lamps, a few yellow leaves. The road winds along at the base of immense sandstone and granite mountains with tombstones decorating the slopes and no forests in sight. The young Chinese who accompanied us explained that the Chinese refused to allow their dead to be buried in the cities, and every city is surrounded with tombstones. "If you are on your way to a city, you know at once that the city is near when you see the dead." His sepulchral voice was perfectly calculated to disarm us. The motor-car splashed through the mud, throwing up great black bow-waves and leaving a black wake, like avenging angels, flying through the air.

National Central University is about twenty miles north of Chungking. It has been savagely bombed, and some of the students and professors have been killed. Among grey open fields, among cedars and yews, the young students lived in small plaster-and-mortar houses, but the grey choking clouds drifting close to the earth made them looked more worried and less carefree than they were. The boys wore Sun Yat-sen uniforms and the girls wore blue gowns. Not all of them looked well-fed, and many were pale with weariness; but what was most surprising was their long swinging strides as they walked under the avenues of trees.

Most of the classrooms are small underheated plaster rooms— a blackboard, rows of chairs, nothing else. I imagine the students in Russia in the sixties resembled the students here. They are the elite of the country, the chosen vehicles of the future greatness of China; and therefore they work like trojans, throwing their whole lives into their work. Their eyesight is bad. At night they work by the light of rape-seed oil-lamps; during the day they work by the light of a weak sun. The impression of terrible responsibility and a perfect acceptance of that responsibility is unalterable; and I have never felt before how greatly I have underestimated the power of reconstruction in China. Those students, some of them so obviously suffering from tuberculosis, belong to a generation which has lived and starved through the war-years, and they are determined that the future generation shall not live and starve as they did.

I met a girl student on the campus and spoke to her. She was thin, with a greyness in her skin which spoke of arduous study and perhaps of tuberculosis. Her eyes, very dark, were old, and yet her face was young. She spoke in almost perfect English. She had been a guerrilla in Manchuria. She had been wounded. She came down to Chungking, and then feeling that the war was not being waged in the capital as it should be waged, she returned to the north. It was only when she was wounded for the second time that she decided to return. She was studying physical chemistry, and hoped one day to be in charge of a factory—it didn't matter what kind of factory as long as it was productive and useful for the country.

"We are all working in China. This is all that we think about. There are students here who believe in communism and others who believe in the party, but we have no time for arguing. We carry on because we believe that above communism or above the party there is always China."

She spoke about her adventures.

"I was sad when I came down. There were so many rich people, and besides I was friendless. When we were fighting, we knew everyone. If we wanted money or arms or bandages, we always found them; but it was more difficult in the capital. I met the Generalissimo. He is so great that I wept for three days because of the terrible tasks which face him. And then too he is very handsome and looks very young. But the terrible tasks! No one else in China has so great a responsibility. I believe in him and pray for him, but not everyone in China is like him . . . You know I was wounded. We have no hospitals in the north, but hospitals are not necessary. I stayed for three months in Japanese-occupied territory, and though the Japanese passed every day they never found me."

"What do you want to do when the war is over?"

"I shall go back to the north and start a factory in Manchuria. The earth is so rich there—and then I shall marry and have children."

I spent some time in the hydrology department. On the walls there were maps of the Yellow River, the scourge of China; and I was not surprised that most of the students came from the north. There was a young Dutch professor of hydraulics, who spoke about the lives of the students with more hero-worship than I have seen in the eyes of a professor before.

"They live on nothing and they work like madmen," he said. "I gave them an examination a little while ago. One of my best students fainted during the examination. I found that he had been studying for sixty-four hours without stopping, without having any food. He finished the paper—the whole paper—in about half an hour, and then he fainted. This is the kind of thing we are faced with—students who continually sacrifice their health for the sake of knowledge. And yet what use will be their knowledge if they are dead before they practise it?" He was filled with fear

92

for the students. Their food was bad; almost all of them were penniless. There were a few rich Szechuan students, sons of landed proprietors, but the entrance examination was unusually difficult and only the best students were capable of passing. It was the second best University in China, the best being the Associated Universities in Kunming. He had visited the Associated Universities and wondered why they were less famous abroad.

"A student will think nothing of travelling from Pekin to Chungking or Kunming. He knows that the best professors are here, and that the blue-prints for the future of China are being made in the Universities. Our professors could obtain well-paid appointments in the Government or in private industries, but they too know that the future of China lies in their hands. Two-thirds of the students here are taking science subjects, and the Minister of Education, Dr. Chen Li-fu, is even attempting to make it difficult for students to study the humanities. We have enough natural humanists in China, but we haven't enough scientists. There were more trained hydraulic engineers in China three thousand years ago than there are today. That's why they are working so desperately hard—to catch up with lost time."

The professors' dormitory was dark and damp. A long low building, with a corridor leading off into small shuttered bedrooms, each with its pallet bed and little else. Sometimes whole families lived in these small rooms, where the rain crept through the broken tiles and the paper windows fluttered like flags in the chill wind. It was cold. A mist rose over the Yangtse, and it was impossible to see the river from the steep cliffs. And here they worked and lived and sometimes died, not fearing for the future, quietly making plans for a renovated China, dreaming of the sun among the winter mists, planning steadily and with forethought for the day when the war should be over.

"But they are so tired, you understand," the Dutch professor told me. "They are weary after four years of war. They have been bombed, and will be bombed again—National Central University has seen whole buildings go up in flames. I know the Minister of Education. He is doing everything he can for them, but even so prices are rising, the rice is not always good rice and the birth of a new child may mean ruin to many of them."

He took me to the library. It was getting late, and the students were already reading by the light of rape-seed oil-lamps, each student with his own green lamp. The students looked cold, but they were rapt in their books. They looked hungry, but the books carried them into a strange land—a land where everything was rigorous, scientific and perfectly proportioned to its appointed end. All round the small low building books were crowded; there were books in Chinese, German, French, English—in every known language. And as I walked round, listening to the hum of whispered breathing, the faces of the young students golden in the light, everyone quiet and intent upon the book before him, it seemed that the whole building was a hive of seething activity. In those young minds a new China was being made.

And then home, in the darkness, the black cliffs shining in the headlamps. The car was crowded with students who wanted to spend the week-end in Chungking. All the while they sang and talked, so charming in their youth and the bright audacity of their conversation that I realised at last why Bergery spoke so often about the young in China. "They will build in faith." "But what if their faith misleads them?" "It doesn't matter—they are the toughest creatures in the world." But in the dark motor-car, winding along the rocky road which leads to Chungking, it was difficult to think of them as tough—they were like the young everywhere, who live neither in the past nor the present but in the refreshing river of the future.

January 20th . . . I HAVE been to see an official of the Ministry of Education. Like many other officials I have met in China, he looks extraordinarily young and has the manner of a boy, yet he is over forty. (Bergery said: "Add ten years to the age of any Chinese you meet, and then you will probably be right.") He wore the customary blue Chinese gown, patched and darned, with holes at the elbows. There were thick lenses in his glasses. I asked him what he thought of the future of education.

"It is not a fair question, for I should answer that it has never been brighter. At last we are dealing with education with every ounce of strength. You must understand that in the days of peace, every University could go its own way; but now every University follows the pattern set by the government. You may think this is dangerous, but on the whole the dangers are offset by the advantages. In the old days the Universities carried on according to their own lights, but today the common experience is pooled. There is a great hunger sweeping over China—a hunger for education, and there are not enough scholars and too many students

—not enough equipment and too few books. We carry on, and the future has never been brighter. but the present is a time of experiment."

He was head of a department in the Ministry of Education—a department which was struggling with inflated prices and the knowledge that at any moment the last egress from China might be closed.

I told him that shortly before the war a friend in Singapore had flown to China and arranged with the Commercial Press to send a million copies of Chinese text-books to the colony. He knew my friend and spoke feelingly of the Chinese in foreign countries who still looked to the motherland for education.

"If only we could pay our scholars better," he murmured. "You see, we are a country of scholars—and they have always starved. Yet they are the acknowledged leaders of the country. When the guerrilla wars broke out, it was the Chinese professors who were asked to lead the recruits, and sometimes a Chinese professor of philology would be asked to conduct a siege or an attack against a Japanese railway line. It didn't matter whether he knew anything about military matters—he was a scholar, and he was expected to know everything. Professor Wen Chien-kung led the guerrillas in Shansi. Professor Chang Yu-kuang led the guerrillas in Shantung. Professor Yuan Mo-han led the guerrillas in Chahar. And so in all the other provinces where the guerrillas are fighting—the professors are elected to the places of honour and the greatest danger. Of course it is a tradition in China that the professors should be called upon at any moment to conduct military operations, but today we can no longer afford to let them disappear from the schools."

He was gaily optimistic about the fighting in Burma. It was unthinkable to him that China should be cut off from the outside world.

"And if we should be cut off?"

"We shall continue in the old way—we are theoreticians of the moment, and we dare not think more than a few hours ahead."

He spoke of the long journeys of the Chinese students across the interior. Sometimes, caught in a Japanese nest, they had to fight their way out; and usually they were unarmed. The students in Wuhan University at Hankow walked to Kiating in Szechuan in 1938. About a hundred perished on the journey. They were bombed and machine-gunned; they lost the greater part of their scientific equipment but managed to preserve their library almost intact. They lived in a temple, where the golden gods still shone down from the altars; they were not well-fed . . .

And so, through all this tragic exodus of the Chinese race, through danger and ill-health, without medical equipment, often starving, the students came to the south-west. The young official smiled—the gentle deprecating smile of the cultivated Chinese.

"It was worse in the Sung dynasty, and it was still worse when Confucius was living."

January 23rd . . . I AM surprised when people tell me that Chungking is not beautiful. Even if this viscous grey mist lasted throughout the year, I would still be happy here. "But wait a few more days," they tell me. "Wait until the thought of green fields in spring becomes like a nightmare. In the old days the Chinese loved the mist and the rain, and they would journey from one of the old capitals—Loyang or Sianfu—just to experience the pleasure of walking through the mist and seeing suddenly, high above them, a high crag mossy with evergreens. But not now—the poetry has gone, and we curse the mist and the rain and the muddy streets as we curse the Japanese."

I am beginning to wonder. At first I hated it; and it is true that walking in the evening down the long winding road which leads from the Press Hostel to the centre of the town, while motor-cars swirled past in the blue mist and the red lamps shone in the valley below, I began to feel so weary of the undifferentiated greyness that I almost wept. The smell of wood-oil, the poverty of the beggars, the enormous black motor-cars, the swarms of people moving like one person, the riches strewn in all the brightly-lit windows and the poverty cowering in the moist alley-ways—all these became wearisome beyond endurance. And then suddenly and unexpectedly a child in a blue cotton frock would pass slowly down the street carrying on her back a child who was hardly an inch smaller; and the quick gravity of the child and her perfectly shaped features made life tolerable again. China is rich, too rich in her children, and yet there is hardly a child who is not graceful and even beautiful. I have seen in Europe—in the ghettos of Cracow, for example—many deformed children, and there are many deformed children in China; but I have never seen a country where the children are so full of vitality. I have seen children, especially the children of rich parents, who looked as though they were dead to the world, without life, the sap no longer flowing through them. But here, even when they are quite silent, their faces are filled with the most intense expressions of amusement, enjoyment or melancholy. "This is because we are so primitive," said R. "Our children are in the Stone Age still." And a little while later, he added: "The parents pay no heed to them unless they want them as labourers. They are left to their own resources, the parents go to work and the other children would starve if the elder children did not tend them. And so they learn early, too early, to fend for themselves. Have you noticed that all our children have the expressions of middle-aged persons?" It was not true. The children had the expressions of children, delighting in their childhood, though it is harder than any childhood anywhere else on the earth.

On the way to the British Embassy, there is a wasteland, where the buildings have been torn down by bombs, a long stretch of yellow mud littered with rubble. According to R. this place was the headquarters of a gang of child-robbers and cut-throats. He was extraordinarily bitter about them. "They will do anything for money—they will rob, steal, pilfer, murder." We went there once late at night. Hidden in the remains of a house, the children were playing; and it was true that they were members of a secret society, and perhaps it was true that they robbed a little. They were orphans, and yet for some reason they had no desire to enter an orphanage. Instead, they formed a society and clubbed together. Whatever they earned was placed in a common pool and once a month they gave themselves up to an evening of leisure. They danced, they made incredibly long speeches, they played cards, smoked cigarettes and read the newspapers aloud. One child, perhaps he was eight years old, was making an impossibly serious speech when we arrived—an interminable political speech, calling upon them to sacrifice themselves for the country, to devote their lives to the reconstruction of China and many other laudable objects. He was desperately serious and even pompous; and he would never have ceased speaking if the student had not begun to put questions to him. He answered them all with becoming gravity. He was obviously the star-turn, and the other children were a little in awe of him. The candles guttered out. New candles were brought. In the light of the candles the children's faces glowed redly, almost unbearably beautiful. A girl in a bright-red dress was calmly feeding a baby with oranges,

97

stuffing them in the small mouth and throwing the peel over her shoulder. And sometimes, when she thought we were not looking, she would take a bite from one of the oranges and eat it swiftly; and then, noticing that we were watching her, she would blush in confusion. The speeches continued. In our honour the children decided to order a bottle of white wine. They did this quite secretly, without telling us, and I am convinced that they made the decision by means of signals which neither of us observed. They poured out the wine in small white porcelain thimble-cups which miraculously appeared; and in return for their hospitality, the young student and I were called upon to make speeches.

"How long should I make a speech?" R. asked.

"About half an hour," they answered, "and your friend because he is a foreigner should make one for an hour."

And so they listened, quietly and gravely, while R. exhorted them to serve their country, obey the Three Principles, to help the weak and never pilfer. It was a strange series of commandments, but they cheered ecstatically; and in the corner the babies slept, and the girl in the red print dress still blushed in confusion whenever she saw us watching her. She was beautiful, with enormous black eyes and a long oval face—a child madonna.

"What is so curious is that the most terrible stories are told about them," R. said, when we returned. "There is a story that much of the opium smuggling is done by the children, and that they have even killed other children and opened their stomachs and filled the stomachs with opium and arranged immense funeral processions, and the opium has been taken across the river." It cannot be true. All night I was haunted by the dark eyes of the child in a red print frock as Confucius was haunted by the Duke of Chou. There is so much goodness in these waifs of Chungking that I begin to believe again, as I used to believe many years ago, that it would be better if the world were given over to children, and anyone reaching the age of twelve should be painlessly executed. To watch the children of Chungking is an education in expediency and beauty. They live with terrible intensity; at night they lie in small heaps in doorways or underneath the great piles of timber near the river; and yet they do not live for themselves but for each other. And that curious mixture of maturity and childishness in their faces is so beautiful that it sometimes becomes unbearable. At night, in the shadows, sleeping in the cold mist, shivering in their brilliantly coloured rags, they dream of the sun.

January 24th . . . THIS evening, I am looking down at the lights in a valley from a house near the Soviet Embassy high on the hills overlooking the Yangtse river. In the mist the electric lights have a white opacity. There are thousands of lights stringing like a necklace over the valley, and you can almost discern the shape of the land by the curvature of the necklace. Occasionally a motor-car winds through the valley, or a man walks with lanthorn in hand through the muddy alley-ways. You follow the lights like someone bewitched, so splendid they are in their violence or disorder. King Alfonsus of Aragon besought God to set order among the stars, but there is order enough in this lack of order. We have amused ourselves by giving names to these stars in the valley. There is the Dragon, the Serpent, Hi Ho the Lord of the Sky, Prince I who shot the sun with his arrow, and there in the corner, where the lights are faintest, there is the greatest of all constellations, spreading out rays of white fire, almost perfectly symmetrical, the Constellation of the White Horses of Chungking. There are two horses, facing in different directions, and they are so clearly imprinted against the dark valley that they seem to be alive; and in a moment, or even less, they will start racing across the valley.

The conversation turned to horses. I told them that in my childhood, in the south of France, I saw an enormous white horse higher than a house and yoked to an immense chariot rumbling through the corn-fields. It seemed to move with terrible slowness, and yet with a kind of fixity of movement and determination which was terrifying. The horse seemed indeed to be straining against invisible obstacles—and yet, what impressed me even more than the horse was the shape of the chariot, the two tremendous rayed wheels and the curved flare of the chariot. There was no charioteer, and I have forgotten whether there were any reins. Years later, I saw in a cameo the identical horse and the identical chariot described as the caravan of Mithra; and believed from that time that some ancestral memory from my forefathers in Provence had led me to dream of the celebrations of the sun.

Bergery told a story of a horse he had seen in the Polish-Russian wars at the end of the first great war. Warsaw was deserted. The women had been compelled to retreat towards Germany; the

99

soldiers were advancing to the north. Aud suddenly as he drove through the deserted city, a wild horse, perfectly white, with foam dripping from its mouth, plunged out of a side-street. He had no idea in which direction the Polish army could be found, and a sudden inspiration led him to follow the riderless horse into the fields north of the city. He followed it, and reached the Polish army headquarters in half an hour.

But the best story of white horses was told by T. He had been living in a small temple at Hangchow. Previously he had been living in a small temple in Japanese-occupied territory. There was a price on his head; he had entered the monastery to avoid capture by the Japanese, and there, disguised in his grey robe, tonsured, the nine bluish-red pastilles burnt into his bare yellow skull, he had prayed and meditated cross-legged in a deserted alcove. No one paid attention to him. The monks occasionally spoke to him, but they knew that he was a soldier in disguise and for some reason suspected him of playing on their sympathies. They knew that he killed men, many men, during the wars. He had studied philosophy in Pekin, and one evening, exhausted by his meditations on Buddha, he began to meditate on the famous logical apothegm of Kung Sung-lung, who attempted to prove that a white horse is not a horse. T. meditated quietly. There were moments when he thought he had achieved a solution to the problem. There were other moments when the solution failed him. After twelve or thirteen hours of meditation, a white horse suddenly appeared to him, whether in dreams or in reality he could not say. It was a horse with peculiar marking, like the markings in jade, on its face, a face which was somewhat stylised, like the faces of knights on the chess-board. And whenever he meditated on the problem, the horse appeared, sometimes galloping against perfectly blue fields, sometimes walking sedately in some imperial procession, sometimes quietly galloping down a grey dusty road. When at last he escaped from Japanese-occupied territory, he went to recuperate in another monastery near Hangchow. One evening, as he was walking in the grounds of the monastery, a solitary riderless horse flew past him. It was obvious that the horse was quite mad. It was bucking and struggling. People were shouting outside the monastery wall. A group of monks, fanning themselves gently in the garden, were surprised out of their wits by the horse, which suddenly broke in among them, knocking them over like ninepins, stamping and raging, and snorting

100

wildly, while drips of yellow foam like washleather poured from between its teeth. T. knew the horse was mad. He threw himself at it, caught the bridle and was surprised to see it grow suddenly still. He walked it round the gardens. It was quite tame, and he said he could have made it do anything at that moment. Some villagers came through the monastery gates. The horse had killed some children in the village street; it possessed, they said, a perfect mania for destruction and deliberately trampled down everybody within sight. It was at that moment that T. noticed that the horse he was leading round the garden resembled in every respect the horse he had seen in his meditations.

"What happened to the white horse—was it killed?"

"No. It took me a long time to convince them that it was not dangerous. You know that the Buddhists refuse to kill living things. They begged that the horse should be allowed to remain in the monastery. But three weeks later it died, quite suddenly, in the courtyard, at the spot where some days previously it became quiet in my hands. I do not believe in the transmigration of souls, but I find it difficult not to think that the horse had not been human, and I began to imagine the whole life of the horse—I could imagine almost every detail, and sometimes even now I wake in the middle of the night and think about it, staring into the darkness until it seems to ride out of the night and feed from my hands."

But the end of this story is even more curious than the beginning. When T. had finished speaking, and the cakes were being handed round, we suddenly looked up to the wall. There, mounted on a bright yellow-embroidered scroll, there was a painting of the Yuan dynasty showing a perfectly white horse with red nostrils and a great sweeping blue tail cavorting in a field of coloured flowers. The painting was painted with the precision of a master, every curve of those rich and powerful flanks, every detail of the finely-drawn but prominent eyeballs, every line of the mouth and the splendid forehead so perfect that we were hushed into amazement; but what was still more extraordinary was that each of us recognised in the horse painted five hundred years ago the horse we had seen in our waking dreams.

January 26th . . . THE white dawn. The wind blew the clouds away, and at the moment when I looked through the window the sun was rising. Everything was white, a pure incandescent white such as I have never seen before. I imagine this whiteness may be visible in a Russian winter, when the snow lies thick on the earth and the trees are covered with rime; but this was a whiteness like milk, white and blinding. The river, the great block of the Y.M.C.A. building which towers over Chungking seen from the south bank, the tower of the Roman Catholic cathedral, the river and the sampans—all were white. Bergery saw it and talked about the thick mist, but though the mist was there and seemed indeed to be as thick as it has ever been, we saw the north bank clearly all covered in this rich whiteness, as though dipped in white paint. A few minutes later the clouds covered the sun, and slowly the light faded from the city. And for the rest of the day we have lived in a dreary darkness, through which the pale yellow headlamps of motor-cars peer fitfully. In Chungking al is mist and greyness unrelieved. And the river is a heavy pool in which darkness gathers in streams like thick grey hair.

I imagine a small village, perhaps a village in the north of Russia near the Arctic circle, where the sun never appears. But once, thousands of years ago, a forester, coming out of his forest after trapping hares, saw a rift in the clouds and was almost blinded by the spectacle of the burning sun. He turned to the village deep in thought, his mind filled with the vision. No one believed him, yet the vision was recorded in the histories of the place. They speak of this vision still with bated breath—a golden sun against a blue sky framed in white clouds.

This evening, as we returned from the north bank, Bergery said: "This cloud stretches half-way to Kunming. There must be a village somewhere in Kweichow where half the sky is covered with thick clouds and the other half is covered with sunlight. There, like a terrible line drawn across the sky, lies the limit of the clouds, a thick grey line like a rope which the people worship. I would like to see this village—the village where the sky ends."

I have made enquiries. It seems that this cloud, which stretches over Chungking all winter, does end somewhere in a place which is fixed and permanent; but unfortunately this place is among high mountains and has only been seen from aeroplanes. This place is somewhere in the Tibetan mountains, and a traveller who has passed over it three or four times says that it ends above a high precipice, where there are green dragons . . .

102

January 27th . . . INTERMINABLE discussions about East and West, but where is the dividing-line? I have lived for years among the Chinese in the South Seas, and though there are acute differences, they are not analysable and the same differences exist among ourselves. The passion for making distinctions. And yet the Chinese are so like the people of the West that all the geography-book definitions fail. I have seen in a book on human geography the statement that the Chinese have thick black hair, almond eyes, small hands, thin bones and are generally smaller and slighter than the people of the West. Everyone of those statements is demonstrably false. Nearly all Chinese children, for example, have light brown hair which grows darker later; though many retain brown hair for the rest of their lives and some have hair with a golden hue. I have rarely met a Chinese with almond eyes, though it is true that on the Chinese stage slanting eyes are the characteristics of the gods and of beautiful maidens. That they have small hands in the south is perhaps true, but there are giants in the north; and the northern climate together with *kaoliang* have bred a race which is roughly the same height as the Europeans. To make generalisations about the Chinese people is something so dangerous that it should long ago have been regarded as a sin of scholarship or taste. Their customs and their history are not ours; their ways of regarding life are not ours; and they often have different motives for doing the same things. A Chinese outside China is as assimilative as any foreigner, and I am beginning to believe that there is only one thing which really distinguishes him from the rest of the inhabitants of the world, and that is the Chinese landscape. We are creatures of the landscape. Our minds are shaped according to the countries we have lived in. The mind of an American of the northern coast is like the coast itself, craggy with rocks and bitter with longing for the West; there are great flowering trees in the minds of those who have lived in Oregon, and sunlight broods heavily over the minds of the West Coast. So in China there are precipitations of yellow earth in the brains of the Chinese; there are rocky crags and temples and herd-boys blowing pipes and sampans flowing down-river in the luminous mist. Our minds are landscapes; and though we would often prefer to forget the landscapes which have given us birth, we can no more escape from their dominance than we can escape from our sins.

Our minds are landscapes, and those who are blessed above all men are the natives of the South Seas, who see life flowing prodi-gally in the seas, the forests and the skies. If I had been born in Malacca or Bali, I might have been a great philosopher; I might even have been great enough to know that it is not worth while to be a great philosopher. The philosophers who live in Paradise know that the pure enjoyment of the moment is the greatest philosophy; and therefore every naked child under the Malayan palm-trees may be a greater philosopher than Hegel or Spinoza.

> O the mind, mind has mountains: cliffs of fall
> Frightful, sheer, no-man-fathomed. Hold them cheap
> May who ne'er hung there. Nor does long our small
> Durance deal with that steep or deep. Here! creep,
> Wretch, under a comfort serves in a whirlwind: all
> Life death does end and each day dies with sleep.

But in the South Seas each day dies with an awakening so prodigious that I imagine the Malayan child can hardly sleep for joy of expecting the dawn of a new day.

January 28th . . . THIS evening, while we were talking about the possibility of a long war, Bergery rose from his bed and went to the window. After a while he said: "One should live like Moses, stretching his arms towards God, standing above the plain of Raphidim in unbelievable agony and torment, until the moon rises and the stars shine again. Assuredly they will shine more brightly if we pray."

February 1st . . . BUT what is so extraordinary about Berg-ery is that he has seen everything—everything without exception, and remains the most completely humble person I have ever met. He has been a war-correspondent for so long that the sight of blood or the evidence of torture awakens no physical pangs in him, and he has killed his own nerves; and yet, by the most terri-ble concentration of effort, he has been able to re-create in his mind a purely *logical* sensitivity which has nothing in common with the sensitivity of the flesh. His face is heavy, and reminds me sometimes of the face of the central figure of the Elephanta caves—dark, drawn and terrible. This at least is what I think when he is not present in the room; but when he is there the suspicion
104

of a gaunt bitterness vanishes, the heaviness disappears, the *terribilta* is nowhere to be seen. Only in the way in which he weighs his words, ponderously dreaming, calculating every nervous twist and fibre of the words which he loves so much, do you notice the background, the long years, the wandering, the knowledge that is always there that perhaps the wandering is in vain. He is married, but he never talks about his wife. There are even children, to whom he has referred only once since we arrived in. Chungking. He is completely self-contained and always seems to occupy the least possible amount of space. And sometimes, watching him as he reads the *National Herald,* I have a suspicion that he is not a man who has experienced every war of the last thirty years but a man of the future.

It is impossible to record in writing the *weight* which he gives to words. When he says: "China is the mountain," the words at first mean no more than they appear to mean. Later, the reverberations of the voice suggest endless dissociated meanings, and you begin to imagine a pyramid of meanings only to find later that the meanings he intended to convey included so many more pyramids, each one superimposed on the other, that the effort of keeping pace with him becomes confusing. He loves China with almost the same breathless adoration with which a lover loves his first mistress, and this is perhaps because China was his first mistress and his early formative years were spent in Manchuria. In the cold, windswept valleys of Jehol he first saw the imperial splendours which he has been searching for ever since. They left on his mind an impression so absolute that he still regards them, as I regard him, as belonging to the future. And this evening, sucking at his pipe, frowning so that dark brown lines appeared on his brown forehead, he began to talk of the young Chinese he had been seeing in Chungking with exactly the same delight as he talked of Jehol.

"They have come to this stage of the history of their country with a complete knowledge of their future, and it is the first time they have possessed this knowledge. They know that they will become a great power, and that just as it took Germany ten years to recover from the war, and Russia fifteen years, they can expect to be great within twenty years of the end of this war. They have planned their future so industriously that they have no time for anything else. They have no time even for recriminations. They have not forgiven Roosevelt for sending scrap-iron to Japan; they have not forgiven Churchill for closing the Burma Road. They are dangerous. They are the most dangerous race on the earth. And they are dangerous only because four thousand years of traditions have implanted in them a tolerance and an abiding love of goodness which will one day shock us out of our complacency. A war does not shock people out of their complacency. It increases complacency. But the time will come soon, perhaps very soon, when the example of the Chinese scholars will be the example which we shall all be unconsciously following. Voltaire admired Confucius above all men; yet Voltaire was the father of the French Revolution. The coming revolution will be fathered by the Chinese themselves, and perhaps it will be fathered by them without their knowledge and certainly without their permission. The revolution will come. It will be a revolution as terrible as any in the world's history; and it will owe its origin to some Chinese scholar, working quietly and in poverty in some remote valley in China, and through him the veils will suddenly be lifted from our eyes and for the first time we shall see clearly. I tell you, China is dangerous for the peace of mind of the world. Imagine China after twenty years of peace. Imagine every small village in the interior with its own electric light, every farmer with his motor-car, every rice-field with its tractor—and behind all these four thousand years of conscious history. In twenty years a quarter of the human race, having suffered the greatest crimes known to man, suddenly leaps into consciousness of its own strength. Do you think it will have little effect on the rest of the world? Do you think it will sit there, supinely obeying the dictates of the foreign industrialists and allow itself to be exploited by others? Do you imagine that a race which once imagined that it possessed the whole world will allow itself to suffer any more indignities? But what is so extraordinary and at the same time so understandable is that the Chinese of this generation are determined to set an example to others. *They are the race which has suffered.* Therefore they are determined that the knowledge they have derived from suffering shall not be wasted, and this is true only because the knowledge we derive from suffering is the most precious thing we possess. They have mapped out their future. They have decided to become a great industrial power, and at the same time all that we mean by American industrialism is foreign to them. The scandalous labour conditions of the treaty ports will not return, perhaps because Rewi Alley has done his work too well. The

106

scandalous impositions of foreign interest-bearing securities will not return, perhaps because we know already that it is dangerous to place a foreign race at the mercy of the stock-market. What Mexico accomplished, China can accomplish with still greater ease. And so for them the future is not dark, but so bright that it is blinding. That is why the young students work through the night by the light of rape-seed oil-lamps. That is why you see on the walls the one word 'Reconstruction'—a word whose history is as old as the Chou dynasty. Of all the countries in the world I have the greatest hope for China, not because she is numerically stronger than any other country, but because the old traditions have never died and the old books are still read by scholars and soldiers alike. If I could live another twenty years, I would prefer to live them in China; and if I must die, I would prefer to die in China. The greatness of this country is terrifying, and this is what I mean when I say that China is the mountain."

Into the early hours of the morning he was still talking of China, her prodigious history, her incalculable expenditure of treasure, her vast knowledge and incredible patience. But I suspect that Bergery's main argument belongs to the sphere of art, and it is really because China has produced the greatest artists that he believes her to be invincible. When he talks of China, emotion enters so quietly that at first it is a vision. He is still the young lover adoring his first mistress, incapable of finding fault with her and so enamoured of her that he would follow her to the ends of the earth.

February 2nd . . . A YOUNG girl with a pitcher stepping carefully down the Wang Lung Men steps. It was dusk, the grey dusk of Chungking which is shot with yellow. She wore a blue gown and her hair was oiled and smoothed close to her small head. All round her the crowds were hurrying to the ferry-boat; and on the stone roadway above motor-cars were screaming and the orange vendors were shouting their wares. We had no eyes for anyone except the girl. She walked slowly, dreamily, unconscious of the crowd, stepping firmly and delicately and at the same time a little timidly, as though she were afraid that the pitcher might be broken. She was Ruth descending the steps towards the well, so ignorant of her beauty that the rest of the world might not have existed for her. And all evening Bergery has been talking about her.

February 3rd . . . AT AN International Peace Conference I met a young professor of English in the Military Academy at Shantung. Today he called on me, and we spoke about Dr. Sun Yat-sen, the founder of the Chinese Republic. I asked Professor Chen Hsi-fen whether he could recommend a good book on Dr. Sun Yat-sen to me, but he shook his head and said there was very little of value, the majority of the manuscripts are lost or hidden in Japanese-occupied territory. There are a few popular lives and a few serious studies of important developments in his thought, but nothing comprehensive has been written in Chinese. "It may be that we are too near to him, and therefore we have not come to a position where we can assume a proper perspective," he suggested. "The Vice-Minister of Propaganda has written a life of the Generalissimo, which is complete enough, but no one has attempted a life of the Founder of the Republic. It will come, perhaps, after the war, or perhaps it will never come, for we know every detail of his life almost by instinct." I was surprised at this, thinking of the innumerable lives of Lenin and Churchill which have appeared in the last few years, and I suggested jokingly that he should write a life in Chinese and I would have it translated into English. Rather to my surprise, he immediately assented. The life is going to be written, but neither of us knows when the task will be ended.

I am continually struck by the extraordinary memories of young Chinese. Professor Chen knew many of the Founder's speeches by heart. He explained the most complicated details of that most complicated life with a clarity and an understanding that was almost alarming. The Chinese have an affection for Dr. Sun Yat-sen, which they have possessed for no other leader of their country. The pale face, which peers down from innumerable walls, half-smiling and dreaming, the face of a scholar who knows precisely the limits of his power and of his charm, the face of a man whose vision was never abrupt but continual, so that he resembled in his greatness the immense rivers which flow through China, is so striking that I can never pass it without wondering whether it will not immediately come to life.

Professor Chen quoted for me one of the early proclamations of the Chinese Republic:

"We will remodel the laws, revise the civil, criminal, commercial and mining codes, reform the finances, abolish re-

108

strictions on trade and commerce, and ensure religious tolera-
tion and the cultivation of better relations with foreign
peoples and governments than have ever been maintained
before. It is our earnest hope that those foreign nations who
have been steadfast in their sympathy will bind more firmly
the bonds of friendship between us, and will bear in patience
with us the period of trial confronting us and our reconstruction work, and will aid the consummation of the far-reaching
plans which we are about to undertake, and which they have
long vainly been urging upon our people and our country.
With the message of peace and goodwill the Republic cher-
ishes the hope of being admitted into the family of nations
not merely to share its rights and privileges, but to co-operate
in the great and noble tasks of building up the civilisation of
the world."

The proclamation was written by Dr. Sun Yat-sen shortly after
he had assumed the Presidency. "But no one believed him outside China," said Professor Chen sadly. "It is only now, after four
years of this terrible war, after the attack on Pearl Harbour and
the attack on Malaya, that people are beginning to believe that
the Chinese have a contribution to make to the present civilisation."

February 5th . . . CHUNGKING is a new city, but even now
you will find traces of the ancient city founded more than two
thousand years ago. There are crumbling walls and archways still
left standing. There are old houses, which have escaped the
bombs, and which bear on their façades the remains of golden
intaglios. Coming out of the dark side-streets in winter, you are
surprised to see high above your head a delicate carving of hinds
and deer, or of serpents and tortoises cut out of white marble.
Sometimes these carvings are scorched by the flames, or broken
by the shock of bombs, but even now they retain the splendour
of line which characterised the carvings of the early years of the
Ch'ing dynasty.

Along the main streets the small streets branch off into rubble.
Rubble is everywhere, and the shop-fronts are little more than
façades; and as you go through the shops, out into the courtyard
on the other side, rubble faces you again—a broken wall, the
blackened stem of a chimney, six inches of bricks with a green

109

moss growing on them. The solidity of ancient China is absent here. Everything is flimsy, and you expect the slightest blows of the wind to knock down these shops which consist of a single plaster wall, on which someone has described in Chinese characters which are so clumsily written that they are almost illegible, the names of the proprietors. It is curious to notice how many of the shops advertise themselves as coming from Shanghai—and yet it is not so curious. The values of Shanghai have been transplanted to Chungking. To get rich quickly, to have a beautiful mistress (or at least a mistress who compares favourably with Hollywood standards), to be able to give dinners in which shark's fin, already almost unobtainable, will be served as a delicacy, to ride in motor-cars and be able to say that your income can be measured in millions are the hallmarks of the most exquisite taste. The old Chinese scholars have temporarily vanished, or they are hiding in small hotel bedrooms no larger than a cupboard. There is no sign of the greatness of China here. Instinctively, on the road to Changsha, we perceived that greatness; but in the squalid restaurants, where the table-cloths are torn and stained, and the paper decorations set up for Christmas have grown tawdry and dusty with age, and sleek black motor-cars like immense eels float past the plate-glass restaurants, there is is even less greatness, for there is less vitality, than in Singapore. But all these things are illusions, or rather in the centre of the town they are true but they do not represent the spirit of the place. Outside the city, in the valleys approaching along the Chialing river and down by the Yangtse, the dynamos can be heard humming late into the night, and in the morning you see the workmen in blue overalls marching quickly through the mist and the yellow fog to relieve the workmen who had worked all night.

The sound of the dynamos at night, and that other sound, inexplicable and perfect—the sound of the sleeping city. A policeman on sentry-go, dressed in dead black; a ricksha-puller sleeping between the shafts of his ricksha, a beggar huddled in a doorway, and high above you the black windows. The marble palaces of the banking quarter are like palaces in dreams, enormously high and rigid; though during the day they are tawdry beyond words. The gilt letters written over the doorway of the greatest bank in China were damaged by bombs; they have never been repaired. But at night those gilt letters, broken and stained with the green mildew of the city, are beautiful beyond words. There are great
110

hoops of gates near the British Embassy, remains of the once powerful bastions of the city; but now they are shelters for beggars and cigarette sellers, places where prostitutes gather, and the imperial inscriptions written above the gates are almost illegible. Opposite these gates there is a bus-station which reeks with purple fumes of wood-oil vapour; but standing there at night, looking up at the round barrelled gateway and the broken skyline beyond, you have an impression of the strength of high walls, their remoteness and inconceivable solidity. The old China was strong in appearance, and majestic beyond the dreams of men; the new appears weak, and its majesty and strength lies in the heart of the people.

February 6th, Tigers . . . A YOUNG child in south-west China is dressed in a tiger-cap, a close-fitting cap of velvet and silk, with coloured stones, a mouth of gold wire, eyes of glass and ears of white rabbit-fur. The tiger-cap is drawn carefully over his head to give him luck, and there is nothing so curious as to see the fierce snarling head of the tiger superimposed on the face of a small laughing Buddha. The tiger-cap is perhaps animistic, and goes back to the time when the Chinese worshipped and feared the animals in the northern forests, but all the stages through which Chinese religion has progressed are demonstrated in the clothes of the child. He wears on the cap a heavy silk ornament showing three Buddhas standing upright. Round his neck a heavy silver wire, the two ends joined together with the formal emblem of a phœnix, safeguard him from the devils of the Taoist pantheon. He wears on his small wrists a thin jade ring, the sign-manual of the Confucian scholar, who prized purity over all things. When he is very young, he is wrapt in embroidered red silk, the colour of the Han Emperors, and it is only when he grows older that he enters the drab blue world which surrounds him on every side. In winter the blue cloth looks grey, and too often it is smeared with dust and mud; but to come out of a side-street and to see a small child carried in the arms of his mother in the most resplendent red silk is like a sudden shock on exposed nerves—a shock so beautiful that the colour lingers for hours on the unwilling eyes.

There are still tigers in Szechuan, just as there are leopards, lynxes and baby pandas. You will see the faces of tigers painted in bright colours on the walls of shops, and in the small second-

111

hand shops by the river, you will see the most terrible masks of tigers in all their glory. There are tigers with golden eyes and livid green eyes; there are tigers with tusks; there are tigers with the faces of dragons and tigers with the faces of buffaloes, and all of them carved out of wood and painted in the brightest colours imaginable. Perhaps it is the misty winter which is responsible for the thickness and brightness of the paint. There are no half-tones. With a savagery unimaginable outside the Easter Island masks, the peasants of Szechuan have drawn portraits of their gods.

I have bought a tiger-mask. His eyes are oblong, his mouth is a perfect circle enclosed by six tusks on each side. He stares with ghastly malevolence from my walls, and I wonder whether he is protecting me or whether he will descend from the walls and throw himself like a poltergeist round my room. In my dreams a headless tiger prowls over the Yangtse, but I have no courage to remove him from the walls and throw him into the river where he belongs.

February 7th . . . COMING down the Wang Lung Men steps this evening, I had an impression that I was in Elizabethan England. The masts and ratlines were etched against the misty blue river. Half-naked coolies, with immense yellow chests, were carrying casks of cement up the three hundred steps. The masts of ships were flowing past, and the noise of the city came down the stone steps, muted it is true, but still so vibrant that they resembled the calls of the London street-vendors. Here, as at Greenwich and Battersea, houses are built on piles. Here at low-water small mat-sheds are erected, and by the light of red candles you can buy horseflesh and rice, barley and rice, those yellow chickens which dangle from strings with their entrails hanging out, headless pigs and the bleeding heads of pigs killed only a few moments before. You can sit on a baulk of timber and watch the world passing in the candle-light, and you notice—though you must have noticed it before—that everything looks more beautiful in candle-light, and even the blood dripping from the mess of bones in the pig's neck is resplendent. There in the corner you will notice a tea-house, where thin transparent glasses are filled with bright green tea, and leaning against her husband's shoulder a weary girl who can be no more than seventeen unbuttons her dress and feeds the half-sleeping child on her lap, and you are

112

surprised to notice that in the candle-light the colour of her breast is bright gold. Over there is a young merchant with pince-nez who smokes a cigar and plays endlessly with the gold chain of his watch, and from time to time he looks towards the blackened roof of the ferry station, sighs and watches for the green light of the approaching ferry-steamer. But the ferry is delayed, and the green light is still shining in the mist on the farther shore.

Through the tea-house small boys come running with the evening papers. The papers are dark brown in colour and miserably printed, but their faces shine like apples and their bare shoulders move with ease and ingenuity among the crowded tables. They cluster round an old man with a wizened forehead, who holds a long-stemmed pipe to his mouth, and they wait anxiously and desperately while, from the folds of his voluminous grey silk gown, he extracts a brown fifty cent note so frayed that you expect it to fall to powder in his hands. A blind beggar enters, led by an extraordinary beautiful girl in pigtails. He sits down quietly on the only available chair, mutters into the ear of the girl—for the blind are as secretive as the deaf—and waits for his tea to be served, and all the while he taps his stick. The waiter pushes through the dense throng of tables. He is a short man, but powerfully built, with a heavy moustache and immense antennæ consisting of three or four hairs wound together, springing from a raspberry mole. I have never believed that there was a yellow race, and I have never seen yellow Chinese before. He is bright yellow, not gold, the bright pasty yellow which you associate with anæmia and jaundice, and he is yellow from the roots of his hair to the creases of his rolling stomach. He lifts the pewter teapot above his head, and a stream of perfectly white or silver water pours from a height two feet above the cup, resembling the trajectory of a silver bullet. He does not smile. He is an automaton. When he hears a voice demanding tea, an incomprehensible sound is vomited from his moustache, and he makes his way with the deadly aim and earnestness of a sleep-walker across the room. He has no preferences. The young prostitute with the oily and ringleted hair is served almost at the same moment as the famous banker, who was recently appointed to the highest post in the Stabilisation Board. The sound of the small tea-house is like an inferno, or like that rumbling which I am beginning to associate, ever since I first heard it in Barcelona, with the sound of subterranean dynamos working at full pressure. There is no pause, or

113

rather a pause is the signal for an increased volume of sound. And all the while, like a deadly monotone, a half-naked beggar whose legs have been cut off above the knees and whose sores are still covered with bright green scabs, whines at the entrance of the shop.

Over the dark misty river the green light of the approaching paddle-steamer comes nearer. You notice it, and at the same moment fifty other people notice it. They stream out of the tea-shop like viscous lava, flinging decayed notes on the rush tables, pushing and shouting, the young girls clutching their babies and attempting to safeguard them from the pressure of the surrounding crowd. The landing-stage is like a maze, guarded at both ends by policemen with bayonets and green papier-mâché helmets. You struggle down one side of the maze, and the wave of struggling people pushes you towards the other. The wooden gates are opened; you throw yourself down three feet into the utter darkness of the ship's deck, muttering under your breath at the youths who have jumped over the rails and taken the only available seats. A small yellow candle burns in a socket nailed to the iron funnel. Everyone is good-tempered, and everyone is weary with the day's work; and watching the black water and the occasional spurts of silver spray which come from the paddle-wheels, admiring the yellow lights of the city as they recede in the distance, you begin to compose yourself for the struggle ahead. On the farther shore there are no tea-houses; there are small half-naked boys whose bodies shine bright red in the light of the bamboo torches they hold in their hands, and steep rocks, and perilous pathways along the water's edge. You brace yourself for the inevitable shock which comes when the ship's fenders break against the wooden deck of the floating stage. You pray humbly and earnestly that the sound of the screaming child will not everlastingly fill your ears, and you admire in the darkness the curve of a girl's neck and the flowing beard of a scholar. A boy, with the face of a dryad, offers to take your baggage up the steep cliffs. You argue with him, but you know that there is so much charm in his movements and in his smiles that you will inevitably accept his price; and when the shock comes, and you are climbing the steps cut out of granite rock, holding a flare in your hand like a blood-red banner, you know that now as ever you are not in Chungking but walking at night among the ghosts of Elizabethan England.

February 8th . . . WE HAVE been walking among the graves. Some impulse of melancholy must have led Bergery to take this path along the south bank of the river, among the crumbling houses, winding through interminable dank streets, where the open gutters are filthy with all manner of refuse, until finally we came out among the fields where the humped mounds of the dead resemble green beehives and a few red candles are glowing through the wintry afternoon. On the day of Pure Brightness the Chinese come to pay their respects to the dead, but this day is in spring and usually when there is a bright silver moon in the sky; but even on this afternoon, which differs from no other afternoon, peasants were coming with their small offerings of candles and painted eggs. There is a tradition in these things. You hold the candles in both hands and raise them three times above your head with a quick and almost a jerking motion, while you mutter prayers and gaze fixedly at the graves. On some of the graves there are small sticks from which frayed banners of coloured paper dance in the wind; but on many of the graves there are bowls of desiccated rice. The wind tosses the banners—a cold wind, which makes us shiver under the branching elms. There were few stones to the graves. Perhaps the Chinese recognise that the dead should bury the dead and keep no other memorial except that which remains in their hearts, or perhaps with the increasing cost of living it is no longer possible to employ stone-masons and calligraphists to make elaborate carvings.

And so we wandered among the graves, ill at ease and sick at heart, fearing the encroaching presence of the dead, while the wind roared on the fields which were more desolate than Egdon Heath.

February 9th . . . LOOKING down from the high rocks, the air still and clear, and watching the small boys riding their Tibetan ponies bare-back along the shore, I was reminded of a novel I wrote years ago about Mongolia and of the two boys Mishka and Petka whose insolence and beauty were the motive of the adventure. I had imagined the adventures of the boys without ever having seen them, and until this moment I had never known why they clamoured so insistently into the fabric of the story, so that even Ungern-Sternberg and Valentin Tikhonov, who were intended to be the heroes, were compelled to resign themselves in the background. But looking at these boys, remembering their

115

faces as I have seen them every day since we arrived in Chung-king, I realised why the boys of the story came from far eastern Siberia and possessed Mongol blood in their veins.

I know nothing so hopeful for the future as the grace and strength of young Chinese boys. They have suffered terrible hard-ships, they have walked barefoot from nearly all the provinces of China to enjoy the imaginary riches of Chungking. During the day they accept with good grace the jobs which are offered to them. At night they huddle together under mat-sheds or in de-serted houses, thin, undernourished, comforting themselves with the comradeship of the dispossessed. In other countries they would choose for themselves a leader, a man who could train them to rob and steal. Here in Chungking they are entirely inde-pendent, living their own lives, completely self-contained. In the bitterest weather you will find them smiling—and surely, in the whole of God's earth, there is nothing so beautiful as a young Chinese smiling.

February 10th . . . I HAVE never taken a bus ride in Chung-king before, and perhaps the experience is not one to be repeated. I was in a hurry to reach the Press Hostel at Liang Lou K'ou, and there were no rickshas available. Besides, I had wasted a good half-hour in the spotless white dairy near the banking quarter, drinking fresh milk and smearing my toast with the thinnest imaginable smear of butter. It was an unexpected delight, for I had imagined that milk and butter were unobtainable in Chung-king. The bus started a good five minutes' walk away. You queue up between iron ramps, which were once painted green, and you wait patiently until the bus appears. You are cramped inside the iron railings, while an extremely attractive Chinese girl attempts to push her umbrella into your eyes—for it is raining bitterly, the ricksha-pullers have put on their armour of brown bark of some fibrous tree and the motor-cars are splashing waves of mud on to the pavement. You wait patiently. It is five minutes before the bus roars to a standstill and you begin to clamber into it.

There are so few motor-buses in Chungking, and they are driven so recklessly, that each journey demands the absolute maximum of passengers. A bus which was made to contain fifty with difficulty is crowded with over a hundred. The springs scream. You start slowly, so slowly that you have no idea that you have started until a vicious jerk throws all the standing pas-

116

sengers on to the floor, and when you rise you are surprised to notice that nearly all the faces of the people who were leaning against you are covered with mud. The bus conductor stands on the running-board, and the doors are wide open, so that the pelting rain has unrestricted freedom of entry. Suddenly the bus conductor decides to demand his fares. He squeezes himself into the bus, bangs the door violently, pushes his way with the momentum of a steam-engine into the farthest corners of the bus and begins to demand two dollars fifty for the fare. The fare would be quite reasonable if there were any comfort, but you begin to feel that the conductor should pay you for the honour of entering his miserable bus. At every turning—and there are many turnings —you curse aloud. You can hardly breathe. If you die, or if you have a heart-attack, nobody will notice it, for you are lost in a sea of people all breathing heavily, all despondent, all sliding backwards and forwards with the movements of the bus. You are exhausted beyond endurance. You want to sink down on your knees and pray; but there is no room to pray. You want to hang suspended in the air, drawing up your knees, floating above the heads of the other passengers supported by the leather strap. But someone else is supporting himself on the only leather strap within reach. You become sardonic. With the greatest difficulty you peer out of the window, and you are amused and contented by the expressions of the people whose clothes have been splashed with mud from the bus or who are drowned in the purple fumes of petrol vapour. You are even delighted when the bus lurches violently, mounts the kerbstone and almost passes through the plate-glass of a shop window.

February 11th . . . IN A house off Liang Lou K'ou I have met a living Buddha. There was a Korean, and three or four Mongolians, but I was more interested in the living Buddha, who wore a loose Chinese gown and a small black skull-cap, and except for his rosary resembled any one of a thousand Chinese you can see in the streets of Chungking. His face was perhaps a little thinner and a little darker; his eyes were small and very black like olives and he smiled with such serenity that it was impossible not to smile in return. I bowed very low, and it was curious to watch how the others who were present also bowed low, making a slight genuflexion. An old Chinese, whose thin frayed white beard resembled a white feather in the wind, seemed to be overcome with emotion and for a long while he gazed into those burning black eyes. There are, I believe, seven living Buddhas in China, Mongolia and Tibet, and according to the *hutukhtu* "there are others whose names are not known". The living Buddha spoke a few words of English and smiled happily when he said "good-morning", although it was already late in the evening. Except that he remained incredibly still, he was not unlike the other Chinese in the room; and his voice was softer and gentler than the other voices. He ate delicately, but with more gusto than I had thought possible in so holy a man; and when he smiled there was a trace of melancholy still in his eyes.

There are still a few rooms in China which are well-decorated. The merchants, the landlords who have possessed property in Szechuan for many generations still possess sufficient money to decorate well, and they have exquisite taste. The room was papered in gold; there were comfortable chairs; a wood fire roared cheerfully in the chimney. Servants entered soundlessly, and the curtained lampshade alone was enough to remind us that civilisation was present. All the graces of life were visible, and nothing was lacking for our comfort, and yet, and yet the presence of the living Buddha made a mockery of them. So quiet he was, and with such insolence did those dark eyes measure our pretensions. All the time he seemed to be saying: "This is not life, but a mockery of life. The only life is to pray for the sins of the world."

February 13th . . . PROFESSOR CHEN suggested that I should interview Dr. Sun Fo, and obtain his permission for the life of Dr. Sun Yat-sen that we are writing, or rather, since this is a misstatement, the life which he will write and I shall revise if revision ever becomes necessary. We received a message from Dr. Sun Fo that he would receive me at his country house just outside Chungking at ten o'clock this morning. I was late. We could not find the house, which is perched on the top of steep hills, and besides the chauffeur insisted on believing that the house we should go to was a house some thirty miles away. It was windy and rainy. A fog crept over the city, and we could hardly see more than a few yards ahead. We climbed the steep hill, and arrived covered in mud.

In a large room, facing the river, with a blue carpet and blue chairs, a room with almost no decoration at all, we talked about
118

the life. Dr. Sun Fo wore a blue suit and looked younger than I had imagined, very alert and at the same time shy and self-effacing. He looked very like the photographs of the Founder of the Republic. The telephone bell rang. He disappeared behind the blue curtains and returned some moments later, saying that he had received a telephone from the Legislative Yuan, of which he is president, but though he would have to leave shortly, there was no urgency—where were we?—oh yes, there was a recent investigation of the Sun ancestry, which tended to prove that the Sun family came from Kansu, where they were known as princes under the Ming Emperors. He was not absolutely sure that these investigations offered a complete proof of the history of the family, but they were almost complete. "In China our ancestral temples are the sources of history. Our names, and often the details of our lives are recorded in the temples, and sometimes these temples are in distant provinces and we may never go to visit them. There may be four or five temples for each family, since each family during the last thousand years has moved across China." He spoke about recent researches in the life of the Founder of the Republic. Much of the material has been lost in the fire at the Commercial Press in Shanghai—the "fire" was a euphemism for the deliberate Japanese bombardment—and still more is carefully hidden in Japanese-occupied territory. He was anxious that the life should be the life of the man, written so that men could see him as he was, and he spoke a little wistfully of the complexities of the political career of a man who after being President for a few days deliberately took the road of political exile. In becoming President of the Legislative Assembly he followed his father's choice, for Sun Yat-sen had insisted that the country should be governed by law and a duly elected parliament possessing the rights of recall and referendum. As President of the Legislative Yuan he fulfilled the functions of Lord Chief Justice, and yet he looked absurdly young and resembled a scholar who has entered a government organisation, though he would have preferred to continue his days in a University. In the blue suit, against the blue curtains and the blue carpet, he seemed to bring with him that curious sense of self-effacement which I have noticed so often with Chinese scholars. A few minutes later it was time to leave, and we slid down the muddy slope to the car, while the guardian wolfhound bayed in the mist and a few sol-

119

diers with bayonets at the slope watched us with the air of conquerors standing guard on the hill.

All the way back to Chungking we were fighting the mist and the rain, and we thought of the young scholar, the descendant of princes of the Ming Dynasty, who carried on his father's traditions.

February 14th, Chinese New Year . . . AT NIGHT, when it was very dark, it began to snow. We stood out on the rocks looking over the Yangtse, the great hulks rolling in the strong tide, and suddenly it seemed that an immense whiteness was descending from the heavens. In this darkness whiteness is unaccountable. It looks ghostly, there against the steel-rusted sides of the riverboats moored at anchor. And then too the snow is so incongruous in this city, where everything is hard as rock, where no benedictions are expected; and we remember: "The last things to fall from heaven were bombs." But peering through the darkness, walking through the slush and mud, slithering and groping in blackness, we see the ghostly glimmer of the snow in the vanishing sky, and suddenly everything appears strangely tender and luminous, there are more lights than we ever expected, and somewhere over the other side of the river beyond the Wang Lung Men steps people are singing. It is a ghost night, and we walk down to one of those moored hulks, where we are going to dine, with the expressions of people who are lost in a magical and entirely unbelievable world.

From the deck of the boat we can see the sampans still moving down-stream. They are few, of course. At this hour of night most sampans come close to shore. But here, the twinkling lights of the ship dancing on the water, the Wang Lung Men steps illuminated by fairy lights, we feel closer to tears than at any moment since we left Changsha. "I'm damnably homesick," Bergery says, thinking of a white village on the New England coast which he has not seen for twenty years. I think of Mary Tavy and Tor Point, a stream rippling in Cornwall, the long walk from Saltash to Antony. The hawthorn hedges are bright yellow; larks are singing; some soldiers are firing at the butts; and in this Cornish summer, so heavily scented that you feel the air like a weight of flowers, there is no hint of snow. Yet surely the snow comes from England! A black sampan, throwing a black shadow like a scarf, goes down-stream to Ichang, and suddenly we remember that we
120

are standing on this old hulk, from which the engines have been removed, whose strakes are white with barnacles and whose funnel has been cut down because someone wanted an extra foot of cast steel. "Malaya is falling. They have taken the engines out of this old junk," Bergery says bitterly, but for the moment the fall of Singapore is still remote. White-coated Chinese stewards move about on deck. The cabins are lit with the blue-pointed flames of acetylene lamps. Everything is white and chromium-plated; there are even painted silk shades on the electric lamps, and this is really surprising, for the Chinese and even the Englishmen in China seem to possess an unaccountable love for naked electric bulbs. And sitting there, looking at the perfectly white starched table-cloth, the cut glass, the flowers in a silver vase, we seem to be curiously at home. These things, so small in themselves, protect us from the elements.

"And if Singapore falls, what then?"

There is silence. In the captain's cabin, a wireless is going on. The six "pips" of the time-signal, and then: "This is London calling——" and something about Singapore which we dare not listen to, for we have known it already. Here, in the Yangtse, among high rocks and screaming gulls, Singapore takes its place in history.

The Chinese are not bitter. Now that the end is in sight, they know better perhaps than ourselves the cost for the future. They have complained against the Colonial Government which refused to enfranchise the Chinese; they complained more bitterly against the Government of Burma, because no Chinese troops were allowed to enter Burma six months ago. But the rancour has vanished. The young Chinese intellectual at the head of the table raises his glass:

"We have friends in Singapore. Let us drink to their health now and for ever."

When we return it is still snowing. The gang-plank sways in the wind.

February 15th . . . ALL through the morning the air held an ominous sweet stillness. Snow lay on the mountains—the whole city was white. The sun shone, not grandiloquently but faintly through rifts in the clouds, and the earth now white and tender no longer possessed the terrible hardness which I shall always associate with Chungking. There is something implacable in this

121

rock upon which the city has been built; as though the toughness of the inhabitants had been communicated to the landscape.

On the foreshore we found the pony-boys and bargained over two small white Tibetan ponies with curling manes. They were soft and round-barrelled, with intelligent long heads, and their skins were still powdered with diamonds of snow. They were gentle to handle. I have seen them try to bite their guards and buck when a young woman from the city tried to mount one, but perhaps that was because she was wearing expensive furs and concealed herself in a mist of cheap scent. Besides, there was no hint of snow a week ago . . .

We ran races over the rocks and the snow, the wet skins of the ponies gleaming. They raced with all their strength; and though Bergery's long legs were in danger of being knocked by the rocks which grow to all sizes and circumferences on the foreshore, and though neither of us rode as skilfully or gracefully as the small boys who crouch on the ponies' necks with arms akimbo or aloft in the air, we were content with our ride. In the frosted air, the snow still a quarter of an inch deep, we knew the invigoration of speed and the solace of an ice-cold wind. Chungking resembled a birthday-cake from the white spire of her ugly cathedral on the skyline to the white caves in the rocks.

February 17th . . . COMING out of a side-street in Liang-l'ou-K'ou, where two roads meet high above the cliff-edge and the airfield on the Yangtse, I came face to face with the General-issimo. He wore a black *ma-kou* (one of those short black patterned coats which all Chinese wear when they reach the age of scholars) and a long blue or maroon skirt. His moustache is turning white; his cheek-bones are high and sharp; his face thinner and smaller than I had imagined. He walked gracefully with squared shoulders, and as we passed he turned to a short fat little man who hobbled at his heels, and said something in a voice so sweet and feminine that I stopped dead on my tracks and listened for dear life. But afterwards there was silence . . .

I had seen him before on the famous day when he addressed the Ministry of Foreign Affairs and upbraided them for being—I have forgotten their crimes but I know they were many. It was the day when Quo Tai-ch'i left the Ministry. We were walking along the road which runs parallel to the river. The Ministry of Foreign Affairs is a small brown building half buried by the
122

debris of a shattered skyscraper, whose broken stumps cling to a ledge of rock twenty feet away. We were walking through the courtyard when suddenly an immense motor-car drove up, guards sprang out, the doors opened, the Generalissimo sprang into the car and was driven quickly away. He appeared then to be heavily guarded; and muffled in a brown greatcoat, he resembled the figure that I have always had of him—mysteriously gentle, ruthless, the spirit of the Han revived. And then that other day when a fast motor-boat surprised ours and threw up so great a wake that we were half-drowned; and reclining in the back of the stream-lined blue motor-boat, smoking a cigarette, wearing a trilby hat and a military overcoat, the figure we have seen so often larger than life was magically reduced to human proportions.

I have asked K. who knows him well what he thinks of the Generalissimo. K. giggled, pulled at his moustache which has been grown in imitation of the Generalissimo's, and burst out into a long hymn of praise.

"But what do you really think of the Generalissimo?" I repeated. "After all, he has himself deprecated the tendency to treat him as a god."

"He is a very great man . . ."

"Yes, I know, but what do you really think of him?"

Half an hour later he told me:

"You have seen him in that fast motor-boat which takes him across the river from one of his houses among the mountains to the headquarters of the Party. The boatman is a wounded soldier, and sometimes—especially on a moonlight night—the Generalissimo will sing on the water. I assure you, he sings with especial sweetness, and sometimes they sing a duet, and sometimes Madame Chiang sings. He has a great love of singing." He told me of the German military adviser who lives on the south bank, and who is still paid regularly for his services in the past. "The Generalissimo is the man in China with the longest memory," K. continued. "He never forgets those who have fought him or those who have pleased him. When you meet him, you will be surprised by the depth of light in his eyes. He is great and gentle above all men, more merciful and compassionate . . ." In another five minutes he was declaiming from the Generalissimo's speeches; and once more it was necessary to ask him to be more definite. He burst out in surprise:

"But don't you regard Churchill as a god?"

"Certainly not. We know all the mistaken interpretations he has read into the life of his distinguished ancestor Marlborough. We know nearly all his faults, and it is possible to criticise them openly in Parliament. We regard him as the best man for the job, and the wisest. But we don't speak about him in hushed voices."

"But we do—we regard Churchill as almost superhuman."

"I think you are foolish and mistaken. Surely we know by now that it is dangerous to think of men as gods."

"It is a danger we have very nearly fallen into," K. admitted. "You must remember that for a long while we possessed German military advisers; and American Methodism has also added to this peculiar attitude of reverence for our leaders. Then too the Party is extremely powerful in China, and there is little or no organised opposition to the Party. The Party is the seat of all power, all industry, all effort. You must understand that we are grateful to the Generalissimo for everything that he has done for us, and we show our respect by regarding him as almost superhuman. In the Political Training Centre, which he has inaugurated for Party members, that feeling is perhaps greatest; but it exists among us all, and though it is true that he deprecates it, it is also true that others encourage it. How much does he know? No one knows. A little while ago the *Ta Kung Pao* wrote: "There is a halo of sanctity and silence around the Generalissimo." The newspaper was suspended for three days, the manager made a personal apology, but still no one knows. He is a military leader, the greatest since Tseng Kuo-fan, but we are not sure that he is a great administrator. And so we live and dream of the war, knowing that it is better to be well-led in war and best to have faith in a good man."

He was speaking with great simplicity. It was night, and we were descending the Wang Lung Men steps in the mist. Far away, down-river, a small motor-boat was throwing up a great white wake. Was it our imagination, or did we really hear the sound of high-pitched singing coming from the boat?

February 20th . . . A LETTER from Malaya. "Everything is good here, and we feel that we are fighting the Japanese in good heart. One or two of your favourite bookshops in Bras Bassah Road have disappeared; there are a few other buildings you will no longer recognise. We have complete faith in the army. The

124

heat is terrible. For some reason, it has been hotter since the Japanese landed in the north than at any time since living memory. The merantis are out in my garden; and though I miss my daily swim in the Chinese swimming pool, which has been taken over by the army, I am grateful at the opportunity of defending this territory. Imagine me in my singlet and white shorts, with a tin helmet three sizes too large for me, a revolver at my side, a trailer-pump in my back garden, six or seven bank clerks sleeping in my shed, and an alarm nearly every night. The trouble is that whenever they drop incendiary bombs, a wind springs up. But we make up for all the distasteful business of putting out fires and gathering up charred corpses by watching dog-fights. I have never yet seen a British plane coming down in flames, and I have forgotten how many Japanese aeroplanes we have seen bursting into fragments in mid-air.

"Please remember me to my friends in Chungking, and tell me please how you enjoy life in the Free China capital. I have a very confused picture of Chungking, chiefly derived from films showing bombardments. You see the river, some rocks and great spouts of black smoke—not very satisfying material for my imagination. (1) Are there skyscrapers, (2) Are there restaurants where you can order whatever food you like, (3) Are there any pretty girls, (4) Are there any great industries, (5) Are there any beggars, (6) Are there rickshas, or do you drive about in cars, (7) Is the New Life Movement having much effect, (8) Do you see the sun, (9) What about the cost of living, (10) Is there anything left of the Japanese bombardments?"

It is too late to answer the letter, but if I could send a letter to Singapore, I would reply:

(1) There are skyscrapers, but they are mostly big banks and government offices. There are even electric lifts in some of the buildings, and they are very massive indeed.

(2) There are four or five good restaurants—the "Daisy" and the "Moscow", both owned apparently by Russian émigrés, are exceptionally good. There are a few tea-houses, and an immense number of shops where you can buy anything you like except motor-cars and motor-car accessories, and perhaps it is impossible to buy aeroplanes. There are drug-stores, where rather doubtful drugs can be bought. There is even a dairy, where you can have excellent milk at exorbitant prices. There are three million cigarette shops, and a few fruit-stalls. It is the end of the season for

125

oranges, and though they are still very sweet, you will find that about one in three has been cunningly designed to appear like an exceedingly good orange, though in fact it is exceedingly bad.

(3) There are many pretty girls.

(4) There seem to be few great industries in the city, but there are innumerable small-scale industries in the outskirts. There is an excellent electric generating station, and the Chinese are extremely proud of having camouflaged it so effectively. I will let you know more about the industries later.

(5) There are twenty million beggars, and nearly all of them squat on the Wang Lung Men steps. I am very well acquainted with all of them. They are suffering from every possible disease, but there are a certain number of diseases which they all possess. They are all, for example, suffering from venereal disease, trachoma and tuberculosis. Some of them carry their mothers on their backs; others carry their children—it is a matter of taste. They murmur in such plaintive voices, and their diseases are so terrible, that I have given money to all of them, and I have always regretted it.

(6) There are rickshas *and* motor-cars. If you have friends in high government offices, you may ride occasionally in a motor-car. Otherwise you walk or take a ricksha. If you walk, you will suffer from the cardinal sin of envy, and you will not be surprised when motor-cars pass you and splash you with mud; and you will reserve your spleen for the occasions when an ignorant ricksha-driver cuts your head with the end of the ricksha-shaft. You will observe also that all the roads are steep; that shoe-leather is expensive, that the ricksha-drivers are exceedingly good fellows, who curse the lack of sunshine and the presence of motor-cars as much or even more than you do, and that too many pretty girls ride in motor-cars. Petrol is scare. The trouble in Burma will make it scarcer for some time to come. Finally, you will observe that the streets in Chungking are deliberately planned to stretch your temper, and like the oranges they are cunningly designed. You think you are walking up an inclined gradient towards the brow of a hill. You are always quite wrong. You are walking up an inclined gradient which will lead you to another inclined gradient, and this in turn will lead you . . . You should remember also that there are no comic-pages in the newspapers, partly as a result of the shortage of paper and partly as a result of the fact that there is nothing comic to report.

126

(7) I have no idea.

(8) No.

(9) It is rising.

(10) I do not know why people talk so much of the Japanese bombardment. Many people have been killed, and it may be true that Chungking has suffered proportionately more than any other capital except Warsaw. But if Warsaw or Singapore were built on rock, you would have felt safer; and we feel absurdly safe under the ten-mile-thick canopy of cloud, with a ten-mile-thick carpet of rock underneath our feet. It is true that the old city has been destroyed, and perhaps it was prettier than the present city, which has nothing to commend it æsthetically. I had hoped to see bamboo groves and gardens hidden behind high walls. I have seen the Yangtse, and perhaps the Yangtse is more terrible and more beautiful than anything I had ever hoped to see.

W., who sent me the letter from Malaya, was one of the heads of the Kuomintang organisation in Singapore. He was fat and completely charming; and if the Japanese catch him, he will certainly be killed. At a time when the Colonial Government disapproved of the Kuomintang and even considered it as a secret society, he took me to the Party meetings, introduced me to his friends who possessed works of art, taught me the little Chinese I know and impressed upon me that of all countries in the world China was the most humane and considerate to strangers. Surrounded by his twelve children, everlastingly smoking his pipe, he smiled gently at the immensity of our naval base and the peculiar air of officialdom which made us at times so perplexing to him. He was like the Knight of the Spirit, in Kierkegaard's *Fear and Trembling*—the perfect bourgeois who concealed the soul of the wisest philosopher.

I pray for him above all others. In his delight in simplicity, in his charm and gentleness, in the sweetness of his manner and temper, he was greater than anyone I have ever known.

February 23rd . . . It was one of the characteristics of W. that he refused to believe anything about Chinese civilisation until he had tested it against his experience or his great knowledge of China's history or literature. He had studied under Hu Shih in Pekin; and he believed that the Chinese had sadly over-estimated the strength of their culture in many directions, and underestimated it in others.

127

One evening, in his small white house near the seashore, we were discussing the Chinese attitude to life. Without knowing much of China, I had said: "What is so terrible is that Chinese civilisation is so peaceful; you have a hatred of war which goes deep into the soul. This is what makes it so remarkable that the Chinese fight so brilliantly."

He sucked at his pipe thoughtfully, staring out towards the islands.

"On the contrary," he exclaimed, "the Chinese are an immensely warlike race. You hear of our poetry in praise of peace. Have you heard of our poetry in praise of war?"

And then he began to sing in that queer singsong falsetto voice of the Chinese scholar a poem of war—a poem in praise of war. In that extraordinary voice you could hear the thunder of horses and the snapping of armour. He recited another, quieter and more determined, an elegy perhaps, or a muted hymn of praise. "We have many others," he concluded. "We are a warlike race because we have seen so much of war—there is not a square inch of my immense fatherland which has not been stained with blood."

From that night onward we began to translate the poems. There were poems in horror of war which were nevertheless full of a curious satisfaction in death; there were poems in praise of war, and even poems in praise of the enemy. There were the long and masterly poems of Tu Fu, where the rhythms are cunningly contrived towards a mounting horror of desolation, and there were those shorter pieces which are rarely preserved in anthologies, for the later Emperors did everything in their power to make the Chinese race submissive and peaceful. During the T'ang dynasty 22,000 poets wrote 48,900 poems. These are figures I remember, as I remember that the earth is 93,000,000 miles from the sun—for the pleasure and awe which derive from their immensity. But what is most remarkable is that the greater majority of the poems were good; they were received into the canon; they were entered into the official compilations, and short lives of the poets were compiled. But they are too many, and unless, like Socrates meditating in the sunrise, we see the whole universe at our feet, the treasures of China will never be revealed to us.

Today China is buying time with space, and we may console ourselves that time is a mercantile product. Others have paid the

128

price for those four years of massacre and rapine. Still more will pay it in the future as unquestioningly, asking in a world where understanding has vanished, not that they should be understood but that they should be helped. For four thousand years the Chinese peasants (who later became soldiers) have hated the arts of war. They were reasonable men encamped on the shores of a yellow river. Spring, summer and autumn they loved, and winter except in Pekin was a bitter penance to be endured because it contained the seeds of another year and a host of ceremonies. Yet they began as huntsmen and their early poems are indistinguishable from war poetry—the enemy a wolf or a dragon. In the supreme bewilderment of modern war they are returning in their tens of thousands to the consolations of poetry, but the enemy is no longer a wolf or a dragon. The enemies are high-explosive shells and the untamable rapacity of the Japanese.

Poets moreover are still springing up among the grains of rice. They have been hardened by suffering and their verses are incised with the same nervous lines which mark their care-worn faces. The poems of modern Chinese poets contain no bitterness. Behind the flame-throwers and the poison gas they see the villages of their childhood, the rice flowing like rivers and the faces of the village boys flooding the valley like an eternal springtime. This happened, they say. All my family has been destroyed. The wells have been poisoned. God alone knows who is responsible, but who can destroy my memories of childhood? Those who have been defeated in this war speak most often of their homeland. The poetry of Louis Aragon resembles him in its nervous insistence on the beauty of French names; and the anonymous Czech poet who wrote:

The prophets have not foretold all:
In the voice of the war, we heard the Resurrection,

was speaking as though he were familiar with the undiscovered fatherland. Too many Chinese poems are concerned with a sweet melancholy. It needed a beastly and voracious war to make that regret so palpable that it could be touched.

Not all the Chinese war poets were warriors. Lu Lun was a scholar whose ancestors for four generations had been connected with the imperial court, and his four sons followed after him.

129

There is no evidence that he saw war at close quarters, but the richness of his imagination is something quite unique in Chinese poetry. In "Dark night: the wild geese fly high", he composed that rare thing—an ode in honour of a Chinese victory. The ode is extremely short and the strands of meaning are many; it is condensed, but the images are neither congested nor confused, and the poem possesses a hardness and sharpness of vision which were unknown in Chinese literature before and have rarely been excelled since. The monk of eight fingers died only a short while ago: he was the master of the present Buddhist abbot of China, and had burnt in the altar-flames a finger from each hand. The war poetry of today is influenced by Russia, for Chinese poetry fits easily into the stabbing scheme which was invented by Mayakovsky.

The record of the struggles with the Huns is indelibly impressed upon the literature of China. Li Po speaks of the soldiers looking back towards their distant homesteads, seeing only "an endless white road of sorrow". From the same border city Tu Fu dreams of a girl and the dream suddenly ends in a sob:

> *O the tears of warriors streaming down like rain!*

He can think of nothing further to say. The poem ends as it began, in a note of regret, but there are other poets who demonstrated the vigour of the Chinese soldier. Yo Fei, the famous general, prays for the day of his release with unmatched feelings. The poet Shen Shan, himself a warrior, remembers the texture of things—a squirrel's fur, the thickening of a horse's mane in the frost, the glint of armour and the impact of wind on the pennons in the van. The imagery is swift, the pen races the thought, the heart beats time, the invention never falters, but beneath and around all this there is an atmosphere of tender pity, of universal friendliness, of how mellow a wisdom, how golden a simplicity.

No Chinese poet could have written the Anglo-Saxon song which inspired the Franks to battle. In Chinese poetry each word has a shape of its own, and every poem seems to have been written in the hard crystalline light of *The Phoenix and the Turtle*. On the subject of war I can think of only one poem in English which possesses the peculiar condensation of Chinese poetry. It occurs in Hardy's *The Dynasts*:
130

Yea, the coneys are scared by the thud of hoofs,
And their white scuts flash at their vanishing heels,
And swallows abandon their hamlet roofs.

The moles' tunnelled chambers are crushed by wheels,
The larks' eggs scattered, their owners fled,
And the hare's hid litter the sapper unseals.

The snail draws in at the terrible tread,
But in vain; he is crushed in the felloe-rim;
The worm asks what can be overhead . . .

I

GENERAL YO FEI (XII century)

FULL RIVER BED

My hair bristles in my helmet.
Standing in my porch I see that the pattering rain has ceased.
I raise my eyes to the skies and shout with the vigour of my
  ambitions.
At the age of thirty fame and great deeds are nothing but
  earth and dust.
Eight thousand li away lie the clouds and the moon.
Do not tarry: the hair of young men grows white with empty
  sorrow,
The shame heaped on us in Chingkung is not yet wiped
  away.
When will the sorrow of the Emperor's subjects come to an
  end?
O let us drive endless chariots through the Ho-lan pass.
Now our sweet ambitions are directed upon the flesh of the
  Huns,
Laughing we thirst for the blood of the Hsiung-nu.
O let everything begin afresh!
Let all the rivers and mountains return to us
Before we pay our respects once more to the Emperor.

II

LU LUN

THE DARK NIGHT OF WILD GEESE

The arrows of Chimpoko are tipped with hawks' feathers,
Our pennons gleam with swallow-tails.
They wave alone above the armies,
And a thousand companies raise a single shout.

In the dark forest the grass is frightened by the wind.
At night the general stretches his bow.
In the early morning he finds a white feather
Hidden amid white stones.

Dark night: the wild geese fly high;
The Hsiung-nu are fleeing, fleeing.
We pray for daylight and a cavalry charge.
A great snowfall conceals our bows and knives.

In the desert our broad tents are filled with food:
The western tribesmen praise our victory.
We drink and dance together in iron mail,
The thunder of drums moves the mountain rivers.

III

LU LUN

ON MEETING A SICK SOLDIER

The way is long; the body over-burdened.
Foodless he journeys the thousand li to his home,
Tearing his hair and sobbing before the city walls,
While the autumn wind pierces his golden scars.

IV

SHEN CHAN

TWO SONGS FOR GENERAL CHAO

(i)

A coat of squirrel fur, dancing girls,
Wines from the palace and silks belonging to the Great Khan.
But the old general on the eastern front fights keenly:
Though he is seventy, he will fight to the death.

(ii)

The wind on Tien Shan slashes the autumn like a knife.
South of the city their horses shiver, manes shrinking.
The old general rattles the dice,
And wins the fur coat belonging to the Great Khan.

V

LI PO

THE BRIGHT MOON

The bright moon soars over the mountain of Heaven,
A bright moon gliding over an ocean of clouds,
A shrill wind screaming ten thousand li away
And a sound of whistling from the Yu-men gate.
Now the sons of Han are marching along the road
And the Tartars search the bays of the Blue Sea.
This is an old battlefield:
No one ever returned from here.
Gazing at the horizon, the soldiers
Stare towards their homes.
Their hearts are filled with fear and trembling.
Tonight, from the high towers, they see
Only an endless white road of sorrow.

VI

WANG CH'ANG-LING

THE YOUNG WIFE

The young wife, upon whom grief has not yet come,
On a spring day paints her face and climbs the emerald
*   tower.*
Suddenly she sees the willow-buds bursting along the paths
And sorrows that she has sent her husband to the wars.

VII

LU LUN

ON SEEING CHANG'AN IN SPRING

The east wind blows over the green rain mountains.
I see a thousand green houses in my dreams.
When shall I arrive at my homestead?
Spring falls on the river. How many ever return?
Over rivers and plains float the curling clouds;
Palaces and castles stand in the setting sun.
Who remembers the scholar in a world at war?
Grey-haired, I stand alone at the pass of Ch'in.

VIII

SHEN CHAN

Behold, the horsemen are galloping along the Szechuen road be-
*   side the snow-white sea,*
Sand stretches like prairie grass, so vast, and the yellowness of
*   sand meets the sky.*

Here in Lun-tai, in late autumn, the wind howls all night.
A river-bed of broken stones as large as kettle-drums
Is thrown up by the wind, and everywhere the air is full of stones.
The Huns pasture their fat horses in the yellow grass.
Westward, among the golden hills, smoke and dust are flying.
The Han general collects his forces against the Western enemy.
All night he has not removed his coat of mail.
All night the army marches, weapons touching.
And the wind's muzzle is a knife slashing the sky.
The manes of the horses are icicles, strings of cash turned to ice,
Five-petal flowers among the smoke-clouds of sweat.
In his tent the general dips his pen into ice.
Ah, if the Huns had heard of it, would not their courage fail?
We—we know that they have no love for our short swords.
We—we know that the army awaits tidings of victory.

IX

THE MONK OF EIGHT FINGERS (1841–1921

THE SONG OF A SOLDIER

At thirteen I followed the army and garrisoned a border
    town.
Five thousand iron horses marched together.
At the Great Wall a battle was fought: all perished.
My heart has now no desire to be pictured in the Hall of
    the Clouds.

With broken banners in my hands I beckon to the setting
    sun:
Heroic souls, follow me back to your village homes."
And suddenly a skeleton arose and talked like a man:
"Honourable Sir, take this letter to my father and mother.

"Tell them I am an exile, a ghost among new ghosts;
Tell them I am far from home, a wanderer——
For they have no reason to know whether I am alive or
    dead——
And tell my wife not to suffer for my sake."

135

X

TU FU

THE CHARIOTS GO FORTH TO WAR

Chariots rumble and roll; horses whinney and neigh;
Men are marching with bows and arrows at their hips.
Their fathers, mothers, children, wives hurry to say fare-
*   well.*
Raising clouds of dust over Hsien-yang Bridge,
They stamp their feet, weeping, among bundles of
*   clothes:*
They block the road and their lament soars to the sky.

And the passers-by listen to the soldier:
"We are conscripts.
Since the age of fifteen we have defended the northern
*   rivers.*
Till we are forty we shall serve on the western front.
We leave our homes as youths and return as grey-haired
*   men.*
Along the frontier there flows the sea of our blood.
The king hungers for territory—therefore we fight.

"Have you not heard, sir,
How through the two hundred counties of Shantung,
Through thousands of villages and tens of thousands of
*   hamlets*
Thorns and brambles are laying waste our country?
Sturdy peasant women swing the hoe and drive the
*   plough:*
For the corn has gone to seed, the dykes are filled in,
And men are slain like dogs and women are harried like
*   hens.*

"You, sir, enquire of me, how dare I complain?
It is winter now, and we are drafted to the western front,
The magistrates are clamouring for higher taxes.
If only I had known the fate in store for boys,
I would have had my children all girls,

For girls may be married to the neighbours
But boys are born only to be cut down and buried
    beneath the grass.

"Do you not see, sir,
The long dead ancient bones near the Blue Sea bleached
    by the sun?
And now the lament of those who have just died
Mingles with the voices of those who died long ago,
And darkness falls, and the ghostly whimpering of
    voices."

XI

TU FU

My boyhood was passed in the northern city.
My youth I wasted in the wars.
My body hustling among the horses' hooves
Eager to snatch from the earth a seven-foot grave
Was decorated with a beard of porcupine quills.
Now white clouds hurry over the Lung Pass,
Red clouds below.
Never shall I return until I am discharged,
Never shall I see my wife in Fengtien,
She who sings and dances to the lute,
She who sings on her Mongolian flute
Songs of warriors attacking the palisades.
O the tears of warriors streaming down like rain!

XII

LI PO

My country is in ruins, only the mountains and rivers
    remain;
In the spring city, only grass and the mossy trees.
Lamenting our time, the flowers shed tears,
In regret of parting the birds startled my heart.

The beacon fires continued for three months,
A letter from my family is worth ten thousand gold coins.
So often have I scratched my white hair in despair
That soon I shall no longer be able to keep a hair-pin.

Today, Chinese poetry has hardly changed. There is the same delight in fighting and the same weariness, the same melancholy and the same bright colours. The past is always very close in China, so close that it overlays the present. I have asked a Chinese what he thought of the present wars. "It was worse at the end of the Sung dynasty," he replied; and as he spoke, he seemed to be speaking from his own recollections. "We are conscious of being travellers in this land," said another Chinese. "We do not believe that we are permanent—only the family is permanent." And a little while later, in a voice of such deep melancholy that I wondered whether it was possible for a man to speak under so great a strain, he added: "In the present wars, even the family——" There was no need to say more. With the decline of Confucian ethics and the invasion of the Japanese, the family has undergone greater trials than ever before. Perhaps it is true that from now on there is no permanence, except for the Chinese race.

February 27th . . . I HAVE written nothing since I came to Chungking except a short play in verse on the subject of the Wang Lung Men steps. I cannot get them out of my mind. They cut the rock-face in two, you can see them from every vantage point on the south bank, and at every moment of the day they change colour. They are like white silk in the morning mist; but a little while later, when the water-carriers come to feed their pails, they turn suddenly black and glint like wet black marble, and again in the afternoon when a pale sun shines feebly through the clouds, they are shadowed with purple lines and people walk down the steps in bright clothes, and you see them from the opposite shore like angels descending to the wells.

They have been practising for some festival or other. This afternoon a great yellow dragon wound its way slowly up the steps, emitting fire, coiling its great folds like a concertina. There were lanterns in his eyes, though it was daylight. Inside the dragon boys wearing only blue trousers rolled up to their knees were crouching in mysterious attitudes of worship. I remained still; fed with my thoughts; for the river is so much like a dragon that

138

it was difficult not to believe that the dragon had come to life, plumed with feathers and breathing fire. But when the dragon reached the topmost steps it surrendered ingloriously, the boys stepped out and the yellow skin lying on the stones looked tawdry. A moment before I had thought it the most powerful thing in the world!

The dragon, the stone steps, the river flowing so powerfully between the banks. . . . And then, too, the blind beggar who came down the steps one morning, a beggar who must have come from the north, for he was powerfully built and his great naked shoulders coming out of the mist looked like the shoulders of some god. Had Ulysses come to Chungking on his pilgrimage? So, in the drama, I imagined an old beggar coming down the stone steps at midnight, when the last ferry-boat had gone, and exchanging reminiscences with a soldier and a girl. He had lost his daughter in the rape of Nanking. In the morning a storm arises, and a ferry-boat is thrown upon the coast in a fog, the only survivor is a small girl with a ring on her wrist. The old beggar believes it to be his daughter, and the soldier consoles him:

This whiteness is the purity of your souls.
As a boy wears a ring of jade
To remind him of love for mankind,
So the white falcons of his wrist
Lead him to the promised land.
Early the sons of Han
Were imprisoned in the fields of grain,
And earlier still the grain comes to them
Through the mouth of the Mother,
Who toiling like Ruth in the plain saw the distant
    kinsman,
And sleeping at night at his feet she remembered
The winnowed husks, the grain and his sleepless love,
So we who are living must never forget
The sighs of the peasants and their urgent demands
For the fruits of their labour.
Now over the earth there come
The whispers of the dying; and children in brothels
Speak a language known only to the soldier.
For when the innocent girl opens her eyes
And sees in the revolving mirror

The curving back of the soldier,
How shall her eyes scatter like diamonds
Corinthian columns, orchards and kisses?
Listen, the words
Are planted on the lips of St. Eulalia.
They grow in green towers, pillars of fire, cloudy
    branches,
Roses of magnificence, meadows of edelweiss, immortelles,
But there in the dark room where only the shadows
Remind you of China, the soldier bends to his task
The weight of generations of murderers.
Why did she come here? Choosing the path through
    the brambles?
Or taking the narrow path by the rice-paper windows,
Where the peasants are baking cakes and the champing
    horses
Spoke of a freedom still unperceived.
Why did she stand near the temple in the evening,
    wondering
Whether the aeroplanes flying low were herons or eagles?
Why did she wait for the soldier? Were you expecting
    a crown?
Did you come through the boles of the trees? No, we
    came singly,
Expecting no offering. Peace was no crown. We were
    weary,
And there was no health left in us. Only in the morning
    we saw
The spears of the beloved coming to meet us. And then
    the vision
Of peace in the snow-white pillow, the white kingdom.
For us there is no glory.
But afterwards, in the crystal light, she leans on her
    elbow,
And sees through the snow-thatched roof the roads in
    the air,
And clouds shaped like heroes. Shall I kill myself?
No, I must work. This is my freedom.

BEGGAR

                        Who is this girl?

She who suffered and died, one whose form and features,
Race and speech I know not, one whose eyes
Soft, mitigated by divinest lids, build in faith
The virtue we are searching for.
Three years ago she was a child, eager
To exchange a bruised knee
For a mother's caress of hair.
Then we who found her, sought her
Not here in the ruins, but in the hidden pathways
Where the brothels are forgotten and only the tombs
  of the ancestors
Shine on the white hills. This was our suffering.
Let us sleep now.

February 28th . . . THEY were sowing the winter rye high
up in the green hills. Ducks—the brightest-coloured ducks imaginable—were wandering over the fields, and the small boy clinging to the buffalo did not shiver in the cold wind which came
from the second range of mountains. There were pine-trees sighing in the wind, whose leaves are beginning to shine with the
colour which steel would have if there were any greenness in
steel. The small kernels of rye lay in the old man's hand, so plump
and white that you would have said they were a small family of
white mice if you had seen him gazing at them from a distance.
And slowly they began planting. I know nothing of farming; I
do not even know the way the seeds are dug into the ground, or
how they are reaped, and so I watched him carefully as he rolled
his sleeves and dipped his hand in the water. The hand seemed
to stay there for a long time. He was bent down, ankle-deep in
the soft slimy water, in which his blue coat open at the neck and
his round shining copper head were imperfectly reflected—an old
man, but his body was young and lithe, and there was no great
pain in bending. The old woman followed him with her basket.
He lifted handful after handful from the small bamboo basket,
and when at last every inch of the field had been covered, and
his hands and his body were splashed with mud, he looked up to
the sky and sighed. It was like watching a primitive festival, for
at that moment the sun came out through the heavy clouds and
for the first time the grey muddy field shone gold in sunlight.
Afterwards we followed them to their home, the small brown
141

cottage half-buried among the pines. When they were near the house, they came to a small stone shrine the colour of old bread, very brown and no higher than their waists. There were two gods within the shrine. The paint had peeled from their faces and their gowns, which were once gold, were a still darker brown and pitted by worm-holes—as though the gilt bread had been nibbled by mice. The old woman took a red spill from the basket, lighted it and pressed it in the little mound of grey ash within the shrine. They stood there for some minutes. They did not light any more spills. And after a few moments, while they gazed intently at the impassive gods, they went on their way, the old woman swinging her empty basket and the old man striding forward as though he possessed the whole earth. And after them came the small naked boy clinging to the horns of the buffalo, his face bright red and all his body wet and shining from the rain. . . .

March 1st . . . EVERY morning on the ferry-boat there is a man who makes a speech and attempts to sell things. Sometimes he sells books, sometimes patent medicines, sometimes little bright packages of cosmetics or hairpins wrapped up in coloured paper. It is always the same man, a small grey face with a yellow forehead, hair clipped close to the skull, a pair of spectacles which are bound together with pieces of tape. In his squeaking high-pitched voice there is no trace of emotion, and he seems to be saying: "This is what I am paid to say—it's obviously nonsense, but I won't cease till we reach the other side." The small ship gathers speed. The feathers of the paddle-wheels throw up great white fountains, the heat from the engine-room is stifling, a cold wind blows across the estuary and still he speaks in his monotonous high-pitched voice, and still no one pays any attention to him. The great white wall of Chungking looms over us—ahead of us the intolerable stairways. We prepare our bundles: the chickens, the rolls of blue cloth, the bamboo bags filled with produce from the mountains. We are near the shore, but the current has driven us down-stream, and it will be a long time before we reach the landing-stage. The man with the broken spectacles knows this. He pays no attention to the people who are queueing up before the gangway. He smiles knowingly. He knows that he can break through the walls of their patience, he knows that they are bored by the interminable journey, he knows that in the end they will surrender to the brief moment when boredom disappears and

142

money is exchanged. The landing-stage creeps nearer. You can almost see the oranges shining in the stalls at the foot of the Wang Lung Men steps, but they are hidden behind mat-sheds and it is only when the mat-sheds are split open by the wind that you can see them clearly. The soldier on the landing-stage is preparing to open the gates through which you will pass. The old man continues in the same monotonous voice, but already people have come to buy his wares. He is like an automaton. He does not smile, and even when he is changing your money, he is declaring the excellence of his hairpins. . . .

March 2nd . . . IN THE house of the American Military Attaché—surely the warmest and most carefully-decorated in Chungking—you sit round the fire, wine is poured out, the uniformed servants slip past on noiseless feet. Here is everything you want—good butter, books, whisky, the choicest wines. An atmosphere of complete repose. You can hear the wireless in another room, and as though from a long way you can hear someone speaking into the telephone: and it is obvious that a young man is making a rendezvous with a girl. You look round the room, the doors are painted white, there are curtains, cushions, a strip of Chinese embroidery on a table. A long-legged youth is declaiming against the Japanese while leaning comfortably against the fireside. We have been discussing Changsha, but already the battle is so remote that we have only the vaguest idea of what we are talking about. The Philippines, Malaya, Burma—they are present in our minds, but only as even the most innocent of us are eternally accompanied by ghosts. The ghosts do not raise their voices. The servant in the white mess-jacket enters to announce that dinner is served, and it is only at that moment that the American Military Attaché announces that he had himself taken that extraordinary photograph which hangs upon the walls. It is a photograph of Chungking—Chungking in flames. It shows towering columns of heavy black smoke rising over the city, twenty or thirty of these columns, and each one nearly a mile high. The shadow of the smoke lies on the river, which seems to be broken by the weight of the smoke hanging in the air. It is obviously a bright day, for where there are no explosions the city is dead-white, like powder. And suddenly, as we all look at the photograph, the defensive mechanism of our minds crumbles like the smoking, powdery city, and the ghosts of the Philippines, Malaya, Burma, the islands

143

in the South Seas, raise their voices. All through dinner there is a hush. We ask polite questions, we discuss for the ten millionth time the differences between American and English words and their meanings, and we all know that we want to return to the fireplace and the photograph of bombed Chungking.

There is a chill in the air when we return. The fire has gone out. The photograph seems to be in movement; we can see the flames and the black smoke-clouds climbing, and we have only to shut our eyes to see the Japanese aviators sweeping in formation over the defenceless city. You can hear the sickening thump of the bombs and the screams which break the silence between the raids, and then in this silence the Military Attaché speaking: "But the most terrible thing of all is not in the picture—people were trying to reach the safety of the south bank, there was a large boat and the Japanese bombed it. When the Japanese had gone away, there was no boat and no people struggling on the water, there was no sign of wreckage and not even the white trace on the water which shows where bombs have been—*there was nothing at all except their screams.*"

March 3rd . . . THE Dutch Chargé d'Affaires has invited me to stay with him in the pine-woods. We met in Chungking at the Bank of China, but the bank took such a long time to complete his affairs that I was on the point of turning away when he suddenly appeared, hopped into the car and we drove off towards the motor-ferry. I knew nothing about the motor-ferry, which lies up-stream, where the river curves into a great shining bay. We waited for the first cars to pass over, and then glided smoothly across the river in a lovely stillness. The sounds of traffic in the city did not reach our ears, but we heard the birds and the cries of small boys playing in the sand. It is low-tide and there is sand everywhere, and you begin to realise why the upper reaches of this prodigious river are called the Golden Sands. The Chargé d'Affaires talks in a quiet serious voice of Nanking. He is one of the few who remained behind after the Japanese entered. He cannot believe that anything that happened to Rotterdam can be worse than the Japanese treatment of the Chinese in Nanking. "It was terrible beyond words—not terror that can be understood, not terror enforced on the population by order, for no orders were given and consequently no orders were obeyed. It was not the inhuman terror of the Germans who count people mathematically,

144

and say: 'So many people must be executed, so many tortured.' Nor was it the terror of the jungle, or even of madness, or of the uncultivated. It was not naked terror—for it was terror wrapped up in uniform, and bearing bayonets and carrying revolvers. It was in a sense a kind of negative terror, the terror which comes through the sudden knowledge that your skins are terribly thin and at any moment you may be hurt. Imagine some animal so tender that the slightest movement, a breath of wind, will produce such pain on its skin that it squeals in terrible agony. This is why the Japanese committed those skins of theirs to the most terrible punishment. They suffered atrociously. They screamed with horror. And all the time, afraid that they would be hurt, surrounded by their enemies, they committed the most inhuman actions that any soldiers have ever committed. The siege of the cities of Holland in the Middle Ages pales into insignificance beside their siege of the human decencies in Nanking. They committed crimes which not even the wildest Germans could commit, and they committed them in anguish and fear, in mortal terror, screaming in cold blood."

We discussed the reasons for the peculiar apathy of the Japanese towards their own soldiers. I had seen the funeral pyres at Changsha; and there were curious stories of how the Japanese would murder their own soldiers when they were wounded. The Dutch Chargé d'Affaires nodded. He had heard of it thousands of times before, but I was unprepared for his answer. "There are too many fish round the coast of Japan."

"What have fish got to do with it?"

"Iodine content too high. They live on fish—here there is almost no fish. When they come to China, they have to change their diet—with all the consequences that entails. They are brought up in the simple faith—to love the Emperor, to die for the Emperor and become saints in Heaven after they have died. And the first thing they see in China is the cultivated scepticism of the Chinese —not only the intellectuals, but also the peasants have this scepticism. It is rooted in them. But for the Japanese, without faith, the world does not exist. And so they break down into a state of terrible remorse and dissatisfaction."

We had crossed the ferry. We were climbing up the immense hair-pin roads which have been cut out of the mountains. On one side, sheer cliffs towering into the clouds; on the other side, a drop to the pine-forests and the river below. The road was quite

145

new, the mark of the pickaxe glittering still on the granite walls. And the small motor-car, whistling along the yellow road, seemed to be possessed of ten thousand demons of speed. We raced towards the clouds. At intervals we would see the wide bay of the river, like an estuary among sands, shining like a silver shield. It was like a journey in a switch-back railway, twisting and turning for ever between the rocks. And then we came out into a broad flat road at the bottom of the valley, the same road which I had travelled a few days before with Bergery, but at this hour it was bathed in an extraordinary greyish-blue light, and even the clouds hanging low overhead possessed this extraordinary colour. There were storms ahead; we could hear the rustling in the pine-forest, and the sighing of the wind on the distant mountains. "We'll have to hurry," he murmured; and leaving the car at the foot of an immense lane of steps shaded by pine-trees, we walked up to his small house, which is sheltered on all sides by the pines.

It was one of those houses which had been built many years ago by some of the early merchants in the treaty-port: all wood and white-wash and mosquito-netting. Inside a small fire was roaring. There were comfortable chairs. The wireless was on, the blue valves glimmering in the faint light. A portrait of Queen Wilhelmina, a photograph of an extremely beautiful Dutch girl on the mantelpiece, Dutch cigars and a few bottles of Chungking gin. It is not a very potent drink, and we drank near the fire, while the wind raged outside and the noise of the wind among the pines was like a hurricane.

We talk about Batavia and Soerabaya. For a moment we are living on the sun-drenched coast of Java, looking out towards the islands. The B.B.C. news bulletin comes on. There is continuous fighting, but already it is becoming clear that Java is in the same position as the Philippines and Malaya—the green forests and the white cities are being stamped out by the small dark Japanese.

"And what happens?" I ask.

"We shall carry on—from the remote forests. It may take years, but in the end the islands will return to the House of Orange."

And suddenly, while the wind tears through the pines and the roof creaks under the weight of wind and rain, I have a vision of flying from Soerabaya to Den Pasar in Bali three years before. It was a cloudless day, a perfect day for flying. For hundreds of miles we flew low over virgin forests, thick matted forests which showed no earth between the dense green branches. And sud-
146

denly, as we approached Madura, the forest gave place to a small volcano, biscuit-coloured, and in the centre of the volcano a green lake and small puffs of pure white smoke. It was perfectly peaceful; a few birds circled low over the green lake—cormorants and egrets, and we watched them as we banked over, wondering at the stillness and beauty of the mountain lake. So they would fight in these impenetrable green jungles near the sea, and sometimes a submarine would come through the sea-lanes, and sometimes they would be attacked by wild beasts.

March 4th . . . WHY did I come to China? Why does anyone come to China? There are moment in China when the dirt and poverty of the people make one suddenly decide to take the next aeroplane to India, and then a moment later a girl on a white donkey passes slowly along a dusty road, or a pair of pigeons rise high in the sky, or at night a courtyard opens silently, lamps are lit, you hear the click of tiles and the whispers of women down some deserted alley-way; and then the amazing vitality and beauty of these people, whose arts are so ancient that they have long ago forgotten the origin of their simplest customs, surprise one with their fine excess. There are moments when you have the impression that everyone in China is consumptive—they die quickly, but in the short period of their life they burn with a fine flame. The small boys at the landing-stage who come to take your luggage—they look eight years old, but they are probably fourteen—burn with the same flame as the countrywomen who come into the city with bamboo baskets piled high with vegetables. The boys, especially, are handsome and quick in their movements, and they will tell you that they belong to a gang led by a boy of sixteen and that all their money is turned over to the gang. And as you follow them along the rocky pathways beyond the walled houses on the south bank, listening to the patter of their feet on the rain-soaked rock and watching them in the blazing light of the bamboo torches you carry, they seem to possess so much wisdom and beauty that you wonder whether any children in any other part of the world would equal them, though these are half-starved and they stagger under the weight of their burdens.

China was made for the night and the dawn. A few days ago we began to live in a house near the Canadian Mission Hospital, far away from the main traffic of the river. You reached the house

147

by a long winding path over the foot-hills, climbing among steep fields of rice, small battered whitewashed houses, duck-ponds, tombs. We would cross the river from the north bank under a full moon, and it was not always a pleasant journey, for the boatman would think nothing of stopping in mid-stream and refuse to take us to the other bank unless we paid another ten dollars, and sometimes, knowing that we would have to walk for miles along the rocky coast, he would allow the boat to drift down-stream. But always the nights were beautiful. The shape of a curving roof against the stars, the songs of the boatmen, the small red fires in the boats along the shore, and the great white cliffs of Chungking would console us for the solitary journey. And even the gravestones, so gloomy and white in the moonlight, and even the dogs grubbing the earth at the root of the recently-made graves, were not real—they were reality raised to a higher pitch of excitement. So we walked alone at night, listening to the children and old men breathing under their poor matchwood sheds, while the moon rose and the great sweep of the river disappeared into a silver distance. Sometimes, too, but very rarely, there occurred the happiness which a Chinese poet of the Sung Dynasty described in a long-forgotten poem:

I am old. Nothing pleases me any more. Moreover, I am not a great scholar and my ideas have rarely travelled further than my feet. I know only my forest, to which I always return.

The blue fingers of the moon caress my lute. The wind tosses the clouds and ungirds my silken robe.

You fool! You ask me what is the supreme happiness on earth. It is to listen to the song of a young girl as she passes along the road after having asked you the way.

March 5th . . . WE HAVE been walking among the hills on the south bank. The sun is out, there are great white butterflies slowly wandering up the slopes of yet uncut winter rye, and the sky is blue like a thrush's egg, and there are warm furry gusts of air from every rock. We have been climbing the Tu Shan, a great green pepper-pot flanked with groves of pines; and the pines are in leaf, and everywhere the earth is scented with the spring—a smell compounded of milk and musk and the petals of the small white nameless flowers in the grass.

It is spring, and the loveliest time in south-west China, where

148

there is no autumn and winter comes suddenly out of the darkening north; and no real summer, for the heat comes out of the sky, drenching you in a boiling yellow liquid. But spring there is, when the winds of the Yangtse freshen the white sails and the mountains fume no clouds. In the desolate blue transparent sky spring descends softly and unmenacingly, with a submerging sweetness which is reflected from the rough stones and the green tombs. Szechuan blooms only in spring. The liquid stream of the sky sometimes descends in showers, and the nights are longer and colder than visionary dreams; and not so cold that we do not climb out over the rough-stone banks and watch the fires. Spring is the time of fires and meteors—at night. But during the day such a softness in earth and shadow that we wander tranquilly over the hills, where four thousand two hundred years ago the Emperor Yu met his bride.

We climbed over the hills where we have been earlier in January, and walked towards the source of the river, avoiding the small villages and making for the pagodas. There was a pagoda all covered with green moss, and after walking across a moor with ancient quarryings all solitary and primeval, the solemn pagoda shone suddenly like a jewel in the valley below, through a sparkling wave of sun and dewy haze. The haze of spring is a continual enchantment. The haze floats over the river, disappears, emerges among the cliffs or floats down-stream among the waves of the river, flying like a pennant from the small tug-boats and the camouflaged gunboats under their green mat of leaves. The tender, dreamy haze of spring has changed the rocks of winter into yellow flames, and we have already forgotten those days when we climbed down the slopes of the south bank into the waiting ferry-boat, among the reek of horses and their droppings, in the silt and the mud, with the rain . . . yes, we have forgotten the rain, we tell ourselves over and over again, yes, we have completely forgotten the rain.

Bergery has been reading everything he can lay his hands on about the history of Chungking. He is half appalled and half delighted by the age of the place. He does not begin in revolutionary times. He begins at a time when Szechuan lay under an immense blue sea, which suddenly and as the result of precipitating earthquakes turned into an immense river which flowed through Yunnan and down the central valley of Indo-China into Malaya, meeting the Pacific somewhere near where Singapore

149

now stands. He talks learnedly of the Emperor Wu, who was second Emperor of the Chow Dynasty, who made a member of his family the Duke of Pahtzekuo, and when in 340 B.C. Shi Huang Ti of the Tsin Dynasty, who burnt the books of Confucius and conquered the whole of China—but I have forgotten what Shi Huang Ti accomplished in Szechuan and I remember only the story of the bandit Chang Hsien-chung, who murdered forty million people in the province at the end of the Ming Dynasty and enjoyed his murders so much that he attempted to invade the province of Kweichow and repeat the performance. . . .

We passed through a small village, cruel under the overhanging eaves of dark rocks, where the children looked pale—and Bergery asked: "Do they ever go in the sunlight, which is so near?" and he invented a story of the children of Szechuan, who are so accustomed to seeing a dark cloud overhead that they are afraid of the sun, and perhaps even regard the sun as an enemy, and suffer terrible punishments if they ever step into the sunlight —but at that moment, climbing over a buff of bare yellow rock, we saw some children playing in the sun, their great black eyes shining with excitement as they tried to push a small black pig towards the crest of the rock.

We walked along narrow streets where the crooked pavements were no longer terrifying as in winter; for in this bright sunshine it was impossible to imagine the filth which came running over the stones two months ago. The air was sweet. The plum-blossoms, like a million white birds sitting on the branches, scented the air; and there were small buds of magnolias and high up on the hills a faint redness of poinsettias. We lay down on a hill near the Canadian Mission Hospital looking at the river below and the valley behind, every field neatly cultivated, the green lettuces sparkling and the small shoots of Indian corn greener even than the lettuces, and we wondered why this city, whose name in Chinese contains the character for "love," should be so terrible to us still. There was no sign of the bombardments, though the grey-biscuit walls of the hospital have traces of black explosions. It was very still, and very beautiful—the haze on the rivers, for the two rivers met at our feet, and the ghost-white sails of the sampans gliding tenderly up-stream. And sometimes we could see the small beetle of a ferry-boat churning a white wake in the green river, puffing up grey smudges of smoke and hopping into harbour. Then millions of much smaller beetles would make their
150

way up through the markets which are strewn all over the sandy coast when the river is at low tide, and then suddenly they would burst through the other end of the market and climb immense and innumerable steps towards the vestiges of a city wall. We could see far-off mountains thirty miles away, and occasionally the brilliant pale glitter of a pagoda, whiter than any marble, on the crest of one of the mountains. And later the sun rose higher, drawing the scent from the earth, while Bergery shaded his eyes and looked down the immense yellowish sweep of the Chialing river, following the flight of a blue pie or the hovering of eagle or hawk. And all Chungking lying below, its white sails unfurled, ready to weigh anchor and float down the Yangtse like a giant white bird, splendid in her whiteness reflecting the sunlight, so splendid that we forgot the tawdry grey spire of the Cathedral and the grey canyons of the streets and the guilt and the suffering which lay deeply embedded in the city. The city, like the country, lived. It was China and would be China for ever; it would never change, and no bombs could destroy her. Down below, among the green circular tombs and the dusty roads where children and old women were following invisible pathways, a small lake lay in the shadow of maples; and seemed indeed to hover like a lake in the sky before our eyes, not blue, but green with duckweed, with the most brilliantly coloured ducks paddling in the strange shapeless black roads which in the green lake, made a fabulous duck with a green sheen of wings and a copper-coloured head and half-visible copper-coloured webbed feet struggling through the duckweed. The wind brushed the feathers, or an eagle-shaped cloud descended on the green lake, and the duck became transformed into a reddish-purple animal, with no sign of copper-coloured head and no webbed feet at all. This was magical country, and so beautiful. The long tufts of the pines, and the blue mountains, and the small brown plaster and bamboo houses already cracking and crackling in the heat, and the eagle-light wheeling of the perfectly blue daylight, and the ghostly whiteness which crowns the plum-blossoms like slowly melting snow—only the snow does not melt, but with delicate crystals remains streaked on the reddish branches. And in this heat, looking down at the curved roofs of the flaring temple which rose from a courtyard below, I heard Bergery speaking of Changsha, and the sky did not darken but seemed to increase its devouring and beautiful light.

151

"I have been thinking of the boy—do you remember the boy we saw on the banks of the Liuyang river? I would like to write a story about him. You remember how he described the attack, how the Japanese were crossing the river at night, and he heard nothing, and suddenly one of his men said that a whole regiment was crossing by the water-wheel, and there was not enough ammunition to keep them away. It was not the beauty of the boy which made me notice him, but the way when he described these things he seemed to be springing on his toes, and at any moment I expected him to soar into the air, and perhaps disappear. There are people who seem to be able to make a leap into the infinite, who seem indeed always about to make this leap, and we remember them because we are afraid they will disappear. I dreamed last night that he was dead. I knew in my dream that the army was farther north, but I dreamed that he had died exactly where we saw him, among the rice-mounds, leaning against a tree, wearing the blue cotton uniform which had been washed so many times that it was nearly white, and as he died— oh, I have forgotten what he said, but it was something so beautiful and unexpected that I shall always remember his expression. I knew then, as I have known unconsciously for many years, that I shall not escape from this grief."

I did not know what was in his mind, for the sky was still clear, the small boats were still riding their sails into the ghostly wind and the plum-trees were still flooded with white birds; and everything was quiet among these yellow rocks. He continued:

"Probably you have never read Virgil. No one in your generation reads Virgil, and perhaps it doesn't matter. But at the end of the Fifth Book of the Æneid, there is the account of how Palinurus dies. He knows that he is fated to die, and perhaps he knows that it is impossible for him to die heroically. I will try to translate it. 'And now the dewy night had almost reached the middle of her course, and the weary sailors, stretched along the hard benches underneath the oars, relaxed their limbs in peaceful repose; when the god of sleep, gliding down from the ethereal stars, parted the dusky air and dispelled the shades; and speaking to Palinurus, he said: "Palinurus, son of Iasius, the seas themselves carry forward the fleet, the gales blow fair and steady, the hour for rest has come. Recline your head and steal your weary eyes from labour."' Palinurus listens to the voice, overcome with sleep, remembering that he is the helmsman and that the fate of
152

the company of Æneas depends upon his watchfulness. But believing the voice of the god, Palinurus at last obeys, and while he sleeps the god seizes him and plunges him in the waves. Later, when the ships were being driven against the rocks of the Sirens, Æneas, realising what the gods have accomplished, suddenly cries: 'O, Palinurus, who hast so much confided in the fair aspect of skies and sea, naked wilt thou lie on unknown sands—

> *nudus in ignota, Palinure, iacebis harena.'* "

As he said these words, Bergery's eyes were grave to sadness; and repeating them slowly and softly, it seemed as though he was attempting to raise the boy from his grave by an incantation. Since he returned from Changsha, there has been a settled sadness in his face and in his eyes. As we came down the hill in the sunshine, he said: "I think I admire the Chinese more than any other race. It is not that on the whole they are more beautiful than other races, or that they have more vitality, or even that they are more human. It is simply that I am beginning to understand them better than I have understood any other race. Their army is not always well led. The soldiers are too often underfed and squeezed by the officers; but that they should live and fight *in spite* of everything that makes life so terrible in China—this is what is wonderful." The sun was still shining on the plum-trees. Below us the stone city was spreading out its white sails.

March 7th . . . WE HAVE been to see Dr. Wang Wen-hao, the Minister of Industrial Reorganisation. A Dutch friend had given us a letter of introduction, and he begged us on no account to spend longer than a quarter of an hour with the Minister.

The Minister lives in a new house built over the Yangtse, a small white courtyard where a few trees planted in stone vases gave an air of the countryside, and round the courtyard are small white buildings. The sun was shining. The river was pure white in the faint morning sun, and in this sequestered corner of Chungking began to acquire a charm which I had thought completely lacking in the city, the charm of something small in a city of giants. And the office of the Minister was equally small—hardly larger than my bedroom on the south bank—and there were no decorations except a few maps on the walls. Through the window he could look out at the Yangtse, the small black sampans and the coolies, the great black masses of people milling up stone steps—the industrial reorganisation of China.

He was a small man with a brown face, deeply sun-tanned. His lips were thin, his forehead high and his fingers as he laid them on the blackwood table resembled the fingers of scholars, and you expected to find long white nails in golden sheaths. A terrible motor accident some years ago had very nearly broken his skull in two, but there was no sign of injury and the small face turned towards the light possessed an extraordinary calm. He was a scientist, like General Yu Ta-wei, the Minister of Munitions, but he had thrown himself into the task of Chinese industrial reorganisation with something of the passion of a religious enthusiast. Yet he did not look weary. There were hardly any papers on his tables. In his long maroon gown, he looked perfectly at ease, smiling quietly, his hands folded on the table; and as he listened to Bergery's remarks an occasional quiet laugh would break the monotonous voices of the conversation.

Bergery asked him about the effects of the closing of the Burma Road. Dr. Wang Wen-hao laid his hands on the table, palms upward.

"It is disastrous," he said quietly, so quietly that we could barely hear him. "In A.D. 126 the explorer Chang-ch'ien opened the road towards the West. As you know, he crossed the Tarim and the Sogdhana, and visited the kingdom of Samarkand and penetrated into India. Today the road is closed, and for the first time since Chang-ch'ien left China, we are cut off from the world except for the small supply routes through Russia. The future is dark. We are reorganising our transport and our industries on the basis of self-sufficiency; but our means are limited and we cannot see far into the future."

He was not optimistic. He complained a little against the British, who had not installed sufficient machinery in the oil-wells nearer China; he complained—not bitterly, but with a kind of proud intolerance—against the lack of success in Burma. It was clear that he regarded Burma as the crux of the transport situation, and would have been prepared to sacrifice a province of China rather than that communication with the outside world should be interrupted. He pointed to the maps on the wall. He showed us the centres where the greatest production was taking place, and when Bergery asked gently about the oil-wells in

154

Kansu, he made it clear that their development was as nothing in comparison with the development of oil-wells in Burma. He spoke about the difficulties and the successes of Chinese industry, the extraordinary stratagems to which the Chinese were reduced in an effort to maintain production, and though he mentioned figures, they were not for publication, and though he believed fully in the recuperative powers of Chinese industry, he was clearly disheartened by recent events in China.

"But we shall go on—we shall send out more and more expeditions to find out whatever metals remain in the Chinese earth. We have the scientists and the workmen, and though we are fighting for time . . ." He shrugged his shoulders. We had already been talking for an hour. He came down the steps to the doorway, looking very slight and extraordinarily young in his maroon gown, and as we shook hands he said: "Have no fear. The mistakes of the past can be rectified, but we can no longer afford to have mistakes in the future." He smiled; and while the car drove off, he stood there waving, and we wondered why so great a man should waste so much time on us. Almost alone, he had reorganised the basis of Chinese industry. The young students going out to the north-west, the factories along the river or buried among the mountains owed their origin to him, and more than any man except the Generalissimo he was responsible for the continued resistance of the Chinese people.

I remembered the slight figure outlined against the bare branches of trees later in the evening when Bergery was looking across the silver river under the moon.

"Did you notice, though he was very short and almost insignificant, there was something so clearly shining in his eyes. They were like the moon . . ."

I do not know what had come over him. A dog barked. Between the rows of dull trees a fog was ascending. In the rice-fields there was all the moisture of ploughed lands, the heaviness of labour and growth and grain-bearing, the sweet scents of autumn strangely transformed to winter; one could breathe them only on the bright edges of the world, on the rim of the desert or in the centre of a great kingdom.

March 8th, The Smells of Chungking . . . I DO not know why, but I associate the smells of Chungking with England. The terrible heaviness of Malaya is absent, and instead all smells and

155

sounds seem to be muted, softened, made richer by the mist and the rivers. There are places where the smells are unbearable: refuse-pits, gutters streaming with filth, as in the narrow road which winds up to Huang-ko-ya behind the hills. There you will find dead dogs and rats creeping with yellow vermin; and there, too, you will find winter flowers growing in secluded gardens. But it is in Chungking, or rather on the outskirts of Chungking, that you smell England. There are loads of rice hay which are not entirely different from the loads of hay which you will come across at the winding of a road in Cornwall. There are motor-buses which smell like French motor-buses, perhaps because they both use wood-oil; there are small country cottages smelling of wetness, tobacco and hemp, and this, too, is like England. Down by the river there is everywhere the smell of fresh pinewood and charcoal, a smell which for some reason I associate with Hampstead Heath. And I have walked down a small country lane after the rains, while the sun sucked up all the wetness exuding from the rock and a faint rainbow was etched out on the sky, and then it has seemed that all England was ripening under the sun, and I had only to turn my head to see the first white berries on the hedgerows. . . .

March 10th . . . LAST night, returning from Chungking, the boatman took me three miles down-stream. It was very late, the moon was covered with clouds and the river so dark that perhaps he was in danger of losing his way. I remember that the small boat moored at last on a sandspit and there were great rocks high overhead, and it rained dismally, and I heard his oars creaking in the rowlocks long after he had gone away. I climbed along the rocks. I could see nothing except a faint silvery-blue gleam on the river and the lights of Wang Lung Men steps. No boats passed. It was dreary and miserable, and because the sun had been shining in the morning, I had taken no overcoat. I thought of Bergery, sitting up alone in the house, reading or writing by candle-light (for there is no electric light in this small walled house in the country), and I wondered whether he had awakened the servant and whether they were climbing down to the beach to fetch me.

I wandered for hours. It was difficult to see, and the rocks were precipitous. People were sleeping under mat-sheds, thin crusts of bamboo ten inches high; and sometimes in the shelter of the rock
156

there were beggars and small children sleeping fitfully. They did not stir as I passed, but I heard them coughing. And then the dogs barked. I had come to the outskirts of a village. I was pursued by the Furies. They barked and snapped and jumped out of the darkness till I almost cried out for mercy against these avenging angels of silence. And still everyone was asleep. At a large walled house at the end of the village, I knocked on the gate. After a long while an old man came out, and it seemed to me that I was listening to him for hours as he hobbled across the cobbles. He opened the gate and raised the lantern to his eyes and said nothing. He stared into the depths of the landscape, and sometimes his lips would move, but he said nothing. He was shivering in the rain, his eyes were wide open and the little tassels of his cap gradually filled with rain and turned silver. And so he stood there, watching the night, long after I had gone.

I slept in the shelter of a gravestone, looking down over the milk-white mist and the faint rain. There was a small plum-tree in front of me, and though I slept on and off for a few minutes, I was conscious of the presence of the plum-tree all night. I did not dare to touch it. It was perfect as it stood there, and I wondered whether its flowers would open with the dawn. But in the dawn the tree was black and chilly, without buds, and the inscriptions on the gravestone were unreadable, and I walked back to the small white-walled house in the hills feeling like someone who had trespassed upon the night. And even now I can hear the dogs barking, barking, barking. . . .

March 11th . . . I HAVE been thinking of Anna von O., for whom I once possessed a terrible affection. I could not live without her, or see anything at all except through her eyes. She wrote with greater skill than anyone I have known, and possessed a gift for satire so devastating that her books were almost too painful to read; and the long story she wrote about the German Consulate in Baghdad had annoyed the Germans so much that they offered a reward for her capture dead or alive.

She was one of the first foreign correspondents to enter Spain, where she adopted a small Spanish boy. One evening, in October, 1938, Hidalgo de Cisneros, the Commander-in-Chief of the Spanish Republican Air Force, brought the boy from Moscow, where he had been staying. I remember the first time I saw the child. He lay in the centre of the enormous bed, looking terribly weak

157

and small, like a featherless chicken, and long after midnight the tears were still streaming down his face. Anna was also crying. She had been looking forward to him for so long, she was so over-worked and the terrible strain of her life in Paris, the work with the Freedom Radio and the savagery of the French police, that she lived in a kind of nightmare, not daring to go near the child for fear he would suddenly howl in the heart-rending voice of a child who had no idea where he was or what was happening to him.

But the next day he revived. He would walk out in the Luxembourg Gardens carrying a doll, or trailing a little wooden horse in the dust under the chestnut trees. He became as brown as a berry, the weariness wore away, he was full of a gay impudent life, with large dark eyes which possessed incredible depths. He wore on the left lapel of his coat the small winged badge of an officer in the Spanish Air Force, and his small round face, the smell of bath-water, milk and woollens which seemed to surround him wherever he went and the way he would swing into the saddle of the bi-cycle I bought for him one winter's night are things which I have never been able to forget, and hope I shall remember always.

Tonight, at seven o'clock, in a warm room, drinking sherry, I learnt for the first time that Anna had been herded into the *Cercle d'Hiver* among all the other refugees, and it is difficult to believe that she was not holding Juan tightly in her arms.

March 12th . . . In a few days I shall become a professor in a Chinese University. Years ago in Singapore, I met a Chinese scholar who spoke of the Universities of Pekin as though they alone possessed a passport into the future. He would describe the laboratories, the lotos pools, the blue-gowned students, the wealth of books and the glory of old Chinese architecture, and he would say: "You are wasting your time here—you should go to Pekin, which will soon be the intellectual capital of the world." I could not take him to the Naval Base, and he could never understand my affection for the extraordinary harbour where five races worked uninterruptedly under the heavenly sunlight building great docks out of mud, and high walls where previously there were only mangrove swamps. I showed him my book *Singapore River* in manuscript, and though he recognised himself in it, he would say only: "There is nothing here about Singapore, and everything about China." Perhaps it was true. We smoked long
158

into the night, looking over the muddy reaches of the sea, and from time to time he would switch the conversation back to the subject of the Chinese Universities, where he had been a professor. "They are only beginning, you understand. Everything is there. When there is civil war, and even when there is war, the Universities continue. All that is best comes from the Universities. And now——" And then he would go on to talk of the vast plans of reconstruction which were in the hands of the Chinese Universities. The youths and young girls who came out of the Universities were building a new life and a new civilisation out of nothing. He has no words to express his admiration of them. "In my youth we were fearful, we obeyed orders, we followed the ancient traditions, which were good and just. But these—these young people, without any traditions, throw themselves upon the world. They are rockets, burning in the night, and they give so great a flame that I am continually dazzled by them. . . ."

March 17th . . . Four o'clock in the morning. We had been sleeping in a small house facing the Chialing river, and the sounds of the mahjong players could be heard through the walls, and suddenly there were the sounds of cries, sharp orders, a terrible sound like an interminable wailing. The police had come to arrest the mahjong players, and the young poet woke up with a start and rushed outside. When he returned he was pale, and his smooth black hair was covered with glistening globules of rain.

"What happened?"

"They came to arrest them. I wanted to see it."

"Why?"

"It's interesting, and besides—I want to know everything that goes on. I am trying to write about China. I must see everything."

He spoke of the young girls and the old men mounting the steps in the rain, their hands tied behind their backs with black ropes which have been soaked in tar, and he began to wonder what would happen to them. "They may be able to bribe themselves out, and they looked rich enough to have food provided for them in the prison. But what was terrible—really terrible—was to see an extraordinarily beautiful girl mounting the steps in the rain, with her hands tied behind her back, and the policemen saying coarse things to her. I don't play mahjong, but do you know, there is nothing else to do now. All amusements have been stopped. The films are not worth seeing. We are cut off from the world. Everything is so dear, and now there is only gambling to relieve the monotony of life."

But at four o'clock we went out into the rain. It was pitch-dark. We carried torches made of bamboo strips cunningly wound into the shape of hollow turnips, and inside a small greasy red candle burnt and spit with a yellow flame. There was a wind, and we had to shelter the lantern with our bodies. As we climbed down the steep steps, the faint candle threw immense flickering shadows on the walls—shadows of beggars and sleeping children, shadows of old women and young girls; and they slept through the rain and the continual beating of hammers from the small shipyard near-by. In the great darkness a small paddle-boat lay moored off the landing-stage, gaunt and grey, the rain shining a little on the iron roof.

And still we had to wait. We waited for a long time, in a solid mass of people all sweating in the rain, while the night thickened and candles flickered continually down the stone steps like will-o'-the-wisps, for we saw the candles, but we could not see the people who carried them. It was over an hour before a faint watery light began to streak across the sky. We sat on the iron deck of the boat, waiting patiently, listening to the squeal of ungreased wheel-barrows high up on the rocky streets. We began to distinguish the pale faces of our fellow-passengers, the little girl holding a hen by the feet so that it continually knocked against the iron deck; the Taoist priest with the face of the mediæval mystic and the hair wound into a greased top-knot; the babies asleep against blue-veined swollen breasts; the lovers gazing into the darkness and holding hands. The smell of sweat and rust, garbage and stone. And then suddenly, in the cold morning air, the light begins to grow; the white river birds torment us with their screaming; a small boy comes on deck to feed us with salted rice-cakes, and the deafening roar of the city begins to grow out of all proportion to the city's size. There are curious intervals when the roar dies down, inexplicable silences, but we have no ears for the city now, we are gazing across the river towards the first jet of sunlight which falls on the white pagoda high up on the cliff-side.

And now with the increasing day a mist rises, white and tender as the mist in Chinese paintings, and over the summits of the grey-blue hills a white shaft of sunlight penetrates the clouds, and in this frail sunrise we bathe gratefully, knowing not only that the
160

mysterious Chinese darkness, blacker than ink, has perished, but that all the frozen particles in the air will soon disappear into a faint warmth. Hot tea is poured out. Vegetables are loaded on to the galleys. The steep plates on the deck are thick with rust and curve dangerously as we walk on them, but already a great rumble, like the coughing of a dying man, is making the plates shiver and sending up streams of white smoke and froth at the sides, and already we are setting out—towards the gorges, the grey rocks, the golden sand and the mysterious small cities. And suddenly, in that curious intoxication of morning which makes China so strangely different from all other countries, we see the gaunt rocks assume fantastic shapes, they are grey lions, purple dragons, and the frail scenery appears to be painted in deep brown and ochre on an interminable blue sheet of silk.

The delicacy of the Chinese scenery is most noticeable in the early morning, when the rocks are still insubstantial and the dreaming air still broods in an enduring sleep. Above us the city towers, washed clean by the night and the rain, and while the sun climbs still higher the granite rocks burn with a kind of luminous flame. And still, though the river hovers in faint pastel colours before us, the city retains the primitive contrasts of black and white. Small rafts are passing us; soon they will be followed by larger rafts consisting of hundreds of logs bound together, and in the centre of these rafts small log-houses are built and the great yellow sweeping oar rides on the stern, guided by a small boy. But there is little traffic on the river, though thousands of boats, with small red fires burning, are wedged against the shore; and the smoke from the boats is already turning the white city into the colours of the river. Soon the city disappears. We are gliding up the river, silently, hardly disturbing the water-fowl; and look-ing over the rail we see that there are only two or three feet of water in the shallow river. We are gliding away from a dream into another dream; a dream which is eternally repeated in China whenever the sun shines in the early morning.

But the wind coming from the west across the mountains, a wind as cold as ice, brings with it the scent of the grave-yards and the dust of the previous day; blows out the patched sails of sam-pans and throws up small white columns of foam against the sides of the rocks. It is not a heavy wind; it seems to be bursting out of the restricted spaces of an invisible tunnel and to play fanwise on the water—but it is cold. You take shelter by stepping away

161

from the rail, or by disappearing downstairs, where in a small cabin lined with stools, the port-holes grey with mud and dust, people are lying down like so much baggage, and here and there a squat silver Szechuanese pipe, with its long silver stem and box-shaped water-bowl, can be heard like the continual sucking sound of water near a well. At first you think they are opium-smokers, so engrossed they are in their pipes; their lids fast-closed and their faces screwed into the shape of meditation. But they are not opium-smokers, there are no dancing-girls smoking with old men, and though even the children smoke cigarettes and it is not unusual to see a child of three with a cigarette in its mouth, nothing is happening which could offend the most timid spirits.

Upstairs, thousands of things are happening at once. The waterfowl are screaming; thousands of sampans with ragged white sails patched with somebody's blue trousers are bearing down on us; the sand is glittering—level reach upon level reach of sand; the fields are changing colour—have changed colour, for there are no more small knolls of grave-yards, and in their place there are great clumps of silver-blue cypresses, green willows, oaks on the horizon, walled houses and terrible rocks rising like immense teeth from the river-bed. Through all these things, with a clanking of chains and spitting fire and smoke from the funnel, the small paddle-boat passes without the least trouble; and the eye painted on the bows does not quiver in the least. We are deliberately and quite consciously travelling through a dream. At every moment the landscape changes. Here are fields of winter rye. They have disappeared. Instead of the immense hill fading into the sunlight which you noticed a moment ago, there is only a high white rock carved with Roman figures, to show the height of the tide in former ages, and a small temple with a gold roof, colonnades and a small encircling wall. The temple has gone. You are fighting your way through steep gorges. You feel like water—you are being poured through the narrow neck of the gorge and you will find yourself in the darkness of some dreaming stomach. Nothing of the sort. The gorges disappear by magic, there are no more hills and once more you are basking on level shores of glittering golden sand; and you watch the man swinging the long coloured pole at the bows like someone mesmerised, forgetting that in a moment he will order you off the boat, for the river is so shallow that she can no longer proceed with passengers.

We wade ashore through four inches of water. The sunlight

162

plays on the water; and waving lines play on the curved strakes of the ship. You notice with a feeling of surprise that the paddle-boat is floating in three and a quarter inches of water, and you ask yourself as you climb on the rocks what will happen if a gust of wind turns the boat over. For every year there are accidents on this river; so many ships have been lost that passengers are officially warned to be fatalistic; and though the sunlight shining mistily on the bamboos and the cedars shines with a light which seems to be reflected, and though you have noticed the most extraordinarily coloured rocks just beneath the surface of the river—rocks which are bright green or bright orange, veiled with velvet moss of all colours—you are sufficiently conscious that the dream might end at any moment to realise that there is no safety on Chinese rivers. Do you want evidence? You have passed seven junks with only their masts and a part of their bows sticking out of the water. Some of these junks are green with age, small boys bathe from them and they have become an accepted part of the landscape, and even their number does not terrify you in this mist-frail morning. But while the paddle-boat carves its slow passage between the small rocks and the shelving sand, you are glad you are on dry land.

As though the scenery were determined to make you believe that you were dreaming, you notice that there are no seasons. There are rice and barley, horse-tooth beans, winter rye, green radishes, clusters of bamboos in all colours ranging from the innocent green of the young shoots to the stately brown of old age. There is no sunlight; it is all moonlight—with a golden moon. How long it will last you have no idea, and you do not care; the river alone will bear you along through the wondering enchantment of the strangest moonlight you have ever seen.

We sit and talk under the awning, watching the small white temples to the earth gods as they sail past, very white against the green hills. You pay no more attention to the extraordinarily beautiful cedars on the distant hills than to the rafts wheeling in a white mill-race or the flicker of the coloured pebbles in the river disturbed by the iron paddles. Everything is reduced to the level of a single enchantment; and as the sun grows hotter and the fumes from the funnel crowd down upon you, the enchantment does not lessen—it increases by infinitesimal degrees of prestidigitation. The "perilous seas forlorn" are three and a quarter inches deep, and Ruth is still wandering in tears amid the

163

alien corn under a marble pagoda. But it is the small white temples to the earth-gods, and high up on the hills the bright yellow walls surrounding the farm-houses which attract our attention. There are places where thousands of barges are moored, and other places where the air is sweet with the blue-grey smoke of lime. All along the left bank of the river there are lime-kilns, where white cliffs of chalk can be seen among the bright green cedars. Small boys hover over the red fires under the brick-kilns, and there are so many of these fires that our progress down the river is lit with these incandescent flames. Occasionally there are villages. You recognise them first from the distance by the great sloping wall down which the merchandise of the villagers is slipped into waiting boats. There are coal-mines, potteries, basket-makers, innumerable farms, and you have no need to wander in the villages to see the things they manufacture; for everything is prepared for you along the river-bank, and every sampan is being heaped with merchandise before your eyes. The green cedars, the white rocks and the blue river under the towering skies are things which you know you will remember, even if the strange shapes of the sampans with their high sterns and long sweeper oars did not make it inevitable that you would remember the journey. And meanwhile the birds, great white river gulls with yellow beaks and wings as silver as the wings of herons, coast around the after-end of the paddle-steamer, where food is being cooked and an enormous copper cauldron is seething with soup. The landscape has changed beyond recognition. It is no longer Chungking, or anything approaching Chungking, and it is only when the haulers come again into view that you realise the hardships of the land. The ship they are drawing is far out in mid-stream, and they themselves are wading thigh-deep among the loose stones; and though the river is low, there are whirlpools and high rocks in mid-stream, so that sometimes they have to bend and strain against the thick ropes of palm fibre slung across their chests. A man stands amidships beating a wooden drum, standing on a platform which makes him visible to the world. The long slings are jointed to a sliding crown on the mast-head, and when the mast is bending and creaking with the strain, he puffs at his pipe and renews the tattooing on his drum—but it is a different tattoo, sharper and more insistent, and almost like a cry of pain. The haulers wait. They stand there in the water, seeming naked, mopping their sweaty brows and cursing the de-
164

lay; and then once more they crawl on all fours, resembling otters in a stream, only their heads visible above the level of the glassy river.

I have been watching the haulers for a long while until it seems that I am myself a hauler, wearied beyond endurance by the weight he carries on his back. I am straining fiercely against the current; my feet are bleeding; I am hungry for rest and weary of toil. For ten, twenty, thirty years I have walked down the side of this river, until I recognised every stone and tuft of grass; and the weals on my shoulders have healed only because they are tired of festering, and even the beauty of the river has no meaning for my eyes. I am sick of the river, and yet I know more of the river than the foreigners who travel on the steamers. I know its changing caprices and the face of its storms, its hollow echoes and its merciless confusion of beauty. I know that it will not pause if I drop dead. I know that there are kites and vultures overhead; and graves on the slopes of the cedar-clothed hills. I know no end to suffering. Ai-ya! Ai-yee! Ai-ya! Ai-yee! Ai-ya! . . .

And suddenly, turning among the hills and the ravines, we saw the sun stretching down between high green cliffs, a mist floating lightly on the gorges. We are already in sight of Peipei. The wind turns sharply as we leave the gorge we have been travelling through behind; and coming at last to an estuary, with green hills on one side and a sandy, stony beach on the other, with red-brown houses perched on the granite rocks, and field after field of cedars, we know we have come to the end of the journey. The steamer will go on, but it will leave us at the landing-stage. The sun shines. There are thousands of small booths on the shore, and the deserted river is once more filled with small boats bobbing on the immense glassy wave which our bow sends towards the shore. I have been looking for the University—it is not large, a few small whitewashed buildings facing the village and perched above a sandy cliff. I would not have noticed them if my companion had not pointed them out.

March 18th . . . Peipei is a small town, consisting of three streets joined together like two letter L's, yet in all Szechuan it is hardly possible to find so many educational institutions. There is an Academy of Music and ballet-dancing, the Kansu Medical College, three or four middle schools, the Sun Yat-sen Institute for the Advancement of Culture and Education, the bureau of the

165

School of Compilation and Translation, the headquarters of the Geological Survey and the Geodetic Survey, a school of science and three or four other schools, and not far away there is the building where the Legislative Yuan decides upon the laws of China. And yet, when you first come to the village, there is no sign of all these institutes of learning. You see small fields among the mountains, ripening yellow wheat, brown glistening paddies, green seed-beds and vegetable plots climbing the rolling green hills. There are few trees, for here as elsewhere China has been denuded of her trees by the ravages of house-builders; and there are few children. The spring crop of wheat, barley, rapeseed and peas is being gathered; the horse-head beans are purple; the cabbages are still tender green. You walk down the main road, dusty with a luminous bright dust, passing the ghosts of rickshas whose wheels are patched beyond recognition and whose hoods are ribbons of greasy yellow cloth, and in two minutes you are out in the country. There was a village here in the T'ang Dynasty, and perhaps long before; and it is difficult to think that the village can have changed. The same blue-yellow ducks were floating on the ponds, the same sycamores and elms were sheltering the rice-fields from the wind, the same goats and pigs and fowls were scrabbling in the mud on the edge of the fields. The air is sweet, as always in places where the river opens after being constricted between high rocks; and though the houses are poor, and the peasants look poorer, you are surprised to notice the number of distinguished scholars who walk away from the village street with their cotton bags filled with the purchases they have made in the crumbling shops.

The scholars here are poor, desperately poor. Their loose gowns are patched with ill-matching colours; their shoes are down at heel. A motor-bus roars past, swallowing them up in purple wood-oil vapour, but they do not care. They have been here for years; they have taught in the schools, translated the classics of foreign languages in the Bureau for translation and compilation which was founded more than eighty years ago, and they are still poverty-stricken. Early this morning, when I came out on to the great square facing the river, I saw hundreds of middle-school students exercising in the rain. They formed fours, bent their knees, lunged out with their arms and ran round the square like young gods, or rather like young goddesses, for afterwards I noticed that they were only girls. They wore white trousers and thick woollen
166

sweaters, and they raced with an ease and a grace which I would have thought impossible so near to Chungking. I have seen nothing like this in the capital. Their breaths came in white bursts and the rain fell on their upturned faces, and they looked so young and graceful that for a moment I imagined I was again in Bali. Afterwards, they broke ranks and wandered schoolward, their hands deep in their pockets, striding with perfect freedom like goddesses through the rain.

March 19th . . . IT IS still raining, and the white walls and grey tiles of the University have turned black as soot. Here the buildings are low and small; the mud lies thick round your ankles; in the cold unheated rooms the students shiver in the wind coming down from the mountain. They look ridiculously young, and yet they do not walk with that extraordinary grace which I saw yesterday on the field. They have come to years of responsibility, and perhaps their studies are harder. There are students from every province of China—the broad cheek-bones and broader foreheads of Mongolia, the dark eager faces of Kwangtung in the south, the beautiful ivory pallor which I shall always associate with Soochow, the red cheeks of Hunan and the lithe beauty of Pekin. I came over in the ferry this morning in the sweeping rain, plunging through mud down the slopes of Peipei, past the enclosed bamboo matting of innumerable sleeping-sheds, amazed by the skill of the boatman who knew every reef and found his way through all the currents. A mist was trembling on the green hills; the gorges on either side were invisible. Alone in the boat with the boy ferryman, I felt like one of those boatmen in Chinese paintings of the Sun Dynasty, who find themselves lost amid encircling hills and an encompassing mist; and dream of the lotoses which they could pluck if they were not so busy singing on their lutes. The mist hid everything except a trace of green, and on this smooth wake the exertions of the boy seemed unnecessary and even vulgar, for there was no visible current, and nothing by which we could measure the movement of the boat. We came ashore nearly a mile from the University, and I walked along the river-bank, straining to see the land on the other side. There was no land. The river is rising. Occasionally, very faint, there was a silver gleam like the spin of a coin in the sky.

The Chinese mist is a thing which you see otherwise only in dreams. It is not a fog; it does not lie like a thick cloak on the

167

land. It is eternally moving and very soft, and so fragile that you can brush it away with your hand. If you wait for a while and look in any direction, it will disperse for an infinitesimal fragment of time, and more often than not it will return again thicker than before. The white walls of the University, hardly distinguishable from the surrounding farm-houses, I saw when I was half a mile away; but it disappeared until I was close under the eaves. There was a small garden full of flowers, a flag-pole flying the Chinese flag, uncurtained windows, no sound. It began to rain, but the rain did not disperse the mist; and the small white doves flying on the branches of the cedars looked heavy like lead.

But inside the class-rooms everything was as I had expected it to be. As though determined to make the grey sky disappear, the girl students wore their most colourful gowns, and even the drab blue gowns of the men students shone in this dusky twilight. But what was even more delightful was to notice that though they were shivering in the cold, they looked well fed and there was no sign of the greyness of the faces of the people in Chungking. I gave my first lecture, feeling very nervous, wondering whether they could understand a word I said, and watched them as they walked out in the rain with a feeling of elation. In their smooth jawbones and fine eyes there was a keenness which I had not yet noticed in China, and I was delighted at the thought of staying among them. I looked at my watch. It was ten minutes to eight in the morning. I felt that I had spent the whole day either wandering in the mist or talking to students.

March 20th . . . NEARLY all the books in the library were lost when the University moved from Shanghai. I have been browsing in the library while the rain falls in torrents outside. Outside, a few wet pigs, black and steaming, swelter in the rain, and the silence of the room is broken only by the bugles which announce the hours. One of the librarians, who wears a tattered black gown, was the son of a Duke who received his dukedom under Yuan Shih-kai. He is a scholar. He looks out timidly through thick eye-glasses at thin rows of books on the shelves and sighs deeply. "You should have seen the library in Shanghai—ah, that was something to talk about." I console myself that there is a complete edition of the *Encyclopædia Britannica,* and if necessary I can read it right through. The rain falls, and in a small
168

room leading off from the library someone is singing in a high fluted voice a Chinese poem about the rain.

March 21st . . . The sun shone for a while this morning, and I watched huge clouds of smoke rising from the grasses. D. has taken me to see the farms which belong to the University. Pigs and sheep are kept; there are sheep browsing in the meadows, and the cows are calving. I have been to four Universities, but I have never seen a farm so close to the place where scholars study, and the rightness of this arrangement is so pleasant that I can hardly tear myself away from the fields to attend my own lectures. "There are fifty different kinds of citrous plant," D. tells me. "We are experimenting on new kinds of tea-leaves; we are making vinegar and preparing plans for increasing the productivity of our fields." He is young, with a tall forehead, and though he stoops like a scholar, he walks with quick easy strides through the mud, delighted because I have fallen completely in love with the duck-pond and alarmed whenever I show my ignorance of Chinese fruit. "Oranges came from China—the original sun-kist oranges came from Szechuan, and these lemons——" He crushes the leaves of the lemon-trees between his fingers and holds them to his nostrils. "Our lemons are sweeter than yours, and our potatoes are sweeter, and everything is sweeter." He is so pleased with the fruits coming from the Chinese earth that he is almost prepared to swear that olives were first known in China. "At first we wanted to have the agricultural produce in the hands of the students, but they had no time, do you understand, and there was labour trouble, and the students' food is not good enough for hard manual labour, and so we employed local labour. They are not the best material for scientific farming, but what else could we do?" He was annoyed beyond measure when he noticed evidence of blight on the winter cabbages. "They were good a week ago—useless now, except for manure." And all the while he was rubbing the sharp-pointed glistening leaves of the lemon-trees between thumb and forefinger, shouting with sheer joy at the productivity of earth. "Soon the hills will be covered ten feet high with Indian corn; there is nothing so good as a hot Szechuan summer with the Indian corn sprouting so quickly that you can actually watch it growing. And then this part of the world, do you know, it is more productive than anywhere in Europe. We have two, and sometimes three crops of rice, and every inch of the land

169

is cultivated." He talked about the hookworm disease which attacks farm-labourers who wade knee-deep behind their ploughs. Their bellies become swollen with the worm, and their legs are distended as though they were suffering from an elephantiasis of varicose veins. "The University is studying it—we are trying to find ways to prevent it. We are experimenting all the time." It was not strange to hear these words. I had heard them before in Chungking, but here at least they were wholly convincing. This small University, with its pathetically simple and inadequate equipment, is conscious of its own importance and experimenting all the time.

March 22nd . . . THE butterflies came out, for today is summer and a thick white summer mist lies on the green fields. We can breathe again; and the journey in the ferry-boat from the hotel to the University is no longer a journey across the streams of Lethe.

I walked through rice-fields to the house of the dean of the faculty of arts, a famous painter who is slowly recovering from malaria. We wandered through the University farm, past the cage where the black pigs were snoring, past the trellis of vines and the clusters of yellow bamboos, which look as though at any moment they will burst into flower, until we came to the open fields and the cedars. There is a small brook running over muddy stones which we leapt across; and then wandering up and down between fields and forests, turning by the bare rock which the University has excavated for an air-raid shelter, we come at last to a plain between mountains upon which the shadowed light of the summer clouds throws purple wings. Here we may be ten thousand miles from the noise and dirt of Chungking. The trees gleam freshly; there are rice-fields in whose changing colours we see the green sprouts and the clouds with equal precision. And walking along the raised earth-bank between the stepped fields which shone like luminous lakes, it seemed that summer had come with a clash of cymbals.

Nearly all the professors of the University live in farm-houses. These farm-houses are as old as ploughs, their floors are stamped mud and in high summer, when the mosquitoes breed in the damp fields, they are death-traps for strangers from the towns. The dean of the college of arts caught malaria the previous year, and has never recovered. In a large room, with fretted windows

170

which look out on a wide stone courtyard, with its small library of Chinese and foreign books and scrolls hanging from the walls which he painted himself, there is an extraordinary atmosphere of tranquillity and ease. The sounds from the courtyard come muted through thick walls. The farm-girls are bathing beans in water, perhaps in order to increase their weight for the market. A dog is barking behind the bamboo grove; and the shadowed mountains rising beyond the gate sparkle with the light from the inundated rice-fields. Children can be heard, and the soft sound of a broom sweeping the threshing-floor. We are lost in admiration of the scene when at last he comes in, leaning on his stick, smiling weakly and courageously, for we know that he has risen from his sick bed to see us. He is tall and thin, with blue rings under his eyes, and powerfully veined hands. He wears the inevitable scholar's gown, and all at once he begins to speak about the pictures, quickly gazing at the monochrome illustrations as though he were attempting, in this infinitesimal fragment of time, to clothe with colours the mechanical reproductions of the great works of the Chinese past; then he sighs.

"The best books on Chinese art have been written by foreigners. It is a great pity, and yet it is quite understandable. For us the task is too difficult—there are too many books to read, and too many paintings to see before we can trust ourselves to write safely about our own art. The scholars are more fortunate. They have a few, a very few paintings, but often they are the best; and they can write of them more intimately, because they can see them more frequently. There is Binyon—a giant among essayists on Chinese art. I recommend this book to you. You must read it if you want to understand Chinese art."

He talks gravely, with careful precision of accent, and his hands are continually weaving strange patterns. We tell him how much we admire a painting of sunlit mountains hanging on the walls; and immediately he orders a servant to remove the painting and wrap it carefully in paper. With the greatest difficulty we refuse the gift. He has brought with him some blue flowers which he proceeds to set in a small brown vase near his writing-table— a writing-table which is covered with three or four ink-stones, three curiously carved boxes of seals, lecture notes and students' exercises and English, Japanese and Chinese books in amazing confusion. The flowers fill the scented air with a still stronger scent, and we inhale their perfume at the same time as he begins

171

to talk of the French impressionists. He finds in Cézanne and Matisse and in a few paintings by Van Gogh the same characteristics as he finds in the painting of Chinese artists in the great dynasties. "Their art resembles ours in their pursuit of the inner form. Cézanne, above all, has so much in common with our Taoist painters that I am thinking of writing a monograph upon him from this point of view alone. And their adoration of light——" He takes out of a locked cupboard the post-card reproductions he has bought in the British Museum. They are poor things, but almost the entire University library on foreign art was lost in Shanghai, and he values these coloured post-cards as others might value painted reproductions. He shows me a painting by Van Gogh and compares it with a scene from a small collection of Chinese paintings cut out of a Japanese magazine. "You notice the similarities—the tremendous insistence on the real form, the careful elaboration of the sunlight. You notice how the impressionists show the mountains *absorbing* the sunlight, living and breathing and praising the sunlight with their whole hearts, and how the shape of the mountain is no more than the shape of the sunlight. Look carefully. Look how we paint our trees, and how Van Gogh paints his trees—or, better still, look at the small house under the cliffs in the Chinese painting and compare it with the house in the south of France by Cézanne. They are not the same. They could not be the same, but notice the similarities—the study of significant form." Clive Bell's famous phrase slipped out of his mouth before he was aware of it. He smiled wryly. "In understanding the painting of our own country, we have a lot to learn from the West," he smiled.

High above the mountains small green clouds were floating, and these clouds reminded him of a long scroll he had painted the year before. He painted according to the way of the ancient Chinese masters. It was a long horizontal scroll, which he unfolded carefully, revealing many views among rocky mountains. There were mountains which we recognised—for the gorges near Peipei have been painted nearly as often as the limestone cliffs at Kweilin—and some which we thought could only have occurred to him in dreams. There were beetling cliffs, rain-storms, drooling cascades of water, men rowing in boats under the eaves of forest hills, great cataracts and mountains and temples hidden in bamboo groves. It was a surprising achievement to have arranged a complete continuity between such different scenes, and he was not unproud of his work. "I spent eighteen months painting that tree," he said, pointing to a small tree which rose from the ledge of a high crag. But what was still more remarkable was the extraordinary harmony of colours in the scrolls. He used only black, blue and green with here and there the faintest scratch of pale red, and this pale smear was so brilliant among the attendant blues and greens that it seemed almost to be crimson. He was afraid that the painting might have been improved if he had employed only one colour. "The use of blue and green is decadent —our greatest painters painted in monochrome, and could give you the impression of more colours than exist in the spectrum." We followed the landscape as he unrolled it before our eyes. A storm had come up. The fishing-boats were taking to shelter, and the poet talking to the girl had also taken to shelter, leaving the girl behind. Clouds rose behind the eminences of cliffs. A savage wind blew the bamboos headlong. But soon—the careful fingers silently unrolling the scroll—the rain passed, there was light and sunshine again, and every blade of grass was singing. We no longer knew which was the real world. We walked home in the dark. Very faintly in the undergrowth we saw the blue gleam of fire-flies.

March 23rd . . . I HAVE been annoyed all day. I found in the library the Penguin edition of *Antony and Cleopatra*, and read it right through in the two-hour interval between my classes this morning. Towards the end, when Cleopatra begins to lose all hope, she confides to Charmian:

> *My desolation does begin to make*
> *A better life; 'tis paltry to be Cæsar:*
> *Not being Fortune, he's but Fortune's knave,*
> *A minister of her will: and it is great*
> *To do that thing that ends all other deeds,*
> *Which shackles accidents, and bolts up change;*
> *Which sleeps and never pallates more the dung,*
> *The beggar's nurse, and Cæsar's.*

Even though "dung" is apparently the reading of the Folio, I cannot believe that Shakespeare wrote it. When I was younger, I read it as "dug", and the meaning was completely perfect and almost mathematical in its precision. Yet now, whenever I read

173

it again, I shall see this miserable word "dung", which conveys nothing, which is empty of all significance except a childish pleasure in dirt, a word which has nothing in common with the force of *merde*—a silly, stupid, passionless, inchoate, harmless and vulgar word beyond all the words in the English dictionary.

March 24th . . . THERE is a glider-field below the town, a smooth square of tussocky grass which will be inundated when the river rises again. The small gliders are towed out by soldiers holding long elastic ropes which are suddenly set free, and the glider rises in the air, beautifully poised, dipping its wings which shine in the white sunlight—but alas! it never flies high. I saw thirty or forty glides this afternoon; they were all the same, and each glider landed at the same place. I am told it is too dangerous to fly high; there are wind currents in the mountains and along the gorges which defy the most expert flier, and now back in the hotel bedroom I can think only of the soldiers in worn brown khaki uniforms who resembled the haulers on the river even to the sounds of their voices—Ai-ya! Ai-yee! Ai-ya! Ai-yee! T. says it is the common language of China.

March 25th . . . THE electric light goes out at ten o'clock, but the hotel provides mirrors. I have found that if I light two candles, I can make them shine nearly four times more brightly by a cunning arrangement of mirrors. Tonight there were rats. They came and looked in the mirrors, quite fearless. They were not disturbed by the sound of a girl singing in the next room, nor by the wailing babies in the room two doors away, nor by the lamentations of the bride who had lost her husband a few hours before. They were calm and fearless and perfectly behaved.

I worked steadily, correcting papers, preparing lecture-notes and wondering what strange destiny had brought me in war-time to this small hotel which fills me with a quiet horror. The hotel is shaped like a Chinese house, with a courtyard, where every morning the boys throw their pails of dirty water; so that even on the sunniest days the grass is drenched, and a curiously unappetising smell comes from the drowned roots of the trees. At night there are mysterious sounds—creaking beds, strange tappings, terrible sighs. At one o'clock, when I was going to bed, a tremendous rapping echoed on the doors. At once all the mysterious sounds of the night disappeared, and gave place to this heart-

174

breaking repetitive rapping sound. There were no voices. No one answered the rapping, but the walls shook under the blows and I could hear people turning over in their sleep, complaining drunkenly and dreamily against the desolation of their peace. And then the sounds became fainter, and I imagined an old wanderer, footsore and famished, who had come to the doors late at night, growing weaker and weaker, until at last he fell unconscious in the rain.

Through the torn paper windows in the moonlight I saw a cat leap after a rat twice as large as herself, and the sudden appearance of the cat and the rat flashing across the white roads was like the sudden explosion of lightning, not terrifying, but so strange that it was some minutes before I could accustom myself to the real world.

March 26th . . . "WHERE do we go from here?" He is a Mongolian student with a nervous intelligent face, and the finest eyes I have ever seen; he was worried and homesick, like so many of the students, and he could see no way out. "We are surrounded by enemies now, and though it has happened before, it has never been so dangerous. In the old days the Tartar tribes could conquer China with bows and arrows, but bows and arrows are not deadly weapons like machine-guns. Now we are surrounded by machine-guns, and simply because we are cut off, we have no real friends in the world." And then again: "Pity and sympathy are not matters for international politics. Really, it is the fault of the powers that China is in the position that she is in now; and yet they do so little for us. If they could send us the scrap-iron they sent to Japan. . . ."

They do not often talk about these things. We are isolated; and there is something so heart-breaking as this isolation is seen through the eyes of the students that I wonder whether anyone will ever see it as I see it now. Here we are doubly isolated. In this remote valley between two gorges, so near to Chungking that we are almost a part of it, but so far away that only the faintest rumours of what is happening in the capital reach our ears, we live in a world which has been cut off from foreign countries for nearly four years. The latest numbers of the foreign magazines in the library are dated 1936. There are no more than one or two books dated 1937, and nothing afterwards. Great masses of Japanese magazines lie on the shelves—they are unread, the pages un-

175

cut, but they are more recent in date than anything from England or America.

This afternoon I went to the Kansu medical college. There must have been thousands of opportunities during the last four years for my countrymen to present them with medical and chemical magazines. There is nothing. The equipment is running short, and even the test-tubes and glass beakers are so few that I am amazed that any valuable work can be done. The college stands on a steep cliff; it is built of stone and resembles a feudal castle which dominates the landscape, and from there you can look down upon the plunging torrents of the gorges—and on the other side of the river the slate roofs of the University are shining in the watery sunlight. It is an extraordinary view, the hills with their tawny grasses which they wear like bear-skins, the blue river running below between white stones, the gorges in the distance fuming with smoke and mist and the gorges near at hand like dark entrances into another world. But what was most remarkable was the single tree on the top of the hills overlooking the gorges, a tree which was struck by lightning many years ago and yet stands there still, dominating everything and so perfectly proportioned to the landscape that it takes your breath away.

March 27th, Market-Day . . . Two hundred years ago, when Macartney came as envoy to the Ch'ing Emperor, he was told that China was self-sufficient and had no need of the produce of other countries. Here, on market-day, the self-sufficiency of China becomes so certain that you wonder why anything more than a few steel rails are imported. Here are leopard-skins brought down from the neighbouring mountains, immense blocks of rock-salt, enormous baulks of timber; in closed pens there are ducks and sheep, great slabs of black pigs, innumerable fresh-water fish. There are crabs and ray-fish, bottles of wine, some red, some white, some dark brown; there are rolls of blue cloth and a few rolls of coloured cloth which have been smuggled through the Japanese lines; there are pewter-pots, ploughshares, copper basins, so many kinds of knives that I have lost count. They all come from the surrounding countryside, and the craftsmen who made the tools are often the men who wait patiently in the market-place. I have watched an old woman haggling for half an hour over the price of a square yard of blue cloth. She succeeded in getting it at a price she could afford, but not before she had
176

related her whole family history and discovered a remote relationship between herself and the weaver. Even the large industries are represented on the markets. The cotton-mill, the small iron-foundry, the coal merchants and the boat-builders are all here; and the old women who sell handkerchiefs and hair-pins are almost lost in the vast crowds who assemble in the streets. Tomorrow the place will belong to them once more, and they are conscious of their importance in the community; but today they are eclipsed by the peasants who have come down from the mountains, and the beggars who are so numerous that one wonders how they can still exist profitably.

And as though the noises of market-day were not sufficient, more and more paddle-steamers come to berth at the landing-stage. The hooters and steam-whistles tear the air to shreds. An old French missionary, with an enormous beard which resembles a spider's web, wearing a frock-coat and a rusty clerical collar, walks through the crowds reading his missal, ten times larger than life. He does not see the crowds. The white river-birds floating above the house-tops have no existence for him. Once, when he looked up, he saw a young girl unbuttoning her gown and presenting her breast to a baby who resembled all the seraphim and cherubim in heaven, but he hastily averted his eyes. Like a ghost he walked through a crowd so packed with vitality and pure joy of existence that one felt that he must vanish in a wreath of smoke. But no; he walked straight onward, content like St. Bernard with his missal, praising the pure glory of God and in eternal fear of witnessing the glory He has accomplished on the earth. The vitality of a Chinese crowd is so intoxicating that I can never feel it as something remote from me. It clamours on the mind until you surrender of your own will; and even then, when the market-place is so crowded that you can hardly move, and the cries of the ragged children are so loud that you can hardly hear what is happening, your surrender is incomplete until you have lost yourself completely in the crowd.

It is a good-natured crowd, and even the beggars are well-behaved. They await your gifts with interminable patience, saying nothing, the outstretched hand speaking in whispers. It is not a beautiful crowd, unless you believe as I do that a patched garment of fifteen different colours is more pleasant than anything except a white gown trimmed with red or green. The faces of the peasants who come down from the mountains are rough and an-

177

gular; their eyes are smaller; and there are occasions, particularly on stormy days, when their roughness approaches to brutality. The Szechuanese are a race apart. They are colonisers, sent into the province after the massacres of the late Ming dynasty. They came to a country thick with vegetation, where even the sites of the towns were unknown and the forests spread over all. They have ransacked the province, cut down nearly all the trees, planted opium instead of rice during the years of the war-lords and lived to regret their poverty in one of the richest provinces of earth. The typical faces of Honan and Hunan can still be seen, but they are becoming rarer and a curious uniformity is descending upon them. In a hundred years' time, according to Z., who is an anthropologist, the Szechuanese will become a single race with its own peculiar characteristics.

It was evening when we left the market-place. Along the broad banks of the river a few old women were crouching down over the red candles which they stuck in the ground. Dark clouds raced over the mountains, and high over our heads a red star was moving swiftly through the clouds. At first I thought it was an aeroplane, but Z. laughed contentedly: "It is a sign that someone has died," he said. "Whenever anyone has died, we light a hollow lantern and let it drift into the upper air. Sometimes we light three or four of these lanterns, and sometimes people have said that they have seen the souls of the dead departing through a rift in the clouds."

March 28th . . . Peipei is not a typical village, because it possesses a zoo, has an excellent mayor, contains eighteen educational institutions, a hospital, four or five good bread-shops and a theatre. The zoo lies on the hills above the hotel, surrounded by cedars and bamboos and approached by a broken stone pathway which winds towards the monkey-house. There are leopards and tigers, white rabbits, three monkeys and the most beautiful peacock I have ever seen. Here, under the bamboos, tea is served in porcelain cups and black sunflower seeds in little paper packages accompany the green tea "like brother and sister".

This morning, in the rain, we wandered up to the monkey-house, for according to Z. there is nothing so delightful as visiting a monkey-house in the rain. It may be true, but the paths were slippery and the smell from the tiger-cage was increased by the rain. The dripping bamboos, the clouds slowly forming among
178

the cedars, the small boys sheltering under the eaves and the howls of the monkeys gave an impression of such terrible remoteness from everything we were accustomed to that I wondered whether Z. had not gone out of his senses. "No, this is quite natural," he answered. "A Chinese likes to wander about in the rain. Sounds are sharper in the rain; the earth smells sweeter; the shapes of things are more distinct, and the drops of silver water hanging from the bamboos are so exquisitely proportioned that it is only in the rain that we are perfectly content." He sighed. The monkeys were no longer howling, but a wind was growing, and as he watched the waving branches of the bamboos he was like one of the monks in an old Chinese painting I have seen—a monk in a red gown who sits cross-legged in the spray from a waterfall. We walked to the tiger-cage. The tiger was old, but still graceful, and he blinked at us from between his muddy paws with the somnolence that comes from feasting. All round the bare cage were heaps of bloody bones. It was like a charnel-house, and I turned away, but not before Z. had announced in magisterial tones that the red of the fresh meat was necessary for the appreciation of the scenery. "In Chinese paintings you will often find a daub of red in the most unexpected place, and what could be better than finding it here, for surely this is a painting. Look at the birds flying in the rain. There is no sun, but their colours are sharper and their cries are more penetrating. You are an ignorant barbarian. You do not know that China is only tolerable in the rain."

April 3rd . . . I AM puzzled by Z. He is a graduate of Harvard and Heidelberg; he is one of the best anthropologists in China; he holds three appointments concurrently; and he wears his immense and almost intolerable learning with the ease of a young boy carrying his satchel to school. Indeed, he resembles a young boy. The first time you meet him, you are aware of a certain organic over-refinement of features, and you think perhaps that he is a charming young girl disguised with a slightly professional air. He looks seventeen. He is really forty-five. He laughs delicately; he holds his tea-cup delicately; he smiles with the intoxicating sweetness which I have found only in China; he talks in a low voice which is purely English, though he has never been to England; and he takes so much pains over my education in Chinese literature that I am beginning to wonder whether it would not be better for the future of China if I quietly disappeared, for in gaining an anthropologist China has lost a great poet.

He has killed men and enjoyed killing men. He told me this morning that he was quite sure that he had killed fifteen men in cold blood, and he had delighted in the experience because it had proved that his mind was strong, though his body was as weak as a girl's. He had fought near Mukden, at a place not far from the ancestral home of his grandmother, and all the while he was fighting he was thinking of his grandmother. He told me all this without the slightest impression of braggadocio and with the most charming sincerity. "The first man I killed was quite young. He was the son of a puppet governor, and I remember that all the time I was planning to kill him, I was thinking: 'You are so handsome that nothing would please me better than that you should become my blood-brother. We could live together in some deserted monastery in the hills, and we would be happy like lovers.' He was so handsome, you understand? There was Manchu blood in his veins, and there is Manchu blood in my veins, and yet I killed him. For three days I wept." He murdered a Japanese general. He had no thought of escaping. He had written his will, and death seemed very close to him. But in the confusion after he had shot the general at point-blank range, he noticed that one of the general's aides was motioning to him to go away. He felt ashamed. He wanted to surrender himself, for everything was prepared and there was no point in living any more. "But what was the use? Fate had decided that I must go on killing. I must be an avenger, and yet all the while I never felt that I was avenging my country—it was as though something quite different was making me act in this way, something that I could not understand, and there was neither heroism nor cowardice in these assassinations."

It was raining again today. We walked up to the zoo, to admire the plumage of the peacock spangled with diamonds of rain.

"But if it is a Chinese habit to wander in the rain, why is it that today we are the only people here?"

He smiled with an expression of infinite compassion:

"There are very few real Chinese in Szechuan," he explained. "To be Chinese means that you are born in the north and are descended from generations of scholars."

180

April 4th . . . I DO not know why I have delayed so long in meeting the dean of the faculty of law. He lives in a small house facing the river, which is also the headquarters of the magazine which is edited from the University. More than anyone I have met he resembles the Chinese scholar of my dreams. He is lean and thin-boned, and his hair is turning grey; his fine eyes are continually lit with little dark flames, and he speaks precisely, with a minimum of gestures, as befits a famous lawyer. At one time he was a judge of the Supreme Court under the Pekin Government. In later years, when he ran a school in Shanghai and lectured at the University, he was counsel for the defence in the Court of the International Settlement when three Chinese gunmen were put on trial for the murder of a Japanese consular official. At that time his life was worth nothing. Threatening messages came from the Japanese, who ordered him to throw up the case. He refused. With a passionate devotion to justice and an equally passionate devotion to his country, he continued to act in their defence.

The small room was colder than any room I have ever been in. Through the concrete floor moisture seeped. There were papers everywhere—bound copies of the magazine he edits reached almost to the ceiling, and there were no other ornaments to the bare room. There were paper windows which were torn to shreds. He wore European clothes which were torn at the elbows, and his shoes were down at the heel; and yet, so great was the impression of pure sincerity and even of majesty which he revealed, that it was only long afterwards that I noticed the discomforts of the room.

He spoke about the University with more affection than anyone else. There had been complaints that the University had failed to maintain the standard it reached in Shanghai. Poverty-stricken, it had attempted to remain a private University to the last; but in January this year it was incorporated into the system of national Universities endowed by the Ministry of Education. He had watched the University through all the crises. He had accompanied it overland from Shanghai to Peipei, and he possessed for it the devotion which is reserved only for bachelors who have a passion for learning. But this morning he refused to talk about the history of the University, and spoke instead of the long tragic exodus from the coast. The present Minister of Education had saved it from extinction by giving large sums of money from his own purse in order that the University should be transferred in safety.

"In those days life was cheap, and so was food. We could live comfortably on our salaries, and the students looked well-fed. When we came down the Yangtse, we could buy two hundred oranges for two dollars—as many as we could carry away. Today oranges are eight dollars each, and everything else has gone up in proportion. We could manage the University on ten thousand dollars a year; today a University costs the Government an unlimited number of millions, for the students are fed free, the professors are paid from Government funds and even the doctors and the medical supplies are paid for by the Government." There was no bitterness in his voice. He was happy there, but he was deeply concerned about the professors who possessed large families. "How do they live? No one knows. It is difficult enough for the students, but it is still more difficult for the professors. The President lives in an old farm-house, where the rain leaks through the roof. In the old days a professor could afford a car; today he is penniless, and at the same time he is supremely happy, because he knows that his job is worthy of him."

He spoke for a short while about his defence of the Chinese in Shanghai. I asked him what happened in the end, but he shrugged his shoulders.

"The judges did not dare to pass sentence, but the Chinese boys were held in prison. We arranged that they should be fed, for as you know in Chinese prisons the feeding arrangements are very primitive. But they disappeared—no one knows what happened to them."

Above all, he liked to talk about the history of the University. Fuhtan University was one of the oldest in China, where the age of Universities is still measured by decades. There were Universities in the Ch'in Dynasty, over two thousand years ago, but though the ancient traditions have been carried through, the modern Chinese Universities prefer to regard themselves as newborn. Dr. Sun Yat-sen had been one of the founders of the Universities, but even before the revolution, under a famous Christian scholar, the students had worked for the emancipation of China. Students from Fuhtan had died during the revolution, and it was perhaps for this reason that Sun Yat-sen provided the University with a plot of ground in Shanghai and became an honorary presi-
182

dent. At first the University was supported by grants from overseas Chinese; and though its character was now changing, and it was no longer a University dedicated to the sons of businessmen, the tradition of the founders was still visible in the large faculties of finance and economics. The dean of the faculty of law wanted to see it broaden out. He wanted it to become one of the great institutions for scholarship and scientific experiment; and it was clear that he dreamed of little else except the enlargement of the scope of the University.

"These are times of experiment," he said. "The war has made us more critical of ourselves—and this is a good thing. At the same time we have lost too much to be able to see far ahead with any certainty. One of our best professors was killed in a bombing-raid two years ago. He was a man who had been marked out for president, and we are still suffering from the shock of this loss. So much depends on the survival of a few people——"

We walked out into the garden. It was already getting late, and the moon was rising clear over the hills. The Chinese flag had been removed from the flagpole at sundown, and now everything looked bare and deserted. In the river the last sampans were moving to shore. He picked up a small leaf from a plant that grew in profusion on the edge of his small garden.

"It is a sensitive plant," he said. "You touch it, and at once it curls up in fear. We are like that. During this war we have shown that we have tough exteriors and can fight with the best, but underneath this superficial appearance you must realise that we are farmers and scholars—in three generations the scholars become farmers, and three generations later the farmers become scholars. The fabric of Chinese civilisation was as delicate as a spider's web; and so you can understand that the death of one man can shock us so much that we grow afraid of the future.

April 5th . . . I HAVE been teaching English poetry, and suddenly I have discovered that I know almost nothing about the history of the Border ballads. There are few books here, almost no anthologies, and there is no separate study of the ballad. But quite by accident, in a remote dusty corner of the library, among cobwebs and innumerable ancient scrolls, I found the ballad of Thomas the Rhymer and with great hoots of enjoyment recited it to my students this afternoon:

183

For forty days and forty nights
He wode thro red blude to the knee,
And he saw neither sun nor moon
But heard the roaring of the sea.

I know nothing about the technique of teaching. You stand against a blackboard, you address a crowd of students at seven o'clock in the morning, when it is raining and great clouds of smoky mist are drifting over the flower-beds outside. Because you are afraid that the students will fail to understand you, you write out on the blackboard interminable sentences of quotation and analysis until your elbows grow weary and your coat is covered in a soft powder of chalk. You are entranced by the nervous intensity in the expression of a young student from Shangtung and by the serenity in the face of a young girl in a flowered gown. You try to speak clearly and slowly, and yet, intoxicated by the beauty of the English language and by the curious sensation that they really understand every word you say, you begin to talk faster and faster. The quotation from Katherine Mansfield or Charles Doughty is smeared from the blackboard. You begin to ask questions, and suddenly you realise that everything which the English language has in common with Chinese they understand; but all that is peculiar to English is foreign to them. They are perfectly polite, they make the most graceful bows and inclinations, but all the time they seem to be wondering: "Is this really a language? Chinese is much simpler, and all this talk of stress and rhythms in prose is quite foreign to us, since the Chinese language still works by almost mathematical rules."

I think I have found a way out. The English lyric and the Chinese lyric are very close to one another. If I have time, I shall write a book on English poetry for Chinese students, and I shall deliberately select those poems which approach most readily to the Chinese idiom. Z. agrees with the plan. He loves English poetry with a passion which can only be derived from the fact that he reads it through a mind steeped in Chinese poetry. He chants English poetry as he chants Chinese poetry in a deep fluting voice which pays no attention to syllables or even to rhythm, in the "voice of an intoxicated bird". There is no other way to describe the voices of Chinese scholars when they are singing their native poetry. And ever since we have discussed the plan, he has been discovering new similarities between the two poetries.
184

It was a fine evening. We sat out on the lawn of the hotel, listening to the faint shrill voices of the actors on the Chinese stage near-by, while waiters came with boiling cups of chrysanthemum tea, and small boys played in the grass at our feet. And as the moon grew higher in the sky, and the wind changed, so that the voices of the actors grew louder, he began to sing in that high piercing resonant voice—so Chinese that it was almost impossible to mistake it for English—the words of the Princess:

> Now sleeps the crimson petal, now the white;
> Now waves the cypress in the palace walk;
> Now waves the gold fin in the porphyry front:
> The firefly wakens: waken thou with me.
>
> Now droops the milk-white peacock like a ghost,
> And like a ghost she glimmers on to me.
>
> Now lies the earth all Danae to the stars,
> And all thy heart lies open unto me.
>
> Now slides the silent meteor on, and leaves
> A shining furrow, as thy thoughts in me.
>
> Now folds the lily in all her sweetness up,
> And slips into the bosom of the lake:
> So fold thyself, my dearest, thou, and slip
> Into my bosom and be lost in me. . . .

April 6th . . . WE WERE discussing Bertrand Russell's article on the plan for an international University in the room of the dean of the faculty of law. The wind blew, the paper curtains rustled, the yellowish-green flame from the oil-lamp flickered on the table strewn with innumerable sheets of thin brown friable paper. It is one of those evenings when you expect frost; but outside, beyond the dusky flowers in the garden, the sky is serene and a silver moon surrounded by blue rings rides on the mountains.

It is a scene I am becoming accustomed to in China. To see nature through the waving paper windows, to sit round a small rapeseed-oil flame like a conspirator, to discuss everything without exception and to make vast plans for the future is an occupation which we share with the rest of the world. But here there are moments when we feel that we are not outrageously selfish in our discussions, and our plans are not wholly withdrawn from the world. The steel-bright intelligences of the Chinese professors and students have been tempered in four years of war and suffering, and thirty years of terrible instability. There has been no peace in China since living memory. Only eight years ago the fields where we walked this afternoon were covered with the purple flowers of poppy. Ten years ago the villages near the gorges were paying their taxes sixty years ahead to a war-lord who was prepared to sacrifice the wealth of his whole province rather than lose his interest in the productivity of the land. So these professors and students have a right to speak and to discuss the future, for they have suffered and they are the inevitable leaders of the future.

But no one liked the international University, and yet no one disagreed with Bertrand Russell's thesis. International Universities were necessary. It was necessary that the best minds of different nations should come together, to warn, to cajole, to instruct, to plan out the future. They should come together on a footing of perfect equality, and with absolute fearlessless. They should possess, if possible, diplomatic immunity and should be regarded as of equal importance to the ambassador. The scientist, the scholar, the inventor, the poet—all possessed distinct functions in the community. They could meet at the great Universities of the world, and we imagined that these great Universities would be linked together and that the current of the world's scholarship and learning would pass through them all. "Peace will be possible if the learned men really understand one another," one of the younger professors suggested. A still younger professor imagined a world in which vast sums of money were spent on encouraging foreign travel by all sections of the community. Young English mechanics and craftsmen would be encouraged to spend two or three years in the north-west of China; an American lumber-jack would spend some years among the forests of north China; a stone-mason would leave his shop in Scotland and spend a year among the stone-masons of Ceylon and another year among the stone-masons of Pekin. There would be an enormous increase in travel, and people would come to regard the whole world as their garden. There would be so much travel that war would become almost impossible, because a quarter of the population of England
186

would be dispersed over the rest of the globe; and millions of Russians, Indians and Americans would be working and playing in countries far from their borders. "There will be so many hostages that war will become an impossibility," he declared, "and the world will accept peace simply because the natives of each country have offered so many hostages to fortune. And there will be peace anyway, because we shall have rounded off the rough edges of our national characters, we shall be more tolerant and we shall realise that there is no pleasure in killing people simply because they speak another language, and there is infinite pleasure in meeting them and talking shop. If we can do this—if we can spend in one year on foreign travel the amount we spent on building three armoured battleships, then after a few years we shall come to regard war as an anachronism, and we shall laugh at people who still talk of tanks and submarines in the same way that we sometimes laugh at people who still talk of cavalry regiments."

It was an excited speech, and the young professor was so clearly filled with a vision that we did not dare to interrupt him. Instead of vast naval convoys, he imagined still vaster convoys of passenger ships. The airways would be filled with young mechanics, students and professors, and there would be no end to their travelling.

"No one will be considered civilised until he knows at least five foreign languages. We must make ourselves citizens of the world, and nothing is so necessary as to learn foreign languages. We shall erect statues to Hugo and Berlitz in our market-places, and we shall pray that our children shall be born with a gift of tongues."

Not everyone agreed with the young professor. There were some who were afraid that the distinctive character of the national civilisations would change out of recognition under the impact of an international community of nations. Others spoke mildly of utopianism, and still others criticised the plan because no nation would allow an unlimited number of foreigners to enter its doors. But the young professor continued, ardently and without the least trace of doubt, or of self-consciousness, to show that all our hesitations were in vain.

"You call it a dream, but this is one of the dreams which will become a reality. We know now that civilisations are mortal. We cannot afford any longer to play with war. We shall become in-

187

ternational in sheer self-defence. It is not too late. And then, when we have travelled all over the earth and found it beautiful, we shall no longer think it is necessary to starve in fox-holes, we shall no longer respect generals and armoured cars, and for the first time we shall begin to live on the earth as we were meant to live —in peace and comradeship with all men. It will come sooner than you expect. It will come as soon as this terrible war is over."

And as we went away, we thought of the vision of the young professor, pondering in our minds whether at this late hour such things might not indeed be possible. The blacksmiths, the stone-masons, the skilled electricians and engineers, the young doctors and foundrymen and mechanics—we thought of them setting out on their voyages of exploration, no longer bound to their small factories and hospitals and shipyards, ambassadors of good will to replace the ambassadors who too often had led us into war, the young in all their glory setting out to discover the world!

April 7th . . . WALKING up the steep hill behind the village near the University, we looked down at the green rice-fields and drum-towers, and there in front of us lay the white sails of the sampans rippling in the breeze. They were so white, and they shone with such excitement, clapping their sails and dancing in the wind, that we were for a moment astonished. I have never thought this village was anything but hideous. The narrow streets are covered with stone-slabs which are often broken, and some-times at night your foot slips down into the running filth which creeps below the slabs. The children look diseased; they are thin and pale, and under-fed. The black pigs, snorting lugubriously in the dark shadows, are as menacing as the filth underfoot, and the shops are tawdry beyond words. Though in Chungking a beneficent government has outlawed the tea-shops, there are more tea-shops in this village than I have ever been able to count; and new ones grow like mushrooms overnight. But suddenly, standing among the fields and looking over the curved roofs of the houses, the white sails took our breaths away.

China is a place where beauty appears unexpectedly. The pro-portions of a curving roof, a girl smiling sleepily in a doorway as she whisks the flies away, a child riding a black pig bare-back, three old women walking arm-in-arm through a mist-laden field, the clean curve of a plough as it comes dripping from the earth— all these have the quality of everlastingness. If you search for
188

them, you will never find them. They come so suddenly that you are overwhelmed, and they have gone before you can photograph them in your mind.

April 8th . . . Z. BELIEVES in spiritualism, or rather he believes in his own particular brand of Chinese spiritualism. We were talking about fox-spirits, and suddenly he announced that he had seen one that morning in his own room. He lives in an abandoned watch-tower near the bus-station, where the light penetrates through small T-shaped slits where rifles once reposed in defence of the village against the bandits of the hills.

"What did he look like?"

"Like a fox, but it was quite clear that it was also a beautiful girl. Fox-spirits walk very graciously, and their tails are very large and silky."

"You are quite sure you saw it?"

"Yes—you see, I had been dreaming about my grandmother."

"That explains it."

"I was afraid you would think it would. No, I was not dreaming, though it was early in the morning and I was still in bed. My grandmother was famous for her beauty and she died tragically, and we all knew that she would become a fox-spirit. I told you before that she was a Manchurian, and the Manchurians are disposed to believe strongly in fox-spirits." He paused for a while, trying to make clear in his own mind the extraordinary sequence of events he had witnessed during the morning.

"What happened?" I asked impatiently.

"First, I must tell you that we had a special temple to the fox-spirits in Pekin. It was not very large, and I do not think any of us ever entered it, but we knew it was there and we had a vague idea of its contents. Dust, spiders' webs, a small altar, a stone image of a fox, tapers and candles and perhaps a prayer-mat—nothing more. I had been dreaming of my grandmother coming to sacrifice at the shrine of the fox-spirits, and when I woke up I could see every detail of the small shrine, and at the same time I could see every detail of the room I was living in. The fox-spirit came through the small T-slit in the wall, a very beautiful fox-spirit, the fur almost pure gold and the eyes bright green like emeralds, an enormous bushy tail which seemed to resemble the plumes of a peacock dyed bright gold. The fox-spirit came up to my bed. I knew it was a fairy, and I dared not touch her. I thought she had come to take me away, and I began to think: 'During the whole of the summer I have planned to study the Miao tribes in Hunan and it is absolutely impossible for me to leave the world yet.' For a long while the fox-spirit said nothing. I could see the bright red tongue, the green eyes and the bushy tail. She was talking softly, but I could not hear what she said—fox-spirits talk in very low voices. And then she began to talk with exactly the same voice which I remember in my grandmother, a voice which was very soothing and sweet, and yet so aristocratic that I remember that I always felt confused when she was speaking. She talked of her life among the spirits, and of how tired she was of wandering through the snowy forests. She wanted to come back and live in the family. She wept. She put her paws on my bed and began to lay her head against mine, and her head was so warm and furry that it was almost as though a beautiful girl had come. She told me many things about our family that I had never known. After a while she rose and lapped some milk which lay on the table. She took some sweets, too. She looked at the room critically, advised me to buy curtains and to find some tapestry to cover the walls, and all the time her voice was breaking and she was crying. And then a few minutes later she walked away, and I can still remember the slow padding footsteps of the fox-spirit as she disappeared through the T-slit in the wall."

I must have looked incredulous, for after a moment he said: "You don't believe it?"

"Yes, I believe it."

"You are being polite—*kieh-ch'i?*"

"I believe it, because you have said it was true. I would not believe it if anyone else had told me."

"I am glad you believe it, and you mustn't be surprised at the strange beliefs of the Chinese. At birth we are Confucians, Taoists and Buddhists. Also, the great majority of us belong to the Kuomintang party, which is another religion. But underlying all these religions there is still another religion which is rarely mentioned in discussions about the Chinese, and yet it is more important perhaps than all the others combined. We are animists. We believe there are gods in everything, and at the same time we are a little sceptical. Watch the young housewife when she makes offerings to the gods—the coloured eggs are laid out before the family altar, but she is not sure that they have any magical properties.
190

The food we prepare for the gods we eat ourselves, and the paper money we burn for the dead is no longer inscribed with its value and indeed it is simply punctuated with a few holes to differentiate it from paper which is not money. We believe in the animistic gods of our forefathers, but we are not entirely satisfied with them. But go into the remote villages, and you will find people still worshipping the trees and the rice-crops, and they are happier because they worship these things."

We spoke about Bali where the spirits of all growing things seemed to fill the air, and we agreed that if it were possible to believe in these things, we would all become poets and there would be no necessity to prove ourselves, for the world would be so full of life that we would resemble people who are eternally in their own homes.

As we came down the stone steps to the ferry, a great pile of burning paper was shining with a yellow flame. It was still broad daylight, but the flames shone like leaping tongues and the face of the old woman who peered intently into the flames was also burning with the light of the flames. And we talked sadly of the angels who guarded the gates of the irrecoverable Eden.

April 13th . . . EARLY this morning we rode down to a temple facing the gorges. K. suggested that I might live there, for it appears to be a habit of foreigners to live in a deserted temple facing great rivers. Like so many young Chinese students, K. is a poet who is determined to solve the riddle of modern Chinese poetry. He knows the difficulties, and sometimes they weary him beyond endurance, so that he can almost cry aloud against the pain of tradition and the still greater pain of attempting to invent a new language to express the thoughts of the present age.

"In the old days there were accepted canons of taste, and poets had only to fashion their words according to the accepted canon. Even our greatest poets, Tu Fu and Li T'ai Po, obeyed the canons set down by generations of poets before them. They added new feelings and sentiments, but they added nothing to the structure of the verse, and their feelings and sentiments fitted easily into the accepted metres. Today we must write of things which were unimaginable to the ancients. We must write of armies with modern weapons, of steam-engines, of aeroplanes, of iron-clad ships. Tu Fu wrote about China when the state was dissolving under the pressure of the invaders, but we must write about China made

191

young again by the terrors of invasion. We no longer think in the same way as the ancients. Our standards are different from theirs, and we are no longer fatalistic. This time we shall not absorb the invaders. This time we have no thoughts of self-pity, and the poet who writes about the pity of China will prove himself to be a bad poet. But how can we write this new poetry? The old poetry is in our blood. We know, too, that we shall never in this generation write poetry as great as the poetry of the past—we shall never equal Tu Fu or Li T'ai Po or Chu Yuan. We are living in a poetic desert—that is why T. S. Eliot's *Wasteland* is so popular, and why we read foreign poetry with such hunger. We are discovering all the poets of Europe, we are translating Schiller and Miskiewicz and Herrick and Racine and a thousand others in an effort to find a poet faced with the same problems—and so far we have found no one. In the end a poet will come. He will rise out of the country fully armed, as mysteriously endowed as any of the great poets of the past, and we shall not be surprised when he comes. But this is certain: we are determined to produce this poet, for to us civilisation has no meaning without poetry. Probably he will be a poet from the ranks of the people. He will not be a University professor or even a student. He will speak in a language which we shall find strange at first, a hard, ruthless, terrible language, like the language invented by Mayakovsky in Russia. When he comes, we shall all attack him. We may even kill him with our misunderstanding of his work; but he will survive when we have all perished. And all our wars, all our sufferings, all the terror which comes from our long journeying will not be in vain, because he will record it all in imperishable verse."

I was surprised that he should hope so much from his poet of the future. Great poets are rare enough in all generations, and it was extraordinary to think of him spending sleepless nights as he attempted to fashion in his own mind the conditions of great poetry. It is true that the new language of modern China is not suitable to poets. *Pei-hua* is still in its infancy, and *Wen-li* may never return. Meanwhile there is no correct Chinese, as there is a correct English. And amid a multiplicity of styles and idioms, the younger Chinese poets are lost.

At the temple we found the gods still in possession. They were terrible gods, life-size, covered with cobwebs, with great bleeding tongues three feet long coming from their distended mouths, with

192

dragon's claws and cockerel's feet, feathered, menacing. I am not going to live there.

April 14th, A letter from Bergery . . . ". . . BUT what I have always wanted to know is whether China will take her courage in her hands and follow us across the roads to a new world. Is this hyperbole? It is not intended to be. The spectacle of renascent China is one of the few spectacles which the modern world has to offer me without burning my heart. And yet it must be so. The traditions of centuries will flower, and from China we shall receive the greatest blessings imaginable by man.

"When I was young I dreamed of bringing the tides of East and West together, and from the maelstrom of these two conflicting currents, I imagined a miracle—there would be dry land. I had hoped to see before I die the white crest of the wave of the Orient leaping high in the air and becoming rock—a new nation built out of uncharted seas. It may be so. The East is fluid, and we ourselves are rigid in spite of our inventiveness. Once I thought Indian and Chinese cultures would meet across the Himalayas; but now I believe more strongly than ever that the tidal wave of India and China will meet among the islands of the South Seas, under the palm-trees, in a kind of fairy-land more beautiful than any I have ever seen. Let it be. We are the children of the sun and of philosophy; the enemies of custom; friends of learning and inventiveness; brothers of freedom. If we could only learn from the Chinese to have patience . . .

"Sainte-Beuve remarked of his countrymen that they would continue to be Catholics long after they had ceased to be Christians. I am a Buddhist, long after I have ceased to believe in Buddha. And so are all the Chinese, and what is more surprising is that they are Confucians and Taoists also. And we are all these things because we must have our roots in history. This is what the modern world has forgotten—history is everything, the rest is immaterial. History is the smile of the child, the seed and the flower, the ponies neighing, the audible sigh of the lotos in the early morning when it opens its leaves. History is now and China. It is everywhere. And in it we have our roots, as the flying spores of seed still have their roots in the trees.

"And so, having accomplished a little of what men call history, I would like to spend my days in some remote Chinese valley learning history from the beginning. I am too old, too ill, too

193

stupid, to follow the wars much longer. They have asked me to go to India, where they expect trouble. I shall not go. I shall avoid trouble like the plague. I must clear my mind before I die.

"And do you know, sometimes I have the feeling that we are outside history. During the last twenty or thirty years we have avoided history, we have run away from her, we have run away from all traditions. The revolution of nihilism is not history; and we are all nihilists now. In our own age, when the most precious things of man, whole cities and civilisations, can be destroyed by bombs, history stands still and culture progresses by infinitesimal fragments of experience, or else withdraws altogether. . . .

"I know nothing that gives me greater assurance for the future than the intelligence of the young Chinese students. No group of people outside Poland have suffered so much or so often. The Universities which left the coast and travelled inland, losing their libraries and scientific equipment, continually bombed and massacred, were deliberately attacked by the Japanese, who knew that if the Universities failed, the rest would fall into their hands. We know nothing of this in the West. It is true that friends of mine in Polish and Czech Universities have been killed, the University libraries wantonly destroyed, but the Germans seem never to have realised completely that the Universities of the lands they conquer must be razed to the ground. The Japanese did this, and it is to their lasting infamy, a crime greater than any other crime, since in the Universities lies the heart of a people. I hear of students living on coarse rice, of professors living in small ramshackle farm-houses, and yet these are the inheritors of the oldest civilisation on earth and the future legislators for the whole of Asia.

"Nothing is so important as that the East should understand our history. *Nothing is so important*—except one thing, and that is that we should understand theirs. I hear half-hearted talk of increasing the number of professorships of Chinese, Indian and Russian culture in British and American Universities.

"One evening, at Changsha, I lost my hope for the future, and found it again. Do you remember when we walked together towards the two remaining pillars of the University of Hunan? So great was the impression made upon me that it reminds me of the explosion of a depth-charge. I was weak, and believed in nothing. Now I believe only in your Universities. Just as the prophets and ascetics went into the desert, where they were forgotten by
194

men, and returned bringing with them the glory of a culture new-formed, so I believe that out of the small groups of men who painstakingly set out to understand the nature of the civilisation they live in, learned scholars and young men enthralled with the genius of their country, we shall see the beginning of the revival so long expected. The wars will come to an end. Pray God that they do not find us with only our weapons in our hands! . . ."

April 21st . . . BERGERY arrived this morning, having travelled all night by pony along the river-bank. It was very typical of him, but he looked tired—he had been caught in the rain—and the *mafu* was evilly-disposed, a one-eyed man, with an expression of pure malevolence. Bergery insisted on making the journey, calling the *mafu* by all the names of Eblis; and the *mafu* followed him with surly patience.

I have taken Bergery to see the President of the University, an old man, already a little tired, with the eyes of a young bird. They shook hands, sat down to discuss the future of Universities in China and completely forgot my existence. Bergery looked at the coloured maps on the wall. "We shall have buildings here—and here—and here——" the President kept on saying. I have never seen Bergery look so much the child. He asked questions in bad Chinese, and was answered in the most correct and lucid English. Some students came in. Bergery leaped up and made a low bow, which amused the students and set the girls giggling. He was perfectly at ease, and when the President suggested that he should make a speech in the barn-like amphitheatre, all wooden beams and bole-weavilled timber, he complied at once, asking only that he should first be allowed to browse through the *Encyclopædia Britannica*.

He made the speech in the afternoon, introducing himself with a few words of apology in Chinese. He spoke of the prospects of peace and the place of the Universities after the war. He drew a picture of peace so eloquent that we wondered why the war had not ceased ten years ago, a peace in which students, farmers and artisans were described as the leaders of the future, a peace in which there would be food enough for all, there would be no beggars, no one would be poor, but on the contrary everyone would be so extremely rich that they would be continually dazed by their good fortune and by the fate which allowed them to be born in the world. It was a speech such as I have rarely heard, for

195

it was passionate and scientific at once, and at the same time it was prophetical of mercy and redeeming love. The gaunt head on the rostrum, the long face, the dark eyes and the unmanageable streaks of grey hair which wound round his temples fascinated us; and when it was over I was amused to see the students crowding round him and begging for his autograph.

I can remember very little of the speech. A few isolated phrases, which numbed us with expectation of glory, a few sentences of impassioned hatred against those who had made this war possible, a few revelations about the progress of the war which came to us like the strokes of lightning in a clear sky. And then the extraordinary hammer-blows of the peroration:

"The mania which has descended upon us now belongs to an epoch outside history; and we who live in the world and outside history must find the road back again to history only by the most terrible hardships. You have proved that you are not afraid of hardships, but I must warn you that what lies before you will be still harder. The world is hard; all things—beauty, the grace of children, understanding and learning—are hard, harder than you have ever imagined. I have not come to make you think the world is easy. There is heroism only in combating the enemy, and the enemy lies in ourselves, in our love of ease, our tiredness, our terrible weariness of our responsibilities. But today the war is almost over, and you will have your rewards. Forgotten by the outside world, you will suddenly be remembered. You will live in a flowering land, and by your sufferings you will make yourself known. So it is in the world. The terrors are always followed by peace. The moon shines in the cloud-littered sky on the night of the murder. The way is hard, but there is hope and perfect beauty to be found on the road. I have only one more message—Work, love, the sun, make small groups of friends among yourselves, such groups as can never be broken, meditate."

There was thunderous applause, but I doubt whether anyone understood what he was saying. Fascinated by the spectacle of a famous war correspondent, who was only too obviously ill and excited beyond words by being among Chinese students, they re-
196

turned his almost visible adoration, and begged him to stay. He has not yet decided whether he will remain.

In the evening we talked of his plans. He would like to remain somewhere near the University, on a high mountain overlooking the river, surrounded by books, attended by two or three servants and by bearers who could take him down the mountain whenever he would like a change of scenery. We have not once mentioned the fact that he is obviously dying.

April 22nd . . . HE IS still behaving like a young child. This evening I found him among the shallows near the river, talking with the students. They were perched in the shadow of the rocks, and while he told them of his adventures, they listened openmouthed. But often he would insist that they should tell him of their adventures, and then the tables would be turned, and he would listen open-mouthed to the unsung heroes of the Chinese wars.

In the evening I took him to the village, where there is a school of ballet-dancing. I had told him nothing about the invitation I had received. We walked down a lane, where the ducks shone in the pools in the red rays of the declining sun; and suddenly, as we passed a grove of alders, the small white stone cattle-sheds beside the road burst into music. I cannot explain it otherwise. We were walking quietly, listening to an old woman in the distance who was flogging her pony, when suddenly the air was filled with music from four or five pianos and violins. He was utterly thunderstruck, and so excited that he kept saying: "No, this is nonsense, it can't happen, even in China where miracles are apparently commonplace." Inside the cattle-sheds we found a famous Chinese dancer in black tights, surrounded by her pupils. They were all very young, and some of them were extraordinarily beautiful.

"What are they doing?" he asked from the seventh heaven.

"They are practising a ballet," she answered, and spoke of the ballet school of Kurt Jooss in England, where she had been trained; of Dartington Hall; of Irina Baronova; of the Russian ballet in all its glory and mystery. It seemed so odd to Bergery to find, in a remote village in China, portraits of the women he had seen in the crowded theatres of London, Paris and New York, and he looked at the photographs on the wall with the weariness of an old man who sees the loves of his youth returning in all

197

their glory. The Chinese children fascinated him. "They have no bones," the ballet mistress said, twirling a great ball of twined wire which apparently demonstrated the positions of the body. "I think we shall make a ballet in China as great as anything produced out of Russia. They come to us very young. We train them in music, painting and drawing; we have complete control over their lives. They are like nuns dedicated to beauty, and if you come again to China in five years' time you will see the old Yuan theatre accompanied by a ballet so splendid that you will wonder how it is that you have never seen such beauty before."

She spoke in the language which Bergery could understand, the somewhat hyperbolical language of the recently converted. She told us that it was by the order of the Generalissimo that music and ballet-dancing were being encouraged; that the money, on which all the students lived, came from the Ministry of Education, for they were all too poor to support themselves. There was a small spindle-legged girl with dark eyes and an oval face, who looked exactly like the early portraits of Pavlova. There were three or four small urchins dressed in ribbons who looked as though they were already prepared to take the stage and dance until they dropped dead. It was late when we left. We heard the booming of the drum and the faint music of the violins as we passed down the deserted road.

April 23rd . . . THE new house is ready, and we have taken over possession today. It stands on a hill overlooking the University, a green hill of broken rock surmounted by an immense banyan tree, and beyond the banyan tree, on a small rise, lies the house. There are no curtains; the doors are square, like tombstones, and there is a great hole in the roof which at first I thought was due to lightning, but later learned to be the windows of an old astronomical telescope.

There are advantages and disadvantages in the house. At night the road is dangerous, for there are still bandits. And there are great broken gaps in the road, through which you can fall on nights when there is no moon and the bamboo torchlight has flickered out. There are tombstones everywhere, and these too are frightening, especially that of a young University student who died mysteriously many years ago—a tombstone painted green and standing like a monolith against the clouds.

But there are great advantages. Early in the morning you can
198

look down on the river lying between the gorges, the green-capped mountains, the lazy summer mist rising and falling, the white patched sails of the sampans and the clear air. In the morning everything is fresh and beautiful, dew-dripping, clamorous in the sun. Behind the house there are fields of orange-trees, the dark green leaves shining wetly among the orange-coloured boughs. There are grasshoppers and small toads; and the fireflies are still shining after dawn. The terraced rice-fields are covered with a thin white shield of mist, and there are tufts of mist in all the trees. The dawn is more brilliant than when the mist is gone. What a curious, silent, dreaming and implacable world lies beneath the clouds! We think of the peasants in their bamboo cottages below, as they wade out in the damp, early morning air to their rice-fields, seeing no sun, surrounded in whiteness. And yet our own world on these early mornings is still more mysterious, for we see birds disappearing in the clouds or skimming over them, we see the smoke of blue fires drifting upwards through them, and just as clouds in childhood have the shape of heroes, so when these clouds dissolve into fragments, they acquire the shapes of people we have known.

I have called the house, after a house in a novel I once wrote: "The Hall of the Sleeping Cloud". Bergery has been enjoying himself in the village buying furniture. We have a folding table, six stools, two chairs and a bookcase, for which we paid $300. It is not dear, but we have by no means finished; and last night, we discovered at three o'clock in the morning, that we had forgotten to buy the beds!

April 24th, Market Day . . . IN THE little village there are three market days a week, but every day is different. There are days when you see immense bluish-white slabs of broken salt and round bamboo trays filled with every variety of yellow beans, melons, grapes, sunflower seeds. There are other days—usually stormy days—when you see only immense heaps of patched clothing, rusted locks, silver toys, herb doctors, dentists, quacks. There are an extraordinary number of quacks, who will tell your fortune and discover your ailments by the most incredible numismatics. As we went through the dim-lit cloud-covered streets, we saw an old peasant with his trousers hitched up to his thighs—old, greyish thighs, the colour of mud and swollen with hookworm. He looked weary with pain, but when the street doctor pushed a

199

silver needle into his thighs, his face brightened, and it was evident that the pain had gone. There was a little blood, and the doctor wiped it away with some brown paper. A moment later he pushed a needle into another part of the thigh. The needle slipped out and fell in the mud, but he wiped the mud away on his sleeve, blew on it and once more inserted it into the wound, and once more he brushed away the little flakes of blood with an old torn piece of brown paper. The peasant did not die. An expression of intense happiness came over him; he smiled and shook with happiness, and became still happier when three more needles were inserted into his leg. The sky was downcast, but the little crowd surrounding the street doctor lived in the sunlight.

April 25th . . . THE sky cleared, and the wedding drums could be heard as far away as the University. Bergery was browsing in the library, but as soon as he heard the drums, he ran out, expecting to see the wedding pass through the grounds of the University. But it was still some distance away, winding along the road which follows the river, a road shaded by maples and thick clumps of banyan.

The wedding procession passed outside, framed against the trees, the river and the distant hills. There were so many musicians, servants and sedan-bearers that we lost count. We could not see the bride. Under the quilted and embroidered cloth, she hid in her brightly painted sedan-chair, where mirrors tinkled and flashed in the sun, and roses of blue and green ribbons quivered above the chair. There, too, was her furniture. There were the embroidered pillows and hangings, the quilts and mattresses, her chairs, her tea-pots, her mirror. There were great baskets of sweets, round which the flies gathered. There were her relatives, who stuffed handkerchiefs in their mouths, wailing with happiness. And so the procession passed, to the banging of copper drums and the interminable outbreaks of cartridges and bamboo crackers, and all the while the air quivered and the small white sails of the sampans in the river seemed to remain still, gathered into silence and motionless as the gulls. The whole University came out to watch the procession. The youths and girls playing basket-ball ceased attempting to throw a ball into an iron hoop; the University servant ceased to follow the disorderly sheep wandering along the cliffs; the servants who attended to the black pigs forgot their charges, and looked open-mouthed at the cavalcade which passed under the maple trees. We watched them till they were out of sight, for the colours of a Chinese University in wartime are drab; and the colours of a country wedding are as exciting as flames.

On the chair carrying the bride, or perhaps on one of the chairs carrying her possessions, two pieces of red paper inscribed in gold characters had been seen hanging loose. When the procession passed, the wind must have torn them away, for shortly afterwards we found them lying in the dust at our feet. Bergery picked them up and read out the characters slowly: "Beautiful flower and full moon," and the other read: "Long lives like Peng (the Phœnix) and the same number of sons as Chi."

April 27th . . . Bergery has decided to visit a temple high up on the mountains. This is not the famous temple on Splendid Cloud Mountain, where the Abbot T'ai Shu lives with his Buddhist students, but another. It is small and almost inaccessible, but there are three or four farm-houses in the neighbourhood, and he expects to be able to get all the food he requires.

We left early in the morning, when the thick vapour still hung over the river, followed by bearers and wandering along the shore, at first on level plains of sand, then clambering over rocks and then, since the sun was almost unbearable, we took shelter in a grove of mulberry trees. After nearly three miles of walking, we came to the beach where the small covered boats sail for Pei Wen Hsuan and the rocky defiles of the gorges.

It was one of those days when a strong scented wind, coming down-river, brings you the scent of orange-blossom so keenly that the nostrils can barely withstand the excitement. Bergery was in good humour, joking with the students who had offered to be our guides; and yet not joking, for he possessed too great an admiration for them to let the conversation develop so quickly into laughter. A girl student had crowned him with flowers. Another fetched ripe yellow corncobs from the near-by fields, and as we unwrapped them from the dewy bluish-green leaves, they were so tempting that we began to eat them raw, after first brushing them with permanganate of potash. At the bay, where the sunlight shone so brightly on the river and the sand that we were blinded, we paused for a while, taking breath, gazing at the small white orphanage which lay towering high above us on the cliffs; till at last the salt smell of the river and the hurrying sun told us that we must seek shelter in the boats covered with coir-matting, and slowly we sailed down to the hot springs.

The springs are not the only hot ones in Szechuan. According to a doctor in Peipei, they have medicinal properties; and as we sailed beneath them, watching them smoke out of the rocks in great falls, we put out our hands and received an unexpected benediction of boiling water. There is perhaps nothing so mysterious as the gorges of a Chinese river. Once in the gorges, you are no longer bewildered, for you find yourself in a green lake shadowed by cliffs of all colours—here blue, here red, here crimson-lake and there deep orange turning to tawny brown. Ragged trees, their branches sagging outward and their roots climbing out of the rocky sub-soil, groan and overshadow the lake, twisting and turning according to the prevalent wind. Here there are no horizons, and no sounds. These rocks do not echo; all sounds are muted between them. And in the small village which has grown up among gardens and temples where the hot springs gush out of the earth, the thick clumps of yellow bamboos add to the silence only the whispering of the leaves.

Bergery begged the students to sing for him. He lay at the bottom of the boat, fanning himself, gazing up at the immense depths of bluish white sky above, so overcome with enjoyment that he forgot to thank them. We were perfectly content. The river, the cliffs, the darkening air, the silence and the thick white spiral clouds of smoke ascended from the springs; and beyond them the long road to the mountains. We climbed up the stone steps, passed the open-air bath where boys were bathing naked, and found ourselves at last in a stone-flagged garden, among rockeries and small lakes where the lotoses are in full bloom, the red tips shining like spears and the oily green leaves filled with quicksilver drops of dew.

Three or four hours away lay Chungking. We were actually within the city limits of Chungking, and here was the garden of the hashish-eaters in all its summer glory.

There were small stone tables among the whispering elms. A boy came from a tea-house and offered to bring us tea, to the astonishment of the students who had tried often to have their tea brought out into the gardens and failed. It was growing late. The sun was high above us. We had forgotten the time taken to travel down the river, and soon it was time to climb the mountain or abandon the journey for the day.

202

It was Bergery who insisted that we must abandon the journey. He found a grove of bamboos in the afternoon where we could take tea, and near-by some limestone caves where you could sit in the cool shelter of the rock and meditate on the surrounding whiteness. He found, where the mountain road begins, great blocks of stone on which the Emperor of a certain Han Dynasty had caused to be engraved the ascetic features of Buddhist monks. These stones, half buried among ferns, were known to the students, but they had never seen them. We wandered through temples, where the folding sunlight cast shadows on the gold Buddhas and on the painted eaves and ceilings. A temple had been converted into a school. Along the walls there were hideous posters showing the features of eminent scholars, and it was surprising to come upon the faces of Napoleon, Ghenghiz Khan and Thomas Paine. We listened to the hungry buzz of small children reciting the sounds of the Chinese characters they were learning; and when night fell we wandered among the lotos-gardens, listening to the shrill cicadas and the sighing of the bamboos. It was a night of pure magical expediency, when fire-flies wander among willow-trees, when the river is silent and yet boats still sail down-stream, a night when the cliffs appear to possess whispering lives and the small hot streams in the square mossy channels beside the pathways were filled with goldfish.

"It is a night to die in," said Bergery. "Tomorrow we shall go up to my temple."

He was completely happy. All the weariness which comes over people who have stayed for long in Chungking disappeared, and on his face there was only an expression of perfect content.

April 28th . . . BEFORE dawn we set out. I remember now only the blue hills we saw at the summit of the first cliffs and the girl in the red dress washing clothes in the mountain stream. It was hot, hotter than I have ever known it in Szechuan, and we walked through rice-fields tilted along the slopes, while the water poured through them from the fountains high above our heads. But there was no sign of the peasants. Silence and desolation filled the air, and sometimes there were birds' wings. It was the silence of deep summer, when the earth smells of treacle and the mist still smoulders on the ground.

We were carried by bearers. Their naked shoulders grew silver with sweat, and they walked with a kind of dancing motion, so that we were continually being jerked from side to side; and yet this was pleasurable, for it meant that there were moments when we could see the mountains shining clear in the heavy summer. Here there were thick groves of Indian corn, here there were walnut trees; and under the shade of the trees, while the king-fishers dipped overhead, golden and greenish blue, passing the small earth shrines where a few red candles still glittered, we saw the trees growing thicker and thicker towards the summit of the mountain, passing through so many shades of greenness that we lost count and felt dizzy already with the altitude:

"They never told me Szechuan was like this," said Bergery. "After the war we shall have posters in all the railway stations: 'The Highlands of Szechuan beckon you!'—something like that, and the thousands of people who come will never know that we came up the mountains in the silence, before them."

The scenery was magnificent. Wave after wave of ice-blue mountains, the white river smoking below, the sails of the sampans sometimes catching the light, and the silence of high summer with the humming-birds among the trees, the lakes of rice so still in the heavy morning that they seemed to be caught up in a wave of breathless adoration. And then suddenly the rice-fields disappeared: we were on broad uplands, and there was Bergery shaking his stick at all the imagined glory of the place, and saying: "If one has to fight wars, it is better to fight them in China. The attack begins at dawn—no one knows why, but it always does. And China is the only country in the world where the dawn is supremely beautiful."

It was late in the afternoon before we reached the temple. We were high up, the air thin and sweet; and from there we could no longer see the sampans flickering in the broad sunlight, nor the corrugated iron roofs of the University. The gorges, too, had disappeared. The small temple, of red brick, surrounded by a crenel-lated greyish-white wall, covered with inscriptions, with small outriding gardens and pavilions, shone on the very summit of the mountain, with trees all round disappearing into the grey depths below. A servant came out, bowing low. They said he was an old monk, who had forsaken the monastery to enjoy the comforts of matrimony, and it was surprising to see the young wife and the small child who played there on the summit of the mountain.

We had no time to go in. One of the students decided to re-main there for a night, or perhaps for three or four days; but the
204

sun was already low in the sky and indeed had disappeared beyond the mountains, and even if we hurried it would take two hours before we could reach the University by the quickest route. For a moment we saw the dragon gates open, we heard his tremendous laughter as the books at last burst out of the blue sackcloth bag in which they had been hauled out of the valley; and then there was silence, broken only by the double call of the snipe, the humming-birds, the eagles and the curlews.

Half-way down we heard the moaning of panthers in the forest. Shortly afterwards one of the students turned to me and said: "It is true that the panthers love the heights." Then I knew that Bergery would be happy. He would study Chinese poetry; he would be visited by the monks; he would play with the old monk's child; at night he would listen to the sighing of the pines and the moaning of panthers in the forests.

May 5th . . . J., who has been teaching me Chinese, has a habit of answering my questions only after deep thought. There was a green moon last night, a tremendous moon which covered the eastern hills with a shimmering light, and we sat outside the house, under the pines, looking down on the last labourers in the fields and the beautiful spanned arch which joins the two buffs of land below. It was a scene such as Rembrandt would have painted; for here there were coruscations of pearls and scarlet robes, great avalanches of buried colour, and even more than during the day the whole earth seemed to be breathing.

We were talking, then, of the philosophy of life of the younger Chinese. What did they find in life? What was the background to all this feverish suffering and brutality and terror and beauty which was sweeping over China? The students, I said, lived apart. They seemed to have little contact with the outside world, and indeed it was difficult to believe that the students as they passed through the insanitary village I knew so well had any sympathy for the lives of the inhabitants. J. was ruthless, as are many of his kind. The generation of people who were born before the Republic would soon die out. It was impossible to do very much for them. They preferred their ancestor worship, their filth, their beggarliness, their outworn habits and still more outworn thoughts to the life which the Generalissimo was preparing to give them. There were already plans for the future. But what are those plans? He smiled. In the moonlight, in his blue gown, weaving a

205

garland of snow-grasses, he looked like an apparition from the T'ang Dynasty, who had unaccountably descended upon the mountain.

"It is all very clear," he said, "and there have been many examples in the past. We have suffered more than we are suffering now. We mapped out our path three thousand years ago, and we shall keep to the plan. And yet this time the plan will be put into operation with complete ruthlessness. The plan is simple—it is not unlike the Russian plan. We shall industrialise China. We shall make her powerful. We shall make her respected, but we shall never go to war. Have you read the *Book of Changes?* Almost on the first page you will find these words: 'Let the superior man exert himself with the unfailing pertinacity of nature.' There is a gloss on the words, which may have been written by Confucius— it is the favourite quotation of the Generalissimo, and reads: 'Day by day the heavens revolve, with a constancy that only a supreme pertinacity could maintain. The superior man models himself upon it with the unceasing exertion of his energies. . . .' This is what we believe; this is what we shall put into practice. The tremendous energies of the Chinese race have been squandered in the past, but from now on they will be organised. Have you read the *Book of the Mean?* 'With the highest integrity we shall accomplish our purpose, unfailing and enduring,' or again in the words of Confucius: 'We must race on, unpausing day and night.' I translate badly, but this is the sense of the thing. These words we have taken as our spiritual guides. There is another guide, which you will see inscribed on the walls wherever there is a public meeting: 'The Revolution is not yet accomplished.' If you can remember these things you will have no fear for the future of China, organised as never before, no longer squandering her riches, proud in the humility of her ancient civilisation, no longer unprepared."

And watching him, so elegant and so handsome in the moonlight, it was difficult to remember that he had already been wounded in the war, was an accomplished swimmer and glider, wrote poetry and longed only to be put in charge of a fertiliser factory somewhere in the interior of China. He was obsessed with China. He would talk about her for hours with the tenderness of a lover, and sometimes he would quote from the ancient poets, not because they understood China, but because they also loved her; and then he would wander away alone towards the cliffs and the rice-fields, too overcome to trust himself to speak any more.

May 7th . . . COMING at night from the University along the long winding stone path between the rice-fields, I saw a ghost. Or perhaps it was not a ghost. The cicadas and frogs were screaming—I have never heard them screaming so loudly, and the moon was shining with its great blue rings shimmering and quivering and throwing out immense blue streamers like the streamers which decorate the heads of the courtiers in the T'ang Dynasty; and yet the moon did not shine upon the rice-fields, for they were covered in a thin summer mist. I walked alone. I passed small slumbering cottages, where the only sounds came from the black pigs grunting inside, or perhaps there was a mysterious swish from a cotton dress, and once a boy came out of the house with two pails of water hanging from a yoke over his shoulders. In the silver moonlight the boy shone like bronze, and I watched him as he returned, while the water dripped along his bare arms and shoulders and down his legs; and the bronze changed to glittering silver.

But I did not want to talk about the boy. He was not the ghost, for I felt his hot breath and heard him panting as I passed, and answered his gentle salutation with words which he may not have understood. Nor were the voices of the armed soldiers who called across the mist ghosts, though they are frightening enough at this hour of night, and I am never sure whether these guardians of the night understand my replies. There have been bandits here quite recently, and soldiers stand at the cross-roads of the mountain paths, calling out to all those who pass, and you must answer quickly unless you want to be shot. Your body will fall down into the rice-fields and what is left of it will only be recovered at the next sowing. And then, too, the fire-flies like green moons encircling the reeds by the lakeside—no, they are not ghosts, though at times they are frightening. And sometimes dogs bark suddenly, and sometimes a child starts yelling, and you have no idea in the darkness that you have passed a house. But none of these are ghosts. The ghosts came when I was passing almost the last of the terraced rice-fields where the mist lay unaccountably thick, and suddenly out of the mist and the darkness an enormous silver heron rose at my feet, an immense span of silver wings rising effortlessly towards the moon. And this really was a ghost, for the

207

heron was at least twenty feet high and the wing-span was so huge that it seemed to cover the lake and throw down a terrible black cruciform shadow.

I have told C., who is staying with me. At first he thought I was only frightened, for it is a long and dangerous journey—dangerous because there are so many places where the stone path has been silted away. But afterwards he remembered that at the identical place a few days ago he saw almost the same thing, and accounted for it by a trick of refraction.

"There is no other explanation?"

"No," he said, and went on to talk about the ghost houses and the credulous beliefs of the Szechuanese until I was frightened and told him I must sleep.

"There are worse things than white herons," he said gravely. "There are mysterious tigers, who are never seen, though you can see their pud-marks; there are sheets of flame, which go out when you come near them; there are fox spirits, and once a year at the full moon the carved gods in the temple come out and walk over the countryside."

I shuddered, thinking of the gods with the forked and bloody tongues and cockerel's feet which I had seen in the cobwebby temple by the river gorges.

"And there are axes of ice which fall from heaven, kill and melt away again before they can be seen, and sometimes the moon——"

But I was already past all dreams of horror, and was falling asleep. Vaguely and intermittently I heard the voice droning on as it related all the unimaginable terrors of Szechuan.

May 8th, Boils . . . DURING the last few days nearly everybody I knew well has come out with boils. They attack the back of the neck, the buttocks, the armpits, the bridge of the nose, the hollows of the palms. In this heat we are all sweating, though we lie about half-naked all day. And still the boils come. With the greatest difficulty we succeed in exterminating a single boil which comes up in a great blue weal; we break it, pour boiling water over it and watch the sickly yellow pus draining away, or we squeeze it out until it flows away from the wound like an interminable ribbon of yellow tooth-paste. We smile. We pretend to be perfectly aware that these things are sent to try us. But what is annoying is that no sooner has one boil disappeared than another springs up in a totally different place.

208

I have bought some sulphanilamide. C. has thrown it away. "There is no sulphanilamide except in the hospitals," he says. "It's all doctored stuff, made out of flour and lime—it will only make things worse." I have made enquiries among the students, and I have found none who believes in the products sold by the chemists. They are resigned to their fate, and they know that they must remain underfed and without proper medical supplies, except those which are provided by the excellent school doctor; and there is so pitiably little of it that they remain uncomplaining. I know nothing like this forbearance. I have seen three students and a professor sick with malaria. They toss in their beds in a kind of delirium, they moan and sweat out all the juices of their bodies, but they do not complain. All round us the fields are malarial. There is no quinine, or rather there is so little that it must be preserved for severe cases only. "And what is a severe case?" I asked C. "It is severe when they think you are dying."

Meanwhile the lucky ones walk about covered with bandages which hide unruly boils, dreaming of the day when pure sulphanilamide will once more be obtainable.

May 9th, A letter from Bergery . . . "... I AM perfectly content. I am even beginning to contemplate in the Buddhist fashion, cross-legged under an immense brooding pine-tree, gazing at the sunrise in the morning and losing myself in apparitions of sunset at night. Nearly all my books are here, though I envy you your *Encyclopædia Britannica* in the School Library. The student is still here. He pretends to be learning English, though I have told him that with a language as *sufficient* as Chinese there is no reason why he should waste his efforts on such an unprofitable occupation. Why do the Chinese students have such an admiration for our language? I explain that if he reads our Elizabethan prose he will obtain some measure of profit, but by the time of Milton our language was already in a decline. When he comes down from the mountain, you are to write out for him all you remember of Traherne and show him the plays of Shakespeare in which the fiery prose of our ancestors reaches its heights. For the rest—nothing. We have declined, and so have they. Our days of glory are over.

"You ask me how I can reconcile my days as a war correspondent with an earnest desire to contemplate the beauties of the Chinese language and the Chinese scenery from a high mountain. I cannot reconcile them, and do not propose to. But if you have patience and mercy, you will remember that I have seen more bloodshed than is given to any man to enjoy in a single lifetime, and I am intoxicated by thoughts of peace. There must be some, even in war, who think of peace. I cannot follow the wars any longer. Changsha is the last, unless the Japanese penetrate these corn-bearing valleys of Szechuan; and even then they will fail to see me on my mountain-top. I am intoxicated with peace. In this sunlight I am dedicating myself to peace and trying desperately, more desperately than ever before, to work out a method by which men can once again live in hope.

"I have no trust in the politicians. I have no trust in the generals; nor do I trust the monks and the war correspondents, who after all have much in common with monks. I trust children, students and young women. I have learned from my beautiful housekeeper more than from all the wars I have covered for my newspaper. Even the old profligate monk, who loves flesh more than God, taught me much. The search for a real and fundamental basis for peace may not be in vain, and even Kant in his old age thought it worthy of his study. When the book is finished, and not before, I shall come down from my mountain; and then perhaps, like a spectre of the past, I may wander off to the wars. But I shall not see the wars. I shall be there in the body, but in the spirit I shall be adoring the sunrise from the Mountain of the Scented Blossoms. . . ."

May 10th . . . I HAVE wondered for a long time how the students live. They are mostly poor, though they are not so poor as the students in National Central University, which is nearer to Chungking, and therefore nearer to the smoke and dust of the city. J. has been telling me how he lives. He writes a few articles for the newspapers; his poems are being published in the poetry magazines which are springing up in every city and parish; he earns a little more by acting as a librarian in a small community library in the village; he has a few rich friends among the students who invite him to sumptuous meals, and an uncle in Chungking who remembers him occasionally. "But it is so terribly unfair," he complains. "There are students who are so poor that they cannot even afford to cross the river. Their clothes are the clothes they wore before the war. Even a hair-cut, a notebook, a pencil may be beyond them. Because their food is bad, they lie out in
210

the sun, since someone has told them that they can obtain vitamin C in this manner. Then they get sunburnt and have to go to hospital. For the very poor students, the fates are utterly unmerciful; the girls will not pay any attention to them and they know they are outcasts. What would you have them do? And even when they have obtained their degrees, they have little hope of more than a few hundred dollars a month. Yet they live on the most glorious hopes that Chinese students have ever had. In two or three years they will take part in the reconstruction of our country, and they know that nothing is so important."

It is sometimes difficult, watching the students as they play basket-ball or as they study late at night under the great timber roof of the auditorium by the small leaky flames of tung-oil lamps, to realise how few of them are in good health. I have known a brilliant student of philosophy who had to leave a few weeks ago, because it was only too evident that he was contaminating his fellow-students with tuberculosis. He did not complain. He spoke of returning fully cured after the summer, and if will-power alone can cure him, he will certainly return. When I saw him for the last time he said: "It is necessary that we should have philosophers, and so I must work and read and understand all that has been written on philosophy in China and the West. We must make a bridge between these things," he said, and his eyes were feverishly bright. . . .

No, this is impossible. There have been only a few periods in the world's history when students have sacrificed themselves so completely to learning. The Chinese students of the present generation are not always brilliant, but those who are brilliant are so great that I am continually being awed by them. They say that Chinese education has failed to meet the stress of war; and this is partly true, and in any case it is an inevitable result of the war. The Middle Schools are not good, because the teachers are underpaid; there are whole branches of the Universities which are bad, and should be uprooted. But here and there, in the most unexpected places, you will find students so talented both in their knowledge of science and the humanities, knowing all or nearly all that the West has to offer them, and all or nearly all of what China has given them, that one bows before them. There are professors who are tired, and there are others who have overcome their tiredness; there are students who are sick, and others who have overcome their sickness. And in all of them there is the spirit of an astounding adventure.

May 11th . . . K.F., who was once a banker and is now the editor of an American newspaper, wrote and asked me what I thought of investment in China after the war. I have no idea why he should send the letter to me, though I was delighted with it and still more delighted by the University servant who asked for the stamp "because the face of the man looks very good". What kind of answer can one give? I am not an economist. I see the rich fields, producing two or three crops of rice a year; I see the mountains cultivated up to the line of the pines; the tremendous traffic of sampans on the river. It is clear that this is not a poor country, and it is clear also that industrialisation is coming, as it came in Russia and England and America in a terrible wave which will throw many people out of their accustomed orbits. There is a North-West to be planted; there are mines to be excavated; there is untold wealth under the earth. And yet none of these things are important in comparison with the Chinese students. It is they who will industrialise the country. The young geologists who are being sent out by Wang Wen-hao, the electrical engineers who are damming the rivers and producing hydraulic power in the most unexpected places, the sociologists who are gradually changing the familiar shape of the village community—all these things are surely more important.

I do not know whether it is worth while for the American investor to invest in China after the war, but I do know that it is worth while for him to pay attention to the revolution which is sweeping over this country. The days of *laissez-faire* and incompetence are not over; there are still too many officials in Chungking who gaze at the clock for three-quarters of the day; there are still too many underfed soldiers; there are still too many bureaucrats who frighten one by their enormous pretensions. But there is a Generalissimo who is trusted by all, there are a few good financiers, there are good geologists and engineers, and there are good professors and students. There is a feeling of illimitable hope sweeping over the country, and among the students it shines like a bright flame.

May 12th . . . "After the war," said C. this morning, "the greatest problem will be the soldiers. We shall have to remove
212

them gradually from the army, and we shall have to train them for years. There is little or no vocational training in our army; and the soldiers know little of the world except that which they have seen in the wars. They must be brought back to life, and at the same time they must be made to realise that the country owes them more than it can pay. There is such a terrible anonymity about the Chinese army! They are almost ciphers, and there is no way except on the battlefield that they can show their particular individualities. What shall we do? I think we shall have in every province of China immense Universities under canvas, and in these Universities they will be taught scientific farming, all the more recent advances in agriculture, mining, and even mechanics and engineering. A large number of them will go to the North-West. A few will return to their ancestral farms. They will have to begin again from the very beginning. Many of them will even have to learn to read and write. Think what a problem it is! Seven or eight million soldiers will abandon their arms and clamour for a new life which is worthy of them. It will take years before they are absorbed in the country, and yet when at last they are absorbed, it may mean that for the first time in the history of China there will be a real peace. This—not conquest—is what we are fighting for."

May 13th . . . HE IS still talking of ghosts. He loves them with a quite particular passion, and insisted that we should walk out to the famous ghost house which lies beyond the gable windows of the Sericulture Institute. It is a large house, high up on the sandy cliffs, facing the coal-mines on the other side of the river. You reach the house by a small muddy path which winds down to a creek and then up again through a grove of ancient mulberries. It was surprising to think that the house was haunted, for the blue tiles shone in the sun and the wild garden looked a little like the most beautiful of all wild gardens which I have ever seen, the garden of the poet Antonio Machado in Barcelona.

"Eight or nine years ago a general who had been disgraced and expelled from the army built this house. He brought with him his concubine, and a child by a former marriage. The concubine was beautiful and the child was a pretty girl of about five years. He came to live in the house, furnished it from Shanghai, ordered the mayor of the village to arrange that the electric light lead should be swung on masts over the river so that his house could

213

be illuminated by electricity. He lived there. He would go boating with the concubine and the child. Surrounded by wolf-hounds, he was perfectly safe from attack, though it was known that he feared attack from some soldier, or from the relatives of a soldier he had executed. And then one day it happened. No one knows how. No one knows even when the murderer performed the deed, or whether it was one of his own servants. They were found in bed with their heads cut off some days later, after a thunderstorm, and there were no witnesses, and no one really worried. Our detectives in Szechuan are not like the detectives in Pekin. The bodies were buried, the verdict was 'Murder by persons unknown', and that was the end of the general who deserved his punishment. Yet one thing was curious. The peasants in the village said they had seen a green light descending from heaven on the night of the murder—a sign or a portent. They knew perfectly well who had committed the murder. They had prepared it long beforehand, and everyone knew about it."

The blind glass windows shone gold in the sun. There was an air of broken majesty about the dilapidated house looking down over the sand-dunes, and the blue tiles were falling off, and the garden was beautiful beyond words in its wilderness. We looked through the windows. At first we saw nothing. After a while I saw a wolf-hound with a sleek coat moving out of the shadow and walking slowly towards the window, a wolf-hound which looked well-fed and which refused to pay attention to us, for a moment later it returned to its hiding-place among the shadows.

"If there is no one in the house and the doors are locked," I said, "how does the wolf-hound live?"

"What wolf-hound?"

We walked back slowly from the house of the dead.

May 14th . . . THERE are survivals of customs which have died out in other places. This evening, walking through the village in the moonlight, we came upon some peasants dancing outside the last house in the street. There was a young man stripped to the waist with blue feathers stuck to his chest, and his face painted red; and there was a crown of gold ribbons on his head; and he wore the same slack blue trousers and the same rice-straw sandals which he wore every day of his life. There was an old man in a golden faded gown covered with inscriptions in red, inscriptions which looked a little like Tibetan, but may have been
214

older and even more complicated. There were no priests. There were drums and cymbals, and crowds of small children gazing at the small scented fires on the ground around which he danced. They danced slowly, the old man and the youth, and later a few more came to join them, singing a little, raising their hands to heaven and then dropping them listlessly. Someone had died in the house. The painted-paper house, decorated with ribbons, still wet and shrunken after the rain, lay like the picture of a stage; for the painted roof and the flowers in the window caught the blue flickering light of the fires, and for the first time I realised how impressive these paper houses can be. The colours, like all colours in Szechuan, are hard and garish—bright blues, greens, velvety reds. The door opened. I could see the white unpainted coffin inside the house, and a cock was already fastened to it, limping around the bare unfurnished room at the end of a string. The mourners, in white sackcloth, were wailing and laughing at the same time. They brought food out to the dancers—little yellow rice-cakes, cups of boiling tea, but the handsome youth with the blue feathers stuck to his chest was too delirious, or too exhausted to drink or eat. So the dancing went on, old men beating the cymbals, the youths and maidens sometimes joining in. Once the cockerel burst out into a long moaning whine, a sound which I had never expected to hear from any bird.

We stayed for about half an hour, puzzled and rather hurt by all this strangeness, for we were accustomed to see Taoist priests with black oiled topknots and ungainly greyish-black gowns performing the ceremonies with drums and bells on little platforms erected outside the houses of the dead; or else Buddhist priests, in red or yellow robes, crowned with the Buddha crown, interminably chanting. But J., who knows the more perverse customs of Szechuan better than anyone, is still puzzled and wonders why the youth should have daubed himself with feathers.

The dead man was a miller, who ground down the corn-cobs and sold the powder at a high price. His corn-mill was better than the laborious mill-stones which are the common property of the villagers; and they say he was murdered. Also, that he was loved by the youth and detested by the priests, whom he would chase from his house. I know no other explanation, and now, writing late at night, I can still see the blue shadows on the whitewashed wall and the motionless faces of the children who crowded round and watched the dancer daubed with the blue feathers.

May 15th . . . "CHU HSI in his commentary on the *Great Learning* wrote: 'By long application of our powers we one day reach a point whence we see the whole scheme of things spread out before us; we perceive the realities underlying phenomena, and the relation of accident to essence, and the structure and workings of the human mind.' This attainment can only come as the fruit of positive action. If, in the course of practice and experience, the knowledge we have acquired and the methods upon which it is based prove inefficacious, we may take it that what we valued as knowledge was not true knowledge. The natural processes of the universe and of human life go on unceasingly, and in trying to ameliorate human life by positive action we must realise that such action to be effectual must be similar to those processes in its continuity and tenacity. The whole universe is the scene of such action, and man in so far as he truly acts participates in its immense activity. Let us therefore distinguish clearly between mere motion and the true action that works by a steady advance in an undeviating course, with the timeless inexhaustibility of flowing water towards its appointed aim." Generalissimo Chiang Kai-shek.

May 16th . . . THERE was a rumour that old Mother Chao, the leader of the Manchurian guerrillas, is living in our village. I have seen photographs of her, an old wizened woman less than five feet high, with a broad forehead and penetrating dark eyes. Three of her sons had been killed in the border fighting, but she wept only when the youngest and most handsome died. There are students here who have come from Pekin and who regard Madame Chao with something of the same adoration with which we regarded Lawrence of Arabia. She was already old when the war broke out. Sickened by the behaviour of some of the northern generals, who refused to fight the Japanese, she began a ceaseless war of her own. No Japanese ever found her, for she could disappear with ease among the common people; and more than once she penetrated Pekin. There is a story that after a successful attack against an armament depot inside the Forbidden City, the guns were hidden in a house near the North Gate. There were so many guns that at first no one knew how to remove them, until at last Madame Chao decided that her eldest daughter should marry her eldest son. There was a wedding ceremony, and a great cavalcade of painted sedans and chairs was led out
216

through the gates, and though a Japanese soldier tried to kiss the bride, and there were moments when they thought all would be discovered, they set out successfully towards the Western Hills; and in each chair and every sedan there were guns.

We have wandered all over the western bank of the river, climbing over muddy foot-hills, slipping and disappearing in the sand. The junks are all piled up against the shore, for it is a grey day, and only the red bell-rope tassels of the ponies and their silver harness gleam under the leaden sky. There are retired generals living near the village, and many concubines. There are wolf-hounds more fierce than the wolf-hound I saw in the haunted house, but there is no sign of Madame Chao.

May 17th . . . AT DAWN, when the sun climbs over the hills, the servant girls stand at the doors of their houses, and with three red spills in their hands, lift them towards the rising sun. So did the ancient Greeks kiss their hands to the sun each morning, believing that it was beneficent and innocent of all harm.

And reading Elizabethan poetry to my students, it occurred to me suddenly and with a sense of shock that our own poetry disregards entirely the existence of the heavenly bodies, and we know nothing of astrology or astronomy, and care less for the phases of the moon. Yet, in all great poetry, the sun is a creature of light and also of a breathing immensity, who broods with loving-kindness over the crops and the herbs. As our culture moves farther away from the farmlands, so we can expect poets to write of the sky "like a patient etherised upon a table".

May 18th . . . A TROUPE of actors from Chungking has been performing in the great barn in the village. I am told that every village has such a barn, where interminable performances of ancient Chinese plays are performed to the beating of drums and cymbals; and I would curse them late at night in the quietness of the rat-infested room in the hotel, for I could hear the screeching voices of the boy-players and the whining of the girls, and sometimes as I passed at night I would look through a crack in the wall and see the gaily decorated costumes, encrusted with pearls and silver ornaments, and marvel, and then go home, haunted by the voices of the actors and yet not liking them.

But this was something different. They were plays based on the Taiping Rebellion, written by living authors, acted by the best

217

actors and with all the stage properties sent down on huge lorries from Chungking. Pei Yang and Tsu Su-wen, the most famous actresses in China, were among those who played, wearing costumes which must have cost a fortune at ordinary times and were now beyond price. They acted magnificently, though the play I attended lasted from seven o'clock in the evening to one in the morning. Between the acts there were pauses lasting half an hour, while we sucked sunflower seeds, learning to open them in the proper way; and though weary almost beyond endurance, we delighted in the colours of the stage and the timing of the actors. The Taiping rebels were heroes, and yet not heroes. The Taiping Emperor spoke in a loud voice, the deep-throated throbbing voice in which all emperors addressed their subjects. The Taiping princesses, in gowns of lavender blue, continually kneeling and imploring mercy, continually repeating the time-worn formulæ of the Court, were enchanting; and the ruthless princes, with their bows of deer sinews and their gowns of purple, were even more enchanting. At half-past twelve the palace began to burn. Surrounded by the armies of Tseng Kuo-fan, the Taipings threw themselves in the flames or raised their hands to Heaven at the foot of an enormous Cross which had been planted on the stage, and then I realised that the Chinese genius for stage-craft had suffered nothing by the passage of centuries. The Cross, gleaming crimson in the light of the fires, the face of the princess in the olive-grey gown, so drawn and suffering that it seemed impossible to believe that her grief was assumed, the flickering red flames seen through the windows and the bodies lying along the crimson carpets on the floor—all this was purely Elizabethan, and suffered nothing at all from being acted in the vernacular, without poetry, with only the bare words and gestures of suffering to enforce its moral. For the moral was clear. The Taipings were heroes. They had tried to enforce an equitable distribution of land in the Yangtse valley, they had attempted to supplant the obsolescent Ch'ing monarchy with a monarchy arising from the people, and they had failed because of differences between them. They were Christians. They were revolutionaries. They were the fore-runners of the revolutionary movement.

We went away, filled with the colour and gleam of the stage, thinking of the extraordinarily beautiful features of the chief actress, and wondering at the merciful dispensation of Providence which had brought them to our doors. The rain blew in gusts over
218

the river; clouds darkened the moon. But even under the mat-shed awning of the ferry-boat, cowering in the rain, we could see the fires burning in the imperial palace in Nanking and we could see the jewelled Cross shining in the flames and the torchlight.

May 19th . . . AND today there are even films. That is so extraordinary that half the University has flocked over the river to see a film of Chinese soldiers fighting against the Japanese in the north. There are films in Chungking, but no one takes them seriously. They are pre-vintage American films mostly, and we go into the dark theatres to watch a streaky silver light play on a white screen, for it is difficult to understand what is happening. The film has been cut to ribbons. Once I saw a film played back-wards, and though we murmured a little at the thought that a man on the ground should glide upwards to the saddle of his horse, the audience was not unduly alarmed. The market has apparently broken down, and with the disorganisation caused by the loss of the Burma Road, no new films are coming in.

But this film was excellent. It was shown in the open air with a travelling projector, benches have mysteriously appeared, and we can see it on either side of the screen. When galloping horses cross the screen, the sound of their footprints is made by small boys; when the hero attacks the Japanese bandits unarmed, the same small boys raise blood-curdling yells to heaven. When the machine-guns decimate the enemy soldiers, the sound of machine-guns is faithfully reproduced; and when, at the very end, the hero advances towards the camera, waving his blood-stained sword at the end of which there waves his blood-stained shirt, their joy knows no bounds, and they refuse to go home until it is played all over again. Under the faint moonlight, the faintly-shimmering sheet stretched between the goalposts has caught our emotions and flung them beyond the stars.

I am sorry that our films are fitted for sound. There was more fun, and more imagination in the old films, which should never be called "silent", since they spoke to us with sounds which we could imagine to our hearts' content. Imagination is disappearing from the West; and when films are three-dimensional, and when the heroine can flood the auditorium with the scent of her body, and when even the taste of her food is somehow communicated to our mouths, I shall disappear to some remote back-water of

219

China, and there, among screaming children and old men, I shall watch Charlie Chaplin in all the glory of his silent progress.

May 20th . . . I AM surprised every day by the number of paintings which are still being made. In Chungking I counted over twenty shops where your paintings and scrolls may be mounted, and even here there are three mounting-shops. For a week or more, your painting on thin Chinese paper is plastered flat against the wall, where everyone can admire it; then it is laid carefully on the bench and with glue extracted from the liver of fishes, the pollen of wormwood and the white bitter dung of partridges, a glue so thin and fluid that you hardly notice its presence, the painting is mounted on the slightly-thicker paper, ready to be hung on your walls.

For some reason the Chinese have never liked putting their paintings behind glass. They like delicate slabs of marble, where blackish-grey veins suggest immensities of mountains or of clouds. They like heavy blackwood furniture, which has nothing in common with the exquisite delicacy of their painting. Here, where the bamboos grow in profusion under the green cedars, they have a passion for bamboos, and nearly every painting in the shop contains a few leaves and petals of bamboo. Rarely do you see men walking in these paintings, but often there are fishes gliding in the grey luminous depths of rivers; red crabs stalking the winged moths which lie at the bottom of streams; a saint in a red robe contemplating deserts of white hills; a pony galloping along a stream with its bridle flung up and balanced over its wise old head; but men never, for there is more life in the animal world, and what can one gain by contemplating the figure of a man, unless he be a god?

I have been discussing with C. the difference between East and West.

"You paint women, and think they are beautiful," he said. "We paint crabs, and know that they are good to eat."

We had gone to the village to bargain for some bamboo chairs among the crowded stalls near the river edge; and afterwards we had gone in search of a seal. A seal is important and mysterious. For a long while C. has been insisting that I should have one, and he has even pressed upon me some valuable blood-red paste, with which I can sign my name to all official documents. The paste is really valuable, and is in fact a present from his father,

220

handed down from generation to generation. "It's probably Ming Dynasty, but couldn't possibly be later than early Ch'ing." And then he went on to discuss how we would celebrate the end of the war at his house in Pekin, drinking the old wine that has been buried in the cellars for four hundred years, "but the Japanese may have found it", he sighed, "for they are good connoisseurs of wine, and yet I am almost certain that they have failed to find it—it is buried very securely". At last we found a stone which pleased him, and on this stone my seal will be engraved in the characters which appear on early Han bronzes. He was pleased with the stone. He held it to the light. "It is the colour of the moon on an autumn day in Pekin, when the clouds are low and there is a wind driving down from the hills." In such wise does one buy seal stones in modern China.

May 23rd . . . Two years ago Ernst Toller died. I have been wondering whether his life could have been saved, and whether all of us were not responsible for his death. I used to see him nearly every day while he was in Paris. He would call at the flat in the Avenue de l'Observatoire, looking very tired, speaking of mysterious political connections, always about to leave for Stockholm or London or Berne, always conscious of his past glory.

He was short and paunchy when I knew him and the colour had gone out of his eyes. They were smoky grey, very tired, but still keen and observant, but his face was tanned by the Swiss suns and his hands were delicate and tender, the finger-nails carefully trimmed. He would often move his hands softly and delicately, without any purpose, and I have seen the same delicate flow of hands among Chinese scholars. I am sure that somewhere there must be books on the art of hands which flower and assume all kinds of disguises. And yet, when I close my eyes and think of Toller, I am conscious that his hands were even more weary than his eyes, but they seemed to shine with a light that had long since gone out of his eyes.

I saw him for the last time in February, 1939, at the corner of the Rue Racine and the Boulevard St. Michel. It was raining; there was a battered cap on his head, and he looked worn out. We spoke about his journey to America and England. Neither of us had much hope that the war in Spain could be saved. And as he moved away, disappearing in the mist and rain, he raised his hand as though in blessing, and said: "In the end we shall win," and I whispered: "We must win soon if anything can be saved." "I know my Germany," he answered. "She is mad. She will take on the world, and on that day we shall be saved."

This is the kind of language that we spoke in those days of Apocalypse, failure and triumph. Only two months before, at Les Deux Magots, I had seen Del Vayo shrug his shoulders hopelessly as he talked of the great number of heavy guns which the Germans were manning on the Ebro front. "What will happen?" we asked, and all I remember were the words engraved on rock: "We shall win in the end."

Toller was happiest in Barcelona. Occasionally General Hanns, in command of the Tortosa front, would come and stay in the small room on the top floor of the Hôtel Majestic, and twice we spent the whole night talking together. Hanns was seven foot tall, skull-cropped, always laughing, always intolerably self-controlled. He had been a colonel in a famous German mountain regiment, and for years remained in Germany secretly directing communist propaganda among the soldiers. At last he had to escape to Switzerland. In Spain he was the only foreigner in complete command of Spanish troops.

One evening, while bombs were flowing down on the harbour, he told a story which sent Toller into the seventh heaven of delight. "My soldiers refused to fight, and already we were retreating. I had killed many of my own soldiers with my revolver, but still they retreated, and even my staff seemed about to throw in its hand. I called for my aide-de-camp, and asked him to bring me a bowl of water. And then slowly and leisurely, so slowly and leisurely that they were bemused, I took off my socks and boots and let my feet soak in the water. Guns were howling outside. You understand, I was sick of killing. I had to invent something quickly by which my staff would know that I had no intention of retreating." He paused and gazed at Toller with an extraordinary expression of happiness. "It worked. They didn't retreat any more. The message went round that General Hanns has taken off his stinking socks and has no intention to retire." After a while he said: "You killed too few in Bavaria. If you had killed more, Germany might have been saved this appalling war." And already they were talking about the war which broke out in September of the next year as something so fixed and certain that only a madman would doubt it.

On one of the moonlight nights when Italian aeroplanes were

wandering unmolested over the roofs of Barcelona, I accompanied Toller to the aerodrome. He had promised to take me along with him, but at the last minute our plans failed, and he went to Madrid alone, leaving me with all his possessions, including a letter addressed to the world, which was only to be opened in the event of his death. We were quite alone, and he was telling me what he should say to his wife in America, and once more he began to speak of his vendetta against the Germans in power. I had never understood why Hitler hated Toller with such vindictive hatred, with such violence and with so many promises of a barbarous death. One could buy in Paris copies of German newspapers in which all Toller's movements were recorded, and there was always a photograph showing him resembling an anthropoid ape. Yet he was handsome, and his grey hair falling over his forehead in the moonlight gave him the air of an elderly scholar, not unlike many of the elderly scholars who came to Barcelona in those days.

We spoke about the future. It was August, 1938, a few weeks after the Republicans had crossed the Ebro. He thought they could still hold out, for President Roosevelt had shown signs of sympathy with the Republicans, and an increasing impatience with the non-intervention committee. "But if it fails the battle goes on," he continued. "It will go on, not because men believe in justice or fair-play, but because it is in the nature of things that one terror should provoke another. This is the end of the world as we have known it. From now on naked terror will be fought with naked terror. The Moors who crucify the Republicans, the Fascists who drop the bodies of our comrades from aeroplanes on to our lines, the hostages who are slaughtered, the girls who are violated, demand vengeance. It is as simple as that. And yet it is not so simple. There are some spirits in the world who possess the quality of mercy. This is what I have been trying to describe in my play *Pastor Hall*. I am not sure that I entirely understand mercy, but I believe that it is only through mercy that we can prevent the whole of Europe from disappearing from the map. Europe will die. She may be reborn. It is certain that everything we have loved has gone, and it is still more certain that the peace we enjoyed before 1914 will never return to us. Hitler hates me, because he was once in my power. I could have had him killed, for Bavaria was in my power. I should have had no mercy."

A little while later he went on:

223

"Four times they have tried to assassinate me. Once in Paris, once in Switzerland, once in Stockholm, once here. And yet I am no longer very important to the future of the world. My books still sell, they are translated in many languages, but they are not read. I belong to an early generation, and now there is a generation like Hanns which is physically strong and mentally courageous above everything which was produced in the revolution in Bavaria. We have learned a lot, and those who are old cannot catch up with the young. This is why I tell you that the war of the future will be a war fought by the implacable young against the implacable young, and this is what is so terrible, and breaks my heart. . . ."

We began to talk of the play he was still writing. The manuscript lay on my desk at the hotel, a manuscript typewritten on cream note-paper with the blue insignia of the hotel at the top. He was very fastidious. He spent a whole day in Barcelona searching for good paper to write on at a time when war correspondents were writing on the backs of envelopes and the margins of newspapers. Paper was scarce. One of his most prized possessions was a copy of *Don Quixote* printed on cork sheets so thin that five hundred pages occupied no more space than a small family Bible.

He was feeling his way towards a new kind of literature. *Masses and Men*, which always seemed to me the greatest play produced out of the havoc of the last war, employed a medium of anonymity which gave the characters an almost universal significance. He wanted to develop a medium through which the characters would be universal and at the same time so concrete and recognisable that they resembled people whom we all knew. He had been reading the ancient Greek drama. "Do you believe that life is more important than a great drama?" he asked. "Sometimes life is also a great drama," I said. "But which comes first— life or the dramatist?" I could not follow him on those untrodden paths. Evreinov had said something similar, and left me dumbfounded. It seemed impossible that all the suffering and glory of the world had been created simply in order that an Æschylus should write his plays. He said nothing more; but I suspected then, and still suspect, that he regarded himself as a dramatist lost in the mechanism of a drama he had created. And what drama could be so great? The first of all the revolutionary leaders of Europe, the sworn foe of the leader of the Nazis, the vagabond of the spirit, who was now journeying to Madrid in order that the

224

world outside should have the testimony of a great dramatist that Madrid remained unshaken. He spoke of the wireless with tenderness, and something only a little less than love. "The stage and the wireless must come to terms," he said; and I imagine him sweating to produce a drama as great as *Prometheus Bound* out of the evidence of the modern world and producing it over the wireless.

The aeroplane left at three o'clock in the morning. The last Italian bombers had flown; the holes in the aerodrome were already filled, and the small aeroplane sailed into the night, showing no lights, dark against the background of black snow. I saw him again three months later, when we would often dine together, but even then it was clear that his nerve was going. Every day the German newspapers on the kiosks recounted his movements. He left for Stockholm and returned for a few days in February. Almost his last words, as we parted in the Boulevard St. Michel, were: "If ever you read that I committed suicide, I beg you not to believe it."

He hanged himself with the silk cord of his nightgown in a hotel in New York two years ago. This is what the newspapers said at the time, but I continue to believe that he was murdered. He was weary beyond all weariness, but out of his weariness and hopes for the future he hoped again to create out of the drama of the world a drama which would lift our hearts as they were lifted by *Masses and Men.*

May 24th . . . IT WAS only yesterday that I noticed the immense grave hidden behind my garden. I cannot think how I failed to see it before, for it stands out, with its columns engraved with sleeping dragons, beyond the orange-trees. It is the grave of a mother of a famous admiral of the Ch'ing Dynasty; a great stone square used as a threshing-floor by peasants of the neighbourhood, and on two opposite sides there is a low wall with stone elephants and chargers and a solitary headless knight, nearly life-size, protecting the entrance to the grave. Columbines grow over the arched dome of the grave itself; dogs couple in the rice-straw at its feet, and there are blackberries and small sugar-acorns all round. The shining green leaves of the orange-trees shroud it from the burning sun and from the grave you can look down at the rushing river between its high rocks, the yellow sand, the solitary whispering sampans on the river, the calmness of high summer in Szechuan.

We shall come here often, for there is more silence here than elsewhere. The little stone cottage, where the screaming mill can be seen being turned by hand, watches quietly; and children play unharmed among the nettles. At night the students will come here with their two-stringed guitars; the girl students in their long blue gowns will lean on the parapets of the grave; a few old professors will bathe in the light of the full moon. Certainly, the old admiral's mother has not died in vain.

May 25th, A message from the Mountain . . . EARLY this morning a message came from the Mountain that Marshal Feng Yu-hsiang would be pleased if some of the professors from the University would visit him. He lives in a small house surrounded by a wattle-fence not far from the Buddhist monastery which I have never visited, on a mountain range not far from Bergery. According to rumour the small cottage was guarded by the wildest blood-hounds imaginable, and there was half a division of soldiers hiding in the surrounding woods. But we failed to see either the blood-hounds or the soldiers, for today the soldiers were given a holiday and the "Christian General" was prepared to allow himself to be defended by professors.

It was a long journey under the sun, and we were tired when we reached the cottage in time for lunch. The Marshal resembled his portraits, his great round face beamed with pleasure and he walked among the forests in an old grey Sun Yat-sen coat and with a walking-stick, very much as Pilsudski walked among the forests of Polesie. He is well over six foot, enormously wide, and with the most charming smile I have yet seen in China. He gives the impression of reserves of strength and of the most extraordinary dignity, and at the same time he possesses a quite childish enjoyment of life. We sat down at table, very quiet and dignified, discussing poetry and taking sidelong glances at the porcelain figure of the "Laughing Buddha" on a sideboard which resembled him to perfection. The sun shone. The blue smoke from the kitchen invaded the whitewashed hall, and the murmur of conversation continued in the drowsy afternoon so long that even when everyone else had finished dinner, I was sleepily carving the remains of a chicken on my plate. With the most perfect good manners the Marshal carved an imaginary chicken on his.

And so we spoke of his battles and the great days of the north. When the Southern Army under Chiang Kai-shek invaded the northern territory of China, Marshal Feng Yu-hsiang's army was still powerful. There had been times when he might have fought it out, for no other army in China was so well-disciplined. Chiang Kai-shek's army contained a sprinkling of excellent officers from the Whampoa Academy, two or three good divisions and an incredible number of raw recruits who possessed *exactly one bullet each in their gun-pouches*. If Feng Yu-hsiang had fought, he would probably have driven the Kuomintang Army to the sea, as he had driven the army of Wu Pei-fu to the sea. He did not fight. He became a blood-brother of the Generalissimo, the only person in the whole country who can address him as "ti-ti", or "younger brother". He spoke of the extraordinary veneration he possesses for the Generalissimo, and in halting English he spoke about the necessity of love.

Somewhere in one of the books of Vincent Sheean there is a description of a meeting with Feng Yu-hsiang when he was encamped in Honan. Feng Yu-hsiang is described as a blood-thirsty tyrant whose use of biblical precepts was a sham and a delusion to outwit his enemies. It is doubtful whether anyone meeting him now would come to the same conclusion. Feng Yu-hsiang is sixty-five. He is not ill, but he is loaded with years; and like many Chinese he longs for the quiet of the monastery. The days of glory are over. He will deliver speeches whenever he is asked; but in his heart he hates travelling about in the cloistered silence of a motor-car, and only the dramatic instinct which led him to wear two-feet high-astrakhan caps in the streets of Pekin, so that his appearance could be seen from a distance, gives him pleasure in these days when speeches no longer have much meaning for the hard-driven people of China. He is content in the little wattle-hut on the mountain, and likes to quote the poems of Tao Yuan-ming. When one of the professors asked him what he wanted above all things, he answered: "Peace."

This is not a portrait of the Marshal. This immense smiling giant has defeated us all. We were continually at the mercy of his charm, for the flickering light which shone on the porcelain model of the "Laughing Buddha" shone on his face also. Once he ruled over the whole of northern China with a hand of iron; the Emperor of Manchuria quaked at the mention of his name; a word would send armies south, west and north. Now, writing in my own house, from which I can see the faint red sparkle of his torches high up on the mountain-side ten miles away, he resembles the gilded figure of Tien Kuan who hangs on my walls—three times as large as life, smiling out of the pure enjoyment of living.

May 26th . . . I HAVE been thinking of Epstein, wondering in this place where there is no time for art whether anyone during the war can create things of beauty. I had been dreaming of an immense grey hand, perhaps of granite, which came out of the sky and seized the world and squeezed it, so that only a little dust remained; and perhaps I was thinking of Feng Yu-hsiang's immense hands, or of Epstein's, or the hands of a boy called Daimalen in a novel I once wrote. And now as I think of hands, I remember Rodin's hand of God in the museum in Paris and many more, and all these hands are terrible and mysterious, they come out of the sky and destroy the earth as it is and make something more noble and lasting out of the fragments of dust in which we live.

I spent some weeks with Epstein in Paris. I was learning to sculpt, and wondering why it was that all the faces and bodies I tried to make out of clay resembled someone I had seen in dreams. We would sit in the Café du Dôme, looking out across the busy thoroughfare of the Boulevard Montparnasse, while Epstein talked of the negress he was drawing in a small atelier near his hotel, of Modigliani, of Picasso and a thousand others. He had the serenity which I now associate with Feng Yu-hsiang. He would talk of marble and clay as though they were the elements of his being; and he would summon out of the air or out of music the shapes of intangible beauties and dreams. Once, while we were eating, some music coming over the wireless startled him into immobility and after a while he began to draw on the back of a menu strange shapes and contours which were dictated by the music of Beethoven, saying that a certain relation of shapes which had tormented him for many years had at last become clear.

Once or twice in England I went to his studio in Epping Forest. At that time he was drawing his youngest son and seemed to have surrendered his love for titanic forms and to have found comfort in the half-dreaming and visionary expressions of childhood. But in his studio in London the great titanic shapes were littered in
228

profusion under the skylight, and the great white figure of "Behold the Man" was turned away from the sunken alabaster carving of "Consummatum Est". I admired "Consummatum Est", without reserve, and it still seems to me to be the work which most successfully illustrates our times. Lying prone in the grave, Christ was leaden-grey in the half-light. The extended palms with their wounds, the grey face deliberately carved to show a flat surface, the long robe, the hollows between knees and thighs, the tremendous *weight* of the body which seemed to sink deeper and deeper into the earth, all these were impressive beyond anything which I have seen in sculpture before or since. The weight of the marble, its texture, its resistance and the extraordinary way in which it soaked in the light—all these were the work of the master; and there was such a curious mingling of power and austerity, of reserve and strength that I began to understand why Epstein found so much comfort in the posthumous quartets of Beethoven, where power is quiescent, yet magnificently controlled. He wanted his Christ to be buried in the crypt of some Cathedral in London, where the worshippers could gaze down upon it and feel the sorrow which came from the bitter earth. There was an extraordinary originality in the conception, for the prone Christ possessed all the glory of Christos Pankrator and was yet more terrible in his majesty when he lay still than when, with arms outstretched, he gazed over and beyond the worshippers in the Cathedral at Ravenna or Palermo. I preferred this suffering Christ to the contemptuous Christ of "Behold the Man", whose crown of thorns was a crushing weight of marble and whose expression of quiet contemptuous silence reminded me only of the disappointing heads in the Elephanta caves; and just as the Indian sculptors of the Gupta period idealised a formidable silence, so here Epstein had idealised only the strength of a terrible power and contempt. I did not understand his drawings from Baudelaire, but I loved beyond measure the Virgin and Child in the National Gallery, the tenderness of the protecting gesture of the Virgin and the escaping child.

Once in Paris I was surprised to discover Epstein rapt in wonder before the Burghers of Calais. It was raining, and the stone plinth of the statue was stained with the grey sediment of bronze. In this dreariness of an abandoned garden, he would bend down and look up at the great striding figures with an expression which showed that he had discovered new and unsuspected beauties in the relations of shapes, and in the gaunt carving of the characters. But now, while the Tibetan ponies are racing outside my window, I remember most of all his interminable protests when I said that the Han Dynasty horses we were contemplating in the Musée Guimet were not sufficiently powerful for their frame. "The Chinese have shown more power than almost any other race of artists," he said; and I thought of the brutal Chaldean lions and the half-frightened faces of the African carvings he had once possessed, and wondered whether China could show the same power. I am still wondering. There are hardly any works of art to be seen here now, and the scrolls and paintings which are occasionally shown in the local museums are by no means the best that China has to offer. The glories of the Metropolitan Museum in Pekin are hidden in the granite caves surrounding Chungking, and all that we see are the dregs of small and unimportant collections. I have seen a small stone Buddha belonging to one of the professors which is perfect of its kind, but it is no better than the Buddha I possessed in Singapore. Calligraphy is rarely great now, but we thirst so much for good reproductions that when the colporteur arrives at the gates of the University and lays the black rubbings of famous inscriptions on the grass, we crowd round and buy more than we can afford. And even the native art of Szechuan which was once vivid and grotesque is now no more than an amusing pastime for old men in the evening, who will paste their figures of the gods on their gates in the morning. There is still art in ceremony; and it is still true that the civilisation of China is best demonstrated in the way in which two Chinese greet each other.

I had hoped that Epstein would come to Malaya, where the races are so mingled that beauty had become a commonplace. The children of Malaya, with the blood of Malays, Chinese, Buggis, Balinese, and even of Tibetans, and a thousand other races, would have compelled him to admiration. Even here, in the faces of youths and young boys, there is more life than you will see in civilised cities. Though the land is weary of its rice, and the old peasants are weary of living, children here have a kind of instinct for the pure enjoyment of life; and on three handfuls of rice a day show a great deal of energy. There is a place for a great sculptor in China.

May 27th . . . THE day cloudy; no sign of the sun. The clouds are like grey boards nailed to the mountains. C. is again teaching the Chinese, and there are occasions when we talk in a kind of English-Chinese *patois* which is not unpleasant.

I have been making a list of the extraordinary circumlocutions which were once employed in China. They are delicate and sometimes moving:

"The ice man" means the marriage intermediary.

"A halo round the moon for wind and a moistened pavement before rain" means almost the same thing as "Coming events cast their shadow before".

"On the edge of the pool there grows the grass of spring" means brotherly love.

"The nose ancestor" means the founder of a family, since according to Chinese anatomy the nose is born first.

"Orion and Scorpion" means two friends apart.

"The Twenty-eight Palaces" are the zodiacal constellations.

"Many changes of grass cloth" means marriage.

May 28th . . . THERE was so much noise in the restaurant that we could not hear our own voices. Some soldiers were celebrating the promotion of one of their officers, and they were playing the finger-game. This game must be among the most ancient in the world, and it was certainly in existence in the Han Dynasty two thousand years ago. You clench your fingers and suddenly throw out some of your fingers, and your opponent must immediately shout out the number of fingers you have thrown out, and at the same time you must shout out the number of fingers he has thrown out. You do not use ordinary numerals unless you are a novice; there are strange cabalistic formulæ which are used by those who are accustomed to the game, for the Chinese numbers are like ours in being confusing over the telephone, since so many of them sound alike. The noise was deafening. Three or four couples were playing at once, and they were all shouting together. Wine flowed. We tried to shout above the infernal din of breaking wine-glasses and orders uttered in parade-ground voices, but we were outnumbered and the soldiers possessed no mercy. We fled to a tea-house overlooking the river.

It was quiet there. I know no more quieter place in the whole of Szechuan; for though we talk, something in the atmosphere dictates silence, and the tinkle of teacups is quieter than any voices. They are long porcelain cups, exactly like the cups you see in early paintings, with little porcelain covers. The tea-leaves are poured in. The boiling-hot water comes from a red-hot kettle; and the young man who has invested his life-savings in the ramshackle tea-house at the water's edge moves quietly among the chairs. His wife wears a blue gown and looks more like a Madonna than anyone I have yet seen in China. And so the evening passes while the stars fade out of the watery sky, and somewhere in the distance a beggar is playing on a two-stringed violin.

May 29th . . . IN THE quiet temple, below the flickering butter-lamps, coolness comes with the setting of the sun. Bergery has come down from his high mountain. When the sun is shining, he says, he is perfectly content, but when the grey clouds cover his small temple and lightning crackles on his roof and even the face of the small boy in the courtyard looks pale and worn, he prefers the heat of the valleys, and the movement of the sampans. We sat in the temple all afternoon. Sunset comes soon among these deep gorges and high mountains, and we were content to talk in the half-light long before the sun disappeared behind the hills.

He is delighted with the temple and only wants to install central heating to be perfectly at peace. "Sometimes I go to the monastery," he said, "and I notice the starved faces of the monks, starved for sex, for colour, for light, for anything but their abstruse studies of Tibetan; and then I think life would be perfectly simple in a monastery in China if only there were central heating. Do you know, they have a complete Japanese edition of the Chinese translation of the *Tripitaka*. I look at it, and I shudder, for I know that in those hundred and thirty volumes which have never been translated into English, nearly everything is there. If only I could begin my life again!"

He told an extraordinary story about an Egyptian girl.

"We were excavating south of Thebes, and by luck we uncovered the mummified body of a girl. She had been buried near the entrance of the caves in the XVIII dynasty. I felt then in a single moment that I could record her whole life, that I knew everything she had ever done, I saw all the things her imagination had touched, and my imagination touched her life at so many points that it was impossible to believe that I had not known her. She was extraordinarily beautiful. Even as she lay there, en-

232

crusted with sand, the flesh peeling off her nose, the bracelets green with verdigris, her cloth dress turning to powder, she was unbelievably beautiful. The rouge on her lips and the green malachite on her eyelids were still fresh. She seemed indeed to be breathing. I remember most of all the tight white skin drawn over her cheek-bones, and the small breasts pushing up through the frail cloth of her dress. She lay with her feet together and her arms crossed over her stomach. She was perhaps thirteen, for in Egypt girls mature early, and she had only just matured. I thought of her lovers, her small low-roofed house beside the Nile, and I wondered if ever before men had seen the past so clearly. Surely she was breathing! The dragoman was attempting to cut off the gold finger-rings. She looked so light and beautiful that I knelt down in the sand and picked her up. For a moment, for one solitary moment, she lay in my arms; a moment later I was like someone stark mad, for she had turned to powder, her head had rolled away, her arms and her feet were lying in different places and all that remained in my hands was a little square of faded cloth." He looked away at the dim lohans shining by the light of butter-lamps against the walls. They were made of plaster painted white, with coloured robes, and they seemed to be gazing down earnestly at us, not smiling, but at the same time there was tenderness in the folds of their robes and in the gilt hems of their sleeves shining in the half-light. "I thought of her when I heard the German tanks running down the fleeing peasants of France, and when I went to France and saw all the bloodshed, I became reconciled to death, because I realised that in the end we turn to powder. The Elizabethans could think of death only as a kind of immense suppurating wound, the tissues of the body swelling with unaccountable oils—all dreadful and all profane. But death is not like that. If we could remove the fear of death, we could remove all wars." And then, a little later, he said: "But why, in the moment before her body dissolved before my eyes, should she have revealed all her secrets to me? It was exactly as though she were speaking. Even now, I hope that if my body is discovered in a thousand years' time, people will still be able to feel the colours of the world I lived in when they see my bones. And so I hope that when I am dead, I shall be remembered as a part of the colour of this world."

I have tried to remember some of his *obiter dicta*, but they are not always easy to remember.

"Like Jacob serving for his love, we must watch and wait for seven years. In the old days there were cloisters where those who were weary of the wars could find solace, but now we must find this solace in ourselves. And is it not better that we should pray alone?

"*Discipline!* In the beginning, like everyone else, I thought Hitler deserved well of his country. There was no discipline in Germany; the very atmosphere we breathed was undisciplined, and vice is not pleasant when it comes with every wind. I remember the streets of Berlin as places where men and women coupled like dogs, and at the same time that the most tremendous experiments in social geography and morality were being made, people still behaved like dreamers who had not yet awakened from the war. I was pleased with Hitler. It was good to think that the prostitutes and the beggars would be driven off the streets. But afterwards, when discipline had bitten into their souls, when they were once more adoring the commands of Prussian officers, I knew that you cannot wake a dreamer by placing him in the ranks of an army, for thereupon he enters another dream. And again, after this war, we shall all be dreamers. The shock of the war, its terror and remorseless pathos, will have driven the best part of ourselves underground; and we shall fall asleep, like the Seven Dreamers of Ephesus, and with even less hope of awakening. What is necessary above all things is that we should keep awake. Therefore Christ said: '*Watch and pray.*'

"When a man suffers, he is told that he must no longer carry heavy burdens. In the same way Europe should have been allowed to suffer without any additional burdens after the last war. The whole of Europe wanted to lay down its arms. We were weary of war, weary of blood, weary of murder. But the powers dictated that all these things were still necessary; and so armies were maintained, and though they were small nothing less than the abolition of the armies could have saved the peace of Europe. I shall not live in a time when there are no more professional soldiers, but I know that the world cannot breathe much longer under their influence. We must do away with it all—everything without exception. Less than this is a *scandalon* in the face of God.

"One cannot be gentle enough towards women. If I could have lived my life over again, I would have changed only this—I would have been more gentle. A man has no power over a woman for exactly the same reason that he has no power over the heavenly bodies: they belong to different worlds.

"And then, too, if I could have lived my life over again, I would have stayed more often in China. Once Rousseau prophesied that out of Corsica would come the giant who would lead France to glory. It is perhaps easier to prophesy that the giant will come out of China, a giant who will change our generation until it can no longer recognise itself, a giant so strong that he will break all our outworn formulas about our heads. He will come perhaps from one of the Universities; he will be ruthless and cunning; he will be a peasant, like any one of those naked peasants who haul the sampans up-river. But he will change everything, and the world should beware!"

It was growing late. The gilt patterns on the ceiling shone down on his face long after the butter-lamps had gone out. Outside in the mist the sampans were still sailing towards Chung-king.

June 1st . . . THE summer rice must be ploughed, and so they work knee-deep in the black mud, the old peasant, the buffalo and the peasant's boy. The buffalo resembles one of those shaggy prehistoric beasts, mud dripping from his shoulders, the grey muzzle half under water, only the immense bloodshot yellow eyes sweeping from under the curved ridge-bones of the forehead. And so they walk round and round the small field, the black earth turning under the level of the water in which the perfectly white clouds and the green sheaves of Indian corn are brilliantly reflected; tirelessly, tirelessly, turning up the black mud. The boy wears only a pair of blue sweat-soaked shorts rolled up to the thighs, and he steps beautifully and easily in the thick mud; but the old peasant is ponderous like the old buffalo. I have seen the boy in every city of China: he is always the same, lithe and strong, his face deep red, his round head shaven white and his small mouth continually pursed for whistling. He walks with little quick strides, and his lean yellow shoulders have a habit of rowing, for in his effort to keep up with the other animals in the field, he must use every muscle. So they wander round the field in the blazing sunlight, taking no care of the shade, remorselessly turning up the earth, while a warm, sickening smell of summer sweeps up the river and steam rises from the rice-lakes down the mountainside.

235

The slow plodding of the ploughman is nightmarish: hour after hour he drives the plough through the mud. Sweat trickles down his bare chest, which is the colour of wood which has wasted away in the sunlight; and the white bones shine faintly through the stretched skin. He seems to be unaware of the great heat. A kingfisher dived like a blue bullet across the field. He paid no attention to it; nor did he pay any attention to the sandy curlews on the branches of a banyan. He was content with his field. Sometimes he would pass his hand slowly across his chest, and glance at the boy with an approving eye; but in this terrible heat, the sun nearly vertical, their inky shadows as thick and black as mud, there was no need for words. Suddenly a miracle happened—or rather there were three miracles which followed one another without taking breath. From somewhere near the University a white cloud of river-fowl rose and scattered in the sky, shining like drops of rain, and suddenly they swung low over this field and alighted on the green banks, where parsley grows and a few lettuce; and they stayed there, wings shivering, perfectly white against the green. A moment later, as they were turning the corner of the field, the ploughman lifted the ploughshare from the mud; the mud dripped away, and the white blade, beautifully grained and curved, whiter than anything in this landscape except the birds, flashed in the sunlight, so well proportioned and so sharp that it resembled a knife, though made of wood. A little while later, as though weary of circumnavigating the field in the remorseless sun, the boy climbed on the buffalo's back and produced from somewhere in the rolled-up folds of his trousers a small yellow flute, which he played—and immediately, in a scurry of white wings, the birds flew away.

There are days when these miracles happen in China, but they are not many, though they seem to occur more frequently in summer than in the mist-laden quiet of winter. Soon the rice will be shooting out of the earth, in broad-flung banners of green, and the river will turn a sickly yellow, and the river-birds will fly to Tibet; but in this summer every mountain is a stairway of palisaded lakes, and every buffalo is a creature out of prehistoric heraldry. It was hot. I walked home through the blood-red tassels of the Indian corn and watched the steam from the lakes rising in the pitiless sun; but though this landscape is more beautiful than any other, nothing so affected me as the sudden white flight of
236

the river-birds to the rice-lake, the apparition of the yellow plough so smooth and clean that it resembled a sword long-buried in the earth and the boy riding the buffalo as though he owned the whole world.

June 2nd . . . I HAVE been living out of doors and feasting on the valley. I shall never grow tired of this valley—the green river, the white shingles, the small grey-clustered town on the rocks, and then the two mountains forming the gorges in the blue smoky distance. Today the mountains carried on their shoulders cloaks of brown bear's fur.

I woke up this morning with an extraordinary sense of exhilaration. Everything seemed beautiful. The sky was pure blue, a milk-white mist hovered in the valley and there were more tiny tongues of mist curling over the rice-fields. I would have preferred the house with the golden tiles which overlooks the University, but it gives me infinite pleasure to take the bamboo chair out among the tombs and gaze down at the river. At the back of the small square house where I am living there is an ancestral graveyard; a block of stone, with walls and an altar, all overgrown with green mosses and berries, and along the sides of the wall are mythological animals—Tartar horsemen, dragons, elephants caparisoned in gold. The gold has long since vanished, and the superstitious peasants of the neighbourhood have hacked off the heads of the Tartar horsemen; yet still, in the evening, the tomb seems to be alive.

I have been correcting examination papers, listening to "the wave of the pines", gazing down at the gorges and the white-roofed buildings of the University, watching the reflections of the river-birds in the rice-lakes as they wheel high overhead. And suddenly, this evening, when it was growing dark, the moon appeared exactly above the gorges, very white and round; and the air grew misty and grey, and the cool wind turned each green blade of Indian corn silver. At that moment I felt that I was no longer alive. There was so much exhilaration of pure beauty, so many birds in the air, so much colour in the earth and youth in my veins that I knew that if it lasted a moment longer I would die. Youth! Youth! Beauty! Beauty! In these moments of ecstasy my happiness was torrential. I was a fountain springing out of the earth. . . .

June 3rd . . . THE rain was still falling, sweeping down from the half-seen hills, and suddenly the rain ceased and we went out among the tomb-stones and gazed at the moon. C. would sometimes rub his eyes, blinded by its brilliance. We found the rabbit in the moon, and the old man with the axe, and the Emperor who disappeared from the earth and made his home with the concubine who became the virgin of the moon. There were clouds of frozen jade passing the moon's face, and they moved so slowly that it was as though there was not only a procession of stars but a procession of women dressed in clothes of jade; and all round the moon, for thousands upon thousands of miles, there streamed the blue flames of her aureole.

C. says he has never seen the blue aureole so clearly as in Szechuan. You can see the blue fire throbbing from the moon's centre. But what is so extraordinary, even more extraordinary than this aureole, is the changing colour of the moon, one moment white with the brilliance of snow in sunlight, now yellow and almost golden, now coloured with a green misty glaze like the patina on the ancient black and green vases of the Ming Dynasty. And yet these colours do not change visibly, but seem to follow upon one another with transcendental changes as insubstantial as the moon's presence in the heavens. Somewhere in the valley a girl was singing. Fire-flies, like molten green sparks, flew among the elder-trees and somewhere in the distance there were smoking fires and great shadows over the rice-fields, where the farmers' sons were searching for eels; but we had no eyes for anything except the moon.

June 4th . . . WE HAVE been bathing by moonlight. The river is inexplicably low, the water pale green in daylight, and underneath the high rocks we have left our clothing and sauntered down among the pools. There are currents in this river which have teeth, and tear a man apart as easily as they dash sampans against the high rocks; but this evening the currents were preoccupied and we nestled under the shapes of rock, watching the moonlight flooding down over the breast of the river, while small black boats, almost invisible, were crossing in the direction of the village.

There are days in summer when the river is so inviting that all the boys in the village spend their afternoons in the water, puffing and leaping, their brown shoulders made browner by the sun,

238

though their bellies remain white. They follow the small boats and sampans, clinging to ropes or simply diving like porpoises in the stream; and there are other days when only a solitary bather, perhaps a traveller who has walked for miles over our inhospitable mountains, bathes on the foreshore. But at night, when the moon's eye is wide open, everyone bathes, or else they take their mandolins and row singing on the water, and then their voices come out of the darkness like angelic presences and we see nothing except the black shadows of the boats and their white wakes.

Under the shelter of rocks the water is warm and still. Sometimes a bewildered fish flickers past with a toss of a silver tail, to lose itself in the splendid silences of the evening; for there are few sounds. Our swimmers race down the path of white sand between the rocks and enter the water with a soft sound of gentle rustling, and you hear nothing except the lapping of young limbs in the water, and sometimes a half-caught breath or the sound of distant laughter. Young and graceful, they lose themselves in the stream's silence and seem to belong to the river as they never belonged to the earth, while the moon pours upon them the benediction which the river refuses; for though the river receives them, she does not love them, and she is most beautiful when she surrenders the swimmer on to dry land. It is at moments like these—that moment when the young boy stepped out of the river, dripping silver, and stood outlined against the black rocks—that we realise finally that the river is perfect when it is completely still, and no bather struggles among her waves.

Tonight, treading water softly, our faces shining in the moon's rays, only our shoulders and our black matted hair showing our expressions, for our faces were like stones, we heard the booming of the deer-skin drum in the monastery—how many miles away? Such trick of reflection or acoustics brought the voice of the monastery on the top of Splendid Cloud Hall into the hollow pools beside the high rocks. Other voices followed—perhaps in a village twenty miles up-stream a farmer's son was having an altercation with his wife. The voices rose shrilly in the warm summer night, and perhaps they would have continued had we not on a sudden impulse decided to thrash the water with our hands and feet. Then, as far as the eye could see, the river turned white and fountains rose high above our heads, as we laughed and sang in the moonlight. The last boats were returning from the opposite shore, but we drowned the voices of the singers and the mandolins. And long after we had grounded in the shadows, the water was foaming as at the birth of the first man.

June 5th . . . I WAS walking along the green path which leads to the gorges. On a small buff, jutting out over the river, there is a small stone temple, where red spills were burning and grey ash collecting on stone shelves. And there, just below us, among the rocks, a small crowd of students was collecting hurriedly from all directions and staring at some small yellow object which had been thrown up by the river.

We walked down the cliff wall slowly, for at that moment a cloud had covered the face of the sun and the great thumping heart of happiness gave place to an inexplicable sense of warning. But when we reached the foot of the cliffs the sun came out again, and there in the sand, quite naked, lay a boy with a golden skin and the muscles of a swimmer. He was perhaps sixteen years old, with a round face red with sunlight; and there were still some silver pearls of water in his thick black hair, though there was no water on his body. He seemed to be sleeping, his knees drawn up and his hands and arms thrown out as though he were enjoying perfectly the laziness of summer; and there was a soft yellow smear of sand on one of his cheeks. He was dead. He had been dead for perhaps an hour, for the fishermen had caught him up in their great nets and he had been seen swimming earlier in the morning.

He looked more beautiful in death than ever in his life. So calm and quiet in the sand, and every part of him so perfect. I do not think there was much sorrow in the faces of the students, for the boy had never looked more splendid or more beautiful; and the sun still seemed to redden his cheeks. He lay there like someone expecting the first touch of wind to awaken him from slumber; and when one of the students spoke softly about bringing a coffin, it seemed the highest indecency, and the greatest wrong, that he should not be given back to the river from where he had come.

The sunlight smouldered on the rocks, and as we walked away the shadow of an eagle crossed his sleeping body. At that moment he seemed to quiver into life, and no one would have been surprised if he had suddenly leapt to his feet and flung himself once more into the river.

240

June 8th . . . THE examinations are still going on, the river is still rising, the wind is still sighing through my pine-trees, and we decided to rest and go up-stream to the Hot Springs. There must be floods in Tibet, for the river rose so much at night that we heard the crackling of houses on the waterfront as they were dashed against the rocks; and the boatmen looked wild-eyed this morning, as though they had spent the night fighting the monster.

The beach was covered with debris and patches of soapy foam, and the field where the gliders sometimes rise twenty feet in the air was sticky with deep mud; and we walked dangerously along the cobble-stones, feeling them sink beneath our feet. The boatmen were chary of taking us, and we decided to ride along the ledges of the mountains on the small ponies whose hooves we sometimes hear at night as they strike flint from the rocks. I chose a pony with a necklace of bells, and all the way to the monastery and the springs I took a perverse pleasure in the music of the bells.

It was already afternoon when we reached the springs. We climbed down into the cool limestone grottoes and drank innumerable cups of boiling tea; and sometimes the students composed poems or sang quietly in the soft, melancholy voices which they assume in the heat of the summer afternoons; and then again we descended into the limestone grotto as a preparation for visiting the temple, which is now a library, and where there are trees that sing and Han Dynasty copper vases which produce sounds like the quick sigh of violins. We found the singing tree in the courtyard, below the carved steps which lead to an immense plaster statue of the Queen of Heaven. The tree was an elm, three-quarters dead, which would produce only one sound, a low monotonous sound like the withdrawing of the sea. The copper vase was more captivating. It could produce many sounds, and many patterns of water. It was laid reverently on the stone floor, filled with hot water, and the two shining copper handles were vigorously rubbed by all of us. Then dancing patterns appeared on the water, and a soft fluting sound rose and fell according to the strength of our hands or the tricks we played when rubbing the handles. There were patterns like fantails, and others like snow crystals when they are seen through a magnifying-glass, and still others resembled the jewels in kaleidoscopes. While the patterns formed in the water, a thin spray from the vase hopped and hovered in our faces.

In the cool of the evening we returned to the bamboo grove and the stone tables and the cups of boiling tea. Darkness came, and the striations on the mountains on the opposite side of the gorges turned purple, and then malachite green, till at last the purple rose again and the mountains seemed to be hollow in the heavy darkness. There were no stars, for the heat of the day was so great that the air was water vapour. And so we talked into the night of China and England, and the great changes which are coming, and what the students will do when they leave the University.

I am never tired of wondering what will happen to them. I see them now, still gawky, still unformed, and in two or three years they will go out into a world which as yet possesses no existence for them, so dreamily and with such dangerous lack of interest do they regard the future. Perhaps they are living so intensely for the moment, that they have no time for the future. Perhaps indeed they are so conscious of the threat of the future that they dare not speak of it openly. And so I was surprised when one of the students began to speak of Kansu.

"This is the frontier-land, the wild west, where one day we shall have to go," he said, gazing down at the unfurled sails of the sampans drifting softly down-river. "We are tired of the cities, or rather the cities are exhausting us. You must remember that in the early days we built our cities like clusters of tents, and all our houses were made of wood. They were perishable material, for at any moment we might be invaded or we might want to trek elsewhere, and then we would leave our cities behind us and journey into the vast spaces of China—from Pekin to Szechuan or Yunnan across mountain trails. In the old days the civil servants all made these voyages, and though they complained often enough, for it meant separation from their friends, they knew that it was only in this way that the country could be kept running. But in the Ch'ing Dynasty men remained more in their homes, the love of wandering half disappeared and the country became unknown. Now the country is being explored again. Of course this is partly the result of the war, which has brought the Central Government from Nanking to Chungking; but already there were signs of this exploration before the war. The oil-fields in Kansu. . . ."

I have forgotten exactly what he said, but the tone of his voice and the significance of his gestures struck me sharply; and when

I asked him where he had learnt all this information about Kansu, he said he was leaving at the end of the term to join his brother who was working at a meteorological station somewhere in the northern tip of the country abutting upon Sinkiang, three hundred miles from the nearest landing-ground, among snow mountains where no motor-car had ever penetrated and where lamaism was still in power. He was delighted to get away from Szechuan. "The air is dry there—it is not moist as it is here. The earth is uncultivated there, not over-cultivated as it is here. For days we shall never see a soul; but we shall go out riding and seeing mirages and shooting game and drinking mares' milk, and we shall grow fat with the good things of the land. We shall forget time there. We shall live like gods, or angels."

There were echoes in the bamboos, and his voice received an added richness from the sonorous echoes. Others began to speak, at first impatiently, as if they thought there was exploration to be done nearer at hand than Kansu—students who dreamed of solving social problems, of decreasing the death-rate, students who spoke of the organisation of the village *hsiens* as though these alone represented the *summum bonum* of all effort. I have often thought them untouched by the future, and it is true that the future is so dark for all men that they are content to work well and hard in the present; but this evening the spring-gates were folded back, and the flood-tide of aspirations soared through. There was the student who was taking journalism only because journalism offered perhaps the easiest progress to a degree:

"I am going back to Kwangtung, where my father has a farm. I shall organise the farm on the co-operative system, and when my father dies, all the peasants who are working our fields will become shareholders. We must solve the land question before we solve any other question—the oil we receive from Kansu costs twenty times as much as the oil we receive even today from America, and thirty times as much as the oil which percolates through the blockade from the Japanese. Why should we go to Kansu when the land is so rich—and so poor. I shall introduce new systems of tenure and new systems of cultivation; I shall try to obtain a government post, and superintend all the farms in the neighbourhood. I shall see that in my district the peasants become owners of the land, and I shall do everything I can to destroy our present unequal ownership of land. One day the Government must fulfil its promise. One day the land must go back to the men

243

who work it. In Szechuan the system of absentee-ownership is pernicious beyond words—all the landlords are thieves, for they live on the increased price of rice and the farmers gain nothing. Sun Yat-sen promised that these increases of price should go to those who cultivate the land; but look at the men ploughing the fields. Ill with hookworm, living in miserable mud houses, cultivating the soil from morning to night, insolent because they are uneducated and brutal because they are underfed, what place have they in the land? Yet they are the farmers of China, the salt of this earth!"

The stars came out and grew dim again; we could hear the last of the coal-coolies coming down the mountain. There are great depths of coal here, which are brought down mountain trails in wicker baskets slung on men's shoulders or in the panniers of ponies. The cost of the coal is almost prohibitive: but in a country whose imports have been almost entirely cut off, even prohibitive costs become economic, because necessary. And perhaps it was the sound of the coal cobbles falling from the panniers along the granite ledges of the mountain which made the student who was studying mining engineering to speak out aloud.

"China is still unexplored. There is tungsten in Hunan, and wolfram farther north, and tremendous loads of limestone and coal in this valley. But what do we know of the vast quantities of minerals which are yet unexplored? They say there are few minerals and little oil in China, but we have only begun to explore the crust of this earth. They used to say that there was marble only in Dali in Yunnan; today we know that there are thirty immense deposits in Yunnan. They used to say that the iron ore in Hunan was of second-grade quality; today we know that there are deposits of the first quality. The Government is doing everything to increase our knowledge of minerals. Already there are blue-prints for the economic shape of the country after the war. There will be four great ports: one near Shanghai, another at Tzapu, another near Canton and still another north of Tientsin to take the trade of Manchuria. And from these ports our minerals will travel all over the world. . . ."

The bamboos sighed, and the freshening wind among the pines and the immense cypresses along the mountain-side. Water was rippling in the stone fountains among silver mosses shaded by datura plants; and sometimes we heard the voices of the lovers in the limestone grottos. It was time to descend the stone pathway to the waiting boats; but still we talked about the future of China, the tremendous increase in cultivation which would follow after the war. The four great ports were a vast prize for the undiscovered hinterland: and in our minds' eyes we saw factories rising in deserts, telegraph-poles, steel foundries, great blast furnaces spitting red fire against the night skies. China, the last to enter the commercial race, might find herself among the first. The recaptured islands of the Indies would for years replenish her stocks of prime commodities, and with the return of Hongkong and the greater voice which China will have in the affairs of Malaya and the Philippines and Java, there was no end to the prospects lying before her. "We have come to the cross-roads," one of the students said. "For thirty years we fought the ghost of our past at the cross-roads, but now from beneath the gibbet where our dead past swings, we can look clear-eyed on the future. For us, it is more exciting than the future has ever been." And perhaps, I thought, it was because the future was so exciting that they dared not speak of it.

The river was raging; the waters thundered and spray came off the breaking waves like steam, spray which rose solid and broke off in glancing sharp-pointed splinters in the light of the moon. Once in mid-stream the voices of the river were quieter; and though the rocks were drenched in water, and the gulls were screaming, it was quiet by the small charcoal fire which burnt redly on the boat's bows. We lay down on the sacking under the great curved bamboo screen which protected us from the waves, and sometimes we would lean out and gaze at the rocks beneath the water. The moon shone like daylight. Underneath the breaking waves the hollows of rock were green and dark like sea caverns, and sometimes in these moss-bearded hollows there were small white eggs of rock rocking gently in the waves. We were grateful for the red fire on the bows, which turned our faces into glowing embers, and grateful for the voices of the singing boatmen and the thud of oars. Against the distant rocks at Ch'ingkan-pei the waters still thundered and growled; but in this quietness we gazed up compassionately at the stars, who need no consolation, and heard all around us the deep-throated roar of the river, now soft and mysterious as the flight of birds migrating in the dark, now close upon us like the voice of the echoing thunder in the chasms of mountains.

June 9th . . . C. INVITED some students to the house, and after a vast meal invited them to sing for us in the garden. There was a girl in a blue gown with a violin, a boy with an extraordinarily fine tenor voice and three or four students who performed the accompaniment. All the while the wind sighed in the pine-trees; and the moon shone on their upturned faces, and on those curious round stones which litter my garden and which were left here by the ancient gods. We could hear the waters thundering and a mare whinneying, and sometimes red lights rose among distant rice-fields—and suddenly while they were singing, a small boy led a pony along the path which leads down the mountain-side. It was so lovely that after a moment I purposely kept my head down, for fear that the singers, the pony and the boy would disappear the moment after. And then later, when the students were walking down the mountain-side, still singing, and that last final terrible moment when their voices could just be heard above the thunder of the waters. There are so many moments like these which break the heart with their beauty.

I have been writing in my diary. C. is asleep in the hard bamboo bed which lies against the wall, beneath the painting of Tien Kuan which I brought from Singapore. The moonlight shines on the uncurtained windows, the white moths are tapping against the wall and the dive-bombing mosquitoes fret and roar in the still night. I have been trying to finish a poem which has haunted me for the past week. The table and the floor are littered—perhaps there are over forty versions of the gaudy little thing which has at last emerged from its immense and terrible birth-pangs:

> *O we shall never end this war until*
> *The Persian boy is given back to us:*
> *Fair as gazelles he rode along the hill*
> *Under the archway of Tiberius,*
> *Impatient of summer flood or winter Nile.*
> *Like Alexander young again, he rode*
> *Into the heaving shadow of the peristyle.*
> *No sooner had the arrow sped, a sword,*
> *Dipped in the blood of Kings around his head*
> *Quivered in sunlight. You who are afraid,*
> *Take heed of innocence, for this boy's wounds*
> *Have lips to utter celestial sounds.*

June 10th . . . I HAVE forgotten the exact date, but I remember that a hundred years ago in this month there died in a small white house perched on the cliffs of the Neckar the German poet Friedrich Hœlderlin, whose life was brief, though he lived to the age of seventy. I know no poet who can convey the excitement of pure creation so perfectly or less ambiguously; his verses have the spontaneity of the river which he loved throughout his life, and the splendour of the sunlight which he adored. When he was old, when Diotima was half-forgotten, when insanity had changed the lovely face of his youth into the star-struck face of his age, the world complained that he was mad; but even in his madness poetry flowed from him like an unending fire. In the summer of 1807 he was removed to the small house on the Neckar, and there Waiblinger met him:

"In the morning, when he is most restless and tormented, he will rise with the sun and take a walk with Zwinger. He likes to amuse himself by taking a handkerchief and brushing the hedge-poles or ruffling the grass with it. Whatever he found, even if it was only a piece of iron or leather, he would pick it up and take it with him. All the while he would talk to himself, questioning and answering himself, sometimes with yes, sometimes with no, frequently with both, for he denied willingly."

And somehow, this picture which Waiblinger gives of his old age, fits perfectly into the pattern of his amazing youth. He had burnt himself out, as the Greek gods and heroes must surely have burnt themselves; and in his later voice there was no note of regret. Goethe and Schiller played with the Greek renaissance. Hœlderlin lived in it. Passionately, and perhaps hopelessly (for he must have known that there are tasks which are beyond the range of mortal man), he determined to re-create out of Christian and Greek mythology a new mythology which would be fit for a race of gods.

He loved poetry more than life. For him the poet's task was the greatest and the most wonderful of all the tasks facing men on earth. When he was old and dying, Bettina von Arnim came to visit him, and she would take surreptitious notes of his interminable monologues:

"He who recognises poetry in the divine sense must acknowledge the mind of the All-High as beyond his intellectual law, subjecting all law to Himself. 'Not as I will, but as Thou wilt.' Therefore he must himself build no laws, because Poetry will

247

never allow herself to be fettered, and versification will always be an empty house inhabited by goblins. Law in Poetry is the form of the idea in which the mind must move, and therefore the divine cannot be received into the human mind. The body of poetry is the form of the Idea, and when seized by Tragedy becomes fatally positive, *for murder flows from the divine.*" On another occasion Hœlderlin said that there were two figures of art, two rules of calculation, "the one showing itself on an equal elevation with the god-like, at the beginning inclining towards the end; the other darting from the divine light like a free sunbeam, seeking a resting-place in the human mind and inclining from the end towards the beginning. Then does the mind rise from despair to holy frenzy, in so far as this is the highest manifestation in which the soul surpasses all utterance of words, leading it into the light of the poetic god, where it becomes dazzled, penetrated by a light that withers it, losing its original brilliance in the pure sunlight. But the soil thus thoroughly scorched is on the point of resurrection; it was a preparation for the god-head, and only free poetry can be translated from one life to another."

Sometimes I believe that I am certain that I can understand everything he says; at other times I acknowledge that the pressure of his language belongs to an order of things which is beyond me. In the portrait made during his youth the stars seem to be dancing. But in old age, the lightning has struck him in two places—at the corner of his mouth and at the corner of his eyes. He saw the visible universe with his starlit eyes, and uttered his poems through his star-struck lips, blinded by continual lightning. And yet he remains perhaps the greatest of German poets, and even his immense, intolerable inhumanity becomes sanctified by his sacrifice, for he sacrificed everything to poetry and believed that the world was well lost.

In "Patmos" he attempted to combine the ritual of Greek mythology with the ritual of Christianity. It is a long poem, and it may be that towards the end he lost sight of his original purpose. But in the first three verses, which recount his ascent towards the islands on the coast of Asia Minor, he introduces a note of passion and original colour which is absent in all the German romantic poetry I have read:

Near is
And hard to seize the God.

But *where danger is, there rises*
The Saving One also.
In darkness dwell the eagles,
And fearless go
The sons of the Alps over the Abyss
Of lightly-built bridges.
Therefore since all round are piled
The summits of Time,
And the dear-beloved dwell near, languishing on
Inaccessible hills,
Give us innocent water, O wings give us
That with most faithful thoughts
We may go hither and return again.

Then I spoke, when I was led
More swiftly than I could tell
And far, whither I never
Thought to come, by a genius
From my own home. It darkened
In twilight as I went,
The shadowy forest and
The desiring brooks
Of my Fatherland. Never had I known these lands;
When suddenly in new splendour,
Secretly,
In golden smoke there gleamed
Swiftly awakened
In the steps of the sun
Fragrant with a thousand peaks

Asia appeared to me and blinded I sought
One that I knew, for the broad roads
Seemed strange to me where down
From Tmolus go
The jewels of Pactolus,
And there is Taurus and Messogis
And full of flowers the gardens,
A calm fire. But in the light
There gleams high up the silver snow;
And sign of eternal life
On inaccessible walls

> *Ancient is the ivy and resting on*
> *Living pillars, cedars and laurels*
> *Are the solemn,*
> *The divinely-built palaces. . . .*

I do not know anything in poetry which contains quite the same exhilaration and concision as the first three verses of this poem. They rise to heights, for which poetry was not fashioned. The incantations of the Negritos in Malaya are perfectly conceived and possess the same awareness of divinity; Christopher Smart's poems have the same molten excitement, but they are still, they do not move in adoration as Hœlderlin's poems move, and they possess too rigid a symmetry to contain the wealth of overtones which Hœlderlin introduces in the original German. The first four lines I used to repeat in Spain, when the bombs were falling round Mora de Ebro: they have been a refuge at all times of danger. And perhaps there was nothing surprising in the thought that the bombs were being dropped by German pilots.

I carried Hœlderlin to Spain, and translated—how inadequately? —most of the long poems in the hotel at Barcelona or while we were hiding at the front. I have seen Hœlderlin's grave at Tuebingen, a square stone, on which flowers were always heaped, bearing only his name. When the coffin was being lowered into the grave, the day was overcast but a mysterious solid beam of sunlight penetrated the clouds and shone only on his grave. It was, perhaps, as he would have expected. The trumpeter of the gods was receiving his final benediction.

July 11th . . . BRILLIANTLY fine. The dawn came clear and still, perfectly white in the purple sky. I was sleepless, and looking through the window I saw the dawn coming through a clump of pines, advancing like an army with all its banners flying. I am aware that the simile has been used before; but this dawn was so victorious, so clean and so still that it resembled nothing so much as the tanks of the *anarquistas* advancing towards Tarragona. They were small brown tanks, home-made, bearing the black-and-red pennons of the anarchists; and every man in every tank knew that he would fail to return. The tanks went down the long road to the dancing tune of the Catalan national anthem; and here too the dawn came with music and a cloud of white dust.

I could make out, low over the hill, the blue-tiled roof of the
250

Institute of Sericulture. The great square house facing the river resembles a palace on the Loire. Faint cloud-shapes hover over the lead-blue roofs; and the thick groves of mulberry trees glisten faintly in the blue dawn. The half-moons of silver paddy-fields are beginning to shine with an interior light, and already the peasants in blue clothes, with enormous yellow sun-hats, are beginning to filter into the fields. It has rained during the night. Perhaps that is why the air is mysteriously scented and fresh, and the earth looks as though it has suddenly come into being for the first time—everything new and glistening, and the magical light creeps slowly from the heavens, and seems to shake the dew from the leaves.

It is, of course, in the morning, at the stroke of sunrise, that China is most mysteriously beautiful. The cloud-capped towers and palaces in the sky are still unformed. Great bastions and walls will form over the gorges—but not yet. Skirting the brow of the hill beyond my house, and beyond the garden where the Indian corn is stretching out stiff green leaves, the coppice begins to redden; and I think of the Emperors of China who would welcome, in those great coverlets of blood-red silk, the concubines who were taken by eunuchs through the corridors and deposited at the foot of their beds. The coppice glows with the colour of healthy flesh, shivers in the cold wind, and for one infinitely magical moment is streaked with bars of silver. Gradually the morning is following its accustomed routine. The half-moons of paddy-fields no longer glow with an evanescent light, but resemble more than anything in the world silver shields clattering before the announcement of battle. And now, as the day grows through my uncurtained window, the dogs begin to bark, the great banyan on the brow of the hill—I have seen it standing on the perilous cliff three miles away as though it was within arm's reach, so fierce and tall it is at all seasons of the year—begins to shake in the freshening wind as though there were a thunderstorm or an earthquake, and I go out alone to breathe the scented air and watch the sunrise.

The roofs of the University glitter like ice; there are pools of dew on the rough uncut stones which stand in my garden. The threads of snails are drying in the sun, and from over the barren hills and uplands of the gorges there stretches, like a sheet laid out on the earth, the white flame of the wind. The river is blue, deep blue, the colour of eyes. The woods and coppices on the

251

summit of Splendid Cloud Mountain are turning to fire, and is it my imagination which makes me see high up on the mountain edge the trace of the monastery? The thin leaves of the bamboos are shivering in the breeze, and yet there is a kind of languor in the atmosphere, and perhaps the Emperor and the concubine are still sleeping. These mornings in China are infinitely repeated; and half-ashamed of myself, I begin to wonder whether I shall still haunt these places when I am dead. Does this brightness vanish wholly from the eyes? What a delightful state if one could possess only one's eyes and a faintly receptive brain to absorb all this majesty of cloudland and riverland, these shadowy colours on the grass. Death is so still and learned; one would wish to be for ever in motion, knowing nothing, purely receptive, like the stream which welcomes all shadows as they pass. If the disembodied spirit possesses a memory, it would be intolerable; and if it possessed no vision it would be still more intolerable. One should be buried as the Chinese are buried, in heaped graves which make no pretension of being hollows in the earth; and without a coffin, so that the eyes may look through the grasses and see—

Already the wind has coloured the river with patches of white. The wind here is white, whiter than any of the stones or rocks which litter the river's path. And the bear's fur, slung so negligently over the shoulders of mountains, already it is deeply engrossed in sunlight, already the mountains are quivering with life. The river-gull flies over the wintry coldness of the stream, but soon it will be spring, and in half an hour it will be summer. Dragonflies, butterflies, even spiders are beginning to tremble in the sun's light.

Do you remember the scent of the pines in deodars and merantis in Malaya? or the sweet-smelling hop-fields on the road to Dover? the eucalyptus trees in our garden in South Africa? Do you remember the glistening rock at Paarl, from which the small Dutch town derived its name, for the white rock resembled a pearl and could be mistaken for no other object? Do you remember the groves of beach-trees and junipers at Chandi Mendut, where one boiling summer day we saw in his beehive cave the sandstone Buddha who is more majestic than any Buddha in India? Do you remember the black snake coiling in your path in the house we once possessed under the shadow of Simonsberg, and the acanthus lilies which flowered so thickly on the ridges and valleys of the mountain? Do you remember the glassy stare
252

of blue Windermere, and the snow on the mountains of Westmorland? There is no need for you to remember, for they are all here between the gorges and the river, and it is as though everything in the world that was beautiful is accumulated in the mist-laden mornings of China.

July 13th . . . I AWOKE before dawn to see the rain like a falling curtain before my window. The dog was barking. I could hear my servant pattering downstairs, but I could not see the river. Even on the blackest nights the river shines; but shrouded in the summer downpour, there was no sign of the river or even of the landscape in which I live, only impenetrable purple darkness and the occasional flash of foam-flecked water—the river perhaps, or a tree lit by invisible light from below, but certainly, I thought, it cannot be the river. The rain falls silently in Szechuan. The Chinese are a magnificently uncomplaining race, but I would have wished to hear some complaint against the rain. Mute were the fields, dumb the hamlets, silent the woods. And still downstairs I could hear the nervous pattering of my servant, and there was no one else in the house.

I went back to bed. When I woke up, the landscape was mirror-colour, silver with rain. Live streams of water ran along the branches; every grass was bending under its load of rain. There was again no colour left in the earth: even the mountains were inundated, and silver. Swift and tangible, like silver steel, the silent rain beat upon the roof-tiles in never-ceasing anguish. It would never end. It would go on for ever, as long as there were clouds in the sky, as long as there were flooded lanes and towns to be submerged under the weight of rain. The village, the University, even my grey pines had disappeared. It was one of those days when one can stay in bed, surrounded by books, with a good conscience.

But at nine o'clock my servant came in and announced that we had been robbed. Everything had gone—everything except my books, the bookcase, a camera which I kept in my bedroom and two trunks which lay under my bed. My boots, bought in Rangoon, had gone. My shirts, even the enamel basin in which I washed, a suit of clothes, a chair, the curtains, all of C.'s clothes, my shaving-brush, my mirror—they had all gone! Impossible to think that the robbers had come in this poisonous rain! And she kept talking quickly: "They tried to attack me—an old thin man

253

and his son, must have been his son—they tied me up. Come and look downstairs. Everything gone!" It was like a refrain. I went downstairs. It was clear that the robbers had come through the window. The room of a C.N.A.C. pilot downstairs was in confusion. I picked up a knife which lay on the floor near his door. It was very sharp and had been used apparently to cut the leather bands of his trunk. We kept a boy, who looked insane but who worked with passion.

"Where's the boy?" I asked.

"Down in the village. His mother is ill."

I looked at my watch. C. would come back soon if the rain cleared. I hated the thought of telling him that everything he possessed had disappeared, and cursed him for spending the night in the University. I walked round the house. The grass was trodden down near the window, and a straw sun-hat with our boy's name clearly painted on it in black was lying just outside the door. It was drenched with rain. The servant was weeping, but I had never liked her, and there were heated arguments between us and the pilot about keeping her. He had suffered more from the robbery than we had; it was perhaps a just revenge for wanting to keep her.

So we waited. No one passed. The rain kept coming down, and the sunless day crawled on: bleak and dull, with no hint of the cessation of the rain. Then it began to clear a little; more light shone on the thatched farmsteads half-way down the mountainside, and even—miracle of miracles!—someone was attempting to light a fire under a woven bamboo screen. I could see the blue smoke ascending a little way above the sides of the screen, so bravely and so ineffectively, for a moment later it was crushed in the rain. No one came up the mountain path. In the kitchen the servant was preparing breakfast. She looked older and more ugly than ever, the small pale face under the discoloured blue turban.

She told me three or four times what had happened. At four o'clock in the morning the robbers had come—the old man and the boy. They had assaulted her, struggled with her, and she had fought in defence of the house, and she had failed to awaken me. At ten o'clock the pilot came. He was soon in tears. C. came at eleven; but by that time we had found out that the robbers had gone in the direction of a village three miles north of here. It is a famous village, the centre of all the thieves' industry in this

254

hsien, a village where they watch you surlily as you pass, seeming to be calculating how much your dead body is worth.

And still the rain falls. Like an immense waterfall, which falls in softly waving curtains, each curtain losing itself in the next, subtly communicating its presence to the one that comes afterwards, the rain tumbles from the clouds. Stark and dripping, the trees stand forth. We are left alone in an old house among the debris. And on the floor, like a threat or a menace, another knife as sharp as the first has mysteriously appeared.

July 14th . . . THE University office has presented us with Mausers. There were six of us last night in the house, with Mausers lying across our knees. The house no longer possesses the air of an old observatory; it is a besieged fortress. We are prepared to give as well as receive.

By the light of candles, the rain dripping outside, we talk softly into the night. C. wears his singlet and baggy grey trousers. His muscles shine and quiver in the candle-light. He has seen the superintendent of police in the village and arranged to have the grounds patrolled by gendarmes. And there in the rain, in the padded cotton coats, walking among the bushes and the Indian corn, we can see one of the gendarmes quietly spitting on his hands.

We felt like Storm-troopers.

"Did you ever see Hitler?" C. asked.

I nodded. There was a long pause. The rain was still falling. We had crept up into the attic, to see whether any of the lost property had been hidden there—impossible to believe that it had been removed entirely during the night; and we were covered in dust.

"Did you ever see Hitler?" C. repeated, and suddenly one of those memories which crowd round me at the moment of sleeping rose up in my mind and refused to be silent.

"Yes, I saw him twice."

"When?"

"Once in Munich, and then in Vienna. I had tea with him in the Hotel Vierjahrzeiten."

C. gives a yelp of excitement.

"Is it true that you once tried to murder him?"

I don't know how the rumour has gone round the University; it may have come from Chungking, for I have no recollection of tell-

255

ing anyone here. None of us are proud of our activities in Vienna, but C. insists that the story should be told, and we sit there, facing the window, occasionally glancing at the gendarme who shivers in the rain.

"I reached Vienna three days before Hitler," I began, for it seems that one cannot begin these stories in any other way; and besides I am a little proud of having forestalled Hitler by three days. "Most of my friends hated Hitler, and we took part in processions in the streets which began the moment when Schuschnigg had announced the plebiscite. There was an extraordinary tension in the air, and though we knew that Hitler had grown angry beyond any anger he had known before, we did not know that he would march in. The evenings were quiet; the days were full of anxiety. And then he came, with his army wagons, which broke down probably because they were ordered to break down by the High Command; and the soldiers in field-grey marched through the streets of Vienna, and many men were arrested, and we saw them being driven in the direction of the Kanzlerei, very pale and white in the March sun.

C. nods his head. He has seen cities invaded in China, and he knows this dull apathy better than anyone.

"Then we discovered that there were arms in the house I was living in. There were little Hungarian revolvers, Mausers, pistols, and about twenty rifles. For some reason they were taken out of the cellars and placed in my bedroom, and perhaps it is because I was drunk with the excitement of the times that I had no particular fear at seeing them there. I had walked with the Stormtroopers into the Kanzlerei on their triumphal march by the light of smoking tapers; I had made friends with a few of them; I was fair-haired and blue-eyed, and perhaps that was why I was not afraid. More and more guns came to my bedroom until the room resembled an arsenal. We made plans to shoot Hitler in the Mariahilfestrasse when he passed down on *his* triumphal procession. All the time, in the cafés of the Ring, we were discussing how we should take Monarchists, Royalists, Social Democrats and Communists over the border. We interviewed the British Consul in an effort to find a method by which Freud and Madame Dollfuss could be taken over the frontier, but Consuls are never particularly helpful and he threw cold water on all our suggestions. They were very practical suggestions, and the French Embassy did succeed in removing Madame Dollfuss two days later. We had decided to shoot from the street. We would walk out with the guns in our pockets or under our coats, for there was a strong wind, and the Storm-troopers had no time to search everyone; and there was one of us who had decided to shoot from a window. Altogether there were eight of us, and only one was a Jew. On the night before Hitler's procession, we sat round my bedroom, discussing what could be done. We could only wait. At one o'clock in the morning we heard that Storm-troopers were searching the street *from both ends*. We decided on flight. We would take the guns and go elsewhere, for there was a street opposite our house which led to the Ostbahnhof, and there was no sign of Storm-troopers in this street. We took the guns. It was a cold starry night. We carried the larger ones under our coats. We could see the Storm-troopers in our street, but they were a long way away and they paid no attention to us; but as soon as we got into the street facing ours we noticed that there were Storm-troopers there also. There was a telephone-box just near. The Storm-troopers were coming nearer; it looked dangerous—very dangerous—and we decided to put the guns on the floor of the telephone-box and keep watch, so that when the Storm-troopers had passed, we could retrieve them and still carry out our plans. Some of us returned home; others went on; and both those who had gone home and those who went down the street towards the Ostbahnhof say that no one came near the telephone-box. But two hours later, early in the morning, when there was a light frost on the ground, I went out to the telephone-box. There was no sign of the guns."

"Is that all?" C. asked, more disappointed by the ending of the tale than the beginning.

"Yes, that is all."

We look down at the ghostly river, break open the Mausers and gaze at the blue gleaming steel inside. The burglars have not returned, nor are they likely to return, though C. talks happily of the kind of greeting they will receive.

July 15th . . . THE plot thickens. C. has been warned that he must not continue to annoy the burglars. The maid-servant is still under arrest; a servant from the University has been arrested, too. As he was being led away past the farm-buildings, he is reported to have shouted: "They are after us! You must hurry— avenge me!" We console ourselves with the thought that blood-

257

and-thunder does not only exist in the pages of Shakespeare.

C. has been talking about the proverbs of Szechuan. They differ a little from the proverbs elsewhere.

Joy is the mother of sorrow.

The scream of the eagle is heard when he passes over; so does the name of a good man survive his death.

The dragon bears a dragon, the phœnix a phœnix; and the offspring of a rat knows how to gnaw a hole.

In drawing a dragon you only draw his skin, not his bones; knowing a man, you only know his face and are ignorant of his heart.

The melon merchant declares his own melons are sweetest.

In a melon patch do not tie your shoe; under a plum-tree do not adjust your cap.

Guard your mouth like the mouth of a vase; guard your thoughts as a city is guarded.

A man who has never had enough is like a serpent trying to eat an elephant.

The towers near the water get the moonlight; flowers and trees in sunny places first get the spring.

July 16th . . . Last night the prisoner was brought up to the house. He came slowly, dragging his feet, in patched clothes, his head sunken on his chest, his arms bound with black twine behind his back. As soon as he came to the house, he threw himself on the ground, kissed our feet and begged for mercy. I felt sick. C. kicked him away with his feet, not gently, but at the same time without hurting. And so we stood there, while gendarmes with brightly gleaming bayonets surrounded us, looking down on the thief who has stolen our property and the property of so many students that his thefts are past counting.

The old amah in the house is his mistress; the boy who occa-

258

sionally helps her is his adopted son. For years the students have been complaining of theft in the dormitory; and in prison the amah has confessed that we were robbed by her and by this old man, and the man himself has confessed, though he has now retracted his confession. The students have formed a council of war. The old man is taken to a shed overlooking the house, while we remain in the moonlight under the pines, listening to the distant sounds of muted questions and answers. The man is denying everything, and we are now once again where we were when the amah woke me up and told me that the things had been stolen.

The trial is conducted with complete dignity, and at the same time with utter relentlessness by the students. They are poor; they cannot afford to be continually losing their property; and they are determined that thefts shall cease. A dim light comes from the half-open door of the house. C., who has lost nearly everything he possessed, leans tranquilly against a pine-tree and plays on his flute. "It is no good," he murmurs. "The old man knows our strength, and he knows that we shall not shoot him. The stolen property was taken to a village three miles away across the mountain road. By now it may be in Chungking—anywhere!" And then once more he plays on the flute.

And so the trial goes on, far into the night, cross-question, muttered answers, always denials. He has signed nothing. Why don't they let him go home? On the old crafty face there is an expression of weary triumph; the rain falls, but the blue fire-flies are still galloping among the bushes and only a whippoorwill rushing among the orange-trees frightens us. Our guns lie quietly in our pockets. At dawn, with nothing accomplished, the old man is led down-hill.

July 17th . . . A MESSAGE from Marshal Feng Yu-hsiang, inviting me to stay with him on the mountain. I have accepted. The trial and the thefts are becoming wearisome beyond words.

C. has been to see the head of the local secret society, whom he describes as the gentlest cut-throat he has ever seen; quite young, faultlessly attired in a lavender-blue gown, pale-faced, his hands covered with jade rings. He is the son of the former head of the secret society and wields great political power. He has promised to investigate the theft, though he swears that the secret societies have no part in it. What is more promising is the expression of his annoyance that a foreign professor's belongings should

259

have been stolen. The curious sign which appeared etched in our doorpost this morning is apparently a reminder that I am under his benevolent protection. I am looking forward to meeting him at a party which I have promised to give as soon as the stolen property is returned.

We have decided to leave the house. I think I shall regret this, for houses are desperately difficult to find; but there is no alternative. Letters have arrived at the University—anonymous letters threatening C. The University authorities have done all they can, but we are too far away from the University guards to be well-protected. "Under the shadow of the Marshal," says C. regretfully, "you will be perfectly protected." We are not in need of protection, but throughout the afternoon we have been preparing to evacuate.

July 19th . . . WE HAVE been climbing up Splendid Cloud Mountain nearly all day. Early in the afternoon we passed through the village of Ch'in-k'an-pei, among white stone houses and immense banyan trees. The sky was molten. The sweltering heat of Szechuan rains down from a small copper-coloured sun, sending all the villagers asleep; and no one walks on the mountains. The red earth between the rice-fields shines like a smooth shield. Even Liang Tsong-tai, the poet who is leading me up the mountain, complains of the *quality* of the heat, though he pretends that in his native Kwangtung the sun is stronger.

"The heat here is like a bath-house—it is all fumes and steam," he complained; but in truth, though the heat is wet, and you feel exactly as though you were in a stifling Turkish bath, there is no smoke, no fumes, no clouds. And inside the houses the old peasants are asleep.

I have no passion for Splendid Cloud Mountain. It is too near, and we see too little of the sunlight because we are surrounded by mountains. The green mountains hem us in on every side. But as we began climbing the mountain, along a paved road where every other stone retained the characters inscribed upon it when it first became a gravestone, out of the dark village into the flooding sunlight, we achieved the exhilaration of people who are sunstruck and who walk for miles in the burning heat because they are unconscious of everything except the blinding radiance of the countryside. Liang Tsong-tai, in his leather sandals, his shorts and his green shirt, flaunted his magnificent physique, and his bare

260

arms worked like pistons; but already he was tiring and his small eyes looked worried. And so we climbed up, silently, wondering whether we would reach the green heights high above us, taking shelter under the tormented tung-oil trees, whose green berries are beginning to burst into fruit. And slowly we watched the river, which was so wide when we crossed it a few hours ago, disappearing until it was no more than a thin milky line etched among rice-fields. To the right glinted the shadows of the fire-forests which sweep up to the very summit of the mountain. Behind us lay the nestling villages, the rapids, the rice-fields and the river.

"I can walk for fifty miles," Liang Tsong-tai announced.

I did not doubt it; but I was sick of walking, and the bearers who are carrying my luggage were turning pale under the sun.

"This summer I shall walk from Chungking to Kweilin," he announced shortly afterwards. I did not doubt it, but I would have preferred to remain silently contemplating the landscape from the frail shadow of a tung-oil tree.

All the way up the slope he spoke of his prowess at walking. It was admirable, but I noticed with satisfaction that he was beginning to breathe heavily. The sun was disappearing behind the opposite mountains. Even then the heat remained. The stone path blistered our feet, and we lost our way once.

"There are villages in China which are forgotten by everyone," Liang Tsong-tai said, "and perhaps this is one of them. Tao Yuan-ming, a great Chinese poet, once described a fisherman who discovered a village where everyone dressed in the costumes of a preceding dynasty and everyone was happy, but when he went to find the village again it had disappeared. I have known in Kwang-tung villages which have never seen the income-tax inspectors, because they are secluded among the mountains. Perhaps this is one of these."

When we turned at right angles, crossing a small stone bridge, the village had disappeared; and perhaps indeed it is one of the secluded villages of China, for I have never seen it again.

It was growing dark. Tall trees grew above our heads. Occasionally a peasant would walk slowly in the quiet of the evening to his farmstead, or a village girl, half-asleep after her long siesta, would take a stroll. But there were few signs of life on the mountain, the trees were growing wild and we made our way up some precipitous steps, dank with leaves, and found ourselves in an enchanted garden of tomb-stones and small greying obelisks, the black leaves high overhead. Soon we came to a broad high road, the main road leading to the summit of the mountain. Temple bells were ringing. We heard the beating of a deer-skin drum, followed by the reverberating and ominous silence which follows always, as a sign of its accomplishment, the beating of the drum. Then suddenly, long before we had expected to see him, we saw an immense giant, shaped a little like a bear, standing in the middle of the road. He was performing exercises with his feet, according to the rule of Chinese boxers everywhere, kicking an imaginary opponent and laughing at the top of his voice. He had not seen us. It was Marshal Feng Yu-hsiang, once lord of the whole of North China and still one of the leaders of the country.

When we were some distance away, we bowed, but he paid no attention to us. The red earth road shone in the sunset. When at last he saw us, followed by the two bearers, sweating and panting as we climbed the hill, he laughed with all the strength of his immense lungs, a laugh which reverberated in the forest and frightened the birds nesting in the trees, so that they rose in a flurry of white wings.

He wore a blue uniform, without medals or any sign of rank. He walked with immense strides, and yet delicately, conscious of his great strength. He was particularly gentle to Liang Tsong-tai, for though Liang was small and muscular, he was no match for the Marshal, who was tormented by the thought of hurting people, even when he shook hands. It was nearly night. He led us to a small pavilion which looked down over bare uplands to the villages in the valley. Under the eaves of the pavilion, inscribed in gold on a red board, was the inscription: "The Pavilion for Regarding the Moon".

The moon rose. Lights shone in the valley. The river disappeared under the shadows of the bank. There were a few monks in black gowns enjoying the spectacle of winged shadows descending on the green valley. Very faintly, like a small white square in the distance, the University collected fragments of the remaining light.

The Marshal was talking of poetry.

"Is it true that the young people in the University still read my poems?" he asked.

Liang answered truthfully: "They read them with great enjoyment, but they are trying to write different kinds of poems."

"My poems are simply poems written by an old soldier," the Marshal continued. "I have no claims to be a poet."

"Yet you have invented something which did not exist until this time," Liang replied. "You have invented a poetry which reflects the feelings of the people."

The Marshal was particularly pleased with the answer. He beamed from his immense height and spoke to the young monk standing by his side, who disappeared and returned some moments later with cups of tea, biscuits and bread.

The night grew darker. The valley disappeared, and only the white birds sailing slowly over the uplands caught the faint light of a forgotten sun. A pale moon came out, and immediately everyone became excited. "The Moon-regarding Pavilion" was fulfilling its purpose. We talked in hushed voices, and I noticed the young monk who had been talking to Marshal Feng standing by my side. In the moonlight he was very beautiful. He was not well-fed and wore only a thin black gown, and I saw the protruding ridges of his ribs and the shape of the sunken stomach, and his bare feet in sandals shone in the moonlight like his face. He was talking about Buddha and Ananda, the cousin of Buddha, and of how they watched the moonlight riding over Benares; but I forget the story and remember only that he spoke later about T'ai Shu, the abbot who lived in a temple higher up on Splendid Cloud Mountain, and the peace and quietness of the monastery. Later in the evening I learnt that he had been an airman before he became a monk. After leaving his monastery in Hongkong, he accompanied T'ai Shu to India and obtained the rank of *bhikkhu* or law-giver; and now, peering through the night, where the shadows were green and grey, he looked too young to sacrifice his life in meditation, and as the moon rose higher over the waves of hills, he seemed suddenly to turn to stone, to become as monumental as the granite hills or the great oak-trees, and still he remained young. His dark eyes were vigilant in the night. He listened to Marshal Feng Yu-hsiang discussing poetry with Liang Tsong-tai, and yet he appeared to be abstracted from the scene. The moon came up, a silver ibis in the desolate starless sky. We left the pavilion and walked towards the monastery, hardly talking, for the night was alive with strange visitations of moonlight. Occasionally he would point to one of the open catacombs where monks had once been buried, though like the tombs where Charlemagne's knights were buried in Alyscamps, nothing is left of their bones. Rising above the forest trees the stone stupa containing the bones of the founder of the monastery shone in the moonlight. Occasionally we saw men lurking among the trees—monks perhaps, or soldiers guarding the life of Marshal Feng Yu-hsiang, and once we heard the roar of a leopard in the hills.

Nearly a thousand years ago the monastery was famous. During the T'ang Dynasty the famous artist Wu Tao-tzu carved on the walls of the monastery a fresco depicting the pains of Hell; but there is no sign of the fresco at the present day, though the remains of an earlier monastery in rough sandstone, an elephant god who has long since lost his trunk, an urn in the garden, can still be seen. The young monk was still talking of Ananda. Another monk passed, wearing a yellow robe which fell over his left shoulder, leaving the other bare. Through the deserted lanes beneath the tall trees only the birds and a few wild-cats with startling green eyes appeared to disturb the silence. The Marshal's soldiers were looking for us, and we returned to his camp.

Hidden in a grove of bamboos, surrounded by a wattle-fence and reached by stone steps, each one of which retained the inscriptions of ancient tombstones, we came to "The Hall of the Empty Heart". Here in the small stockaded courtyard lit by tung-oil lamps, the soldiers were busy with tables and chairs. The Marshal had decided to write a poem in praise of the moon. Paper was brought out, ink-slabs were swilled with water, a boy with a horsehair whisk stood behind the Marshal and brushed the mosquitoes away. In the silence there was only the faintly perceptible sound of ink-brush and paper.

He waited in silence. The young monk had disappeared to make arrangements for Liang's stay in the monastery. The Marshal had unbuttoned his coat. Occasionally he would gaze up at the moon and start chanting in a deep bass voice. Black letters appeared on the moonlit page, thick black strokes which were written in so firm a hand that one expected them to turn into tortoises, rhinoceros-horns, anything you pleased. Tea was brought out, enormous wide handle-less bowls sprinkled with what appeared to be silver tea-leaves, though later they were recognisable as chrysanthemum petals. Everything was enormous. The Marshal was enormous, the bowls of tea were enormous, the characters on the white page and the bronze kettle of boiling water—they were all enormous. Once again the Marshal looked up at the moon in the sky, baying like a wild-wolf, his eyes closed, his great hand still stretched over the table and holding the poised black brush. The poem was finished. The secretary slipped it away and carried it into a remote room behind the stockade. And as we drank and listened to the cicadas, the Marshal of China, who was born the son of a baker and who assisted the Kuomintang into power, began to sing again in the wild tempestuous voice which comes only from the northern plains, a voice so melancholy and so deep that we began to grow uneasy, afraid that it might be prolonged and still more afraid that it would assemble the ghosts of the forest from every side. And swiftly, as though he remembered that we were tired, he dismissed us and returned to his own room, followed by the boy who still waved the fly-whisk above his head.

July 20th . . . I AWOKE early to find that the Marshal had disappeared to Hot Springs. Liang Tsong-tai came down from the monastery with his French translation of Tao Yuan-ming's poems, and we have been going over the poems with the Chinese original in The Moon-regarding Pavilion. The sun shines on the valley, on the great white river and the green plains of rice-fields on the slopes; and there is a white mist like puffs of smoke from a steam-engine hovering over the gorges. While we were translating we heard continually from the forest the doubt call of a snipe.

Liang Tsong-tai believes that the four greatest poets in China are Chu Yuan, Tao Yuan-ming, Tu Fu and Li T'ai-po. We propose to translate them all, but this morning we are beginning with Tao Yuan-ming, who loved wine and retirement, and who wrote in a style which has passed through emotion as ashes pass through a fire. There is a dryness in his simple verses which is pure genius, a love of solitude which is never melancholy but always vigorous, a contempt for riches and glory which is itself a desire for both riches and glory. In a hard morning's work, with the sun beating through the eaves of The Moon-regarding Pavilion, we have translated six poems:

I

I have built my house among the habitations of men
And yet I heard neither horses nor carriages:
Would you know how these things come to pass?
A distant soul creates its own solitude.

I pluck the chrysanthemums under the eastern hedge.
Calm and splendid lie the mountains of the south.
The smoke from the mountains glitters in the sunset,
The birds return in flocks to their nests.
In all these things are secret truths
Which no mortal words can express.

II

In the month of June the grass grows high,
Around my cottage the black branches curl and sway,
The birds delight in their sanctuaries
And I too am happy in my humble lodging.
I have ploughed the soil, I have sown the seed
And once more I have time to read my books.
The small road is impassable to carriages:
My friends must return in their sedan chairs.
In an agony of happiness I drink the spring wine
And pluck the lettuce growing in my garden,
And while a sweet wind freshens the trees,
And a fine rain comes gently from the East,
My thoughts fly idly over the history of Ch'u
And my eyes wander over pictures of Mountains and Seas.
With a single glance I embrace the whole Universe.
If you have not happiness now, when will you have her?

III

The bitter cold year comes to an end.
In my cotton gown I look for the sun in the porch.
The southern orchard is bare, without leaves.
The rotting branches are heaped in the northern garden.
I empty my cup and drink to the dregs,
And when I look to the kitchen, no smoke rises from
*   the hearth;*
Books and poems lie scattered beside my chair,
Yet the light is dying and I shall have no time to read.
My life here is not like the agony in Ch'en,
But sometimes I suffer from bitter reproaches.
Then let me remember, to calm my distress,
That the sages of old suffered from the same melancholy.

IV

In the quiet morning someone knocks at my door,
Throwing on my clothes, I open the door myself.
"Who are you, coming to my house so early?"
An old peasant coming with the best intentions,
Who brings me wine and a bowl of rice-soup,
Believing that I have fallen on evil days.
"You are living in rags under an old straw roof,
But you seem to have no other desire.
All the rest of the world suffers from ambitions.
You too must learn to delight in the dust of chariot-
        wheels."
"Good man, your kindness wounds me to the heart,
But my soul is fashioned otherwise than theirs.
Perhaps I shall learn to walk in the dust of their wheels,
But to be false to myself—how shall I expose myself?
Let us drink and enjoy the wine you have brought
For my path is already laid out and cannot be altered."

V

A guest resides in my heart,
Our interests are not altogether the
        same.
One of us is drunk:
The other is always awake.
Awake and drunk—
We laugh at one another
And we do not understand each other's
        world.
"Trembling, trembling with fear!
O folly of the earth!"
"Be proud and alert,
Then you will approach to wisdom.
Listen, you drunken old man,
When day dies,
Light a candle."

VI

I must return. My fields and my orchards
Are invaded by weeds.
Why should I not return?
Since I have made my soul the slave of my body.
Why should I wait, moaning dreadfully.
No, I shall not waste my sighs on the past,
I shall lift my spirit towards the far future.
I have not wandered too far from the path.
    Still I know
I am once more on the road to my home.

Lightly, lightly, the boat glides lightly,
My gown fills with wind and flies in the air.
I discover the road as I go forward
And curse the faintness of sunset and dawn.

Ah, then, my door and my house will appear
    to me,
I shall exult and run like a boy,
The servants will press forward to greet me,
My children will be waiting before the door.
The three pathways are almost overgrown,
But the pine-trees are still green,
And the chrysanthemums still spread their
    blossoms.
I take the children by the hand and enter,
Wine is brought to me in full bottles,
I empty the cup and lean on the window
And joyfully contemplate my favourite branches
And joyfully savour the peace of my cottage . . .
Sometimes I wander in my garden
Where there is a door which is rarely open.
I lean on my staff at my leisure
And sometimes lift my head and look around.
Idly, the clouds climb the valleys,
The birds, weary of flying, seek for their nests.
Light thickens, but still I remain in the fields
Caressing with my hands a solitary pine . . .

I must return!
I shall have no more friends to amuse me.
The world and I have broken apart.
What have I to do with men any longer?
I shall forget my self in the peace of my family,
And the hours will pass, and the music of my
*   lyre . . .*

And the peasants say that spring is coming,
And in the western fields we must seek out our
*   ploughs.*
I shall ride out in a carriage
And drive over the sharp hills of my estate.
I shall row a small boat into the wilderness
*   of leaves in search of a quiet grotto.*
The trees, splendidly gleaming,
Climb higher with the coming of spring,
And the fountains and the springs
Steal from their caverns of rock.
Ah, happy is life in the spring,
But my life is slowly coming to an end.

How long shall I stay in the world?
Why do they not leave my heart in peace?
Why do I torment myself so vainly?
Shall I stay? Shall I go?
I have no love for honours.
I have no love for riches.
Paradise is beyond all my hopes.
And therefore in the clear daylight
I shall walk among my fields and among my
*   flowers,*
Singing a little and sighing
And climbing the mountains of the East,
To the accompaniment of a liquid stream
Chanting a few songs,
Till the time comes when I shall be summoned
*   away,*
Having accomplished my destiny, with no cares
*   in the world.*

When we had finished, it was noon. A white mist hung over the river, but the shadows of the pines on the slopes of the mountain were black, black and purple, the colour of a funeral pall. There is such a heaviness at noon in summer that we have been expecting a funeral, or at least a thunderstorm. But there is no thunderstorm. Bells rang from the monastery, and meanwhile Liang Tsong-tai kept repeating: "Tao Yuan-ming is the greatest of all Chinese poets. He is the 'ash of song'. In him all experience has been refined into disillusionment. He is great because he is a supreme master of verse, but also because he is a supreme master of disillusion. We are all disillusioned in China, and simply because he expresses this disillusion so completely, and at the same time so effaces himself, he is our greatest poet." It may be true. I realise that our translations have nothing of the music of the original. The lines in English have nothing of the sweetness of the Chinese, nor their *sultry* flow. They are poems of autumn even when they describe high summer, and in their peculiarly stark assonances they seem to suggest a world which has almost completely departed.

Liang spoke of this later when we were having lunch. The enormous difficulty of understanding ancient Chinese verse! The three thousand years which have passed since the beginning of the Seven Kingdoms have altered everything in China: the race has changed, the customs and ambitions have also changed, nothing is left the same except the language which has survived everything. Yet the language has also changed in the most subtle and incomprehensible ways. The ideographs remain the same; perhaps even the interpretation remains the same; but each ideograph is overlaid with three thousand years of experience and gestation. Where was the end of it all? He did not know. Sitting at the end of the table, majestic in the sheer dominance of his height, Marshal Feng Yu-hsiang, wearing cotton pyjamas, smiled mysteriously as though he knew.

Later . . . THROUGH a forest of green pines and silver eucalyptus-trees we walked to the monastery. It was early in the afternoon, the immense green trees silent above our heads, the birds silent in their nests. In the brilliant summer light the tombstones of the dead monks, tombstones which resemble stone coffins placed on their sides, look almost as mysterious as at night, the river flowing white and deathly silent below, and the black
270

shadows rustling among the trees, and high up on the mountain slopes the long low bark of a leopard. We walked quickly, gazing up in the high branches at the pink squirrels and the great inscriptions painted on blood-red boards, inscriptions which spoke of the ancient history of the monastery and the names of the saints, and the prayers for peace that were offered there. In the silence and the heat we were stepping back two thousand years to the time when the monastery was first founded.

I think it was the heat, the extraordinary *depth* of the heat which made me feel sick with that strange sickness which comes when the mind is working at tremendous pressure. When I was young, I would leave the shipyard in Birkenhead and take the tunnel to Liverpool, spending the afternoon in the Hornby Library, an extraordinarily beautiful Italianate building which had been erected behind the library. Here were all the books in the world that I wanted to see. There were paintings and sculptures, editions of rare books printed by Morris, an Aldine *Psychomachia Polyphili* with excellent and unbelievable engravings of gods and goddesses wandering through a dream. I would go without lunch, and sheer starvation would produce somewhere around six o'clock a sensation which cannot be very different from an epileptic fit. Surrounded by so many beautiful things, excited beyond measure by the beauty of engravings and even by the beauty of the initial letters in the ancient Italian books, streamers of light and heat would go mounting along my spine, to burst into a succession of explosions in my brain. The exhaustion after a heavy morning's work, the semi-starvation and the excitement never failed to produce an unexpected result; for the experience was entirely unexpected, although it happened with great regularity every Saturday afternoon.

Walking on the summit of Spendid Cloud Mountain, in the heat of the afternoon, the same experience occurred after an interval of more than ten years. I was conscious of the most terrible clarity. I could see everything—every single pine-needle, every grain of silver bark, every changing colour of the blue sky. But what was still more extraordinary was that I saw clearly the shapes and faces of two people whose indistinct presences had troubled me for six months. I had been thinking for a long time of writing a novel about China. It would be a novel in many volumes, perhaps ten, and it would contain the lives, sufferings and triumphs of a Chinese family through the years. And sud-

denly they were there! Their names, their features, their clothes——
They passed us. They almost brushed our sleeves. I saw Rose in
a white Chinese gown trimmed with a red and black hem, her
black hair brushed backward over her forehead and falling in
two pigtails down her back, and a little way behind her was
Shaofeng, her brother, taller, his face the colour of light-brown
wood, with thick eyebrows and a long serious mouth. His hands
were large, and though his legs were no longer than Rose's, he
gave the impression that he could stride down the mountain twice
as quickly as his sister. Faintly, but still real, walking a little behind them, came their father, wearing a grey gown and a white
goatee beard.

What they were doing on this mountain I could not tell, but I
am certain that they lived here. They were more real than ghosts.

July 25th . . . I AM still haunted by these figures, and as
soon as possible I shall write down their story. This heavy mountain air is like wine, and it is only in the evening, after sunset,
when we walk down the lanes carved out of the mountain that the
excitement of thinking about these people disappears; and then it
is perhaps because Feng Yu-hsiang is twenty times larger than
life, and all other thoughts are obliterated.

He carries a swordstick, and at some distance behind us there
is one of his guards. His English is good, and he has a passion for
pointing to things and giving their English names. "A lime-tree"
—said very slowly, every syllable clearly pronounced, and afterwards a tremendous burst of laughter which echoes against the
rocks. Down below the river winds swiftly between the gorges,
there are villages and hamlets and small men working in distant
fields, but they are so small that they resemble children's play-
things; and it is easy to imagine that we are in a land of giants.

It is in these hours when we wander among the coppices,
speaking of the past and the future, that I have learned most to
understand China. Feng Yu-hsiang is not a great dialectician; he
knows little enough about Chinese painting or art or calligraphy;
he is at heart a recluse, and perhaps he has never entirely believed in the efficacy of his wars. For years he had the best army
in China, but he rarely speaks of it; and that serenity which
shines from his face is the serenity of the Chinese people when
they are at peace. He is China, and like the Chinese he is crafty,
272

ingenuous, melancholy, hard-working, subtle, evasive, dominating, capricious, loving and hating by turns.

This cottage, which lies on the outskirts of the monastery, is typical of an ordinary Chinese cottage in Szechuan. There are fowls in the dusty courtyard; long-suffering asses come carrying blue-white logs of charcoal on the wooden saddles across their backs; there are strings of red pepper hanging from the eaves, and great haunches of pork drying in the sun, until they are the colour of black lead, with here and there patches of greenish-red verdigris. The lavatory is a little evil-smelling hole in the ground where all the blue-bottle flies congregate. And all day long you can hear the cicadas and the double call of the snipe, and the great golden eagles wheel above us, flashing in the sun or dipping silently and mysteriously into the purple shadows of the forest.

This evening he spoke about the campaigns in Burma, where his best generals were lost. He spoke without bitterness, though he clearly believed that the British failed to use the opportunities that were open to them. He asked many questions about Singapore, and mused silently about the collapse of the East Indies. He had not expected it to come so soon. The war of tanks and aeroplanes is not altogether to his satisfaction. He complains that there was more nobility in the ancient wars; and in his first campaigns the Chinese were still using lances and arquebuses, and bows and arrows were not yet entirely negligible. He has never ridden in a tank or flown in an aeroplane, which he considers idiotically dangerous; and he thinks longingly of the old days when the villagers obeyed the ritual of the seasons far more than they do now. He is an anachronism, but he is also a portent of the future; for the world must come back to this simple ritual of life before it goes to destruction.

July 26th . . . EARLY this morning we went to the monastery. I could not recognise Feng Yu-hsiang in the military uniform, the blue neatly-creased uniform and the flowing blue cape. He wore no medals or insignia, and he says that he has never worn them, perhaps because he is sufficiently aware of his importance in his country's history, but as we strode out under the palms and the silver eucalyptus-trees he looked as though he was about to invade a beleaguered city. We were welcomed at the gates by the *fa-hsi,* the doctor of law and the second-in-command of the monastery, a man nearly as tall as the Marshal, wearing only a great orange-coloured gown folded like a Greek toga and leaving his left arm bare. There were bows and salutations. Like mice, the little grey monks hurried across the tiled courtyard. Soon the elders of the temple approached down the steps, where the yellow-gold flag of the Buddhist trinity waved in the wind; and behind the carved doors of the temple, we could see the innumerable coloured silk curtains which float down from the high-timbered room.

The heat was appalling. Although it was still early, the sun glittered on the tiles, on the grey lichen-covered stones, on the painted roofs of the temples and on the grey-black gowns of the monks. They are all youths. They walk quickly, with the little running steps of people who are not accustomed to cities. They crowd round the Marshal, looking with slightly-myopic eyes at the extraordinary giant who has suddenly appeared among them. They crowd into the schoolroom, where he will give an address. The proceedings are opened with a Buddhist hymn. The abbot smiles from his chair facing the youths, and as he smiles he caresses the silk sleeves of his gown or touches the jade bracelets on his wrist with an expression of benediction. They are an extraordinary couple, the Marshal and the Supreme Abbot T'ai Shu, the Buddhist pope of China, but they have more in common than they perhaps imagine, and they smile at one another from time to time with expressions which do not hide a slight mutual contempt. The Marshal has been known to draw blasphemous ink drawings of monks riding donkeys with their faces turned to the donkeys' tails. He likes the monks, but he finds it difficult sometimes to understand why they are so many and so badly-trained from the military point of view. The prayers and hymns come to an end. The crossed flags of China and the Kuomintang Party on the dais gather the sunlight. The monks cheer his opening sentence, in which he says truthfully that he is delighted to be among them, reminding them that they have shared melons together in The Moon-regarding Pavilion half a mile away. And then he continues, his voice rising and falling with the precision of a trained actor, speaking of China and the unity of China, the accomplishments of the war, the necessity of loyalty to the Generalissimo, the continual awareness which is necessary if the war is to be won. The monks have a place in this scheme of things. Unlike the monks of a previous generation, they are well-educated. They have a function to perform, and they must never

274

forget that their learning must be put into the hands of the unlearned farmers and artisans. He tells them stories of the Generalissimo. He recounts his own adventures. We have entirely forgotten that he was once the military leader of the whole of north China. He is a country gentleman who has come to visit the monks living on a nearby estate. And then, when it is all over, when the Supreme Abbot has begged him to enjoy a vegetable lunch and when he has refused, we wander out into the sunlight, while the birds chatter in the enormous oaks which range in countless tiers above our heads.

We have returned to the "Hall of the Empty Heart". The military tunic is removed. In shorts and singlet and bare legs, we sit down to our northern meal. But first there are certain sacred obligations to be remembered. The macaroni must be stirred and mixed with a liberal sprinkling of pepper. The onions, which are enormous and coloured with deep veins of purple, must be solemnly chewed, for he believes quite rightly that they serve as a preventative to a whole series of deadly illnesses, including gout and tuberculosis. He must also exercise his legs, for at the age of sixty-five there is a great temptation to grow fat; and so he rises from the table, leans one immense powerful arm on the trunk of a great bamboo and begins to swing his legs backwards and forwards, gazing up at the blue pigeons and the rice swallows who are unaccountably lingering in the branches. This accomplished, he sits down to his meal. We are entirely alone. The guard of honour, and even one of the cooks, has accepted the invitation of the monks to dinner. The sun shines. We are driven from one patch of shade to another, for the sun is entirely overhead. After dinner he does his boxing exercises, and a small boy from the orphanage comes to present still another pound of blue-red juicy grapes, which are bathed in permanganate of potash and eaten with relish. Some books are brought out. He writes a poem, chanting the tones in a monotonous high-pitched voice; and all the while he is gazing at the fluffy white clouds overhead and their dark blue shadows on the folds of the hills. There is quiet and contentment. Lazily he turns over the pages of a book—a book which possesses a peculiar significance, because it is the only present he has ever accepted. It is a book printed and painted by hand in the Ming Dynasty, showing green reeds, swallow-tails, birds perched in the sedge of a lake, innumerable coloured birds, painted so freshly that it is almost impossible to believe that it is many hundreds of years old. The birds glitter on the pages, flash their wings, cheep and fly away. And when the last page of the book has been turned, he walks slowly upon the stone pathway, where the inscriptions of ancient graves may still be seen, and disappears into the remote recesses of the wattle-cottage.

The afternoon is prolonged into an interminable silence. A white-tailed egret perches on the sunken milestone in the road. From the distance you can hear the drumming of temple bells. A flock of white birds, rising from the distant rice-fields, flickers in the sun with so blinding a light that we are dazed. Very faintly in the river we can see the steamer coming from Chungking.

July 27th . . . IN THE heat we hide in caves. There are caves everywhere, and all of them are very ancient. Since the T'ang Dynasty, and perhaps even before, there has been a monastery in these hills; and in the T'ang Dynasty it was even hotter in Szechuan than it is now. So we hide from the midsummer heat in these shallow hollows of the cliffs, where there are inscriptions carved in gold and red, saying that "Abbot Ch'ing-tai ordered these caves to be made for the comfort of his friends". And here, among empty graves and wild willow-trees, where the bamboos are so close that we have to break a way through them with our shoulders, we shelter from the sun.

It is in the evening and the early morning that Szechuan is best seen in summer. Every evening there is a haze like faint strips of blue silk: in the morning the haze is thick, milky-white, impenetrable, like a cotton garment. The thicker the haze the hotter the day. But this evening there were no wraiths of silk dissolving into the green-and-blue downlands; there was a thick opaque mist, not white but steely grey, and the lightning flashed low overhead. I have never known thunder so loud or lightning so blinding. The hills echoed; we heard the panthers roaring in the forest, and the quick scurry of squirrels. We could not see more than a few yards outside the window. The thunder was like a huge fist punching the earth, and the lightning did not come in single bursts but in continual rolls, which flickered interminably long after the sound of the thunder had ceased, folding in garish blue-grey folds among the boles of trees. At those moments we could see for miles. We could see the river, the sampans moored on the shore; sometimes we even thought we could see people
276

sheltering from the rain, and hear their curses. The lightning magnified. It coloured everything deep blue: even our hands, the white covers of the Chinese books on the table, the bronze candlestick, the greasy black-wood table—they were all blue.

And still the panthers roar in the forest, and still you can hear the faint whistling squeal of the squirrels.

July 29th . . . MYSTERIOUS visitors arrive. They come early in the morning, which is the only time that the journey from the gorge is tolerable; they come with leather cases, and in the cool silence of the Marshal's bedroom their low voices can be heard like the rumour of a distant stream.

This evening the visitors were no longer mysterious. We sat in the courtyard of beaten earth, while the chickens scuffled in the dust and the only sound came from the flickering of the horsehair fan which the orderly waved over the Marshal's bald head. We spoke in English. We discussed the future, the Japanese, the arming of the Chinese armies, the terrible lack of equipment and food among the Chinese soldiers.

I asked him what he thought the Chinese would do to the Japanese. He answered at once:

"We shall leave them alone; we cannot contaminate ourselves with such vermin. We shall punish a few, but the rest have been misled; they are poor people, and we should sympathise with them." And then, a little later, laughing gently: "We will take Tojo round China in a cage. The amusements of the Chinese peasants are not so great that we can afford to miss this." He has a horror of monarchy in the East. When I suggested timidly that the Ch'ing Emperors had in the early years of the dynasty deserved well of the country, he very nearly exploded. "No monarchy! No monarchy! We Chinese have finished with monarchs for ever." And then again: "We are not slaves." He said this in a tone of terrible indignation. "The Japanese thought we—the Chinese—could be made into slaves. How is it possible? How is it possible that they thought such a thing? We are not slaves. We fought the revolution to free ourselves from slavery. Did they think we fought the revolution for fun?" His contempt for Pu Yi, who was for four years in his power, is terrific. "A little man, a very little man—did he think he could rule China?" It was amusing to think of the diminutive Pu Yi and the giant Marshal together. "I have never seen the Emperor. Why should I see him? What business is it of mine to see the Emperor? Should I bow before him?" He made a mock bow and burst out laughing. Really, there were things that were incomprehensible, and one of the most incomprehensible was that the Ch'ing Emperors had held China in fief for so many years. "No, never, never, *never*, will there be an Emperor again in China."

We discussed peace terms. With enemies, according to Chinese custom, there are only two methods of behaviour. One could deal with them harshly by extermination, or one could leave them alone in their shame. Although still a member of the Supreme Military Council, he was not speaking officially, but he made it clear that the Japanese were beyond everything else stupid and should be dealt with as stupid children. They should be punished; but to remove them from the fair land of China seemed punishment enough. "We have to rebuild China; we cannot afford to waste so much time on the little dwarfs."

The sun went out at last. The visitors, who are among the highest in the land, disappeared, and we were left to the dust and the softly-waving bamboos. After dinner he began to sing, while puffs of smoke rose from the freshly-made tea and the fly-whisk still flashed menacingly above his shaven head. In the moonlight the deep-throated songs coming from the immense chest had a curiously hypnotic quality; and the great round copper-coloured head itself seemed to be suspended in space. He sang for half an hour, an interminable song of huntsmen on the Mongolian frontiers; then suddenly and without saying a word he went to bed. For long afterwards I heard the voice and saw the copper-coloured head bellowing at the moon.

July 31st . . . WE HAVE been talking again with the monks in The Moon-regarding Pavilion. A young monk has been reading to Feng, but tiring of the high-pitched fluted voice of the boy he asked an older monk to read; and sat there on the parapet, quietly content, shaking and nodding his head from side to side as the story progressed.

He is a little tired. During the afternoon he wrote his memoirs; they are already in four or five volumes, and still have not come down to the time of the Kuomintang March to the North. But what is extraordinary, according to the professors at the University, is the quality of his prose. It contains some of the rough-
278

nesses which may be expected in a soldier, but it is virile and perfectly adequate to the theme. And now, as he grows older and more experienced, the prose improves continually. But he is more proud of his poems.

He is not a great poet in the normal sense in which poetry is considered in China. It is simple and exhortatory; it speaks of familiar things without great art, but with perfect understanding of the minds of soldiers. When the monks had gone, he scribbled a few lines on the edge of a newspaper, consulted the rhyming dictionary, and ordered the orderly to bring a sheet of rice-paper. There is silence. The fire-flies are everywhere, but even the retreating footsteps of the monks add to the silence. And suddenly he looks up. "Can you hear the fire-flies?" I can hear them, but very faintly. The sound is like the faintest click of the loom. Underneath the tall grasses there are curious snail-headed worms with green lights on their tails. They are not pleasant when you see them closely. "Can you hear the fire-flies?" he repeats. "What does their sound remind you of?" The sound is so brief, so intermittent, that it is impossible to think of anything similar. "It is like the first sprinkle of rain in a day in early autumn," he announces, smiling, and continues to write his poem. It will be called, I am sure: "Fire-flies".

Before dinner, we wander in the direction of the monastery. He is amused at the thought that I am unmarried. "In China everyone is married," he announces, and thereby confirms my belief that even the sagest of men are not always truthful. "It is a crime to remain unmarried. I shall have to find a wife for you," he sighs, and begins to talk of the extraordinary things that happen at the death of virgins. There was a monk in Pekin who feared women more than he feared the devil; he would never approach them, and though they adored him, he held them in derision. When he died, as an emblem of his virginity, thirteen pearls were found in the dust of his ashes.

He asked me what kind of wife I would like. I answered at length, describing a sunburnt oval face, long rope-like pigtails, long legs, long fingers, a deep singing voice and square shoulders and a fine carriage. He sighed in despair. "You want too much, and that is the great fault of youth. You could have one or two of these things, but not all. The Chinese are a more sensible race —they get what they can find."

August 1st . . . I HAVE been ill for the last few days, and tomorrow I shall leave reluctantly for Chungking. I should prefer to stay here, and I shall be still more ill in Chungking; but there are no doctors, and the journey must be made.

We have been celebrating my departure by an immense feast. All through my stay here I have worked far into the night, waking up a little before lunch. The Marshal goes to sleep an hour after sunset and wakes with the first birds, who can be heard chattering long before dawn. But this morning, in preparation for the early boat tomorrow, I awoke early and we sat under the shade of the bamboos, discussing the intricacies of the English language. He asked me to show him the greatest poem in the English language, for it seemed necessary that one should know at least the greatest. I found one of the songs of *The Tempest* and went through it slowly. He did not entirely understand it, and kept on shaking his head and crashing his immense fist on his bare skull, crying out: "Ah, what a mutton-head I am!" and then smiling with perfect glee.

He is not a good pupil. According to his aide-de-camp he has been learning English for thirty years. Every morning, when he was on his campaigns, an old missionary would enter his tent and they would go carefully through the prepared exercise for the day. Outside the tent a notice was written in huge characters: "THE MARSHAL HAS GONE TO HIS GRAVE." When the lesson was over, this notice was taken down and another was put up: "THE MARSHAL HAS BEEN RESURRECTED FROM THE GRAVE." He agreed that the story was quite true, but he knew no more English then than he knows now. He liked to speak English with the British Ambassador, Sir Archibald Clarke-Kerr, and when I presented him with a feather-pen which once belonged to the British Ambassador, he was as pleased as a child. "I shall keep it always, and even write with it." He waved the pen in the air. I could see already the terrifically robust signature written with a feather-pen, from which all or nearly all the feathers have been bitten off.

He thought that it was possible that if I could modify my demands, it might be possible to find a bride for me. For the first time in my life I was implacable. He was, or pretended to be, grief-stricken. "There should be as many marriages as possible between the English and the Chinese, for they are so much alike." "And the Americans?" I asked. "The Americans are good, but the Chinese and the English have more similarities." We went through the list of similarities. We have both produced great poets, we have both chopped off the heads of our kings, we have both produced great painters, we are both hide-bound with custom, and if any further proof of our similarities were needed, it could be demonstrated by the fact that the British and the Chinese annoy each other to perfection. He was pleased when I told him that one of his paintings could be sold in London for £100 for the Chinese Relief Committee and promised half a dozen paintings, and he was delighted when I told him about the battle of Changsha. "We must help each other always—the British and the Chinese. We are good people. We have so much in common."

I think this is true. The more I remain in China, the more extraordinary appear the similarities. And while the candles gleamed in the courtyard and the great bald head surmounted by the waving fan swung from side to side in the half-light, it is true that he reminded me of an old country squire in the Midlands of England, with the same sonorous voice and the same intransigent belief in the greatness of his country. And then, once again, like a wraith, he disappeared in the darkness.

August 2nd . . . WE CLIMBED down the mountain early this morning. Sometimes, when I looked down these hills, it seemed impossible to believe that there was any life in the valley. The tuberculosis, or the excitement of living in these heights, has given me an extraordinary sense of isolation, an isolation *which contains everything*. I have no envy for Bergery. One can think more clearly and taste life more sweetly on the heights; but it is dangerous to live there for long, and even if I have to exchange a mountain for a hospital, I shall be among men. It is not the silence that is fearful, but the terrible *downward view* upon the world. It is this which makes it so easy for airmen to bomb defenceless women and children without compunction, and there would be a different story to tell if they bombed from under the ground.

On the heights everything is clear, even in the darkest weather. While Liang Tsong-tai was here, he recited in Chinese his own translation of Goethe's poem *Über allen Gipfela ist Ruh'*, and it was then, I think, that I noticed for the first time the falsity of the theme. There is peace, certainly, but it is not the peace of the earth. It is peace abstracted from life and the love of created things. Bergery may save his soul alive by living among peasants

281

on his high mountain, but I would lose mine. In Chungking I am more alive. The seething mass of people, whose faces are like the faces in Dürer's engravings, whose habits are still mysterious to me, though I have lived among Chinese for five years, whose children fill me with delight, these people are alive and they have long ago discovered the secret of peace. They call it the *Tao*, and make it more mysterious by inventing a beautiful symbol for it. They live warily and uprightly, with tolerance and forebearance for all the sins of the world; and they understand life better than our novelists. It is good to be among them. Once more I confirm my belief that if China could have fifty years of peace, the world would be compelled to follow suit, if only because we dare not play recklessly with the examples of demi-gods.

But this morning, coming down the hill into the warm blue aqueous air of the valley, surrounded by an armed bodyguard (for we had left the Marshal defenceless in his eyrie), I began to believe for the first time that I was really suffering from tuberculosis. A white heron rose over the marshy rice-fields—a real heron, unlike the hallucination C. and I have seen near my old house. It rose slowly, with a tremendous wide flapping of wings, shining silver in the low sun, poised interminably over the yellow blades of rice. It flapped its wings, but did not move; and was so beautiful that it left a taste of some terrible sweetness on my mouth. Still, still, unmoving, yet moving, rising gracefully and falling again, yet unmoving, seen against the clear blue sky and the grey uprush of the mountains, it hung there for eternal deserts of time. And did not move. And did move. The Still Centre. No, there are no words to describe its beauty, though Shakespeare's "The Phœnix and the Turtle" must approach it. And even when some prisoners, shackled and bound with iron rope, were pushed roughly past us on the dusty road, it still shone there, an image of permanence while the world flowed through my hands. I have never seen anything to compare with its beauty.

Later . . . THE river was low. The steamer came with a loud puffing and blowing of the stern-wheel, throwing off great smoky streamers of wave, and pitching in the wake of a steamer which had passed up-stream a few moments before. The great planks of the gangway sagged under our feet; everywhere there were cries, sudden stampedes, terrible explosions of wrath, as we pushed our way past the crowd coming down. (The Chinese disapprove of
282

queues; there is more fun in the rough-and-tumble of a combat every time you enter a public vehicle.) Smoke rose from the exhaust-pipes, covering the water with threads of silver; then dispersed again, flew up among the white gulls, and disappeared into the crystalline air.

I have known such mornings in France, in a remote provincial railway station, when the air is clear and the only emotion remaining in the world is the emotion of expectation. A young monk, in a flowing black gown, bare sandalled feet and a black umbrella which hung on the crook of his arm, climbed with me in the boat. Occasionally he would come down from the monastery and talk with Feng Yu-hsiang, but more often we would wander alone through the forest. He had been an airman in Hongkong before he became the secretary of T'ai Shu and a doctor of the law. He accompanied T'ai Shu to India; and between flying an aeroplane and contemplating the goodness of the Law, he seems to have obtained the serenity for which Bergery would give his right arm.

The river flowed away. The purple moss-covered rocks, the green peppers growing on the banks, the cedars and the fiery bushes of bamboos were a more delectable sight than anything God had to give to the earth. These paddle-steamers glide; you are not conscious of movement in the glassy water, and like the heron we progress by infinitesimal gradients of infinity. Great white sails flash by; heavily-weighted coal-barges oared by children whose ankles are deep in the water float by a miracle on the water, where the cliffs of the gorges crowned with the pinnacles of temples and pagodas are reflected with greater precision than in the air. Gulls wheel round us; the hot-plates in the kitchen aft steam off fire and thick waves of shimmering smoke; the boilermen come out, three-quarters naked, their trousers tattered and their muscles alive with silver oil and black coal-dust, to breathe for a moment an air in which all impurities have long ago been dissolved. The Chialing river has none of the magnificent turbulence of the Yangtse: it is life-size, and not particularly loved by the gods, and therefore we can contemplate it with ease, noticing only that we are foreigners on its smooth surface and have never belonged. And what then? A new and altogether unsuspected cliff, a promontory streaked with silver and gold above level plains of white sand, and then when the cliff has gone, as all cliffs must disappear, more and still more cliffs raise their heads above the horizon. The Buddhist lama says that the whole world is illusion, suffering is illusion desire is illusion; we are all caught in the web of illusion. And it is good and just that he should talk this nonsense leaning against the stern-gunwales and gazing up at the flocks of wild gulls. *It is all illusion.* The girl feeding her baby at her swollen breast, the old women cackling, the old man sucking reflectively at his silver pipe and the child who has opened his coat and found a place on which he can rest his head, a place near the old man's heart; they are all illusions. It is when we get near to Chungking that the illusion vanishes. Smoke-stacks crowned with green wreathes to hide them from the Japanese airmen—these are not illusions, nor are the great floods of small boats moored against the shore, nor the rock that has tumbled over into the water from the crag of the promontory which you can see half a mile ahead. The mountains are getting higher, greyer, darker, more majestic. The hum of the white city begins to echo on the silver river; and as at last, weary of travelling and of all beauty, coming to the close and evil-smelling streets of the capital, crowding past beggars and prostitutes, merchants and the decayed fish and animal bones which hang in the unswept shops, one gazes with the monk who has lived so long on the heights, gazes with an expression of terror at the turbulent world around him, and almost without knowing what he is saying, he exclaims: "The Japanese should have bombed the city into ruins. It is filthy beyond any words, or any hope of salvation." It is not true, but when you step from paradise into the dust and heat of Chungking, it is understandable.

August 3rd . . . THE heron pursued me in my dreams last night, and early this morning, before sunrise, I wrote this poem:

> *Through the waters of the night*
> *Comes the heron of my delight,*
> *Dreaming of the winter snows*
> *And the milk that ever flows.*
>
> *And the heron sings alone*
> *And the horn of plenty fills*
> *With the sweet, unchanging tone*
> *Of the songs he hourly spills.*

Who shall pluck the golden bough?
Who shall set the heron free?
In what summer and what snow
Did the heron come to me?

Who shall bind the heron fast?
Who shall hood the falcon's eyes?
From what meadows of the past
Flows the milk of paradise?

Through the waters of the dark
The heron sings like any lark:
Palely as a dream he goes
Through the winter and the snows.

Through the forests of the sea
Pale swans are gliding noiselessly:
Softly, softly through the night
Comes the heron of my delight.

August 4th . . . I HAVE been again to the hospital, but the film is still wet and it is difficult to see the marks of lesions, if there are any. This is the second film; and seems identical to the first. The doctor was enthusing about sulphanilamide. Three years ago nearly all his patients suffering from pneumonia died. "It is the disease which attacks our soldiers most. When you are undernourished, when you are fighting and sweating and living in the open, pneumonia comes so naturally that we become accustomed to the symptoms. A million people have died in China of pneumonia since the war, and they still die of pneumonia; and it is no longer necessary." He spoke of the National Health Committee, which was doing excellent work, though there was inefficiency there as elsewhere. But on the subject of the local sale of drugs, he was violent in the extreme. "On the coast our doctors were among the best in the world, but what is so tragic is that they have succumbed to the general atmosphere. They do not heal. They think only of money." He shook his head sadly. "They have forgotten their training, and those who should be the first to help their country are among the last."

August 5th . . . IN THE courtyards, in the streets, in the small alleyways, the heat comes out of the earth and falls from a cloudless sky. There is no moment when you are not pervaded by the heat. In the South Seas the heat is liquid: here it is solid. It comes in blasts through the wide streets, heavy with the scent of dust and jessamine; it comes through the windows of your bedrooms and clings to you as you lie stifling and naked in bed. It is merciless, and it kills.

A few people still walk in the deserted streets, a few ricksha-pullers still struggle wearily up the high roads, but nearly all of them are asleep under the ricksha awnings. And even while they are sleeping, the sweat still oozes from their yellow skins and stains their blue clothes black. Soldiers in China often walk hand in hand. This morning I saw two young soldiers in thick padded cotton uniforms. They were walking down the Street of the Seven Stars, laughing and joking, while the sweat streamed down their faces in torrents; and suddenly they looked at one another and burst out laughing again, and decided to hold hands no longer. In this heat the touch of hands is like a burning.

Early this morning, when I woke up, the dormitory was in darkness. Although the thin sheets wrapped round my body were wet with sweat, it was still cool; and suddenly the sun burst through the green chimneys beyond the river, and we were flooded with heat. "Look, it is coming—take cover!" someone shouted. There was a rush to the bathroom, and we have taken turns to bathe for ten minutes in the luxury of cool water, while the heat seethes and bubbles in splendour all round us.

In this dormitory there are men of all the provinces of China, and of all trades. There is so little accommodation in Chungking that we crowd in wherever there is the smallest available space. There are mattresses on the tables, on the floors, on cupboards, in passage-ways. In the courtward there are mattresses on the sun-baked stones. The rich merchant who is divorced from his wife could easily afford a room in a hotel, but he prefers this house, for by a miracle there are no mosquitoes here. We are high up. A wind comes through the open window, and he mops his face in a bandana handkerchief and scowls at the sun.

August 6th . . . It is in the evening that the heat becomes terrible. Shops shut early, but the doors are left wide open, or rather they are removed from their frames and laid on the pavement. The doors become beds. Everyone who possesses a right over a portion of Chungking's pavement sleeps out of doors. In the evening a thick treacly soup of heat exudes from the walls and the earth. Now is the opportunity. It comes out, exactly like a sticky treacle, creeping over the almost naked bodies in the road.

There is more gambling, more crime, more debauchery in the heat of summer than in the wet cold of winter. The spirit of man is defenceless against the gruelling heat; and he can only pray and hope against the murder he may commit, or the murder that may be committed against him. Tempers are easily frayed. All afternoon an old woman was screaming in the courtyard; in a small shop near the river a girl with a hatchet was explaining volubly why she had murdered her husband. He was not murdered, but he was gravely injured; and the blood ran in streams from the crown of his head.

Where will it end? We do not know. The heat gathers like a crouching lion and springs upon us unawares.

August 8th . . . IN THE centre of this courtyard there is an old palm-tree, the leaves cracked and verminous, and here and there among the drooping branches a few grey stains of mildew. In the shadow of this tree a cross-section of the whole life of Chungking passes before my eyes. Here lovers come, and children, and a great flapping white goose who cackles monotonously as it strides up and down the courtyard. Sometimes the children play with the goose, and burst into laughter at its curious waddling stride; or they throw rubber tyres—no one knows where the rubber tyres have come from—in the hope of lassooing it. It pays no attention to them, for it is as strong as a wolf-hound and holds them in the greatest contempt. In the evening it disappears, and then the courtyard is filled with beds and naked children lie on embroidered mattresses and lovers shelter in the shade of the palm-tree.

Yesterday they were lovers, the bare-shouldered boy who works in the smithy and the small girl with glistening pigtails who works in the tobacconist shop half-way down the street. They were happy, sitting on the steps and looking down over the river, where the smoke of the small paddle-steamers rises and a small pagoda shines down from the hills. But today they are enemies, they sit on different sides of the palm-tree and no longer hold hands, turning their faces away, each one sheltering in one of the shadowy wings of the palm. The whole courtyard knows they are

287

lovers: they sleep on beds very close together, and early in the morning they can be heard laughing and shouting together. I have asked a professor who lives in the courtyard what has happened. He bursts out laughing. "In this heat—love—only a fool——" And a little later: "In a week the storm will burst and they will love one another again."

The heat has made life still more naked. It is always naked in this courtyard, where the most intimate affairs of life are carried on publicly. Children are born, they are suckled, they are weaned, they marry and they die before our eyes. The wind freshens—a faint rustling of my diseased palm-tree, no more. And then silence, the furtive rustling silence of the sickly heat, while we hold our breaths, fondly believing that if we make no movement at all the heat will forget us.

In the morning the sun comes up along the Yangtse. The fever is over. After that fitful sleeping, the doors of the furnace are opened and the nightmares disappear in streams of fire. Very faintly from the centre of the city we hear the cries of the street-vendors, and then the great hushed silence which inexplicably precedes the work of each day; but the furnace is alight, the doors of the furnace are wide open and we walk like the three prophets into the flames. And so every morning, hardly daring to breathe, we look for the dark cloud with the feather of some lighter colour which will wash away all this burning. But the skies are cloudless, opaque and blue; and the birds are silent, and we too are silent, not daring to complain.

August 9th . . . NIGHT lay over the city, covering it like a blanket. In the dim starlight roofs and houses shine blacker than ebony; but as one by one the faint white stars come out, the houses also turn white. Inexplicable passage from dark to light.

August 10th . . . IN CHUNGKING there are all the modern conveniences, though some of them are in an unrecognisable form. There are tall buildings, there are even lifts, there are black shining limousines, there are flower-vendors, dairies, steamships, contractors, government officials, bank clerks. And now suddenly a new convenience has suddenly appeared—every street has its ice-cream shop. There is an ice-cream shop in the street I am living in. In small rooms, painted blue, with electric fans whirring pleasantly, in a temperature of 80° we drink iced lemonade.
288

Oranges and lemons are plentiful in the province of Szechuan, but they ripen in winter and the price has gone shooting up through the last three days. On Monday an orangeade cost fifteen dollars; on Tuesday it was twenty; on Thursday it was thirty. So does everything rise, and we sit in corners discussing the inflation.

"It has come to stay," C. announces, with a worried look in his eyes. He has just bought thirteen hundred electric fans and proposes to hoard them. "What else can I do? We are all hoarders now—the banks are the greatest hoarders of all. The Government cannot stop it. It must go on, because it is in the nature of things." It seems an unsatisfactory explanation, and we discuss the history of prices in China during the last few years. "When I first came to Szechuan, the peasants distrusted us—we were 'down-river men', meaning that we were not Szechuanese and deserved in their eyes no better fate than the fate they proposed to administer to the Japanese. They did not like the Government. It was better and stronger and more capable than the provincial government, but the provincial government was theirs and they felt they possessed a kind of proprietary right over their war-lord. The Generalissimo changed this. He is careful in the use of force, but when it is used, it is used effectively." He thought for a while and then continued: "These things change. When we came, though they distrusted us, they allowed us to buy at reasonable prices. Rents were the same for all. Now there are three rents: a rent for the Szechuanese, a rent for Chinese and a rent for foreigners. They are not conscious of doing evil. It seems very natural in their eyes, for they regard trade as something holy and secretive, and among themselves exchange prices by inserting their hands in one another's sleeves and silently whisper the prices by squeezing with their fingers on the forearms. But at first—for the first six months—the Chinese prices were very much the same as the Szechuanese prices. We could buy as many oranges as we could carry in a basket for a dollar. Rice was ridiculously cheap. House-rent was ten, twenty or thirty dollars a month—and we thought it excessive. Then they gradually came to realise their power. They knew we were here to stay for many months, and perhaps many weary years. They decided to get rich. They decided that we should pay for our occupation of their territory. The Szechuan gentry decided, at a secret conference, to produce a state of affairs by which the ancient war-lords would once again re-enter their patrimony. They will fail. Even with the help of the secret societies they will fail. They are in league with the banks, and they will deliberately raise prices so that the soldiers, the officials and the professors will find life difficult. The soldiers, the officials and the professors will go away and never want to return if they succeed; and then perhaps purple poppy flowers will once more grow over their fields. But they have forgotten one thing. They have forgotten the Generalissimo. They have forgotten his army and his air force, and above all they have forgotten that in every province except Szechuan and Yunnan men have forgotten their ancient acrimonies and a national consciousness has been born as long never before."

I do not know how much to believe of all this, but there is certainly some animosity between the Szechuanese and the "down-river men". Meanwhile the fans are whirring pleasantly, and an extraordinarily beautiful girl in a print frock comes to take away our glasses.

August 15th . . . THE atmosphere has changed since I was here last. In February and March we were afraid. We were not afraid of Japanese aeroplanes, but of the defeat of armies. It is a time which the Chinese already call "the time of the collapse of armies", and while the Philippines, Malaya, the Dutch East Indies and Burma were falling, there was an air of hysteria over Chungking. We lived in a double darkness, for the fog also covered everything. During those early days of defeat, we spoke much about the A.B.C.D. front—America, Britain, China and the Dutch. Now we talk less about A.B.C.D., perhaps because we have come to believe that God helps those who help themselves. It is extraordinary to realise that we are isolated, almost completely isolated from the rest of the world. A few camel-trains descend through the north-west from Russia, a few aeroplanes arrive from Calcutta—and this is all. We are at the mercy of ourselves; we cannot expect help for many months; we are separated by vast oceans and unclimbable mountains and great deserts from our nearest allies. *And this isolation has proved a strength.*

The chalk-marks on the wall with the interwined flags of Holland, America, Britain and China are fading from the walls; the portraits of the allied leaders, which are to be seen in nearly all the cafés, have grown old and dusty with age; we no longer refer so trustingly to the co-operation of the allies, though we know it will come. But how long? No one knows. And simply because no one knows, the best among us have decided to tighten their belts still another notch and fight it out again. The spirit of the Doomed Battalion has returned.

August 16th . . . THE thunder was twitching, and the movements of the distant clouds were like the dying wings of a bird. But still there was no rain. One half of the sky was perfectly bright, the other half as perfectly black. We console ourselves with the thought that there has never been such a drought in the history of Szechuan, and one day the wind will turn.

Still a few shops are open, and still a beggar or two limps by. He is asleep, of course. No one can walk about these streets without falling asleep. Like soldiers who sleep during their longest marches, we are all somnambulists. The ricksha-pullers, the actress who rides past in an immense grey-and-blue limousine, the lorry-drivers, the officials, they are all asleep. The girls wear flowered print skirts, the men wear shorts in spite of the mosquitoes. The dogs in the gutters, the birds in the branches, the boatman lazily fanning himself in the river—they are all asleep. It is at night that we begin to awake.

August 18th . . . D. WAS at Columbia. "And do you know why I returned?" he asks, pouring out the last ounce of bootleg whisky which came up—ever so mysteriously—from Calcutta. No, none of us know why he has returned. "I was happy there," he went on. "I was invited to join a great fraternity, I was petted by everybody, I even obtained a Ph.D. But I could not stay in America." The suspense is getting unbearable. None of us know why he could not stay in America. "I liked American girls," he adds calmly, as though he expects us all to be dumb-stricken by his confession, "and on the whole their faces were pleasing, and sometimes they could talk intelligently, but their legs—my God!— *their legs!*" It is impossible to convey the malignant derision in which he held their legs. "But American legs are famous for their beauty," we object in chorus. He smiles. It is the smile of wisdom faced with the implacable youthfulness of the unwise. "But look at Chinese legs," he exclaims in triumph. "They are smooth, white and they *flow*. So many generations of Chinese girls have carried water from the wells. They are proud of their legs—that is why they have slit skirts."

291

He begins to talk about Pekin. For ten years he lived there, and he finds it difficult to accustom himself to this city of fog. Here there are no tamarisk trees or peonies, no chrysanthemums, and the scent of the lilacs and the yellow briars in his courtyard in Pekin are absent here. Only the baking splendours of a Chinese summer and the crash of the sunlight as it comes over the hills are the same. He talks of oleanders, the boughs of cryptomerias, the muffled drumming of soft feet on the unpaved earth in the *hu'tungs* as though by talking about them he could bring them clearly before his eyes. He delights in the splendours and anomalies of the capital.

"There was an Englishman there who kept monkeys, and every kind of wild beast in his garden. There were stags and snakes, even a small baby camel, three or four peacocks, a red-eyed pheasant, five kinds of ferret and six kinds of eagle. He lived alone in an immense compound, and no one came to see him because they were afraid that they would be bitten by the immense shaggy wolf-hound at his gates. Then he disappeared. We heard nothing from him. Letters were undelivered, and the milk lay untouched at his doors. I went to investigate. I spent a whole day with a gun examining the house for signs of his murder, and even dug up a newly-made path of cement. No, he had vanished. And then, just as I was going out, I noticed that there was a baby wolf-hound at the gates. The baby looked exactly like my friend the Englishman." He winked at me. He seemed to say: "It's quite all right—if you live long enough among animals, you become an animal." D. smiled. "Pekin is wonderful," he sighed. He went on to talk of the graces of the people, the shopkeepers, the servants, the coolies, the water-sellers—they were all wonderful.

"One of my servants was a Manchu princess. She was so beautiful that I could not let her come into my house when there were guests—they would all fall hopelessly in love with her. She ate arsenic and powdered pearls, smoked opium, gambled, committed all the seven deadly sins in turn and remained beautiful and virginal all her life. She died young. Once, when I was away at the western hills, she disappeared. We found her in the Canal some days later, and there was no explanation of why she had died. But what was terrible was that even when she was drowned, she was beautiful—more beautiful than ever, and all the people who had loved her in Pekin came to see her in the mortuary. The arsenic preserved her body for three months, and for three months

292

they came to gaze upon her. And when we buried her, one of her lovers dug her body up again." He smiled. It is clear that he loves Pekin, loving the city with the kind of love which people in the Middle Ages reserved for the Virgin. Z. suggested that it was good enough if one were born in Suchow and died in Hangchow, but D. gazed at him with pity so profound that he almost wept. "In Pekin," he said, "the servants behave like courtiers; for they know that life is not only a means for getting money. In the shops the assistants will discuss the price of whatever you want to buy over a cup of tea and relate their whole life histories in impeccable prose. Here, if you buy, they are rude to you. It is only if you refuse to buy and curse them as knaves that they treat you politely. God, what city have I come to!" But a moment later a girl walked past, and he had forgotten his loathing of Chungking in contemplation of the white legs flashing and flowing beneath his eyes.

August 19th . . . D. HAS taken me to see an actress. This is the second time in my life that I have met an actress. (Just before I left Singapore I wrote a wireless play and Marie Ney, who was then staying in Singapore, was asked to take the part of a French girl in occupied Paris. We discussed the play, but when it was being broadcast I was flying over Sumatra on my way to China. Ever since I have regretted that I did not hear her voice, so deep and resonant and lovely beyond all words.) "She's only a slip of a girl," D. remarked at the foot of the immense dark stairway which led to the pent-house on the roof. It is the darkest stairway I had been up. Outside, you could hear the voices of the street made hideous by the tunnelled reverberations of the walls, for there are no windows and sounds come through the sunken courtyard and up the winding stairs, where at any moment a gunman will leap at you from the dark walls. . . . But in the pent-house everything was light and gay. An enormous bed lay in the middle of the room. Windows looked out over the whole of Chungking, grey mist rising eerily in the distance. And the actress was there, surrounded by her white kittens and white rabbits, an old lame servant, and there were three or four bottles of Chungking gin under the sideboard and scrolls from the highest officials in the land decorated the walls.

"She is only a slip of a girl." She looked indeed like a charming peasant girl, or even a student, in her blue gown. There was

293

nothing to distinguish her from hundreds and thousands of Chungking women except the extraordinary beauty of eyes and nose. The eyes were very deep and sunken, and very dark. The nose was small but curved gently like the nose of Cleopatra, the white wings of the nose flattened a little and the bridge very high. She smiled. It was not a particularly bewitching smile, but it was charming; and after wandering through the dust and heat of the city, she looked cool enough against the background of open sky to make us feel once more in a pleasant humour with Chungking.

She talked about her work.

"It's very hard, for actresses are very badly paid. We have troupes of actors and actresses, who act together, refusing to be separated. We buy a theatre for a month and pay the expenses ourselves, and what profit there is is divided between us. But generally there is little profit, for rents are high and we dare not raise the cost of tickets. So we try to act in the films, but the films are not organised and it is still a kind of game, with all the directors trying to seduce you and all the camera-men inexperienced and all the relatives of all the directors acting as well. We are not yet skilled enough. Many of our best camera-men are caught in Hongkong, and there are others in Shanghai. So we carry on as best we can, trying hard to make ends meet, for we know that we must continue to learn our trade. After the war it will be different. . . ."

She wants to go to America—anywhere where she can continue to learn her trade. "After the war" is a frequent phrase in Chungking, but she believes with all her heart that great films will be made after the war. There will be scenarios by great Chinese writers; there will be large studios; millions of dollars will be invested in the Chinese film industry. She showed us some stills of her work in Hongkong, and sometimes it was difficult to recognise her in these pictures which showed a farm-girl being tortured by the Japanese or a mother sobbing over her murdered baby. They were tragic pictures, so tragic that it seemed difficult to believe that this slip of a girl could have acted in them. She spoke about the two Chinese actresses she held most in respect—Pai Yang and Tsu Su-wen. She had been to see them at a rehearsal that morning, and speaking slowly, in unpractised English, she said: "They refuse to play cheaply. They play with all their hearts—all their hearts. This is what the young actors and actresses must learn."

And then she disappeared. It was late in the afternoon and dust

294

was whirling over the city. She came back a few moments later wearing her rouge and mascara like a queen, utterly unrecognisable. I had not expected it, nor had my companion, for he gazed at her like someone thunderstruck. The peasant girl wore a white silk gown with a brilliant red girdle; there were flowers in her hair, and she was no longer wearing carpet slippers: she was wearing high-heeled shoes which seemed to be made of beaten gold. Her lips were no longer the same lips, nor was her hair the same hair. There were ear-rings of pearls, a very thin gold chain round her neck and enormous sapphires on her fingers. "They are all paste," she smiled, dropping into a chair, "and you know the Chinese are very good at making paste jewels." She smiled languidly. She was Yang Kuei-fei, the great beauty of the T'ang Dynasty, and she knew it.

"Why don't the Americans make films on Chinese subjects?" she said. "They have gone through the whole history of the West; it is time they turned their attention to our history. Each dynasty of China at least deserves a film; and there are enough good actors and actresses from China to act in them. There is so much colour in Chinese history—so many murders and wars and suicides and betrayals." She talked about the costumes of the different dynasties, the long flowing costumes of Ch'in, the disorderly but highly coloured costumes of T'ang, the great splashes of red and black of Han, the Persian colours which invaded the Mongol Dynasty of Yuan and the three hundred and seventy-five colours of Ch'ing. "In those days people knew how to dress. Even the Manchurian costume was graceful, but now—nothing, a blue gown covered with ink-stains."

She was tired, for she had been working nearly every hour of the day. She was studying English, Chinese, the art of the stage, the piano, twenty thousand other things. It grew darker. The lights had gone out all over Chungking, and we lit candles; and in the light of the candles the diamonds and the thin gold necklace and the white silk gown shone more vividly than they ever shone in electric light. Great spinning shadows moved across the walls. The streets were filled with acetylene flares, which burnt the eyes and threw purple shadows on the walls below. Food was served by the lame old *amah* whose ugliness only served to bring the peasant girl's beauty into sharp relief. I was drowsy with her beauty, and hardly heard them talking the common gossip of the town, whether Mme Kung had really left Hongkong at the last moment with eighteen trunks and three pet collie-dogs, while a hundred thousand people would have given their lives to get on the aeroplane, why the Foreign Minister had been dismissed, who was responsible for the rumour that a Japanese wireless had been discovered in Chungking. Once I heard her say: "You really must see Mme Chiang Kai-shek and Mme Sun Yat-sen—they are the most beautiful people in China." But I heard little more. Glasses tinkled. The peasant girl in the white gown was speaking English with a sound like the tinkling of distant fountains. Outside, for the first time in three weeks, there were thunder-clouds in the air.

August 20th . . . THE thunder-clouds hang above us, but no rain has fallen. It hangs like a threat, a menace to our peaceable and fruitful lives. By a curious effect of resonance, sounds grow louder, and the motor-cars rush through the streets with a sound like a tornado in flight. In my courtyard the sounds come to shake the palm-tree, and the children lie awake on the bamboo boards all night. They were so restless that night that at two o'clock in the morning they tied an old rusted tricycle to the goose's tail and howled with amusement. A few heavy drops of rain, the size of pears, fell in the night; but no more have fallen. We are breathless for rain.

Boys wander round the streets, almost naked, crowned with leaves, beating drums and praying for the rain. It must come soon, for there has been thunder on the hills. But if it lasts much longer, we shall surely perish.

August 21st . . . NIGHT! We have been walking through the streets under a full moon, looking down at the half-naked corpses that lie on the pavements. In the moonlight their faces are touched with green; their arms thin and heavily veined; their legs are sprawled out across the pavement. There are old men and young girls, and sometimes small boys nestle in the arms of the old men and babies crouch over the breasts of the girls. Some are so nearly naked that at first they seem to be naked, and others tear off their clothes as the night advances. For they are not corpses, and it is only the stillness of the hot night which gives them the appearance of corpses—that, and the expressionless faces of those who sleep heavily.

For during these hot nights, if we sleep at all, we sleep heavily,

296

like drunken men. We are drunken with the heat, which shrivels the palm-trees and throws a great cloth of mist over the roaring river. The river is the only sound you hear at night. The river is rising. Already it is turning brick-yellow, though the Chialing river is still blue—and there is a wavy line drawn across the Chialing where the two rivers meet. No thunder. The night roars: in every sleep there are great roaring waves—the sound of the sleepers as they breathe heavily.

More corpses; more stretches of moonlit, white road; more naked children who have crawled out in the middle of the road, where there is more wind and the moon is brighter. Still they lie like corpses—some face downwards, some gazing blindly at the brilliant circle of the shimmering moon, some leaning against the walls like dolls carelessly thrown away, and you expect to see eyes made of buttons and the stuffing coming out of their stomachs. And still the night goes on, not changing, heavily breathing, with roaring waves of sleep coming from the slumberers.

Heaven help those who are sick tonight! The heat sucks all energy away. From the steaming foreheads of the dead comes a thin vapour like a spirit. Occasionally you see people walking in the streets, treading carefully among the corpses. Here and there you will come upon the sounds of activity. In a small room off the Street of the Seven Stars, there is a cotton-mill. Pale-faced girls, having wound the thread on the bobbins, draw it up tightly across the slotted frames of laurel-wood. Through a chink in the shutters, you see them bending over the frames, hear the soft clink and shuttle of the woof, smell the heavy smell of wet cotton. The carders are still working, and the lovely humming sound of the wire which beats the cotton into a kind of white silk fit for our pillows and embroidered eiderdowns can be heard in the deserted lanes. But not many people are working, though the lights shine from every house. The Chinese have a passion for sleeping in the electric light; and at other times of the year they sleep easily. The moist damp shadows creep along the wall—an old beggar with a tuft of silver beard, blind and led by a remarkably beautiful boy who looks as though he has stepped out of an Italian picture. There is a green flute, a long-handled pipe and a small tobacco-case shaped like a small walnut hanging from his belt. The blind do not sleep. The shadows come out into the glare of a concentrated battery of electric lamps; and the light is so bright that even the blind man knows he is in the presence of a mystery, and sighs, and would sit in this curious glow which filters through his broken eyes, but the boy leads him on. The thumping of the stick on the stone road awakes no one. In all Chungking there are no sounds like the faltering steps of the blind on a hot moonlight night.

And then the dawn. A grey funnel of yellow appears over the hills; and a few lorries creep out of the silence of the caves of rock and begin to move towards the heights overlooking the city. But now the full horror of the heat is upon us, for many have died during this night. "Lend a light! Lend a light!" A small coffin is brought out on to the street, and we make way for it as one might make way for a triumphal procession. "He died during the night," someone mutters, and at the same time we see the small boy, with arms like matchsticks, who lies against the wall. No one has covered him with matting. The sun catches the small pinched, starved and blue-white features, and he seems to be smiling. "Lend a light! Lend a light!"

August 22nd, Air-raid . . . THE moon rose high over the city, very white against the dark cloudless sky. Late in the evening there was an air-alarm; the red triangles were hoisted on the mast above the Meifung Bank, and the Street of the Seven Stars was in swirling flood—people were rushing in every direction, small carts piled with luggage, rickshas weighed down with six or seven packing-cases, even bicycles were loaded with the family property. The shutters went down with a bang. Motor-cars—too many motor-cars—went screaming into the countryside. There is something merciless in this great river of people rushing down the streets in the dust and smoke of the evening, something terrifying, resembling the Yangtse in full flood. They run, not because they are afraid, but because the sound of the sirens and the great triangles on the high buildings remind them of the past; and instinctively they race towards the shelters. Even if they took no thought of running, their limbs would carry them away.

I went down to the Yangtse, and there among the black swarms of people running down the steps of the Wang Lung Men, the whirlwinds of yellow dust and the silence that reigned over the heads of the people a reddish-white moon was rising over the pepper-corn hills. Soon the moon turned white and black shadows began to dance in the streets and on the river. The green ferry-boat, puffing steam from the exhaust near the paddle-wheels,

298

choked and sighed against the immense length of landing-stage; and the black masses of people, silent only because they were out of breath, began to regain their breath and pour out their pent-up feelings in sullen explosive bouts of good humour. The mothers comforted the babies by whipping open the front of their gowns and offering their breasts—it is the only way, and I have seen the same thing in Spain during an air-raid. And so they wait, packed close on the shadowed steps, laughing and fanning themselves and keeping a watchful eye on their possessions. Till, from the megaphone on the paddle-steamer, comes the voice announcing that there will be no more passages across the river that night; and then some return wandering up the steps, and others bargain with the boatmen, whose frail twenty-foot-long and paper-thick boats lie under the shadows of immense pyramids of unstripped logs.

The moon! The moon! I have never seen a brighter or a larger moon. It comes slowly up-sky, white with markings of rubbed silver, immense and brooding, larger than any moon you have ever seen. The kites, flying across the face of the moon in chains, seem to take half an hour to perform the chaste ceremony. I have been watching the moon for so long that I find the steps deserted at last, and there is only a policeman in shining black who comes quietly to my side and shakes his head. "The shelters are crowded —you and I——" We are alone. We shall watch the aeroplanes alone in the immensity of the dark city.

For everyone has gone into hiding. Under the stone steps are immense caverns; and through the stone steps it seems as though we can hear the people breathing and sighing in the dusky damp half-light underneath. And then silence, silence so deep that it could be felt and touched and perhaps even seen.

We walked slowly through the street. In packed caves underground the people were taking shelter from the moon, but we walked among the silent houses, where there were no lights, where cats and dogs and wild rats were alone in showing signs of life. I walked slowly, because for the first time the city seemed to be superbly beautiful—immense canyons of buildings shining white and black in the moonlight, the edges of the buildings clear-cut against the deep blue night sky, and the starlight shining in the puddles of water and the immense white moon already mounting over the housetops. A few ricksha-pullers lay asleep at their shafts' ends, but otherwise the city was deserted, or seemed to be deserted; for the policemen and soldiers at the street corner hid in deep shadow. I left a policeman and walked on alone, drunk with the beauty of the white city and the white moon. As I turned the corners, the bayonets of the soldiers followed me, swinging in a wide half-circle low on the ground. I was puzzled a little. They did not challenge me. And I passed on, while the rats leapt from half-open windows and scurried with flicking tails into the shadows. Only occasionally I heard movements inside the houses. And still, every turn and every corner, there were the soldiers whose bayonets swung round, glittering blue in the moonlight that penetrated the shadows.

Then the aeroplanes came. They swung down very low over the city, the sound of the roaring engines echoing in the deserted streets. Like night hawks, their wings glittering in the moonlight. I do not know why, but I was not afraid. I remembered a story I had read many years ago of a man walking through a bombarded city, not mad, but entirely alone and detached from the world; and I remembered walking through Mora de Ebro and wondering at the ruins. But here there were no ruins—or rather the ruins were already buried under the stone-white façades of the buildings which shone so brilliantly in the moonlight. The aeroplanes came low—impossible to distinguish their markings—black against the immense white moon—four aeroplanes which swung up against the frosted white clouds and seemed to hang there poised, waiting for the moment when the key of their bomb-racks would be slipped off.

In the Street of the Seven Stars there are still a few remains of the ancient walls. An immense barrel-shaped gateway leads to Lin Tse-harng. Though I passed it often it had never seemed to be so beautiful as now, the plaster melting away, the inscriptions rusted with age, the inner wall plastered with government offices and crowded with cigarette-stalls. A few policemen were sheltering there. Still, as in a dream, their bayonets followed me, moving slowly along the line of my path. The aeroplanes flew away, only to return; and once more the ancient crumbling walls shook under the explosions of their engines.

A British subject in China has, or should have, the right to call upon the Ambassador at moments of great crisis. I wandered along to the British Embassy, where there were dug-outs, though rumour had it that the previous Ambassador had never used them. There were guards with steel helmets, young soldiers with
300

pink faces and light-brown hair walking up and down the small alley-way outside the Embassy with the soft clink of footsteps like the rattle of guns.

"There is an air-raid," one of them murmured. "What the dickens are you doing here?"

"It's a fine night——" It was useless to tell him that the last time I had been near a shelter was in Barcelona on a day when the shelter was flooded with three feet of blood, torn flesh and broken bones.

We walked up and down the small alley-way together. The immense white moon, like a million-horse-power searchlight fitted with reflectors, still shone in the heavens, crowding out the light of the stars.

I told him that whenever I passed a street corner the bayonets followed me with mathematical precision.

"Did they shoot?"

"No."

"They should have done. They are ordered to shoot anyone who wanders about the streets after the last alarm."

"Then why didn't they shoot?"

There was no answer. At twelve o'clock came the all-clear, and from a thousand holes in the ground the people of Chungking came to see the blazing wonder of the moon in all her glory, riding overhead and snuffing out the stars.

August 26th, Conversation with a Korean . . . THERE are few Koreans in Chungking, and those who remain are either scholars or officials. Korea has produced few famous writers, and her history since the occupation by the Japanese has been unknown by the outside world. Korea is the "silent kingdom" of the Japanese. It is far away, and the customs of the people are different from the customs of the Chinese, and the heart of the people can rarely be heard beating. For a few hours this morning I think I heard it beating.

He was small, and his face was the colour of yellow leather, very bright, as though he suffered from jaundice; and his hands were like a woman's hands, and he spoke quietly and with terrible nervousness in a language he had never mastered. Yet he was a Korean revolutionary, and perhaps the greatest of all.

The small room in the hotel looks over the Chialing river. The Chiadine Hotel is the best and most expensive in China; better than the South-western Hotel in the Street of the Seven Stars, and better than the terrible square building which is being erected in Min Seng Lu by the Chinese Army for its distinguished guests. Here you are high up; you can see the junks and sampans floating down-river; you can see the hills and the pagodas against the clear air. Downstairs there is an enormous circular room with a fine painting of Sun Yat-sen in his black gown against the wall; and there are scroll-paintings of flowers and birds hanging against the pillars. It was here, among blue-holstered chairs and polished floors, that I met the Korean for the first time.

Later we went to his bedroom, which was rather smaller than a boot cupboard. It would have seemed larger if there had not been so many pieces of Korean furniture. A servant came and brought tea, but the Korean pushed his cup away and gazed at the curious chests with hammered bronze locks which lined the wall. There were many chests, all different, and it seemed curious to find them there.

He said that chests like these were made only in Korea; neither the Chinese nor the Japanese had influenced the Koreans in making them, though the Dutch seamen who were wrecked on the Korean coast in 1632 may have helped to give them their particular shape. They were very tall; the wood was pink or bright red and well-seasoned; the brass-bound locks, the mother-of-pearl set in the wood, the brightness of all these pieces of shining bronze dazzled me, and I looked hungrily at the scrolls in Korean handwriting on the walls.

"We are wine-drinkers, we do not drink tea," he explained, gazing at the empty tea-cup. "And there are many other things which distinguish the Koreans from the Chinese. How old we are as a race no one knows, for though the old capital of Korea was once the capital of the Northern Han Dynasty, our traditions have come from another mould altogether. Perhaps we are descendants of the original inhabitants of China, but this too is unlikely; like the Japanese we are a mixed race, with the blood of the South Seas and the Siberian steppes and the yellow plains of China flowing through our veins."

He spoke of the Japanese treatment of the country.

"There are countries in the world which have been invaded for a few years; there are countries and empires which have disappeared from the map, but there is no country like Korea. You know something of the occupation of China. Imagine a similar
302

occupation after thirty years. All traces of our original ethos are being carefully wiped out. We have no existence except the half-existence which the Japanese allow us. Our children are taught Japanese: they are taught nothing about our Emperors and our achievements in art and learning. They are taught to despise everything that is not Japanese, and every morning they must salute the Emperor kneeling. The Japanese can do what they will with our women and young girls. . . . Imagine for thirty years a country which has lived under threats, and knows no other kind of existence. When the Japanese earthquake destroyed a quarter of Tokyo, they laid the blame on the Koreans and massacred them; and if they lose the war in the Far East, they may massacre us again. There is a Korean Revolutionary Party which has been trying for years to smuggle in arms to the revolutionaries inside the country; but arms are difficult to get, and, like the Chinese guerrillas, we find it easier to get them from the Japanese. Sometimes we can buy them from the Japanese. . . ."

I have read recently that sometimes in Russia guerrillas in occupied countries are able to buy arms from the Germans. I could not understand it, and asked him for an explanation.

"But nothing is easier to explain, my dear fellow. What is required is an understanding of the psychology of the Fascist soldier. He is not fighting for something he understands; he is fighting because he is ordered to fight—with the result that he is terribly bored, and wants money for women and above all for cigarettes. He wants money at all times—money to send home, money to buy food, money for a bath. A Fascist must have, and always will have, a peculiar idea about the value of money, and he will surrender or steal in order to have it. What is one rifle more among the enemy? He cannot think that the rifle he sells will kill him. Oh no, my friend, you do not yet understand the Japanese."

He drew a picture of Korea so full of bribery, jobbery and corruption that it seemed unreal. And yet this quiet, nervous voice was the voice of a man who had been many times in Korea in recent years. I asked him how he envisaged the end of the war.

"There are two weaknesses in the Japanese," he answered. "One is an internal weakness, an inherent instability in the social system of the Japanese. The factory-workers are near to Communism, the artisans are near to state socialism, the merchants believe only in the credit system, the Navy believes only in the

Navy, the Army only in the Army. Ultimately, the Japanese lack the small-group system of the Chinese and the Koreans; they idealise the large group, forgetting that the large groups have conflicting interests. The internal structure may collapse. Then there is the war situation. They are drunk with victory now. It is better that they should remain a few more years drunk with victory. . . ."

"By that time they will have made Manchuria and the South Seas among the richest industrial centres of the world."

"No matter. The rot has already eaten into their bones. In Korea there are vested interests fighting against the vested interests in Manchuria and Japan proper. The time will come when they will break out—not in open warfare, but in something much more subtle and terrible. They will break out into the disease of separatism, and their strength will be lost. It will be easy, then, to pick off the separate states one by one."

I am not sure that I agree with this thesis. The minds of revolutionaries frighten me, for they see subtleties which remain invisible to me. But the tremendous vitality and beauty of Korea is something that cannot perish from the earth, and the recent understanding between the Koreans and the Kuomintang augured well for the future. I thought of a Korean dancer I had seen in a theatre at Paris—the lovely oval face, the perfect black eyes and the slim body which seemed to give an independent life to the silk clothes she wore, which were made of blue and white strips of cloth, in which there were embedded precious stones.

An hour later, when I left, he followed me to the door. "A country that can retain its revolutionary fire *for thirty years* . . ." he murmured, and there was a long pause. "Such a country does not deserve to die."

August 27th, Conversation with a Manchurian . . . HE WAS, and is, the descendant of princes, and on the finely-carved face there was no trace of the peasant. Nearly every Chinese is descended from peasants, and is at most three or four generations removed, but the tall Manchurian leaning negligently against the wall had the air of the palace courtyards, that air of patience and calm and finely-tempered decision which characterises those who, for generations, have led lives of luxury. It is many years since he has led a life of luxury. Like the Korean he has worn many disguises, though it seems impossible to believe that they were

304

successful. The small moustache, the long fingernails, the dappled silk gown with its faintly-embroidered eagles and serpents—no, it was difficult to imagine him walking alone and barefoot along the Manchurian passes.

It was his birthday; it was also the birthday of his father. The small silver wine-glasses, the silver chop-sticks chained together with little silver chains, the tablecloth (which is an European invention, and detested by launderers, for unlike the Europeans we are accustomed to let greasy bones and slabs of gravy discolour it until by the end of the dinner almost the whole table is coloured blue, red and grey by the things we have spat out of our mouths) —all these things were of the finest quality and could obviously have appeared only on his birthday. His father stood there like a rock, a rock with a majestic beard three feet long and the colour of Elijah's. The Manchurian bowed before his father, before his guests, before the painting of his mother on the wall, and declared that no one should leave the table until he was drunk. Cushions were provided underneath the table; more silver wine-glasses appeared, for there were five kinds of wine, some green, some red, some white, some purple, some the colour of old blood. It was this, the famous *hsiaohsing*, which completely broke our reserve. It was not ordinary *hsiaohsing*. There was a bite in it, so that you coughed almost as much as you cough when you drink their infamous white wine. It was *hsiaohsing* in which fat pig and a few other curious additions have entered, and it was the special property of the young prince and his father. They alone knew the formula: they alone knew how to entertain their guests like princes.

It was not—except for the wine—an expensive meal. There was fish and crab baked in sour wine and three or four small meat-dishes, and a grey syrup of shark's fin soup, but the father explained that nearly all these things had been brought from the cellars, where they had been stored for the last two years. Some of it was brought down when they retreated from Nanking, for like many people here they were living on their reserves. There were the inevitable toasts, and before the dinner was over we had decided that we loved each other so much that we should have to meet often, and still more often. Afterwards, a little drowsy, a little florid, a little bewildered by the unsuspected beauty of the room which had appeared so barren before, we spoke about Mongolia, Manchuria and all the North-East provinces.

Neither the Chinese nor the people we are pleased to call Manchurians like to refer to Manchuria, which has a suspiciously Japanese odour. Since 1934 it has been officially known as the North-Eastern provinces. And it is here that the revolutionary movement against the Japanese has reached its highest vigour. There have been moments when the revolutionaries were not always at peace with the central government. Sometimes, for reasons of its own, the central government suspected that they were attempting an autonomous solution of the problem; at other times they suspected that the Communists were too much in the majority. They were not happy about Manchurians; nor were the Manchurians, who hid in the tall *kiaolang* grass, continually sniping against the Japanese and carrying off their arms, at peace with themselves. Occasionally the subtlety which inhibits all revolutionaries led to warfare among themselves; but this was rare, and they have fought the Japanese continuously and with a passion of courage which will one day be known. According to the prince (who was the most plebeian of princes), the Communists murdered the son of Madame Chao, and for the while there was civil war in the North-Eastern provinces, much to the delight of the Japanese. Then there was a secret meeting, a pact was signed and war broke out afresh—but this time against the Japanese alone.

"But what is more remarkable is the solidarity of the people. The mines have to be worked; like the French, the Poles and all those who are imprisoned in Europe, we have learnt the art of sabotage. The Japanese are not getting all the coal they want from Manchuria. Their steel is unaccountably weak—it is easy to reverse the order of some of the treatments to which steel is subjected. The Kwangtung Army in the north is good as a fighting army still, for they are continually fighting us!" I was delighted with this last remark and told him so, whereupon we decided to be blood-brothers and everything he possessed was to be put at my disposal for life and everything I possessed was to be put at his disposal for life. "Yes, we are good fighters," he continued in a more sober mood, "and this is particularly so because the earth is hard, we are big-boned and taller than the Japanese and"—his voice dropped a little, as though in sadness—"there are few Manchurians left—it is a country colonised by the toughest of Chinese." I had not expected this, and he went on to speak of the colonisation which went on throughout the last years of the Empress Dowager as something inevitable and not to be quarrelled with. He was himself a pure Manchu; like many other Manchus he had been disinherited by the Revolution. As a child of three or four he had been carried by peasants in a bundle over the walls of Nanking to escape the blood-bath. There was no bitterness now. "Against the Japanese, how can we afford bitterness?"

"We have made plans for the future of Manchuria," he went on some minutes later. "In the future Manchuria and the coast of Chekiang will become the great industrial centre of China." China was unexplored; there were unimaginable deposits of the lesser and rarer metals in Hunan, phosphates and aluminium in Kweichow and Yunnan—a great aluminium belt stretching south across the Shan States into further India—and everywhere there were signs of development. "The Chinese were great artisans in the past; they will be greater still in the future," he concluded, and as we went away, I thought of the tremendous hopes surging through the breasts of the Chinese, of their philosophy and their triumphs. In this small family, which gave every appearance of wealth and yet was poor beyond the dreams of avarice, hope glowed like a single flame—and was in fact the flame of the ancestors.

August 30th, Conversation with a Kuomintang Official . . . HE LOOKED like a boy, although he was at least thirty-five according to his friends. In the neat blue Sun Yat-sen uniform, with its high starched collar, he looked like one of those boys I had seen so often at Changsha; resolute, quiet, calm and walking with immense swinging strides. Often these boys have the mouths of women and the eyes of old men. They can be seen walking arm-in-arm up the streets at night, bound to each other by a love stronger than sex, talking softly and sadly under the moon. They live in the world which lovers live in; so complete, and with no frontiers except the heart. . . .

He was tall and big-boned, but still it was the face of a child, a child whose hair was continually falling over his forehead, and there were unruly little dimples in his cheeks which gave the impression of someone who had found the world amusing. He had not found the world amusing, for when the Japanese occupied part of the coast of Chekiang, he had remained in charge of the resistance, had signed death warrants, executed people with his own hand, lived like an outlaw and a king, and he had escaped death so often that there were days when he no longer cared whether death took him. He sat on the table, swinging his feet, talking about the Bavarian Alps and the little village of Zell-am-Zee in Austria, which we both knew well. "I am going to Sikong next week," he said. "I won't return for three or four years. I have always wanted to go there—the high mountains." I said something about the serenity of the upper air and the beauty of the frozen world where shadows come sharply out of the sun. "I am going, too, because it seems to me that nothing is so important as the unity of China. There are places which must be put under our law. Only once before, in the Han Dynasty, have the young men of China felt the rightness of their law. We are imperialists in that sense—we cannot alter ourselves. All that is China must become Chinese."

We talked about the Tibetan monks who were teaching young Chinese priests the culture and language of their forefathers on the high mountain near Peipei. According to some, they were to be the advance of Chinese imperialists in the west. He laughed.

"The Chinese are imperialists—yes, but not in that sense. Manchuria we must have; Korea will always be part of the Chinese economy; but Tibet is too far—— When the Generalissimo speaks of our old frontiers, he does not mean Ceylon, which once paid tribute to our kings. There are natural frontiers, inhabited by people of Chinese descent, and these must come again into the fold."

I asked about Inner and Outer Mongolia. He shook his head; and though it was clear that both Mongolias formed part of the Chinese inheritance, he made it clear by his silence that they were not prepared to fight against Russia.

"One half of Siberia was occupied by people of Mongolian origin twenty years ago; but this has changed now. We do not want Siberia, and even if we wanted it, we should not get it. The Esquimaux are of Mongolian origin, and so too are the Red Indians and the Aztecs—it doesn't mean that we can take over these countries."

He spoke about the new training which was being given by the Kuomintang. It was hard and relentless training, and had much in common with the training of the Communist Party members in Russia. He seemed to be a little frightened by its intensity, and by the lack of intelligence among party leaders. "Everything that is not in the party manuals is distrusted; there is little room for free thought. But things are changing every day, and soon it will become tempered with more wisdom."

He, too, spoke of the future with tremendous enthusiasm. If the Kuomintang and the Communist Party could come to terms, there was no reason why China should not have a century of peace. Peace! It is an intoxicating word in China as elsewhere, and as he mapped out his blue-prints of the future, he looked once again like a young boy—a young boy who has stolen into an orchard and returned with forbidden fruit.

September 3rd . . . IN THESE last days before the beginning of term, I have been seeing ten or twenty people daily. Chungking is alive with enthusiasm, and it is difficult to know where to begin in summarising the conversations I have had with the leaders of this country. There was the director of the orphanages, the young Chinese who has just come down from the North-west to examine the situation of the Chinese Industrial Cooperatives in Chungking; there was the Economic Adviser to the Supreme Military Council, the secretary of Yu Ta-Wei, the Minister of Munitions, the Banker whose name cannot be mentioned and thirty or forty more.

Perhaps it is not possible even to begin, and certainly it is impossible to give more than a rough estimate of what they are thinking and doing. Chungking is a heroic city, where thousands of workers live in unhygienic small rooms, crowded together, diseased sometimes, more often devitalised, sustained by the thought that China is once again about to take her place in the world, sacrificing everything to the common weal. The word is rarely enough mentioned nowadays, but it is demonstrably present in the thoughts of the Chinese.

The headquarters of the Orphanage lies at Chiu Chin Middle School, past Liang L'ou-k'ou and the Press Bureau. There are about twenty buildings surrounding a deserted campus, where a few goalposts still remain as evidence of the school which once lived in this shady hollow. There are trees and motor-cars and vast numbers of clerks come and work eight to twelve hours a day in small rooms so dark that electric light permanently shines from naked electric bulbs. Here are the homes of thousands of things besides the immense girdle of orphanages which stretches right across unoccupied China. There are micro-films, aeronau-

309

tical surveys, magazines are edited here, bulletins are issued on two hundred different subjects, and somewhere in this neighbourhood live the Generalissimo and the head of the police, Tai Li.

As we walked through the long room where a hundred girls were busily filing information on the subject of orphans, the director began to speak of the unimaginable horror of the long exodus from the coast as it affected children. They were the chief sufferers, for disease caught them easily and few people paid attention to children.

"We are trying to build up a sense of community among the children," she said. "The orphans are loyal to each other and to the orphanage. In the days in Pekin, in the great orphanage on the Western Hills founded by my father, everything they wanted was given to them. It was a model orphanage, and six or seven children would be under the care of a foster-parent, a woman who had lost her children, a widow or even a woman who still wanted to look after children though her own children had grown to manhood. Here it is less easy. Huge sums of money are coming in from England and America, but there are so many orphans that it does not go very far. We are a country of orphans, and it is desperately necessary that these children should grow up to adult life without too much struggle. It is difficult to feed them well, difficult to clothe them, difficult to educate them. We have too little food, too few clothes, too few teachers. . . ."

We passed an enormous filing cabinet where the details of the lives of the children were recorded. Girls in dark-blue gowns were poring over small squares of paper which summarised the lives of the children.

"And there are too few doctors," she added a little while later. "This is one of our greatest troubles, for every child suffers from small ailments; and yet we have rarely enough trained advisers to cope with them. Even bedding wears out. Nothing is permanent in China except the orphans—yes, we are a nation of orphans."

I went out into the dusky courtyard. It was getting dark; and there were few people under the trees. A policeman stood at the high gates. Motor-buses passed, crowded to the roof with people returning to the suburbs. And as I walked out into the light and dust and heat of a Chungking evening, I was haunted by the words of the woman who for so many years had guided the destinies of the orphanage of China: "We are all orphans."

310

September 6th . . . WE HAVE been wandering over the steep hills of Peipei, wondering what lay beyond. The mountains above the gorges are so high that daylight comes here only for a few hours, when the sun hangs directly overhead; but there was no sun today, and already we are on the verge of winter. There is no autumn in Szechuan. The dead leaves fall from the trees, the streets are thick with mud, the grey awnings over the shops sag in the heavy wind, and there is no hope in the face of the land. Or rather there is immense and permanent hope, but we are like people imprisoned in the grey weather, not knowing where to turn.

We had crossed the range of granite hills which lies above the river. We had come to villages whose existence I had never suspected; villages where there were no rivers, and where the old men sitting out of doors seem never to have heard of that majestic river which flows at the feet of the University. Here the water comes up through wells or small silver mountain streams the colour of salmon leaping. And though they are only seven or eight miles away from the Chialing, they live in a world of their own, with customs which are different from ours, and even their faces, sterner, stronger, redder than ours. C. has been speaking about the forced immigration which took place at the end of the Ming Dynasty. "Once, when we first came to this place, we went out over the hills and came to a village buried among great cliffs of rock and great forests. It was a village in which even the headman was ignorant about the war. They knew nothing; they lived entirely remote from the world. And though, by some magical means, they were aware that the Ch'ing Emperor was no longer in power, they still burnt incense before his portrait and still carried on the ceremonial of the times. They had not heard of Chiang Kai-shek, though they had heard vague rumours of an uprising in the north. When the first revolutionary armies penetrated Szechuan, the elders of this small village forbade people to leave. They were afraid of the war-lords, afraid of having to pay taxes sixty years in advance. And so they grew up happily, separated from the rest of the world, perfectly content—for their fields produced good rice, good wine and good herbs. They had everything they wanted. Why should they enter the world?" But everything had changed now. It was a village like other villages, with its soldiers in blue-grey uniform, its shrines to the earth-god, its wine-shop where wine is poured out of great casks bound with

311

flax and lacquer, and there was even an officer who lived in a small house on which the twelve-rayed white sun of the Kuomintang shone against a sky-blue background. In only one thing did it differ from other villages. Before the shrine of the earth-god there were no candles—there were bronze vases filled with flowers.

September 7th . . . THIS evening, after classes, we walked out across the fields again, crossing the mountain road where the mud-stained ponies come with their great bamboo panniers of coal-dust and charcoal. It was late, but we wandered off into the darkness, for the sun had been shining and we were happy to wander in the moonlit night.

C. has been trying to find a house for me. We found a beautiful house, surrounded by an enormous spiked wall, overlooking a mountain stream and a clump of bamboos. There were partridges and perfectly white egrets wading in the pool, a few stone tablets dating from the latter part of the Sung Dynasty. It is impossible to imagine a lovelier place in summer, or a more desolate one in winter. Today it looked at its best—the waving bamboos, the egrets, the deep pool, the houses banked against the mountain-side in the distance and the forest of pines running along the contours of the mountains. In the moonlight the house looked like the house which all scholars dream of possessing. In such a house Tao Yuan-ming had composed his elegies; in such a house Su Tung-po composed his odes.

But we wandered on along the mountain path, and decided to return only when it was very late. Unfortunately, we took a short cut down the muddy bank, and coming past the courtyard of a timber-roofed house set in a grove of alders, we discovered ourselves surrounded by armed men and barking wolf-hounds. Rifles were pointed at us; the dogs leaped at our throats. We were glad we had taken short sticks with us, for undoubtedly they saved our lives. We were examined roughly by men who looked as though they were bored and therefore would take the greatest pleasure in cutting our throats. But at last, our pockets having been searched and our bodies roughly handled, we were allowed to go on—saved only by the metallic badge which bears the name of the University and which we wear on the lapels of our coats.

"What kind of house is it?" I asked. "Is this the headquarters of a military station, or have we come upon a band of thieves?"

C. shook his head sadly. At first he refused to tell me, but at last he admitted: "The house belongs to one of the great banks. They are hoarding cloth, waiting for the price to go up, when they will sell it on the market. Probably there are a million million dollars' worth of cloth stored in the house."

September 8th . . . NEWS trickles slowly in these remote villages of China. We tell ourselves that we are a part of Chungking and are ruled from Chungking, but news is nearly always late. A Communist paper arrives early in the afternoon; the Government papers arrive the next morning. But there is little news in the Communist paper, which is heavily censored. The English papers, the *National Herald* and the various bulletins issued by the various press-attachés in Chungking arrive weeks and sometimes months late. There are professors and students here who do not read the papers, and know little of what is happening outside; thereby they save valuable time.

There is a wireless mast over the roof of the University, but the wireless set has long ago fallen into oblivion. We live, not on news, but on rumours. The most extraordinary rumours are believed until the moment arrives when a still more extraordinary rumour arrives. There are wireless loud-speakers on the streets of Chungking, but there are none here; and perhaps no great harm is done, for no one in Chungking listens to the wireless speakers —they are too loud, and there are too many other musical instruments in competition with it. And after all, there is a great virtue in rumours. They are more human than the impersonalised news which appears under date-lines in newspapers. It is coloured and tainted by the person who spreads the rumour. And surely these rumours are less extraordinary than the real news. When I think of the Russian armies advancing, the attacks and counter-attacks in Africa, the defence of the guerrillas in the north-west, then it seems to me that all news, however small, however insignificant, is extraordinary beyond words; and I wonder at the Chinese Universities which live their quiet lives separated from the world, and at that moment it seems that the greatest news of all is that they should be allowed to continue and plan quietly the rebirth of Asia.

September 9th . . . I HAVE been to see the mayor in the hope of finding a house. He is a short man, with a face of dull leather and small eyes; but he holds himself with great dignity and carries on the lapels of his coat the emblem of a silver greyhound, which means that he has been appointed the mayor of a *hsien*, the autonomous or nearly autonomous unit of Chinese civil administration. We have been talking in the mayor's parlour, where the rifles are stacked in rows and gendarmes enter from time to time to lay reports on the black-wood table. China is still in the state of "military tutelage" according to the principles set out by Sun Yat-sen; and the effect of the military is visible in nearly every detail of civil administration.

We talk about the past, when the mountains surrounding this village were infested with bandits. The mayor's brother had marched against them less than ten years ago and executed them out of hand. They were deserters from one or other of the warring armies that swept backwards and forwards through Szechuan.

"It is not all over yet," the mayor said, gazing up at the ceiling and blowing out great puffs of tobacco. "There are still a few bandits, and we punish them mercilessly." He spoke about the last bombardment of Peipei, which occurred when Lin Yutang was living in this village. "We had to build everything up again, reestablish everything. There was no panic. There are many hills in the neighbourhood, and many shelters; but everything had to be built up from the beginning. This is what is heart-rending." He was proud of his administration and prouder still that the Generalissimo had come often to inspect his plans. "Peipei is a model village," he explained. "The Government proposes to carry out experiments, which may later be copied by other villages throughout the land. There are so many centres of learning here, and we are not far from the headquarters of the Legislative Assembly and the Ministry of Education. Experiments in education, in civic health, in the training of the young . . ." The list was endless. "But we are not satisfied, we shall never be satisfied until everybody in this village has enough to eat and has the best medical care."

He is a good mayor, but his problems are almost insoluble. There is heart-rending poverty here. On the clayey banks of the rivers there are people who live under mat-shed roofs like beasts, and the haulers who come up-river, leaving behind them a trail of blood from lungs or chafed ankles, are in no better plight. And prices are mounting, mounting. But at night, as we crossed the river, seeing the banked smoke fires of the furnace, the chimneys
314

of the mills and the lights burning in the dynamo house on the water's edge, we felt that he had reason to be proud.

September 12th . . . THERE was a storm tonight. We crossed the river in one of the small University ferries, while our umbrellas were snapped by the wind out of our hands and the storm lashed the waves. We could see nothing—absolutely nothing, and all the time the boat was filling with water. It took an hour to cross the river; usually it takes at most twenty minutes. And then, afterwards, when we had dried ourselves and lay back in what comfort can be derived from hard bamboo beds, we congratulated ourselves that the summer was over, for there would be no more bed-bugs and we would no longer be broiled by the sun. Then we spoke about the end of the war. I asked my friend Y. what he would buy immediately the war ended. He thought for a while, and answered in only one word: "Books." I asked G. and K. and L. and several others, and always the reply was: "Books."

This is the great hunger in China. Books are printed and published on coarse paper, but they are not books in the real sense of the word; nor are there any foreign books. We have no idea what books are being published abroad. Occasionally, it is true, we find a book we have not seen before, but the new book, the book with the smell of printers' ink, the pages uncut, this they have not seen. And while the storm raged overhead and the rafters creaked and plaster dripped on our faces, we dreamed of the almost unimaginable bliss of seeing books fresh from the printers' hands.

September 13th . . . I HAVE crossed the river in the mist, wondering how the boatmen could find their way among the rocks, for there are rocks everywhere and the river is low. There is no rule for the river; one day low, one day high; and the changes are so sudden that you may see the small mat-sheds by the river's edge wandering down-stream in a soapy yellow froth five minutes after the river has risen. But by good luck this morning we drifted down-stream and came to earth at the foot of the village.

This little village, with its two muddy streets and great banyan trees, is a paradise in summer, and we are able to forget the coal-coolies who come panting down the mountain. But in winter it is impossible to forget them. They are half-naked, their bodies

315

covered with soot, and there are red weals in their black bellies which shine like jewels, and they sweat even in this cold wind under the weight of their bamboo baskets filled with coal. They come in straggling groups past the watch-tower on the slopes, treading deep in mud, sullen, footsore, with expressions of agony on their black faces; and they have lost all patience and care nothing if they collide against you, smothering you in the black dust of coal.

But the mist is beautiful, and when I see them coming through the hovering shapes of mist which hang over the village, they seem to have come from some other world, in which mist and darkness are thoroughly understandable. They pant and whistle as they run the last remaining stages of their race, the coal-dust dripping from the baskets, the dogs howling at their heels, in-human in their agony, their eyes like red ink splashed on a black page, their bodies trembling in the heat and cold. So in this wilderness they come to the waiting boats.

There are epics to be written of the workers of China. The story of the tin-mines of Kochu in Yunnan is still untold; the story of the North-West must remain for another generation. Here we have only the haulers and the coal-coolies, and today both of them have been shining dimly through the mist, invisible until they are but a few paces away from you, and simply because they disappear so easily in the mist they seem to be as free as the crested sandpipers who swoop low over the river. These are the people who have made China. They have altered the shapes of rivers and the contours of mountains; it is by their agony and sweat that we live. And therefore we accord them the reverence we offer to all labourers who starve by the wayside.

September 14th, A Letter from Bergery . . . "... THE white wings of the gulls seen against the mist suggested to me this morning passages of whiteness leading to still more brightly coloured passages of a still more luminous whiteness. We live here, my dear Robert, in the fog and the mist, cut off from the world as with a knife. The book is nearly finished, a book on the nature of peace and the nature of war. Pray God that those who have the future of the world in their charge will not entirely neglect it.

"It seems to me now that all those who take part in the wars, those who by the power of their tongues, and by the power of their inventive minds, have fashioned out of material things in-

316

struments of punishment, are somnambulists; and what is above all necessary to the future of the world is that the somnambulist should be awakened in time. How many people go through life dreaming! How many people are incapable of living their own lives, but borrow from the tattered fragments of history a piece of life here, a piece there, until nothing is left of themselves, for they are clothed like the mænads in the skins of wild beasts. So Hitler borrows the forelocks of Napoleon and Disraeli, and the uniform of the English soldier, and the philosophy of a renegade Englishman; and believes that out of plagiarism he can conquer the world. But the sin lies deeper. All those who do not live their lives freely in the truth are plagiarists; and therefore they are a danger to the world. If we could live simply like the Balinese whom you love, worshipping the gods, eternally in adoration, there would be no wars. Of this at least I am certain. We must cut the Gordian knot, and be ourselves once more.

"I had hoped, before I died, to see the change of heart of which so many prophets have spoken. There were moments in Spain when I lived in the Apolcalypse and saw all the angels like snow-flakes descending from heaven. The snow fell on the faces of the dead but did not awaken the living. *Innocence* is the greatest vir-tue, and by 'innocence' I mean our capacity for good, for being good, for always and permanently adoring what is good in our hearts and in the hearts of others; a kind of chastity which differs from our human chastity in perpetually propagating itself. That innocence exists I know from the faces of children, and from many other things. The way in which we forget the hardships and terrors of life—surely this is a sign of our innocence, and without innocence we would all be suicides. There will assuredly come a time when innocence will rule over us, when we shall no longer be ashamed of the curious evolutions of the sexual instinct, and we shall understand—as we have never understood since the age of archaic Greece—the beauty of the temptations that assail us, providing only that those temptations are innocent. Death will lose its power to frighten us; we shall accept it as a part of life, *and perhaps the greater part;* and it will be no more to us than a change of clothing, or as the change of weight which overcomes a swimmer the moment he dips into the stream. And just as faith moves both through intelligence and through some inborn in-stinct, so shall we discover that this state of innocence, which is

317

common among children and animals, will be found also in men of the greatest intelligence, as already we have seen it in the minds of Leonardo, Dürer and the rest. Buddha has only one command: Be innocent. This above all. And lest we forget this innocence which is knocking on our doors, there are birds to remind us. Oh, Robert, the birds come and climb on the trees in the mist, and surely there is nothing so beautiful as the *poise* of those birds. . . .

"This evening, when we lit the fires and the mist lay sheltered behind the paper windows, I watched the maidservant suckling her child. There was no shame, but great beauty as she sat by the fire, stripped to the waist, the great milky-blue breasts so full of milk that the child was almost drowned. There is innocence on these high mountains which none have ever seen in the valleys. Let this be a reminder to us. We must climb higher, or be sheltered from the world, before innocence appears. So the Chinese, for thousands of years, have hid themselves behind the high walls of their family estates, loving privacy because they worshipped innocence. And surely this is what the Chinese have to teach us—that respect for the human soul which even the Christians, by raising it to a non-human plane, have failed to achieve.

"The light is out. I sit and muse by the fire, dreaming a little of the world of light. Out of scattered experiences, from the bloody fields of Spain and Verdun, Changsha and Africa, I see the flowers on the tombs of the heroes. These flowers must be allowed to grow in all innocence, lest we perish. I was dreaming a moment ago of the deserts of Africa, and it seemed suddenly that the golden sand turned into coloured flowers. Is this a dream? The birds and the flowers must be our guide, for when the earth is beautiful, then men also will be beautiful. I like the Arabian myth by which the stars are named after birds and flowers. It is surely better than our own, which peoples the heavens with war-like heroes.

"I am looking forward to seeing you at the Buddhist Requiem on Splendid Cloud Mountain in the next few days."

September 17th . . . A MESSENGER came down the mountain this morning to remind me that the Requiem would be sung in the monastery in the evening. With the messenger came a large folio bound in brown covers—a present from the abbot. The book contained the Chinese text of the Requiem, which is supposed to have been composed by the Sun Dynasty poet Su T'ung-po, but it is unlikely that he did more than change in some way the form of the original Sanscrit. I spent the morning poring over the book with one of our poets. There are whole sentences in the Requiem which he cannot understand, whole sentences of Sanscrit written in Chinese characters according to the sound; and he guesses wildly at these strangely un-Chinese sounds. Best of all the book contains illustrations of the positions of the hands to be assumed during the ceremony. They are like the hands you find in Indian sculptures, long and without bones. But where I saw swans and towers, sudden gardens and stairways, Yang Chih-sing saw tempests and sunrise. You can read anything you please into the expression of the hands.

In the afternoon clouds covered Splendid Cloud Mountain; a rainy wind blew down-river. I have no prejudice against the rain, but a journey down the Chialing river in a rainstorm is not comfortable. The mat-shed awning over the boat drips and the water mounts in the well of the boat. You are uncomfortable and you are unhappy, crowded together knee-deep in water, while the rain lashes the rocks outside. So we crouched in silent misery under the mat, praying for the cessation of rain. It did not cease. The boatman jumped overboard and pulled us over the rapids, and I was glad when we reached the stone steps of the Hot Springs three or four miles up-stream. Steaming clothes are not pleasant, but the boatman was angry with the weather, and I feared to be the weather's hostage to misfortune.

The mist was white, opaque, thick as cream. A few black storm-clouds high in the heavens, and a few eagles monotonously circling among the pines. I did not know that eagles cried, or had any voice at all; but they were whimpering in the mist as, blinded by the clouds, they flew low over the invisible white earth. A sensation of being continuously on the edge of a precipice. The sedan-chair-bearers almost naked, for the mist weighed heavily on their clothes; and sometimes the mist so thick that it was impossible to see them. Then the mist cleared, and the magnificent rippling brown back and legs of the boy in front would emerge from all that whiteness. Splendid Cloud Mountain is a holy mountain. While they were carrying me up, almost unconscious for the misery of low-drifting clouds, I wrote this poem:

After the sunshine come the mists of rain:
The shadowy horses stand and grope in vain,
And the white glimmering fragments of mist sweep by,
While angels and monkeys scream from the deep abyss
Lifting their scattered hands against the sky,
Where perilous hands are hidden in clouds of ice
And we are left to our cold obscurities.
Buddha has fallen; no sound from the risen Christ
Echoes from the deep caverns of the treacherous East.
Now angels and monkeys, snowflakes and winter mist
Are hurled into the abyss, and smitten
By the soul's voice driven through stricken crowds.
In all the holy books and sermons written
When was the holy mountain free from clouds?

Later . . . I REACHED the monastery long before the ceremony began. Bergery was there, with a white spaniel and three
or four small urchins he had picked up on the road. In the bare
tiled refectory, the monks came on slippered feet to see whether
we were comfortable; and spoke of the ceremony with hushed
voices, wondering perhaps whether it was right that a foreigner
should be admitted.

The sun had long ago disappeared, and when at last the ceremony began by the light of butter-lamps and a few incongruous
pale blue acetylene lamps, we had forgotten the events of the
day; for a Chinese temple is made for the night. We seemed to
have been living among the silken curtains of the temple for all
eternity, and only the distant barking of Bergery's spaniel suggested a distant world outside.

At the head of an immense table the presiding priest took his
position. He was dressed in a flowing red robe, the colour of
brick-dust, squared and patterned according to no known law;
and on his head he wore the five-faced Buddha crown on which
little embroidered figures of Buddha standing upright in the attitude of someone giving his blessing shone in the blue and yellow
light. Down the sides of the white table priests sat bowed over
their instruments, the books open, their hands playing lightly on
the strings. They were all young. Unlike the presiding priest, they
wore their customary black gowns. And suddenly, while the wind
320

fluttered the hanging curtains, the priest began to intone, and his fingers would describe the paradises to which the soul of the dead man had gone.

"O listen to the voices of our hearts! As swift as an arrow flies the golden crow, as swift as the shuttle flies the jade rabbit. The living and the dead live in worlds apart. Where can their faces be seen or their voices be heard? The first stick of incense is burnt to summon the ghost of a man.

"O listen to the voices of our hearts! In the distance the mountains with their many colours can be seen, but no murmuring waters can be heard. The flowers are still in bloom, though the spring has gone. The birds are not startled by the approach of footsteps. The second stick of incense is burnt to summon the ghost of a man.

"O listen to the voices of our hearts! All life is a dream, everything is fragile and dies. Only the way of Buddha offers a path to resurrection. The third stick of incense is burnt to summon the ghost of a man.

"O listen to the voices of our hearts! O Kings and Emperors of all Dynasties and Kingdoms, you who have been enthroned on high with mountains and rivers under your jurisdiction. Your reigns have lasted only a moment, and from far and wide the complaints of the people have never ceased. The cuckoo cries down the peach-blossom moon; the branches of the trees are dyed red with blood. May all these lonely ghosts of ancient kings come to attend this sacrifice.

"O listen to the voices of our hearts! O Lords and Generals, you who have raised gold tripods weighing a thousand *chin* and have created a great wall of flesh and blood. In vain you have sweated your horses, and in vain you have aspired after great fame. Alas, where are your fighting horses? The earth sighs, and wild grasses grow over the battlefields. May all the lonely ghosts of Generals and Lords come to attend this sacrifice.

"O listen to the voices of our hearts! O poets and scholars, you who have worked industriously embellishing sheets of white paper. In vain you have worked by the light of glow-worms and in vain you have worn dry your ink-wells. Alas, you have left nothing behind, and your souls long for their homes. May all the lonely ghosts of scholars and poets come to attend this sacrifice.

"O listen to the voices of our hearts! O beautiful virgins and ladies of the court, whose beauty may be compared with a summer day and whose fragrance is lovelier than cassia. You lose yourselves in the embraces of lovers, but after love comes the breaking of hearts. The trees wither; spring blossoms fade; the trees of your beauty become autumn skeletons. May the lonely ghosts of all beautiful women come to attend this sacrifice.

"O listen to the voices of our hearts! O beggars and thieves, all you who have lost your lives in the long waters or in the mouths of leopards and tigers! Your souls wander neighbourless in the world, and there is no justice to right your wrongs. Alas, the crows are cawing in the evening; rain falls, the autumn wind carries everything before it. May the lonely ghosts of the wronged and the injured come to attend this sacrifice.

"O listen to the voices of our hearts! O lonely ghosts of all places, O prostitutes and thieves, warriors and merchants, virgins and concubines, sailors and elephant-tamers, all you who have suffered and sinned, come to attend this sacrifice. . . ."

Even when they had finished singing these psalms the ceremony was not over. The small bells were ringing, the monk with the Buddha crown was folding and unfolding his beautiful hands, while the robes of the monks continually swayed softly; and slowly, but with ever-increasing momentum, the singing gained power and authority, rose higher, became piercingly sweet or suddenly subdued to a whisper—a whisper which could be heard, as the deer-skin drum is heard, twenty miles away. A few monks prayed on the bamboo fibre hassocks on the tiled floor, but those who sat at the table were not praying, and seemed indeed to be receiving the ghosts of the dead with their voices. The aged monk at the head of the table removed his crown, his robes were taken from him by a serving boy; and in the dark robes he continued to sing. A curious chased dish was placed before him; I was told it was a model of Mount Sumeru, on which the earth is suspended. The cakes on the table glittered in the pale blue flares of the acetylene lamps, and a small vase, perfectly white, was suddenly added to the unaccountable riches on the table. With this vase, by running his finger lightly round its rim, the priest blessed the food, and still singing, he began to throw crumbs of rice into the air, after blessing them. This was the monstrous food of the dead, who seemed to be present in the air and perhaps hiding behind the softly falling scarves which hung from the roof-beams. And still they sang, playing on conches and horns and flutes, their long bony fingers strumming the strings of violins. They were no

322

longer conscious of the world. The priest was lost in abstraction and gazed with half-closed eyes at the shape of Mount Meru inlaid with silver. The white vase shone, and the singing continued to the end. When the end came, showers of rice were being thrown to the waiting dead, voices were rising higher and higher, and still there was no sign that the music would come to a conclusion. Suddenly, as though in the middle of a theme, it ended; and at that moment we knew that we had seen the shadow of paradise before our eyes.

The horror began when we went to bed. In one of the large rooms on the wing of the monastery, there lived a former governor of Pekin, who amused himself in defeat by counting his beads and writing elegantly on white paper the poems he had written in his youth. There were two or three beds in the room, and the ex-governor was kind enough to supply biscuits. I shall remember this night for a long time. The sense of horror and loneliness began when he started talking of Pekin. There was a single rush-light. The walls were crumbling, the bamboo laths showing through the plaster; and I suppose the immense shadows we threw on the wall had something to do with it. Occasionally we heard "the wave of the pines", the soft sound made by the higher branches of the pines in the mountain wind, and then—still more occasionally—the hollow, vibrating tunelessness of the deer-skin drum. It was still dark and cloudy; strange shapes began to form outside the windows; the wind began to tear through the thin paper panes. The ex-governor, in his blue silk gown, walked up and down the room.

"It could have been saved, it could have been saved," he kept on repeating. "If the capital had been Pekin, and not Nanking——"

We sympathised with him. We ate his biscuits. We purred gently when he explained how he had increased the amenities of Pekin, which the Japanese are now tearing to pieces; and when he spoke of the huge ferro-concrete buildings which were being erected on the outskirts of Pekin, we sighed contemplatively and wondered whether anything would be left when at last we arrived. In 1937 he had lost his kingdom. Too proud to ask the Central Government for help, he lived in the monastery, perfectly content, growing fatter each day, and each day a few more wrinkles appeared on his brows. Occasionally he was solaced by the presence of his daughter, who was allowed to remain in the monastery against all the rules of the order.

Bergery had known Pekin in the days of her glory. He lived quietly in a small house inside the Forbidden City, planting stone-white magnolias and carefully tending three or four shoots of rhododendrons specially imported from Yunnan. He had had a heart-attack as a result of following the Abyssinian war, and he lived very quietly and secretly. He had met the governor occasionally, and they began to talk about Pekin as lovers will sometimes talk of their discarded mistresses. And so they continued, while the mosquitoes chirred in the yellow-washed room, and occasionally a flake of plaster would fall from the walls.

There was something terrible in this conversation of vanished glories. They would say: "Do you remember Prince Tao Belah in the summer after Wu Pei-fu ran away, and left everything to Feng Yu-hsiang? That was the summer of the great drought." It was like a nightmare. First one, then the other, would begin a flow of reminiscences, each one more sickly than the one which preceded it; till I had a vision of Pekin in all her glory suddenly falling into powder and leaving no more evidence of its existence than a few stones. I remembered Xanadu. It has been discovered at last, but not by the Chinese. Japanese archæologists have unearthed four or five enormous stones, a few inscriptions, the black hollows in the earth where wood has lain. Now there were only black-beetles and rubble. . . . "I never had time to count my art treasures," the governor was saying, and when Bergery asked him whether they were safely buried, he almost burst into tears.

When we went to bed, it was long past midnight. The sky had cleared, and the mosquitoes delighted in the warmth. It was as though millions of mosquitoes had suddenly entered the room, whirring their black wings and drowning the sounds of voices. At night the sound of someone chewing biscuits can be pure horror. So it was now, in the silence that followed the last of these terrible memories; and when the rush-lamp was put out, and we went to sleep under beautifully embroidered silk quilts, the night became more intolerable than ever, for we were all dreaming of the vanished glories of the past. It was then that the horror began or perhaps it was a quarter of an hour later, a horror which made us sick to death, and showed our worn faces the next morning like the faces of people who are about to be executed, or have been executed already.

324

I do not know why bed-bugs in Chinese monasteries are worse than bed-bugs in Chinese hotels. I only know it is so. They lived in the blankets, in the thin seams of brocade, even inside the silk covering; but at night they swarmed over us. In the morning they would die, but they made the very best use of the hours that remained to them, and they crept under our pyjamas and made sleep impossible, and life no longer desirable. They were quite remorseless, and they were quite impossible to find. All through that night, while the deer-skin drum could be heard beating at intervals, they assaulted us from every direction, and though sometimes we would catch them, and a small silken bladder of blood would be squashed between our finger-tips, they had nearly always escaped when we searched for them. They have gone before you feel the scratching pain. They raise horrible red blisters on your flesh, they jump easily from one end of your body to the other, they slip between your fingers, they crowd in your hair and walk solemnly over your face, producing the most comical and the most terribly unexpected lumps on lips, nose, ears and eyelids. And you fight them all night, with never a moment's rest, until you are exhausted and you lie back, surrendering to them, but then they climb all over you and once again you begin the unequal contest. You no longer have the feeling that you are fighting an animal smaller than a finger-nail. You are Beowulf fighting with Grendel. Not one animal, but a million animals, and all of them have hairy arms, and all of them bite. I cursed and groaned, and shortly afterwards I heard Bergery and the governor groaning, and the rustle of the quilts, and sometimes one of them would get up, walk to the window and return slowly to bed. The beds were against three sides of the wall. A faint moon rose, and the mosquito-nets shone like white ghosts floating above the bodies of my friends. They said nothing. All night, there was this interminable terror, and when dawn came, we were fast asleep and the bed-bugs were having the time of their lives.

A monk came in when the sun was high in the sky with a message from the abbot, and some flowers which he had gathered with his own hands in the garden. We dressed and shaved slowly. There were weals on my shoulders and a red road across my chest and stomach. One of Bergery's eyes had swollen to an enormous size. Only the Governor of Pekin was apparently untouched, but he looked weary beyond endurance, pale, no longer fretful, but as though the life had been washed out of his dark bruised eyes. We

325

went out into the garden, where the white mist settled still on the flowers, and the most heavenly blue sky brooded over the temple eaves.

"The requiem for the dead . . ." Bergery murmured, thinking of what had happened the night before; and looking at his swollen eyelid, the size and colour of a small red pear, I burst out laughing. The abbot was coming to meet us. In one hand, carefully and tenderly he held an enormous fan.

September 18th . . . IN CHINA autumn is the season of the dead, but autumn mornings are more beautiful than other mornings. The river lay below us, white in the misty thickness of green pines and evergreens, and the yellow gorges glinted in the sunlight. A few white-sailed sampans were gliding along the river, and through Bergery's opera-glasses I watched the wind softly blowing on the billowing sails.

There are mornings in China when the earth seems to be sighing, and other mornings when the earth seems to be breathing contentedly after the battles of the night, and the clash of the moon is forgotten in the vapours of mist. I do not know why, but I find that as I grow older, beauty hurts more. This morning, at high noon, as we were walking over the raised mounds between the rice-fields, we were both so overcome by the beauty of the place that we were weeping. There is something intangible in the beauty of a Chinese morning. The blue sky sparkles more brilliantly in China than anywhere else—sheets of blue powder stream across the heavens, each powder-point glittering with crystal light. The earth shone, the green of the new rice vivid against the blue sky, and there were deep green pools of shadow under the trees.

Bergery talked for a long while about the Requiem. He looked older, there were dark lines on his forehead and his flesh looked worn, saggy about the cheek-bones, the hair in violent disorder.

"Stevenson lived to forty-five, Proust to fifty-one, Chaucer to sixty—it's surprising how long authors live," he said, and suddenly returning to the old subject. "I should hate to have the Requiem sung when I am dead. I should feel that it was impossible to remain dead, and I would come to life on the wave of one of their trumpets and look at the high priest throwing bread-crumbs in the air and burst out laughing; and then I would watch their beautiful hands, and cry out of sheer impatience, because my fingers will never make those lovely patterns." Immediately after-
326

wards he returned to the subject of writers. "I don't know how they live so long. The strain in a great writer must be terrible, for the great writer penetrates the characters of others far more than actors penetrate characters. To live so many lives, to live them simultaneously, to be always at the beck and call of the creations of your imagination—no, that is terrible! Think how they lived! Stevenson in Samoa, Heine in his mattress grave in Paris, Proust in his cork-lined *apartment*, Spenser always remaining humble towards my lord of Leicester and yet hating him from the bottom of his heart, Chaucer shedding tears of wrath over the villainies of the people. . . . No, the writers have the worst of it. Life deals with them with splendid effrontery, cursing their existence and making great literature out of their sufferings."

He was enormously enjoying himself. He insisted that all writers were physically weak, and their physical weakness implied a greater mental courage and a habit of revenge. The really important thing was to realise our limitations. He began to talk about death. He said he had read somewhere that one man out of nine dies in agony. "We die instinctively now, like beasts, but in the eighteenth century men died all over Europe with grace. We have lost the art of dying." He said he would like to be buried without a coffin, on the spur of one of the granite rocks overlooking the river, at high noon, when the eagles and snipe are wheeling over the green crown of the forests. "The old writers, all my generation, are dead," he said. "A new generation will grow up after this war, and they will have none of our traditions, but they will look forward, as eagles look in the sunlight, caring nothing for the past which has misled them. A new generation will appear without a conscience, but with a deep respect for the past—a respect which will grow in the measure of their failure to understand it. Do you remember the stone Buddha of Chandi Mendut? Perhaps we loved it more than the original worshippers, because we failed to understand it and yet it was so overwhelmingly beautiful that we were defeated by it. So it will be in the future. The young will come and inherit their kingdoms."

I am beginning to think that Bergery is shuffling out of his past and living only for the moment; and perhaps for this reason he understands the war more fully. It is difficult to explain the charm of his voice, the gentleness of his manner, his continual animation and his great sorrow. So men must have lived on these same mountains at the end of the T'ang Dynasty, when the Court fled to Szechuan, remote, imperturbable, seeing everything from the perspective of their high mountains.

When we returned the abbot was waiting for us. He carried in his hand two small jars of scented herbs, which he asked us to tend carefully in his memory. Shortly afterwards we left the monastery, and came down the mountain-side in chairs, and it was strange to think of Bergery cooped up under those softly-flowing curtains, carried in a chair on the backs of two sweating coolies whose brown shoulders shone like molten copper throughout the journey down the mountain. At the foot of the mountain we parted, Bergery to his castle on the cliff edge higher up the river and I to the University. All that night I wondered whether he had reached the house safely. It grew dark early. With high mountains all round us we could not expect to see more than a brief sunlight each day. But it was only when I reached home that I remembered his parting words, for somehow their significance had been hidden from me while we were talking. "Come soon—in the winter it may be too late."

I do not know how long he has to live, but I am oppressed by the thought of his death. He will not die as other men die; and I am sure he will not hang himself like Toller. He will go out in a blaze of glory, but in what manner and in which month I have no idea. All that was best in the old Europe existed in Bergery: if he survives he will be able to give us a clue to the future.

September 20th . . . We have been hardened in Soviet Russia, and though we have cursed those who permitted such ghastly brutishness, at least we have looked into the eyes of death and learned to love life as never before; and we have overcome the weakness of our hearts. We are glad to do our difficult part and see our soft hearts writhing with the pain of longing, and grow harder and more mature. We often pray that we may survive, but still more we are ready for death. We are ready to step on those thousands of hidden mines, we are ready to be shot by cunning bullets from well-hidden Soviet snipers. We are ready for everything, and the gentle atmosphere of our homes seems remote as though it was a partly forgotten dream. We look upon the European nations as though they were part of an unreal life we shall never more encounter on this earth.

I have copied this from a quotation published in the *National*

Herald, translated from a German war correspondent's report of the war in Russia. Of all that has been published since the beginning of the war, this is the most revealing statement I have read. The war in Spain was not like this, nor was the beginning of the war in France. But since Dunkirk, since the moment when the Germans attained a pure hegemony over Europe, the atmosphere of the nightmare, which no one believes, for he knows that he has only to wait for a few more hours until the dawn, has continued with ever-increasing velocity. From Chungking, this kind of war is understandable, for we live ourselves in the atmosphere of a nightmare, in darkness and astonishment; but not once in the battlefield of Changsha were these things present to our minds. But surely the Japanese think in this way!

As the war continues, prolonged beyond the endurance of its protagonists, so must this element of the nightmare enter more profoundly in the minds of the strategicians. How does one fight against an enemy who believes that he is sleeping, walking, as Hitler says, with the certainty of a somnambulist? The war of swords is only a part of the necessary war. The war, by which one strips the illusion from the enemy's eyes, may be more important and more formidable than the war by which he is defeated in the field. And what if we ourselves have illusions? Must we fight an implacable war to remove the blindness in our own eyes?

In the long run half of our war is against the enemy and half against ourselves. The nightmare of continental Europe has spread until it touches the whole world. What if suddenly men should wake up, tear the veils from their eyes and notice for the first time the frightful things they are doing in their dreams? The war which kills the enemy kills also the victor unless, at the very last moment, he can tear the veil from his eyes. He is right to fight, and perhaps he has a right to destroy whole cities, but he has a still clearer right and a more urgent duty to realise that he is living in a nightmare, which is not necessary in the sense that the dawn and the sunrise are necessary. Perhaps something will be born of this travail. Perhaps we shall wake up, as opium-smokers wake up after a long night of exhaustion, sweating in every pore, having cast out for ever the drug which oppresses us. But many opium-smokers die by the wayside and many fail to sweat out the drug. But what if the nightmare should kill us? What if we, or the Germans who invented it, begin to believe in the nightmare to the exclusion of everything else? Will the world perish? Or are people too strong to be exhausted by a drug whose power surely is less than that which the Japanese, who try to drug all the Chinese in the occupied areas, profess that it possesses?

In Germany—the nightmare. In Japanese-occupied China—opium. There is little difference between them, for both paralyse the nerve centres and lead to a deadening of the emotions which are natural to healthy people. The three hundred and fifty millions who live in the Fortress of Europe, which is only a fortress in the sense that it allows the giant immunity from the law-giver, and the countless millions under Japanese domination in the East are in danger of losing their nervous systems by a systematic effort of brutalisation. No conqueror in the past has wielded such destructive weapons before. But the danger only begins here. The nightmare has no boundaries, and it is the Germans who are probably most conscious of it, for at least they have time to think and grieve, while the rest of Europe is too concerned with the battle for its own existence, and the Chinese are too concerned with their implacable vendetta against the Japanese to succumb to the drug. Therefore we may expect the nightmare to be a double-edged weapon. "We look upon the European nations as though they were part of an unreal life, which we shall never more encounter on this earth." But do the European nations, struggling for survival, think that they will never more appear on the earth, when they have no other ambition except to dominate the nightmare? And so I imagine that they know in their hearts that even the longest night and the longest nightmare cannot endure for ever, and when the dawn comes even the Germans will throw off the dream with a shrug of their shoulders, hardly believing that they have walked over precipices at night. And this perhaps is the most dangerous point of all, for the nightmare which filled them with terror during the night will be forgotten as easily as though they had only been weeping. How does one exorcise a nightmare from a nation's soul? And still more important, how does one remind a nation that nightmares are dangerous and in a certain sense may be considered as crimes justifying the penalty of death?

St. Paul said that the sufferings of the present time are not worthy to be compared to that glory. But surely in this age they are worthy of all glory, all tears, all penitence. We cannot calculate sufferings. We cannot make a calculation of this man's sin and this man's terror. Mathematics is useless here, and must remain useless until we can measure the value of a single tear. There may come a point—it was a point which was reached three or four times in the Middle Ages—when the pure spectacle of suffering becomes so overwhelming that the masses of the people will turn into religious fanatics, and the flagellants may yet appear in the streets of Moscow, London and New York. But it is more likely, and indeed extremely probable, that they will appear in Germany; and perhaps it is true, as I once suspected, that the flagellants arose as an unconscious effort to revive in reality the sufferings that the people of Italy had experienced during the *nightmare* of the Black Death.

We can only fight and pray. Later, there will come a time of reckoning, but in the final instance it will not be a reckoning with the people but with their souls. The nightmare was already evident in Germany before the war. I felt it in the Ringstrasse in Vienna in March, 1938, when the continual maniacal cries of "Sieg Heil!" reverberated with the unmistakable accents of people who have no idea what they are saying, and whose faces the next morning showed signs of an immature awakening. But the real awakening will be something more terrible than anything that happened in those early days. It will come suddenly, as an avalanche comes. It will come with feverish force, with the sense of a sudden illumination. At that moment we may expect the veils to be lifted from all our lives.

Bergery believes that we must worship or die, but I prefer to believe that if we wait patiently there will come a splendid sunrise. I like to think of the Duke of Chu, who was so anxious to carry his golden principles into action that whenever he saw anything that did not tally with them, he would look up in thought till day gave way to night; and if by good luck he found the answer, he would sit on waiting for the dawn.

September 23rd . . . ONE of those days in autumn when a thick white mist like flakes of ice settles on the river, and you know that there will be no clouds and the sun will shine on the fields of winter barley. I walked out in the mist, seeing the grey trees intangible in all this whiteness, the sun above burning a great hole in the white cloud overhead like a hayrick on fire. Then one by one the houses on the opposite shore appeared, very bright, like the whites of eyes, and the river below, golden in the faint sunrise, like a mouth. The illusion of watching the appari-

331

tion of some beloved face with clearly defined features continued for perhaps five minutes, but at last even this illusion disappeared in a moment which was still more miraculous—the mist dissolved, there was a liquefaction of blood, and suddenly the blue river, the yellow gorges and the immense sky swung out of the mist, trembling with dew, glittering with a thousand points of liquid light, so vivid that you could almost hear the clash of cymbals as the whole earth danced into life.

And then in the evening another miracle. Crossing the river at night, under a faint moon. A few naked haulers were still wading knee-deep in the river, dragging the long hemp-ropes attached to the masts of the sampans, their bronze bodies shining in the faint moonlight. Some trick of the light made them appear larger than they were, so that they resembled archaic gods on their way to perform a sacrifice. But there was still another miracle in store. High up on the beach great baulks of timber floated up during the floods lay motionless and quiet. The moon came out, and I remember that at that moment the naked haulers looked smaller than ever, for they threw small black shadows; but the young poet Yao Pen, who was by my side, pointed to the great white baulks of timber shining in the moonlight and whispered: "The bones of the earth." And for a brief moment it seemed as though they were indeed the bones of the earth, huge, terrifying, monstrously enlarged by the moonlight. And I remember I thought: "If they perish, the earth also will perish," but later, as we walked across the deserted beach I remembered that in the morning I had seen the young earth dancing in all her finery, and it seemed curious and strange that we should have seen her in such differing disguises at such short intervals of time. Tomorrow, perhaps, there will be clouds over the whole sky, and we shall not see the earth at all.

September 26th . . . DISCUSSING Chinese poetry and calligraphy. The ecstasy which is so easy to reach when writing Chinese characters. The intoxication of pure form. Today I wrote the simple character for "jade", and my teacher said that it was exactly in the style of Ssu Tung-po, and I remembered that at the moment of writing the character I had in my mind the vision of a great lake, with willows and some dark red trees planted among them, and somewhere on a hill-top a great walled palace with yellow roof-tiles. Perhaps I knew, but I had forgotten that Ssu

Tung-po was once governor of the great lake at Hangchow and planted many willow-trees there with his own hands. But I am still mystified by the only example of my Chinese calligraphy which looks even remotely respectable.

September 27th . . . I HAVE written to Bergery, telling him the story of the death of the great Chinese poet Li Ho, which I learnt today. When the poet was dying, he saw in broad daylight a man dressed in purple, riding a crimson dragon and holding a tablet on which were inscribed strange hieroglyphics like ancient writings or like the signs made by lightning in the sky. Li Ho could not read the words on the tablet, but suddenly he left the bed and bowed low to the young man riding the dragon, and he murmured weakly: "I am reluctant to leave my mother, who is old and sick." Then he heard the man who was dressed in purple laughing and saying: "The god has built a tower of white jade and wishes you to immortalise it in writing. It is very pleasant in Heaven, and the life is not hard." Then the poet wept, and all around him saw him weeping, and thereupon he gave up the ghost. And then a mist rose from the window of his chamber and some people heard the sound of flutes and departing chariots; and when they heard it, the mother forbade them to moan, and they remained silent for a while. Then they knew that the poet was indeed dead.

September 30th . . . A LONG procession forming in the town. A grey day. No clouds, but a kind of grey pall over the sky like lead or like brains after they have lain for a few hours on a battlefield. There were puddles everywhere—perhaps it rained in the night. A soldier, in an old brown uniform, beating a drum, and the procession very silent and still, as though not walking but gliding—a procession in a dream. I followed it down to the river, thinking it was part of the autumn sacrifices, though I should have known by the expression of the faces that it was something still more important than a sacrifice to the gods. A few boys were shouting, someone was weeping and somewhere in the centre of the crowd a man was moaning and complaining in a tired voice. At first I did not see him, but when we were half-way down to the beach I heard many voices complaining and noticed that they came from a group of four men, naked to the waist, their hands tied with rough cord behind their backs. Their bodies were not brown like the bodies of the peasants, but pearl-white and thin, the flesh touching the white prominent bones. They seemed to be drugged. Suddenly I thought: "Yes, this is a Buddhist ceremony. They are going to offer a sacrifice to the river." We were very near the beach. One of the men, shorter than the others, with a great hairy black mole just below his underlip, was struggling and attempting to break the cords which bound his wrist. From time to time he shouted, or rather barked, in a voice which was half-way between a cough and the bark of a sheep-dog: "I am not guilty! I am not guilty!" And immediately afterwards he cursed and sat down on the stones, refusing to get up. The soldiers wore black and carried shining carbines. They lifted him up very tenderly. He was no longer cursing. In a kind of dull stupor, walking a little behind the others, occasionally throwing up his head, his mouth twitching nervously, he followed them to the river's edge. Then the crowd was told to move away, and only the children continued to speak excitedly, pulling faces and jeering at the condemned men. The river seemed to be still, and suddenly the wind dropped out of the immense white sail of a sampan in mid-stream.

We waited. We did not know why we waited. It was like watching a play. The soldiers stood at attention. The prisoners also stood at attention. The soldiers moved away, and the prisoners edged a little towards the river—but I have no idea what happened afterwards. I think I noticed first the scent of powder, not acrid, but slightly sweet, and then a little later the gasp of astonishment and fear and understanding which ran through the crowd, and long after that the sounds of the rifle-shots. I turned away. There was some sound of moaning, and then a long silence. When we were perhaps fifty yards away, we heard the sound of scuffling, and that was the most terrible, for there were no voices, only the slither of stones and human bodies and no cries of pain.

In the city there are already notices saying that three famous bandits and a murderer were executed by order of the mayor. The orders had been prepared beforehand, and the ink was still wet and running a little on the paper.

October 1st . . . A FAINT sun, high above the clouds. Stalingrad still occupies our thoughts. I have asked one of the students about the progress of the war in China, for he has just come through the occupied area. It is still, of course, possible to travel

334

from Pekin to Chungking, and often the Japanese are delighted to be rid of the Chinese in the occupied area, but according to the student fighting is continual, relentless, and yet so restricted in its shape that it is difficult to record its pattern in news bulletins. There are lines which each side have taken up. They are determined to maintain these lines. The Chinese are waiting for heavy guns and airfields, for though airfields can be built by coolie labour, there are not enough coolies to make them, and there are no bull-dozers. Yet, without artillery and without many airfields, the Chinese continue fighting the ceaseless guerrilla war to which they have been trained.

He spoke of starvation in Shanghai, starvation in Honan, starvation in Kwangtung. Everywhere starvation. A curious story. When he was crossing the frontier he came to the centre of the no man's land, where nothing grows. "It was like T. S. Eliot's *Waste Land*. No farmers, but the rice had been planted years before and had rotted. All black. But sometimes, among the blackened rice-crops, you see a hoe or a plough or a dead bullock exactly as they were left years ago." There is a belt ten miles deep where nothing grows, and he thinks that years later, when they make an aerial survey of China, the belt will still be visible, though the earth has been replanted. "When I was crossing the border, I knew what it was like to live in Eliot's *Waste Land*. And perhaps there are many other waste lands in the world, in Poland and Russia." He had been robbed on the journey by a Japanese soldier—nearly everyone seems to have robbed—but he bore no bitterness. I can see him still, jauntily crossing the waste land, delighted at the spectacle of a hidden hoe which revealed the presence of an ancient farmer who has long since disappeared from the world.

October 3rd . . . THE sun came out this morning. We went to the hot springs which lie in the gorges about two miles north from here. I know nothing quite so beautiful as this river, and we have been discussing how after the war we shall make a film of China around this river. The film will be in technicolour, the story of one of China's rivers through the seasons. It will begin in the early morning, when the sun is beginning to ripen on the granite hills and the boatmen are awakening under the thatched roofs of their sampans. There will be sea-gulls whistling among the pebbles, and the soaring black flight of the evil kites—

335

"the kites", as one of my students said, "with the perforated wings". And then the camera will follow the boat-boys as they strip and dive in the river, and the gulls creeping down from the sky when breakfast is being prepared on the small earthenware stoves in the bows, and the old men smoking pipes, and the young girls washing in the lea of the boat, and then the camera will follow the night-watchman, who has been beating a wooden gong at all the watches of the night, and comes down at last to the river to see that everything is in order among the moored boats. And sometimes, when the river has fallen, the half-naked boat-men will push the boat solidly into the water, with all its freight of children and screaming women, and there are other times when the river rises suddenly and the boats are dashed against the high rocks before anybody has awakened. The film will show all this. It will show the mist and the clouds, and the sodden heat of summer and the shivering boatmen as they crouch over the fires in winter. And the silence—the long silence that follows the break-ing of the fast, and the smell of old rice, and the scouring of the wooden rice-bowls, and the appetites of these men who work even harder than ricksha-pullers. All this must be shown or sug-gested. Then slowly, accustoming themselves to the shock of cold water, with the mist still hanging over them, they push the boats out into the river, uncoil the hauling ropes and take their places and wrap white slings round their bodies and begin to haul, shouting: "Ai-ya! Ai-yo! Ai-ya!" though there are no sounds in the world except those which they have learnt to speak from their childhood which can imitate the terrible force of those words. And then the film changes. High up on one of the gorges there is a small temple, painted red and gold. The sunlight travels down the pillars, the monks awake, you watch them hoeing vegetables in the gardens, you see them at meditation, you see the abbot striking them when they fall asleep and their confusion when they wake. And the face of the great Buddha, hidden in a tall glass case, smiling among butter-lamps, and the sacristan ringing his bell, and the mournful prayers to welcome the sunlight, and the palm-leaf hassocks, and the mortuary tablets, and the loveliness of the view from the high gorges into the valley. And then a sea-gull, whose flight the camera follows, will bring us once more to the river, the patched sails of the sampans, which are all colours —blue, green, red, even bright yellow—sampans seen from great heights as I have often watched them, entranced by their silence
336

and the slowness of their motion—sampans seen among the rocky torrents as I see them nearly every day, entranced by the terrible bow waves which are thrown up, and the naked haulers half buried in the blue river, yet still straining doggedly at the ropes, still shouting "Ai-ya! Ai-yo! Ai-ya!" and then again the silence as the heavy boat slides into the main stream. And all the villages they pass, the smoke and the dust and the small red fires burning at night. And the old bearded overseer, gazing at the river with expressionless contempt, smoking his long-handled silver pipe, and then again in the evening the young boys swimming and the sunlight fading out from the land, while their white shoulders catch the last dying gleam of the sun.

Perhaps this film should be taken on the Yangtse, but the Chialing is a small river and it would be easier to make a unity of the film. I say the Chialing is small, but there are days when it is monstrous, when it is wider than the Thames at Westminster and creeps over the foot-hills, and there are other days when you can almost wade across it. We always know when it rains in Tibet, for the yellow water comes running down, and sometimes there is a small bore, a pillar of water running towards Chungking. And we know too when a river boat is passing without looking up, for it sends such a wave against the small boats which carry us across to the town that we are almost thrown overboard, and the boatman balancing himself on the spur of the boat sways backwards and forwards as though he were hanging from a pendulum dropping from the centre of the sky.

And there are other things in this film. I would have the camera floating like a bird over the gorges at every hour of the day; it would swing down upon the sampans in the blue misty evening, and rise to follow the sunset over the mountains. In the evening, as the sun creeps up and down the valleys, setting light to the pine groves and the green clusters of bamboos, the mountains turn all colours—now they are blue icebergs, wave upon wave of blue icebergs disappearing into the faint blue of distance; and then again when the sun rises, the tips of the mountains catch the light like wooden roses ignited with petroleum, blazing from mountain peak to peak. Or again, the dust whirling in tall columns on a summer afternoon, or again the rippling of the wind coming over the waters, and one by one the torn sails of the sampans billow out, or again the white mist, tangible almost, a solid sheet of white, descending and rising over the valleys. In China the wildest scenery is compassionate; and perhaps this is the reason why the Chinese remain in this inhospitable land. There is a blue glitter in the sky which I have seen nowhere else; and there are clouds whose savagery is indicated by their shape—they are dragons and headless crows and vast engines of destruction, with lightning riding on the cloud's hem. I would have in this film all the sounds of China—the hollow drone of the deer-skin drum, the queer whistle of the wind against the jutting edges of the gorges, the bells of high monasteries, the mumbled prayers of the old women lighting red tapers on the stone shrines which stand at the entrance of every village. Sometimes the bearded god in these shrines is painted with gold leaf, but more often he is crumbling stone; yet greater reverence appears to be paid to the aged gods than those who are decorated in all the finery of startling colours. The Szechuanese, like the Hunanese, have a passion for pepper; and with pepper goes a love for bright colours. Yet in the whole of this province there are no more than twenty or thirty houses decorated with yellow tiles and painted eaves. There is something dead in this province, and something deathly in the air; and perhaps the explanation lies in the murder which took place towards the end of the Ming Dynasty, a murder which can be only equalled by the Mongols. The story is familiar to all. The governor of the province became a homicidal maniac. He gave orders to his bodyguard to kill everyone, men, women and children; and as evidence of their obedience he ordered that the fingers of the slain should be given to him. He himself murdered eight hundred of his concubines. His bodyguard swept down on unsuspecting villages and exterminated everyone; and it was said that forty million people were killed in the space of a few years. People left their farms and hid in the high mountains, but the mountains were inhabited by leopards and tigers, as they are today, and so they died. For a hundred years the trees grew freely where previously there were farmsteads, and perhaps this homicidal maniac came as a blessing in disguise, for the earth could renew itself for a brief space, till at last the Emperor in Pekin, hearing that a whole province had been depopulated, ordered that the villagers of the southern provinces of Honan and the northern provinces of Hunan should take part in a forced emigration to the rich woodlands of the south. And that is why, even to this day, Szechuanese contains many dialect words which are to be found in the north.

338

But the film would only suggest this. It would show the shelving rice-fields by the river's edge, the women in blue trousers wading knee-deep in winter fields, guiding the black buffaloes through the brown mud. It would show the white clouds reflected in perfect miniature on the lakes of rice and the homecoming of the villagers in the smoky evenings. It would show the dragon-boat festival, when golden boats race one another in the flood-tide, and small cups of leaves and sweet rice are thrown on the waters in memory of Chu Yuan, the loyal minister of the State of Ch'u. And it would end as the last splinters of light disappear in the summer forges and a grey wind ruffles the sails of the beached sampans, and small red fires appear on the bank. In China the rivers are still the most populous roads. Men and women carry nearly everything that is small, but the rivers carry the granite piles and the great loads of rice. So the film would contain the whole of China; it would reflect the soul of China as nothing else, not even the fast-disappearing religions reflect it. The rivers have a life of their own. Like the Himalayas, they are perfectly impassive and care nothing for the lives of the people who live on its banks; and therefore they have achieved a kind of greatness and they are indeed the gods of the place, but the gods are so unapproachable that no Chinese worships them. He worships the earth only, perhaps because the earth is closer to him and somehow less impassive.

I should like to see this film. I should like to see many films on China. The people are superbly photogenic, and though the landscape is too tenuous, too frail almost, the people stand out against it as the enormous decorative kings of Chinese drama stand out against the painted backcloth of their dramas. No one has yet explored the possibility of the film industry in China. Until recently actors and actresses were regarded as the lowest classes of society. But in the house of a film actress in Chungking I have seen stills taken in Hongkong which are more dramatic than anything that I have ever seen in Hollywood. The Chinese are essentially dramatic. You have only to walk down a street in a village on a hot sultry day, when nerves are frayed beyond endurance, and you will see a family taking part in a heated discussion. They lift their arms, they appeal to Heaven, they roll their eyes, make sudden vicious movements and call upon the bystanders to witness the perfidy of the offending member of the family; and yet no blows are struck. Gesture, the most minute flicker of a long sleeve, the most grotesque faces and the most appropriate positions become the vehicle of an enchantment which makes everyone happy. A ricksha coolie knocks down a policeman. He makes the most abject bow. He runs to the assistance of the policeman, he howls with grief, he receives all the policeman's kicks with the greatest equanimity; but when at last the policeman has explained the exact details of his pedigree, when the bystanders are waiting with blood-thirsty impatience for the blow which will cleave the ricksha-driver in two, both the policeman and the coolie burst out laughing. Tragedy is so common in China that it has become a habit of gestures, which the old Chinese stage perfectly understood and raised to the highest power of communication. The Chinese will always be the world's best tragic actors, for they have known tragedy more intimately than any other race; and simply because they are such great tragedians, they will always be good comic actors. I have seen unbelievable cruelty among the peasants, but I am told that it is rare in other provinces, and I can well believe it. The portrait of the Chinese gentleman, with his almost superhuman equanimity, still remains; equanimity is still the greatest virtue; and the Generalissimo is a living example of that superb equanimity which has come down through the ages. And in this film of China I would show the faces of the peasants, faces which are deeply engraved by the weather, but are almost expressionless, faces which can be seen in the villages along the river and in the gods in the temples, faces which are somehow withdrawn from the world, not only because they are weighed down by the terrors of existence, but also because they belong to the race which possesses a ritual of gesture through which even tragedy may be exorcised.

October 6th . . . No SUN. I have been dreaming again of Bali, where there is much Chinese blood. I remember being taken along a woodland path, through a maze of small wooden houses, until we came to a clearing where small girls about eight years of age were dancing the infinitely complicated dances of Bali. They wore the golden head-dress that all Balinese dancers wear; and yet there was on their childish faces an expression of such divinity that in the smoking light of torches they seemed indeed to be goddesses walking the earth. Their eyes were closed. Cymbals and drums were being beaten. The forest came nearer, and we felt closed in, impenetrably surrounded by the dark cedars.

340

And still the dancing continued; the painted faces were silent; the thin bare arms held flowers above their heads; hens fluttered; and in the silence we could hear the dancers taking breath for a divine conversation. The movements of their fingers were expressive of the bewilderment of the night. And then—and then, in the mounting clash of cymbals, they began to sing. . . .

I remember all this perfectly, and I know that there are temples in China where the same sense of the divine nature of man is understood and celebrated by the priests. In the whole of the Buddhist church there is only one great ceremony—the ceremony for the dead. But the world is shattered almost beyond repair, and there are too many dead. We need a ceremony for the living.

October 7th . . . No SUN. There will be a few days of sunshine before March, but they will not be many. Here at least it is better. In Chungking there is rain, petrol fumes, yellow rock: there is no sign of grass.

I have been writing here, between bouts of sickness, the first chapters of the long story of China which will probably be called "Love and Peace". I began it in the summer, only a short while ago; but already it is winter. At night, after classes, in the deserted hotel bedroom, among rats and lice, it will be written. And while the thick white mist rolls up to the gates of the hotel, surely it is better to think of China in the summer, and the figure of Rose, Lifeng and Shaofeng walking under the bright cedars. Their lives will be the life of China, flowing tumultuously across the country, lives which are never-ending because China is never-ending. All the reverence I have for China will flow into their slim figures.

Perhaps it is true that one writes best in illness and filth. These small unwashed cubicles in the hotel are the home of red-bellied rats who nest in the bathrooms under the great earthenware tubs. Occasionally the bath-boy will throw boiling water over them. They do not die. Scalded, their bellies turn bright pink. There are more rats in this village than I ever dreamed possible.

October 8th . . . No SUN. I am still writing "Love and Peace", but I am too much in love with the English prose classes at the University to spend much time over it this evening. The candle flickers, and the rat has gone away. This morning, for five

341

minutes, a pale sun shone through the clouds. There is a greyness in the countryside which resembles the greyness of a dying man.

October 9th . . . WITH my students I went to Hot Springs. The lotoses and the willows are dead. Only a few leaves of the lotoses emerge above the silent pools. Above us the mountain was shrouded with mist. No sky, no sun.

October 10th . . . THIS morning J. said: "In China winter is a time for contemplation. In the north we lie on our *k'angs,* smoke cigarettes and work at our lessons. All the best books have been written in the winter." It may be true. I hope it is, but I am beginning to dread the passage across the river every morning, when a cold wind rushes out of the gorges.

My friends, the geologists, are going up to Kansu by air. "There is milk and honey, and perhaps more minerals in the earth than anyone has ever known. We shall be completely isolated, but the air there is dry and we shall no longer suffer from a Chungking winter." They look pleased, though they are a little afraid of bandits. They have reminded us of two phrases which are common in Szechuan. "In Szechuan the dogs bark at the sun." "Young man, do not go to Canton; old man, do not go to Szechuan."

October 11th . . . AMONG students and professors it is possible to forget the mist and the rain. Coming over to the University early in the morning under a varnished paper umbrella, it is curious how the atmosphere of mist and turbulence departs in the quiet of the class-rooms. The lecture over, the mist crowds round us again. And looking at these students, knowing how weak they are and what they have already suffered, it is curious that they should have come to Szechuan, for they hunger for the sun. But the sun protects us from Japanese bombs, and the University has suffered sufficiently. More and more it seems to me that the choice of Chungking as the war-time capital is one of the greatest gambits of a government in power.

October 12th . . . JAUNDICE. Fainted twice in the street, and was carried home. I looked in the mirror. Quite yellow, and deep blue rings under the eyes. A feeling of weakness, but how exciting the moment when you fall asleep and all this weakness disappears. Suddenly strong, you go running after dreams.

342

But I object to jaundice on æsthetic grounds. One should not have bright yellow hands and yellow eyeballs. One should not have blue rings round the eyes. One should not feel incapable even of reading—that is the worst.

October 20th . . . I SHALL ever be grateful to the professors of this University, especially Liang Tsong-tai. There have been constant visitors, and we have now arranged a beautiful trick against the god of diseases. My carrots and potatoes are brought in a thermos-flask; and though I empty them out of the flask with the greatest difficulty, it is good to eat and feel the strength returning again. But what worries me so much is that the English prose class has only just started.

October 27th . . . No CLOUDS, or rather clouds everywhere. No sky, no sun.

1943

April 15th . . . Winter has passed, and spring comes round again. The small flakes of rice in the rice-fields vanished, the heavy red mud of Szechuan changed inexplicably to dull yellow and green, and once more the sails of the sampans going up-stream are white. This winter was like the travel of an aeroplane through heavy clouds; no sign of the sun, and often we were freezing round small charcoal fires. There were tunnels of grey air through which we tried to find our way; but it was all un-necessary. If we had had patience, we should not have com-plained.

I am less sorry for the students and professors than for the farmers. Even in the winter fog, they ploughed knee-deep through their rice-fields. The swollen hook-worm veins of their legs grew larger; under their immense straw helmets they seemed to be bowed down to the earth, and you saw them in the distance, moving slowly against the ashen grey of the fields where no plants could yet be seen; and as they walked homeward they did not sing. All through the winter I thought of that journey to Kweilin, when suddenly the white towers and pinnacles of the place shone through the mist as we approached; and of the wealth of that city which is so much wealthier than ours. There you could buy pig-skins, ivories, tiger-skins, small lacquer buddhas; there were shops full of jewellery and still more shops full of bales of cloth. We are poorer here. There is less wealth in Szechuan, for com-munication is difficult; and in these outlying villages, communica-tion is almost impossible.

But spring has come! There was a day when the mist disap-peared so dramatically that one feels it will never return. There are good auguries, too. On Chinese New Year, there was snow for the second year in succession, and we feel sure that the war will end soon. New buildings are going up on the University campus. Even in the village, there are signs of returning prosperity; but perhaps it is only because there are more men smoking their long pipes in the tea-shops, and more girls in light costumes walking under the alders.

Already there have been air-raids or air-alarms, but we face them with more confidence because we have seen the sun.

April 17th . . . THE small shoots of brilliant yellow rice are coming up through the muddy fields. The Indian corn is three inches high; it will grow to ten feet before the summer. Dogs did not bark in the winter. Now, as you pass the small farms with their single thatched cottage where the pigs and dogs root in the long shadows, you hear the pigs grunting and the dogs howling all night. Silence has gone from the world.

K., who stays on a farm, told me this morning of the mysterious death of his farmer's chickens. He swears that they were killed by ferrets, for the blood had been sucked from a wound in the leg and they lay stiff and cold in the courtyard. But the farmers say that there are no such things as ferrets, for no one has seen them. They come at night, gliding like shadows, invisible because they are so small. "But it was ferrets," K. says, with conviction. "Ghosts go for your neck; only ferrets go for your legs."

April 18th . . . THERE has been a murder in the village. We know little about it, but many of the students have seen the dead body of the girl, and half the village knows the name of the man who killed her. She was married, but unfaithful, and she was killed by one of her lovers. "No, it is not pleasant," says K., "but she seems to be smiling and not in too great agony. If you have never seen a dead body, you should have a look at her." It is no use telling him that I have seen too many, and want to see no more as long as I live.

But the murder is interesting, for the whole village has changed overnight. Old women whisper in corners. The old man from whom I buy lumps of greasy brown sugar lives next door to the house where the girl was murdered; and he is on tiptoe with excitement. Even the coal-coolies seem to have more life today and come running down the mountain, swinging their panniers and
346

smiling. The murder is a sacrifice to the god of winter, or perhaps to the sun. It has cleared the air, and I am half grateful for that curious secretive flow of life which it has produced.

And angry with myself for being grateful.

April 19th . . . I HAVE been to attend a meeting at the Legislative Council, which occupies a building some distance away from here. I had met Dr. Sun Fo, the son of Dr. Sun Yat-sen, shortly after my arrival in China; but I was still more impressed by him today. He wore a brown maroon gown, and as he stood in front of the portrait of his father there seemed to be such an extraordinary likeness that it was as though Sun Yat-sen had come to birth again. Something of the same thing happened when I saw him before; and it was curious to see the miracle completed.

There were over two hundred members of the Legislative Council present. They were men from all walks of life: farmers, scholars, merchants, editors, writers. They were of all ages and of all classes. They had not been elected, but were chosen partly by the Government and partly by Dr. Sun Fo himself, and though the election is undemocratic, it has given a fairly representative body of legislators to China.

I asked T. K. Chuan, the editor of *Tien Hsia*, whether it would ever be possible to have a purely democratic system in a country of nearly five hundred million inhabitants. He is himself a member of the Legislative Council, though he has made few speeches. "It is not entirely representative," he admitted, "but every kind of opinion is represented on the Council. We have members representing the occupied part of China, members representing labour, others representing capital; there are members representing the Government, and other members representing the Universities and Research Institute. It is like England—in war-time a thoroughly representative legislative chamber is impossible." There was one sense, however, in which he admitted that the Chamber was totally unrepresentative—there was only one woman in it. "She is the woman with the greatest responsibility in the world," I suggested. "She carries on her shoulders the weight of nearly three hundred million other women." He laughed; and when, a little while later, we met the extremely attractive representative of three hundred million women, it was difficult to think of that tremendous responsibility reposing on her slight shoulders.

The legislators meet in an old farm-house so securely buried

347

among the forests that no airman will ever be able to find them. There were reading-rooms, offices, a library as large as the University library, there were small rest-rooms where the legislators could dream in comfort of the effects of their laws; everywhere there was a feeling of activity. The legislators admitted there were difficulties. A large part of the functions of the Legislative Council had been taken over by the Supreme Military Defence Council. Government departments introduced their own laws; and sometimes these laws conflicted with those introduced by other departments. There were three or four officials who spent their whole time attempting to codify the laws. Still worse, the laws of the realm could be promulgated, but no one could be certain that they would be carried out. The voices in the assembly rose to a hum. A bill on the control of medicines was being passed. The legislators were leaning forward, intently listening to the young doctor who was speaking. There were a few people talking in subdued voices at the back of the hall, but everyone else was listening. The bill was passed. On the dais, with the photograph of Dr. Sun Yat-sen below the crossed flags of the Republic, Dr. Sun Fo was sitting at a table covered with a red cloth. The meeting came to an end. Dr. Sun Fo passed through the gangway, and came out into the courtyard, along the stone elephants and ancient lions and the fig-trees. Another meeting of the Legislative Council was finished.

Afterwards, we lunched with Dr. Sun Fo in a small wooden house high up on the spur of the mountains. It was raining; the forests were thick with damp and smoky vapour; down below the rice-fields glittered in the faint sun. Servants came to take our coats, policemen inspected us carefully; but inside the dining-room, by the warm fire, while the pictures and scrolls gazed down from the walls, a magnificent host in a maroon gown answered questions without pause. The Chinese are a little perturbed by the appearance of an anti-Chinese book in America. The thesis that Japan should be allowed to retain the balance of power against a renascent China had infuriated some and saddened others. It seemed a poor consolation for seven years of bitterly contested war. I explained as best I could that the freedom of the press in England and America involved the lunatic fringe; they could say what they liked, and it was better to allow them to talk nonsense if it so pleased them; and I begged them not to take such statements seriously, even if they were written by University professors. I hope they believed me; for I can think of nothing so tasteless as the thought that China should be deprived of her hard-won liberties. Then we went on to talk of the scrolls written by the famous poet Su Tung-po of the Sunny Dynasty which hung from the walls, and Dr. Sun Fo discussed those characters which he admired best.

A Chinese scroll is often a work of art, every detail of the calligraphy worthy of the attention of the connoisseur, for the art of the calligraphist lies in minute details. Most difficult of all are the characters which seem the easiest, the characters which have only a few strokes and those, too, which are most commonly repeated. We discussed the scrolls at length; and we were lost in admiration of his collection.

We discussed, too, the possibility of translating some of the great Chinese Classics. Since Legge translated the Thirteen Classics, it has been commonly believed in the West that nothing else remains to be translated. We counted up the list of books—extremely important books—which remain to be done—*The Dream of the Red Chamber,* the *Histories* of Ssu Ma-chien, the famous Commentaries on the *Annals,* and there are a thousand more books which are worth translating.

"The West is only beginning to understand China," Dr. Sun Fo said. "This is where the scholars must help us. If we can find means by which these books can be translated—books which many Chinese know by heart, though the West is ignorant of them—the West will be in a better position to judge us. We are a country of scholars, and we should be known by our scholarship. We must see that these works are understood by foreigners."

He was generous in suggesting ways in which the books could be financed; and promised every possible assistance. And as we walked back through the damp forest and over the muddy stones between the rice-fields, it seemed to us that we had the keys of understanding in our hands, and they shone like bright gold.

April 20th . . . IN THE smoky glare of three candles, the old man was telling the story of the Three Kingdoms. The tea-house was crowded with old and young, sweltering in the heat of the evening as they crouched on the wooden benches, gazing steadily and fixedly at the face of the old man shining in the candle-light.

349

The three candles, in old cigarette-tins, were placed on the table before him; and from time to time he would touch them lightly with his fingers, move them a little or simply shadow his face from their light, and it was clear that he was manipulating the lights according to the progress of the story.

"Then Chu Ko Liang advanced without trembling under the ledge of the cliffs and made as if to surprise the warriors hiding there. He counted their sleek horses, each one with its tufted mane bound in silk; he counted their bridles and banners, and listed in his mind the wealth of their saddle-bags. And still they were sleeping under the elder trees, and their guards were sleeping, and their horses were sleeping. So he advanced cautiously, knowing that the tinkle of each stone might give his position away. He unsheathed his double-handed dagger, and crept forward, whispering prayers to the Lord of Heaven, and having come within three paces of the largest of the men, he noticed that they were stirring. Nevertheless he went forward. He crept stealthily. And he was about to——"

At that point he ended and banged two cigarette-tins together. It was a masterly display of the story-teller's art, and yet he seemed unconscious of the mastery. He was an old man, very thin, naked except for the blue trousers tied to his waist with a soiled white waist-band; and the bones of his throat and chest shone white in the candle-light. It was evident that he smoked opium, for his low voice and the sudden twists and turns of his head belonged to a man who was still half submerged in his opium dream. We sighed. So well had he told the story that we were impatient to hear the end; but first there must be a libation to the gods! He came round with another cigarette-tin perched precariously in his claws, shuffling barefooted over the loose boards of this deserted shop; and so we search in our pockets and look for those soiled bank-notes which shopkeepers will refuse. He does not see us. He is blind, and afterwards a small boy will lead him away along the river path. But this is his glory! We dare not let him go until the story is finished, and perhaps it will never be finished and he will linger in the village till the end.

It is dark in the village. The shops are shuttered; the dead chickens and the dead pigs are hidden behind wooden shutters. Only in this corner of the village is there a little light. Tea is served, and the old man returns to his dais, shaking the cigarette-tin and smiling with satisfaction. He hawks up his spittle and
350

coughs loudly, gazes unseeing at the rafters and quietly returns to his tale.

"But when Chu Ko Liang had advanced another three feet, it seemed to him that the men lying there were only phantoms; and when he had advanced another three feet, it seemed to him that the men lying there were only shadows; and when he had advanced another three feet . . ."

But already we have burst out laughing. The small boys in the front row clap their hands and the old men at the back shuffle their feet in applause. Chu Ko Liang advances up the mountainside. Chu Ko Liang brandishes his sword or eats a whole mutton at a mouthful or spits three men on a single skewer and roasts them over the monastery fire. It is all the same story, but the variations in the story are endless, and these giants who once strode over Szechuan were still striding over these hills, and they were far more real than our lives.

At night the way back to the University is dark. We take our candles in the bamboo lanterns and make our way past the cesspits until we reach the river road. Y. is silent, thinking of the story which has affected him almost to tears.

"Why on earth did we invent printing?" he complains. "A real story-teller should be like that—every tone of voice, every movement of his arms should be expressive. Did you notice how he manipulated the candles? When anything terrible happened, he slid the candles along the table and it was impossible to see his face. All that darkness—his face—the eyes and the white teeth— how effective it was! What can the poor writer do which is half so effective? We write, we make little black marks on the page, but this man tells us everything, we know everything, we see everything— wonderful."

I tell him that I have seen Hitler demonstrating the same use of light in Nuremberg. He stood at a table with a switchboard, and every time he mentioned the National Socialist Party the lights burnt pure white, but when he mentioned the international conspiracy of Britain, America, Russia and the Jews, the lights were blood-red.

"It is a trick as old as the hills," I suggested, "and this is proved by the fact that Hitler only knows those tricks which are as old as the hills. There are better tricks."

"Can you mention them?"

"Yes, but the blind story-teller knew them too. He knew when to pause, he knew how to shape his stories, he knew how to obtain his sympathetic audience. These are difficult things."

And Y., who is one of the most famous writers in China, sighed softly in the darkness and murmured: "Who should know that better than I?"

April 23rd . . . IN THE courtyard the children have been screaming all afternoon. They are poor and under-nourished, their skins are pale blue and neither their father nor mother pays much attention to them. They live in the house near the gate, which lies over a cesspool where the rats congregate from the four corners of the earth. And so they screamed. There was no reason for their screaming. Or rather they screamed because they were ill and under-nourished, because their skins were blue, because there was lice in their hair, because they were sick of suffering. It is a sound which can be heard often in China, and only one sound is worse—the sound of a woman screaming.

T. says that all this will end as soon as sanitation comes to this village. But when will sanitation come to this village. Night soil is used on the fields, and every morning as I come across the river, I see the open casks of night soil as they are taken to the fields. In Peipei the soil-pipes are buried underground. Here in the village there are open drains, where the rats crawl and the green flies hover in clouds. The children cry because their intestines and skins are sick with disease; and only the strongest survive.

"We have proved," says T. sadly, "the story of the survival of the fittest. Only the fittest could survive the agony of Chinese life." He smiles wearily: "There is even a department of sanitation at the University, but what can we do against the vested interest of open drains? It will be a long time before they disappear."

The child is still screaming. It is impossible to work, or even to think. The terrible cold quivering voice of the child is only a response to suffering; but as soon as I have told myself this, I know that it is no longer true. There are good nurses and good doctors in China; the pity is that there are insufficient.

Later . . . THE child is quieter now. There is no more strength in his lungs. Occasionally he sobs, but he sobs in a language which I can understand. Now in the silence and the darkness I have put this child in a poem:

The child in the courtyard of his panic fear
Must stare into the windows of his soul
Or shake the bars, or break the flaming spear
In fear of fire—the fire Prometheus stole.
And now I hear the child's cold quivering voice
Echoing down corridors where the walls are silent,
As tombs within the rocks of paradise
Are said to shelter angels in the crevices
And precipices where the threatening eyes of eagles
Drip like the dripping ice upon the salient,
Where barbed wire tears on skulls and is but the more valiant
Than the dark stars which tear our threatened lives to pieces.
Delirium of the age! Must children cry
Like shaken leaves upon an ageless sky?

April 24th . . . THE school doctor has opened a small surgery half-way up the hill, and on the door of the surgery there is a notice: "Those who cannot afford to pay the doctor's fee, will be treated free of charge." There is nothing else, but for this, and for many other things, the University has taken him to its heart.

I had to see him this morning about a blood-poisoned finger.

"I put the notice up because I saw three-quarters of the village suffering from disease. They must be treated, and it's so easy to treat them. A little scabies, a little goitre, a little—but they are very many—unhealed wounds. They allow their wounds to go on. They see a herb doctor or an acutipuncturist, and expect them to cure everything; but the herb doctor can cure only a few things, and there are fewer still which can be cured by the acutipuncturist." He sighed, for he knew that the villagers would be suspicious, and then he added in that quiet voice which I have come to know so well: "If you see anyone who is sick, send him to me."

He is still young, and soon the whole village will be flocking to him. His wife, whom he married only a short while ago, is a trained midwife. He comes from a Christian medical University on the coast, and knows his job better than most, and in his quiet manner and in the extraordinary *certainty* of his treatment, I have never met a doctor so impressive.

The University has on its staff a Chinese herb doctor, a short, bald, wiry man whose knowledge of herbs, of Chinese boxing, of building houses, of half a dozen other things is equally impressive. If you have tooth-ache, he will give you a herb which will soothe it in five minutes. For complicated ailments, he will take your pulse; and he swears that there are eighty-four gradations of the pulse-beat which can be readily discerned by the trained doctor. He believes in animal magnetism, and can by sheer will and force of character induce an electric current into your arms. Last year he made out a long prescription of Chinese herbs to cure my jaundice. The medicine was bitter and had the consistency of black syrup; it contained the dried legs of frogs and the skin of field-mice; but the jaundice disappeared after three days and has never returned.

The problem of Chinese and European medicine will never be solved, for the Chinese believe firmly in their herbs. Their *materia medica* has been tested out for four thousand years; and though it has been found wanting in some things, in others it has admirably served its purpose.

"I do not claim to cure everything," he said. "I do not claim to cure cancer, but I think it would be good if Western and Chinese medicine were studied together—and perhaps too we should study Indian medicine seriously. The Harvard Yenching Institute has been studying Chinese medicine, and finding the most extraordinary similarities between the use of Chinese and Western herbs. There is the bark of a tree which grows in Szechuan; we have used it for centuries against fevers, but it is only recently that the bark has been analysed and found to have nearly all the properties we associate with quinine. There are many other curious similarities. . . ."

My tooth was aching. I bit on the herb, and in three minutes the ache had gone.

April 25th . . . In the palatial Maifung Bank which has been erected on the outskirts of the village, the tellers in white silk gowns are softly fanning themselves. There is the continual click of the little black abacus, which lies on the low blackwood desks; and yet banks in China have a discreetly personal air. An old soldier in uniform comes to bring you a glass of boiling tea; the bank manager, who resembles a coolie and shaves rarely, so that he resembles a scholar, comes through the folding door, looks out at the low drifting clouds and returns a moment later, probably to write a poem. There are scrolls on the wall, and they differ

354

from the scrolls in the houses of the professors only in being painted on paper of curious, variegated colours. I prefer white, but the Government and the offices in Chungking seem to prefer marbled patterns of green and blue, or curious mixtures of spotted gold and brown, so that the paper resembles the hides of fantastic leopards; and on these extraordinary coloured strips of paper, there are full-blooded inscriptions, quotations from the classics or summonses to war.

To understand the uses to which paper has been put in China would need a lifetime's work. Paper of all kinds—the almost granulated paper which comes in immense rolls to the University, so bad that it decays in days of foul weather, to the creamy bamboo paper which is still manufactured up-river for bank-notes—there is no end to the variations of paper in China. You buy it in rolls; and when the roll has been flattened out, a great sheet measuring eight foot by four is displayed before your eyes. Nearly all paper-shops for some reason are small, and it is impossible to see the whole sheet as it lies on their narrow shelves; and perhaps this is only one more trick of a trade which is over twelve hundred years old in China. Paper is sealed, and marked with the emblems of the manufacturer, not in the watermark, for even the bank-notes have no water-marks, but along the edges of the rolls. . . .

We were discussing paper as we walked through the village in the morning. Z. knows paper well, for his father is one of its chief manufacturers, and he spoke of sizing and silicates and soda with enviable passion. It was only afterwards, as we were descending towards the river, that we noticed the old village pensioner who shuffled slowly over the great square facing the river, and sometimes he would stoop down and pick up a sheet of paper and taking it carefully to a small red brick-kiln, he proceeded to burn it; lest the gods of literature and learning should be displeased as it lay idle in the grass.

April 26th . . . THE weather is boiling; it is the first foretaste of summer. Late in the afternoon we wandered down to the river, I in shorts and W. in a beautiful creamy white silk gown. The wind rippled on the silk in exactly the same way that it rippled on the smooth river.

He was obviously very worried, and began to throw the small greenish-red pebbles which line the bank into the stream.

"What is so terrible," he complained, "is that Chinese culture is

355

no longer represented abroad. While Hu Shih was still Ambassador in America, the scholars were proud—they were well represented, and all that is best in China has flowed through the hands of Hu Shih. But there is no one else—there is only Lin Yutang, who rarely comes to China and seems to be out of touch with her youth and her scholarship; and Pearl Buck, who made so many mistakes in *The Good Earth* that they are past counting. *Tien Hsia* no longer tells foreigners about our lives, and no one except a Chinese can speak worthily of China. Our modern novels are untranslated; our poetry is unknown; even our scientists are relegated to the back pages of the learned journals. The West has vested interests in itself—it is frightened of the Indians and the Chinese." He paused and threw a large jagged stone in midstream. "We shall have to fight for a place in the sun after the war."

"You mean you will have to fight for it by war?"

"Perhaps not by war, but we shall have to fight. We are still half regarded as coolies—our soldiers are praised, but no one writes worthily about them abroad. It is all superlatives, without understanding. And then, too, our civilisation is praised, and again there are superlatives; but so little understanding that one can only weep. The West is proud; China is proud; and these two different kinds of pride will never meet."

There were no more stones left to throw. We walked back slowly in the direction of the University. We were silent. I was struck by his use of the word "proud", and remembered a story told me by a high official in the Chinese Foreign Office who was sent to a mission in Burma. At the post-office in Rangoon, he lined up at the end of a queue, and a burly red-headed Englishman, one of those Englishmen whom he most admired, followed him at the end of the queue; but the Burmese clerk refused to serve anyone until the Englishman was served, and in despair the Englishman went to the head of the queue. Afterwards the official of the Chinese Foreign Office talked to the Englishman over coffee at the hotel.

"I can't help it," said the Englishman. "Someone has put such dam' silly ideas in their heads. They think we are lords and masters! Do I look like a lord and master?" and the Englishman burst out into wild, happy laughter, stroking his red moustache and glaring ridiculously at the Chinese. "But the truth of it is that we have gone too far. We had to impress 'em, don't you know. Well,
356

they're impressed now, but there's no more room in their skulls for any other impression. Numb-skulls!" he roared. But that was not the end of the story, for it turned out, to my Chinese friend's amazement, that the Englishman was one of the world's greatest authorities on Chinese ivories and would have given his left arm to avoid the incident they had both witnessed. And as we walked back, thinking of Chinese literature and art, and of how little it is known abroad, and thinking too of those remaining prejudices which divide the East and the West, we wondered whether we could ever foresee a day when these misunderstandings were cleared up.

"The real trouble is that you don't understand us, and we don't understand you, because neither of us takes the trouble to learn the spiritual histories of the other. If we knew that, if we knew the springs of action and the ideas which lie at the root of your thought, we should begin to understand you. . . ."

April 27th . . . We were looking at the map on the wall, showing the battle-lines all over the world. There were many lines in China, a few in Burma and a thousand more in the South Seas. There were flags of all colours on the map, and the grey-blue seas, the reddish hills, the white deserts and gaunt green plains on those excellent maps published by the Chinese Foreign Office seemed to be alive with people—you could easily imagine the whole course of the war, and at the same time you could see the earth in all the glory of its rainbow colours.

The thin professor, looking up through very bright, thick lenses, began to draw lines on the map with his fingers. Then, in a very quiet voice like someone concluding a lecture in elementary geometry, he said:

"It's exactly the same—nothing has changed. It was the same last year, and next year it will be the same."

We thought he was wandering off into one of his well-known day-dreams, but suddenly he talked gravely and still in the voice of the geometrician: "Drawn perpendiculars to all the battle-fronts and all possible future battle-fronts." He paused for a while, amused by our expressions which showed clearly that we thought he had gone mad. "And what you find, gentlemen, is the geometrician's dream—all lines converging to a single point. What is more, gentlemen, the lines converge on two of the most ancient

357

cities in the world—Chungking and Vienna. *Austria and Szechuan will be the final battlegrounds of the war.*"

We look out of the window. Nothing has changed; the lawn with its tulips, its beds of sensitive grass, its pigeons and dogs slumbering in the heat are still there. The sampans are still gliding down-stream, and smoke still rises from the factories on the further bank. For a moment, for almost a minute, we took pride in the thought that the earth we were standing on would be the scene of gigantic battles in the future. The river would be stained with red, there would be no houses and no sampans. For miles around there would be desolation. And then suddenly, when we thought of the high mountains and the gorges and the snail-like Japanese crawling along the mountain paths which are so tortuous that they are called in Chinese "pathways like the intestines of sheep", we wondered whether it was possible for the Japanese to come near us. "Ah, the Chinese landscape," said another professor, a geologist. "It has defeated us, and really it will be surprising if it doesn't defeat the Japanese." And in a softer voice, thinking of the bitterness of the land, he added: "Poor devils!"

April 28th . . . ALL round the University there have been growing up little tea-houses and restaurants. Yesterday there was a plot of broken ground, where chickens wandered and a few broken bottles lay scattered over the earth. Today there is a thriving restaurant, quite new—with new lamp-brackets, new stools, new tables, even new china bowls. In a few days all this newness will have vanished. The wooden planks will be blackened with smoke; the yellow pine will turn grey on the tables. Soon the bowls from which we eat *pei tsei, mien* and *Tsou-k'an* will be chipped at the edges, and the girl in the bright blue gown who serves us will no longer look young; for though one can become rich by owning a restaurant, the sulphurous kitchens take toll of health.

Six months ago the girl was young, and there was an adorable sparkle in her golden-black eyes. Today she is middle-aged; her hair falls in wisps over her forehead; her gown is unbuttoned, and she no longer cares for her appearance. It is true that her husband bullies her, but the kitchen, where the dead chickens hang on strings, bullies her more. One of the students, who loves her with an entirely platonic love, has decided to set fire to the restaurant to preserve her beauty, and we half wish him success.

358

There are restaurants in the village where the cooks have salaries at least eight times the salaries of the professors. The world
is becoming a place where people eat; for the main task is to
preserve one's strength till after the war. But the food is getting
poorer and more altered every day, rents are going up, and one
thinks twice before buying such elementary things as candles.
The students who have worked so long by the dim light of candles of rape-seed-oil tapers are already showing signs of great
strain. And still the prices go up and no one knows where it will
end.

May 3rd, A Voyage to Singapore . . . WE WERE sitting on the
rocks with our legs dangling in the water. Small fishes like tad-
poles crept between our toes, and the milky-blue water eddied
swiftly on the verge of the rocks. It was one of those evenings
when thoughts which are long dead are suddenly revived.

The boy in the white shorts and the blue sailor sweater was
swearing mildly. "Soon there will be no Chinese civilisation left
in China," he complained. "We are all becoming Westernised
and losing our souls. And the worst of it is that the Japanese are
the inheritors of our civilisation at its greatest. T'ang art, T'ang
costumes, T'ang customs, T'ang furniture, T'ang ways of living—
the Japanese saw that they were good and kept them, but we
have forsaken them. We wear a comic mixture of Chinese and
Western dress: we are at least half Westernised."

"It is not true," said a younger boy, who was gazing placidly at
the green and blue depths of the pool. "The Japanese have taken
over little pieces of Chinese civilisation, but they have understood
nothing. They are more brutal than the Chinese can ever be, and
more innocent of courtesy than any race on the earth. Perhaps
this is why they have such complicated rituals—like raging leopards who perform rituals over the body of a dead deer."

For some reason we burst out laughing. The boy, however, was
almost crying.

"But it is exactly what happens," he complained. "The leopard
does perform such a ritual, and so do the Japanese. I have seen
them. I have come from Singapore. Where else could I learn all
that I know about them?"

We did not know where he had come from, for people come by
many roads to the modern Universities. They come from the
deserts of Mongolia, from the white mountains of Sinkiang, from

the forests of Indo-China and the tea-plantations of Burma. It was the first time that a student had come from Singapore.

"Where I come from," he continued slowly, and in a voice controlled by instincts of deadly cunning, "the Japanese have no knowledge of Chinese culture. In the first three weeks of their occupation they killed over twenty thousand Chinese. They did not kill men only; they killed babies and young girls and old women—there was no respect for age. They killed everyone in uniform, and all those who were well known. They rounded up the people hiding in the rubber estates and bayoneted them to the trees. They cut off heads, and the heads were placed above the notice-boards written in Chinese as a warning. They buried wounded Australian soldiers alive. They were drunk with power."

He was silent for a while, and went on in a lower voice.

"There is no Singapore any more. There is an island in the South Seas called Shonanto—the south island of the Showa Emperor. In the old histories they speak of an invasion by the Majapahit Empire, and how there was so much blood spilt in Singapore that the earth turned red and refused to grow rice. But this is worse—the earth is crimson now. There were ninety thousand Australians and Englishmen who surrendered. Those who were left have been taken to Thailand to build roads. They have little food, and almost no clothes. They are worked harder than any coolies. The Japanese have tried to erase from people's minds the thought that Malaya was once occupied by the English. Sometimes I would go from Singapore to Johore. The causeway was blown up by the British, but it is now repaired, and there are two sentries on the Johore side of the causeway and one at Woodlands Gate. You must bow as you pass them. Sometimes they will ask you where you are coming from, and if you reply 'Singapore', you are slapped in the face and kicked to the ground.

"Singapore has changed hardly at all, for very little was destroyed. The Cathay building is the headquarters of their propaganda, and the banks are all Japanese now, except the Overseas Chinese Bank which for some reason has been allowed to continue. But though nothing has changed, and the weather is the same, the whole spirit of the place has changed out of recognition. Singapore is over-populated; for no one dares to live in the surrounding villages. At any moment the Japanese will enter a shop and take whatever they please without paying for it. There are loud-speakers everywhere, and the Chinese boys are so accus-
360

tomed to hearing Japanese songs that they whistle them all day. The pay of a Japanese soldier is $26 a month, but he can steal another $300 with impunity. They killed us when they arrived first; now they try to tell us that the Japanese and the Chinese must combine together against the hated British—and a little Eurasian, with a spiteful tongue, writes excellent leaders in the *Shonan Shimbun* explaining that everything will be lost if the British return.

"The Japanese have controlled prices in theory, but in practice there is no control at all. A yard of cotton costs $13, and you are only allowed to buy three yards a year. You are allowed eighteen *kapang* of rice a month in theory, but in practice you can only obtain seven or eight. There are Chinese junks which smuggle sugar from Java; they are brave men, but they are tortured to death if they are caught. They force water into your nostrils until your lungs and your stomach burst, they squash lighted cigarettes against your genitals, they kill you slowly and at their pleasure. Or else, in an open space in the rubber-fields, they charge you with bayonets—men, women, children, it is all the same. I have known a man who was left for dead after one of these bayonet charges; he had three wounds in his throat and four in his chest, but he was young and strong, and so he recovered. They have killed the teachers in the Government. They killed everyone who wore any sort of uniform—even if it was only an A.R.P. uniform. The officers carry short daggers unsheathed. If they take a dislike to you, they will plunge the dagger in your chest.

"All this I have seen with my own eyes, and I have seen nothing of Japanese civilisation. They have forgotten whatever culture remains in Japan. They live in the houses left by the Europeans, they sit at tables and no longer crouch on the floor. They smoke Western cigarettes, for millions of tins were left behind, and they eat Western food, for millions of tins of food were left behind. They dance with the Chinese girls at the *New World* and the *Great World*, and they have cowed us with fear of their revenge. No one is fighting them; there is no secret organisation fighting against them, and no aeroplanes come to give us hope and faith in the allies. We have forgotten the English flag. Everywhere we see the Japanese flag—the red spot of blood on a white ground.

"They pretend to love the Indians and Malays; they have hated the Chinese. There were eighteen Japanese shops in Johore Bahru, and we used to think they were spying on the Naval Base. They

361

were not spying on the Naval Base; they were working with the Malays and making tracks through the Malay forests for their armies. The Sultans are stripped of power. The Tungkhu Makhota, once Crown Prince of Johore, is a retailer of watches—most of his cars have been taken away from him. The Japanese spies in Johore have been given high positions, but they have lost their friends. And at night the lights burn at the head of the wireless masts in the Naval Base, and this is the only thing that reminds us of England.

"There are no Englishmen left in Singapore except dead ones. Sir Shenton Thomas and General Perceval are in Formosa. A few heads of Englishmen, impaled above the notice-boards, are no longer recognisable, but they were Englishmen once, and when I saw them first, they had light-coloured hair; but now the hair has grown darker with the rain and the dust. The English will come— we are certain of that, though the newspapers speak only of great defeats and the wireless continually drills into our ears the incompetence of the English, saying that they must have been incompetent indeed to have lost Malaya. We know that they will return because ships are sunk in the Straits of Malacca. Many ships have been sunk, but only one was reported in the newspapers, and that was because there were Malays on board. The Japanese are trying desperately hard to treat the Malays well. We have always said the Malays are treacherous, but they have exceeded their treachery during this war. When the English soldiers were hiding in the forests, still fighting, it was Malays who revealed their presence to the Japanese. In all the fishing villages on the coast, there are notices signed by the Japanese High Command giving the rewards which will be offered for information; and the Malays accept the rewards and go out carefully to find the survivors. They are wealthy now. In the future they will be poor again, for treachery never pays.

"And so Yamashito still struts about the streets of Singapore. Singapore is the great central base, where the Governor-General of the Indies lives in Government House. The Emperor sent him a sword from the hand of Tojo himself; and he wears the sword at the theatres and cinemas which he attends—a small man with a heavy beard who inspires fear only because with a single stroke of a brush he can order all the Chinese in Singapore to disappear from the earth. Lim Boon Keng is the head of the China Association; but he is old and grey now, only a puppet, and he dares not

362

offend them. But strange things happen still. Once in March, 1942, we heard explosions from the Naval Base for three hours, or more. They were very loud, and we prayed that a saboteur had set fire to the ammunition left by the British. . . .

"They wear shorts and khaki shirts with a white tag over the left breast on which their names are written. These are the soldiers. There are marines in green, and sailors in white—and many warships. A few Chinese work in the Naval Base, but all the time the Japanese have been trying to encourage the Malays. There are still rickshas—the Chinese are still coolies, and we dare not go out at night for fear that we will be arrested and sent out to build airfields in the Andaman islands or in Siam. Life is insecure. You can bribe a Japanese, but it is dangerous—he may accept the bribe and then push his bayonet through your stomach. Women dare not go out alone, and we are all poor, for salaries have been drastically reduced. The English banks were closed; no money could be taken out, but money owed to the bank had to be paid. Once the oil-tanks on Bukhit Timah road were set on fire; they burnt for three days, and the fire was so brilliant that it was like moonlight—but they took their revenge. Once more there was slaughter. They lost the oil-tanks in the Naval Base, and it seems that when they lose oil blood must pay.

"I have told you all this because you said there were some good things in Japanese civilisation. You say they have respect for the past, but the statue of Raffles has been taken to the Museum, half the Museum has been transported to Tokyo and Raffles Library is closed. You suggested they have respect for China, but they only teach Japanese in their schools. From the night when the nine aeroplanes came over, and we saw the anti-aircraft guns of the *Renown* and the *Prince of Wales* turning the sky red, there has been little hope in Malaya. We were sunk in despair. They have reiterated so often the story of their conquest that we half believe what they have to tell us; and we are so bemused that we dare not fight them. But faintly, very faintly in our hearts we have hope that they will return. If the British landed in small groups along the coast near a Chinese village, they would be helped and they might be able to start a wave of revolt. But God help them if they landed on the coast near a Malay fishing-village."

He said many more things as we gazed down at the green pool near the rocks. He hoped that when the British return, the old system of colonial administration will have vanished for ever; and the old administrators will also vanish. It was believed by the Chinese in Malaya that the Japanese decided to strike when they did because they learned of the trials for corruption in Hongkong and Singapore just before the war. They knew their power. Their system of espionage was perfect, and there was no Chinese army to fight against the Japanese until the last moment.

"You lost the most beautiful islands in the world," he said, turning to me, "through treachery of others and because you did not understand the Chinese and the Malays. You could have had the Malays on your side—Raffles would have them on your side— and the Chinese would have fallen into your arms. But when the islands are returned again, remember that we are brothers."

May 15th . . . I HAVE been spending a week-end in Chung-king, looking at the new plays. There is a play on the life of Mozart in which my friend Tsao Yu is acting the name part. The stage-settings are the best I have seen in China, great billowing folds of coloured silk, a part of the palace of the Hofburgs in Vienna all white, gold and ivory, the little room where Mozart is composing his symphonies and the larger room where he died and where Alieri comes to visit him on his death-bed. I have never seen such prodigious acting. Mozart dominates the stage; he roars and blusters; sings divinely; makes love with the most formidable bows; plays on the violin; storms the chancellery of the bishop near the Stefansdom; and brings the house down with the tempestuous fury of his acting. *This is Mozart.* It is Mozart in Chinese, and I understood only one word in ten. But what a prodigious performance! what extraordinary command of the stage!

I have never seen anything like this for sheer beauty of expression. Mozart comes in, sits down at the harpsichord, which possesses no keys, dusts the air with his scented handkerchief, takes snuff, scowls at the music, laughs with a tremendous cracked voice and sits down to play a minuet or a cradle-song for the Viennese maiden *who speaks Chinese with a Viennese accent.* He is all of Mozart and he is all of Vienna. His gestures are calculated, and the sweetness of his voice is calculated, and even in his passion he is calculated with the terrible sophistication of the Viennese. Tsao Yu has never been out of China; yet this is the Vienna I have known and imagined before Hitler came to paint it red and black with swastika flags. His fingers run on the keys, and somewhere behind the stage a gramophone plays; but the illusion is so perfect, the manners of the Viennese *Mädchen* are so carefree and at the same time so sophisticated, and Mozart himself so completely dominates the stage that the music seems indeed to rise from his fingers and his lips. There is a scene where the girls try on their crinolines. They are no longer Chinese girls; they are the resurrected ghosts of the past, living and dreaming before our eyes, cajoling, threatening, making eyes—above all, making eyes. They are fair-haired, and truly nothing is so beautiful as a face with Chinese eyes and fair hair. They dance. They caper. They throw their arms round the neck of Mozart. They sing plaintively when he has gone, and when he returns they are still singing. They laugh and dance in circles round the room, and even when Mozart is dying, they are still laughing. Mozart lies in a great four-poster bed, writing his requiem against time. He struggles for breath, leaps out of bed and fights with the musician who has come to torment him, and dies peacefully at last, an old man, though his heart and his body are still young.

I confess to a passion for plays in which there is music. The music of the play was carefully chosen, the dresses were carefully chosen, the *décor* was still more carefully chosen. The same settings could never be used for another play; and we were grateful for this, since the Chinese stage with its single back-cloth is used until it is worn out. This was something new, fresh as the morning, springing out of the excitement of the actors and their worship for Mozart. And even when we went back stage and saw the crinolines swinging up on wires until they rested half-way up the walls, saw the moment when the women actors removed their noses of white wax and smiled at us with their noses which were no longer Viennese, even then the excitement of the play echoed in our hearts. Tsao Yu was wrenching the cotton hairs from his face; he resembled a clown or a leper, in a mask of white grease-paint, but he was still Mozart. He dominated the green-room as he dominated the stage, and though he was almost weary to death, for he had been acting continuously for five hours, he began to discuss the play. Yes, the stage designs were the best he had seen in China. They had cost a hundred thousand dollars, and God knows whether the backers would see their money again. An old Austrian had taught them the proper gestures, and a musician from the Chungking Symphony Orchestra had supervised the playing of the gramophone record. Everything was delightful except the cost of the play and the weariness of performing night after night. . . . And so we went out, into the deserted streets, where the rain shone on the bleak pavements and a small quivering light in a side street told us of the presence of a restaurant. We ate noodles and chicken soup. Afterwards I watched Tsao Yu disappearing into the distance, a short, slight figure in a soiled blue gown, a scholar who differed hardly at all from any other poor scholar to be seen in the streets of Chungking; but for five hours he had held three thousand people spell-bound.

There were other plays in Chungking. There was, for example, *Tao Lien,* a play upon the Chinese Red Cross which Tsao Yu had written. It opened with a scene in some desolate part of China near the battle-front, you hear the chink of mahjong tiles and see the paper windows torn to ribbons in the wind. There is an air of uneasiness and discontent, of weariness and staleness, and at once you think you are in Russia at the time of the Tsars. The play moves slowly. You hear of distant attacks by the Japanese, but the Red Cross remains unruffled, more interested in the pursuit of mahjong parties than the cause of the war. And all this is explained to us at the moment when a new supervisor arrives to change the whole shape of the Red Cross station and instil new life into the members. The scene changes to a house still nearer the battle-front. A woman doctor goes out to attend the wounded. Her son is dangerously hurt. And still, like a benevolent angel, the Government supervisor keeps the reins in his hands. The Red Cross station is full of life, but always at the background we are conscious of the mysterious depths of depravity which have their origin in the weariness which comes from a too long war. The play is a tract for the times, a warning and an encouragement: all that is good and bad in the field hospitals leaps to our eyes. The Japanese come nearer. The battle becomes more intense. The hospital itself is under fire. You see the wheels glinting as the machine suddenly begins to perform at high pressure; and in the end you see the victorious Chinese Army passing below the window, while the lady doctor exhorts them in a passionate speech of revenge. There are faults in this play. The themes were too many, and there was altogether too much nebulous action. But the excitement of the attack, the trumpets, the Chinese flag waving wildly outside the window, all these consoled us for the inevitable unevenness of a patriotic play. The more I see of plays in Chungking the more I am convinced that the great dramatist of the future will be born in China. The Chinese have a natural instinct for self-dramatisation; they love colours and movement, and understand the architectonics of action. They have action in their bones, and at the same time they are contemplative: it is out of such material that great drama is made.

May 18th . . . MALARIA has come. The sun-baked earth, the festering pools, the low tide and the heavy white sulphurous mist which descends upon the river at night and lifts only with the coming of the sun, the green lakes of the rice-fields and the weakness that comes from dysentery—for we all suffer from dysentery nowadays—have combined to send a wave of malaria through the University. Flies in millions congregate around our desks. Bed-bugs climb under the mosquito-nets, crawl over your body at night and mount towards the apex of the net in the morning; and though you catch them, there are twenty again the next day.

We have taken our beds to the duck-pond and soaked them in the green messy water, and though the bamboo looks clean now and the ducks flying over our bamboo beds are beautiful beyond words, the bed-bugs remain. We tried an experiment this afternoon. We poured boiling hot water over the beds. This killed the bed-bugs, but sickened us, for the water turned red with blood. We have tried everything. We have taken our beds to the river, praying that the fast-flowing current will take the bugs with them down-stream. But the bugs are tenacious, and perfectly happy in the interstices of the wooden bed-frames. They are the colour of the wood and no eye can see them.

The legs of the students are covered with weals. Kept awake in the night, they are sleepy during the day. They have no rest from the insects, and since each insect carries poison they have no certainty that they will come through the summer unharmed. At high noon we are so weak that we lie gasping on our beds.

May 19th . . . K. ESCAPED from Hongkong three months ago. He came to the University with the clear intention of leaving it as soon as possible and joining the Chinese Air Force. For the last three months he has been talking happily of his training in India and America. He is strong and handsome beyond the average, very tall and thick-boned, with a mop of silky black hair over his forehead.

"Aha, I shall go to India and America—no bed-bugs—good food —and a chance to wipe the Japanese from the skies."

He talks always of "wiping them from the skies", delighted with this suggestion of a brush sweeping across a blackboard.

But today he was in tears. He has been to the medical examination and been turned down for tuberculosis.

"I am perfectly well—there is no trouble with my lungs—I am stronger, much stronger than any other student here," he keeps on saying. "I am Chinese—we all have spots on our lungs—what crime is it?" He is sobbing near the river and one of the students is afraid he will throw himself in the water.

May 20th, Conversation between two Chinese . . . "WHAT is the best thing that the English brought to China?" "Everything they brought is bad except Shakespeare's songs."

May 28th . . . THE term is coming to an end and the examinations will soon be here; but for three or four days there is a lull while we prepare ourselves for the agony of final preparations. We had gone down to the shore, watching the yellow sun as it slid over the rim of the mountains, and in the half-darkness under the shadow of the rocks we sat whispering and sometimes singing about China—an inexhaustible subject, but one which is most fitted for conversations late in the evening under the shadow of rocks.

The tall student with the unruly hair had gathered some frogs in his hands, for there were many frogs jumping up from the river. Still small, they shone silver in his hands and croaked continuously.

"In Pekin," he said, "there are frogs ten times larger than this, and no one dare kill them, for they protect the rice. And yet they are dangerous and people have been blinded by them." He paused dramatically, for though everyone else knew that the frogs were larger in Pekin, and also that they were poisonous, my incredulity was only too obvious. "If you touch their faces—it is only polite to call the scabby mass at their shoulders a face—they discharge a kind of white pus, which is collected by Chinese herbalists as a cure for digitalis. It is also a poison. They have sex glands, dark black, on their fore-paws, and with these sex glands they press the female in order to make her more fecund. . . ."

368

The subject of frogs was almost as inexhaustible as the subject of China, but by devious routes we returned to Pekin.

"It is Pekin now," said the boy who lay negligently along the rock gazing at the faint stars. "It is not Pekin any more, for Pekin means the northern capital, and the Japanese prefer it that way. If you call it Pekin, the soldiers slap you on the face."

As though there were some mysterious connection between the name of the capital and the murders done by the Japanese, another student broke in:

"I was travelling on the Pekin-Tientsin Railway this time last year. It was dark, very late at night, and I was afraid. The Japanese Secret Service men began to board the train. They asked us where we were going, examined our luggage, prodded us with bayonets. They stayed in the train with us, cross-examining us, with their pistols loaded and the safety-catch off. There was an old man in the corner pretending he was dozing. You know the mysterious effect which descends upon you on a journey by train at night—everything seems unreal, and it is best to doze when the Japanese Secret Service agents come on board, for perhaps they are not real. And even now, though it happened before my eyes, I wonder whether it is real. They began to cross-examine the old man sharply. He was not afraid: he answered their questions, but it was clear that he was guilty of some crime. Suddenly a Japanese officer bent over, took out a long thin knife from his pocket and thrust the knife up his nostrils, jamming it home with the palm of his hand. The man died—without a sound, silently, though blood came from his eyes. We were travelling very fast. The windows were opened and the body of the man was thrown out, and the silver knife was still in his nostrils. At the next station the Japanese descended. And now I am looking up at the stars, and I remember looking up at the same stars as the train travelled between Pekin and Tientsin."

There began a whole crop of stories about Secret Service agents. The boy who had escaped from Singapore—by what mysterious roads and with what torment of spirit must be left imagined— spoke of the secret agents whom the Japanese had found in Singapore among the Chinese and the Indians. The police station had been extended. It was nearly three times as large, and there were five times as many secret agents and detectives as before. They delighted in torture, if only because detective work was boring;

369

and they hated their masters and knew that they were hated by their compatriots.

"More mysterious things are happening in Singapore than ever happened in the Legation Quarter at Pekin," the boy said. "Perhaps this doesn't sound so strange to you, but we were brought up with the thought of the Legation Quarter as the most vicious place on earth. People died mysteriously in the Legation Quarter —people died and disappeared, but we knew who committed the crimes. In Singapore, they die and disappear, and no one knows who committed the crimes. There was a wave of murder after the occupation—the prisons were opened, and the murderers went back to their trade of murder. The Cantonese and the Hakkas are not friends. I lived next door to the family of one of my friends. He was a student, young, handsome, brilliant, like many of the sons of Straits Chinese. He lay dead in the garden. I went into the house. All his sisters were dead, the servants were dead, the father and mother and one of the grandparents lay dead upstairs. I do not think the Japanese killed them, though perhaps they may have done. They were killed, I think, by my friend, because he could not bear to think of his family living under the Japanese occupation. And who is to pay for the crime? Is it the Japanese or my Chinese friend? One day a Chinese agent in the pay of the Japanese came to our house. It was then—then that I understood for the first time how easy it is to murder. I could have murdered him, I could have murdered my whole family to prevent them from being polluted by his presence. This is what I find intolerable—that Japanese should be able to make the Chinese act for them."

They told many more stories that night: about the English doctor who disembowelled the daughter of a European Minister in Pekin, about the Consul (there appears to be a fatality in Consuls) who went insane after a shrapnel wound had penetrated his skull, about Doihara and the Shamanists, about the Boy Emperor and the flower-girl, about the Annamite in the Legation Guard who pulled a Chinese boy from his bicycle and about the feasts and murders which took place behind the high walls of Pekin. All this has passed away, as the swift-flowing river at our feet has passed away; but this evening, while the stars came out like little squares of transparent ice, they seemed real enough. The memories of the Chinese are long, but after an interval they are coloured by present emotions. The terrors of war are not perhaps greater than the terrors of peace: only more numerous. "There are places on the world's surface which are so terrible," said the Chinese boy, "that it seems difficult to believe that they can ever be occupied again. They say that the buried cities of Indo-China were left to the jungle because a terrible crime had been committed in them. Perhaps it would be better to leave Singapore to the mercy of the trees. . . ."

June 3rd . . . THE blind old seal-carver still wears glasses. He sits behind the counter of his little shop, and sometimes he takes off his glasses and gazes up at the sun. He can see very faintly—the difference only between light and shade. The faint incisions which he makes on jade are for ever hidden from him; and perhaps it is not necessary to see, for the sensitivity of his fingers is *three-dimensional*. I have watched him pass his finger-tips over a seal-carving of my name and tell me exactly to what depth, and in what shape, he had carved the letters. He has a long single strand of grey hair which trembles from his upper lip like the antennae of a moth. "These are in the characters of the old bronze seals," he said, as he gave me the carving. "They are the best. China was great then." I do not know why it is, but every peasant in China knows that his country was greatest in the Han Dynasty and speaks of past greatness with the terrible sincerity of those who know that it can never return again.

And as we walked down the dusty road in the broad sunlight, where everything dazzled and a clammy warmth came from the moist asphalt in the street, it was pleasant to touch and look at the jade carving done so delicately and with so much passion by a blind man who will never see his handiwork.

June 4th, The Moon . . . THERE were two immense rings, one faintly blue and the other golden, about the moon this evening. And from the outer edge of the farthermost ring streamers of shimmering blue light were continually being driven across the blue sky. I am told by my students that the most extraordinary things happen to the sun and the moon in China. There are rainbows round the sun sometimes, and what is more peculiar still is that they are not concentric but have different centres and cross one another, and the order of colours of the rainbow is often completely reversed. If you go up Mount Omel, you will find "the flames of Buddha", a great cliff filled with mist with rainbows ceaselessly playing on the surface; and in the midst of all these rainbows your own shadow can be seen magnified many times larger than life.

But I am content to watch the blue rings of the moon in Szechuan, and perhaps it was stupid of me to quote Vaughan's lines:

> *I saw Eternity the other night*
> *Like a great ring of pure and endless light,*

for the student immediately exclaimed: "But that's Chinese poetry —it's not English." I assured him it was English, and luckily managed to find it on the printed page for him. And then we went on to discuss the extraordinary similarity between Chinese and English poetry. There are Elizabethan love-songs which have so Chinese a flavour that it is almost impossible not to believe that they are translations. And so all evening we recited poems to each other, and wondered whether the Chinese poets were English or the English poets Chinese. There is, in both languages, the most effortless betrayal of sentiment: nothing is hidden, and the poet is fearless against the world, believing that everything he says is sacred, as indeed it is. But is there any other part of the world where the poets are so similar?

June 5th . . . ONE of my students has shown me a letter he has received from Bergery. He had written to ask Bergery about some particular difficulty, which has no place here; but towards the end of the long letter Bergery explained his own conception of life.

". . . Have you noticed how often in Chekhov and Katherine Mansfield the wrist flickers round, there is an infinitesimal movement of the hand on the clock-face and all that was dark before becomes instantaneously bright. The world is changeable, and we who live in her are as changeable as the sun and moon. I beg you not to despair. The moon and the sun are not living creatures; they have no courage; they do not lie awake at night, nor do they love. Yet they are splendid above everything else in the world, and we should do well to imitate them. Imitate all that is beautiful. Imitate (for this is more natural) the dancing things of the world, the stones in the river, the flowers in the earth, the pollen of trees. Not Solomon in all his glory was as beautiful as these . . .

372

"There are names that are singularly lighted up in my imagination, and I would have you attend to them earnestly. Among your own poets there are Chu Yuan, Li Ho, Tao Yuan-ming, Tu Fu and Li Shang-yin. I would wish you to know as much of these poets by heart as the human memory can hold. In England there is Shakespeare, Mallory, parts of Chaucer, most of the older Keats and everything of Smart's, even his doggerel translations. I would have you read Traherne's *Centuries of Meditation* and know them by heart; I would have you write some passages of commentary on the best works of my friend T. E. Lawrence. All that is bitter, all that is explosive in English prose is good: our best poetry for that reason is written by Englishmen and our best prose by Irishmen. . . .

"And there are other things I would talk about if there were more time, but my life is coming to a close and yours is beginning. This is as it should be. But let me confess once again that I can see no reason for the world except its beauty. *Geduld ist alles.* Have mercy and courage, and everything will be given you in double measure. . . .

"I believe in God, the angels, the saints who comfort us and our own immortal bodies which torment us. I believe in China—in her youth and her glorious opportunities in the future. (Be tolerant of the West, and remember that we are too young to be well-mannered; and do not judge us by our embassies.) I believe in England, and her tolerance, which is deeper and more understanding than you might think if you considered only her traditions. I believe in the tremendous spirituality of the Indians and the generosity, the almost unbelievable generosity of my countrymen. I believe in Hell, Heaven and Purgatory in that order, and yet have no more fear of them than a man who descends a mountain path at night has fear of the tombstones on the way. I believe in youth above all, and therefore I desire that you should believe in yourself and refuse to despair. Praise God, yes—and never despair. Look at the morning and the evening stars, the flowers and the animals: among them, and there is no reason to voyage farther, you will be safe. . . ."

June 6th . . . AT THE foot of Spendid Cloud Mountain there is a small village of huddled roofs and great banyan trees called Chin-k'an-pei. Somewhere in this region is the Pekin Mining Syndicate, but rather more important than any syndicates are the small houses covered with vines and approached only by long avenues where a few distinguished scholars have retired. This afternoon we called on an old scholar who is famous because in a book of a hundred pages published more than thirty years ago he made a reasonable attempt to synthesise the philosophies of Taoism, Confucianism and Buddhism.

It was one of the smallest houses I have ever seen, a single room which he used as bedroom and study. He wore an old tattered gown and a grey patched skull-cap; yet he was not poor. He was absorbed in his studies—those studies which would lead him in another ten years if he survived to write another small book of perhaps eighty pages on the religion of the Chinese. He was thin-boned, and had once been tall. His skin seemed paper-thin in the light coming from the paper windows. His white beard, like his clothes, was torn in places; but the great jade ring on his wrist, his courtly manners, his sharp beaked nose and the small black eyes peering from behind heavy lead-coloured spectacles suggested an enormous capacity for sustained thought. We talked about his first work—that small pamphlet which had changed a little the opinions of the scholars ever since.

"But scholarship is dying," he said. "The old order is dying—that is true. Yet scholarship is so precious in itself and as an example to others. In the West you have put your trust in scholars who are scientists, and perhaps that is legitimate; but I would prefer that there should be some good scholars who remain." He apologised for not speaking English perfectly and confessed that he had neither read an English book nor spoken to anyone speaking English for forty years, yet he spoke perfectly. "You have a good few scholars still in the Universities—there is a scholar who has studied the Chinese calendar in all its phases, having read 80,000 books on the subject, in your University. Perhaps he will write a book of 300 pages, or even of 400 pages, for all these things are important. People speak too much—speaking is an excuse for not thinking—and they study too little. Before the revolution we thought carefully before we spoke: today we think little, and talk too much. I cannot read the newspapers. There are *speeches:* there are *battles:* there is no *thinking.* In the old days Chinese scholars were chosen by the Emperor. On them there was imposed pure trust, and rarely did they misuse the trust. They lived frugally, governed honestly, wrote little and were content with the world. Our military commanders were scholars, Tu

374

Fu and Su T'ung-po were scholars and officials—even Tao Yuan-ming was an official. This was a world in which the behaviour of scholars was the hallmark of everyone's existence. Then how could we fail?"

His room was even poorer than the rooms of Chinese scholars in the University; he was talking a language which they alone still understood. There was the table, three or four ivory brushes, a tattered scroll on the wall, a jewelled fly-whisk which, since it was high summer, he was occasionally flicking against our clothes; there was the cheese-cloth mosquito curtain and the thick-soled slippers under the bed, and here and there on the walls, cut out from the scrolls which he had once possessed and considered insufficiently dignified to grace his bedroom, were *single characters of Chinese*, written boldly and elegantly, with tremendous passion and effrontery. It was as though the calligraphers at the moment of writing had seized the secrets of nature. There were perhaps twenty of these characters written in different styles and at different epochs; and it was clear that the old scholar believed that in the whole history of Chinese handwriting no characters as good as these had ever been painted. Later, just as we were about to leave, I noticed what appeared to be a bronze umbrella-stand behind the door filled with rolled-up scrolls.

It was then that the room became charged with excitement. One could not ask him—even as a favour—to show us the scrolls. One could only hope that he would notice their presence before we had gone. I felt sure that they were good; and they were better than anything I had ever seen before—copies of T'ang Dynasty paintings, a painting of a monk, perhaps Bodhidharma, in a red robe, a single curlew on a swinging branch painted in thick monochrome like tempera, some golden birds and some court ladies dancing at the foot of the throne, and four or five other paintings and a few pieces of calligraphy.

"The rain has got at them," he said sadly, pointing to the yellow spots, "but perhaps it is better like this. The world no longer appreciates good painting or good government. The world is covered with high clouds, and we hear only the murmur of the rivers and see nothing clearly. All that is good in China is past; and I am too old to hope for a resurrection."

June 7th . . . MARSHAL FENG YU-HSIANG is staying at Hot Springs. We walked among the deserted lotos-ponds in the rain, while the trees shone like jewels and the great yellow building which clings to the cliff wall shone like a fountain. Suddenly a wounded soldier came limping along the wet road. The Marshal stopped and gazed at him for a long while, with a curious wondering expression in his eyes. When the man came near, the Marshal bowed very low and smiled; and the wounded soldier smiled; then they began to talk in low voices like conspirators dreaming together. The talk went on for a long time. The rain dripped on their shaven heads, and on their clothes, and they were entirely unconscious of the rain. When the soldier had gone, the Marshal turned to me and said: "It is curious—I have led many armies to battle, but I have never been wounded. Perhaps I would understand better if I had been wounded."

We went back to the small villa he occupies near the lotos pools. He sat on his bed, joking and laughing, laughing sometimes until tears came to his eyes. Cross-legged on the bed, he no longer looks tall; he is reduced to human proportions until you remember that Buddha sits cross-legged behind the glass walls of his altar. We talked about the poverty of the Universities and of the soldiers, who are often terribly underfed; of the thieving and hoarding which are sweeping like a plague over China. He nodded silently. After a while he began to invent new names for all the foreigners he had known in China, for there are thousands of possible names which correspond to the sounds of a foreign name. He roared with laughter, but as we left he remembered the soldier limping along the muddy road and begged us to buy something at the shop which the soldier has opened—"anything, just a trifle, two or three dollars only". We walked out in the rain, and at a turning in the road we came to a small shop where biscuits and fans, rolls of towel-cloth and ink-stones with green inscriptions lay in profusion. The soldier was there, staring at the mist and the river. We talked about the Marshal. "He is so good to me, so good to me——" the soldier kept on saying, and his eyes filled with tears.

There is no point in this story. People *are* good to each other; people do weep and greet each other courteously in the rain. There is a lack of sophistication in the Chinese character at its best which is dangerously near to the most complete imaginable sophistication. There are people who say that the Marshal must be incredibly sophisticated and that his simplicity is a disguise, the disguise of the robber baron who is regarded as one of the
376

saviours of his country because he possessed a good advertising agent. It may be true. There is no judgment of these things. But J., who came with me, said afterwards the only words which have any meaning: "They were walking in the rain, they bowed to one another and afterwards they wept for the misery of the world."

June 8th . . . THERE are things in Chinese poetry which are impossible in English poetry—we cannot string together a list of nouns, and say that it is poetry. Today I came across two lines of Chinese poetry, one from Tu Fu and the other from another T'ang poet, Wang Tsang-ling. The first comes from a poem called the "Jade Flower Palace", which describes how Tu Fu came upon a deserted palace where the grey mice scurried among the roof-tiles and in the dark rooms there were ghostly green fires. But he does not say "in the dark room there were ghostly green fires". He says:

> *Dark room ghost green fire*
> Yin Fang Kuei Ch'in Huo

and since the first word is one of the most mysterious in the whole of the Chinese language, the line possesses from the beginning a singular force of resonance. There is no grammar, no verb, no adjective, no noun. There are only ideas jammed together by the power of association and meaning; and you see the poet wandering through the deserted courtyards, seeing the ghostly green fires more vividly than if there had been half a dozen adjectives. This is poetry reduced to essentials.

The second example is from a soldier's song:

> *Great desert wind dust sun colour dim*
> Ta Mo Feng Chen Shih Tseh Hung

You may translate this, if you please, as: "Over the wind and sand of the great desert the colour of the sun darkens." It will not be an accurate translation; it will be fifteen words long, and eight words longer than the original, and it will not help you to understand the crystalline gravity of the poetry. But it is the best we can do.

I do not know whether translation is ever possible. A novel may be translated, perhaps. A legal memorandum may be translated.

Journalism may be translated. T., who ekes out his University salary with voluminous translations, replied grimly: "Until recently the Chinese Government was always prepared to accept the text of its laws in the French version, but they have decided to go back to the ancient Wen-li way of writing. That at least was clear." And he added: "They say that in French everything can be said without ambiguity, and perhaps in the Wen-li language there is still less ambiguity—I do not know. But I do know that the laws of the Commonwealth of England should be written in pure pictograms. I was once arrested in England, and lost a fortune on the interpretation of a single word which could have been drawn in two strokes of a Chinese brush."

June 9th . . . I go round this campus like a ghost. I know every pebble, every flower-bed, every mud-brick building by heart. I know where the crocuses are planted, and where the sensitive plant ends; I know the byres, the sheepfolds, the piggeries, the place where the white eagles come to bask in the sun. I know all this as I know my own childhood; and it is quite certain that I shall leave at the end of this term and go to Kunming. I have not told Bergery. He will complain of being left alone; and if I ask him, as I shall, to accompany me to Kunming, he will say: "I am perfectly happy on my mountain. Go and spend your wild oats in Kunming (which has a terrible reputation), and leave me in peace." I shall not go in peace, and it will be so difficult to leave him that I shall go like someone blinded and amazed.

There are rumours of fighting between government and provincial troops in Kunming; of bandits and highwaymen on the Kweichow road; of seventy-two dangerous bends on the road to Kunming. I shall go, nevertheless; for though I have great loyalty to this University, the greatest University of all in China is in the south-west.

This evening, as I came across the river and climbed the muddy hill which leads to the campus, the moon shone on the white flowers beneath the flag-staff. The flowers shone in a kind of luminous brilliance which I have never seen before—it was half-ghostly and half-frightening. "We call it," said T., who has not an atom of poetry in him, "the moon-flowers shining in the snow."

I do not know how I can tear myself away from this place. The small cramped class-rooms, the colonnades round the campus, the muddy road to the library, the long walks along the coast of the river, the basket-ball players and the small tea-shops at the edge of the field: they are too much a part of my life for me to be away from them for long. And this moon shining on the ghostly flower-bed makes it more difficult than ever to depart.

June 15th . . . MOTOR-CARS still come to the hot springs, but God knows where they get their petrol from. There are sleek black limousines which look for all the world like streamlined seals. There are women walking in dresses which seem to have been made only yesterday; and there are fat profiteers looking like innocent caricatures. But there are also young girls and boys lying on the grass, and eagles spiralling high above their heads with bronze-coloured wings: there are small boys like *cherubinos* and small girls like dolls. There are temples which are now schools, and as you pass the walls, you hear the zzzzzzzmmmmmmmm of their continual repetition of the sounds of the Chinese characters. It is one of the most pleasant sounds in the world, and not to be forgotten; for it is as continuous as the river, and sweeter than the song of the golden oriole on the branches of the willows.

Bergery was waiting for us on the steps of the temple, leaning against the stone balustrade. Although it was warm he was covered in a heavy tweed coat, and there were three layers of muffler round his neck. He did not look ill, for his face was sunburnt; but he looked weak, and his weakness showed in the long thin hands as white as the stone wall, and the way he spoke. There was an unexpected heaviness in his words; he spoke with a kind of weighty insistence on their value, and sometimes his voice would break almost to tears, a broken cracked voice coming from the great head, from the soft lips, from the blue eyes, from the tangled autumn-coloured hair.

It occurred to me then that autumn had come, though it was ripe summer: an autumn of heavily-laden branches with downward-sweeping leaves, an autumn of silences. He was still tall, still immense; he still dominated those shining green-roofed temples and green lotos lakes, but he was slowly withdrawing into the shade. There was a museum in the temple behind us. It had been used as a library, and Bergery had objected; but today there were no cheap paper-backed books on the shelves—there were scrolls, stone lions, griffins, turtles bearing on their backs unicorns of a former age. There were ancient axe-shaped coins green with bronze mildew, and three or four precious examples of T'ang

Dynasty pottery which had been found in the caves above these rocks. Bergery developed a theory that a great town had once occupied the gorges; but the rocks had crumbled, leaving only the stone slab with its figurines of Taoist priests which can be seen on the rise of the mountain road. The temple at the top of Splendid Cloud Mountain is known to have existed in T'ang times. Surely this was a great place of pilgrimage, and he himself was the last of the pilgrims. Outside on the green lawn an extraordinarily beautiful child was suckling a baby. "There is peace in the gorges," he murmured.

We wandered down towards a small hotel which hangs over the roof of the gorges. From there you can see the blue-sailed sampans slowly moving down-stream. We noticed some enormous rafts on which houses had been built; and piled high on the rafts and all round them were bright-yellow inflated goat-skins.

"This must be the Kansu oil," he said. "They are floating it down from somewhere near the source of the Chialing river."

The oil passed down-stream, silently, into the gathering dusk. There were blue shadows under the ghinkho trees, and the girl who had been suckling the baby came into the hotel to rest a little from the last explosions of the summer heat.

"And when it is over, when all this war is over," he said, "people will still come here to rest from the heat. The lovers will hide at night in the limestone caves, and the truly adventurous will climb the mountain to the temple. There are no places in China which are sacred to peace; but there are quiet places where war may be forgotten. The Chinese are accustomed to war; therefore they have made oases of peace, and perhaps all that is great in the culture of China is no more than a terrible reaction to the commonplace of war. After the great wars there have been great painters, great musicians, great dancers. Kubla Khan sent his armies to Szechuan through Yunnan and Kweichow, but the arts of the Yuan Dynasty were almost as great as the arts of the Sung. War is not necessary, but war is the revenge which the world takes on itself, while art is the revenge which the artist takes on heaven. For the Chinese the blue sky is the source of all goodness. Let us be satisfied with these simplicities."

He was talking like a prophet, like a man who knows that he cannot live but must make terms with life. He spoke slowly and effortlessly, with terrible deliberation choosing his words. And suddenly he would stop and look at the white gulls floating against

380

the green river, or at the young girl still suckling the child. For him there can have been little difference between them.

"The Chinese have few amusements," he said a little later. "There are no cinemas in the small towns, as there are in America, nor is there electric light, nor is there central heating. All those things that the Americans prize are absent here. The Chinese like heavy furniture, the colour of the face of a child in candle-light, the touch of hands, the 'wave of the pines'. Their needs are simpler than ours; and this is only because they are more complex than we shall ever be. They play with their children, and never tire of this play. They are happy only when they are touching another. If D. H. Lawrence had come to China, he would have found all he was looking for—and he would have found a natural courtesy which is lacking, as it must be lacking, in the Australians or the American Indians. China will grow, but she will retain her sense of touch, her dignity and her lovely authority. There is shame in China, but it is different from ours. There is love, and that too is different from ours. There are many things which we can never understand, but if we could penetrate to the heart of their shame and their love we should know all the secrets of this land."

Someone began to tell him stories of the Szechuan villages, stories which made our blood curdle at the thought of the untamed rapacity of the peasants. They would skin dogs alive, and let them run loose with their skins hanging between their legs. Sodomy and incest were common on country farms; the haulers were homosexuals; there was no law for the protection of the young, who are made to work as soon as they can stand. These stories produced no effect on Bergery. He had known China before the revolution; and seeing it now, broken and corrupt, carved up by the Japanese, with an underfed army and a top-heavy bureaucracy, he was still hopeful, still gazing with those luminous blue eyes towards a future which seemed clearer and more sharply defined to him than to anyone else.

"Why should I give up hope?" he complained. "The villagers are cruel, but life is still more cruel to them. Sometimes I go to see the Abbot T'ai Shu on the temple at the top of the mountain. I am plagued with mosquitoes as I talk with him, but I dare not kill them, for my friend believes that they may be the lives of men who have died. I love all life—even that which is cruel. And if you tell me that a Chinese child works as soon as it can stand, which would you prefer—the pampered American child who has no character until the age of eighteen, or the Chinese peasant boy whose character is engraved on the lines of his face, a character which will change but which will always preserve the characteristics it possesses at the age of nine? I have no right to speak for China; I have only a right to speak for the love I bear the Chinese."

It grew darker. Lamps were lit. On the green table-cloth faint grey clouds floating over the gorges were reflected; and there were Bergery's great hands, pale to transparency, drumming continually on the cloth.

"Which would you prefer?" he continued. "Would you prefer life to come flowing in all its untrammelled strength, or would you see life as it can be seen in Brooklyn or Broadway? It is dangerous to dam the springs of life, and this is what the Chinese have never done. They cannot. They *are* life. They have not been poisoned yet with machines. . . ."

"The poison will come," I objected.

"But those who have this tremendous feeling for the pure form of life," he answered, "will transmute the poison into a rare metal. The Russians have done this. The Chinese will do it in even less time. We are apt to think of the four great powers as Britain, America, Russia and China. Unless we are careful the four great powers will be these, but stated in the reverse order."

"You really believe this?"

"Not entirely. The Chinese with power might realise that the power was useless. They would throw it away in a tremendous fit of laughing. What does a Taoist, or a Buddhist, or a Confucian do, when power falls into his hands?"

A little later he was speaking about the Chinese armies in Changsha.

"In the first round of the war in the Pacific, we all blundered. We blundered tactically and strategically. We knew, and yet we did not know. We thought in our blindness that the war was like all other wars; we had few military attachés to the Chinese in the field. We had no military attachés attached to the Spanish Republican Army. We thought the plans of war had been worked out—a few more tanks, a few more aeroplanes, nothing else. But war has changed, as life has changed. From now on we shall be in a continual state of change; and only those who are weak and sensitive will be able to adapt themselves to the violent changes

382

of the next fifty years. Change!—the whole world changing before our eyes, revolutions of custom and tradition, the dissolution of the elements and the new elements appearing like the heads of ghosts from the grey porcelain bowl in which all these things are mixed together—the witch's cauldron. There is going to be a time of change so vast that none may escape it. Britain will change out of recognition; once more America will search for her West; Russia will turn East; China will be flanked by great industrial centres on the sea-coast and deep in the interior. In the centre of the world will be India. Oh, if only we had time to prepare for it! But we have no time, no time—— The blue-prints we made yesterday are antiquated today. Only those who are wanderers of the spirit will survive.

"The wanderers survive; those who are rooted perish. This is the lesson of history, my friends. The crowns of Athens are given to the victors, but the victors pass on, and soon they have forgotten Athena and Artemis as they chase Bellona in the woods of Etruria. The victors pass on! They are no longer here, though their voice lingers for a little space. They have gone more quickly than the seasons or the fall of a pear. They were here yesterday; you saw their sturdy bronze limbs, but already they are only a memory. Today the victors are the Germans: tomorrow the victors will be the British and the Americans, but the day after tomorrow—— The victors have gone. There were vine-leaves in their hair. But there are others who remain—the girl suckling the child, the ploughman in his fields. The tradition is in the hands of women. Men have formed no tradition ever, for they are wanderers whether they will or no. Yet they survive, and the women perish." He sighed, and called for some more sweet wine, but though we heard the rattle of bottles in the corner, the wine was long in coming. "I say that we are wanderers, and it is better so. There was truth in this statement until a few moments ago. But now at last, after millenniums, we have come to an earth where wandering is no longer possible. There is no virgin earth left for us, and there is no place where the print of our feet has not been. This is the great revolution. For the first time in the history of the world we must find comfort in ourselves. We cannot escape ourselves. We cannot hide. We can fly in aeroplanes, travel in steamships, burrow under the Antarctic, but always we shall be accompanied by ghosts of ourselves—our friends. Listen! At the end of this war we shall have known everything. We shall be able to

383

control the tides, climb the highest mountains, bring rain from the skies, grow children perhaps in test-tubes. There will be no adventure left for us. What shall we do, we who are so accustomed to adventure? We must find, before it is too late, a worthy task for our lives, and we must find it now, in the middle of the war, in the silence that follows the crash of bombs. There is no time to be lost. And this is why China is important, for her philosophers for the last four thousand years have attempted to define the nobility and love of man. China is more important for her philosophers than for all her armies. She is more important because of her books than for all her swords and machine-guns. She is important to us now, at this desperate critical period of her life and ours, only because of her philosophers. . . ."

Bergery was exhausted now. The windows were open, and we looked down at the gorges filling with dark liquid light. Bruised clouds floated overhead, and it was no longer possible to see the hills on the other side, though sometimes a light gleamed swinging along the pathways. In his great tweed coat, muffled in scarves, Bergery was uttering his last testament, and hoping to be heard. We said nothing. In another room a small child was crying; and we heard the tinkle of knives in the kitchen as the fat maid-servant cleared up the dishes, and heard the call of the river-birds still floating over the gorge.

In the candle-light the great face seemed larger, more luminous and more carefree. One by one the scarves had fallen from his throat, and the great fur gloves he laid on the table at the beginning of dinner had been accidentally removed by the maid-servant. There was nothing more he wanted to say. There in the gorges the last wild birds were flying over an inky dark sea.

June 20th . . . I AM writing this in the aeroplane on the way to Chengtu. Small white clouds are rolling among the mountains; a grey-blue mist hovers on the horizon. The small Junker plane rattles in the wind, but we are sailing smoothly and intricately above the blue iceberg mountains. For a while I thought I had seen these blue mountains before, and wondered where. They are not like the bleeding-red hills of the cordilleras; they are not white like the Alps, nor greenish-yellow like the foot-hills of Switzerland in spring. They are blue like the sea, a luminous deep blue, never ending. And these blue mountains of Szechuan, with their regular waves, still seem to be in motion. Unchanging like
384

the sea, and yet for ever changing, they climb against the horizon and show the bellies of the waves in the sun.

The scenery has changed. There are fields of yellow rice and small hamlets; a river like a stream of milk. Cool, cool—the air, and underneath us everything is burning in a furnace. And still on the horizon there are waves of blue mountains, exactly like the blue mountains I have seen from Splendid Cloud Mountain. We passed over Peipei and followed the gorges; then turned north towards the great yellow fields and the open hearths; for truly this country is like a furnace, where liquid steel is hardening and the glow from the furnace doors. . . . And there are eagles, buzzards, kites—impossible to count them. The waves of the sea have disappeared. We passed a walled village where the grey cathedral spire climbs up above the red roof-tiles. Then once again the mountains, climbing higher and higher. . . .

Chengtu is the walled yellow city in the distance in the middle of a green plain. Utterly unlike Chungking. The earth flat, and springing green, the blue mountains enclosing her, and the great wall dividing only at the presence of a river. The wing dips down. The lemon-shaped airfield, the small red buildings with the same red-rusted drums of oil piled in great pyramids which I saw in Kweilin. The trees are different, the colour of the roof-tiles is different, there are no rocks as in Chungking—everything as smooth as the palm of the hand. Down, and then up again, as though the pilot knew that we wanted to see the city in its immensity, this city which was once the capital of southern China —*hsiao Pekin*—little Pekin—the greatest capital of the south. But the walls are broken in places, and the yellow wheat and rice are being gathered, and here and there among the fields are vivid blue and silver streams. It is the country which shines magnificently. The little rubble-heap of the yellow town is softened by the shadows of willows, but there are few great streets—a rabbit-warren, grey and brown, with nothing to commend it. Mercifully the airport is outside the town.

June 25th . . . I HAVE been staying on Hwa Shih-pa Campus. I have seen nothing so restful since I came to China. Under the broad midsummer sun, the cows graze in the green fields, the jackdaws flourish their wings and the great curving roofs of the Chinese library reach to heaven. It rained this morning. I walked barefoot over the flooded grass, splashing up silver splinters of rain. There were blue pigeons on the trees and great white clouds fanning the sky. Here, for the first time since I came to China, are University buildings which have the dignity which learning requires. They are heavy and solid; they have not been bombed except by accident. Under these willows and beside the sweet wells, learning can accomplish its destiny.

And perhaps, too, it is the quietness which makes this place so peaceful. There is no river at the foot of the steep cliffs; we are outside the wall of the town. I am no longer sharing a damp, concrete-floored room with a coolie, watching the paper windows as they are drenched by the rain. Here are all the comforts of European civilisation; and too late, I have decided that it is difficult to live without them. I think of Bergery perched on his small red table on the cliff-side, and then of this warm room, papered white, with a Han Dynasty vase on the mantelpiece, paintings, comfortable chairs. I was astounded when I first came to this University. The trim green hedges, the lotos lakes, the neat houses with their lawns, the young girls playing tennis and the boys lounging in the shade of elms—do these things happen? I had forgotten them, living in a world where poverty was the custom and riches were despised. One cannot live here for long; but for a moment—a *brief* moment—it is right that they should be enjoyed.

The world is far away. We are not in the world. The earth is flat, and this too is important, for ever since I came to China I seem to have been struggling up and downhill. Here you can ride bicycles, and perhaps it is this that is so surprising, for no one would dream of riding bicycles in Chungking. There are thousands of bicycles; nearly every student seems to possess one. There are reaches beyond the dreams of Chungking: everything is dearer; fortunes are being made every day; I am still wondering at the student who told me that he had been given a birthday present by his father, a bicycle costing $30,000.

But here at least one can recuperate. The silence of these huge willows, the great block of the campus stretching, it seems, for miles, the bright new hospital buildings, the leper colony, the wireless masts—they are all here. There is an atmosphere of applied Christianity, for half the professors on the campus are priests; and yet, behind it all, there is a curious sense of desolation, as though the place had been cut off from the world. A few
386

aeroplanes, like wisps of hay, fly overhead, but Chengtu is living quietly in its dreams. It will not always be like this.

We lay in the grass, watching the ducks waddling in the pond. The young student with the tousled hair and the thick eye-glasses is speaking reminiscently of the past:

"I didn't want to come here," he ruminated, "but the standard is lower in the Christian Universities at Chengtu than in the national Universities. I came down from the north. I was sick. I couldn't make the grade." His voice dropped, as a stream will drop below the level of the earth. "We are not in the war—that's what is so terrifying. We are living like lords, as though the war had never happened." He pointed to the obscenely ugly, yellow clock-tower, half Chinese, half Western, which rose above a clump of dwarf willows. "The city has been bombed, and the Governor of Szechuan who lives here had the foresight to drive some large main streets through the town, but the Japanese do not hate us. They have bombed every other University, but I suppose they think the Christian Universities are too scrupulous and too inefficient to be dangerous. Why is it? Our class-rooms are good—they are not farm-buildings, and yet we do not reach the grade of the other Universities. Are we taught badly? We have good scientists, the best Agricultural School in China and the best school of dentistry, and yet the feeling that it is all a waste of effort, leading nowhere, taunts us continually. . . ."

He had wanted to go to the great National University at Kunming, which comprises the three Universities of Tsing Hua, Pei Ta, and Nankai. He had dreamed of studying there all the way across the mountains of the north, and when he failed in the examinations, he had contemplated suicide. He regretted now that he had not taken agriculture. Nanking University's agricultural department had been transferred to Chengtu, and he spoke excitedly of Frank Dickenson and Professor Buck, who had between them revolutionised the agriculture of China.

"They are experimenting with everything," he said. "We have cows from test-tubes, yes—there are actually cows from test-tubes on this campus. They have examined Chinese agriculture thoroughly, and the course in agriculture is not easy: agricultural economics, agricultural statistics, methods of farming—every kind of imaginable course!" He was delighted with the fame of the agricultural department, but the agricultural department was not his own, and though he began to speak of the experiments in the

387

production of tea and cereals in Fuhtan, my old University, it was clear that his heart was set on watching the rise of Chinese agriculture.

We began to talk of human sewerage. Even in Chengtu, which is cleaner than Chungking, there were open sewers, and every morning the coolies came to the houses to collect the sewerage for the fields.

"It is one of the things that they have discovered in this University, though the Chinese peasants discovered it many years before. The land grows old. It is necessary that there should be organic nitrates to keep the earth living. There is only one way to do this, and the Chinese and the Mexicans have done it for generations, and even in the Middle Ages the Europeans did it. There is a balance between man and the land: the food he takes from the earth must be returned. They have discovered that without these organic substances, the earth perishes. Once people thought that plants required only inorganic substances—water, carbon dioxide, mineral salts—but we know better now. We do not yet know how plants grow, but gradually, with all the accumulated experience of the Chinese farmers behind us, we are beginning to learn."

We sat there, gazing idly at the blue-green ducks in the pond. Suddenly we looked over our shoulders, and we noticed a small cow, with all the delightful ungainliness of the young, wandering among the hedges. She was white, very silky, and the bones shone through the silk. The student jumped up, delighted beyond words.

"Here she is! She was born in a test-tube," he shouted happily. "The first cow in China who was born by artificial insemination."

July 1st . . . THE days pass quietly. Every morning I go to the Library and quench my thirst for books. There are five hundred books on China, and I am determined to tear the guts out of them. When I am tired of reading, I dream of the extraordinary vicissitudes of these books, which have travelled halfway across the world until they reach the corner of Tibet, or else I wander upstairs towards the Museum, where Tibetan bronzes rub shoulders with T'ang Dynasty paintings. There is an atmosphere of quiet and reflection; no dogs are barking, no children are howling. Under a glass case a Tibetan mask no longer looks savage. There is grace and dignity in the attitudes of the Buddha, in the small medallions and the huge bronzes.

388

Half a dozen Universities are now in Chengtu. The Christian Hwa Shih-pa University has been here for forty years, but Yenching University has at last travelled down from Pekin, and Nanking University and Ginling Women's College have both made their way from Nanking. They are strangers here, and their libraries are small; but they are sturdy, and in the opinions of many of the students their presence will increase the strength of Hwa Shih-pa.

Today, as I was coming out of the library, I met a research chemist whom I had known in Chungking. He, too, was appalled by the prospects of the Christian University going before the other Universities arrived.

"I am not being cruel, and I have many friends among the Christians, but they do not teach with the rigour which our time demands. They have not lost interest in teaching. They know the theory of teaching well, and they have produced brilliant research on the borders of Tibet and Szechuan, but they do not understand our students. Our students are rough. They are labourers. They must be drilled. They must be made to work until the blood pours from their eyeballs. But the missionaries are Christian kindness personified; they deal gently with the students; they pretend that our students are exactly the same as students abroad. You need a different technique when teaching in China. You can demand anything of the Chinese student—even the impossible, and it is only then that he will respect you. Or rather he will respect you if you drive him hard, and he will also respect you if he knows that you are a good scholar. But the missionaries are not scholars, and they do not drive our students hard."

His own work had been brilliant. I had heard before tales of the ingenuity of Chinese research scholars, who make X-ray plates from isinglass, test-tubes from any piece of molten glass they can find, whose copper wireless connections are made from the shavings from old guns and whose microscopes, damaged during the long epic journeys across China, have been patiently reassembled by men who have never learnt the trade. From dyestuffs and soapnuts they have invented new colours; and they are still experimenting upon ways and means of keeping these colours by the use of vegetable dyes. Even here, among all this apparent wealth, the resources of the research scientist are meagre in the extreme. Little was coming in, either for the scientists or the hospitals. The new Canadian Minister to Chungking was helping the hospitals

389

which were founded by Canadian money, but very few were helping the scientists. He was not bitter. In this backwater, among the weeping willows and the clean campuses, he thought he could defeat nature at her own game.

July 2nd . . . THERE has been excitement in Chengtu for some days. There have been many legends, and much has been written in the histories about the burial of an early Han Dynasty emperor near the East Gate. The work of excavation is now in progress, and though for some reason it is secret, and there are police guards and screens around the grave, while the Museum and the Academia Sinica keep a watching brief over the finds, it seems that the body of the Emperor has been removed, and there are only a few traces of the original occupant. I had imagined a tomb like Tutankhamen's, but in this hollowed square underground there appears to have been only a mud altar on which the king lay above a bath of mercury, and there are still signs of the mercury in the tomb. There are almost no furnishings left, and only a few parts of the body of the Emperor remain.

I talked to Chen Te-kun, the administrator of the Museum, about the finds and the future of archæology in China.

"Perhaps there are great things which the robbers overlooked, but it is unlikely. In Kansu and on the great caravan trade-routes across China we may still find some things; but the humidity of Szechuan turns everything to powder. Perhaps we shall find more bones from Anyang; perhaps we shall find in Szechuan and Tibet evidence of the great glory of our kings, and perhaps the tomb of the first Emperor of the Hans will reveal forgotten civilisations. But it is all unlikely. The earth of China is used for growing seed, and the farmers have reverence for their ancestors only to the third generation."

It was his museum in which I had wandered when I was tired of turning over the pages of books. There, in a large and purely Chinese house, ornamented with painted gables, with a great curving roof of gold tiles, the objects found on the Szechuan-Tibetan border were displayed with extraordinarily detailed explanations and descriptions in glass cases. I have never seen a museum so well arranged.

"But the trouble about the Museum," he explained, "is the simple one which arises when you consider the shape of the ancient Chinese houses. This museum is on the second floor, under the
390

curving roofs—and the curving roof is terribly wasteful of space. We have not yet developed a modern Chinese architecture. Perhaps we shall have to throw away the whole conception of the Chinese house, and build anew. We have no right to copy the Western shape, but we may be forced to, simply because concrete and steel obey the shapes that have already been discovered in the West. Here we waste space and keep design; it would be better if we could save the space and still keep our cherished designs." Then he added: "Have you noticed that the modern tendency in design in the West is to open up the house to the sun? In China we cover our houses with a deep roof to protect them from the burning heat."

The administrator of the museum is still young. With his Tibetan bronzes and Chinese paintings, he possesses one of the finest museums in the world. It stands out among the tawdry buildings which surrounded it, flashing its green and golden tiles in the sun. He was proud of the building, proud of the careful arrangement of the objects in the Museum, prouder still of the Border Research Society which was still attempting to piece together the extraordinary history of the relations between China and Tibet. It was another professor from another University altogether who said: "In a hundred years' time even Tibet will be industrialised. This is why the work of the Border Research Society is so important."

July 3rd . . . Sometimes, in reading about the ancient history of China, a few words from some long-forgotten book of classics become more revealing than any connected interpretation. This morning, opening at random the pages of Legge's monumental translation of the Chinese classics, my eyes fell upon the words:

"The people are the stars. Among the stars are some which love the wind, some the rain; the course of the sun and moon brings winter and summer; the wandering of the moon among the stars brings wind and rain."

This remarkable fragment appears in the Confucian *Book of History*, in a chapter called "The Great Declaration". It seems that when the Shang-Yin Empire collapsed under the military rule of the Duke of Chu, some portion of the state ritual of Shang-Yin was incorporated in the text of the new, enlarged ritual of Chu. It is possible, as Legge suggests, that a proper interpretation of the opening clause should be: "The people are like the stars", but later on in the same declaration there are the words: "Heaven sees as our people see; Heaven hears as our people hear." Here is the oldest known statement on the Chinese attitude to nature. The Emperor was never more than the intermediary between man and heaven, the "only one", the single link which owed its power to the restraining forces of Earth and Heaven. But it appears that in the Dynasty of Shang-Yin, the people were also in heaven. . . .

July 4th . . . IT IS raining. The muddy streets of Chengtu, between their high walls, are never ending. There are a thousand streets, and to go from one side of the city to the other, you must turn at right angles at least fifty times. In sunlight, there are parts of Chengtu which are splendid beyond words. There are huge barrel-shaped gates leading through the immense walls; and in places the walls have been broken down, revealing the great earthen fortifications beneath the stone brick tiles. But now, in the rain, small boys are bathing in a perfectly green river, among ducks and wild herons, and the egrets play on the banks. The bridges across the river groan under the weight of lorries, and sometimes the boys would look up from their games and splash each other, white against the forest of silver rain.

We were walking down a deserted street, where a few dead willows alone protected us from the rain. Suddenly my companion said: "You know, of course, that printing was invented in Chengtu. Somewhere here—within a few feet of here—the first printing press was established." I remembered vaguely that at some date in the T'ang Dynasty a printing press had been set up in Chengtu. I had forgotten that it was the first; and as I looked around, hoping to find some memorial to the small hand-press which has since revolutionised the world, I saw only a small courtyard, a few frail trees and some ragged children playing in the gutters. My companion laughed. "What do you expect? Chengtu is so rich, and it has been invaded so many times that all the memorials of the past have vanished. This city has been sacked so many times that we have lost count. We were sacked in 1917 by the Governor of Yunnan; we were sacked in 1921—— But why should I go on? We are accustomed to being sacked, and my forefathers were originally peasants from the north-west who aided the destroying armies. Then we settled here. This is the rich, red basin of Szechuan, perhaps the richest agricultural district on earth. Can you wonder that the governors of distant provinces have come and sacked this city?"

We wandered back through the rain across the University campus. It was growing late, and the flaring roofs of the buildings shone in the liquid sunset. We went towards the huge block of medical buildings which were designed by an artist who had attempted to integrate Western and Chinese designs. In particular, there was an enormous white concrete water-tower surmounted by a green-tiled flaring roof. It seemed to be perfectly proportioned to its setting. Unlike the other buildings, it stood out against the skyline, very tall, the white bastions of the concrete wall reflecting the green of the willows, while the green-tiled flaring roof dominated the scene. There are the ruins of walls and gates in Chungking, but the brilliantly painted joists and shining tiles of the roofs on the campus at Chengtu belong to the world I had half imagined in my childhood, a world of lotos pools and gardens, of jade girdle pendants and the sonorous voices of the chamberlains—a world which I thought had been destroyed altogether.

July 10th . . . I HAVE just read in the newspapers that two men I once knew in Paris have become the leaders of a provisional German Government in Moscow. Willi Bredel was short and red-faced, he had been wounded in Spain and he would talk with an extraordinary air of authority about the developments of the Spanish front. He had been a Labour agitator in Hamburg; he had jumped ship and made his way round the world; he had returned to Germany, been arrested by the Gestapo and escaped to fight in the Thaelmann battalion in Madrid. We would walk up the Boulevard Montmartre together, for we ate at the same restaurant, and in broken French and still more broken English he would talk of the course of the fighting. He knew everything. He was in touch with the refugees, with the men still fighting on the front, with the men like Modesto and Lister, who bore the brunt of the command; and he was always hopeful. He was bitter, and sometimes cantankerous. He was less than five feet in height, yet he had wielded great power among the labour unions in Germany, and he was accustomed to power. He wrote brilliantly. His short stories on the life of the German peasants and workers smelt of the steel-works, the ship-yard and the soil. He had made three trips to Spain since he was wounded; and he always spoke of Spain as though it were the country of the future. He would prophesy: "Spain is the first to suffer, next will be France, then Yugoslavia, then Poland, then Rumania. . . ." It was all beautifully worked out. I never understood why he attached so much importance to Yugoslavia, but it seemed at times to dominate his mind like an inhibition.

I saw Erich Weinert more rarely. He was ill from his wounds, very pale, and he leaned on a stick. He was still young, about thirty-five, but in those years he had put in a tremendous amount of revolutionary energy. There was a price on his head in Germany; he complained that he was followed by spies, which is not surprising, because there were times when refugees in Paris were followed by spies from four or five different nations. He was the pure intellectual. He wrote in a style which possessed none of the harsh brilliance of Willi Bredel; it was calm and assured, and his mind was as quiet as his style. If he becomes, as he may well become, the President of Germany, it will be the first time that an intellectual has had power over that country.

July 11th . . . MEMORIES of Germany. . . . The whole day, in the library, walking among the fields and beside the banks of streams, I have been absorbed in memories of Germany. Beer in the Englischer Garten in Munich, Hanns Johst defending himself vigorously against the charge that in *Schlageter* he wrote the words "When I hear the word 'culture', my hand reaches for my Mauser", the paintings in the exhibition of *Entartete Kunst* and Kokoschka's weeping willows, the red flags in Vienna, the long road shaded with lindens to the Starnberger See and the blue lake unruffled at high noon. The *gentleness* of Bavaria, and the flowering gentians, the sweetness of the air as it flows over the rye-fields of Augsburg, the high towers and crenellated spires, the fat *Mädchen*, the man who sold me tobacco at the corner of the Brennerstrasse, the mock salutes and the guns hidden under settees, the old men hobbling to the war memorial and the old women sheepishly laying flowers on the graves.

July 12th . . . FOR some reason, long after the event, we were discussing the bombing of Tokyo. The old Chinese professor in the brocade gown nodded his head vigorously as though he seemed to be in full agreement, but suddenly he began to speak, and I realised for the thousandth time since I came to China that a man who nods his head may be expressing the most profound disagreement.

"I was in Chungking during the bombardment," he said. "I have no wish that the Japanese should share the same fate. Nothing is so terrible, nothing is so remorseless, nothing so revolting to the soul as a bombardment. The soul cannot suffer in peace such indignities. Only now, two years afterwards, can I think coolly of what happened, and now I praise God that China for centuries refused to harbour such things. The Chinese knew all about poison gases fifteen centuries ago; we invented an aeroplane, and quite rightly executed the inventor; we are the only nation which has thought continually of peace. I have no malice against the Japanese, who killed my parents and my brothers. I have pity, but it is not Christian pity, I'm afraid—it is the pity that burns."

He asked me about Barcelona, and since we were drunk with the headiness of the subject I spoke of the girls lying in the mortuary at Barcelona looking as though they were sleeping; of the dead child which Toller and Marthe Huysmann found in the cathedral square; of the soldier who seemed to be bowing to me at Mora de Ebro; of Lister and Modesto and Cisneros and all the unsung heroes of the Spanish war.

"It was a popular war?" he asked.

"Yes, the people rushed the Montanes barracks in Madrid, armed themselves and killed the traitors."

"And their generals?"

"Their generals were stone-masons, carpenters, musicians like Gallen, a few members of the ancient general staff like de Rocca. The president was a doctor."

He smiled then, and pointed to a portrait on the wall.

"So is ours," he answered, "for Sun Yat-sen is permanent president of China." And then softly, lest he should be heard: "What crimes are committed in his name!"

July 13th . . . THIS campus frightens me. All afternoon I have been gazing up at a tree outlined against a blue sky the colour of old grass. The tree trembles in the wind, the crested woodpecker comes to the branches and sets the leaves swinging, and there is so much peace and contentment that we have all forgotten the war. It is amusing to see the missionary wives riding in shorts on bicycles over the campus, past the white and brindled cows, the willows and the orchards, cycling so slowly that it is impossible to believe that they are ever hurried. Life in Chengtu follows its accustomed paths; the sun shines, and after the rain we walk barefoot in the soft grass.

But where is the war? There are two aeroplanes in the sky, resembling minute golden cockchafers. Meanwhile the yellow-crested woodpecker drums on the trees.

July 14th . . . HE WAS an old man and he had served China well. He knew more about the border of Szechuan than any living man, and his gaunt figure striding up the foot-hills of Ta-chen-lu had been like a portent in the days before Europeans travelled there regularly. He is old now, but there were a few Buddha heads and trophies in the house, and he was proud of them as a man should be proud who has dedicated himself to their service.

"But do you know what we are fighting against?" he murmured, sucking at the ebony pipe. "We know many places where if we dig a few inches in the earth we shall find buried history. There are perhaps two hundred such places near Ta-chen-lu alone, and yet we cannot dig them. The Chinese reverence the earth. If you cut the earth with a plough, the earth does not misunderstand; she knows that the peasant must have his livelihood. But down below, four or five feet below, there are demons who can never be appeased. If they find us cutting the earth, they may even kill us. We must be surrounded by armed guards. It is with such accomplices that we discover the treasures of China."

He was a Christian, but he had thought so much of Tantric Buddhism that at any moment we expected him to perform miracles. I asked him whether he believed in the bear-men whose footprints have been seen on the Himalayas and about the Chinese priests who would walk naked in the coldest weather. He smiled gently: "There are many things more miraculous than that —things which even I, who have seen them, find difficult to believe. I have seen men walking on the air, I have seen men sinking slowly into the ground, I have seen the *richis* dancing on the snow-mountains." He went on at great length to describe the extraordinary marvels he had seen, then he smiled again: "You know—walking on the high mountains—it is easy to believe what you see."

396

July 15th . . . A CARD was brought up, but I did not recognise the name. I was busy, and asked the caller to wait; and even when he came into the room, lithe and handsome, wearing a white silk shirt and those long light blue trousers which are favoured by Chinese artisans, I could not place him. He reminded me of someone I had known, and when he smiled the resemblance became uncanny.

"Who are you?" I asked.

He mentioned a name which I did not recognise.

"It's the same name on the card," he said, and I could only answer: "I recognise the first character, but the other is very strange."

He laughed: "It's a kind of prehistoric and fabulous rabbit—Chinese names are really extraordinary."

A little while later I remembered. His brother had told me about him. I had shown polite interest, and forgotten the matter; and now I began to regret my forgetfulness, for the extraordinarily handsome youth with the flashing teeth and the enormous dark eyes was talking about his adventures. He had escaped from Pekin.

"For a while I stayed in a monastery near the frontier. It was terrible, for the monks no longer obeyed the Law, though the abbot was a good man. The abbot had no control over them; they flouted him, and mocked him behind his back. I cannot tell you what it was like in that white-walled monastery during the winter, with the Japanese prowling in the grounds, for they used parts of the temples as bawdy-houses; and all the while the abbot was praying and performing his office. Sometimes the monks would quarrel over women; they would fight, tear each other's clothes off, and in the evening they would be reprimanded by the abbot who would take out a little red rod and beat them lightly over the shoulders. Then the next day they would fight and quarrel again. . . . It was terrible. All through the winter there were women shivering in our cold courtyard. Sometimes they would die, and sometimes the Japanese would bayonet them, and all this in the silence of the monastery. In the end I left. I joined the guerrillas. Then I joined a propaganda unit. I was wounded in the first battle of Changsha. I opened a jeweller's shop in Kweilin, and all my jewels were bombed. It didn't matter—jewellery is a stupid thing for a young man to worry about. I taught in military schools. I have been mapping out the country around Ta-chen-lu, and now I am trying to go to England or America."

He spoke of all these things very simply, as though it was no longer possible to believe that they had really happened to him. There was a great red gash over his chest still visible through the light silk fabric of his shirt. Handsome, delightful, with all the vigour of the young Chinese, he set out that night to conquer a new world.

July 16th . . . I REMEMBER at Fuhtan a performance of Tsao Yu's play: "Twenty-eight Black Words". It was one of the earliest of the plays directed at the Japanese. There was the villain who looked and behaved exactly like Doihara. There was the boy who wore spectacles and who appeared to be quite mad until the last act, when it became clear that he was the head of the Chungking secret agents. There was the father who was a traitor, and yet not a traitor; there was the stupid servant who was really extremely clever; there were four or five young Chinese, and there was a scene at the end beside a monument, in which my stepson, carrying a basket of flowers and decorated with grease-paint, stole the show.

I had been thinking of this play while J. related the recent arrival of spies in the quiet campus of the University here. There were four pro-Japanese spies, and they had slept for many nights in an apartment near the girls' dormitory. The girls sheltered them, believing that they were refugees; they fed them; found them quilts and mattresses and tried to arrange that they should be sent to Chungking. The charity organisations were helping them, but no one knew where they lived. One night they were arrested, tortured and shot. It was as simple as that. J. shuddered: "But what is so terrible is that we can no longer be sure that the refugees are genuine. How shall we tell? We are not capable of seeing into everyone's soul." He was a little frightened, and as I listened to his quiet voice in the shaded room, some of his fear was communicated to the atmosphere. He went on: "There are bandits everywhere in China. There are a few in the cities, but they are disguised as merchants, but it is on the main roads that you see the bandits. They have guns, arms, weapons. A whole army of them were captured by National Government troops in Kweiyang last year. This is what we are fighting against—poverty

398

and illness, the rigours of a long war, the people still wandering and unable to live, and we are fighting the Japanese."

He told an extraordinary story of some bandits who entered Chengtu a few weeks before. They were stopped by a policeman on the bridge, and because he refused to let them pass, he was knifed in the back and thrown into the river. By good luck he was not yet dead. He managed to swim to shore, and get in touch with the gendarmerie, but the bandits had fled. The policeman was given a funeral attended by the Governor of Szechuan, who made a speech extolling his courage and loyalty to the state. "But the bandits still come—you will meet them on your way from Chungking to Kunming. They are not the descendants of the old armies of the war-lords: they are the children of the inflation and of the prolonged war."

It was a sad picture that he described in this room where the lamplight came through frosted glass, and it was impossible to see clearly—a picture of China at war, mounting prices, bandits, incompetent officials, an underfed and unarmed army which was numerically the greatest in the world. He was a student of history. He believed that the good Chinese earth could hardly support the massive populations who lived on her, and therefore wars were necessary in order that the best should survive. It seemed an untenable theory, a theory born of despair, of the great indifference of the rich and the poor cunning of the poor. But in this half-light, with rumours of banditry and sudden execution all round, it seemed the only theory which would account for the terrors which are let loose on this beloved country of China.

July 17th, Conversation with an American . . . "I CAN'T understand why the Government allows the Chinese Universities to continue," he exploded, puffing until the little red berry of his cigar shone as brilliant as the morning star. "The way I see it is— it's just waste! Chinese students coming to American Universities in war-time! My dear sir, is the Chinese Government aware that there is a war on?"

The young Chinese in shorts, sitting cross-legged on the floor, smiled benevolently. It is clear that he was not in the least amused. He smiled, with that terrible archaic benevolence which is the birthright of the Chinese.

"And what is more," said the American, "I told your Minister of Education exactly what is on my mind. He is a sensible man,

399

your Minister of Education. I'm sure he agreed with me. . . ."

"You are quite sure?" the young Chinese asked gently. "You see, I happen to know that he has spent the greater part of his family fortune in trying to keep the Universities going. He is the man who did more than any other to help them to survive."

It was no use. "I told him that in America our Universities are dead against letting youngsters come along and take subjects which have no use for winning the war. Yes, sir, we are going to win the war, and the Universities are going to help us. Breeding cows on the campus! That's what I see here. What use is that to winning the war——"

"They are Mme Chiang's cows," the young Chinese objected.

"I don't care whose cows they are. Agriculture, eh? Cows and sheep and wild pigs—what use are they? Make bombs, aeroplanes, train pilots, learn to use cold steel, my lad—that's the way to fight wars."

"Have you ever fought in a war, sir?"

"No, sirree—but I am at the service of Franklin D. Roosevelt, President of the United States——"

"President Roosevelt has said some very nice things about the Chinese Universities."

"That may have been some time ago, my lad, but now—look at it with unprejudiced eyes. The Universities are going on, training sixteen-year-old students to read the Chinese classics, and a little bit of Wordsworth and some of the old poets, and perhaps a bit of elementary physics, and some chemistry, and French, and the English novel—whatever to God that is—and Western History. What in heck is the good of teaching these nobodies Western History? I'd drill them and send them into the army, by God I would!"

I am afraid the young Chinese burst out laughing, rolling over and over on the floor. The American was annoyed. He was puffing furiously at his cigar, so that the little red berry resembled one of those winking station lamps which you see on frosty evenings. "By God I'd send them to the army. . . . Playing about on the campus, and doing no good to anybody on God's earth. Discipline, sirree. That's the word!"

But the Chinese, who is a colloid chemist, was laughing so much that we thought he was in danger of collapsing. The American, who might easily have been an Englishman, went away in high dudgeon, and he could not understand the parting words of the Chinese: "We are trying desperately to build a civilisation out of our ruins, and do you expect we can build it with coolies? We can, but we must train them first!" There was no answer. A door slammed, and the Chinese was still rolling about the floor.

I learnt something of his history later. He had organised the students who fought against the Japanese on the outskirts of Pekin. He had been wounded. For months he stayed in a peasant's cottage in the Western Hills, trying to recover from his wounds and at the same time to escape. There was a price on his head. The Japanese surrounded the cottage, bayoneted the peasant and his wife but failed to find him. He escaped with the help of the guerrillas. He worked for a while with C.I.C., the huge organisation which Rewi Alley has created to provide an arsenal of democracy in China, living on a pint of beans a week in the frozen winters of Lanchow, where if you spit, the tinkle of the falling ice can be heard for fifty yards around. Three years ago he joined a famous University in the south-west, but prices were rising and he left his wife and three young children in Chengtu. He was twenty-eight. In the last five years he had experienced twenty times as much as the American had ever experienced in the safety of his government office.

July 25th, The Leper Colony . . . In a small black octagonal building just outside the University, the lepers were playing with their children. There were men and women; they wore light blue clothes, and looked hardly at all different from the Chinese walking under the shade of the willows outside. They were fanning themselves, for the heat was terrible. And sitting on the wooden benches with their children at their knees, smiling and whispering together, it was curious to think that they never went outside the wooden gate. They were prisoners. They could see the wireless buildings, the low-roofed buildings where Dr. Frank Price has established his theological school; they could see the green walls of Chengtu and listen to the boats on the Min river, but they do not see these things clearly. The grey-haired doctor smiled at them and they smiled back. He was fascinated by this disease, and he had spent almost his whole life attempting to understand its problems. "We are trying the sulfa drugs now——" he said, and then shrugged his shoulders. "It's too deep-rooted— it goes right into them, and nothing except chudanagra oil seems to do any good, and God alone knows why that works so well.

401

One day we shall hit on a solution. It will be, I think, a surprisingly simple solution, something that has been under our eyes for generations." It was a mysterious statement, and I wondered what lay behind it. Had he discovered, or half-discovered, a solution to a problem which has mortified physicians since the time of Genesis? He pointed to a strapping young boy who showed no signs of the disease. "He was full of it three years ago—it's gone now. We don't know when it will return, we don't even know whether he is cured, and he is staying here for a month or two more to be under observation." He looked a fine specimen of young Chinese manhood, and it was difficult to think that he had ever had leprosy. "There's his mother over there," the doctor said, pointing to a woman whose face was like a white wound. "I am afraid she will never recover."

July 26th . . . STEPPING into the anatomy laboratory by accident, I saw a pale head leering at me from the trough. The head was not white, but greyish-blue; there was a perfect row of teeth and the eyes were wide open. There was only the head, and it had been balanced very carefully on the wooden trough, so that anyone entering the room would see the brilliant smile.

I spoke about the head later in the afternoon to a doctor from Canada, one of the most brilliant surgeons that China has ever seen. We were drinking tea from porcelain cups; there were egg-cakes and three or four different kinds of sponge. There was even milk in the tea, and white crystallised sugar.

"But the great difficulty—the greatest difficulty of all—is to get bodies for dissection. The Chinese hate to be dissected. Our medical students are praying for bodies. In the old days we could always have the bodies of criminals, but unfortunately executions are comparatively rare nowadays. What can we do? We must have bodies. We ask people to let us have their bodies after they are dead; we are prepared to pay for them, but hardly a soul agrees—even the poorest prefer to die whole."

"But the dead soldiers?"

"Soldiers die, of course—chiefly of starvation in China, but they die. The trouble is that they don't die very near here. There are four or five hospitals here, but we all want bodies. The nurses from P.U.M.C. are working here, and many of the best doctors from Pekin Union Medical College have arrived. This is the best hospital in Free China, but where can we get bodies?"

402

He looked very sad.

"If you die in the next few days before your return to Chung-king," the doctor asked, "it would be a kindness on your part if you could let us have your body."

"Certainly," I said.

But ever since making that statement, I have been afraid that I shall be waylaid.

July 28th, A Letter from Bergery . . . ". . . ALL this summer it has been fine. There are bluish-white clouds, great drifts of clouds and birds overhead; there are flowers on the slopes of the mountain, little green flowers with white cups, little red flowers shaped like our heart's-ease and small grey-green primulas and alpinias. This is a naturalist's paradise. I sit and read in bed out of doors, looking down on this peaceful valley, while the mist rises effortlessly—effortlessly from the gorges. Oh, and there are leopards and squirrels and green adders with yellow shining eyes in the grass, and a small fountain where I bathe in splendour. Here on the heights, as you promised, there is peace. For me this heat, this intense torrid golden heat draining out of the sun, is something so splendid that I cannot understand why I have ever taken shelter from the sun. The girl in the red trousers' complains. I have asked her to be near me, but she prefers the quiet shade of the temple; and besides she is for ever suckling her child, and she is ashamed. But how noble she is! Plump as a fine pear, with backward-sweeping glossy hair, smiling always, walking like Ruth in the orchard, splendid above all animals and so strong and robust that the wind and the rain must be in ceaseless torment when she appears.

"There was a time when I despised men. When we left Spain I despised the Senegalese who barred our path. I despised, and no longer despise, English politicians, but German politicians leave me with a feeling that the sacrifice of intelligence has been too great. I did not love men in the last few years of Europe. But now—now—now, on this mountain-top, I have such a hunger for loving, such a terrible thirst to throw my love over the whole world, such delight in the sun, such terror—yes, terror of living, since everything is so beautiful and so fine that I can hardly bear another moment to remain on this mountain-top. I must go back to the world. The monks are not my friends, though I love them; but I cannot live their life of ritual and I only half understand

403

them. I must go back among common people, the young girls, the young boys lying under the shelter of leaves, the boys in the fishing-villages of Spain, the girls in the white chalets of Switzerland, the men and women of the world. I shall not go among ambassadors and officials any more, for I cannot live in the world which is inhabited by pieces of official notepaper walking on two legs. There must be freedom, and perhaps there is this freedom among the soldiers. . . .

"Do you know, Robert, that extraordinary moment which occurs during convalescence when the blood, so heavy and lukewarm, suddenly stirs and rushes like a fountain? For days you have felt heavy and depressed, for days you have thought only of death; but now, at this moment, this terrible moment, life rushes back again into your veins. This is the supreme happiness. When I was a child I would commit a small sin for the pure joy of confessing it in the confessional. So now I am amazed at the thought that perhaps I have been ill for the sheer joy of having these moments of convalescence.

"I will go to Chungking shortly. I must pick up the threads. I won't live in one of those rooms in the Press Hostel where the boards are paper-thin and you can hear your neighbour thinking. I will tour all the battlefields of the world, see everything, write as honestly and truly as I can of the things of this world. I am dismayed with our journalists. They had the opportunity to write as men never wrote before: they had adventures such as no men have ever known, and yet they write in the same post-Hemingway style as ever. They are children—and yes, perhaps, this, the worst of all wars, is a war of children, who have no idea where they are going. We talk of our rights and freedoms, we do not talk of our duties. We are children of caprice, in whose hands too much power has been placed. Let us begin again. I am still young. I must see the world, or die on a remote mountain-top in China, forgotten by everyone and out of touch with the world.

"Thinking I was dying, I wrote a will, but now I have torn it up. My family knows where my property can be found; and it is curious to think that nearly everything I possess has been left in Paris, Vienna and Pekin. But it is good to travel unburdened. I shall wander over the world with a tooth-brush in my pocket, and try like Walt Whitman to give comfort to the wounded. Do you agree? A life of wandering—the war—and yet to be at every moment humbly and dutifully at the service of heroes. . . .

404

"The world has grown so intolerably tense, so charged with hatred, so filled with happiness gone astray and fortune misplaced that I imagine an old man, an idiot, deformed, perhaps an old soldier, coming after a long visit to the South Sea Islands into the world at war. What will he say? He will look at the corpses hanging on the barbed wire, he will glance pitifully at the shattered houses which are the tombs of old women, he will stifle back a sigh at the prospect of so many innocents massacred or perhaps he will throw himself down naked on the earth like Job and complain against the Creator. No, he will not be like this. He will be a man full of compassion and mercy that he will go round the hospital wards tenderly comforting the people who lie on the beds; he will gather flowers and place them on the graves of children, he will strive with everything in his power to remove the causes of suffering, however light they are. He will be a servant of humanity. He will love gently and simply. He will bow down before God, and without understanding, he will know that it is all the will of God. He will be called an idiot; his deformities will be pointed out by all who are evil-minded, and perhaps it is necessary that he should be deformed, so that people may recognise him. . . .

"In my mind I have always thought of Christ as a young boy, like the Christian Orpheus you can see on the walls of the catacombs with a lyre in his hand and sheep dancing in the foreground. There is nothing more beautiful than a young boy. And so I believed in Christ almost as a mother believes in her son, or as a woman believes in her lover. But now I remember the stories that he was a hunch-back and it was therefore difficult to nail him to the cross; and perhaps it is true that a man must be deformed like Kierkegaard or Christ to do good in the world. . . .

"In the old days there was chivalry, and if an idiot boy fell in the water, there were thousands who would spring forward and rescue him. Even today there is chivalry among the Allied Powers, but how long can it remain? I have read of German pilots circling round our own pilots as they descend by parachute and shooting them. I have read of Japanese soldiers beheading the brave Australians for no greater crime than their surrender at Singapore. What kind of world is this? It is as though we were reading the histories of the tribes, not of the nations. You are right. We must build cities. They are the chief glories of man. . . .

"And so now, as I think of returning to Chungking, I want you

405

to believe that it was good to stay on the mountain-top. 'The girl in the red trousers' has been writing a letter to her mother; she dips her brush in the ink-stone and like any child she sucks the brush with her lips. She looks like a cannibal, with black and white lines etched all over her lips. But how beautiful she is as she springs up and catches the baby in her arms, and strides down to the fountain and throws him into the great rush of blue water. I can hardly leave her; and the old renegade priest, her husband, chewing tobacco on the steps of the temple, sometimes kneeling on the hassocks, but more often making love to his wife —no, this is what is so difficult to leave. In war we are segregated, at the mercy of every wind that blows, but here on this mountain-top there is too much freedom, too much even for those who admire and love freedom above all things. I pray for the living and the dying, for both have freedom. What is terrible is death, and it is terrible because there is no longer any freedom. She has come back. She has bathed her face in the water, but still there are a few marks of the ink. . . ."

There were a few more words to the letter, but they have little importance. I have written them as they stood in his cramped handwriting, where all the t's resemble l's and every w is an m. In a postscript he asked me to meet him in Chungking in the middle of August. There were letters and messages for professors at Chengtu, a drawing of Kuan Yin which had been presented to him by a priest and a lock of the child's hair. I have a curious feeling that he is dying. There is a finality in the letter which terrifies me. I think of him in the temple at night, reading by the Buddha lamps, the settled sadness of his smile, the heavy face carved out of granite on which weariness gives place to the delight of a child.

This evening I caught myself thinking he was already dead. I imagined his burial on the mountains and the face of the young girl. I imagined his whole history, and even wondered whether he had lived in vain or outlived his usefulness. But I know that whether he dies or lives, having seen his face, the rest of my life is only a waiting.

July 29th . . . A TELEGRAM arrived at 6.30 this evening. It was written in Chinese, and under each Chinese character there were pencilled numbers of code, for the Chinese send telegrams by the most complicated numerical code in the world. It read:

COME QUICKLY BERGERY DYING ASKING FOR YOU
BRING DOCTOR NOTHING SO URGENT.

It was signed by "the girl in the red trousers".

July 30th . . . I AM writing this in the crowded motor-bus.
There are no seats. We sit precariously on our luggage, struggling
against the wind, the rocky road, the sudden lurching and the
violence of the countryside. It is still raining. We have been climbing and winding among steep grey hills, and the great red plains
of Chengtu are far behind us. There are small hamlets, where
peasants crowd over little green wisps of flame; and once or twice
we have passed men in ragged uniform, with rifles on their shoulders, and as we scudded past they have turned their backs. The
fat girl screamed "bandits". She was probably right, but no one
cares, though we go on to discuss the large army of bandits that
has been seen around Mount Omei. I curse myself for not having
climbed Mount Omei, the most sacred Buddhist mountain in
China; I am angry because I have not seen the temple dedicated
to Tu Fu, or that other temple, greater and more mysterious,
dedicated to the hero of the *Story of the Three Kingdoms,* Chu
Ko-liang. But it is no use thinking about these things. I have enjoyed the comforts of Szechuan, and life will be harder from now
on. I am glad.

There is nothing to see. The rain pelts the canvas roof of this cat-
tle-truck, and we are being bounced inextricably together. A wide
pagoda flashes past, so beautiful and still that even the little
banker's clerk with the wad of American money which he is going to exchange on the black market in Chungking is awed into
silence. In three hours, if we are lucky, we shall reach Niechang,
where sugar is being hoarded by the merchants who are determined to beat the Government monopoly. There are sweet-cakes
there; nougat; crystallised fruit. There is even a hotel. We have
passed the wrecks of three buses already. "At Niechang," said the
bus-driver, "there are all the comforts of the world. . . ."

August 1st . . . I DO not like Niechang. It is an insufferable
city to wander about in. It consists of two roads at right angles,
and somewhere in the neighbourhood there is a distillery where
urine and sugar-beet are combined to produce alcohol. I liked the
distillery. It was clean with a robust German cleanliness; it looked

a little like the inside of a ship and it was managed by a scientist who wore a maroon-coloured gown and who wandered about in the immense building like the gentlest of Chinese scholars. His factory is immense. There are gardens and orchards, small timber-roofed houses where the workmen surround themselves with the most exotically beautiful children and a small pond in the middle of which (perhaps this is inevitable) there is a statue of Queen Victoria. But Niechang itself. . . . Everyone is rich, everyone appears to have a motor-car, everyone is plump and silly, and the garrison commander has long teeth, speaks French with an insufferable accent and bows like a Polish cavalier. The hotel is full of bugs, the streets are full of beggars and lepers, and the shelves of bottled crystallised fruit are an offence to the good taste of the Chinese. You smell sugar as soon as you come to this town. I do not like this town. I have spent thirty-six hours in it, because the damned bus has broken down. I do not wish to spend another second here.

August 3rd . . . BACK in Peipei. Temperature 103°. There was an apologetic little note from Bergery waiting for me at the hotel. "It was nothing, of course, and you must not be frightened. They all panicked because I was spitting blood, but it's all over now—the last stage of the convalescent. I am up and about again —not very strong, but I feel that the real convalescence is happening now. The girl in the red trousers has just bathed my face, and she has brought a basin of water. 'What shall I do with it?' 'Put your wrists in it.' 'And then?' 'That's all—it is cold water from the fountain. It heals.' I have obeyed her, and soon I felt the cool water springing through my veins. Come when you can. B."

August 4th . . . THE servant came down from the mountain in the early hours of the morning. He was very calm and said very little, except that Bergery was dying, and would I go up. He wore a blue shirt streaked with sweat, and though it was already broad daylight he carried a lantern in which the tung-oil flames still shone in wreaths of black smoke. The sun shone. The river was pale green, and the mountains above us were also green, and even the sky seemed to be tinged with this colour. In the heat we staggered up the dusty mountain paths, occasionally resting on deserted tombstones or in the shade of the tung-oil trees. I do not know why it is, but the shade of the sparse tung-oil trees is prefer-
408

able to that of the pines: cooler and more refreshing. It was past noon when we came to the small temple high up on the spur of the mountain. Smoke came from the roof: and I knew then that he must still be living.

I ran most of the way across the spur of the hill, while the servant grumbled. He had bought some rice, sweet bread and biscuits in the little village at the foot of the hot springs; and now the weight of these things caused him to suffer abominably. He staggered along, breathless and uncomfortable, and I could hear the hiss of his breathing when I passed through the gates of the temple.

Bergery lay in bed, his face very white. The young girl, wearing only red trousers and a thin blue milk-stained blouse, was fanning the flies from his face. All the while he was coughing up blood. He smiled when I came in, waved his hands and immediately began a fit of coughing. He turned his face away to the wall, where the gilded buddhas and blue-green frescoes of dancing girls reflected the light. Meanwhile the young girl ran away, only to return a few moments later with a basket of enormous blue grapes.

"Everything is happening so quickly now," he complained. "I am losing blood, but that doesn't worry me so much as that I am losing hope."

I told him that we could easily fly him to a sanatorium in India.

"Last year I seriously thought of going to a sanatorium, but the Indians wrecked it. I don't blame them, or rather I think I understand them. In every civilisation there is a moment when the people take their revenge upon the machines. It happened with the wreckers in England, and it will happen again with the Germans after this war. I wonder if it is true that the Indians sympathised with the Japanese! I doubt it! They tortured British airmen, they derailed trains, they burnt factories; and surely it was nothing more than a sudden, instinctive and overwhelming hate for the machines. And it is better that it should happen now than later."

He looked out through the lattice-work of gilded doors and smiled at the expanse of blue iceberg-like mountains. After a while he said:

"It is a pity I am dying. I might have been of some use. I have seen more wars than most people, and travelled more, and perhaps felt more, but always I was conscious of the vanity of things. This is what spoilt my life. Once or twice in my life I had power;

409

but I threw it away, because I did not believe that power was good, or even that it was necessary. I'm the last of the Liberal journalists. Those who came after me were mostly youths, without the ability to think, though they could describe well enough the exteriors of things. In the old days we believed the Liberals were descendants of the *homines liberi*, who built the city states of the Middle Ages and fought against Emperors and Popes. We believed in the European tradition, but what do people believe in nowadays? We belong to Europe. I was born in New England, but I am still a European—nothing can change that. I cannot escape, even if I wanted to. There is no escape for us. And though we use the word 'destiny' rarely, we know that it is our destiny to remain always good Europeans."

He lay back exhausted. He was sick and ill, but there was still the same extraordinary blue light in his eyes. They were shining now, as he lay back, his head against the monstrous stuffed pillows, his hands spread out in front of him. Against the golden fret-work of the temple and the crumbling gods he looked theatrical; and the blood on the counterpane was surely grease-paint. He was a little conscious of this, and hated it.

"The Liberal is the only free man," he continued. "He values life, and yet he is prepared to die for the sake of his freedom; and he orders all those who cherish freedom to strive with their lives not only for the sake of freedom, but against any particular freedom when it destroys the love of life in people's hearts. We have only one aim—that people should love life. *The world is a place where people must learn to play in.* I believe that we should adore life, and that it is there only to be adored; and the dance of life is something that truly exists, and without it our lives have no meaning."

The little girl was chewing grapes and spitting out the seeds. From time to time Bergery looked at her. There was a curious sympathy between them. The child was very young, slender and thin, but graceful in her red trousers. A few chickens came through the open doors. I heard pigs grunting behind the temple, and the sound of mallets in the forest, and all the while I was conscious of Bergery's enormous head and the transparent blue eyes.

"It is more difficult to die when you love freedom. For the Germans it must be easier," he said after a while.
410

We began to speak of the early years which followed the last great war.

"In the Ruhr were sown the seeds of the revolt—and surely it is true to say that the Germans have revolted from the European tradition. They substituted a tradition which belongs to the steppes—there is nothing so much like Hitlerism as the shamanism of the Mongols. And indeed, when you look at Hitler, have you noticed how extraordinarily Mongoloid he is? Poincaré and Hitler! Both Mongoloid, and both throw-backs to the times when the Huns were besieging Europe. Oh, don't laugh! Nothing is more possible according to the anthropologists, and surely nothing shows us more definitely the tragedy of our past. Europe cannot change. Even if men have free-will, nations possess it rarely. We are the children of destiny, and our destiny is Europe."

I thought, then, of the extraordinary strains which possessed the blood of the man who was dying on a high mountain-top in China. He was Huguenot, but there was Swedish, German, Irish, English and American blood in him; and perhaps—though I have forgotten—there were French, Italian and Portuguese strains. His fair hair lay on the pillows like a cluster of bright feathers; his eyes were an impenetrable and yet transparent blue; his nose and chin were Huguenot, finely carved, but his round forehead was Irish. Everything that had made Europe was concentrated in him, and when he spoke of Europe, he gave the word an assured resonance which echoed in the rarefied mountain air of Szechuan.

I asked him whether I could arrange for him to be transported to Persia, for it was clear that there was something in India which displeased him.

"But why Persia? I have finished with Persian studies—there is nothing except love poetry and a few well-written memoirs by the Emperors. I could have wished I had time to study Sanscrit again—it is the richest of all languages. I am learning Chinese. Why do you plague me with these civilisations of yours?"

He began to speak of his progress in Chinese. A monk came from the monastery on Splendid Cloud Mountain twice a week. The monk knew no English, and they would talk of Chinese poetry and philosophy all day from early morning to late at night. Bergery could read Chinese, and he remembered many poems, but he spoke the language with difficulty. "One must spend two hours with a tutor every day," he once complained, "and how can

411

I spend two hours every day in the middle of New York?" He laughed when I pointed to the books in the headpiece of the bed. There was a Bible, a Shakespeare, Malory's *Morte d'Arthur, Alice in Wonderland* and the poems of Antonio Machado. The rest of the books were reprints of Chinese classics.

"So it has come to that!" I said. "You speak of European culture, and in a sense you do everything in your power to represent it, but you have only five books from Europe on your shelves."

"You find this surprising?"

"Yes."

"But isn't this inevitable? I am a European, but I am also a man living on a high mountain. I can take with me only what is essential, and surely nothing else is essential. The Bible, Shakespeare, Malory represent the past, and Antonio Machado represents the present. I would like to have read Stephen Spender's *Ruins and Visions,* but how can one get books here? I am told that Louis Aragon has written some good poems, but where can I get them? Certainly not in this mountain-top in China.

"I have always believed that Aragon would be a great poet," he continued, "and it is satisfying to know that my belief has been vindicated. He played with all the early movements. He was Vorticist, Dadaist, Symbolist—and surely a great modern poet would have to pass through all these things. I wish I could have written some poetry. Nothing else. Fifty pages of good poetry that would be remembered, or even a single poem." He smiled wearily. He began to cough again, and the bright-red frothy blood leaping from his mouth as from a waterfall frightened me into calling the red-trousered girl into the room.

"It's nothing, it's nothing," he said between choking coughs. "The priests have given me something against the pain. You'll laugh, of course. A piece of blue paper with the word 'Buddha' inscribed on it in blood a thousand times—my blood, my Buddha. I wrote the words myself. And is it so stupid? It gave me peace, as any mechanical task would give me peace, and then too the old priest smiled and that itself was worth all the pains of composition. And besides, the Chinese character for 'Buddha' looks remarkably similar to the American character for dollar. It was exactly as though I was writing a cheque for a million million dollars of life."

It was then that he smiled, sadly and terribly, knowing that life could not be bought. "There is a destiny in every man," he had once said. "His intellect comes from his race, his heart from the earth where he lived, but his health comes from his ancestors." I could see that he cursed those ancestors, those loose-living descendants of Huguenots and princes; and now for the first time I realised that he was dying—dying simply and horribly, as all people die, alone on a mountain-top, with an ugly monkish servant and a girl in red trousers.

He said once that he wanted to be buried on the mountain-top, without coffin or inscription; but he insisted now that he should have a wooden cross. He wanted the monks to celebrate a Buddhist requiem in his memory, and he wanted to cause no suffering to the girl who attended him. His books were to be returned to his wife after the war—she could dispose of them as she pleased.

It was late in the afternoon when I left. He insisted against all reason on accompanying me to the door. In the sunlight his cheeks looked healthy enough—they were bright red, glowing like some molten metal. As he pointed to the distant mountains shining in the ruby sunset, his hands looked vigorous and I noticed that they were more beautiful than when I had seen them last. He must have noticed how I gazed at his hands, for he said:

"You remember the hands of the priest in the monastery who conducted the Requiem? There was perfection of grace in those hands, surely. One can adore with one's hands more easily than with one's knees, and surely the hands are the most beautiful things in our body. Look at the hands—the proportions of all four fingers, their sizes, the way they speak of the experiences which each one of us has undergone. . . ."

Even then, like a good host in a Chinese house, he insisted on accompanying me a little farther, past the temple gate, past the crumbling stucco gargoyles, past the great stone vase, the datura trees and the small shrine to the earth god, where the weather-beaten goddess resembled to an extraordinary degree one of the Queens on the Royal Porch at Chartres.

"The Earth God," he smiled. "The Chinese are so sensible, for there is no other god it is so necessary to propitiate."

For the last time he spoke of his plan, when he recovered, of settling down in one of the valleys of Szechuan with a few kindred spirits. They would build an oasis in the middle of war, and like the Chinese they would defend themselves behind high crenellated walls. . . . They would cultivate the earth and carve on the high mountains all the poems that best deserved to be re-

413

membered. "We must carve them so deeply that even if the barbarians should one day pass by the foot of the mountains, they would have no time to obliterate them. Whatever happens, our traditions must be preserved. Our Cathedrals can go, our most historic monuments can be destroyed by German bombs, but God help us if we forget our great poets. And if everything should perish, a traveller a thousand years hence would find these poems inscribed in a strange language on our mountains, and from these poems he would be able to reconstruct the whole of the European tradition. And what does it matter? In a thousand years' time we shall all be of one race. We shall have Chinese eyes and black hair; we shall be slimmer and shorter than we are now; we shall be more graceful in our movements. The East and the West are already in the melting-pot in Malaya and the Indies. How long will it last? No one knows, but certainly it cannot be more than a thousand years. And then perhaps, since we shall be all of the same blood, there will be peace."

He was silent, then, for a long time, gazing down at the blue valley, the mountains like icebergs and the mist. I knew he would have liked to descend the mountain. The girl in the red trousers was shivering. She held him by the hand and begged him to return to the temple, for a rainy wind was coming up.

"It is dark down there," he said. "There is more sunlight on the mountains, and I would prefer you not to make the journey."

"I must give my lectures tomorrow," I objected.

The sun was setting. It caught the golden fretwork of the temple gates and the lamps of hollow glass swinging from the temple beams. I went down the slope. After a few moments I looked back: Bergery was still standing there, his shoulders shaking with the terrible force of his paroxysms of coughing. I shall not see him alive again.

August 10th . . . I FEEL certain that Bergery died on the night I left him, but no news has come from the temple. And this is perhaps as it should be. He is one of those who prefer to disappear, one of those who have a passion for hiding behind the screens which life so often and so generously provides. This is not his first death. He has died many times, not only in the sense that he has been reported dead in the newspapers. I remember a railway accident in Germany when the train flew off the rails and

414

together we went up and down the ranks of the overturned carriages, pulling out here an arm, there a foot, there the head of some old man who had perished in his sleep. All the while there was an extraordinary impassivity on Bergery's face. There are men who, because they cannot stand the sight of blood, become surgeons. Such a man was my friend Auguste Souchy, the leader of the anarchists in Spain, who was credited with the assassination of more reactionaries than any other anarchist; and yet he lived simply in Paris, with his wife, in an attic of the Rue Boileau. He who hated murder practised it because it seemed to him a necessary right, and because he believed that the reactionaries were stifling the life of the young. In the same way Bergery, because he believed in freedom, gave himself no opportunity of practising it. When Hitler complained against the reports of British and American journalists in Europe, Bergery laughed sardonically in his face: "It is the first time we have been credited with good sense." He learned languages as other men read books. He was determined that in whatever part of the world he should be sent, he would be able to make his way. He was often tempted to write books, but he always refused. "I belong to the moment of time: the man who writes books has perhaps a year or a century of fame; but it is the moment with all its complexities which baffles and fascinates me." He was generous and suffered fools gladly, especially those who, like St. Francis, were fools of God. He loved priests, old women, the canals of Bruges, tapestries, the Louvre at night and the British Museum on a hot August day, when the galleries are crowded with school-children. He loved everything that was European, and believing that Crete was the beginning of our civilisation, he regretted that he was not sent to Crete during the invasion. "Everything in Europe comes from Babylon and Crete." And so he is dead. It will make little difference to the world, yet thousands of people will have been subtly altered by his presence. He was forty-nine. He looked younger. In his handshake there was still the vigour of youth, and his eyes were bright and blue like the Swiss lakes. Only the two red patches on his face, which gave him the appearance of an actor who has forgotten to wash away the grease-paint, spoke of his sufferings. Perhaps his sufferings were not great, but he bore them with the patience and delight of youth. "To die without suffering," he once said; "that is the greatest imaginable horror."

415

August 11th . . . STILL no news of Bergery. I have been listening in Liang's garden to the gramophone. The sky dark blue with silver stars. Liang has been playing the Gregorian chants, the voices of the *castrati* rising in the midsummer air; and yet in this plain song there is much that we fail to understand. Perhaps these songs are the emblems of Europe; they are what Bergery means when he speaks about the "European tradition", giving the words a force and precision which they rarely have on the lips of other persons. These songs are sung by the Catholic Church, but not very different songs were sung in Athens and in the great colonnades of Karnak in Egypt. They are songs of grief and divine joy—and perhaps grief and joy are the characteristics of our civilisation. The torn body of Adonis is gathered by Aphrodite; the mænads who tear the lamb to pieces see the Lamb made whole in holy worship. And so it seems to me now that divine grief and divine joy are the threads upon which the texture of Europe has been woven. Under a sky thick-clouded with stars, we hear the voice of Europe in a remote valley in China.

Later we played the records of the *Mass in D* which I brought from Singapore. These voices, rising and falling, the male and the female voices alternating, die mysteriously into the heart of a revealed brightness, where everything is known and forgiven, where everything is understood and no sigh of tremor or conflict remains. Where else shall we find the music of Europe? The nervous intensity of the *Grosse Fugue,* which for some reason to-night I associated with the ceaseless flutter of small white birds on cherry-trees, is so close to the soul of Europe that even if everything else perished it would be possible to construct the whole of Europe from these notes alone. Opus 127 in E flat major is a song of grief; the *Heilige Dankgesang* is a song of heavenly relief sung by angels who have seen the dark wings of evil disappearing in the rays of a divine light, so quick and so mournful is its annunciation of joy. But greatest of all, because it conforms to everything in which we believe in these years of war, are the final heart-rending notes of the *Dona Nobis Pacem.* Here, as perhaps nowhere else in Beethoven, do we hear the notes of a redeeming prayer. The certainty of peace, the certainty that the supplication was about to be answered as eagerly as it was offered, the certainty that peace lies beyond and behind everything, lovely beyond words, more beautiful than flowers, and the other certainty that a heavenly kingdom exists in which peace has her place and

416

war has no place, comes like a shock on exposed nerves in time of war. In Singapore I have played it during an air-raid, knowing then that the music would outlive the words of bombs; and suddenly looking up to find the other listener in tears. There are songs of Beethoven and Hugo Wolf which have this effect on me, but I have never wept over *Dona Nobis Pacem*. The mounting tempo of that music, like the slow floods of spring, torments me and yet it does not open the walls of tears. Bergery said: "In this generation tears are never very far from our eyes—and how could we expect it otherwise? No other generation has suffered so much, and no other generation will suffer as much. *We are the generation who suffer*. And this is our greatness." It may be true. Others may believe that the Hundred Years' War in Germany, the Napoleonic Wars, the Wars of Genghis Khan brought frightfulness to an even higher level; but why should we torment ourselves with degrees of murder? A nation cannot suffer more than a man, for a nation is only the sum of its men. But in Beethoven we see for the first time in music the heavenly sum of suffering which is distinct from all these.

Yesterday, when one of my students asked me what I would preserve if only one European book survived, I answered: "The Works of Beethoven."

August 12th . . . Bergery often spoke of inscribing the texts of the great European poets on the mountains of China. This afternoon, having heard nothing of Bergery's proposal and not having met him, Lin Tungchi suggested that we should choose a hundred poems from Chinese literature and another hundred from European literature, and inscribe them on the mountains. There are bare cliffs quite near here where the poems could be inscribed; and I know a hill in Westmorland where we might do the same thing.

But where shall we begin? The whole of the *Iliad*? The whole of the *Divina Commedia*? The whole of *Faust*? I had almost forgotten these, and Lin Tungchi had almost forgotten the *Li Sao*, which is only a quarter the length of *Paradise Lost*, but still too long to engrave on a mountain. We discussed the magnificent monuments carved out of hills by which the Americans seek to commemorate their dead statesmen. "It might have been better," he said, "if they had carved their great books instead."

We know now, even more than in 1918, that civilisations are

mortal. They have their flowering periods and die, they grow according to known laws, and their deaths are inevitable. European civilisation. as we know it today, may continue for five hundred years—scarcely longer, for we are on the threshold of a final mingling of cultures. Today the ancient culture of China is nearer to that of Europe and America than it has ever been. Indian civilisation is still almost unknown; but it will soon be known, for already the gates are breaking down; and New England, which brought us the forest philosophers, may yet see Chinese philosophy in its midst. These three cultures are those on which we shall live; and since the fate of the world lies on our understanding of them, it may be that in the history of the earth the roads which are being cut between India and China are more important than all the terrible battles which are being waged in the West.

So we shall carve these poems on the mountains of Szechuan. We shall carve them so high, and in letters so small, that the soldiers will pass them by. Civilisations depend on the mercy of soldiers. And then perhaps, in ten thousand years' time, when another Constantinople has fallen to the Crusaders and nothing is left of the civilisation we are fighting for today, a traveller in a remote valley of the Chialing river will chance upon these inscriptions and laboriously translate them into the known languages of his land.

August 12th . . . BERGERY died two days ago. He did not die on the night when I went up the hill. The servant came this morning, before dawn, when the sky was still shining with stars. He told me that Bergery had asked to be brought out in the open, on a bed, and he spent the night gazing at the stars with his eyes wide open. The servant, who watched him all night, said there was so much confidence in his expression and so much sweetness in his smile that it was difficult to believe he was dying. The wind blew. The "wave of the pines" on the mountain-tops, like the sighing of waves in Irish bays, can make men mad or content according to their ear for music; and so I was not surprised when the servant told me that Bergery was quite calm, as though in a deep trance, except when the wind blew through the pines, and then it was as though he had seen the high gods, for he would smile happily and begin to sing in tune with the wind.

All the way up the mountain I tried to reconstruct in my imag-

418

ination the circumstances of his death, but as usual, when I try to reconstruct these things consciously, the circumstances are quite otherwise than my imagination would foretell. I imagined that the bed would still be outside the small temple. I imagined that he would still be gazing at the stars. I imagined the small girl in the red trousers fanning the flies from his face. I found none of these things. The girl had been sent away. Bergery lay inside the temple, near the altar, and there were nuns and monks praying at the foot of his bed. Nor was the sun shining. It was grey and misty; and everything seemed about to dissolve into decay. A great unpainted wooden coffin lay near the door. He had asked to be buried without a coffin, but the whole monastery had come following the coffin the day before—it was one of the high-shouldered Chinese coffins which are sometimes painted bright blue and decorated with gold-leaf patterns of flying birds. It was quite empty, except for the cock which was tied to a cord and which sometimes perched on the great lion-like shoulders of the coffin. They were praying and beating bells. A young monk, who had only recently entered the monastery, and whose bare shaven head showed the bright red weals of the incense which had been burnt into the skin, stood alone without speaking or praying at the head of the bed. He was handsome beyond any monks I had seen on these mountains; and it was clear that Bergery had taken a special liking to him. The praying came to an end shortly after I arrived. There was mist on the mountains—great patches of mist which swirled past the doors of the small temple, hiding the pines and sometimes opening to reveal a faint light shining in the valley below. One would look through tunnels of clear air, seeing the river flowing sedately below; and then the mist shrouded every-thing, and you could see no more than a few inches ahead. He had given orders that he should be buried on a great scarp of the mountain looking over the river, and there we carried him in the late forenoon, the monks supporting the coffin on their shoulders. Even the Abbot T'ai Shuh, the reverend holiness to whom all Chinese Buddhists look for support, accompanied the procession down the hill, waving the mist away with his fan. It was bitterly cold; but the grave had been dug already, and the hard earth shone silver at its sides. It was not a deep grave. I was thankful for that, but at the same time, on this small scarp overhanging the river, I wondered whether Bergery's weight, the heaviness of that overloaded coffin, might not one day break off this scarp and send

419

the coffin hurtling into the river four thousand feet below. I think he would have liked the idea, and thought of the rocks snapping and the coffin careering blindly into the river, Bergery himself standing upright with arms outstretched and *flowing* like a mountain stream. There was only the briefest ceremony. Bare-headed the monks stood round, and the utterly sickening sound of earth falling on the wooden coffin-lid was muted by a sudden wind which waved through the pines. I recited the prayers of burial according to the Church of England. I had not noticed until that moment the small dark Taoist priest with the oiled topknot in his hair and the burning eyes, but he too recited a prayer; and then there were the chants of the monks. A few mountain flowers were strewn over the grave. On the small cross someone had inscribed his name in Chinese and the date of his death; and underneath were the words: "He loved China." Kneeling down in the hard mud, I wrote in pencil on the wood:

> *"Near here died Johann Sebastian Karl Bergery*
> *on August 10th, 1943, aged 50.*
> *He loved men, and strove for peace."*

August 13th . . . THERE is no longer any reason why I should stay. I have been invited to join the South-Western Associated University at Kunming, and I have already given in my resignation. I cannot live in a place which is haunted by Bergery. And there is so little sun in Szechuan, and the mountains hide the sky, and there is fever on all these marshlands. Every time I look up at the mountains, I expect to see Bergery coming down; and that black scarp of rock which looks over the river already seems to be falling. Bergery should never have come here—I have told myself this twenty times a day for the last ten days. He could have lived in the *provençal* sunlight of Kunming; and there, interpreting the East to the West, he might have brought himself an even greater fame. He was not famous while he lived only because he had no desire for fame. Now that he is dead, he will become famous as certainly as the moon rises in the sky. He left papers and letters behind. There was one to his wife from which I have made here a short extract: "You wrote to me in Paris, saying that the child was ill. I flew over, and you wept because I did not stay. But, Mary, other children were ill—millions of children, and I had to serve them. A journalist must always be travelling away

420

from the things he loves. You did not know—you could not know
—that for me to live in Paris and enjoy everything that was so
beautiful was itself mortally dangerous. Forgive me. I am a wanderer. I should never have married. I was too restless to learn
how to be silent by your side. Woman loves; man suffers—perhaps
that is why women always want to possess too much, and men
make war. . . ."

August 19th . . . The last few days in Chungking. No
clouds, the sun very hot; and the dust-laden streets like furnaces.
Perhaps we shall go tomorrow—no one knows. I have been wandering in the centre of the city, unable to resist the sun, and this
afternoon I went down to the foreshore to watch the sampans.
There was no wind; the white ships crept down-stream like white
caterpillars, so fat they were, and so slowly they moved. There
are places even here where boys bathe, though the river is the
colour of a yellow cloth soaked in water. The small black ferry-
boats wander like water-beetles on the yellow river, and above
them the sky arches, terribly high and remote, shaped like a
parabola. I lay flat on my back on a rock while the dragon-flies
flew out of the river, and it was strange to think of them arising
from this muddy stream. Some more children came to bathe, slipping out of their dusty rags, and immediately they lost their air
of urchins and became like gods, shining yellow in the water; and
their black matted hair on their foreheads gave them the appearance of having stepped out of a Chinese play. They were splendid.
They swam seriously, chased after dragon-flies, whispered among
themselves and formed wild plots in an effort to catch something
bright red which was floating on the surface of the water. Through
half-closed eyes I watch them from the big slab of rock where I
lay. I could hear the waters thundering, the cries of the children,
the red dragon-flies whirring in the bright blue sky; I could feel
the heat simmering downward from the heavens. I did not see all
that the children were doing. They had divided into two groups.
They were swimming into places where I thought the river was
dangerous, but in the heat and the shadow of the rocks I did not
move. There they were, the two white lines of childish heads and
arms and buttocks on the greyish-yellow river—two arrowheads
pointing towards the small bright red object floating on the river.
And someone reached out a perfectly white childish arm and
lifted the limp red thing high above her head, squealing with

421

delight. I thought they had found something of value, a piece of cloth perhaps, and when they returned they all clustered round the young girl who held the thing to her breast, and they whispered excitedly, and spoke of it with tenderness and great interest. She laid it in the sand, in the shadow of the rock where I lay, while the sun bathed my face and steam rose from the shoulders of the naked children, and suddenly I looked down and saw them squatting in a ring, grave-faced, looking at the damp red body of the small rat, whose skin had been eaten by the fishes in the river. But for them it was not a rat, nor was there any blood soaking in the sand. It was something mysterious and beautiful, which they watched gravely and tenderly; for the sun dried it, the white tendons became firm and sometimes the limp red legs would twitch under the impact of the strong sunlight. The voices of the children playing with the dead rat made me immensely happy, for they seemed to come from a world I have long forgotten, a world where everything is interesting and beautiful. They stood up. They dressed slowly in their patched rags of blue cloth, and they carried the rat tenderly in their hands towards the city.

August 20th . . . B. has been explaining the intricacies of *teh-kuanyin*, a tea which he has brought back from Fukien. It is impossible to define its taste, as it is impossible to define the taste of Grand Marnier; but the heavenly satisfaction which comes over you when you have drunk it is something which I have never known before in the same degree. The sunlight splashed the little blue cups on the bamboo table. The ritual of pouring the tea backwards and forwards between the teapot and the kettle was accomplished with perfect propriety; and when at last every portion of the ritual had been performed, we drank silently and impassively, without the faintest trace of emotion, as the gods in Olympus drank ambrosia.

In Fukien merchants have been known to ruin themselves in collecting tea. They gamble for the sake of winning a fortune which they can translate into a collection of tea-leaves; and as they drink tea, they sigh like lovers. But this tea, which comes from a single mountain in Fukien called the Iron Mountain, is so rich and fragrant, suggests so many conflicting tastes and possesses so heady a flavour that I am quite content to sit there drinking cup after cup, until I have lost all sensation and have become simply a vehicle for drinking this golden tea. The sun-

422

shine shines on B.'s fat face, and in my mind's eye he becomes a laughing Buddha and I forgive him for his official manner and his execrable English prose and begin to wonder whether he is not indeed the fat laughing Buddha I have seen on so many altars.

"To sit in Fukien drinking this tea. . . ." He smiles tenderly at his blue cups, the red teapot, the bamboo table, and he passes his flabby hands over the warm teapot with a tenderness which surprises him, for immediately afterwards he gets up and goes to his bookcase and says: "I am translating the ancient Chinese tea classic. If you want to understand China, you must understand their passionate love for tea." The sun shines on the lawn of the English garden, and I have not the heart to tell him that the book has already been translated.

At night I can still feel the taste of *teh-kuan-yin* on the roof of my mouth, I can still recall every detail of the beautiful blue cups he has chosen with so much good taste and after so many journeys; and I think of him in his small plaster house, sitting alone, drinking the golden tea, his round blue eyes shining with the light of heaven, as he sings in a drunken voice—for this tea has been known to make many men drunk with heavenly wisdom—all the bawdy songs of Rumania and Russia he can remember.

August 21st . . . He was a famous poet, an actor, an airman, a guerrilla—I have forgotten how many things he has done in his short life. He was short and graceful, with long delicate fingers, and he allowed his finger-nails to grow longer than I thought possible in this extraordinary city, where nothing is comfortable and everything is sharp and rough-edged. As he spoke the white finger-nails drummed on the blackwood table, and I noticed that the polished finger-nails were the same colour as his tall forehead, and shone with a translucent light. He spoke in a deliberately careful English and he would make little circles of his lips in an effort to pronounce w's and u's; and these little red circles gave him the appearance of a baby, a very sophisticated baby, a baby who had seen everything in the world and was not in the least surprised at the thought that nothing was worth seeing.

"I studied dramatic art under Meyerhold and Stanislavsky. This was in 1921, and you must know that winters in Russia are not like winters in Pekin. They were wet and miserable days, and we would go to the palace wrapped in furs, shivering in the wet snow, and on a stage which consisted of three or four steps lead-

423

ing nowhere, a trellis which had been erected in imitation of the city wall and perhaps some ancient carpets stolen from the palace of a Grand Duke, we would perform a play about the revolution. I believed in the revolution, then. And later when I came to Hankow and joined the Government, I still believed in revolution, and worked for it with all my strength. I flew aeroplanes over Chiang Kai-shek's lines, I fought among the guerrillas, I wrote poetry in praise of the revolution; but the revolution failed, Borodin returned to China, Sun Yat-sen died and once more we became wanderers. I acted in Hollywood and New York. Even there I think I was considered as a revolutionary, for after six months I was refused a permit and I came back to China. It was easy to live then. I became a female impersonator. I collected an enormous collection of Chinese antiques, particularly those relating to the early Dynasty of Shang-Yin—oracle bones, bronze urns, spears and arrow-heads. I lived in the deer park near the Western Hills. I was wealthy. I acted for Chang Tso-lin, and at the same time I hid revolutionaries in my house. And yet I did not believe that a revolution was possible, and when Chiang Kai-shek marched northward in 1937 I laughed aloud—it was absurd to think that anything or anyone could unify China. This was the world I lived in. I was content. I possessed everything I had ever wanted to possess, I was considered courageous, I had a beautiful wife and two concubines, I had many friends and an interest in some of the Pekin money companies. What else could I demand of life? But all the time I knew there was something missing. I had not found it in the revolutions; it was not present in Pekin. When the Japanese came, I stayed behind. I had friends among the Japanese officers, I could act for them, I delighted in having them to my house, for they could discuss Chinese painting better than many Chinese. And still I knew that something was missing. Then a message came from the Generalissimo inviting me to come to Pekin. I thought it was a trap. I had publicly stated that I considered the Kuomintang to consist of incompetent officials who possessed no thought at all for the future of China. I decided to leave Pekin. I was no longer interested in life—everything was so easy. I expected that as soon as I reached Chungking I would be thrown into prison, and I welcomed the possibility with all my heart and soul. I would be happy in prison. I would be reduced to essentials. I would die, and that would be a final blessing on my unsatisfactory life. But when I reached Chungking and I was taken to the Generalissimo's headquarters I was told that I was to prepare propaganda pieces for the Chinese Army. I was not interested. The Chinese soldier bored me. He was evil and cunning and uneducated, and he was often reduced to a state of bestiality. I ignored the order. . . . The Chinese are very patient. I was paid regularly. I was given sums of money for stage costumes, and I gambled the money away or dressed my mistresses in beautiful clothes from Shanghai and Hongkong—for in those days it was still possible simply to order clothes from Shanghai. I lived at a terrible speed, simply because I did not know what to do with myself. Messages arrived from the propaganda bureau of army headquarters. I ignored them. One day I amused myself by drawing up the scenario of a play—the coarsest and stupidest play about drunken Japanese officers, about opium and white slave traffic, and I made my mistress act the part of the Chinese slavegirl. She acted well. I decided to perform the play. The soldiers liked it. It was coarse and rude and tough, but it possessed some unanalysable quality: I do not know how it came to possess this quality, and perhaps this quality derived only from the actors. I was sick with terror when the play was produced, though I had produced it myself. I thought it terrible. I thought they approved politely, with that terrible politeness of the Chinese gentleman who disapproves, but—no—they really liked it, they saw their own weariness reflected in my drama, they recognised the cultured and stupid Japanese officer, they saw their own rude solidity in my Chinese peasants. I was a producer and actor again. I gave up female impersonators for Grand Guignol, and found that the Chinese audiences entirely approved of it. I became famous again. I changed my name—because I was sick of fame. I wrote more plays, each under a different name. I acted in nearly all of them, and took my company to the front, and saw my best actors and actresses killed by Japanese shells and bombs. My mistress was killed. I began to write with a greater knowledge of the stage and at the same time with a greater knowledge of real life. For the first time in my life I grew hungry for experience, for previously I had been hungry only for excitement. I lived. And since then I have spent nine months in every year travelling to the front with my plays, and one day I shall write a really good play about the war in which the experiences of all the actors and soldiers I have known will be distilled. I am beginning to live. . . ."

He wore a plum-coloured gown, a green jade ring hung from

his wrist, his high forehead shone in the light of the single naked electric light bulb. He looked terribly *alone,* and as I watched his hands playing under the electric light it occurred to me that they were playing a complicated game, or perhaps performing a ritual, which would always be foreign to me. No one has yet written about the lives of the Chinese, and never since the Elizabethan age have we known anything comparable with the resolute lives of modern Chinese poets. I asked him what he would do after the war. He looked up with a surprised stare; and it was as though the electric light bulb had caught him off his guard.

"I shall go back to Pekin—to the deer-park," he answered, and there came to his face a look of frozen terror, and I knew then that he dared not think about the end of the war.

August 23rd . . . AT DAWN the white mist hangs clear on the Yangtse. The grass is still green on the slopes of the pepper-pot mountains, but it is turning yellow and already a few soft patches of yellow appear beneath the pine-trees on the opposite bank. In the morning you hear the small carts taking human manure into the countryside, and a little while later the first rickshas trundle down the stone street, squeaking and groaning, and little clouds of yellow dust pour from the ungreased axles. When I first came to Chungking, the tyres of the rickshas were brown; now they are bright red, and patched in so many places that one wonders how much longer they will last on these granite roads. The heat at night is still terrible, but at dawn there is a short interval of coolness, and I woke up early to see the long banners of red and yellow in the eastern sky, and the last blue star quietly disappearing in the milky haze.

From somewhere I heard the sound of a single galloping horse, and the hollow air echoed with the horse's quick trot. There was hardly anyone walking in the streets, though a few bamboo beds were arranged on the pavement; and there without any covering, running with sweat, half-naked, and quivering a little at the silent approach of dawn, children and young girls were sleeping. But the horse's hooves grew harsher and louder, they struck flints from the earth and the hollow buildings re-echoed the hoof-beats and amplified them. A Taoist monk passed with quick easy strides, the oiled top-knot gleaming under a hair-net. A beggar hopped across the road. And still we heard the hoof-beats, and we could almost see the flash of the steel stirrup and smell the cool leather
426

harness. The young girls woke up, arranged their hair, lifted naked arms towards the sun; and almost they greeted the morning sun with a kiss like the ancient Athenians. The heat grew. We could feel its pulsations as the blue sky grew darker, no longer streaked with the faint silver of the pure dawn, but rich with the aftermath of the glowing spears of the sunlight. The rider was coming nearer. The hoof-beats were deafening. The girls woke up, they walked swiftly to the wells and though still half-asleep they began to murmur in soft voices, speaking of their dreams; and small boys followed them. In summer the aged sleep more, and dawn in China is a world of the young. The steps, covered with yellow dust—the desert of Gobi is somewhere near Chung-king—turned black and silver with water. Birds wheeled over the Yangtse. The first meat-sellers, with their smoking wooden casks, began to plod silently down the street. A little girl of seven, so beautiful that my heart caught in my throat, was solemnly painting red circles on her cheeks and admiring herself in the well. And then, then, when the noise of the hoof-beats was so loud that I thought an enormous train with banners of golden smoke would pass down the street, pushing the houses down like skittle-bones, thundering into the future, a horse appeared at the end of the street and the small boy wearing only blue trousers and yellow sandals was beating her furiously, his arms akimbo, and for some reason the sound of the hoof-beats grew softer and lighter, and it was difficult to believe that this is the horse which filled us a few moments ago with apprehension. But immediately afterwards, when the horse has disappeared, I think of it as an immense creature out of heraldry, foreshadowing a new dawn.

August 25th . . . I HAVE been to say good-bye to Sir Frederick Eggleston, the Australian Minister. He lives on a cliff edge overlooking the Chialing, in an enormous brown stucco house; and all day long military lorries thunder past his house. We came up the steep circling roads in his car, which was surmounted with a wreath of flowers perhaps ten feet long, for later in the day he proposed to place the wreath on the tomb of Dr. Lin Sen, the President of China who has just died. All the small children and all the blue-coated soldiers (who are not very different from children) gaped as we passed; for though they are accustomed to see cars, it is rare to see a motor-car crowned with lilies.

Of all the Ministers in China, Sir Frederick Eggleston is the most popular. He lives quietly in his great house, rarely going out, surrounded by Chinese paintings, quietly performing those acts of friendship and understanding which are more important in China than diplomacy. You will find professors and merchants sitting at his table; an official of the Kuomintang will be discussing the paintings of the Wei Dynasty with a little school-mistress; and when the wine is served on a silver platter and the Minister is beaming quietly at the young soldier, who is arguing forth about the iniquities of the Burma campaign, you have a feeling that the civilisation of our forefathers has been restored; and the sweat and dirt of Chungking have been forgotten. In this great room, with the blue carpet, its rows of bookcases and the great black head of a bronze Indian prince gleaming from the wall, perspectives become sharper and understanding is enriched by the quiet splendour of a balanced mind. He sits there in a great chair, one gouty foot stretched forward, and behind him like a curtain all the yellow smoke and dust of Chungking rise into the air. He is courteous to the young scholar who sits tongue-tied in the corner; and he is apt to show the merchant who has been speaking grandiloquently of the fortunes he has made and will still make that he prefers the company of scholars to those of the money-makers. He is simple and sincere, and perhaps it is his pure sincerity which makes him so beloved to the Chinese.

I do not know why it is, but the rooms of the wise have an increasing light. There is a splendour in this room which I have seen nowhere else in Chungking. Some blue flowers in a silver vase, the painting of a horse over a fireplace, the little blackwood tables, the silent footsteps of well-trained servants conspire together to make an atmosphere where no one feels at a loss. The courage we have lost in the sweltering heat of a Chungking summer is restored to us, and we begin to feel once more the singing of the blood in our veins.

We were talking about the tremendous changes which must take place in the art of diplomacy after the war, and he half agreed with me when I said that we can no longer afford the dangerous experiment of allowing career diplomatists unrestricted freedom to represent their countries. Diplomacy was the art of too many disguises, and I confessed that I found it difficult to understand why poets and philosophers were not given the privilege of representing their cultures. The Chinese sent Dr. Hu Shih to America; Roosevelt has sent many professors and at least

428

one pet to South America, and indeed there was an American tradition by which professors were elevated to the highest rank. I suggested that T. S. Eliot would make an excellent Ambassador to China, and after the war Blunden should be sent to Japan. We had both been reading Sir Nevile Henderson's *Failure of a Mission,* and I had been shocked by what appeared to be the most casual admissions of incompetence. He said very little, but what he said was so wise and illuminating that I began to hope that he would stay for the rest of his life in China, where wisdom is still regarded with deference and delight.

Afterwards, as I came down the straggling path between the pines, I asked my companion from the Chinese Foreign Office what he thought of the Australian Minister. "He is a man who inspires love," he said. "I believe that the Generalissimo respects him more than he respects any other Minister, and though he sees him rarely, he talks about him often." The sun shone on the broken columns of a bombed building. Down below there was all the seething quagmire of Chungking.

August 25th . . . I AM beginning to have an affection for this city, where I have been more miserable than anywhere else. In a few days, perhaps in a few hours, I shall leave it for ever, and I shall have few regrets. The tempest which broke over China made Chungking the capital of an empire; and by some trick of fate the city was endowed with all the characteristics proper for such a beleaguered country. The white scarp looking forward over the Yangtse possesses such grandeur and permanence, and there is so much suffering hidden behind those rocky walls, that I begin to believe that the city has entered my blood, I am a part of its dust and mud, its sufferings, its sunlight, its terrible virtuosity. Out of this rock men have made fortunes, and others have seen for the first time the nature of an implacable, hostile war, and found their souls fasting. The terror of the desert. . . .

> *What are the roots that clutch, what branches grow*
> *Out of this stony rubbish? Son of man,*
> *You cannot say, or guess, for you know only*
> *A heap of broken images, where the sun beats,*
> *And the dead tree gives no shelter, the cricket no relief,*
> *And the dry stone no sound of water. Only*
> *There is shadow under this red rock,*

(Come in under the shadow of this red rock),
And I will show you something different from either
Your shadow at morning striding behind you
Or your shadow at evening rising to meet you;
I will show you fear in a handful of dust. . . .

But T. S. Eliot's *The Waste Land* is not for this generation of Chinese. There is hope in the white rock, and much sordid fear. There are bankers whom one would cheerfully murder, because they hoard rice. There are professors living quietly in plaster houses, where they spit blood on the tiles and shiver in the damp winter, but keeping alive by the sheer virtue of dreams. There is heroism and degradation, as there must be in every imperial city; but the heroism outweighs all else. I have known guerrillas who have tramped from Manchuria across heaven knows how many mountains, believing that in Chungking they will find the hard core of national resistance, and some of them have been disillusioned and others have found that they too were complacent, and still others have gone out from this city like Tobias with the angel, armed with the courage that will create victories. The dead lie on the pavements; the living are not always alive; there is death-in-life here as everywhere else. But one day that immense ship of rock will sail down the Yangtse with all her sails unfurled, and those who watch her from the bank will know that she is only sailing towards her own possessions; and this ship of mud and silk and broken hearts will be equipped with imperial splendours.

I have not lost my heart to Pekin or Hangchow or Cambaluc with so much ease as I have lost it to Chungking. Under the brown fog of winter, in the burning sunlight of summer, in the torrents of spring and the mists of autumn she stands four-square to all the winds of Heaven. She possesses a curious magnificence. There are people who have met the Generalissimo who say that his features are like rock, beautifully carved; and there is fine carving in Chungking. You will not see it in the roads, which are lines ruled across a bombarded city, and you will see it only occasionally in the great plaster-and-stone houses which look like excrescences on the bulwark of rock; but you will see it in the faces of the people and particularly on the faces of the children and the young. You will read their hopes and sorrows, their fears and torturing doubts, as they climb heavily up the innumerable
430

stone steps, as they squat in the shade near the sand, as they walk briskly in blue cotton drill down the dusty roads. They possess what seemed to Bergery a perfect virginity. Though they were overwhelmed by sorrow, they were untouched by it. They lived their lives openly, for no secrets are kept in China; and it is through what the Germans call *das Offene*—the open windows—that we see Heaven.

There is romance in every stone of Chungking, for every stone has demanded its measure of blood. I have known this sense of romance in Vienna when, in a small room overlooking the Kartnerstrasse, I watched men plotting desperately against Hitler; I have known it again in Paris when Del Vayo spoke of the heavy artillery which the Germans were bringing up against the Ebro—"and yet we shall fight to the last man and to the last inch of territory, for we know we are in the right", and then again in Singapore, when out of the mud-flats and lagoons of a deserted kingdom men raised with the sweat of their limbs a great naval base whose misfortunes were common to all the islands of the Indies, or that other day, late at night, when sailors marched in perfect order from destroyers after the *Prince of Wales* and *Renown* had gone down. There are only a few moments in life when romance becomes a thing so near and tangible that we see it in all its glory. It is only by an effort of the imagination that we can see clearly those things which have most touched our lives, and yet these things are remembered in our dreams, at those quiet hours of night when our forefathers and the ancient legends of our country come clear into consciousness, like lights burning in an empty street. I heard the flutter of the wings of romance once when a man I had known intimately attempted to make himself emperor of a small province carved out of the Himalayas, and perhaps this feeling was no different from the days I spent in Bali, when I saw men walking with the dignity of kings and with such assurance that it was unnecessary to imagine crowns. Once in Poland, crossing the cobble-stones under the lovely cathedral of St. Mary, I heard an old professor, weary with teaching, prophesy that there would be a war and that Poland would be crushed beneath the German armies; and while the gulls screamed in a perfectly blue sky and the bronze shadow of the statue of Miskiewitz prevented us from moving on, I heard him saying, in tones of such certainty that it was clear that all doubt was removed from his mind: "The dead will arise." They will arise in China also. The broken-

431

fingered peasants who carved with dynamite and finger-nails the holes in these rocks, the drowned sailors in the yellow flood, the blue-coated soldiers who starve and fight, the weary peasants who grow rice from rock—it is certain that they will never die. They will not be remembered, for though the Chinese carve on their ancestral tablets the names of their fathers and grandfathers, a merciful Providence has decreed that the names of the ancestors of earlier generations may be forgotten; but in the memory of this race the white rock of Chungking will have its place. In a thousand years men will dream of this rock; they will see the sampans in the flooded rivers and count the steps leading up to the heights, and they will remember dimly, as lovers remember faces in their dreams, that this was one of the places where sacrifices were offered on the great pilgrimage of the Chinese race.

And this evening, walking through the dimly lit streets near the water-front, listening to the cries of children and water-sellers, so great an exaltation came over me that I nearly wept. The sun had gone down behind the rocks. I heard horses galloping, the distant roar of motor-cars, I saw the lovers huddled in doorways and the bamboo beds were already being brought out into the streets. Smoke coiled from the red joss-sticks inexplicably rising from the cracks in the pavements; and there were echoes of bells and drums and high-pitched singing, for somewhere in this neighbourhood a Buddhist priest was praying for the dead. The evening is like a mantle thrown over the shoulders of the sleeping city, and so tenderly is it thrown that the city is almost unconscious that evening has come. A water-seller passed, spilling great fountains of water on the pavings. A vague mist blurred the trees, where the kites were folding their wings. Suddenly through a gap among the broken houses I saw the pagoda on the south shore high up above me, white and shining in the starlight, impassive and remote, and yet brought so close to me by some magic of refraction that I could have touched it with my finger-tips. Like a candle glowing at night or like the face of someone long forgotten, it shone on the south bank. I turned away. Through the dark streets rats crawled, and a few late pilgrims made their way homeward, and a few motor-buses shone yellow in the streets. Around a lamp-post bats wheeled, or perhaps—for they resembled birds— they were swallows celebrating in their dancing flight the presence of the flickering gaslight. But no, they were bats, for one touched me on the cheek and frightened me so much that I

432

jumped away; and I went up the Street of the Seven Stars, thinking of Bergery and how much he would have enjoyed the night. I knew then, though I have known it before, that I have stood on Pisgah. I have seen the promised land of milk and honey, the great future of this race stretching into the distance. As Moses descending from the rock wore on his face a brightness from his converse with the God of Israel, my city shone in the thick darkness, the streets, the sleeping children, the steamers lying quietly in the river, the steel hearts of the people—all were shining. I know that I shall not leave this city without a struggle. I shall dream of it all the days of my life, and sometimes turning a corner in some road in America or England, I shall be reminded by a tower or a flight of steps of granite, and once more I shall think of Chungking. There are days when I have only to repeat the name of the city three or four times to find myself on the wings of an exaltation; and though there are other days when I hate the city with a kind of abandoned intemperance of temper, for its cruelty, its cunning and its terrible poverty and undisguised strangeness, those days are soon forgotten. Like a castle on a white rock, with banners flying, or like a ship, I shall see her always. And if I should grow blind or dumb, or if (which is much more probable) I should starve to death, I shall comfort myself with the thought of all those maimed and weary travellers who built out of ancient ruins so perfect a symbol of their immeasurable confidence.

August 26th . . . . THE gulls played about in the air, balancing themselves against the wind, then sweeping around and downwards with the wind behind them. The river bright yellow under the gulls, and the mountains soaring in a perfect white sky, till the rain came—but the rain was lifted away by the wind, and high above us we could see the skirts of the rain wheeling into the heavens. The wind! The wind! Through all the streets the wind blew fiercely, so that even the water-sellers leaned back against the wind and the naked children were blown from one side of the road to the other. Shutters banged, a balloon was whirled out of a child's hand, and suddenly it grew cold—we were freezing. The sky turned black exactly as though someone had drawn a heavy line with a Chinese brush on the bluish-white sky.

The gulls screamed. The wind roared, and thick pellets of rain descended heavily on the bamboo beds which were being brought

433

out of the houses in the dimly lit streets, streaking the yellow boards with great splashes of black. The rain was ice-cold, terrible. A single drop on the hand was like a wound. The rain fell with terrible force, beating the wind. Lightning cracked open the sky—there were mysterious blue kingdoms behind the black cloud. And then, right in front of me, less than twenty yards away, a drop of gold fire dropped out of a fire, broke through the roof of a house and illuminated a single room inside it. There was a scream—the longest and most high-pitched scream I have ever heard; and then silence. And still the gulls screamed.

The storm grew in intensity. For days the heat has been so great that we can hardly breathe. The white stone glittered with heat yesterday, blinding even the ricksha-drivers who refused to take their passengers, but slept in the shadow of the rickshas; but today we are blinded by continual thunder and lightning, and deafened by the roar of the river. The telephone has been cut. The electric light has failed. We creep into corners, thinking of the bleak and windswept city which lies half-submerged before us. But even now, when the thunder is so close that we are deafened, we hear the scream of the gulls.

August 26th . . . THERE were days in Malaya when it rained like this, but only in Malaya. Life comes to a standstill, and in the middle of summer in China we warm ourselves over charcoal fires, envying the Chinese of Pekin with the little porcelain stoves which they carry in their hands or in their long sleeves. The dawn is bitter and cold, and the evenings are frozen. We expect to see ice in the streets, frost on the window-panes.

No paddle-steamers have crossed the river since yesterday evening. The flood comes. We are beginning to be immersed in our exile and to sympathise with the peasants of Honan. This is a visitation. A few days ago boys played in the streets of Chung-king, praying for the rain. With blue trousers rolled up to their hips, with green garlands on their foreheads, and ropes of green leaves over their bare shoulders, they danced through the dusty streets, beating drums and invoking the god of the rain. At the corners of streets they filled their buckets and splashed one another, until fair skins shone silver; and so they danced and sang through the dust-laden streets, under an unchangeable blue sky. Well, their prayers have been answered. There is more rain falling in the streets than I ever remember in Malaya, for there are
434

no great conduits here to take the seepage. The road here is so steep that the rain is like a waterfall, swirling in a mad white race. A child was drowned outside my window. Three people in the neighbourhood have been struck dead by lightning, and the Chinese servant in the house says that their names were inscribed in blue characters on their faces by the lightning. There are no signs of green. Everything is grey, like the rain, or silver like the immense explosions of lightning. T. explains carefully that it is here that two rivers meet and the humidity of the air differs over the two rivers. Besides, there are mountains. . . . We say nothing, but for the first time in my life I am afraid of the rain and I can almost see the green dragon with the silver claws and the golden eyes who whirls in the heavens.

August 27th . . . The rain is clearing. Patches of blue sky. Already we can imagine the heat, when the sun presses down on the rice-fields and holds the earth in a gelatinous silence. But not yet, not yet. We are in China, where patience is the only virtue.

It was strange this morning to see one of the great chimneys opposite the house crumble into nothingness. The rain had soaked through the mortar which a thousand Japanese bombs had failed to destroy, though everything else in the ancient building had been destroyed. And so wearily, at last obeying the god of thunder and rain, it fell slowly, so slowly that it resembled a chimney in a slow-motion film.

But the children are playing. They wade up to their knees searching for treasure, a bamboo cage of drowned chickens, an oiled umbrella—there is treasure everywhere. They squeal with delight, splash one another, swimming in the soapy yellow rivers, invincibly daring. The motor-cars scream past, splashing them with falling veils of silver water which look inexplicably beautiful; and the wood-oil vapour of the motor-buses seen through these fountains of water shimmers like a summery rainbow.

It is still cool, though there is no wind. This evening I looked over the river and I could see every detail of the pine forests below the pagoda; and the river was bright yellow like a softly waving scarf. There is so much clear brightness in the air that we are beginning to believe that the rain was worth while. The air is silver, and we breathe in great gusts of it, wondering at all the freshness that reminds us of spring. But today or tomorrow, we know that we shall be parched with the coming heat.

435

August 28th . . . We leave in three days. T. is still collecting "tickets". He must obtain authorisation from Garrison Head-quarters, the Foreign Office, the Transport Bureau and half a dozen more. He is terribly afraid of forgetting one out of the many authorisations that we must possess before we go south. He is being sent down on an official mission, the car is an official car and the petrol is being paid for by the Government; but my presence in the car makes it fifty times more difficult. I have had three photographs taken, but I must have three more. I must have my visa countersigned by the police and may have to pay duty on my baggage. Most of my luggage consists of books, but T. thinks they will have to be left at the Customs stations until the police have passed them.

"Why? Dangerous thoughts?"

"Good heavens, no! But there is nothing about books on the list of dutiable articles, and they will want to make sure."

In the heat we are both beginning to become surly and bad-tempered.

"It will be worse in Kunming. You are on a plateau a mile high, your blood runs thin and you lose your temper on the slightest occasion. You will be near murder so often that it will become commonplace, and you will be in a country where murder is very common. The tribe people will murder you for a dollar and think nothing of it. We may be held up by bandits—there are at least three large groups of organised bandits between Kweiyang and Kunming. Are you good at shooting?"

"No."

"You will have to learn. If you see anyone with a gun on the road, shoot. There are also wild animals."

"There were leopards at Peipei. They are quite tame. They would feed out of my hand."

"The trouble with you is that you are not taking the journey seriously. Before 1927 there was no road across Kweichow—nothing but mule-tracks. Well, the peasants still believe that they own the place, and if we have a breakdown on a dark night, they will think. . . ."

"The car will disappear and we shall have to walk?"

"You will not walk. You will be kidnapped. You may be spared, but I shall not, because I am an official in the Chinese Government."

"Do they hate the Chinese Government?"

436

"No, but they don't always recognise it. They believe the country belongs to them."

He talked about the Miao race who once possessed a great empire in the south-west; but they possessed no written records and it is impossible to re-create their history. As in Hunan, they were dispossessed at the end of the Ming Dynasty and their territory was given to the soldiers. They have a great love for bright colours, and they could hide themselves well in their mountain fortresses, and even today there are Miaos who live on the summits of high mountains, dreaming of the day when the plains will once more belong to them. They are tin-miners, silver-miners, farmers, peasants, motor-mechanics, and they have a fine sense of loyalty to their own race and they will murder you for the pleasure of murdering a stranger. The Miaos and the Lolos of the south-west make excellent churchmen, for they have a passion for community singing. You will like them."

I wondered whether I should like them, or whether it was possible to like them, but he said no more. He has gone to Police Headquarters in the hope of finding still another "ticket".

September 1st . . . EARLY in the morning, when it was still dusk, we climbed into the car and began the long journey to Kunming. The streets were deserted and swept clean by the night's rain. Chungking at dawn is all whiteness. The great towering buildings of the Government offices in the winding streets looked as though they were built of marble or ice; and the silence was like a benediction, so cool and pure that we felt we were travelling far away from the towns. The birds were chirping, small boys were sleepily climbing the streets towards the newspaper offices, and a few girls crowded round the wells. There are wells everywhere in Chungking, but you notice them only in the morning. I have passed through the busy streets in the afternoon, thinking that all the water came from the river, for the streets were full of water-carriers splashing great black slabs of water on the dusty pavements; but high up, by Liang-l'ou-kou and in many dusty side-streets, the small metal-rimmed wells sparkle at dawn. Then they are forgotten, or perhaps they are hidden from the eyes of strangers. Now the dawn was coming quickly, a blinding whiteness streaked with saffron, and soon the heat would be climbing up the stiff white molten sky, and soon we would be racing through the countryside, under the pines.

437

In the little grey touring-car we crouched forward, the brown-metal drums of petrol perched behind us, and at any moment we felt that they would topple down and we would be crushed under them. T. was whistling like an errand-boy. He was delighted to leave Chungking; but seeing her in the clear morning light so fresh and sparkling, I was afraid and wondered whether even then I would be able to tear myself away from her. We whirled out past Liang-l'ou-kou, seeing the grey spit of the airfield down below shimmering in the summer light, a single aeroplane like a grey moth settling its wings; and then up through the red dusty roads under the cliffs, where caves have been dug out on the level of the road and small wooden gates have been built across the neck of the caves and soldiers in blue uniforms with gleaming bayonets stand on guard. What do the caves contain? I had seen them thousands of times before, and perhaps it was some trick of the light which made them appear singularly curious in this care-free morning. Did they contain drums of oil? Did they contain the art treasures which have been brought from the Imperial Palace of Pekin? Chungking is honey-combed with caves, and everything is buried underground. Sometimes, walking at night, you can hear underfoot the roar of buried dynamos. The wealth of an empire is buried here . . . but these reflections were forgotten as the small car roared over the precipitous road, and once again we saw the Yangtse down below between a cleft of the hills. I have never seen the Yangtse so splendid. There were tongues of white mist in the air and every tree was burnished with dew, but more splendid than anything was the silver river shining like an incandescent flame, pure silver under the mist, blinding us like a mirror on fire. Small bullock-wagons rumbled forward; we passed under a marble *pai'lou* and a sweep of red carnelian-coloured hills rose beyond the rice-fields—red like blood—but already the yellow dust was beginning to whirl in the air, and the blue motor-buses coming from Chengtu threw up enormous yellow clouds like the smoke from autumn bonfires. It was one of those mornings when everything is on fire, and even the sprinklings of dew on the branches blaze with wild starlight. The air was pure and clean, but the dust was coming nearer. We passed down a wide yellow road, and saw the wind coming up from the river, blowing the dust in our faces. The magic had gone. It was morning, no longer dawn.

Some soldiers came wearily up the yellow road. They must

have been marching all night, for their clothes were streaked with dew. They wore brown steel helmets, which come down over the ears like German helmets; there was dust and dirt on their faces—they looked mortally tired. Suddenly bugles played, they lifted the Chinese flag above their heads and they began to march towards the city with quick spirited strides, while the drums boomed from somewhere at the end of the long marching column and the silk flag ran silver in the wind. They were well-made, these soldiers. Their faces were brown; their shoulders were square; there was flesh on their legs and they carried their rifles without effort. But behind them, straggling in small groups, came those who were ill. There were soldiers who were pale and fleshless, their faces the colour of onions, their feet bleeding, their hands hanging listlessly at their sides. Some were being supported by their friends; a few were being carried on green stretchers, with tarpaulins stretched over their faces, so that I thought they were dead. But they marched on, in piteous little groups streaked with red dust, silent and uncomplaining towards the city. They had marched for many days, and perhaps they would march for many days more. It was curious to notice how silent they were. They marched on in the growing heat, between dark-green patches of summer rice, fallow and meadow and clumps of thick black bamboos spread out in a dull, hot diagram under the glistening sky. But the city stood white and glaring below them, and in the deep hollows of shade they would find contentment and rest.

The road went on and on, winding among small coppices and tumble-down villages; motor-cars roared past; white clouds streaked across the golden sunlit sky. Aeroplanes lay hidden in fallow fields, in spaces so small that it was impossible to imagine how they could be lifted into the air, and the dew sparkled on the cotton-netting and the dead leaves which concealed them from the air. The mountains on the further side of the river rose sheer out of the milky haze; they were brushed with pine forests and cypresses, but the summits were clear blue rock, and as we edged sharply down the winding road towards the ferry, it seemed as though the mountains were racing to meet us, their blue fire glinting in the sunlight.

I have never known a day like this in Chungking; so clean, so sweet, so clear was the air. The dust did not suffocate us, and everything amused us, everything was bright and still and fine.

439

It had rained a little during the night, no more than a few drops, but enough to give a glitter to every stone and blade of grass in the fields. Among the fields, under bamboo groves, stood small stone barracks painted over in large black characters with the legends of resistance: "From those who are wealthy—money; from those who are strong—strength." "Down with the militarism of the Japanese militarists." They were simple legends, and I have seen them thousands of times before, but today they acquired an unsuspected meaning, for it was unthinkable that this lovely countryside should fall into the hands of the Japanese. A soldier, wearing a blue padded cotton uniform, came out of the barracks with a fluttering yellow chicken under his arm. We saw the flash of a knife, and was it our imagination which watched this silver knife flashing across the whole countryside? "Down with the Japanese militarists." But the earth was sweet with grain, the sky was broken and blue among the swiftly-moving clouds and patches of sunshine lay on the ripening fields. The small touring-car purred. We were going steeply down-hill, after our long detour from Chungking, towards the ferry. And here the river was wider than ever, shining silver between the blue mountains, and small black sampans loaded with cobalt jars, cabbages, great baulks of orange timber, crates of yellow-and-gold chickens passed up-stream. But the ferry was slow in coming. We sat on the running-board, smoking, waiting for the ferry and admiring the mountains, which were the colour of blue ice or a field of hyacinths.

Once in Spain, travelling from Barcelona to the Ebro front, I have known the same excitement of sunrise, when the earth appears to be bathed in molten metal. There was the same shining in the air, the same air of continual and effortless expectancy, the same delight in pure being, the same feeling that the people were living their lives in an atmosphere of pure freedom. The sun shone with blinding radiance, yet one could almost look into the face of the sun. But what was so curious was that even the landscape seemed the same; the same reddish-yellow earth, the same aeroplanes hidden in the fields, the same small clumps of deep green trees. Where in Spain there were vines, there were patches of deep green rice, but there was little difference between the colour of the uniform of the soldiers, and the broken chimneys and bombed buildings would have looked strangely familiar in Spain. Even the river, though twenty times broader than the

Ebro, looked familiar, and I began to search for the stumps of the stone bridge which Italian airmen and Asturian dynamiters had destroyed between them one day in May.

From a small shop on the rise of a hill a boy brought a wooden pail of boiled eggs. The broken egg-shells lay in the dust at our feet: in the shining egg-shells we could see the blue mountains faintly reflected. There was nothing to do. The ferry was a great lumbering animal, shaped like a whale, driven by a small puffing steam engine at its side. It came across the river gently and menacingly, the only thing in this blue landscape which seemed to contain a spirit of malice; and when at last the motor-car was berthed securely on the tarred floor of the ferry, still we had to wait; and we were glad for the sake of those moments of splendour when, in the silent haze of the morning, we could watch the mountains undisturbed by the throbbing of the steam engines.

Small boys were fishing in the river. From a small boat moored against the shore a net rose sharply in the air, dripping with water and silver with small fish. Army lorries were moving down the road on the opposite shore, until there were seven or eight lorries waiting patiently at the ferry. And high above the lorries, beyond the clumps of bamboo and the grove of cypresses on the blue mountains, a sudden puff of white smoke announced the presence of a quarry. And smoking there, in the shadow of the small touring-car, the world seemed to be perfectly at peace and the appearance of the white cloud only added to the illusion of perfect contentment. Far away in the north a yellow haze shone above Chungking.

And so we rode down the shaded roads towards Kweichow. There was hardly anyone on the road—a few bamboo-shaded shops selling cakes, home-made wines and cheap cigarettes, a few stray dogs, a few small girls carrying mysteriously-quilted babies on their backs. The sun shone on the yellow road and on the green bamboos, which sometimes, even when there was no wind, would shiver, turning unaccountably white and silver. We slept that night in a field, under the shade of a great oak, while the stars wheeled in a perfectly blue sky and the fire-flies came out and the frogs croaked in the marshes near the village.

September 2nd . . . Slowly the landscape began to change colour and shape. The hills near Chungking are shaped like waves, but the hills on the border of Kweichow are made of sterner stuff. They rise sheer out of the earth, veined with granite, with vertical strata showing like pointers to the sky. There are few trees on the hills, except scrub. This morning we drove slowly towards a pass in the mountains, driving towards an immense range of mountains which shone yellow and blue and orange. On the summit of one of the tallest hills there is a protuberance which suggested the face of a knight in armour; but though we drove at fifty miles an hour, the face never appeared to grow larger. Even when we were underneath it, it seemed to be exactly the same size, the blue visor, the steel-black helmet, the gaunt grey shoulders shining in the strong sunlight. I have never seen a mountain like this, for we were both mesmerised by its terrible strength and majesty. No one had told us of the mountain, and we watched it with a kind of fascinated terror, wondering whether there would ever be a day when it would not stand in our way.

But at midday we found ourselves panting in the high mountain air. We were two thousand feet up. Down below blue rivers wandered among patch-work rice-fields, small villages clung to the slopes of rock, smoke rose from a spinney and we could see a long line of soldiers wandering across the fields in the distance. We were high up on a plateau, with the blue-faced mountain above us, looking down on the whole length and breadth of the earth.

There was no sign of anyone. Birds called, but very faintly, from the spinneys of scrub-oak. A yellow fly-catcher whistled close to our ears; a heron dived straight up into the air from a few feet away, and in this miraculous silence, full of birds, we rested in a small pavilion which looks out over the interminable pasture-land.

It was very hot. Puffs of smoke and steam came from the red chalky walls of the mountain road. T. unbuttoned his coat, lounged in the thick grass under the pavilion's shade and began to talk of his years in the army:

"I think the memories of soldiers must be almost non-existent," he said. "In the early days of the war so many terrible things happened that we could not believe them. Terrible crimes were committed by the Japanese, and sometimes terrible crimes were committed by the Chinese. One evening, during the battle in southern Hunan, we found a Japanese encampment. Everyone was sleeping—including the guards. We crept close to the encampment, thinking there was an ambush, prepared to use every
442

hedge as a hiding-place if we were discovered. And then, at a given signal, we rushed in, surprised because no one gave the alarm, surprised at the amount of ammunition which lay all over the camp and perhaps still more surprised by the complete silence that reigned over the place. You must know it was only a small camp, hidden under a great mountain, and close to a perfectly white river, which stretched for miles at the foot of the mountain. Well, we rushed in, screaming at the tops of our voices. The Japanese offered no resistance. They are fatalists; if they know that there is no escape, they do not fight. I ran into the commander's tent. A smoky lamp was burning. The commander was sleeping there with a girl. One of my soldiers pushed a knife into the commander's back, and he pushed it so deeply that he thought he had killed the girl. Outside, there were sounds of firing. I went through the commander's papers. It was summer and very hot, and I suppose I was drowsy; and after a while I noticed something moving. It was the girl. She was wounded. A great blackish-red fountain of blood was falling down her side from one of her breasts. She stood there, quite naked, staring at me from the other side of the bed. She was smiling a little. She was perfectly white in the light of the smoky oil-lamp, except for the blood flowing down her side. I could not help admiring her. She said nothing, but I think she was smiling, and suddenly she fired. The bullet missed me by a hair's-breadth, and I can still feel its little consoling whisper as it passed by my ear." He paused, took out his pipe and looked down at the great blue-green valley. A motor-lorry was chugging up the winding road; great puffs of smoke were rising from a clump of trees in the valley—it was lunch-time, and the labourers were returning from the fields.

"She fainted after that, and I left her there after removing the revolver from her hands. She fainted over the dead body of the commander. But the surprising thing happened afterwards. We killed every Japanese in the encampment and lost only one of our own men. I had been going among the tents, busily searching the dead; for in guerrilla warfare information is more important than a few bodies. Before dawn I returned to the commander's tent. She was still there. She was awake, dressed in a pure white kimono and surrounded by Chinese soldiers. They were talking to her through signs. She was laughing a little, that curious evanescent laughter which is near to tears. She was amused by them. They tried to comfort her. A medical orderly had bandaged

443

her wound. The smoky lamp still glittered on the dead body of the commander who lay face downwards on the bed; but they had completely forgotten the presence of the dead commander. They sang for her. They wanted to please her, they wanted her to laugh and forget the war, they wanted to be liked by her. And though she was always surprised by them, it was clear that she was touched by their behaviour."

He paused again, and looked up at the sky where the heron was still floating in whirlpools of air.

"What happened?" I asked.

"She joined our guerrillas," he replied. "She dressed as a common soldier. She looked after the wounded. She shared all our privations and learned Chinese. Sometimes she would sing for us, but not often, and sometimes she would disappear for a few days, and we never knew where she went. Then she would come back, exactly the same as before, smiling a little, very self-possessed in her blue military uniform, looking like a young boy. She died in our camp hospital from blood-poisoning after tending one of our wounded soldiers."

This was all: he smiled faintly, and far below us a long serpentine line of soldiers crawled beside the rice-fields.

We wound through the interminable pass through the mountains, wondering what could lie on the other side, and we were surprised by the sudden overwhelming beauty of the dark valley. A river ran downward through the red hills. It was a pure blue, rippling quietly over the stones. High above us the bushes were striped like zebras in the sunlight. Bright red dragon-flies made little flickering flights over the pool—for though it was a river, it was hedged in with enormous feathery bulrushes and seemed so silent in the noonday that it resembled a pool.

T. stretched a muslin net on the water to trap the insects floating down, and he lay on a white stone, peering at the small black and bright red creatures which fell into his net. There were faint-green animalculæ with iridescent fins and small black eyes; polyps resembling bubbles of frothy soap and curious little creatures with legs which resembled diminutive carnations. I know nothing about zoology, but T. was beside himself with excitement. In this lazy morning, the sun still high above our heads, I was content to watch the dragon-flies. Sometimes they would alight on the water, a puff of wind would throw them over and they would lie

444

still, very still, as though dead, and the wings would grow heavier and become submerged—the red wings turning to a darker red. But sometimes a miracle would happen. They waited there silently, collecting all the strength in their spent bodies, and sometimes they would leap out of the river again, the bright red veined wings dripping water.

"It's extraordinary," I said, turning to T., whose legs dangled in the cool water and whose head was half-buried in the muslin-net. "How much strength do you think they possess?—they can leap out of the water, even when they are drowned."

T. smiled, picked up a small greyish-yellow puff-ball smaller than a finger-nail and threw it lightly into the air, so that it fell a little way down-stream. It fell awkwardly, floated for a moment and then disappeared among the stones at the bottom of the stream.

"It was a kind of amœba," he smiled. "Nothing can harm it—it is invulnerable. It is only as we grow more complicated that we become vulnerable."

"And the birds?"

"They are less vulnerable than we are. We all have our Achilles' heel, but the insects——"

He gazed down at the blue flowing river. It was an hour before I could get him to go on. He was gazing at all the invulnerable and perfect things in the river.

The sun shone, and still we were coasting beside the blue river. It followed us everywhere. Wherever there was a road cut out of the mountain-side, there was also the river. Sometimes the river passed under delicate bridges, sometimes it wandered through villages, intensely blue, between the level shores of white sand. We are both sunburnt, and we shouted deliriously whenever we lost the river and again when it was found.

"You should stay here," T. said.

"Why?"

"Your eyes are blue."

"You are talking nonsense."

"No, there is really a race here with blue eyes. It is quite inexplicable. Perhaps they are Turkis who somehow reached one of the villages in southern Szechuan—they have blue eyes and black hair."

As we passed through the small stone villages—we were no

445

longer in the country of bamboo and plaster—I looked eagerly for the Turkis with the blue eyes. But there was no sign of them.

And still the river followed us. Perhaps it was less than a foot deep, for every round pebble in the stream shone and flickered in the glorious sunlight. The villages, the bridges, the fishermen with their heavy brown nets, the small boys bathing naked—all were perfectly reflected in the river as in a mirror. And the white clouds sailing so high between the fringes of mountains, how perfectly they were reflected, each particle of sunlight in the cloud having its appointed place in the river. There were bridges with delicate stone pillars, great weirs, small bamboo groves, forests of scrub oak. In their green depths we would have wandered if we had had time. And after the mountains—long green level plains, as flat as billiard-tables, the road drawn with a ruler through the forests of green rice. But the river had disappeared, and we were no longer elated by the strange persistence of the river.

And yet, even in these plains, there were mountains, the strangest mountains I have ever seen. They rose sheer out of the earth, chalk-white, very high, with a few trees on the summit, the naked whiteness of their sides shining in the sunlight. There was one immense mountain which had been split in two, but the two halves were separated by a rice-field. Every crust and indentation of the mountain was reflected in the glistening white flank which rose half a mile away. The mountain had shot out of the earth in primeval times; it had been struck by lightning or a star had fallen into it; millions of years later the earth had turned to lava, and one half of the mountain had floated away. And for miles on either side there were level plains.

It was dusk when we came to Tsung-yi, a small grey village straggling down a hill. Somewhere near Tsung-yi there is a famous University which is almost completely cut off from the world, living in the paralysing isolation which affects nearly all Universities in China; but we had no time to visit it, it was already growing dark—and darkness comes more suddenly as you go south.

We stayed in a C.I.M. mission house, where for something less than $200 we were given the best meal I have had in China. Oranges, marmalade, biscuits, jam, fruits, corn-cakes—there was no end to that extraordinary meal. The missionary was gaunt and worried; he seemed to be wondering whether it was worth while

446

to stay in this isolated small village, among the reeking smells and petty jealousies of a forgotten town, for he admitted that it was difficult to make converts, and he had little hope of extending the field. In the small white-washed drawing-room, with wicker-chairs and carpets, a small library, three or four black-wood tables, we played the gramophone records I had brought from Singapore. A great wolf-hound barked outside, and through the windows we could see the stars wheeling brightly across the sky. We were sunburnt and perfectly content—the old missionary with the grey face of an ascetic, his young wife, the director of one of the departments of the Chinese Foreign Office and myself.

I have never understood why foreigners coming to China have such scorn for missionaries. Their lives must often be harder even than the lives of Chinese professors. There are stories of mission-aries who have become great land-owners, there are stories of Protestant missionaries who have encouraged their converts to hate Catholic missionaries, and stories of Catholic missionaries living in filth, in degradation of the spirit, the more terrible be-cause it is self-assumed.

I asked the missionary what he thought of the future of mis-sions; he was not too hopeful. The Chinese respected them, if the missionary himself deserved their respect; but in the villages far from the towns it was difficult to convince the peasants that Taoist magicians were no guide to salvation. They would come to the missions at the last resort, when they were dying or when they were no longer allowed to enter the magic circle of the Chinese priests. He was a man of nearly fifty, with the worried ascetic face of a prophet, and it was odd to see him in the small house at-tended by a pretty wife and surrounded by the small valueless curios which he had bought in some distant part of China, in-stead of wandering through the countryside, dressed like St. John in camel-skins and with a staff in his hand. There was comfort in the house, but no ostentation, and I would have liked to have asked him why he read *The Flowers of St. Francis,* for he was a Protestant missionary, with all the fervour of a Catholic priest in some southern country in Europe.

He said grace over meals, but he showed no other signs of wishing us to accept his religion. He was gentle and quiet, lost in dreams. I could not help thinking of him afterwards when we climbed up to our cool bedrooms, where everything was simple and unadorned, and where a special sweetness of herbs came

447

'from the white beds ranged against the wall; for his presence could be felt in every part of the old house.

We lay in bed, listening to the moths flopping along the walls and over the unshaded lamps. Long after the light had been turned out, T. woke me out of a drowsy half-slumbering.

"I forgot to tell you a story."

"Yes."

"It's about Kweichow. There was a Catholic priest living in a small coal-hole, a little house no bigger than your fist——"

"Surely it was bigger."

"Don't interrupt. He was living in this dirty coal-hole, and dying of some terrible disease—leprosy or perhaps syphilis, for, you know, syphilis is quite common in these parts of China. He was dying. He was a skeleton. He had no proper bed-clothes. He lay on a broken bamboo-bed, covered with a heap of rags, and he gave no sign that he hoped for any release from his misery. An old Chinese woman came to attend him each day; she left a little rice-porridge by his bed, and perhaps a few leaves of cabbage, and perhaps some salt. The dogs often ran away with his food, and sometimes it would be stolen from him by a Chinese beggar. He did not complain. Three doors away lived the Protestant missionary in an enormous house with a courtyard, a great fat stupid man who rode a motor-bicycle and distributed tracts to the winds, saying that God would assuredly find a place for them in the hearts of the faithful, or something of the sort. He knew the old priest was dying. He could have helped him easily. But he did nothing. He waited till the old woman came and told him that the priest would not survive another day. Even then he waited. He knew that the priest would survive two days, for he had lived on almost nothing since he had come to China, and he was spare and strong above most men.

"The great eyes of the dying priest shone from the bed. With his hands folded on a crucifix, the priest was staring at heaven.

"'I have come to offer you consolation,' said the Protestant priest; but the Catholic said nothing. 'I have brought you food,' said the Protestant, 'and a warm quilt and my own hens have laid these eggs. I have come to begin a friendship.'

"Still the Catholic said nothing. He was raving silently. His great eyes were wide-open and he seemed to see things that have never been seen on earth before, and sometimes his lips moved and almost he uttered words from those thin parched lips.

448

"'I have come to ask you to enter my church,' said the Protestant. 'You must know that Rome is iniquitous. She is the red-robed Whore of Babylon. She is everything which is unclean . . .'

"Still the old priest did not move, but his hands were fastened more tightly round the crucifix and he seemed to be conscious of the old woman who had just entered the room and who crouched by his bed.

"'I have come to offer you the consolations of my religion with a pure heart. It has burdened my conscience that we have never spoken before. You were hard, harder than most men. You spoke Chinese too well—I suspected that the gift of tongues had been given to you. You dressed in rags, you were too proud to beg, you never took a holiday in the hills or spent a week-end in Chungking. You were callous of suffering. When people were dying in the hospitals, you blessed them, but you did not write home to France asking for medicines. You knew nothing of modern surgery or even of the most elementary principles of sanitation; and I remember that when you wounded yourself, you wrapped up your wound in pieces of paper. You said you would worship God in the hollow of a great pit, even if you possessed no more than a few grains of rice, and if you were naked. You were . . .'

"The priest said nothing at all. He did not look at the fat missionary with the dog-collar, he did not look at the haggard old woman who attended him, he did not look at the diseased dogs licking his plate. He smiled triumphantly, clutching the worn crucifix and uttering psalms; yet no words came from those dry cold lips.

"'For days you have lived on my bounty,' the Protestant continued. 'The old woman who waited upon you was my servant. I ordered her to spy on you. Without me you would have died of starvation. Every grain you have eaten was mine, and yet I gave it to you lovingly, because I hoped you would enter my church.' He laid his hands on the priest's bony hands, and stared accusingly into his eyes. He saw the dribble running through the old priest's matted beard, he saw the flickering black veins at the neck and he heard the beating of a pulse. But still the old priest did not see him, but stared through him at the angels in heaven.

"The Protestant tried for the last time.

"'Your religion offers you no consolation. I tell you, on my honour, that excavators in Palestine have found an inscription on

449

rock which relates that your Jesus Christ, who was crucified, was a common murderer. There was a Supper, you remember, and the Apostles drank wine and Peter possessed a sword; but we know now that during the Supper, everyone drank too much wine, there was a brawl and Judas was killed. So He was crucified. And the inscription on the rock found in Golgotha goes on to relate that even when He was crucified, he refused to admit his guilt, and cursed all the Apostles for hiding someone among them who had committed the murder. He did not mention the name of the murderer, but I tell you that the name of the murderer is legion, there are priests like you everywhere, and you are all murderers whom Christ cursed from the Cross.'"

There was a long pause. I could hear the moths still, and the wolf-hound was barking. The night watchman was walking down the street with his wooden clappers.

"Is that all?" I asked.

"No. In the morning they found the old priest dead, still holding the crucifix in his bony hands. The old woman, too, was dead. She lay stretched out at the foot of the bed. But the Protestant missionary was not dead—he crouched in the corner, screaming at the top of his voice, his eyes staring, completely mad."

September 3rd . . . WE LEFT Tsung-yi at dawn. The rain drizzled, the windscreen clouded over and the road unfolded in front of us like a long yellow strip of wash-leather. It was warm and close in the small car, and T. was humming at himself, smiling because he had kept me awake half the night with the extraordinary story of the priest in Kweiyang.

"Is it true?" I asked.

He shrugged his shoulders.

"Why not? It could have happened."

"But why did you tell the story in a house where we were perfectly treated? Have you ever known hosts so kind? They treated us like kings. It is absurd to think that missionaries behave like that nowadays."

"No, but they *might* have behaved like that. All the best stories are about things that might have happened."

The landscape turned to lead. The wind drove across the bleak gardens of rice, broke against the small stone *pai-lou* commemorating a long-forgotten widow who remained faithful until death, it tore against the flapping cloth of the hood and sighed through

450

the cracks in the windscreen. The old, sharply-pointed mountains were reappearing, slashed with vermilion. It was wild, rugged, desolating country, where small children cowered under the hedges by the roadside, and famished chickens dived across the road, their feathers wet and bedraggled. We passed through a small village of grey houses, and it seemed to us that from every house there hung disembowelled carcasses of pigs. And starving children. And immense blue lorries stored under bamboo roofs. And green lakes of mud. And a dead horse lay under a wind-swept tree. . . .

Perhaps all these are the illusions of the miserable grey rain, which takes the life out of men while it gives life to the earth. Perhaps we were half-remembering the comfort and quiet contentment of the white-washed missionary house in Tsung-yi, perhaps we were still half-asleep and dreaming the same nightmare. It was barren land made out of the crust of the earth, which would tilt up at extraordinary angles, so that we imagined we were in one of the circles of mountainous hell. The sharp cliffs were extraordinarily sharp; and as we coasted down the blood-red road we saw another mountain split in two, jagged and misty, and far away in the north lay a small stone bridge. We would have to travel along a thin road cut out of the cliff surface for miles before we reached the bridge; and though the other bank was less than a stone's-throw away, and though we could see people walking on the bank almost as large as the beggars squatting beside the road, it would be half an hour later before we reached the small red-roofed village on the other side.

So we coasted slowly and carefully along the dangerous winding road, the sheer grey cliff on one side, the precipice leading to a winding black river among stones on the other. The mountains seemed to meet over our heads. The rain blew open the hood. We sat there, cold and hungry, waiting for the bridge to come nearer, and sometimes T. had to bend the wheel sharply when a buttress of rock stood in the car's path or when a soldier appeared with a flashlight, beckoning him to slow down.

Nearly all the bridges in China are guarded by soldiers. The bridges are well-constructed, but so many heavy military lorries use the road from Chungking to Kweiyang that they allow only one lorry to pass at a time. As you pass over the bridge, it sags, the wooden boards creak, the wind sings in the wires supporting the bridge. There is a moment of terrible apprehension at the

451

centre of the bridge when you can *feel* its mechanical strain and a sound like a distant detonation; and you look over the side, calculating the distance which separates you from the white stones below, which suddenly and unaccountably resemble bleached skulls. . . .

Three hours later we reached Kweiyang, the capital of Kweichow. The rain lifted. The dusty streets, the small mountains like pepper-pots and still more like pepper-pots than the mountains of Chungking, for they stood up on a level base, ten or twenty small pepper-pot mountains exactly the same size, dark green, with fir-woods and perhaps small temples on the summit, streaming with the last fountains of rain.

September 4th . . . THE car has broken down—a new gasket. But where shall we get it? T. is jubilant. He has just seen a cheap gramophone in a shop marked at 70,000 dollars. "The inflation has really begun."

Somewhere among these hills we shall find the Chinese Red Cross, where Surgeon-General Robert Lim lives in a small plaster-and-stone house. But the hills were not enticing: always the same green muddy cones, the same height, with exactly the same trees on them, and exactly the same foot-tracks climbing to the summit. We stay in a squat little hotel on the main street, and we are awakened by the most deafening cock-crows. There are some good shops in the street, better even than most of the shops in Chungking, and the prices are lower, but under the miserable grey sky there is no temptation to buy anything except oranges.

In the morning a missionary comes to present his card. He is very young and looks ill at ease. While T. yawns, he talks of his conversion. He had prayed to be allowed to go to China and he demanded of God a sign; and one day, when he was drawing in the advertising office where he was employed, the director sent him upstairs to get the map of China in the *Encyclopædia Britannica*—and he took this to be the sign. So he has come to China, knowing little of the language, to lose himself in a remote village of Kweichow, and there is no one to help him and no one to fend for him. There is already a kind of bitterness in his heart—the heart of a lost soul.

He is well-built, with a shock of blue-black hair falling loosely over his forehead. His cheeks are blue, though he has shaved, and he wears a check coat and grey flannels, so that he resembles

452

a young undergraduate; but the most noticeable thing about him are his blue eyes. They are not the eyes of a convert, but of a football player. He notices everything quickly—the flight of a bird, the sudden apparition of an old woman in rags who goes hopping down the street, picking up scraps.

"Do you really believe that the map of China in the *Encyclopædia* was a hint from God?"

He was trying to look at a brightly-coloured bird.

"Yes, certainly. I had prayed for many nights for a sign, and none came. I wanted to be sure that it was God's intention to send me to China."

He began to talk about the bandits in the south. There were small groups of deserting soldiers who had banded together. He had gone into the bandit area alone, without ammunition and without food. He believed that everything would be given to him in double measure. He was ill with typhus. He lay in a house one night, when the bandits were coming closer to the village; he heard shots; he prayed and listened to the dogs barking in the forest. He told the story extraordinarily well. He was quite aware of his powers as a story-teller. "And then they came. They came to the house. I was lying in bed, praying. They did not see me. They were trying to find the women—and food. Women and food, those were the important things. But the women had climbed to the bottom of the well and the rats had gone away with the food. They saw me. It was nearly dawn before they saw me. They threw me off the bed, tied my hands, and led me out to be executed. I prayed. There was nothing else I could do, was there? They were quite pleasant boys. They laughed a lot. They pointed to the tree where they were going to hang me. They took my watch. It was getting light. I had given up all hope of help, for the villagers had hidden in the hills, where they have small stone fortresses and reserves of food. I waited. I thought that at any moment I would be killed, and I was not afraid. And then they laughed, they laughed so much that they could not stop. They just laughed. I wasn't afraid any more, and I began to laugh too —I was nervous and hysterical. I laughed because I had seen an extraordinarily beautiful bird in the tree-tops—it was pale-yellow with a golden crest and a red beak. I laughed because they were laughing. I laughed because I was afraid. They began to talk among themselves. A little while later they released me. It was six weeks before I recovered from typhus."

453

He said all this very simply, with the simplicity of a man who has no idea what really happened to him or even what happens to him at every moment of his life.

He complained a little of the high cost of living, the difficulties of building new churches, the extraordinary apathy of the Chinese villagers, who seemed to be perfectly content with their household goods. He complained of Chinese food—a not unnatural complaint. And all the while he seemed to be looking for something, and perhaps he was looking for another miracle which would increase his indefinite faith. He was a football player who had become, by some magic of circumstance, a priest in the wildest parts of China. He was alone in China and very sorry for himself, but no more sorry than a football player who has received an unusually heavy kick in the shins. I could imagine him sitting naked in the warm bathroom of a university after a football match, surrounded by white tiles and fumes of vapour, discussing Plato with all the other undergraduates.

"Yes, China is a terrible country," he said. "It takes the strength out of you. It's like lobbing a football and finding it going wide of the net. A terrible country!"

It was just as I expected. It couldn't be more perfect. It was so perfect that I could hardly believe it, and I ran out of the hotel to watch him descending the cold shuttered street; and what was still more curious was that even as he walked, he was turning quickly from side to side, searching for some imaginary phantom of beauty, or perhaps only for an imaginary football descending down wind against the sky.

September 6th . . . We are still here, the gasket still unmended, the rain still falling from the sky. There has been so much rain that it has been impossible to go to the Chinese Red Cross. T. balances himself on the edge of the hotel sofa, which is all springs, and talks of the war. He has known many Japanese before the war and since he likes talking about them, and talks about them extremely well, he is good company.

"And yet I have never been able to understand them," he says. "A Chinese, an Englishman, an American act in *character*. You can guess what they are going to do, because in their own way they are extremely logical. Make certain assumptions, study them for a few hours, and you know how they will behave if there is a thunderstorm or if there is a fused electric wire or if a murder

454

takes place. But with a Japanese you never know. They are illogical by instinct. Once I was staying in a place called Z—— in Inner Mongolia. There were Japanese business men and soldiers in mufti there. They had come to see some excavations which were being carried out, and there were perhaps seven of them. They were rich and important, they possessed great influence in Central Asia and they were known to be in a position of quite unusual intimacy with the Japanese War Office. They brought their mistresses and concubines, who were always well-dressed—little doll-faces with bright carmined lips and pale cheeks and hands like lotoses. They lived together in the station hotel, though there was no railway station and the hotel was called station hotel for lack of any other name. And suddenly an extraordinarily beautiful Russian girl arrived. She was introduced by the hotel manager as a Russian princess, a great dancer, and he made her dance for them in the hotel wearing an extraordinarily handsome costume—gold sequins, pearl breast-plates, great gold bangles on her arms —you know the kind of thing. They would make her dance on the tables. It was an extraordinary spectacle—this girl with the flowing yellow hair and the glittering spangles and the Japanese business men and army officers with their wives. They all watched her. It was impossible to take their eyes away from her. She danced with bare feet, almost naked, extraordinarily beautiful and attractive. And yet she was perfectly cold to them, she treated their advances with terrible contempt, and afterwards she would disappear, no one knew where. We set out to discover where she came from. We thought she might be living in the caves, or in a gipsy encampment, or perhaps she was the mistress of one of the Russian employees in the mine-fields. They paid enormous sums to spies. They followed her, but she always eluded them. At last, after three or four weeks, one of the Japanese officers, a thick-set man with a small beard—he resembled the stage Frenchman—managed to make an assignation with her. He disappeared early in the evening. The other Japanese became nervous. You could see them in the hotel lobby, staring through the black uncurtained windows, waiting for the Russian girl to return. They smiled nervously, stroked their moustaches, whispered in corners and looked at the clock. Still the Russian girl did not return. They ordered drinks. They made their concubines dance on the tables, and they even dressed up their concubines in the same way. They began drinking in sheer despair. There was nothing they wanted

455

except to see the Russian girl, and they stayed there, getting more and more drunk, waiting for the footsteps in the sandy courtyard outside. There were no footsteps. The concubines danced on the tables, and they drank vodka, and they sang terrible songs of despair to one another. And then, when it was nearly dawn and a white fog was filtering through the windows, and they were quite drunk, an extraordinary thing happened. They took out their swords and began to strike at the concubines on the tables. They were like maniacs. They struck blindly, cutting them into pieces; and when they had killed the concubines they began to strike each other until they were all dead or nearly dead. In the hotel dining-room there was blood everywhere, little heaps of bloody flesh on the tables and more heaps of bloody flesh on the carpets. And at seven o'clock in the morning the little stage Frenchman of a Japanese entered the salon with the Russian princess on his arm. He was going to announce that they would be married. He saw the blood on the floor, and the knives and swords lying all over the place, and he began to attack the Russian girl for no reason at all. He killed her and then committed *hara-kiri* in the centre of the room, very slowly, never once taking his eyes away from the dead Russian girl. And this really happened, and to this day I have no idea why the Japanese behaved like this. A fever had come over them, and it seems as though they can never stop when they begin to kill, as though some prehistoric instinct, the memory of some other great holocaust overcomes them, and they must repeat the venture in exactly the same way that the lemmings must leave the coast of Norway. . . ."

He was silent. The hard springs of the hotel sofa were becoming altogether too uncomfortable, and this small smoky hotel in Kweiyang looked exactly like the hotel he had invoked in Inner Mongolia.

"Is it quite true?" I asked dubiously.

"Everything is true—every word of it. They killed without any reason, they did not know why they killed and yet they could not help themselves. That is why the Chinese pity them."

He went on to discuss all the differences between the Chinese and the Japanese: how the Chinese love big things and the Japanese love small things, their differing delicacies and loyalties, their extraordinarily dissimilar family lives. He had studied them carefully. He had gone to Japan whenever an opportunity offered

456

and compared them with the cunning deliberation of a connoisseur comparing two fragrant wines.

"And this is how we should regard people, even our people," he concluded sententiously late at night. "We should regard them as wines. Each wine has a different bouquet, and different foods should be accompanied by different wines. And yet all are indispensable. There is no wine in the world which is not indispensable for our enjoyment, and in the same way every people is indispensable. *We are none of us expendable.*"

It was a comforting philosophy, but as we climbed the rickety stairway, it seemed to me a particularly Chinese philosophy.

September 7th . . . It is still impossible to reach the Chinese Red Cross, and we have been waiting impatiently all morning for one of the Chinese doctors who has been invited to dine with us. He was a famous doctor, a research chemist before the war who had taken part in the early guerrilla movement; but he did not come until late in the afternoon, when T. was out of temper. To spite him, since the motor-car was already prepared, T. suggested that we should go on, leaving him to eat alone in the fusty hotel.

But we were glad that we stayed. The doctor was short and fat, bubbling over with laughter. He seemed to take a malicious delight in everything—in the hotel furniture, the bell-boy, the torn table-cloth, the insolence of the frowzy maid-servant. And he talked about the Red Cross with the same malicious tenderness. He liked the Europeans who had come to serve the Chinese Red Cross with a kind of paternal affection, but they were such queer animals, they behaved in such extraordinary ways and he could not understand the complex and sometimes contradictory reasons which impelled young medical graduates to come out to China.

"I had never met people like them before I came here. There were Jews, of course, extraordinarily skilful Jews, who could easily have obtained appointments in England or America, but they preferred to live and work and die in this wilderness. Yes, they died. There was an English girl who had lived for many years in India, where she studied *yoga*. She was a normal girl, happy and carefree, living for her work. In coming to China, she seemed to have reached the height of her ambition. And so she was perfectly content and everyone tried to make things easy for her. On one thing only was she secretive. She kept an Indian

457

sword in her bedroom, hanging over the bed. It was a sword with a queerly-shaped blade and a fine handle, a little like one of those swords you see in Malaya. This sword hung over her bed every day, no one was allowed to touch it and we believed that it possessed magical properties, or at least she thought it possessed a kind of charm which would safeguard her and watch over her through the days of her life.

"She stayed with us for a year, doing important work on blood analysis. She became very friendly with a young Jewish doctor, but she did not allow their friendship to interfere with her work. And one day the Surgeon-General ordered us to prepare a group of doctors to go to the front, and she was among those who were chosen. I have never known a girl so delighted. If the height of her ambition was to work in China, a still higher ambition was to work at the front and tend the wounded. She was radiant with happiness. She was like a flame, absorbing the atmosphere around her, dancing with life and vitality. And then she was struck down with meningitis. It can be a very painful death, and her death was very painful, for at first we could not recognise that it was meningitis—it was unthinkable that she could have the disease. And so in a few days she died. We buried her high up on the mountains. We carried the heavy wooden coffin up the rocks, stumbling a little because it was a windy day, and there was rain in the air, and we wanted to get the ceremony over quickly. It was too painful, you understand. The coffin was lowered into a shallow grave, we read some prayers and suddenly the young Jewish officer ran forward a little, crying as though he thought he could summon her back from the grave. In his hands he held something wrapped up in sheets of some newspaper or other, and he threw this package into the grave and went away sobbing. And we came down the mountain, stumbling in the wind, and we knew that the package contained the sword, and we were all heavy in our hearts, and some of us were crying."

He spoke of the organisation of the Red Cross after dinner, drinking small thimble-cups of *hsiaohsing* wine. He admired Surgeon-General Lim and would speak of him as though he were a god, elaborating how he had built up the Chinese Red Cross from its beginnings. In the early days of the war soldiers died unnecessarily, and no wounded soldier could expect to live. There was no sulphanilamide in those days, and the drugs were so few that they could only be used sparingly. There was no quinine, no sulphur ointment, no bandages. The medical orderlies were untrained, the ambulances were used for more important things. And slowly, against the weight of many members of the Supreme Military Council, the Red Cross had been formed. There were now training schools, where medical orderlies received the most modern training. There were great stores of drugs—millions of tablets of quinine, hundreds of thousands of pounds of sulphanilamide, enormous reserves of bandages and reagents. Tragedies happened. Sometimes they were so badly packed that they deteriorated. Sometimes they were lost or stolen; and they would find drugs bought at enormous expense by the Government sold in the chemists' shops in Kweiyang.

If he could have had his wish, the young doctor would have taken over all the chemists' shops in China. "Bad drugs are being sold in every city. They will give you sulphanilamide made of corn-powder and aspirins made of chalk." I reminded him of the story of the extremely brilliant English missionary lady who had left Chengtu the previous summer to live among the aboriginal tribes of the Tibetan foothills. She cut herself accidentally, and though she possessed a full medical equipment she had died in agonies a few hours later. She had probably taken sulphanilamide, thinking that she had no further cause for worry. The doctor nodded. The same thing had happened even in the army. It was happening in every village of China, and it would continue to happen until the chemists were placed under government inspection. "And even then," he said wearily, "it may still happen. We need a new broom in China. There is so much wretchedness and unnecessary misery."

He spoke of the soldiers who came to be examined at the Red Cross in Kweiyang. They had marched from some distant province, they were covered with lice, they were weary and footsore and half-starved; but after a few days in Kweiyang they put on flesh, their hearts beat more loudly, they could march again with long easy strides. Thousands of soldiers passed through his hands. Some were ill, and these would enter the hospitals. Others would be taken down by convoy to the Burma front, and still others would have to march along the long dusty winding roads.

"What is so extraordinary is their recuperative power," he said. "I have studied Chinese soldiers throughout the last five years, and I have never known such animals. Many die. Too many die.

But there are soldiers who are wounded by Japanese bombs, who lie in the open for days without food, shelter or medicines—and they survive. There is something in their blood which makes for healing, but even today we have been unable to isolate it. Their powers of survival must be greater than those of any other soldiers in the world."

Outside in the street some soldiers were marching, a band was playing, the blue, white and red flag of the Chinese Army waving proudly before them. An officer marched on a white charger. A band was playing. It was raining, and the rain splashed up from the feet of the Chinese soldiers, who wore only their padded cotton clothes, small brown hats and thin rice-straw sandals. They marched gaily through the mists of rain; and thinking of the long march into Burma or India before them, the young doctor repeated:

"Their powers of survival must be greater than those of any other soldiers in the world."

September 8th . . . We left in the driving mist and the rain, having seen little of Kweiyang, for in truth there was little to see. The small touring-car is lighter now, for we have consumed so much petrol that there is no need to carry more than one great drum in the back. The small green conical mountains flashed past in the mist of the rain. The road was quite straight. Every half-mile there is another conical mountain. T. has tried to make them exciting for me by recalling the battles that were fought from these strongholds by the aboriginal tribes; but their deadly monotony palls. They are *exactly* the same height; they have the same angle of inclination; they are all slightly flattened at the top; they all have winding grey tracks along the sides; there is the same clump of trees on the summit. They are more wearying than the rain and more unsatisfying than the Kweiyang hotel.

Soldiers pass. They wear great yellow straw hats, and from each one of them fall curtains of rain. Some of them have taken off their blue-grey puttees and walk barefoot, splashing in the mud; and we see them, bent under the weight of rain, their packs on their backs, the small donkeys laden with machine-guns, the officer on the white charger, and they march straight forward, never taking shelter, eternally on the march. Already, though we are less than twenty miles from Kweiyang, some have been taken

460

ill. They are supported by their comrades with a tenderness which makes our hearts ache. Others are carried on stretchers.

In the mist and the rain we have come to a waterfall. It is a more beautiful waterfall than I have ever seen, wide-flowing between granite banks, between clumps of oak-trees and great shoots of ferns. It falls slowly, one curtain following upon another and being absorbed by it; till a third curtain falls, and so slowly do they follow one upon another that they seem to be caught in a motionless eternity. And the rain falling somehow makes the waters more luminous, like the immense towering waterfalls of Chinese paintings in the Yuan Dynasty; and it seems as though the only light in the world comes from these shadowy waters. Far below, among blue and green stones, the small turbulent smoking river runs between high banks. We lean forward, anxiously watching the progress of the falls, our faces streaming with spray, and we are so fascinated by the sudden spectacle that we are in danger of falling over the immense precipice.

There is no sunlight, but a faint rainbow glitters over the falls. Birds sing in the bamboo coppice. There are veils of rain, great clusters of spray, the terrible roar of the falls. And suddenly, in the distance and the rain, we hear the band of the Chinese soldiers we have passed a few minutes before.

We are staying at An-ning. We arrived early in the morning, when the sky had cleared and we had passed the last of the cone-shaped mountains. There were level fields, and small white-walled villages, and suddenly we came to an immense white ring, pure white, glistening in the aftermath of the rain. It was extraordinarily beautiful, the low white wall, the fields, the Chinese drum-tower, the peasants in blue gowns walking down the dusty roads. As you come closer, you notice that the wall is ruined, with great cracks opening as a result of a subsidence in the soil; and the golden signs on the drum-tower, which sparkled two miles away, are tawdry neglect. But the low wall is beautifully constructed, following the lie of the land, advancing towards small outposts retreating wherever art and nature suggest that a retreat is necessary; and so low that a child looking for cob-apples could jump over it with ease. There are no crenellations which give glamour and magnitude to so many walls in northern China. It is a wall for a busy village, and nothing could be more perfect.

The air is beginning to lose its heaviness. We can breathe freely at last, for we are climbing towards the south-western plateau; and we stand up in the small car. There is a headiness, as of some light wine, in this fragrant and perfectly-transparent air.

We pass through the ruined gateway into a narrow street lined with shops so small that we wonder how the fat merchant we saw walking sedately down the dusty road between the limes can enter them. There are elaborate carvings over the shops, gold-painted; and for some reason they have been painted by a skilled craftsman, so that we seem to have come at last into a place where Chinese calligraphy is publicly exhibited at its best. A great multitude of people surge down the muddy roads; coolies shouting under their heavy bales of rice; an old bearded mission-ary bobbing up and down in the crowd, trying for some reason to attract our attention, until he too is lost in the crowd.

It is market-day. From every small village in the countryside small carts have arrived. The streets are full of people in their best clothes. The merchants wear bright blue gowns, but from time to time you notice their sparkling white silk trousers flashing between the side-slits of the gowns. The women, with silver and gold bangles, are everywhere. There is gold woven in the fronts of their dresses, and their hair is piled up in little wings over their foreheads, oiled and combed. Small booths line the streets, and each booth appears to have its attendant cat tied with string. Little bare-legged girls wander down the lanes between the booths, leading their goats, their fowls and their blind; for there are not enough dogs in the world to lead all the blind beggars of China. The blind beggars, playing their one-stringed violins, are perfectly content to be led by these little girls, whose faces are wise beyond their years. I watched a snake-charmer hovering over his coiled snake, the snake's blue tongue flickering, the little beady yellow eyes remaining perfectly still, and all the while the girl was explaining to the blind man what was happening. And the old blind man smiled, perfectly content.

It was market-day, and all the gramophones were playing. There were at least twelve gramophones in the little street lead-ing to the West Gate. They screamed and roared above the noise of the traffic, above the bands of the soldiers marching magnif-icently into the village, above the cries of the barkers and the sly screams of the lovers in the dark, overshadowing lanes. The Chinese have a passion for sound. They like to surprise you with the explosions of fire-crackers, but the western invention of the
462

gramophone has offered them a new enjoyment which compares favourably with all the sound-machines they have invented in the past. Set twelve gramophones with loud-speakers in a row, use loud needles and if possible a radio amplifier; and they will be delighted beyond measure. It is a matter of no importance what the gramophone plays. T. thought he recognised a jazz tune, three high-pitched excerpts from Chinese operas, a Japanese love-song, the "Peasant and the Soldier", a sea-shanty from *H.M.S. Pinafore* and some old Chinese folk-songs. And if the Chinese have a passion for sound, they have also a passion for bright colours, especially on market-day. The booths were covered with gold and silver tinsel. Inexplicable pink ribbons descended from windows, and though they would grow lighter in colour as the day went on, for the sun was hot and volumes of dust were whirling in the air, they looked bright enough in the early morning. And everywhere there were fortune-tellers. There were fortune-tellers who could tell your future by examining the shape of your face and the years of your life by examining the length of your nose or your jaw-bone; there were fortune-tellers whose only possessions were a mirror and a scroll on which was depicted (wrongly) the circulation of the blood-stream in the human body. There were fortune-tellers who examined your palms, and others who nodded over the fumes of some potent poison. There were open-air barbers gently coaxing the wax out of hairy ears by means of silver spindles. There were doctors with curious dragon-bones, dull grey and violet, on their tables. There were dentists who pulled out your teeth with skewers, and men long practised in acuti-puncture, who could relieve your rheumatic nerves by gently inserting very similar skewers into your thighs. There were cobblers, tailors, cake-sellers, rice-sellers, little spirit-stoves where the most delicious pancakes were being prepared, there were fat merchants, gamblers, stout housewives. In the corn-market a group of soldiers were gambling with dice in a shaded corner. There were flies. There were sweet-meats black with flies, yet the children bought them with the soiled blue bank-notes they clutched in their small fingers. And everywhere there was an air of irresponsible gaiety.

We might have expected it—it was not an ordinary market-day. T. introduced me to the mayor, a small man in a Sun Yat-sen uniform tightly buttoned at the collar, very talkative and sufficiently full of his own importance; yet there was a kind of gentleness in his eyes which suggested that he was a good mayor, who took his duties seriously. He told us that there would be an execution later in the morning. It appeared that an opium-smoker, who had been warned three times, had exhausted the patience of the mayor, who proposed to execute him as a warning to others.

There was a band, fire-crackers were being exploded, small boys ran cheering along the streets, and the extraordinary procession turned out of the long street into the centre of the town. We could not find the opium-smoker. It was impossible to believe that the opium-smoker was the man dressed up in a clown's costume, a long white silk costume into which strips of violently coloured silk had been inserted. He was quite young, with a small moustache, very pale and dishevelled. The small boys cheered him, the band played and sometimes stones would be thrown at him, and then he would glance over his shoulder with an expression of agonised annoyance. There were soldiers at the head of the procession. They walked grimly, almost silently, while the crowds cheered from the balconies and the bugles sounded from the drum-tower.

We did not follow the procession to the end. The opium-smoker's face had been painted white, or perhaps he was pale with the effort of avoiding the stones. He stumbled along, his hands free, his silk gown billowing in the wind. He looked bewildered, and it was clear that a benevolent town council had given him rice-wine before he left the prison. He would turn round suddenly, making little appealing gestures to the children, who can have known little about his fate, though they repeated over and over again: "Shoot, shoot, shoot!" as though it was the most amusing thing in the world. And then, ten minutes later, silence descended over the whole village and we heard the bark of rifles, followed by the winged sound of a single shot. The opium-smoker was dead. The village resumed its normal life.

We are staying in a small inn overlooking the main square in the village. It is raining, and in the great unroofed courtyard men are still talking over their rice-bowls, unconscious of the rain. From upstairs the courtyard resembles a Spanish *patio*, and it needs only a few palms and a whispering fountain to make me think I am once again in Catalonia listening to General Modesto outlining the course of the war in Spain.

It was in July, in 1938, just after the Spanish Republicans had thrown the Germans over the Ebro. In this little country-house near Mora del Ebro; we drank champagne and heard the nightingales singing above the noise of the distant bombers.

"In a few days we shall attack more strongly than ever. We have crossed the Ebro—even the German military authorities did not believe that we would succeed. But we shall surprise them again, and we shall keep on surprising them. They deserve to be surprised!"

He was a thick-set man, with a blue chin and a fine forehead, and he held himself well. He was known to have been possessed of a magnificent heroism in the defence of Madrid, where he rose from sergeant to colonel, and became chief of liaison to Miaja. He was a communist, with a communist's sense of opportunity and a communist's bravery; and he was ruthless against the soldiers who showed the slightest fear. He had been known to shoot men out of hand, and on the same day and almost at the same time, he would share his last crust of bread with a bed-ridden soldier. Legends had grown up about him. He had held up an advance of tanks over the Guadarramas alone, or rather accompanied only by a small boy, who helped him to light the fuses of his home-made bombs. He was adored and hated, and it was not difficult to believe that he possessed some curious quality of leadership which made some men love him with all the passion of their disciplined hearts. But as he spoke there, occasionally beating on the white table-cloth with his wine-glass, his military coat open at the neck and his thick black curling hair flowing over his ears like the hero of some medieval legend, it was easy to believe that the forthcoming attack would be successful, and still easier to believe that Miaja and Modesto between them were a match for the German General Staff.

"But why don't you help us?—Don't you see that it is to your advantage? A great revolution is spreading over Europe, and this crossing of the Ebro is our capture of the Bastille. We—the revolutionaries—are the inheritors of Europe. We have sacrificed too much, and soon there will be a day of awakening. But we must be careful; the enemy is clever; if I thought you came from the enemy I would execute you at once."

I smiled, for the champagne and the nightingales and the great splendour of the dinner were worth an execution.

"And if you fail?"

"We shall not fail. They have guns, but we have faith. It is

465

always like that that battles are won. Think of the young revolutionary Napoleon, think of Cannæ. Here, on the banks of the Ebro, we are attacking the new Bastille."

Rice steamed from the immense wooden cauldrons, the wooden tables shone in the rain, great oil-lamps swung over the deserted courtyard. In all the rooms looking over the courtyard people were preparing to go to sleep. In the small bedroom, shaped like a coffin, where the only furniture consisted of a chair and two bamboo beds, a faint light gleamed from the rape-seed oil-lamp, a flickering green flame.

As we sit on the edge of our beds, drowsily talking of Spain and China, listening to the soldiers who are unrolling their blankets along the covered terrace downstairs, an extraordinary thing happens. A light shines through the torn paper windows and suddenly the door opens, and a girl enters, followed by an old woman holding a lamp. The girl is beautiful, dressed in green and red silk; her face is powdered dead-white, the arching forehead shadowed by the black mass of oiled hair, and the eyebrows delicately curved. In the flickering light of the two lamps she looks like someone out of a fairy-tale. Standing against the wheeling shadows of the wall, perfectly still, smiling a little, showing teeth like pearls and hands like lotoses, she waits for the moment when the old hag behind her will open her toothless mouth and begin bargaining. We both stare at the girl, caught up in the wings of her overwhelming beauty, conscious that the dark night is a wave that has thrown her against these inhospitable shores. The old woman opens her mouth. A settled silence descends upon the courtyard. The girl moves a little towards the bed, her silk dress flickering in the lamplight, moving so gracefully that she resembles an apparition; and suddenly the silence is broken and T. escapes from his dream, waves his arms and says in an unnaturally loud voice: *"Pu hao, pu hao,"* over and over again. The girl disappears, and all through the tormented night I can hear T. sighing, and in the morning he looks pale and dishevelled. . . .

September 9th . . . ALWAYS the soldiers. Soldiers everywhere. Soldiers climbing down the red earth gullies between the ricefields, soldiers drinking at the wells, soldiers marching in long serpentine columns over the dusty roads, in the rain, in the bright sunshine, in the shadow of the wings of clouds. I have seen more soldiers on the road than I have ever seen before. There are

466

soldiers who walk proudly, and others who stumble along, as though impressed by some invisible force; there are soldiers who seem to be running, and others who stand still like beggars in the hot sunshine, showing their scars.

Here and there we come across a few roads where there are no soldiers, but the impression of an interminable stream is inescapable. The colonels ride on white chargers with red saddle-bags, the rank and file follow with the guns, the mortars, the machine-guns which have been assembled on the backs of mules. There are guns camouflaged under leaves, and more guns painted over in bright green and yellow, so that they will be invisible in the Burmese forests. Already we are in Yunnan. The earth rises. Great mountains with pointed peaks lie before us, grey and green in the shadowed watery light; and still the soldiers march among the rice-fields, still they slake their thirst at the village wells, but as we go further the small blue water-proof bags of rice which they wear slung over their shoulders like bandoleers are becoming pathetically thinner; and their lines too are thinning out, and more and more of them are hobbling in the dust and the mud.

They wear immense straw sun-hats or bamboo woven round red paper, so that at times their hats seem to be the colour of the setting sun, and at other times they shine brilliantly like the sun rising in splendour. As the car approaches they scatter to the side of the road. They smile as we pass, throw out their hands with their thumbs pointed upward and shout: *"Ding hao!"* and for a moment, at the thought of this car speeding towards the south, their faces shine with amused envy and delight. We are carrying four soldiers at the back of the car. They came up to us in An-ning, saluted smartly and asked—no, they did not ask, but seemed to be praying that a miracle might happen and that all their days of marching would be over. And sitting there, they look at the eternal slow lines of soldiers passing up the serpentine roads with a kind of tenderness, a kind of maternal solicitude, as though they were saying: "Another car will come, don't worry, everything will turn out right in the end."

All afternoon it has rained, and the great cliffs and bastions of the south-western plateau lie before us covered in the greenish tallow of rain. We climb through mountain passes, only to descend towards the same river again. We count the milestones, the small white bridges, our pulses—and it seems that all are the same. The mountains have sheer cliffs, and high up in the cliffs,

467

unreachable by man, are small black toothless caves. And the trees bend in the wind, and the red road coils like a snake along the immense sloping breasts of the mountains. When shall we reach the end? There are only villages, sheltered under lime-trees and scrub-oaks, where cigarettes and perhaps rice are sold —certainly nothing else.

The soldiers flash past. The peasants look up from the fields, weighed down by the burden of rain. The grey sky against the patchwork of innumerable spear-shaped mountains has a luminosity which dazzles us, yet there is greyness everywhere. From the summit of a great mountain we watched the soldiers on both sides. They paled into the distance, their sun-hats shining red in the rain. They stumbled forward, covered in mud, groping blindly through the rain, weary beyond endurance, their blue coats dyed black by the poisonous rain, more weary than any men I have seen anywhere; and as they passed they smiled, threw out their hands and shouted: *"Ding hao!"*

T. has been watching them with a kind of abstracted air, as though he cannot believe entirely in their existence, or as though he feels foolish, and suddenly his face turns quite white and he looks away at the little grey-and-white birds who make sudden shallow dives among the mulberry-trees. And then in a voice like a groan, while the armies pass in their interminable columns: "O God, for how many thousands of years must the sons of our farmers die on the frontiers?"

September 11th . . . WE ARE so high that our breath comes, in little barks. The mountains have changed colour—they are green and white, standing on the horizon; and the air is sweet like silk, and still there are interminable columns of marching soldiers. We drove through part of the night, and saw the soldiers bivou-acking on the side of the road, the small camp-fires, their sodden clothes, the warm red bodies of the soldiers as they warmed themselves naked before the fires. But in the morning, when we passed Kutsing, the sun shone on the yellow sunflowers, immense fields of sunflowers shining like gold, and though the soldiers still pass and wave their hands, and though the air no longer tastes like silk but like milk, we are obsessed by the soldiers and the dead bodies lying beside the road. We think of the dead walking over all the fields of China in interminable columns like these, and we pray that they are not strangers to their homes. How many sol-
468

diers will return to their farms? Not that dead boy who lay covered in the dust of the roadside. Not that dead boy who dropped in the mud as we passed. "But you saw them by their camp-fires, and surely they were full of life as they stretched out their arms to the leaping flames." "I saw them." "And you loved them, and you were not sorry for them?" "I was sorry for them and I loved them." I heard him reciting some poem of the T'ang Dynasty, and suddenly I remembered those poems we had translated years before in Singapore:

O the tears of soldiers streaming down like rain!

And yet there was something extremely nonchalant in their marching. They had come from every province of China. They were footsore and weary, they were diseased, they were coughing up their blood and there were no medical supplies to relieve them, there were dead soldiers at the cross-roads and live soldiers warming themselves by their camp-fires, sheltered from the rain; and already they were fighting against hunger and disease—the second of the battles to be fought in China. And even here, in Yunnan, in the high clear plateau, they were dying. This is what seemed so monstrous and unnecessary; and yet we knew that there was not enough rice in the country to feed them all, and perhaps there was not enough bamboo in the country for their bamboo shoes, and not all of them carried rifles. And so they passed wearily down the last miles of the weary road which leads to Kunming and beyond, singing, between the sunflowers and the limes and eucalyptus-trees, till they saw in the distance the magical silver ring of the great lake which shines at the foot of the purple mountains.

There were more soldiers than I have ever seen before, and more aeroplanes in the sky than I have ever seen before; and the contrast between great shining blue Liberators in the cloudy sky and the blue-coated soldiers was not to their disadvantage. The soldiers lived as their ancestors had lived thousands of years ago; and they were tamed by discipline and hard living. The aeroplanes, so new and so beautiful, were unbelievably silent and perfect; and it seemed that their perfection lay in their silence in the high, wind-swept sky. For now we were no longer shuttered in by mountain. The great arc of the sky curved overhead, distinct and fruitful, a glittering faint blue, so wide that it resembled

469

freedom. In Szechuan and even in Kweichow you are covered by mountains. In the little spaces of sky overhead you occasionally see the sun; but here there are a million suns, a sun everywhere, and the blue sky broods tenderly over the children living beneath.

I have known such a sky on the plains of Hungary; and one day, standing on Cape Point, the most southerly scarp of Africa, it seemed that the sky was really infinite, one could descend into its depths and return unharmed from the Antarctic or even to Orion. There were a few mountains, grey-blue and watery on the horizon, not real like the mountains in Szechuan; there were clouds and aeroplanes and soldiers and small villages nestling among pines, and everywhere the sweet scent of fresh milk. We had stayed the night in a small hotel in a village whose name I have forgotten, a village of crumbling plaster houses and enormous shadows. We tossed among bed-bugs, cursing the unknown name of the village until our throats were parched with anger; but in this morning—how bright, beautiful and serene was the sky.

And so we coasted along the red roads, between fields of bright green corn and rice, towards the rim of the last mountains, where a curved silver blade like a scimitar shone between the peaks. The sunlight danced on the sword; and every moment of the dance was precious; till at last, coming over the last of the foothills, we saw before us, in all her majesty, the green lake in the sunset.

September 12th . . . The sun very high, shining among the small lakes and the trees and the white bridges; everywhere the scent of limes. I had forgotten the great stone wall round the city, and this morning, as we drove out towards the Burma Road, we watched the sunlight gliding slowly among the purple shadows of the wall. The wall is at least forty feet high; there are great drum-towers at the gates and stone pathways leading from the rice-fields outside, and the stone pathways are full of a jostling crowd of peasants whose dresses are brighter than anything I have ever imagined in China. There are herds of brown cows, innumerable horses and donkeys, gaily decorated carts. Slender girls carry the water-pails up the steep streets, for even here the streets are inclined at an angle. The houses are painted in all the colours of the rainbow: there are yellow houses, pale-red houses, brown houses. There are houses facing the small lake-like palaces,

470

and sometimes, as we pass down the streets, a small door opens on to a courtyard filled with a blaze of red flowers.

And at night the lights shine in the streets, the gramophones blare, American and British officers ride through the streets in jeeps, and there is so much wealth of rippling silks and silver and porcelain that we feel that we have come to another country altogether. And yet the city is not beautiful. Seen from the air it resembled a toy palace, surrounded by glistening lakes; but the small dark evilly-scented alley-ways are the same as the alleyways in Chungking, and there is nothing to distinguish this city from thousands of other cities except its wealth and its position among the mountain lakes. Disappointed and at the same time elated, we walk through the crowded streets, where the ricksha-pullers, in an effort to avoid the stream of motor-cars, drive close to the kerbs, and where the unshaded electric lights blind our eyes. Hungry and covered in dust, we turn down a dark side-street. A signboard, engraved in Arabic characters a foot high, reminds us that within living memory there was a Mohammedan revolt in Kunming. The food-stalls are brilliantly lighted. There are naked electric bulbs everywhere; and the men squatting behind their baskets of flaming oranges, or those great crinkled yellow oranges which are unlike those I have tasted anywhere else, look up as you pass with an extraordinary sense of possession. They do not care whether you buy. T. complains that the Yunnanese love the things in their shops and hate to sell them; and this is why they are rude to foreigners, hating the idea of selling. The oranges are sold by the weight. Four oranges for fifty cents would have been considered a breach of the law before the war, but now four oranges cost fifty dollars, and no one complains. "It is partly the fault of the Americans," T. complains, shaking his head. "They buy anything without arguing about the price, and the tradesmen have no love for selling." In this dark side-street, dark only in comparison with the brilliantly illuminated main streets, the oranges glow with hidden fire, and from time to time someone sprinkles water over them, so that they dazzle like rubies.

Even here, away from the noise of the main streets, there are crowds of people. Throngs of young men in European clothes saunter down the street; there are beggars in networks of rags; old women with silver pins in their hair; attractive young girls in Chinese gowns, white, cherry-red, blue, or in short flowered skirts and small black coats, heavily scented, rouged, with blue eyelids and hair so glossy that it shines silver in the light of the electric lamps. And always the distant noise of the streets, a thunderous roar in the background, a feeling of vitality which I have known in no other city in China, of movement, sudden startling movement, the whole city caught up in a great wave of audible excitement. And suddenly, passing a dark lane, an old woman stands wailing in a courtyard, beating her breasts, tearing her hair, her face outlined in the light of the small window-lamps, and we pause for a moment, listening to the high screams of hunger or despair which rise from the courtyard, but the noise of the city drowns her voice and once more we are lost in the brightly-lit crowds on the side-streets. . . .

September 13th . . . "THE beggars, the beggars!" T. complained this morning, when we went down into the centre of the city after daybreak. It was very cool and fresh, the sky bright blue with milky streamers. A few rickshas trundled slowly up the long steep roads, the flapping rubber wheels of the rickshas licking the cobbled roads. Small donkeys stood tethered to the houses. In a few moments men came out of the houses with great wooden casks shaped like bath-tubs, which they solemnly hoisted on to the backs of the donkeys; and as we passed, we knew that it was human manure destined for the country. But it was the beggars, who crouched still sleeping in the doorways, who attracted our attention. They were covered in filth; their legs red with sores; their bodies emaciated. They slept and shivered in the cold wind, and they lay in positions which I would have thought it impossible for the human body to assume. The sun rose, shining on the gold letters of the memorial arch, on the yellow streamers flooding down from windows, on the grey and green tiles of a Confucian temple, and on the green rags of the beggars. They were all young—some were boys. Sometimes they huddled together for warmth, their naked arms linked together, tormented by hunger even in their sleep, for their mouths would open and close again, exactly like the mouths of fish on dry land. Girls passed them, walking swiftly up-hill to the government offices, wearing blue gowns. The beggars slept until the golden sunlight fell at last into the doorways, and then at last they woke up, picked up their grimy rice-bowls and staggered towards the shelter of some trees.

T. regarded them with pity and tenderness, and yet with a kind of hardness born of many years of disillusion.

472

"Once they were the richest people in China," he said. "They drove the motor-cars along the Burma Highway; they gambled; they squeezed; there were times when they could dictate to the world, and when imported goods were more valuable to China than anything else, they could put a pistol to our heads and say: 'I will carry these, I will not carry those.' When the Burma Highway opens, they will be rich again."

In the centre of the city there was a roar of traffic. Motor-cars, lorries, jeeps, buffalo-carts, small grey asses, wound their way with a deafening roar towards the airfield, or towards the remaining stretches of the Burma Highway. And still, among the great crowds of people on the pavement, you could distinguish the beggars, who wandered aimlessly through the great throngs, with their staves and their rice-bowls, and it was difficult to think that they had once been the richest people in China.

September 14th . . . THE University stands outside the walls of the city, where the red hills rise to the north and groves of cedars stand among the graves. The small mud buildings between the high mud walls have been bombed; and the sparrows and blue magpies noisily chirping among the limes, the motor-cars throwing up great pillars of dust along the road, the screaming children in the gutters and the soldiers busily felling trees have no power to disturb the silence which lies within the mud walls. As you walk through the gates, past the bare-footed soldier who stands on guard, an extraordinary impression of silence comes to you. There are small lakes and pools, grass-grown, with green briars and the yellow flags of banana-leaves near the walls, and beyond them, high above your head, in the distance, stretch the grey-green mountains under a transparent sky. There is nothing to indicate that this is the greatest University in China, except the letters carved in black on a sheet of oak which lie above the doorway; nothing to suggest that those students in blue gowns sitting under the shade of the trees or leaning against the mud walls in the silence of the autumn heat are the future legislators of China. The mud huts are smaller and uglier than cow-sheds; the great tiled library, like a ruined barn, would be out of place in a small Norfolk farm. And yet there is no feeling of poverty. Blue-coated soldiers—the guards of the University—work in the fields. A white mare ambles through the deserted rows of lettuce. A professor, deep in thought, walks across the yellow pathways in a tattered

473

gown, which was once blue and is now the colour of the blue-white dawn, so often has it been washed in the waters of the green lake. Though he is deep in thought, his eyes are bright and his thin face is curiously handsome, and you think you have seen him before, perhaps in some great congregation of ministers of state, until you remember that the man you were thinking of died many years before—a great general who saved the Empire against the rebellion of the Taipings. The professor is a descendant of the general. He carries one of the greatest names in China, and his shoes are down at the heel and his gown is frayed at the edges. He is known for his great sweetness and his kindness to students, who worship him, forgetting his fame and remembering only that he preserves the virtues of the great Chinese scholars.

For this is a place where scholarship rules. All that made China great, her arts, her calligraphy, her understanding, her philosophy, her logic, her benevolence and her wisdom are consecrated here. For thousands of miles the students and professors journeyed to the south-west from the north-east. They suffered incalculable hardships. The books, which they had removed even before the outbreak of the war, were lost during the bombardment of Chungking. Stupidity? Malice? Inefficiency? No one knows. They were lost at a time when great Universities cannot afford to lose books, and they were never replaced. But mud buildings can be replaced. They, too, were destroyed when a flight of Japanese aeroplanes made this University a target for their bombs, but a few days later coolies dug out the red mud on the campus and built new cow-sheds for the students.

Walk through the ill-kept garden, which has all the charm of the gardens you see in Chinese villages, past the flag-pole and the library and the students poring over the notice-boards to the small blue-painted tower behind the University. From there you can see the tin roofs shining softly under the blue sky, the magpies wheeling above the roofs, the blue-gowned students and the professors who wear often gowns of a darker colour. From there the University seems so small that you could almost put it in your pocket—a few small fields of red earth, a small lake, and this lake half-covered with brambles, a few students and professors. Some of the students are bare-legged, for in Yunnan the late autumn is warm; some are dark brown; and some are pale with disease. You can tell those who are sick by the way they walk, slowly, as though they were afraid of expending their energy; and

474

you notice, too, that there is only a very small sports field, with two basket-ball posts, for on the kind of diet which men live on here sport is a luxury which strains the lungs and fills the stomach with questions it is incapable of answering. From the small blue-painted tower with the curving roof you can see the fields outside, those fields which seem to stretch to infinity with their humps of graves. There are graves everywhere, for we are outside the city walls; and it is here that the kingdom of the dead begins. And perhaps it is right that this home of scholarship, where the blue-prints of the future of China are being planned, should be built on dead men's graves, for at once as we enter these walls we are conscious of the great weight of the past, of time flowing like a refreshing river, of youth and old age.

Walk down the hill, past the soldiers sleeping in the sun, the torn blue shirts waving on the clothes-lines, the dogs sleeping in the great heat, their soft white bellies gently pulsating, past the blue lilacs and the dreaming boy whose book lies open on his lap and wander through the library, under the great roof. There are not many books, though a few have been sent recently from American and British Universities—far too few for their self-respect if they knew to what desperate straits the Chinese Universities were thrown by their lack. Wander among the dusty shelves, the chairs piled high with periodicals, the old mildewed gazetteers and *China Yearbooks* and the green-coated *Encyclopædia Britannicas,* and then ask yourself how a University can exist with so rare a collection of books. Look at the title-pages. There is hardly a single book printed later than 1936. Look at the dust and the rats and the much-handled Chinese books, which look as though they will fall to pieces with a breath of wind, and then look out of the windows at the boys and girls who have the future of China in their hands. They are learning in a hard school. They have understood sorrow. They know retreat. But even here, where books and laboratory equipment should be plentiful, where the most modern scientific papers should be piling in abundance on the shelves, there is almost nothing. The librarian comes to the shelves. You notice that he took away a Japanese book on physical chemistry: and you wonder: "There are people here who understand all languages, who have before them the task of creating a new country out of the miseries of the past, and they have almost nothing on which to feed their minds." A rat scurries through the dry dust of the rotting wainscoting,

475

but outside in the fields the dreaming boy still pores over the dog-eared book.

A gong sounds. A pillar of metal hangs from a gallows, and every hour a servant comes and strikes it with an iron hammer. It is a sound not unlike cathedral bells, pulsating with intervals of silence across the green fields and filling the air with wings, each note floating through the air like a globe of bronze. And immediately the students begin to troop out of the cow-sheds, blue gowns rustling in the breeze which comes down from the high mountains. It wakes the dogs and the old white mare ambling through the lettuce-leaves; this wind that comes from the north and bears with it the scent of the gorse and pines on the mountains. And while the students, with their books under their arms, walk hurriedly towards the kitchens, where they will be given a bowl of rice, a few vegetables and almost no meat at all, you can still hear the deep-throated sound of the gong and you can still hear the wind among the cypresses. It is nearly five o'clock. The sun is going down, and as we pass the small mud dormitories, where the students sleep, the frail red sun flames on the mosquito-nets and on the face of the boy who lies in bed, sweating with typhus and his unfulfilled dreams.

You walk out through the gates towards the chemistry laboratories; you peer through the broken windows at a few test-tubes, and your heart begins to sink at the thought of all the unredeemed poverty in this land which will one day be among the richest in the world. Perhaps this is the last generation of Chinese students who will have to face poverty. There is so much eagerness in those faces which you pass in the gathering dusk, so much sickness, so many who walk in thin clothes, for the evenings are cold, though the mornings are like mornings in the hot deserts, and you wonder how many will survive into the years.

"But what they dread most," T. was saying, "is typhus. It is not the pain and suffering which they dread—though the pain and suffering are great enough—but they dread the expense. The hospitals charge $7,000 for a single case of typhus. Translate that into sterling or dollars, and work out how much it is, and then work out how the students can get the money, when their homes may be in the north-west under Japanese occupation, their fathers dead and their farms ploughed under. They dread other diseases, but typhus in Kunming is the worst of diseases. You will have a sick headache; the next morning you have a raging fever, and as
476

you try to combat the fever, your heart begins to weaken under the strain—and it is all due to rats. There are more rats than people in Kunming. They lie dead on the streets, and no one troubles to collect them; but mercifully a cool wind comes down from the mountains."

The wind was playing on the tin roofs of the small hospital inside the south campus; it threw the starlings in the air and suddenly caught the grey wings of an ancient eagle who had been fluttering down-wind with her head deeply embedded in her shoulders. She flew down, the great black eyes shining, and settled on a broken wall, whence she gazed at the world about her. There were small rats playing at the foot of the wall, very young and almost white; and suddenly she swept down, seized a small rat in her talons and flew up again, treading on wind, feathers beating like feather dusters, clutching the wriggling rat; and then perched on a high lime-tree, silent as a ghost. Suddenly an extraordinary thing happened—she began to wave her head wildly from side to side, the feathers half-opened, and suddenly the small rat escaped from her talons, dropped forty feet, and a few moments later we saw the rat running swiftly across the road.

"You see, they are magical rats," T. complained gently. "What can we do against them when even the eagles are incapable of dealing with them?"

He sighed. We walked back to the city, passing the green lake where a few children were boating, crossing the white camel-back bridge which shone like marble, until we reached the house where we are staying. It must be unlike any other house in the world. A famous general built a theatre in the early days of the Republic, painted it blue and green and wrote with his own hand many inscriptions on the walls and pillars. The crossed flags of the Chinese Republic are painted on wood above the stage, but you can still see traces of the earlier five-barred flag which flew all over China before the Kuomintang came into power. The balconies have been boarded up; the green room has been divided by wooden planks, and even the aisles have become small cubicles where the most famous professors live, dream and write of the flowering future. Here in this great hall, the roof falling in, the ghosts of the actors and actresses of the past still present in the air, they live out their lives without any splendour except the splendour of scholarship, forgotten by the world as in a grave.

The lights are turned on. High up against the white ceiling, a small yellow electric lamp gives little light. The gold paint glows, and a mysterious gilded rose between the painted flags begins to glow with a menacing pulsating brightness, for all the illumination in this great hall seems to come from the rose and the long-legged water-bird—heron or seagull—who hovers above the rose. I ask questions about it. No one answers, and when at last I go to bed in one of those small airless cubicles, where the dust lies inch-thick on the floors, I am conscious of the presence of the Rose who broods over my life in the company of a heron and who shines throughout the night like menacing gold.

September 15th . . . I DO not think it is possible to have more respect for the Chinese professors than I have now. This evening we sat on the slopes overlooking the lake, one of the professors began to speak in a quiet, low voice of the long journey from Pekin to Changsha, and then to Kunming. From where we sat we could see the small boats in the lake, the schoolgirls crossing the camel-back bridge, the scented limes and the yellow stucco buildings perched like cliffs high above us; and greenish-white herons rose from the marshes, and the jackdaws cawed in the maples behind our backs. And all the while, like a musical accompaniment to the shifting illumination of the lakes, the quiet level voice continued:

"We removed many of our books before the Japanese came to Pekin, but many of them were destroyed in Chungking and a few more have been destroyed in the bombardments here. In the science laboratories we are still using test-tubes which were sent down from Pekin eight years ago. For a while we could still buy books from abroad. We would send down special messengers to Hanoi, and sometimes we would get the books, and sometimes we would fail; for it was always necessary to bribe the Indo-Chinese officials and we rarely had enough money to bribe them as much as they would have wanted. In Indo-China we first began to feel our loneliness. We had to bribe our way through the customs, and then bribe our way through the railways—there was no end to bribery. And all this was for scholarships!" There was no note of complaint in his voice. For thirty centuries Chinese scholarship has faced difficulties and dangers, and the present wars did little more than accentuate these dangers. "But sometimes I wonder what would happen if we had to march away again. We are exhausted and underfed, and if we set out again we should have
478

to be accompanied by so many coffins that it would be impossible to transport them, and so we should die by the roadside, and even this is not strange to those who have suffered as much as the Chinese professors, the students and the soldiers." He spoke of Tu Fu, the greatest poet of China, who had also died of starvation by the wayside during the wars. "You have seen that starvation is very near to us; you know that we cannot always continue like this, and you will forgive us if sometimes we speak of these things. There is a terrible melancholy in the Chinese race. You have noticed it in the essays written by your students, and you will notice it everywhere in China as the war goes on. The children crying in the streets, the women who beat their breasts and lament openly in the streets, the quarrelling ricksha-pullers and the Chinese poet softly complaining of the injustices of the times—they come from a single root, the terrible perplexing melancholy of the Chinese race." He began to sing in a soft voice in the high falsetto which all Chinese poets employ when they are singing their poems, and suddenly it seemed to me that all that melancholy was centred in the young professor whose hands lay open on his knees and whose shining black hair reflected the leaves of the cherry-tree overhead.

We returned when it was late to the house near the West Gate. As usual it seemed to be deserted; but the ghosts of all the actors and actresses who once danced and sang in this theatre seemed to be more readily visible. The great golden rose above the proscenium arch glowed dimly in the light of candles—the electric current had failed, and from all the paper windows upstairs small smoking candles shone down on the empty stage. The long-legged water-bird was still hovering over the rose, and someone was climbing up the hidden staircase, and at any moment enormous gold curtains would flood down on the stage, the band would strike up, the tables would be loaded with food, the generals would come in their gilded uniforms to take their places in the boxes where we have our bedrooms and from behind the curtain the waxen faces of the actresses would peer in perplexity of delight at the strangers who had come to be entertained. The ghosts were everywhere the ghost of the young tubercular general Tsao Ao, who from this very theatre—how many years ago?—set the whole of China alight with revolution. In those days men still wore brocaded silk gowns, peacock feathers drooped from their hats and jade belts tinkled in the darkness of the auditorium. But now there is only a black-wood table in the centre of the large hall, a table covered with the yellow decaying rags of yesterday's newspapers, a few letters, and the legs of the bamboo chairs around the table have been spliced so often that they are in danger of falling apart from sheer weariness of mending. This is where the greatest scholars of China live. Like the wraith of the great Chuang Tzu, Feng Yu-lan will sometimes sweep down from his high perch above the stage into the darkness of the auditorium, plucking at his magnificent beard, smiling mysteriously to himself, to be followed a little later by Chao Hsun-chang, who stoops a little under the weight of his twenty languages and his vast knowledge of the Mongolian Horde. Here are descendants of the greatest names in China, who walk in rags and are as cheerful as it is possible to be in the sixth year of the war; and there are men whose names are still unknown, though they are powers to be reckoned with in the future of China. They live in these boxes of the old theatre, or in small bleak cubby-holes made out of the panelled aisles downstairs. They do not complain, though the furniture in the rooms consists of a bed, a wooden stool and a black-wood table—nothing more, though there are mountains of books in all languages piled in the corners. Sometimes at night, when a rat crawls across my face or one of the professors is coughing up his lungs, I wake up. "This is intolerable—we are living like pigs—I shall leave for India tomorrow." And then, all through the long night, like a battering-ram, the thought returns: "Is this how one of the great nations of the world treats her scholars? These men are the greatest and most valuable, and they are worth as much or more than the soldiers who lie starving on the dusty roads. They are ill, like the soldiers. They have lived for years in a world where mounting prices are tragedies which we measure by suicides. They live secretly and silently, and no one comes to help them or even to encourage them. They are dying. They are sacrificing themselves for their ideals, and they know that there is so much corruption in the country that even their ideals are at stake." And then in the morning the sun shines through the green boughs of the cherry-trees, the lakes glitter and sparkle, the soft blue sky is filled with small dolphins of cloud, and we know then (though we knew it before) that men can live on air and sunlight and imperishable hopes.

480

September 20th . . . THE rain has begun to come down in earnest. Last night the sky glittered with sharp points of frost; the red and green tail-lights of the aeroplanes fanning the sky and losing themselves among meteors and comets, but when we woke up this morning the earth was embroidered with a grey dripping cloth, and the rain came down in earnest. It does not fall, as in Szechuan, in a continuous fusillade, but in slow sad drops, ice-cold. The Western Hills lay invisible behind a tower of rain, and the grey lake drifted in the smoke of the continuous slow rain. There are trees which rise out of the centre of the lake, only the heads of the branches showing; and they shook there, wet to the inmost pith, lost in the confusion and sadness of the rain, yet struggling desperately, refusing to disappear under the silver waves.

In all its moods this lake is beautiful, and perhaps never so beautiful as when there is no one there. The Hôtel du Lac was long ago taken over by the garrison soldiers. The brown walls are painted over with childish slogans, the yellow-tiled roofs are crumbling with neglect and the young soldier in the baggy clothes and the red-apple face who stands on guard with his bayonet slanting awkwardly over his shoulder, looks still, as he looked yesterday, as eternal and motionless as the craggy rocks which generations of Chinese gardeners have tended in this park.

But the rain brings the scent from the leaves, and there is so much freshness in the air that we know the sun will come soon. The sun is there! It is hidden behind the clouds, but as the rain no longer falls in heavy splashes but in thin showers, we know that the sun will soon appear. We can feel its warmth in the sky, which is changing from Veronese green to blue, and soon it comes out, shouldering through the thick clouds, more brilliant than ever, and half a rainbow hovers over the sky, which resembles more than anything else a blue Delft bowl.

And now the streets begin to fill with people: soldiers carrying empty coffins on their backs and paper umbrellas in their hands, tribeswomen from the outlying districts in their bright blue clothes, with waist-bands heavily embroidered and little black tongues at the back of their cotton shoes, shaped like the curling tongues of kittens. Little boys running half-naked through the mud, dressed in inextricable patchworks of blue cloth; little girls whose long black braided hair still glitters with raindrops, so that for a moment I thought they were crowned with briony; and old

481

women limping, and old men smoking, and the young in one another's arms. Sunlight after rain! In Yunnan this sunlight is more brilliant, more overpowering than anywhere in the world. Brightness lives in it; molten like quicksilver, it fills all the dark shadows which we thought were permanent during the rain, and glows and throws greedy hands in all hollows. A slow cavalcade of donkeys passes under the North Gate, streaked with muddy dust and bearing on their rough hairy backs baskets of blue charcoal. They march slowly and even daintily, past the two soldiers bearing a stretcher, past the school-children making mud pies in the road, down towards the centre of the city, where those blue faggots will be sold; and after them comes a beggar dressed in sheets of sacking, which he will remove by the roadside in a few moments, and sitting there oblivious of all passers-by, he will search for mites and fleas in perfect contentment. Suddenly, from behind the moss-covered ancient wall, a madman appears. He is short and stunted, no more than four foot high, dripping with rain, his hair coated with mud; he comes hopping down the road, half-paralysed, one paralysed hand stretched straight down in front of him, and all the time he makes little quick grunts of terror, hopping and grunting, seeing nothing clearly, for he collides with the water-carrier and grovels in the mud of the road. As he staggers to his feet a blue-coated soldier lifts his rifle and takes aim, and though I know it would be a merciful act to shoot the madman, I am filled with horror. The madman starts to scream. He sees the rifle; and though he can recognise perhaps nothing else in the world, he recognises this gesture, for surely he has seen it thousands of times before. And then slowly, laughing with full-throated pleasure, the soldier flings his rifle over his shoulder and runs to the help of the madman. The terror is over. The soldier follows him a little way down the road, but after a while he tires of the madman's company and returns to his post.

I have nothing but respect for the soldiers of China. I have seen them on the battlefield. I have seen them dead. I have seen them dying. I have seen them marching through cities at night, their helmets gleaming, while their officer rides behind them on a white horse, the long silver sword dangling almost to the ground. I have seen them walking through Kunming, lean, emaciated, their skins blue-white, their hands like claws; and I know, as everyone knows, that medical aid reaches no more than an infinitely small proportion, so much of the British and American

482

money which is sent to them never reaches them. They live like the professors on imperishable hope—the hope that they may one day return to the quiet of a country farm.

September 25th . . . THIS morning, as I crossed the grave-mounds on the way to the University, I came into the middle of the battle. There were aeroplanes flying low overhead, and hidden among the green mounds Chinese soldiers were deploying, their tin helmets screened with leaves. The sun shone as they crawled in the purple shadows of the mounds; and they were laughing and talking, their faces very red and their bayonets bright blue. They paid no attention to me. I was not part of the battle, and since I was carrying books and walking in the direction of the University, I was assumed to be one of those people who have no interest in warfare. Little white bags were being thrown by the aeroplanes. The bombs burst, and chalk dust flew out and no one was hurt. The soldiers laughed with the incurious exciting laughter of the young Chinese; and then they would point to the aeroplanes and hold up their thumbs and shout *"Ding hao!"* while the puff-balls of perfectly white cloud steamed overhead.

Afterwards, when the aeroplanes had passed, I noticed that their whole bodies were draped in leaves, and as they crossed the sunken road in single file it was exactly as though I had attended a *bacchanale*. And when at last I was near the gates of the University, I looked back and saw a young soldier standing on the skyline, with a trellis of green leaves falling from his shoulders. Is this Bacchus or Adonis? What strange part of the world have I come to?

September 26th . . . EVERY night as I work a spider comes to comfort me. He is not like your ordinary spider. He has, it is true, eight thin legs and a small black body with curious encrusted markings. He slides gracefully over the page I am reading and pauses on the word which is no longer legible, though it is the one word on the page which I am trying to read; then he lifts his blank face and stares at me with an expression of spidery insolence which would be amusing if it were not so singularly cunning. I have no idea how he manages to choose this word; nor have I any idea how it is possible to express in English words the calm malignity of his expression. And yet he is a beautiful

483

spider, and the long thin legs under the electric light throw the most delicate of shadows. The thin hair-lines swinging across the page, the ringed white eyes, the insolence of the gestures . . .

But this evening there were three more spiders. They were very small, and they seemed to move with the greatest possible stupidity, sliding from one side of the page to the other. They are not malignant. They have not found the word I am trying to read; and they seem in fact to need assistance. Their mother's milk is still on their lips, and they dance excitedly in sheer joy of living.

There are none of the vast animals which used to decorate my desk in Singapore. There are no flying squirrels rushing through the window and smashing their frail heads against the electric light. There are no foot-long moths for the ants to eat, nor are there any fire-flies in Kunming as there were in Szechuan. The earth, but not the people, have been tamed; the moths are small; the green-flies are without exception incapable of annoyance, and even the mosquitoes have shed their claws. Kunming is civilised. But the black spider with the fantastically thin legs still gazes up at me from the page.

September 27th, The Bulletins . . . AMONG students paper is scarce, but the various agencies of propaganda of the Allied states have been considerate enough to publish bulletins, which can be used by students in the place of notebooks. To be completely successful a bulletin would have no printed matter; but since this happens rarely, we have to make the best of those bulletins which are printed on only one side of the paper. The bulletin of the Soviet Union, which I used to see in Chungking last year, was excellent: it was printed on heavy paper, and it was quite impossible to see the words printed on the other side. The British bulletin is printed on thinner paper, but here and there thicker sheets were to be found. By selecting the sheets carefully, it is possible to produce a notebook suitable for rough notes. The American bulletin is by no means the worst, but it is generally printed on thinner paper than the British bulletin, while the bulletin published by the Chinese in the War Area Service Corps is lamentable in the eyes of the students, for the ink runs through the page and no one but the most poverty-stricken students would use it. This bulletin is edited by professors of the University, who no doubt are quite aware to what purposes their bulletin may be put. They are playing a dangerous game, for the

484

time may soon come when the students will demand that all bulletins should be printed on thick paper and only on one side.

I am amazed by the ever-increasing uses to which these bulletins are put. They may be used as little paper caps for growing plants; children make toy aeroplanes with them; shopkeepers buy or steal them for wrapping up their parcels; a sufficient quantity will light a small fire, and a large number can be sold to the paper merchants for profit. In China there is a tradition that paper should be reverenced; paper is the virgin sheet upon which knowledge may be inscribed. But the time has come when it is so rare and valuable a thing that we are no longer disposed to treat it with reverence. We have for paper the same kind of affection that others have for gold. It is part of our lives; it must be acquired by fair means or foul; it is the repository of all wisdom and all amusements. But so far none of the foreign powers represented in China have realised that they would be doing a very great service to students if their bulletins were not printed at all.

September 28th . . . FOR seven years China has been cut off from the outside world, and only now are microfilms creeping in. T. tells me that Shostokovitch's *Seventh Symphony* was sent to America on microfilm; but no one has yet sent us the details of penicillin on microfilm. There are more American microfilms than British; there are only a few more projectors, and not all the professors know where they can be found. We have no scientific periodicals later than 1938, and the few microfilms that come in are looked for eagerly, with something of the delight of a small child looking to its seventh birthday party.

Our hunger for new books is unappeasable. It is true that there are three or four bookshops in Kunming, where Chinese books printed in Kweilin and Kweiyang on the most dismal yellow paper can be purchased at fifty times their cost pre-war. But modern British and American books are non-existent or in such rare quantities that they must for ever pass unnoticed. I have borrowed three new novels from an American soldier. We shall hold a party. Ten or twenty professors will be invited to attend—not a dinner, for that would cost a fortune, but a tea-party with a few dried biscuits and some flowers in a vase. The books will be placed on the table. We shall gaze at them, but we shall not touch them. They will be sacred until some weeks have passed. Then, and then only, when we have paid our due respects to their authors

485

and the fate which brought them over three continents, shall we open the pages.

Our physicists know little or nothing about what is being done by physicists outside China; our chemists are unconscious of the tremendous strides in chemistry produced by Europeans. We rarely know what is being published in other parts of China; and the poets have almost no knowledge of what the poets are writing in other countries. Yet the book-stores are filled with translations of foreign classics; and though we need books badly, and there is a kind of continual hunger at the pit of our stomachs for foreign books, this return to the classics has much to recommend it. We are wanderers in a strange land, where the printing-presses are few, the libraries almost non-existent, the laboratories are empty of everything except a few broken test-tubes. In the natural geography of their lives, the Chinese professors can see no signs of the familiar landscape. Alone, like Dante in the forests, they know only the leopards, the she-wolves and the tigers.

September 29th . . . It is perhaps an instinct of those who are cut off from the world to think continually about their childhood. For weeks now I have been conscious of a landscape bathed in a blue light, a landscape of tall trees and ivory-coloured statues and a great lake where boats were being sailed by small boys in sailor-suits; and it was only yesterday that I recognised that I had been dreaming of the Jardin de Luxembourg in Paris, and my cousin Alfonse. He had a long gaunt face which still showed the bayonet thrust he had received in the Ardennes; a red scratch going from his left eye to the curve of his lips, and sometimes, especially in cold weather, it would grow livid. I liked Cousin Alfonse for the worst reasons. He was tall, elegant, immaculately dressed; he had an air of command, he manicured his nails to an excessive whiteness, he understood wine and refused to smoke *les petits caporaux,* and insisted on spending the patrimony his father had left him on an incredible supply of English cigarettes. He admired everything English, especially Kensington Gardens and fox-terriers.

As I think of Alfonse, I remember the *Fontaine de Medici* and the hoary green statues buried under the autumn leaves. There are moments when this garden in Paris is more real to me than anything in the world; so fresh and clean are the colours of its grass and temples. For the Senate which today must be flying the swastika flag was to me a temple at the very end of the earth, and the statue of the four pillars of the nations supporting the world first led me to think seriously of peace. In Munich's September the flower-beds were carved up for air-raid shelters; but the garden lost nothing of its power. It was a garden inhabited by small children and old men with the red ribbon of the Legion of Honour, with a few nursemaids and lovers. Like the gilt-tipped railings and the voice of the ancient guardsmen who announced that the garden was about to be closed, it was timeless, like the ages.

And so it is with the rest of the world. The student sitting near the window is still dreaming of Pekin. He dreams of the marble bridges and the yellow dust-storms, and the servants who come out of the house and whisk the dust away from your clothes. He dreams of the Jade Fountain Park and the Western Hills, knowing no greater glory than the presence of Pekin. In Kunming the weather is better. There are no great extremes of cold and heat. There are natural beauties which Pekin can never rival. But here, on the remote edges of China, civilisation came late; and there are no traditions of permanence as there are in Pekin. The green lake, a mile high among the mountains, is like nothing else in China, and beautiful beyond anything in Hopei. Yet they are unhappy. Pekin was their birthright, and without it they are like lost souls wandering in the wilderness.

"What were you thinking about?"

"Pekin—I cannot help it—the snow on the ground and the snow on the high walls. In February or March the snow melts with a roar like an avalanche. . . ."

October 10th . . . Coming over the raised grave-mounds near the University, I noticed for the first time that there were great holes cut in the ground. Perhaps they had been cut so that people might take shelter in them during air-raids, or perhaps the graves had fallen in. But what was extraordinary was that in each of these holes there lay the head and sometimes the neck of a horse. The blood was quite fresh, but often the bones had been licked white by the dogs and pecked by the birds. But where had they come from? It seemed so extraordinary to think that someone had gone carefully to each hole in the night and dropped in it the head of a horse.

October 15th, The Search for Wu San-kwei . . . I HAVE known for some time that at the end of the Ming Dynasty in China, Wu San-kwei assumed power in the south-west, but I did not know that he ruled from Kunming, and I did not know that the last Emperor of the Mings was strangled only a few hundred yards from the place where I am living.

Wu San-kwei had proclaimed himself Governor of Yunnan and Kweichow. From his capital in Kunming, then known as Yunnan-fu, his armies went out in all directions to suppress the tribesmen and to extend his power. He was utterly without remorse, and at one time even thought of extending his power to the north; and with the help of the Lieutenant-Governors of Canton and Fukien, he thought of proclaiming himself Emperor. The young Emperor Kang Hsi of the recently-formed Manchu Dynasty heard of his plans and fought vigorously against them. There was no peace in China during the first thirty years of his reign. Wu San-kwei levied taxes and maintained a court as great as that of the Emperor. He had captured the last Emperor of the Mings as the boy-king attempted to escape along the same forest path through which the Chinese armies penetrated into Burma. He was brought back to Kunming with his young wife and they were strangled at a place not far from here. There is a stone, now covered with the green rags of advertisements, on which his death is proclaimed—a stone set up during the first year of the Republic, saying only that the Emperor Yu-lung offered his life here. His body was taken outside the north wall and thrown to the dogs; and somewhere, though I have not yet seen it, there is another stone commemorating the place where the dogs ate him. As you step out of the North Gate, where the burial-mounds seem to rise in waves of blue-green grass to the infinite distance, the atmosphere of death is unavoidable. Even today people are buried here in shallow graves, and sometimes they are not even buried, but thrown into the great pits under the shadows of the wall. I had thought when I first passed under the barrel-like gates: "A great man has died here and left the memory of his death." Now I know that the last Emperor of the Mings met his fate here at the hands of a traitor.

October 16th . . . ". . . WE WERE climbing the Himalayas, and the blue mountains were clear-cut and edging to green against the sky. We were worn out with climbing, though we

488

were still on the high foothills, and when the snowstorm came we were weary beyond words, and hid in the tents, wondering whether the storm would end. There was isinglass on the walls of the tent; and we could see the mountains through the snow, very clear and white, and they seemed very close. I do not remember very much about these hours, for a kind of sickness had made us faint, and besides—we had had little sleep. I remember I walked out of the tent. I have a curious memory of climbing, though probably I walked only a few inches in the neighbourhood of the tent. I thought it was the end. Everything very still, the snow falling very silently—and then nothing, nothing at all, the eternal reaches of the snow, the quietness of complete passivity. I forgot to tell you I had left my oxygen apparatus in the tent. It is no use, of course, at these heights. We were not yet in the oxygen-region, and in any case we were only suffering from the mountain sickness and the snowstorm. But I remember I was breathing exactly as though I were breathing into the oxygen apparatus—the short quick inhalations, followed by the long slow exhalations. It was sheer joy to breathe. Everything was breath. Breath was continuous—not inward and outward, not inhalation and exhalation, but one continuous stream of breath which neither entered my lungs nor escaped from them, but somehow passed through them. I was breath. This is what the *sannyasis* dreamed and spoke about, but what was so extraordinary was to find that it actually occurred. I—breath; nothing else. That was what was so mysterious and so beautiful. . . ."

He was a Polish professor of chemistry, who had come to China many years ago. He lived, like all the other professors, in small cubicles in houses where the rent went up a hundred per cent each month. There was almost no furniture in the room—a broken-down desk, a few stools, no chairs. The books were in Polish. It had been impossible to sell them. He wore a loose, stained Chinese blue gown, and he was very tall. On the walls there were his own water-colours of mountains, sharp blue ice-crystals which glittered even here in this dark room overlooking a plot of waste land. And he dreamed of mountains:

"After the war, perhaps, I shall go back and climb the Himalayas. The Poles are trained to mountain-climbing, for we have our own high mountains in the south; and the skiers at Zakopane won all the blue ribands at the Olympic Games. The Himalayas—

489

this is the great feat of our generation. To climb higher and higher towards the stars. . . ."

October 17th, Over the Hump . . . HE WAS a young Chinese wireless operator in blue overalls. I had met him first at Kweilin, shortly after the third battle of Changsha. Suddenly, this afternoon, in the busy streets of Kunming, I caught sight of him gazing into a shop window near Bobby's. He looked younger and thinner; his face was darker, and there were a few grey hairs at his temples, though he can hardly be more than thirty. He told me he had become a wireless operator in the C.N.A.C.

You are almost four miles high when you cross the Hump, but you are not yet in the stratosphere. The sky is still blue and the sun is still gold. There are electric storms which paralyse your wireless directional apparatus, and there are clouds which burrow along the surface of high mountains, giving you the impression that you have only to follow the clouds in order to be safe. Many aeroplanes have been lost. There are occasional Japanese aeroplanes to be avoided, and places where the wind-currents are unexpectedly huge: you can drop five thousand feet in a few seconds, and the wings will crumple off, and you will sink like a stone. It is a part of the air which had never been charted before and may never be used again, for there are safer journeys over southern Burma now occupied by the Japanese. Sitting drowsily over the headphones, he would look out on calm moonlight nights at the quiet white wall of the Himalayas flowing beside him—always the same wall, white and never-ending. It was one of the most terrifying things in the world, the white *authenticity* of those huge mountains. They were silent, so huge that they made all experience as insignificant as the life of a termite. They were there, crested with clouds, throwing down immense black pencils of shadows on the clouds revolving in the valleys; and they remained there—they were so huge that it seemed to take hours to pass them, and as soon as you had passed one great cliff of mountains, another and almost identical cliff would appear.

We went into the Nangping Café where the American flying officers come in the evenings, and still he talked about these immense ranges of high mountains which resemble fingers—fingers which will suddenly be thrust out to crush the insignificant aeroplane as easily as we swat a mosquito. "They are very real," he said. "That is what I am trying to tell you. You have the impres-
490

sion of something which is ultimately real: not menacing, only real. There is an American airman over there who has flown over Everest," he added, pointing to the stripling officer in the yellow-leather coat on which the flag of the Chinese Republic had been embroidered on the back. "He thought he would make a detour over Everest. He carried an oxygen plant. He flew over it three times, but unfortunately on his return he was grounded in Nepal. There was a terrible fuss. The permission of the Nepalese had not been asked. The gods would require vengeance for this invasion of their territory. He was arrested. He was taken to the temple, and he prayed there and asked forgiveness of the gods, the gods of the Himalayas." The Chinese boy smiled. A little later he slipped out of the room. In three or four hours he will be travelling beneath the white walls of the Himalayas.

October 18th . . . . . . BUT always in the life of the Universities there is great suffering. I remember at the University of Munich a *Privat Dozent* who would bring in two dry pieces of bread at noon for his dinner. He was desperately poor, and very lean, and he had a large family. A *Privat Dozent* in a German University is paid only by the fees he receives from the students; he is not paid by the University. He was one of the most brilliant professors in the school, and he was marked out for an important professorship, but while he was young he suffered. He wrote a treatise in seven volumes on the brain of the ant. I am being quite serious. It was an important work, and later it was crowned by the Academy. Yet while he was young, he starved.

"In China there is a tradition of starvation among the professors. Confucius was the first to insist that there was no harm in a teacher receiving gifts from his students—he had to live; and Mencius insisted on being treated as though he possessed the rank of a prince. But today we starve. It is in the nature of things. The soldiers starve, the professors starve, the students starve, while the merchants grow rich. It has always been like that. How can we change it?"

October 19th . . . HE CAME up the Burma Road, looking very thin and white, his clothes bleached almost pale-yellow by the sun. I have never seen a man so thin. His legs were like sticks and his face was a skull. And he walked very slowly, tottering like a leaf in the wind. God knows where he had come from or where he was going. Sometimes small horse-carts come trundling along these roads, under the shade of the pines, and you can see in them the white-faced soldiers who have neither expression nor feeling, for they are ill beyond any hope of recovery. They look out at the low reaches of the mountains, but there is no life in their faces, and their skin is paper-thin and their mouths are no more than small holes. But there was still some life in this soldier who came wearily up the road, past the University in the broad sunlight. He wore the thinnest of bamboo shoes, and his clothes too were thin, and you could see the shape of his ribs, and you could imagine the tall youth who left his farm two years ago, strong in limb, handsome, with the free-swinging gait which all those who are young and healthy in China possess. He was dying. I think he knew he was dying, for he walked slowly and paid no attention to the passing lorries filled with the red rusty corrugated oil-drums which speed towards Kweichow; and he paid no attention to the salt-carts and the ponies from whose wooden yokes yellow banners fly exactly as they flew two thousand years ago. He was sick and dying, and he was thin, like a ghost.

He went up the road slowly, paying no attention to us, while the green shadows of the trees sometimes covered him from the sunlight. I noticed there was a great tear in his sleeves, and under his sleeves a yellow bandage frayed with age could be seen. He did not go to the huge North Gate, with its bronze doors studded with iron nails. He sat down wearily under a grove of firs, which look out over a great stretch of distant rice-fields. There is a railway line, humped graves, a playing-field where the cavalry exercise and occasional reviews are held by the Governor of the province, but he paid no attention to these things. Wearily, wearily, he buried his head in his hands, sick to death, utterly weary of the long journey in the dusty road. From a distance he did not look like a dying soldier. You did not see his thin arms, and that terrible white face was hidden in a green shade. He did not sigh. He did not speak. He did not ask for a drink of water. He lay on the stone with his head buried in his hands, and perhaps he was dreaming.

Every day hundreds of wounded soldiers are brought on stretchers along this road. Not all are wounded. Some are dying of dysentery, others of malnutrition, all are thin with that thinness which is seen only in China. They come on their stretchers like dead men, for the Chinese when they are ill cover their faces;

and you will see a sick child carried in a basket with only his legs showing, and you will be wrong if you think he is dead. Sickness is widespread in China. There are not drugs enough in all the world to cure half the diseases of the Chinese. . . .

And the next day the soldier was still there. He had not moved. He had died perhaps at the moment when he crept to the stone. Only the once-green uniform seemed to be a little yellower, and the arms a little thinner, and the face a little whiter. But round his head thousands of black flies were playing.

October 20th, In Search of Wu San-kwei . . . I DO not think we have committed any crime, but this morning we tore down the ragged green advertisements on the memorial-stone which commemorates the last Emperor of the Mings. Though the stone was carved during the Republic, the lettering was pleasing, and it was curious to think of this mountainous road just inside the city wall where he was strangled. Where there is now an electrical works, a court of enquiry was held. It was very brief. Wu San-kwei did not show himself, but hid behind a screen. According to the pictures I have seen, he was a small man with a heavy black moustache and beard, terrible in his anger and pride; and the last Emperor of the Mings was little more than a boy, handsome, like nearly all the Mings, and innocent of any crime except flight. The court of enquiry lasted only a few minutes. Immediately afterwards he was dragged outside, a silk scarf was wound round his throat, and almost before he was dead his body was thrown into a small handcart and taken outside the North Gate. You can still see the place where his body was thrown. A stone tablet let into the side of a sunken road records that he was buried there. Not far away there are *two* monuments to the mistress of Wu San-kwei, who repented of her sins, cast off her robes of silk and lived in a small country house which still stands on the borders of the Lotos Lake.

Many stories have been told of her, and many engravings of her have been handed down. There is, for example, the story that she buried her clothes in the small tower which stands on a hill behind the University; there are engravings on stone which show her in her youth holding an immense fan, her garments flowing as they flow in T'ang paintings. There is another engraving of her in old age, holding a coil of jade beads; and her face is as wizened as the face of an old priest. From the English Gardens, where the students linger under the shade of huge eucalyptus-trees, you can see the white house on the spur of the lake. Ducks are floating in the green slime, and a few reeds wave in the lingering air, and the peasants come in their Sunday clothes from all the villages around to walk in the silence of the trees surrounding the lake. There are Miaos with their bright studded belts and red shoe-tabs, with heavy silver ear-rings and decorated caps; there are the farmers in blue and the small shopkeepers in white; there are students in every variety of patched clothes, and perhaps there are a few who think of the girl who was the mistress of Wu San-kwei, who might have been Emperor of China, who is buried near the Emperor Yu-lung and whose dust is still breathed in this remote corner of China.

October 21st . . . ". . . THE science students are better than the students of the humanities, and this not only because they are offered higher premiums by the Government, but because they have problems to tackle which demand immediate solutions. The best students of China have been coming to Kunming for the last four years, and the best of these are going to the Engineering School. Here are the headquarters of the Academia Sinica, and a thousand other research organisations. There are five Universities within half a mile of each other, and there is tremendous activity in all branches of learning. The best scholars and the best students are here. It follows that it is from Kunming that we can expect the rebirth of China.

"I have been to see the Industrial Co-operatives managed by the professors of the Engineering School. They have a turnover of twenty million dollars a month, and the turnover is increasing every day. Much of their work is being done for the American Army, but a great deal of it follows familiar patterns. The professors are at least the equals of the business men, and as one of the professors said to me: 'If we cannot beat the professors at their own game, we would go out of business.' I think this is a good sign. There is a towering inflation, with every mortal object increasing in price ten times a year; but the professors are sticking it out, erecting machinery, selling lathes, carving timber, buying houses. . . . They are wretchedly poor still, for most of the profit from these ventures must go back into capital and only a little of it is distributed among the professors themselves. But

494

they are showing for the first time in China that they have powers of industrial leadership."

I was writing this in a letter to England, when one of my students came to see me. He had got a job at $500 a day on surveying. He was delighted beyond words, for he had been poor enough in the past and a week at $500 a day would make him rich enough to buy food, a few essential text-books and even a slide-rule.

"But don't you realise," he exclaimed, "the whole of China will have to be surveyed? This is the beginning. And now they are really starting to employ students on a large scale. We can show our merits. We shall no longer have to hide our light under a bushel."

He was delighted beyond words. He had taught in middle schools, spending hours and receiving little pay. Somehow or other—and God knows how much he had struggled—he had made his way through college; and now, at last, after interminable waiting, the undreamt-of opportunities were occurring. He was like a young colt playing in a meadow.

October 22nd, Conversation with a Business Man . . . You could see that he was a foreigner by the cut of his clothes and the elegance of his necktie; but except for these you would have taken him for a northern Chinese. He was tall and inclining to fatness; he had once been handsome, but there were only a few vestiges of his youth remaining. We talked about his mission to China.

"I've come to see about investments," he replied. "I want to have a look at what can be done with this country you appear to admire so much." He became rather patronising. "You shouldn't admire countries, young man—admire people, the really intelligent leaders—great business men and economists—that's where the future lies." And I thought, rather helplessly, that perhaps among my friends at the University there was a future Prime Minister, a future Minister of Finance, but I knew that he would never give them a second glance. I asked him about the investments, and then he said, surprisingly: "We've put a hell of a lot of money in this country, and by God, we're going to get it back again."

I asked him whether he really meant it.

"Of course I mean it. You don't think we can run the world without money and contracts."

"I don't think we can, but do you really imagine that the old ways will work?"

"Can't change. Business is business. As far as I can see there won't be a ha'p'orth of business unless we can get down to brass tacks."

October 23rd . . . I HAVE finished the short stories. I have used the name of my stepson in *The Chinese Soldier* and there has been a slightly acrimonious dispute about his title to the name. I suggested that I should give him a watch in return for the use of his name. He agreed, and reminded me that I had promised him a watch for some other service he had rendered a year ago, and the watch still had not come. "But it is not possible to get watches here—the post office won't allow it, and besides, I really can't afford to buy a watch at inflation prices. I'll try to go to India and get you one." He seemed satisfied, but after a moment he suggested that I should pay him a percentage of the royalties of the book. "How much?" "Seventy per cent." "Why seventy per cent?" "It is the first number that came to my head. We can argue about it. Sixty-five, if you like." (I note here that his English conversation is usually deplorable, but on financial questions it is very acute.) "What about ten per cent?" I asked. I am used to this kind of bargaining on the market-place, but I had forgotten that he had far more experience. "Let's compromise on fifty?" he suggested. We have finally compromised on a sum which must be kept secret, but it is far too great. I hope the watch comes.

October 24th . . . THE postmaster was swatting flies. He is an adept at it, and with the bamboo swat in his hand he dances from one side of the room to the other. And all the while he kept up an interminable monologue—the best kind of monologue—about the immense distances traversed along the ancient roads which divide China from India. The days of the post-horse have returned. There are bandits on the road; high mountains; and sometimes there are inexplicable losses when the mails fail to appear. There are gentlemen in England who send their friends in China copies of the London *Times* which arrive nine months late, after crossing interminable snow-covered mountains. The
496

Ledo road. . . . The Ta-chen-lu road. . . . There are apparently
thousands of roads, and on these roads the post-boys squander
their lives in a remorseless effort to get the mail through. The
romance of mail in China is long-lived. Today the postmen still
wear the green uniform they wore in the Han Dynasty; they
are still efficient; they are ruled sternly by the paternal post-
masters who, if they were bishops, would be known as the lords
of the wildest territories of Asia. . . .

I was thinking of the tremendous progress which had been
made in the administration of the Chinese post office as I returned
home to the University. A letter was waiting for me. It had been
sent air-mail from my Bank in Calcutta. It had been posted on
the twenty-fifth of October, a year ago!

November 1st . . . It was a perfect day for a funeral. As
the long cortège came winding down the main street of
Kunming, it was clear that the old man had lived a life of
classic accomplishment. He had been born before the Empress
Dowager came to the throne—an old man of ninety-three, who
wore a maroon gown and whose long beard reached his girdle.
His portrait in colours came behind the coffin. It was draped with
red silks and placed in a chair supported on the shoulders of his
servants; and for a moment, a brief moment, he seemed to be
sitting there, superintending, with all the accustomed benevolence
of his long rule, the conduct of his own funeral. He was a gentle
old man, and I could easily imagine him running his fingers caress-
ingly through the long silky wisps of beard; but I knew too that
he dominated the family with a rod of steel, and those small
brown eyes of his saw everything that happened. His wife must
have pre-deceased him, for there was no old woman dressed in
white sackcloth among the mourners. But there were men and
women of all ages—children, grandsons, great-grandsons, great-
great grandsons, perhaps a thousand people altogether following
in the wake of the gilt and decorated coffin. There were old men,
doubled up with rheumatism, who seemed to have stepped out of
the Chinese Empire, before Dr. Sun Yat-sen came to destroy the
ritual of an antiquated monarchy; they moved warily, blinking
in the sun, unaccustomed to the traffic in the main road. American
jeeps honked past the swaying procession. The white and red
silks, the green curtains billowing in the wind, the drums and the
trim-bones, the metallic clang of the trumpets, and the long pro-

cession of people in white sackcloth moving out of the shadow of houses into the sun. . . .

November 3rd . . . "BUT where will it end if we do nothing but study?" the student was saying. "Studying is good—I realise this perfectly, and we are helping our country by studying hard. But some of us must go into the army."

All over the University there has been a wave of this kind of conversation. At the end of this term three or four hundred senior students will enter the army as interpreters, and some of them will die. They will go to Burma or Hunan; they will live on the border-line between occupied and unoccupied China; they will return once more to the adventures they experienced at the beginning of the war. Among them are the sons of the President of a major University, a distinguished philosopher and a great general. And where they come from, there are a hundred others ready to take their place.

For years the students have been silent. They have taken little part in politics. Quietly, unostentatiously, they have been preparing blue-prints for the future. But the war is coming nearer, and is reaching towards a tragic climax. China, still surrounded and cut off from the world, sees the Japanese armies still advancing across her land, though they are retreating everywhere else. The successes of the Americans in the Pacific have little enough effect here. There is a kind of sterility in the air; we can do nothing except pray.

And suddenly, as though long-suppressed thoughts had leapt to the surface, the students began to talk of entering the army. They would enter it for many reasons. There is a tradition in China that the scholar makes a good general—they would go as leaders. They would go, too, to try to improve the conditions in the army and to give a leaven to the officers. They would go as interpreters and become acquainted with the British and American soldiers. They would go for a thousand reasons. "And perhaps a few of us will go for the reasons that the Chinese soldiers go—because we hate the Japanese and at the same time because we know that we shall be well-fed in Burma," the student said, smiling a little nervously, as though the confession made inroads on his honour. "Do you know that in Kiangsi the soldiers are prepared to pay $7,000 to enter the American Army? They want
498

nothing more. Their highest ambition is to go to Burma. If you have been well-fed, you can die with contentment."

November 4th . . . You can eat anything, and buy anything you please in Kunming. There are no coupons, no restrictions, no black-out, no unnecessary laws. You may buy a fur coat and a bottle of champagne; sulphadiazone can be bought in the medical shops; an electrical razor, a silk-flowered gown, silk stockings, army boots, guns, oil-drums of octane petrol, diamonds. In the little shops near the Ningpo Café everything—everything in the world—may be obtained. Unfortunately they cost money.

There is no city in the world with a higher rate of inflation than Kunming. Here prices may double in a week, and the thing is so common that we no longer gaze with awe-stricken eyes at price-tabs. Here prices may change more in a day than in a year in America; our scales of values suffer revolutionary changes, and no one murmurs. We are companions of the incredible. We are so accustomed to the impossibility of making our budgets that we have lost the habit of lamentation. The spiral ascends; we watch it with the same sense of fatality as a farmer watches the approach of a whirlwind.

I have been making a comparative list of prices. Two years ago in Chungking I could eat reasonably well for $300 a month. Today I eat less and it costs $3,000 a month. Two years ago one could buy a fountain-pen for $30. Today it costs $700. And so with everything else—a pencil costs $80, which is equivalent to a pound sterling or four or five dollars gold. A typewriter costs $150,000, which is equivalent to £2,000. A small house will cost $3,000,000, which is equivalent, at the official exchange rate, to over £30,000. No one can foretell what the next month will bring in a sudden leap of prices. The spiral goes higher. What happens when it reaches the sun?

November 5th, The Bathhouse . . . I REMEMBER reading that when Mr. Willkie arrived on the Chungking airfield, he was given a hot towel and asked what it was for. He was told that it was the custom in China to wipe your face with a hot towel whenever you were tired, and he said: "This is a very sensible custom. I will try to introduce it into America."

I am not sure that I understand the origin of the hot towel, or why it is so refreshing. The Chinese, living in the north in a dry

499

land, were perhaps the first to invent mechanical means of re-
freshment, and all these things are known to the bath-house
attendants. In small white-washed brick rooms, where the spiders
rule on the ceilings and all manner of insects crawl up the walls,
cubicles containing earthenware baths have found their way to
Kunming. Steam rises from the baths, and through the steam,
wrapped in a towel which is snatched away from you by an
attendant, you walk to your bath like someone walking to his own
sacrificial death. There is a curious air of authority among the
bath attendants. They know most of the artifices of the human
soul, for the valet who waits on his master is further away from
him than the bath-attendant who scratches his back as he lies
in the smoke and steam of his earthenware tub. The bath attendants are merciless. As they scratch your back or twist the
tendons of your ankles they ask you interminable questions: "Are
you married?" "How many children have you got?" "When were
you divorced?" It is difficult to answer these questions. They are
insistent. They try to pull your leg out of its socket, smirk in the
heat, gaze at your wretchedly purple body (which resembles by
this time the body of a new-born baby) and with an air of mod-
esty which is only a secret disguise for the most intolerable
inquisition they begin to talk about your shoulders, the curve of
your neck, the shape of your chin, laughing delightedly as you
squirm helpless in the water which has been dyed black by a
liberal dose of Lysol. You are at their mercy. For nothing—for the
fun of seeing your expression—they will pull at your leg and dip
your head under water. It is part of the game, the madly unheroic
game of being bathed by a Chinese bath-attendant.

Then, wrapped in a quantity of warm towels, resembling an
Egyptian mummy, seated on a low bamboo chair with a glass of
green tea at your elbows, you wait patiently for the final ig-
nominy. A small boy comes and tweaks your toes. He tweaks
savagely. His one aim is to hurt, and he succeeds admirably. He
pulls at each toe until it has left its socket, and he leaves it hanging there with an amused expression on his face. It can be pushed
back later. Your nerves and senses are dumb. You no longer feel.
Another boy is beating you rhythmically in the hollow of your
back, still a third is pounding your thighs, while a fourth may be
cracking his knuckles on your head. You hate the boys. You curse
the bath-house. You swear by all the gods that you will never
return. But afterwards, long afterwards, a faint glow of rude
500

health begins to stir in your veins; the surface of the skin begins to effervesce like champagne; the head glows; the scalp tingles, and even your toes appear to have an independent life of their own. You have been made whole. Once more you are Adam. The small boys, the steaming baths, the spiders and the daddy-long-legs have all had their part in the transformation scene.

November 6th . . . THERE was a time when Kunming was almost a French reserve. There are still shops where the Chinese names are transliterated according to the French fashion; there are still places where Kunming is written K'oen-ming, and perhaps there is no harm in it. There are still a few Annamites in the centre of the city, and I have seen in the private houses of retired generals ormolu clocks and Sèvres china and Louis XIV chairs and terrible Dianas. It is there—in the houses of the retired war-lords—where provincial France exists in all her finery. There are thick carpets, marble fireplaces, gold-handled teacups, little blue bags of lavender, marble-topped tables, antimacassars, lace curtains showing Ariadne in her web followed by Theseus in armour, and there are great red satin bows at the backs of the chairs, and at any moment you expect the maid-servant to enter with a silver tray with rolled-gold handles and thin lace serviettes, and you are surprised when a young man enters in Sun Yat-sen uniform and announces that the noodles are served. The noodles are delicious—little yellow buns filled with sweet and sour sauces, and there is coffee without cream, but with those enormous thin elongated lumps of sugar which you find only in France, Czecho-slovakia and Finland. The war-lord is in excellent humour. He speaks French with the accent of Boulogne. The portrait of his father in a uniform which could only have been designed in the *Brasserie Anglaise* at Boulogne stares down at you from the walls, with its peacock's feathers, sham decorations, moiré silk girdles. But the war-lord is perfectly conscious of the slight air of disdain on his father's face. He knows that in China power is a thing that passes in the night, and all this finery is a desolation and a snare. The peacock's feathers languish, the decorations are superseded, the moiré silk girdles are lost and never found.

There are exceptions among the war-lords. There is a young man in Kunming who owns an enormous estate inside the city, and there you may wander for hours among the trees imagining that you are in some distant province with no city in sight. He

501

has a fondness for blood-red camellias and fast cars; his father was one of the greatest revolutionaries of all, for it was he who broke up the power of Yuan Shih-kai. He is modern to the last millimetre of his tapering finger-tips, and his young wife and children are beautiful as only young Chinese wives and Chinese children can be beautiful. When spring comes he will throw the gardens open to the whole world, for nowhere else in this country of flowers will you see so many camellias, so many magnolias and roses. "I have a feeling of responsibility. I must open the doors—people must come. It is terrible to be surrounded by all this beauty and enjoy it alone." And then too he will send his servant out in the street with a tray of silver blossoms, and everyone who passes will be offered one.

November 9th . . . IN SUMMER the grass will grow high over the graves, but now they are barren. There is grey mud everywhere outside the city walls. And the trees are being lopped by soldiers, who climb up on ropes, and the great mounds of the dead look famished and ill under a grey sky. There is such desolation on these winter graves that the heart almost rejoices at the utter bleakness of death. There is no mercy. Darkness and mud, a cold wind coming down the Burma Road, the silence of the stark branchless trees.

Even the birds have gone, the great crooked black crows who hovered over the library building in the campus. The blue-painted sentry-boxes, so gay a month ago, are streaked with black rain; and the wind descending from Serpent Mountain whistles against the mud walls and tin roofs of the University. Today we are all frozen. The boy who wears only a shirt and a pair of patched blue khaki trousers huddles over his books and dreams of the sun. It is not true that there is sun all the year round in Kunming. There are days when the sun seems to have been swallowed up, as it is swallowed up in Chungking, days when even the ghost of the sun is an unthinkable miracle, and the sleet-rain pours across the Blue Lake in cascades like ice. Is this Kunming?

The rain comes from a towering sky. There are clouds three miles high, and the rain falls from them wth terrific speed. These sudden showers are like snowstorms in high mountains—everything darkens.

I had wandered out across the rice-fields, now flooded and silver-dark; over the railway; down along the narrow willow-clad

502

lane; past camouflaged trucks which looked in this darkness like water-buffaloes; and suddenly seeing a patch of blue sky, as sometimes in a ship after a storm you will see the white clouds through a rent of white sail and wonder at the greater whiteness, I was surprised to see lightning flashing across this thin blue circle of light. Lightning here is more mysterious than in Sumatra. On perfectly clear days, without a breath of thunder in the air, you will see the sky grow suddenly silver with flashes which seem to come from the lake and the hills. But today the storm gathered, and the lightning was *behind the clouds*.

I wandered over a graveyard, smaller and less melancholy than the great stretch of humped graves outside the North Gate. There were a few wooden crosses, now threadbare in the wind; and flowers—not tapers—lay crushed in the mud at the foot of the graves. The Chinese do not plant flowers on graves: flowers are for the living, and the dead are accompanied by the dead through the shades. I prefer the European habit of believing that the dead live and take enjoyment in living things; but as the storm grew louder, and the flashes of lightning, no longer intermittent, spread beneath the clouds, I remembered the boy I had seen in Chungking who lay in a conduit, stripped of his clothes by the explosion of the fire-ball, his body dark blue with deep etched lines of a still darker blue over his chest; and on his face and open eyes an expression of wild surprise. He had lain all night in the raging conduit; in the morning the waters had ebbed away and left him like shipwreck abandoned on the shore. And now the lightning was terrible, forking down to the earth, and sometimes, like the chattering of teeth or the boiling of an immense copper kettle, you hear the sound of lightning striking water. There was no hope for it. I began to run. I saw a horse galloping madly across the fields, the great walls of the city rising above the rocks; and all the peace and beauty of the world seemed to lie in the barrel-shaped gates in the wall where I sheltered, dripping, wildly admiring the storm.

November 15th, The Burma Road . . . THERE is a road leading from Verdun to Bar-le-Duc which is more sacred than the Appian Way. It is forgotten now; the Marshal who ordered the road to be opened has turned the way of the traitors, and the fortresses which were defended at Douaumont have been turned by the right flank of the German Army at last. These fortresses,

503

buried in the forests or standing up proudly beyond the Woevre Plain, are also forgotten, as all wars become forgotten in time, but the Burma Road, which leads right up to the gates of Kunming, will last longer in the memory of men.

If you travel along this road for three hundred miles you will meet the Japanese. They are already in this province, and though their aeroplanes no longer bombard the walls, they are still powerful. But the road is deserted. Very few lorries go down the road, and those clouds of white dust which roar under the avenue of willows and elms are untenanted. Sometimes a donkey-cart jolts down the road bearing its load of sick soldiers; and they gaze at you with pale faces and deep-lined eyes from the wooden cabin. A dog prowls among the burial-mounds. A few scarlet tattered paper flags fly from the summits of the graves. The kites wheel in the heavens. There is a poem by Tu Fu which fits the scene perfectly:

> *I have travelled the road to the Hu barbarians,*
> *There are only the dogs, and the bleached bones.*

November 20th, Blue-print for the Future of China . . . THE elderly scholar in smoked glasses was speaking of the future industrial development of the country. He had the enthusiasm of a youth, and the infectious gaiety of the very old. He spoke with a kind of calculated delight in the plans which he had himself had a part in inventing. He employed phrases which I heard now for the first time, though they will be soon on everybody's lips— phrases like the "Yangtse barrage", "the Gold Areas", "the great aluminium-bearing district of south-west China".

"Many years ago I came upon Dr. Sun Yat-sen's book on the development of China," he said. "I was impressed by its lofty vision and the extraordinary way—it was extraordinary, to my eyes —in which Sun Yat-sen regarded the earth of my country. It opened my eyes to the fact that there may be more wealth under the earth than in the top-soil; and I began to take an interest in metallurgy, mineralogy and geology. These are the great things in modern China; and it is from this point that modern China really begins. We are making plans for the future now. The renovation of the country goes hand in hand with the war. We have selected sites, built the road-beds, studied communications—in our mind's eye we can see the great chain of factories spreading over China.

504

There are fourteen areas for development. There are six great areas for power. And though to you these words may mean nothing, they mean a very great deal to us. We are working carefully. We have made contracts with American firms for the extension of our rolling-stock—all our communications will be got from America. Our shipyards will be multiplied by a hundred; our foundries will be multiplied by three hundred; our cotton-mills will eventually supply the whole of China. In twenty years' time, though we are poor now, we shall be rich; and when that day comes we shall no longer have to import on the scale that we imported before. China, with her tremendous man-power, her skill, her enthusiasm and the richness of her land, will become a great power. And all the time the earth underneath our feet has been unexplored."

The enthusiasm of the young geologists and metallurgists in China is contagious, but this old man, with bent shoulders and smoked grey glasses, saw even further than they. He saw dangers and difficulties ahead—a rich, expanding China producing great mineral wealth and too little food; a country no longer under the control of foreign banks and foreign industrialists, but herself powerful enough to supply credits abroad; a country which by its very wealth, and by its position in the East, must seek for spiritual privations.

"We will be great—too great," he murmured softly. "But we must discipline ourselves for this responsibility. We must be careful. We must know the limits of our courage and the exact measure of our strength. We shall have achieved perhaps a dangerous liberty for which we are not yet prepared. When I think of the wealth buried in the soil of China, when I think of the wealth of our man-power and the courage of our people, then I begin to be afraid not that our country will become imperialistic, but that our people shall lose the last vestiges of their ancient culture. It is not lost yet. We must wait. We must cherish it quietly—this above all."

All over China I have heard this complaint from the old, and sometimes from the young. China learnt the value of mechanical toys from the West; and she knows that they are not important. A battleship is terrifying; but it is only a beautiful toy, necessary perhaps in the age we live in, but of no permanent importance in the history of a civilisation, which grows according to laws which have nothing in common with the laws of the foundry. The Chinese believe, passionately and insistently, that their ancient ways are still *viable*.

"The methods of production have changed, but men have not changed. There is no sign of a change of heart—all the old virtues and vices still survive. But what has changed may change us, and it is then that the danger comes: we must beware that the change is not so great that we are altered out of recognition. It would be better to perish as a nation than to lose our culture."

I know he was speaking sincerely. The great blue map on the table, with the little red stars, indicated the future. Here were water-ways, canals, hydraulic plants, barrages, shipyards, lines of railway. Here were great wheat-belts with tractors. There, in Honan, where famine has raged for forty centuries, the earth was flowering into a new spring. There were junks on the rivers, but there were also specially designed craft—perhaps propelled by petrol engines or aeroplane propellers. The gorges had been blasted; the plains had been made fertile; the immense riches of the Chinese people themselves had been harnessed to the immense riches of the land.

"And then," he groaned. "we will become like America or England. Our sense of values will shrink until it becomes a hard metallic thing—a mass-produced pin." He sighed. A wind caught the blue map and it began to flutter as though alive. "Sometimes I think this is what will happen, and then I remember all the countless generations of suffering that China has gone through, and then I know that we shall survive with our sense of values unharmed."

I went out, down the evil-smelling courtyard and out through another courtyard, wondering at the strange insistence of the Chinese on the dangerous prospects ahead. They were for years an island empire, having little contact with the outside world. Then came the British and the Americans; the unforgivable arrogance of the merchants, and the still more unforgivable arrogance of the legations; the years of riot and disorder, the swift fortunes, the diseases of the West. Opium flowed in from Hongkong and Macao. The gunboats of ten foreign powers were anchored at the estuary of her greatest river. Then came the great silence which descended on China a month after Pearl Harbour, and once more they were an island power, fighting hard, interminably waging war against the enemy and themselves. Hoarding, corruption, starvation—they were enemies enough to break

506

the back of a nation. But the nation was not broken, and in those quiet ill-lit courtyards, where all the lights of civilisation were dimmed, the scholars continued their progress. They will go unrewarded. They will die before their plans are put into operation. They will not see their blue-prints in action. But the way is clear. A vast gigantic power for good is being let loose on the world.

November 25th . . . HE WAS an old man, nut-brown, covered with wrinkles and bare to the waist. He wore a pair of greasy trousers which were once blue, and were now nearly green; and on his feet there were bamboo-straw sandals worn so thin that he could feel every stone, every grain of dust on the ground.

The little desk where he worked was covered with little statues of brightly-coloured clay—green dragons, red warriors, a girl holding a paper umbrella, a yellow snake crawling along a branch of lime, flowers. He worked swiftly—so swiftly that it was almost impossible to follow the movements of his hands. He would roll a strip of clay in his palms, pinch the ends, twist a small petal of clay with the tip of his forefinger, make little snips with his scissors—and there were two hands! The children marvelled. These slender hands looked far more life-like than their own. Some more clay was rubbed together; this time twenty different colours were introduced into the pattern, and this became the flowered dress of a young girl holding a bunch of narcissi, headless and legless. The head was made carefully, a little round blob, three or four little straws of clay for the hair, a faint beak of vermilion for the lips, a tiny stone for the eyes. He tapered off the neck, the nails of his little fingers dug out ears, and he set the head firmly and squarely upon the narrow shoulders. Little red tongues of clay were made into feet, and the miracle was accomplished—an extremely attractive young Chinese girl, ten times larger than life, smiled at us from his tray.

All over China there are street-stalls like this. I have seen models in the round, relievos, hollow and transparent glassware, animals that walk upside down, kittens that remain kittens even when you turn them inside-out, marbles that roll uphill, little houses furnished with all the art of China, even to the imitation Sung Dynasty painting hanging on the wall; and none of these toys is made with clock-work. The delightful, irresponsible and infantile art of the Chinese craftsman does not altogether belong to this world, nor does China belong to this world as completely as other nations. This nation dreams, and will always dream, of impracticable things, and even when the whole of China is industrialised, little boys with skulls bare except for the little wisp of black pigtail bound in blue ribbon which sticks up vertically from the crown of their heads will wonder and marvel at dragons and huge birds like butterflies, and all the dreaming sustenance of the world.

November 27th . . . I DO not know whether I, too, am dreaming. He came out of the dark side-street, naked to the waist, his chest shining with sweat or grease, handsome and robust above the troops of men. There was a singular grace in his movements, and I thought of the young Arab boy who possessed the same grace and the same terrible flowing movement who followed me down the streets of Port Said. And then this god-like figure began to speak in perfect English: "Would you like to smoke some opium?" That was all. Nothing else. I am sure there was nothing else, not even a threat, not even a curse when we shook our heads. He disappeared as silently and majestically as he came.

December 1st, Air-raid . . . THE hooter sounded, and we went out into the street to look up at the dawn-blue sky, whitened by clouds and small puffs of white smoke. It was hot, and the air low down on the lake was misty with haze, so hot indeed that we kept away from the burning walls and walked out in the centre of the street. But the hooters were still sounding, the roads were beginning to fill with people and motor-cars, and the policemen could be heard high above the voices of the crowds shouting that we should make haste. It was impossible to run. We were caught up in the narrow streets leading to the great barrel-shaped gate, thousands of people streaming in their red, green and blue motley into the fields outside.

There have been air-raids here before. There have been times when the city was left gasping and smouldering, and blood ran in torrents in the streets; days of despair and waiting; days of interminable low-flying planes. But today the planes were high, the fighters were out in pursuit, and except for the cloudy puffs of smoke from anti-aircraft batteries and the great black spiral of smoke which rose in the distance, there was no sound of the fighting once you were outside the gate. The heat rained down. The
508

soldiers in their cotton-padded uniforms were sweating and smiling; and as we walked down the valley past the hospital and the green gates, they waited impatiently for the moment when, with heaving shoulders and the help of battering-rams, the enormous rusted door with its green copper-studded nails could be closed and padlocked with rusty chains. There they would stand guard, good-humoured emblems of the strangest army in the world.

We sat under the trees, among the grave-mounds, and the bleeding red pits have been dug into the earth for the greater safety of the living; for crouching low in these pits, many lives have been saved, though the rats come and gnaw at your toes and a dead body may be lying in the mud beneath your feet. There were sounds of distant explosions; a small red fighter plane soared among the acacia-trees, and we could recognise easily enough the whitened teeth of a red tiger. Then the aeroplane disappeared behind flying-buttresses of granite walls; more explosions; the twittering of birds; and suddenly like a great wave the infectious laughter of children.

The children are in command. They are perfectly at ease; they have completely forgotten the bombardments of two years before. The young girl in the blue print frock has stripped to the waist, the better to feed the hungry child, and her golden shoulders seen through the haze of smoke from her husband's pipe are dazzling in this rarefied air. Her father has come up from the country with two rough-haired goats for sale; and the goats, tethered to his walking-stick, browse and graze in the grass at the young girl's feet. Her mother is there, a great fat hulk of a woman, all blubber, shaking with laughter. It is Hampstead Heath on holiday; it is Coney Island; it is the Bois de Boulogne and the Englischer Garten and the Volksgarten in Vienna. There are invisible flags waving over the contentment of the people, who have longed for an opportunity to go out *en masse* into the countryside. Children run races. The most unexpected encounters take place. Every grave-mound is a throne for the quiet people who have come to spend this holiday in peace.

And the country is so beautiful, and they have never had time to see it before. The veined blue peak of Serpent Mountain gleams above the trees; there are shimmering reaches of rice-lakes; a small toy train puffs and blows across the marshland. Horses are neighing, soldiers are marching, men are gazing up at the sky

509

from the battlemented walls. It is all like a dream, or like a child's toy. And news travels fast—"fourteen Japanese aeroplanes have been brought down, and not a single American plane has been lost." This is what one would expect in a child's toy. The gleaming fields, the scarlet-crested woodpeckers, the young girls lying in the grass of the grave-mounds, every track and road for miles filled with people lying on the grass. The fields of the blessed! And surely in the fields of the blessed there are little puffs of white smoke in the sky, and red aeroplanes with tiger's teeth soar over the low-roofed houses.

December 4th, The Walls at Night . . . COMING from the University to the city late at night, I saw three more miracles. I saw a man carrying a small colt on his back, and then, tiring of its weight, he let it fall to the ground, held the halter and then ran after it as it galloped gallantly along the dark road. I cannot think why he carried it on his back, and I cannot think why the sound of the bright hoofs galloping along the Burma Road filled me with such delight.

Then I heard a girl singing. She was alone by the side of the road; there was no one else in sight. She wore a blue gown and her hair was smoothed and oiled, and parted in the middle. In the faint light she resembled a princess who had appeared to startle me from the enchanted woods. As I passed, she was still singing.

Then I came to the walls, gleaming after rain, the immense craggy walls standing against the blue sky, and above them the craggy walls of the clouds, and above them a pale silver slip of a moon so perfect that I caught my breath. And if you ask which is the greater miracle, I must answer that I understand perfectly why a young girl should sing at the end of a road or why a colt carried on a man's back should suddenly race down a wet, shining road. Those things are understandable, but the walls of China are always inexplicable. There were low white-washed walls at An-ning; there are crumbled walls at Chungking; there are walls which have been broken through at Chengtu, and there are a few scattered bastions of walls at Changsha. But the walls of Kunming are better, for their proportions have been carefully calculated to dissemble their power and to mingle with the landscape; they are clear and sharp; they have battlements and small
510

towers against the skyline; and when it rains they are like a ring of water circumscribing the fairy city.

December 6th, The Walls by Day . . . BY DAY, when the sun rises, the walls are pale red, the colour of a painted egg-shell held to the light. They are almost transparent, though they are twenty feet thick, full of mud, and green moss hanging over the battlements, even at sunrise, suggests they are old.

I would like to see these walls from a balloon. The revolving shadows, lengthening and diminishing with the curves of light, would frame the city in exactly the same way that the rain-soaked walls frame it at night. The Chinese have known since the beginning of time that there are gods of the city to be propitiated. You must walk warily by the great gates. But now, in the full sunlight of afternoon, the walls gleaming rose-red and biscuit-brown, hidden here and there by clumps of bamboos and willows, while the golden curving roofs of a few houses higher than the walls stand out against the sky, it is impossible to believe that the walls are evil. These battlemented walls, though here and there you will find vertical slits for machine-guns, are useless now; they no longer protect the city from the enemy. A student said: "We should tear them down, use the bricks for houses and let air into the city." He may be right, though there are better reasons for tearing down these magnificent walls—the gates are narrow, and it is easy to be trapped in the city during air-raids. But if the walls go, something of the particular ethos of the Chinese race will go with them; and I shall no longer feel protected.

In the evening, when the shadows lengthen and the small whitewashed mortuary at the end of the hospital garden has turned black with shadow, and even the little mountain of lime is invisible from the barrel-gates, the wall is alive with running flames of light. The last vestiges of sunlight are reflected by these greenblue walls towering high above me. And at night, black as ink, towering higher than ever, the walls come into their own.

December 5th . . . THIS evening, when I returned through the North Gate, I saw the soldiers standing over a coffin. The lid was taken off, the body of an old man with a grey face and a few wisps of white hair which shone like silver wires in the torchlight was laid on the cobble-stones; and they examined it

511

carefully, reverently, shuffling silently in the mud in their cotton-soled shoes.

No one spoke. It was necessary to establish that the man had died a natural death; and seeing at last that the body was whole, and the papers of death had been signed, they let the small straggling procession go out by lantern-light into the dark. Dogs howled. In the whole of China it seemed that there was none so lonely as the old man with the silver hair who went out into the dark.

December 8th . . . Is THERE democracy in China? I do not know what definition to give to democracy when we talk of Chinese democracy. The people are naturally democratic, and your scholar is the most democratic of all people, if by democracy we mean that splendid grace of spirit which implies that all men are equals. And the peasant and the young soldier and the student are all democratic in their lives: they have reverence for others: they are delighted by the success of others: they work for others, and their selflessness is surely only another name for democracy.

But if by democracy we mean the rule of the elected few over the electing majority, then it is more difficult to reply. The governors of the *hsiens* are not elected; the government officials are not elected; there is democracy only in the senate of the Universities. And yet there is no nation more inevitably democratic than the Chinese, no country where the advice of the elders is more absolute and more trustworthy, no country where men have so keen a respect for scholars. There are evils in China as elsewhere, and those who live and breathe under an exorbitant inflation have perhaps a greater right to criticise their governments than others. But we must first clean up Congress and the Houses of Parliament before we criticise the Chinese, whose People's Political Council stands at the beginning of great powers.

December 9th, The Death of a Professor . . . A PROFESSOR of this University has died. I did not know him, though I have heard of him by repute and I have seen him walking in a discoloured blue gown along the side-streets by the lake. I remember him as a slight stooping figure, deep in thought, with a bundle of books under his arm and a gnarled walking-stick which was waved menacingly against the dogs which haunt the burial-
512

mounds. His hair was grey, and probably he was younger than he seemed; for he had walked from Changsha to Kunming in the great pilgrimage which was led by the famous Wen Yi-to. And now he is dead, and his wife and two children mourn for him, and the doctors who pronounced that he died of relapsing fever know as well as we do that he died of malnutrition and the hardships of the long journey. Food is dear; drugs are dear. If life could be bought with courage, the professors and students of the Chinese Universities would be immortal, but life is not bought with courage and a hundred and fifty students crowd the medical offices of the University each day, and cheeks are becoming thinner, and the grey lines of worry show heavily on the heads of the young.

I do not know anything in the world so important as the survival of the Chinese Universities. They are the pledge by which the East will come into its own. And the professors die for lack of drugs and food, and there is no comfort in their heroism, and those who watch can only marvel.

December 10th . . . I AM haunted by Bergery as Confucius was haunted by the Duke of Chou. He comes into my dreams, still living, still planning and talking, still full of that extraordinary vitality which made everyone adore him. I wish he had come here. These three great Universities in the south-west are the stuff on which he would build his dreams. And he might have written of the heroism of the professors and students, their desperate need for drugs and books, their need for more and still more contact with the outside world, more powerfully than I. There was a quality of menace in his writings. Like a prophet he foretold all. He would write of the importance of these Universities so that ministers and ambassadors would pay attention; writing in letters of fire against the cloud-caps of the world that the East is being born here anew, and nothing is so important as the lives of the young students and soldiers of China, and no price is too great to pay for their friendship. But alas, I cannot write in letters of fire, and this dumb halting prose must suffice.

December 15th . . . I TOLD my stepdaughter this evening that I had heard someone singing in the rain, and that it seemed to be a miracle, so pure was the voice and so perfect the en-

513

chanted forest. She replied: "I was waiting for you. You were so deep in your books that you paid no attention to me."

December 16th . . . I HAVE written five books since I came to China—the two volumes of *Love and Peace* which proposes to recount the adventures of a great Chinese family through the last thirty years, the two plays in verse and the poems which are to be included in a single volume, a book of short stories and a life of Sun Yat-sen. There is a third novel, so bitter that it has been burnt. And God knows how many scraps of poems, and how many epics which may never be written, and how many unfinished sentences and paragraphs in the scrap-books which mount higher and higher each month, until they are in danger of breaking through the ceiling.

I have never known this passion for writing before. In the three years at Singapore I wrote only two short novels, and only a few passages of them still please me. Perhaps it was the Naval Base, which towered over every thought and seemed in those days to acquire an imaginative halo as the great sentinel of the East. I admired Sir Stamford Raffles with the same kind of adoration which in youth I reserved for Napoleon and Cæsar. This man of peace, who fought against diplomats and all the tide of bureaucracy, seemed then to be the last of the empire-builders, the final flowering of the conquests which encircled the globe. The tragedy of his life, his melancholy, his justice and his passion for the Malays was something which I understood; while the officials who ruled over Malaysia seemed incomprehensible to me. And so I lived, happily and calmly, in the shadow of the great docks and gazing for hours at the glittering sunsets of the East. The scent of the casuarina-trees, the small fishing *prahus* along the west coast, the temples and the forests fed my soul and left my imagination free. But there was no need to write. There was so much holiness in the air that one could walk unhindered among the blossoms, and there was need to celebrate the benignity of the gods.

One writes at the moment of regret, or at the moment of fear. In Singapore life was eternal and changeless: there were no fears that it might change, for it was unchangeable, and no regrets at the passing of time, for every day was like every other day, and time did not flow past you like a river, but like the heavens reigned unalterable over our lives. But here, in this swiftly-chang-
514

ing and terribly virile China, where the metal is molten and the people are searching for new gods, or the old gods transformed into a more virile strength, regrets and fears come tumbling into the brain; and the mind, trained for stillness, is tormented by the greatness of the drama which is being played before our eyes. Here no one writes. A tormented devil springs over the page, searching for the phrase which will describe the undescribable courage and ambitions of the great Chinese race.

December 17th . . . IN A white-washed room, looking over a deserted courtyard of stone, the pale-red petals of the mountain laurel. . . .

December 18th, Invigilating at an Examination . . . QUIETLY, wearing blue gowns, they crouch over their desks. Their pens come like the sound of solemn waves against high rocks, an interminable sighing on this long summery afternoon. I know nothing like the quiet concentrated power of these students. You can hear the subterranean dynamos working; you can hear the thoughts whirling in their heads. And now, as they sit there, they are almost unrecognisable, so great a change has come over their expressions. There, with his legs wrapped round the legs of the chair, is the young genius with the tousled hair, the thick crystalline spectacles, the air of an unruly Beethoven. And the young girl with the golden eyes which are heavily veiled with thought, and the boy who still looks like a child and whose maturity I have seen for the first time this afternoon.

Butterflies fly lazily over the meres; the green duck-weed glints in the sun and my crested woodpecker is hammering on the boles of trees. The tin roofs shine with a glassy stare; and there is so much quiet and compassion in this lazy afternoon that I can almost hear the distant sound of cricket-bats at the nets.

I do nothing. I am supposed to watch them, but it will only distract their attention if I walk up and down the long colonnades between the desks. The sighing of the fountain-pens continues; the sound of a page being turned over is like an explosion. And where do we go from here? When you have taken your examination, when you are entitled to add the two letters B.A. after your name, will you be as you are now, thoughtful and quiet in the long summer afternoons, gazing steadily at the object of contemplation and giving at least the illusion of perfect understanding? For this is the saddest moment, the moment when the four years of study are over and you are cast adrift on the world. What will you do? Where will you go? You have no plans, except that China should be better for your existence.

And so the long summer afternoon continues; the drowsy heat mounting from the pools of duck-weed where a small boy is sailing paper boats through a green tide. The flag of the republic is blood-red on the high unpainted mast, and the shingles on the library roof are hidden under the wings of ravens. And what then? When you have left the University, what hopes, what courage, what resources will enable you to build anew, for the ten thousandth time, the fabric of this immense, despoiled and always vigorous country?

I do not know the answers to these questions. I know that they have courage and beauty, and it seems now, in this drowsy afternoon of butterflies and fountain-pens, that these things are enough.

December 20th . . . IT RAINED yesterday, but today was splendid. I do not know what flower it is whose scent comes through my open window, but all the sunlight seems to be in it. It is the beginning of the flower season. On the western hills the rhododendrons are already in bloom. "I saw them yesterday," said T. "They were blue and white, and they looked like the sea in a tempest."

December 21st . . . COMING around the corner of the lake, with the gold and flaring roofs of a small temple behind him, I met Lin Yutang wearing a maroon gown. His face was brown as walnuts, and the silk gown gleamed red and blue like the sea in the evening. He looked perfectly happy. The small intelligent monkey-face showed all the excitement of a mystic contemplating the profound secrets of the universe, and he was almost trembling. He was talking in Chinese, and the words "Chung-kuo" would come out in a sudden rush of endearing epithets. He was glad to be back, glad to feel the soil of China under his feet. Meanwhile the blue lake glittered at our feet.

At the party in President Mei Yi-chi's house we talked about the necessity of translations. China is still unknown in the West. We know so little of her past history that we are always in danger of misunderstanding the present; and the present is no more than an aggregate of its past. The greatest Chinese novels and poems

516

remain untranslated; there are no good books proclaiming the virtues of the Chinese, and their ways of thinking, though Lin Yutang's *The Importance of Living* is valuable as an elementary guide. There are no books on the nature of the historical grammar of the Chinese language except Karlgren's, and for lack of time nothing final has been studied. There are four or five great civilisations still existing on the earth, and China, which is perhaps the greatest of all, remains a mystery to us. We must learn, or perish; for if we fail to understand one another, there will always be wars.

We were talking on these lines in the great ante-room with its plush sofas, Lin Yutang happy at last to be among scholars. He is half a renegade. He had begun his studies in China with some excellent work on philology and then disappeared to edit comic magazines and write novels. He was an excellent interpreter of China to the West, but he was losing his Chinese roots and it was good to see how easily he was resuming them. He was not the greatest of the distinguished scholars present; he was humble, and a little sad; he smiled wanly when his great success was mentioned, and more than once he said: "I must stay in China—I must stay——" and yet we knew he would return. He had addressed the students on Confucius, begging them to return to the ancient virtues; and the students had disapproved, wondering at the strange interloper from the West who had dared to suggest a revival of ancient and antiquated virtues, for there were other Chinese philosophers who could lead them further along the strange unknown roads of the future. We discussed the translation of *The Dream of the Red Chamber*, the greatest novel that China has produced and so far untranslated; we discussed his own brilliant translations of *The Travels of Mingliaotse* and a hundred other things. "Nothing has been begun," he said, "we must begin again from the beginning. We have not begun to translate Western books into Chinese, and nothing of any value has been translated from Chinese into the languages of the West." It was a sad meeting. We were powerless. Here, in Kunming, where a thousand great scholars are starving, the work of translation could have begun if there had been funds enough. We could have gone through the great classics one by one and given them a modern dress; we could have displayed the treasures of China to the West and for the first time we could have made the basis of understanding. Alas, there is no basis. China is still a mystery

517

to us, and perhaps we are half-afraid of this mysterious country, which has developed its arts to a perfection which is almost terrifying.

And so we wandered down the roads which lead to the lake, the golden temples, the brilliance, the sky.

December 22nd . . . I FOUND an unposted letter from Bergery at the bottom of my trunk. ". . . There is a fatality in Europe. We are continually burning our bridges, but the Chinese have made their bridges so strong that they can pass backwards and forwards at ease. The European tradition is broken at several places—there were catastrophes of the spirit along the road. But in China, though the land was in turmoil and the people starved, the spirit remained supreme. And always it was the same."

December 25th . . . TONIGHT the stars came out brighter than ever, perhaps to celebrate Christmas. There was a sky of black steel, there were clouds like dragons and immense spherical stars rolling between them like pearls dipped in quicksilver. We have been comparing this Christmas with Christmases years ago. Last year one of my students was walking barefoot through the Manchurian mountains, another lay in a small village in Honan racked with typhus, a third was in Pekin, skating on the ice and travelling by motor-car to his ancestral temple in the Western Hills. "There was snow everywhere, three feet deep, and people were dying of cold. I went to the temple through an avenue of cryptomerias, and in the evening I began the long journey south. But before I went, I invited a Japanese officer to dine and we made arrangements to meet the next week. I liked him, because he was a scholar and because he hated the Japanese occupation, but it was necessary to lie to him. He was afraid. I was sorry for him. He would walk through the city with his eyes on the ground feeling outraged by the behaviour of the Japanese soldiers, and yet incapable of doing anything. We drank to each other's health. I think he knew that I would never return until the Japanese had left the city. Before we left—my brother and I—he began to cry. He told me that a great Chinese scholar, under whom he had studied, had died in Kweilin. If I knew anybody who was going into Free China, would I write a postcard and send it to the grave? We have not this custom in China, but I promised that I would write down the words which he wanted the old scholar

518

to receive, and I would tell my friends if ever they went to Kweilin. . . ."

It was a strange story, but what was stranger still is that exactly the same thing was requested of a friend who was travelling to Pekin. A Japanese scholar was living in a University near Changsha. He too had heard that his master had died in Japan and he too requested that a postcard should be sent to the grave. And I thought that there are now so many Japanese dead that nearly everyone in Japan is sending postcards to graves; and I thought of the old postmen who never fail to set flame to these cards, so that the words ascend to heaven. In nearly every town and village of China I have seen the small red-brick structures where paper is burnt; and though the custom is dying down, it is still true that paper and calligraphy are respected, and old men still acquire virtue by picking up stray scraps of paper and burning them in the red-brick kilns. But today there was no snow on the ground and all the stray scraps of paper in the roads were being tossed sky-high by the wind. Already the magnolias are coming out: the sticky white buds are invisible unless you come quite close to them. There is a fragrance in the air, as of a fore-taste of spring. The gates of Tang's garden are thrown open, for it is the anniversary of the day when his father, the Governor of Yunnan, began the revolt which ended the career of Yuan Shih-kai on the throne. So the small dusty streets are full of old men who have come to pay their respects to the tomb, remembering their ancient victories; and sitting in this small room, among the cobwebs and the grey rats, I can hear the children in the garden near-by screaming with excitement, although it is dark and the stars are rolling against a steel-black sky.

I walked out in the deserted streets. The sky has never been so beautiful, the stars have never been so close. In the west the bombers are returning. You see them first as little moving constellations of coloured light (red, green and silver), and faintly behind them follows the pulsing yellow glow of the exhaust. They fly so high that they are almost indistinguishable from the stars, which wheel so silently, the Plough climbing up the night and there, on the other side of the lake, a small cluster of stars lying on the horizon like a summit of snow. But suddenly the engines begin to roar and cough again, growing louder and more distinct, the flashlight blinks from the cockpit and you see it coming down low beneath the stars, not hesitantly, but in a swift

519

gliding hovering movement, wheels skimming the trees, the dark nose of the aeroplanes hiding in the foliage, though the tail remains visible. And then the faint crepitation of distant grasses as she settles on the landing-ground, the final triumphant roar of the engine and the sickening silences; for it seems as though something that was essential to the sky has disappeared and will never return.

December 26th . . . IN THIS garden the green squirrels climb high up on the elms, and the white pigeons preen themselves. At night they are locked up in the small white-washed boxes against the wall, but during the day they are everywhere—rolling on the green grass, walking solemnly along the wall, drinking water from the immense corrugated iron oil-tank which lies half-buried in the grass.

In China you will find houses like this everywhere. Behind high walls, cut off from the street, quietness descends in an uninterrupted fountain; and suddenly entering the garden out of the roar of the street is like entering an undiscovered land. There are children playing, a fat Yunnanese maid-servant is bawling from somewhere behind the white-washed plaster house, the sun shines vertically downward, so that you throw only a small black moon-shaped shadow, and in the silence the cooing of the pigeons is no more than a faint pulsation, a reminder that life exists somewhere in this sodden midsummer heat. Is it December? The sun glaring off the glazed tiles gives the green grass the scent of June.

But perhaps there are very few houses like this, for behind the high walls there is an enormous temple, with twenty or thirty courtyards, and tortured black trees which will later bear blossoms of magnolia and camellia stand on marble platforms in the courtyards. Great gilded gods look down in the cool temples at the unswept floors, where no mourners or pilgrims come to offer incense; for instead of the brown tussocks and incense-sticks I have seen so often even in the most abandoned temples, there are steel lathes, dynamometers, wind tunnels, immense electric generators, all the appliances of modern science. The gilded gods smile down kindly. They still hold their tablets and fly-whisks, they still seem to be about to rearrange the delicate folds of their gowns, they still smile mysteriously and efficiently; for there is nothing in the world quite so efficient as the smile of a Chinese

520

god in a temple. Meanwhile the floor throbs with the humming of the dynamos and the young workmen with their sleeves rolled up, in blue overalls and bare feet, calculate the length of polished steel bars with micrometer screws and pay no attention at all to the gods who smile so serenely beside them. There are inscriptions in gold-leaf on the wall which date back to the Great Ming Dynasty, but already the inscriptions are covered with the soft dust of steel filings. There are grooves in the stone floor where pilgrims have knelt in adoration, but there are still greater grooves where the machinery is bedded down. From the ceiling the great fly-wheels, with their leather straps, revolve imperturbably; and the heat and the dust and the shafts of sunlight whirl through the open doorways.

I have known greater machine-shops than this. There were machine-shops like palaces in Singapore, glittering under the hard Malayan sky, where Malay princes walked barefoot along polished stone floors and immense machines, far greater than anything I have seen in China, glinted with dusky oil. In Spain, near Tarragona, I have seen churches filled with motor-lorries and ambulances, while the Virgin peers down from the altar with no hint of disapproval. But here there are so many gods and so many machines that the mind reels. Who possesses the temple? And at night do the gods descend from the marble plinths and make curious images of burnished steel? And what will happen at the end of the war? A crowd of confused thoughts enters my mind. I am drunk with the sunlight, with the wheeling lathes, with the golden smiles of the ancient gods. There are hundreds of temples in this compound. In each temple there are gods. They smile down at the students, they lift their hands in benediction, they are perfectly at rest.

1944

January 1st . . . THE year begins with a blaze of sunshine so brilliant that this morning we were dazzled. The cuckoos were calling in the grove of magnolias outside my window, and the dust rose in golden columns in the narrow streets. The Chinese walls, so black and foreboding at night, are green with creepers and red with the rusty edges of bricks. Day breaks like a clarion. In the whole of China there is no place so perfect as this mile-high promontory in Yunnan.

We went out this afternoon with a young Chinese poet. Small boats were scurrying among the islands like a painting; the eagles foundered in the sky like ships which have lost their anchors. And the sky was high, so high that we lost ourselves dreaming of its immensity. "In China we say that the sky is higher in autumn," he said, "but here it is highest at the new year. You can see through the veils of the sky." He spoke of the Chinese Taoist astronomers who can see the stars in daylight, and of all the curious explorations of the old Chinese philosophers. "The Chinese believed that man had a place in Nature, and it was necessary to find this place; and that Nature is sacred and must not be disturbed. In the West you believe that Nature is the enemy, to be enslaved by your science. It may be so. We cannot tell. But I do know that for generations the Chinese have searched into Nature, trying to understand her secrets without despoiling her, and now at last we must become scavengers—despoilers—men of cunning."

It was curious to talk to him by the side of the green lakes, where the gulls of winter were flying and the black cormorants could be seen flapping lazily from the berthed boats on the sand-

523

banks. There are many, many things in which the Chinese and the West can understand each other; but ultimately there are differences so great and far-reaching—the differences between two ethos which have survived without in the slightest influencing one another, and I began to wonder whether it would ever be possible to understand the East. "For us Heaven and Earth are the two poles of our life, and both are timeless. They are outside the world we live in, and yet in it. They are the concepts by which we understand the world, and shall always understand the world, since it is by Heaven and Earth that we live. And you, how do you live?"

"By Youth and Love. In the West, ever since the beginning of things these have been our ideas. By youth we capture the world; a youthful god is slain, and from his blood comes our freedom."

"In China our gods are all old, and they are immortal—they are never slain. We have no belief in youth."

He was young himself, and very handsome, with the clean jaw-bones and the fine glancing eyes of the northern Chinese, and it was curious to think that he placed no trust in youth.

He went on:

"If we could marry the Chinese to the West—what would happen? I often amuse myself with the thought, for it seems that the children of this marriage would have all your faith in youth and all our reverence for immortal things. A race which had all the virtues of the West and of the Chinese. . . ."

"And what if it had all their vices?"

"I had thought of that, but surely their virtues would outweigh their vices—this reverence, and this delight in youth. Do you know, the Chinese have no love for youth. It is the time of sadness still, the time of marriages dictated by the parents, the time for being soldiers. In children and the old the Chinese see beauty and grace."

"And in young women?"

There was no answer. He had had an unfortunate love-affair, and a settled sadness, like the sadness which would sometimes descend on Bergery, fell upon him. It was growing dark. The small boats were returning, the fishing seines hooked on the prows of the boats; and the sun glinting on the jagged red gash on the western hills seemed to be bleeding. We walked back through the damp streets, where light still quivered on the walls. The jade-white magnolias were creeping over the high walls of the houses, and in this luminous hour all the fragrance of the world seemed to be contained in them.

January 3rd . . . THE white moth, with the faint grey markings, lay on my table at night, warming himself in the rays of the electric lamp. I have never seen a moth more beautiful, for the whiteness shone like silver, the faint grey antennæ continually quivered, and the small black eyes set in the white furry head seemed to be peering inquisitively at the world of paper and fountain-pens and coloured ink which surrounded it; and then suddenly the wings fluttered, there was a tremendous explosion of energy, and the moth began to prepare itself for a sudden startling flight against the lamp-bracket on the wall. But it did nothing. It stayed there, quivering and trembling, the beautiful spotted vermilion body underneath the wings quivering with the same tremendous activity which made the wing-tips invisible. It did nothing except show the beauty of its wings, for a moment later all the energy of the little body subsided. It lay very still, as though dead.

Three or four hours later, towards three o'clock in the morning, it was still there. I thought it was dead. This happened yesterday. Today it lay there, the colour running from the wings until they turned grey and all the silver had vanished. Again I thought it was dead. I picked it up. It was inert, motionless, and even the little black suckers at the end of the feet did not cling to the paper. And then suddenly once again, like Lazarus out of the tomb, it came to life, the colour returned, the grey antennæ quivered, the wings threshed and the body of the moth turned bright red.

Perhaps there is only one moral in this story: there is beauty only in the violent activity of wings.

January 8th . . . FOOD prices are soaring, and we have decided to dig up the little garden at the back of the theatre. We have discovered so much rubble that we have no idea what to do with it; the garden is white with chalky stones, and resembles a magnified bird-house floor. But this evening, when it was growing dark, someone discovered embedded in the earth a huge *makhara* stone, the head of a tawny lion, and a withered hole in the mouth made it certain that it was part of a fountain.

We have been trying to reconstruct these gardens. Where professors are now starving, there were once fountains, parks, cascades, ladies in silk who walked in the evening air.

January 9th . . . SHE is small and slender, and so gentle that one treads carefully in her presence. No one knows where she has come from. The *amah* said nothing, and the little beggar-child who now sits dreamily on our steps has no history and no name. She sits there quietly, smiling up at the sun, watching the soldiers as they pass, continually dreaming. Sometimes, as we come up the steps, we give her oranges; she takes them quickly and hides them craftily in her skirt. She does not trust us, but she smiles at us; and the extraordinary innocence in her burning eyes shocks us a little—her eyes are so large, and they seem to know more than all the books in Tsing Hua library have ever taught us.

January 11th . . . THEY were talking about magic. "But of course the people who know most about magic are the shop-assistants," the elderly professor was saying. "Perhaps not in Shanghai, where another magic—the magic of the dance-halls and the cinemas and cheap prostitutes—holds sway. But in Kunming half the shop-assistants are magicians and a quarter of them can work miracles."

I was astounded. I thought of the pale-faced, drab, insignificant shop-assistants sitting behind the counters where thousands of gold rings are displayed; the pimply-faced girl in the cinema; the too highly painted women in "The Street of Thieves", who sell you stockings at three hundred dollars a pair and a copy of *Life* for five hundred and of *Esquire* for two thousand. It was impossible to believe that they were magicians.

"But don't you see," he continued, "they are bored to extinction. The art of shopkeeping is not one which suggests an understanding of moral principles, and they are far away from any thought of morality. They can juggle with money. Why not juggle with things? They read all the Taoist books—the boy dreaming at the back of the shop is sure to have some magic books in his possession. He will perform miracles. He will hold his breath, obey certain elementary laws and become anything he pleases. You will see the same thing on the river steamers. An old Chinese sitting cross-legged at the bows in meditation—he too is becoming anything he pleases. He is the horse riding the breakwater, the small boy on the buffalo's back, the young girl smiling through

526

the heat-haze which surrounds the engine-room. And they can perform miracles. I have seen a man invite a textile manufacturer to bring a cart-load of silks into the courtyard, sew them together, take photographs of them, and then—whish! this billowing mountain of silk was floating high up in the air. We actually took photographs. Five minutes later, when the silks had all disappeared beyond the mountains, we returned to the living-room. The silks had returned. They were all there, and his wife was complaining that they came through the window, knocked her over, and she was still entangled in them."

Great bombers were flying overhead. In this world of science it seemed that the shop-assistants still possessed their power.

January 12th . . . I HAVE finished the long poem "The Testament of Peace", and it must stand as it is. I cannot alter it. There are parts where I would have preferred it to be more musical, and other parts where the meaning is constricted and tortured into the length of the lines. This poem, on the death of an American airman who was shot down into Kunming Lake, grew out of a single moment of time, but it could not be shorter. I must leave it as it is, and pray that it will be read with the whole breath.

I remember how it began. There was a night of storm last October, and three or four aeroplanes were known to have crashed into the sheer edges of the mountains around the lake. Two or three days previously there had been a dog-fight over the lake between Japanese and American airmen, and *a wing with a star* had been discovered on the sandy shore the next morning; and immediately I formed a picture of the American airman, young and lithe, a perfect representative of the European tradition, for in his veins there ran the blood of Egyptians and Armenians, Chaldeans, Jews and Assyrians, Romans, Germans, Englishmen and Scandinavians—the whole hosts of Europe whose voices he must have overheard in his dreams. Accordingly the poem would be divided into five parts corresponding to the four branches of columns of the European tradition, which are love of altitude, love of rigour, love of community and love of love, and there would be an introductory canto on the lake itself where he had met his death.

I think I like best this introductory canto, where China and Europe are brought together beside the lake. The whole poem is imagined to be a meditation under the burning August sun:

527

I walked into the valley wood in a time of hyacinths
till beauty like a scented cloth entirely overwhelmed me:
motionless and faint of breath I watched the sunrise.
There was no sound of gongs.
But listening there, like someone in a dream,
for the wise verdict of the virgin wind,
seeing auguries in birds, stript boughs, the footprints of lovers,
the small leaf flung on the sand and the wave lifting,
it seemed to me that death came running after,
the lake was frozen over and the birds were dumb.
Numbed in my heart I watched the frail October
on this day in August under a green tomb. . . .

O listen to the voice of love in the dying night,
the hollow reeds murmur in the thick darkness
of flowers and graves beyond our knowing—
crowns of myrtles, violets in streams of light,
the fruit-trees and the silence and the green
impulse which brings all things to the narrowing light.
But in this darkness, alone in the heavenly valley,
O my daughter,
there are no signs or torments for my spirit
save that the flowers will blossom over our loves.
The wind that breaks upon the summer lake
will take my breath away, has taken all,
all but the breath of life that made me one
adoring fountain kneeling before your loves,
a fountain of breath, a fountain of sweet water,
a running sound of laughter.
The acorn dies. Will the great oak remain? . . .

Therefore I desire to be buried in the evening,
there, in the shadow of mountains, green on the horizon,
below the white temple and the heron green,
and may someone carve an effigy of such holiness
that no one before or after will ever equal him,
inscriptions on rock, the fruit of my wild flowers,
those unseen hyacinths growing in the shadow of towers:
saying that I loved China, saying that I was alone,
for no one could love with so great a love
the hosts of the poets and prophets who came to these shores,
528

saying that I loved Chuang Tzu and the fiery bird
wheeling in space for the sake of a luminous freedom,
yet wrote of Christ, since childhood summoned me to
remember
that I was a child of the West, a ghost of the Nazarene;
and tenderly, slowly, into the black earth alone,
with no wooden coffin but naked as I came from the earth,
place me in this holy sepulchre and never remember
wherefrom I am descended and whence I came, and never tell
the spirits of the lake lest they come to molest me.
Then from my blood shall rise the innocent hyacinths,
myrtles, irises, violets, the rose that Christ loved,
all these shall flower according to their season,
yes, all these shall be flowers, herbs for the wounded hearts
of those who lamenting of death are no longer afraid of the
skull.
Through the eyes of my skull shall appear the blue violets,
a smoky puff of blue briony, winter's white flower
the snowdrops of snowfields with their shadows of ebony,
cassia and jasmine shall climb the white tower;
through the lips of my skull shall pour the anemones,
the yellow aconites will drip from my ear
while campion and lilyoak leap from my spine,
and no one will know how I came to these lands.
Sweetheart, the hyacinths are breaking in my heart
And the rose of Christ is flowering in my empty hands.

January 14th . . . LAST night I dreamed of Bergery. I have
been having nightmares, perhaps because I have been working
too hard on revising the poem. When I think of Bergery he was
always ten times larger than life, physically larger, a tremendous
tower of a man, and now in my dreams he was larger still. I saw
him coming up to the coast of France, wading knee-deep across
the sea, and all the time fresh wounds would appear on his
body. His head was not bandaged, but the hair was matted with
blood; and there were wounds on his hands and arms and
thighs. And as he came forward that tremendous forehead and
the great heavy face seemed unchanging; it did not move, and he
did not seem to be breathing. Some terrible mechanic force led
him onward. And then, either in my dream or in a waking vision,
I remembered that he was like my airman in the elegy, and he

was returning from America to his own land. He was bloody and unbowed, quietly undemonstrative, singularly calm; and the mechanic force was so great, and his own power so fearful, that nothing in the world could prevent him from landing on the coast of France.

I do not dream about him often. I think that as soon as the dream begins I involuntarily turn away from him, afraid to see once more on the cliffs of Szechuan that small heap of rubble and the wooden cross. I can see him more clearly when I am waking than when I am sleeping, and it is not even necessary to summon him from the shades. He comes unannounced into all my thoughts and fears. He is the loadstar by which everything is measured, and he must remain so until the end of time.

J. was talking about dreams. "I dream of Hitler and Tojo—I cannot help it. This is how we are made. Mythology begins in dreams, and now a new mythology is growing up. Ten thousand years hence people will still dream of Hitler and Tojo, and even when their names are forgotten they will be a power for evil in the world."

I had written something like this, but I have never heard it so well stated.

January 15th . . . I HAVE more admiration for the Chinese Professors than for almost any other group of men. For six years they have been attempting to uphold the traditional values of Chinese culture, and they have succeeded more brilliantly than anyone dared to believe. They live like Diogenes—wherever there is room for a chair, a table and a bed. They have few books. They are continually on the verge of starvation, and they are almost completely unconscious of the heroism of their lives. They have travelled across China, from one end of the continent to the other, and today the three greatest Universities in China, whose line of descent can be traced back three thousand years, consist of small mud buildings erected on a deserted graveyard. The students and the professors—it is difficult to think of them without emotion, for all that is best in China is crystallised in their presence. They live in small dusty rooms, where there are few or no books and where the paper windows have been torn to ribbons by the wind; and here, almost forgotten by the outside world, they prepare themselves for the final battle which must be won after the War.

This afternoon one of the students told me that a girl student was ill and had asked to see me. The day was very hot, and the gulls and rooks were squawkling high above the campus in the branches of the lime-trees. We walked through the dust of the deserted streets, for it was noon, and no sounds came from the sleeping houses. The student began to talk of his escape from Pekin. It had taken him forty days to travel across the whole length of China. He had been luckier than most, for he found willing helpers all along the road. He had stayed for ten days in Lanchow, five days in Chengtu and perhaps a day in Chungking. On the day before he left Pekin, he invited a Japanese officer to dinner, and they had made plans to visit the Western Hills on the following Saturday. "It was necessary, you understand," the student said. "There are a few Japanese who are courteous, and even a few who are understanding. They know that they have not long to remain in China and they are prepared to help us to escape, or at least not to prevent us. I was sorry for him. I knew he would wait for me, and all the way across occupied China I thought of him waiting there. It seemed so extraordinarily discourteous, and he had never been discourteous to me."

I burst out laughing. It was extraordinary that a Chinese student should pay so much respect to a Japanese officer.

"Oh, they are not as bad as all that. In every group of a hundred Japanese, there is one who is intelligent. It is true that there are forty who are murderers, and perhaps another ten who are soulless officials, mere machines who dedicate themselves to the task of suppressing the Chinese. Then there are ten who are confirmed opium smokers—they have fallen into the trap they have laid for the Chinese. But there is always *one* who knows that he has not long to remain in Pekin, and after the War, of course, no Japanese will be allowed in our city."

He seemed extraordinarily sorry for the Japanese, and I could not help remarking that I had only met one who possessed dignity, and he was a peasant who surrendered at Changsha and possessed the dignity of all peasants.

"The peasants—yes," the student answered. "You see them marching through the streets of Pekin. Some of them are bullies, and have no idea what they are doing, and those are mostly peasants who have lived near large towns. But the peasants who have been conscripted from the country can be recognised at once. They come to Pekin. They are overwhelmed by its beauty. Some Japanese are told that Pekin was built by the Japanese, but very

531

few of them believe this. And so they stare at our palaces and gardens, and wonder what they are doing here, seeing the contempt on the faces of the Chinese who are still fighting, and the contempt of the Chinese who are traitors. Wherever they go they are despised. Wherever they go, they are outnumbered. There is nothing in the whole world quite so horrible as to belong to an army of occupation. They know that they may be murdered at any time, and most of them know that the time is soon coming when they will have to run helter-skelter to the coast. So they bring their *geishas* and pretend to enjoy the scenery, which is so unlike the scenery in Japan that they walk with their mouths open, marvelling like lunatics at the beauty of the northern plains and the greatness of Pekin."

He had been stopped at a village near the frontier by a bearded Japanese soldier who threatened to kill him if he did not surrender all his valuables. He surrendered them with good grace—a few dollars, a few pieces of jewellery, for there was nothing else. Afterwards, when he had surrendered his possessions, the Japanese soldier made a drunken dive at him with a bayonet, and he escaped only because a military car was passing, and the Japanese soldier had sense enough to draw himself up at the salute.

"They are trying to demoralise the Chinese, but inevitably they are demoralising themselves," he explained, and pointed to the blue lake riding among the elm-trees and it was clear that he was half living still in the experiences of his journey.

We walked through dusty lanes, where children were playing the same games that they play everywhere else in the world. With a sharp stick they cut squares in the dust, and marked the squares with magic numbers. Then they jumped or hopped into the squares, squealing with delight. An enormous black pig, the feet fastened to two bamboo-rods carried on the shoulders of coolies, swayed and squeaked menacingly as it was carried down the street. The children paid no attention to the pig. Immersed in their game, they shrieked with delight, and it was only when we had passed that they looked up and shouted after us: *"Ding hao!"* with their thumbs uplifted—the sign with which they greet all foreigners.

"In Pekin the children are silent," the student said. "This is partly because there is so little rice and the rice is so badly distributed, and so they are silent with hunger, but it is also because they feel menaced by the Japanese. The Japanese are everywhere.
532

she had been telling the story of her life), was so beautiful that it seemed as though she had risen through all the generations of Chinese history and no longer belonged to the present age. She was a court beauty in the palace of Huang Ming, the great Emperor of the T'angs. She was the Lady of the Hsiang River, who sighed for the poet Chu Yuan. She was China in all its magnificent turmoil and splendour, its humility and sorrowing pride. For surely it is on the battlefields and in the small squalid houses where the future rulers of China are learning their trade that China is most evident. The merchants who have made fortunes out of the miseries of others and all those who have lost their souls in the insensate money-making hysteria which has swept over the country are not to be counted among the great. The great are here. The soldiers, not always well-fed, marching down the streets with immense pride, the students in their dusty rooms, the professors in their cellars. . . . They have been forgotten, and those who think of China rarely call them to mind. . . .

I had been thinking in these strains, forgetting the darkness which was coming down and the storm-clouds gathering over the western mountains. Outside, the sky was blue, but rent with clouds. Inside the room only the white magnolia in the cracked vase and the girl's pale face shone in the dusky twilight, and they seemed to absorb the light and glow with a pure flame. The girl smiled and whispered something to the boy. Soon a small primus-stove was burning and we were drinking the tea she had brought from Pekin—a pale-green tea which was like some precious liqueur. We drank the health of the students who remained behind, and those who had reached Kunming; till at length, when the storm was driving into the courtyard and we heard the crackle of rain on the tiles, we left and returned to our homes.

January 16th . . . I HAVE been reading what I wrote yesterday, and even now I wonder whether anyone can understand the tragedy of the lives of students in war-time China. Perhaps in Holland, and in the occupied areas of Europe, they will understand. But there is no other nation in the world which has lost its Universities and then set out to rebuild them two thousand miles away. When I went to Changsha I saw all that remains of the once immensely wealthy University of Hunan, and the two Doric columns standing alone in the green plain have haunted me ever since.

There are times when I become wildly impatient. I cannot understand why so little is done for the Chinese Universities abroad. I have heard a Catholic Father speaking in horrified tones of the students who prefer the safety of the Universities to the desperate urgencies of the front line. But where is the safety? The Universities have been bombed almost to extinction. In every University I have been to, even in the Christian Universities of Chengtu, there are visible signs of bombardment. Chinghua University in Pekin has become a barracks and the houses where the professors lived have been turned into whore-houses. Nankai University was bombed to the ground. Today there are very few students who can spend their whole time at the University. They teach in the Middle Schools, write articles in the newspapers, work in the fields and in factories. I have never met a student who was rich enough to spend his whole time at his studies, and I have met many who are ill. In Kunming a mild form of typhus is common, and many students suffer from it. It does not kill; but it leaves them so weak that they find it difficult to concentrate. They go into hospital, raise somehow or other a hundred dollars gold for medical expenses and come out again, looking white as a sheet, with bruised eyelids and trembling hands. Those who have escaped from Central Europe must know the limits of suffering, but they have suffered for only four years. Here there are men who have suffered for six years. And it may be many more years before their sufferings are at an end.

January 18th . . . WE HAVE been discussing Chinese poetry again. There are two schools of thought—those who believe that Chinese poetry, after three thousand years of development, should begin again, and those who believe that it must contain everything that the past has treasured and make terms with the present. I asked K., two months ago, who knows more about Chinese poetry than anyone, whether he could choose two poems which were perfectly characteristic of the modern movement. He told me he has sweated blood in order to make the choice. Should he include Wen I-to's "Dead Waters"? There were young poets like Yao-pen, whom I knew at Chungking, who contained the seeds of the future, but it was impossible to choose among their present works. There were the poets who had written a single poem, there were the brilliant and charming young men like Hsu Tse-mo, whose poetry had been praised ridiculously at their

536

deaths and who had fallen into a kind of temporary tomb. Whom should he choose?

I have copied out the two poems he suggested, though they are long, because I believe that China is best represented through her poets—a belief which the Chinese themselves share to a degree which is unknown in other lands.

AI CHING

SNOW FALLS ON CHINA

Snow falls on the Chinese land;
Cold blockades China. . . .

The winds
Like melancholy old women
Closely follow one another,
They stretch out cold claws,
Tug at our clothes.
Their words are as old as the land,
Murmuring, never ceasing.

Coming out of the forest
And driving a cart,
You, O Chinese farmer,
Wearing a fur cap,
Plunge recklessly in the snow.
Where are you going?

To tell you the truth
I am a descendant of farmers.
From your faces
Full of the wrinkles of pain
I know so perfectly
How people live on the plains,
Passing hard days.

Nor am I
Happier than you.
—Lying in the river of Time
Amid waves of suffering

Which entirely overwhelm me——
Wandering and prison
Have robbed me of the most precious
   part of my youth.
My life
Like yours
Is haggard.

Snow falls on the Chinese land;
Cold blockades China. . . .

Along the river on a snowy night
One small oil-lamp moves slowly.
In that worn-out black-sailed boat,
Facing the lamp and hanging your head,
You sit. Who are you?

Oh you
Snot-haired and dirty-faced young woman,
Is this
Your house
—a warm and happy nest—
Burnt out by the enemy?
On such a night as now
You have lost your husband's protection,
And in terror of death
You trembled under the enemy's bayonets.

Aiee, on so cold a night
Numerous
Our old mothers
Wriggle away from their homes,
Like strangers
Who do not know where tomorrow's
   wheels
Will take them.
—And
The Chinese road
Is rugged,
Muddy.

Snow falls on the Chinese land;
Cold blockades China. . . .

Throughout the plains on a snowy night
Are lands bitten by war.
Numerous men of tillage
Have lost their animals,
Have lost their fat lands,
And now lie crowded
In hopeless lanes.

The hungry good earth
Looks up at the dim sky
And stretches out trembling hands
For help.

Pain and suffering of China
Wild and long as the snowy night.

Oh China,
On this lampless night,
Can my weak lines
Give you a little warmth.

PIEN CHIHLIN

PEKIN

Pekin city: flying kites on a rubbish-mound,
here a butterfly, there an eagle
painted on the blue canvas over Madrid.
Across the sea of sky, what a pity no one can see you,
Kyoto!

O trailing a trail of dust
and leaving all the passers-by in a shower-bath,
flying wheels, you swim in so shallow waters,
yet in so high spirits?

Not so dusty indeed, even they are running away
from something hot at their heels, howling over their head,

539

over everyone's head. Here it is again:
The yellow-haired wind makes a mess of this immense incense-
* pot,*
stirring up the ashes of many centuries,
sending them flying, flying, flying,
driving them into frightened horses, fierce wolves, furious tigers,
rushing, rolling, roaring along the streets,
swooping along your window-panes, giving you a puff,
swooping upon your ears'-eaves, striking off an ear,
or a glazed tile?—

"Dear me! Simply frightened me! Lucky it isn't
a bomb! Ha, ha, ha, ha!"
"Sweet is it? Enough of your fragrant dream?
No rider on your ricksha, yourself lying there as on a sofa,
lucky indeed the tile has eyes!"
"The bird's dropping has also eyes—ha, ha, ha, ha!"

Ha, ha, ha, ha, what's the fun of it?
Hysteria, you understand, hysteria!
Sad, sad,
really sad to see the child imitating the cold man,
young as he is, flying kites on a rubbish-mound,
he also hums the threadbare tune "On recalling the past . . ."
Sad, sad to hear a city of hoary trees
crying vainly,
crying, crying, crying,
homeward! where? homeward! where?
Ancient capital, ancient capital, what can I do for you?

I am a kite already severed from the string,
having stumbled on you, how could I not cling
on your dear willow-branches? You'll be my home, you'll be
* my tomb;*
just send your catkins to every bower, every tower,
never mind if my looks are day by day withering away.

That's rotten, pardon; look here,
Pekin city, flying kites on a rubbish-mound.
Yesterday the weather was really in a nice mess, wasn't it?
Old Feng complains of Heaven every spring, cursed it yesterday
540

because it crowned the city like an immense yellow tomb;
Old Wang said it looked ominous, maybe once dropped asleep
you would never see daylight any more
until the excavations of your descendants centuries later.
But today the weather is really splendid, isn't it?
See the flowering trees posed on barrows for a spring promenade,
and we'll enjoy peonies under vermilion lantern silk
(Are they now enjoying over there pink cherry-blossom?)
It's the doves' flutes that whistle in the sky,
blue silk with white doves, with no aeroplanes—
even the aeroplanes appreciating the view, I assure you,
would not be so hard-hearted as to lay eggs on these glazed tiles.

Pekin city: flying kites on a rubbish-mound.

I am not sure that I always understand Pien Chihlin's poetry, even when as here the translation is his own. In his poetry he gives me the impression of a diver leaping from an immense height into the depths of an immensely deep sea, which he has explored more thoroughly than any diver before. The sea, the air, the mountains and the rivers of China are seen through the eyes of a man so sensitive to the rhythms of landscape that his poems, even those in which the influence of the West is most dominant, have the clarity and depth of a Yuan Dynasty painting. His images are concrete and his people are living in exactly the same way that the images and people of Chinese paintings are living, caught in a casual mood of sustained eloquence and gravity, when they are least conscious of being seen. He will quote a newspaper report, a scrap from a letter, an old Chinese proverb, and invest it with a strange light of contemporary meaning and significance. "Pekin" was written in the enervating summer of 1934, when the Japanese were at the gates, and the mood of subtle hysteria and strength characteristic of the city in the days before invasion seem to me to be caught in a wonderful concatenation of sounds, so that the whole city appears to be living before our eyes. His later manner is more robust, but the traditional melancholy and even the traditional pattern of Chinese poetry remain: in "The Broken Boat" the image of the hair, the disappearing ship and the broken boat itself are exactly the images which the T'ang Dynasty poets would have chosen if they were living in this age:

541

The tide was coming in. The wave lifted to her feet
A piece of a broken boat. Without uttering a word,
She returned to her place on the rock,
And let the setting sun bestow the shadow of her hair
On a piece of the broken boat. Long, and long after
She looked again to the end of a vast sea,
But could not find the white sail she had seen before
The tide ebbed, but she could not send away
The piece of the broken boat drifting out to sea.

The melancholy of the Chinese poets is terrible. It is not for nothing that the people weep, and perhaps the crying children are no more than the poets. China is a hard land, and has always been a hard land, and yet the Chinese are nearly always happy. What is so puzzling is that some of the greatest poetry in the world should be produced by such dissimilar races as the English and the Chinese.

January 19th . . . I HAVE been dreaming of Bergery. It is difficult to imagine that he is dead. Even when I was a child, a great head very much like his startled my nightmares into peace; but what is so strange is that when I met him for the first time, I did not recognize him, though I must have known that I had seen him before. Last night I dreamed of him again. He was walking in the shade of silver eucalyptus-trees, here or in Szechuan, and speaking in a soft voice of the things we both loved. He began to speak about a journey he would like to make, from Ceylon to the Himalayas, when the War is over; and we were together in the dark forests and on the white uplands. "Do you know that in April or March in the Himalayas there are enormous white butterflies which hurl themselves up the snow crevices and die in their thousands? Some instinct, like the instinct which drives the lemmings off the coast of Norway, drives them to their deaths. Perhaps in the eyes of God our wars are no more than the flight of the white butterflies in the Himalayas, and perhaps in His eyes our wars are less beautiful." He spoke for a long time about a journey in India—a pilgrimage to all the sacred monuments. We would bathe in the Ganges, we would walk in the deserted halls of Fatipur Shikri, which Akbar raised and later abandoned; we
542

would see the caves of Ellora and Ajanta, and walk through the *ghats*. We would visit Katmandu and stay a night in the village where Buddha was born. In the forests we would come upon the pud-marks of elephants. . . .

In the morning, when I woke up, I was told that two Indian students had arrived and wanted to see me. One was a Mahom-medan from Aligirh University, the other a Hindu from Benares. They were both students of philosophy, the recondite and rather Alexandrian philosophy which appeared in the flowering of the Vedantas. They were dark, and at first they seemed strangely out of place against the pallor of the Chinese professors and students, and they complained a little of the height—for we are a mile above sea-level and in this rarefied air it is not easy to leap up staircases two steps at a time. They told me that they were the first of a great wave of students who had been invited by the Chinese Minister of Education to study in Chinese Universities.

"Do you know Chinese?"

"No, but we shall learn. It will take us a year, two years, per-haps three, before we can read easily, but all the time we shall be reading translations and learning other things." I agreed that the "other things" were equally important. They were immensely grateful. The best Chinese professors were teaching them; and though they lived in uncomfortable dormitories, and found it difficult to understand how anyone could live on the low standard of living which prevails in Kunming, they were full of enthusi-asm. They talked about India.

"Everything is changing so fast that we have no idea what is going to happen next. Two years ago we thought that Pundit Nehru would be Minister of War and Jinnah would be Prime Minister, but the Cripps scheme failed and we are still bewil-dered. The war has reached India—you notice a thousand signs of war—but there are so many people who are untouched by it that sometimes we feel frightened. The museum at Calcutta is closed, and the best of our art treasures have been transferred to Cal-cutta, and sometimes there are days when it seems that this is the only change in Calcutta. The British Government is scrupu-lously obeying its own laws, and perhaps this is the reason why we find it a little unscrupulous, for neither the Indians nor the Chinese have much sense of law." They were frightened by many things—these Indians. They could not see the future, they could not believe that India would split into two parts and at the same

543

time they saw no sign of a solution or a compromise. It was easier to talk of the Vedantas. One of the students had brought a copy of the *Bhagavad Gita,* and I suspect that he is already thinking of proselytising his Chinese friends, but he was even more interesting when he spoke about the development of modern Indian science. A. V. Hill, the secretary of the Royal Society, is in India. Recently two famous Indian scientists signed their names on the parchment scroll which he brought from London. It may be, as they say, that Indian science is the father of Arabic science, and therefore the grandfather of our own; and certainly the Indians invented decimals and were already conversant with the theorem of Pythagoras five hundred years before Pythagoras was born. But what struck them most was the adaptability of the Indians to the new wave of science which is sweeping over India. The great Tata works are small in comparison with the infinity of white stone buildings which are being erected all over India. Indian education is improving by leaps and bounds. In Bombay University there are thirty thousand students, and though this is due perhaps to the fact that no one in India can obtain a government appointment without a university degree, there is an increasing understanding of the necessity of research, and research is older in India than I supposed. They told me that in 1896 Jagdish Chandra Bose demonstrated short-wave wireless. Modern medicine also owes much to researches in the old system of Ayurveda, and even Galen appears to have inherited a great part of his knowledge from India. India is now resurgent. The changes that have taken place in the last four years are greater than those of the previous forty years; and a new renascent India, no longer forgotten among the Industrial Nations of the world, but vigorous in its newly-acquired youth, is about to take its place in the world. So they said, speaking in pure English, but preserving the quick rhythms of their native Hindustani. They seem to think that we know everything about India. Unfortunately, we know too little. We live on the other side of the Himalayas, in a world where only the headlines ever reach us. Bergery once said: "I believe that the only great result of this war will be to introduce India to China. The war will break down the Himalayas of the spirit which have divided the two most ancient cultures of the world from one another." It may be true. If it is, the two students are the forerunners of a new and incalculable conquest of the world.

I think Bergery was afraid of India. "You kick up a stone, and

544

a million black ants come out. In India fertility is terrifying." He hated the monsoon season, wherever he found it—in Malaya and Java, and even in the Philippines. The sudden cessation of air, the hopeless fight with one's temper and the heat nagging away continuously . . . he hated them all with an impatient and undeviating hatred, and perhaps this is why he chose as his resting-place a high mountain in a remote province of China.

In the summer I shall make a serious effort to go to India. I would like to see Katmandu and the Taj Mahal and Santiniketan and Fatipur Shikri and the caves of Ellora and Ajanta and have a comfortable chair to sit on and a comfortable bed to sleep in and no more of the heartache of seeing my professors worrying their heads off for the sake of their children. I suppose this is weakness, but it would be better to go away and then come back again refreshed. What is so disconcerting in Kunming is the beauty of the place and the terrible poverty of my friends. The magnolias and camellias are out; the white plum-blossom is everywhere, and the trees shine as though dipped in crystallised sugar; there are tulip flowers and azaleas and poinsettias and mountain laurel and crocuses. The lake is a heavenly blue, and the Western Mountain was gold this morning, a pure transparent gold, like a new sun rising over the lake.

January 20th . . . At week-ends the American aviators come into the city. There is a small street, hidden away among the cinemas, where they gather, striding up and down the streets in heavy furs, though the day is warm; they are immensely tall, and the Chinese who pass them have to look up at those fair-haired, gawky youths who stride down the street like gods. For gods they are. They wear a fortune of leather on their backs, and another fortune of leather on their feet. Our admiration is reserved chiefly for those who carry a Chinese flag and some mysterious inscriptions on their back. They are pilots, who may be forced to descend in some deserted place along the Salween river, alone among strangers, and the inscriptions contain advice to the peasants who may find them.

January 31st . . . Mists gather over the blue estuary of time. There are days when we can remember the precise shapes of the past, as bright as the jewels in a stereoscope, when two identical jewels are placed in the frame and they shine with a more vivid

545

light than any single jewel. In Yunnan-fu there are days which seem to have been made to be remembered as brightly as those jewels, when the blue lake shines with the lustre of a perfectly blue sky at dawn, when the air smiles with a savage inanity, so free and intoxicating and blithe. Perhaps the word "blithe" is not used any more, but does it matter? There are few enough words to describe the intoxication of air and the sudden down-rush of the wind, out of the blue sky, with the hawks and the eagles revolving overhead.

I remember leaving Vienna late at night, under the red flags of the Nazis shining like pigeon's blood in a stormy sky. It was three days after we had hidden the rifles in the telephone-box, three days of desperate failure and some accomplishment. R. had decided to ski into Switzerland. On his pale brown face there was a curious expression of certainty. He *knew* he would not be shot on the journey, and at the same time he knew the risk he was running. But his wife was to come with me. He suggested that I should put her photograph on my passport, and the Nazis still possessed a healthy respect for a British passport. "I am sure they won't touch her—they will believe you are newly married." And since his wife was beautiful, and since we both possessed a belief in the stupidity of German frontier officials, we crowded into the taxi after saying good-bye to her mother and waited for the train from the Ostbahnhof—waited—waited—— The mists gather over the blue estuary of time, but I can remember every detail of the station—the struggling porters, the Nazi gendarmerie standing there under the electric lamps, the blue bayonets glinting, the white cords at their collars, the silence of the Nazis and the heavy breathing of the Jews, the white puffs of smoke coming from the wheels of the engine and the still whiter faces of the prisoners who were drawn off the train. Time crept on snail's feet. And suddenly, late at night, as though the train itself was overcome by the thought of prolonged waiting, past endurance, we heard the thudding of the train wheels underneath and found it impossible to believe that we were really moving. It was as though we lived in a prolonged silence, and the movements of the train were some phantasmagoria outside ourselves—a phantasmagoria which was entirely understandable, because it was shared by the enamel basins and the unexpectedly clean beds in the sleeper. We were leaving Vienna. We were going to Switzerland. As in a dream we registered the existence of these two countries, yet found it impossible to believe that the train might lead us away from one and into another. And in the morning the blue lake of Zurich and the white Zurichberg lay outside the train window.

The blue lake in Kunming shines with the same winged blue light as the lake in Zurich. The air is transparent. A few reeds float on the surface. The lake is shallow, and green reeds wave in its depths. Here, too, there are small boats with high prows and battered sails, shreds or ribbons of sails softly reflecting the blue light and the granite walls of the encompassing mountains. And as we rode across the lake in a boat clustered with naked children, old women at the oars, I wondered: "Is this the end of a journey or the beginning? Am I in Zurich? Am I escaping from Austria?" All the way across the lake, I thought of the people I had seen in the train, and yet all around me the gulls were flying, and little boats set out from shore bearing a cargo of black cormorants which would later sweep below the surface of the lake and return with silver fish in their beaks, but their necks are ringed and the fish are taken from them. The hot sun rode overhead. High above us there were small white clouds shaped like the clouds in Florentine paintings. And all the way across the lake the women rowing kept up an incessant soft chant, laughing duskily under their turbans at the huge blue Liberator bombers flying high overhead.

There are times when one can live two lives at once. I was still thinking of Vienna and Zurich, I was still escaping from Austria, and sometimes I was still breathing the air of Spain. In the drowsy summer heat—for it is summer here, though the month is January—the days in Austria assumed a perfect perspective, and the war itself assumed a perfect perspective. Kunming is in the centre of the war. It has been bombed unmercifully, and it is still the main gateway to southern China, the main arsenal of the war against the Japanese; yet the place is so beautiful that we can escape at any moment into another world, where war is unthinkable and peace is taken as something so evident that no one pays any attention to it. And at that moment we began to race a small boat full of American flying officers, whose leather coats shone under the fierce sunlight, while the Chinese flag which has been painted on the backs of their coats added a splendour to the colours of the women who were rowing them to the Western Mountain.

I can more easily imagine a pilgrimage to the Western Mountain than to Mount Omei in Szechuan. The great bluff tiger head of the mountain jutting over the blue lake is so strangely and beautifully carved, the granite rock shining with so many colours, that it is difficult to believe that it is not one of the sacred mountains of China. Pien Chihlin was more interested in the weeds floating below the surface, perhaps because he is a poet and the waving weeds have some message for him which is denied to me. He lay in the bottom of the boat with his head craned over the gunwale, absorbed in the reeds, as Shelley was once absorbed in paper boats; and later in the morning, when the high yellow crest of the mountain lay above us, he made a boat of weeds and watched it capsize in the stiff feathers of wind which unaccountably arose from the west. Then, tiring of the weeds, he gazed at the small fishing-boats where women in bright red dresses were hauling great wheatsheaves of reeds to the surface, for the weeds are natural fertilisers and sometimes you will see them strewn on the bank, brown like immense hanks of tobacco, and then again you will see them carried on muleback into the surrounding farmsteads.

This was the China I have wanted to see since my boyhood. Years ago, in Singapore, a Chinese friend spoke of a mysterious lake high up in the mountains of Yunnan. It was more beautiful, he said, than any lake in Pekin. And though I have forgotten my Chinese friend for many years, I remembered his tones as he spoke of the varying colours of the water, and the great crags surrounding the lake, and the freshness of the air in a Yunnanese winter. It was all true, and yet somehow dissatisfying. The presence of the transport plane and bombers in the sky was so natural and inexplicable, for the war was both present and infinitely absent, that I wondered whether I was dreaming; and in Pien Chihlin's dreaming gaze I suspected the same incontrovertible belief that we were the victims of an imposture; and perhaps we were both thinking of our miserable rooms in the city and the contrast of a lake so green and transparent that it became unbelievable.

"There are cells where anchorites used to pray high up in the mountain," he said, "and perhaps we could live there. It would be cheaper than living in Kunming."

He was making another boat of reeds, but already we were near the shore.

Sheltered by the bamboo hood which covered the boat, we

548

had not seen the small boy who had been rowing in the stern-sheets. Now he came forward, smiling in his blue rags, and offered to accompany us up the mountain. We did not want him, for we knew the way, or at least we knew that we would not lose our way. Yet he insisted so strongly that we decided to take him with us, and as we climbed out of the boat he said proudly to the two old women who had also been rowing: "Since the boat is mine, take care of it while I am away." It was only then that we realised that the small urchin, with the brown face and thin childish arms, was the brother of the two women who carried babies on their backs.

We walked up a small sandy slope, envying the rich who possessed houses on the shore. Except for the high walls and the shapes of the windows, which remain Chinese when everything else is copied from a European pattern, they resemble the houses on the Côte d'Azur, for many wealthy industrialists in China have realised the beauty of the lake. We climbed through evergreens and palms, and came out into an upland of bamboo groves and a gateway carved with the name of Amida Buddha. It was very quiet. A few birds were singing. In a great stone pond goldfish were swimming in water which was almost black with mud. The may blossom was growing outside the yellow-roofed Yun-chi temple, and the scent of the may blossom in the southern wind was so strong that it was almost palpable. Now, though chrysanthemums, mountain laurel and magnolias are passing, the may blossom is in full bloom. On this upland everything was scented. The rocks, the earth, the roads, even the houses seem to give off the faint scent of the small red flowers on the iron-grey trees, and there are moments in this January summer when it appears as though we are living under a rain of scented petals, for the wind blows the frail flowers in our faces. And through the bamboos, as we walked into the temple courtyard, we could see the blue lake below like an immense fringed eye gazing unperplexed at heaven.

We took tea, which tasted of iron, in the courtyard, while the monks in their grey robes and blue trousers watched at a distance. There were rumours that the monks in the temple had been known to hold up stray visitors at the point of a revolver, but it was difficult to believe that these boys, who floated rather than walked among the flower-beds, were capable of inflicting injury. We heard the masons on the temple roofs, the soft thud of mallet

549

against wood, and then again, as the heat descended upon us, there was silence. This is one of the wealthiest monasteries in China. The gods at the gates, unlike those I have seen in other parts of China, are painted with pure gold and look so fresh that they seem to have been born only a few hours ago. There was a purple god with an immense forked sword, leering and baying at the visitors who entered the carved portals; and yet there was an amused expression on those twisted lips, as though in his new war-paint he enjoyed his terrible powers. Inside the temple paint gleamed. There are 108 *lohans* or gods carved out of stucco on the walls. They were not all ugly, though nearly all were deformed. There were scowling *lohans* and *lohans* who smiled through misshapen teeth; there were *lohans* with immensely long legs and another with one arm at least thirty feet high. They were painted so brightly, with so much admixture of gold, that the walls dazzled: and every corner, every niche, every crevice in the high walls was crowded with them. Somewhere, high up on the scaffolding of one of the walls, an artist was painting the face of one of the scowling *lohans*.

There is a tradition that every one of the *lohans* represents a historical person, an anchorite or a priest who is commemorated in these temples. But these gods, who possessed little dignity, painted in the most garish colours, are perhaps more representative of Yunnanese art than of Buddhism. There was a curious similarity about these figures. They had been designed by the same person, or at least by a school which possessed a peculiarly common standard. Before the great doors three immense golden Buddhas stood on high altars. From time to time a country girl came and lit candles before the giant Buddhas.

We went up the sloping road, among the fir-trees, where a few camellias were in full bloom. The lake lay at our feet, green and blue, with softly waving lights reflecting the blue mist of distant mountains. It was one of those days when the air is so luminous and so cool that the effort of walking is transformed into flying. The long slow road, the small marble quarries hidden among the pines, the sweetness of the air—all these were preparing us for the journey ahead. Then stone steps, cut into the sheer granite of the cliff, came into view. We climbed dizzily. The steps were covered with green moss and shaded with palms, and there were a few small rock-temples cut in the faces of the rock overhead where monks must have come to meditate, facing the lake, from

550

earliest times. It was so quiet that a bird chirping seemed an unpardonable invasion of our privacy.

"And when you think of all the millions of people who from time past have climbed these steps and worshipped Heaven by gazing across the blue lake," he said, and suddenly burst out laughing for no reason at all.

It was this, then, that the Taoists had contrived to do so successfully: to see the world and all its immensity, and burst out laughing at the same time, that peculiar Chinese laugh which is so abundant with the abundance of things seen and felt.

"You are laughing because you are a Taoist," I suggested.

"No, I am laughing because I am out of breath."

We had come to the top of the narrow, moss-grown stairway, we were already in sight of the little gilt temples hewn in the rock, the fat-bellied law-givers in their vivid blue and red gowns, the little cupids flying along blue waves of the roof. The temple was delightful. It was so small that no more than two or three people could enter it at once, and it was carefully preserved and newly painted. The Taoist gods were all laughing. They stared across the lake, thousands of feet high above the small boats which danced in the sun-given waters, and they were perfectly happy.

"We are all Taoists," he admitted after a while, "but what happens when a storm breaks on the mountains?" and he pointed to the wreck of an American aeroplane which had once pointed its nose and broken its back against these rocks. "What happens? Are they still smiling their indolent smile?"

There is a legend that a fish that can reach this temple from the lake is assured of immortality. I have no doubt that it is so, but I suspect that we are all fishes and we are all assured of immortality after we have seen these shining Taoist gods sitting on their thrones and gazing with laughter at the silent and placid lake. It is strange if we are not all immortal after such a journey.

"But do you know," he complained as we ran down the steps, "what is terrible is that China is not all like this. If we were thoroughly industrialised I could understand and forgive it, but we have allowed our temples and our houses to grow old, and we have not cared for them as someone has cared for this temple. You noticed there were no priests here, and this is as it should be. It is so good to think that this temple is preserved only by the goodness of Heaven."

551

He was laughing all the way down the mountain. Blue boats rocked on a blue sea. A girl's white dress fluttered among the black boughs of camellias. Once again it was as though we were wandering through fairyland, and it seemed strange that the whole of China was not like this.

"Will you ever come here again?" he asked.

"Of course."

"May I advise you not to? In China, when places are as beautiful as this it is always best not to come twice."

February 4th . . . Y. TOLD me a story of the great writer Lu Hsun, whom he had known in Pekin. Lu Hsun was a small man, and he resembled in every respect a Kiangsi farmer, with a pale waxen face, a drooping black moustache and eyes that appeared at first to be crafty, and it was only later that you realised that they were wise. Often they would go on pony rides to the Western Hills, and Lu Hsun would keep them laughing uncontrollably by describing the lives of the ponies, and how much more intelligent they were than the men who rode them. But I liked best his stories of how Lu Hsun lived in a small bare room inside Pekin (he was teaching at Pekin University), and on the walls there were little strips of paper arranged in no particular order. On these strips of paper there was perhaps a single Chinese character, or a whole sentence, and sometimes he would add a few words here and there, and this was how he built his stories together. He worked very slowly. A short story of about thirty pages would take him a whole year; but it would never be forgotten. I like to think of the room with the strips of paper, some on a level with the floor, some high up near the ceiling; and late at night he crawls from his bed, adds a single character or perhaps even a single brush-stroke to the strips near the ceiling, and returns contentedly to bed.

February 6th . . . TERM has begun again. The little tin-roofed mud houses in the campus are shining with spring. There are more ravens than ever, more than one ever believed possible.

My students this afternoon told me that during the course of the lecture I stopped suddenly, gazed out of the window and remained there for four or five minutes. I have a dim recollection of the event, but I thought it was for a few seconds. I remember that I had been thinking of an aunt of mine who had died recently in

552

France in the family property in Normandy; and suddenly I seemed to be seeing the whole of her life, her childhood, her adolescence, her sisters, I saw her hunting wild duck in the marshes and staying at the château in Polignac, I saw her riding in a landau from Tilly to Paris in the nineties, and all the gaslit brilliance of the nineties—Toulouse-Lautrec, Yvette Guilbert and a thousand others—seemed to dance before the open window looking over the grave-mounds in south-west China. And then suddenly, like the sudden explosion of sound which accompanies the entrance of a train into a tunnel, I heard my own voice saying: "When we consider the work of the later Yeats. . . ."

February 7th . . . THE wounded soldier in dark blue uniform, with the thin crimson badge of the red cross on the lapel of his coat came down the dusty road which leads to Burma. High up above his head, young soldiers were lopping the willows; sometimes a willow-branch would come crashing to the ground like the waving of a green curtain. The soldier paid no attention to the healthy, lithe young creatures overhead: his face was white as chalk, and there was purple under his eyelids. He marched on like a ghost, paying no attention to the traffic, walking in the middle of the road, dreaming like Lazarus of his tomb, and so thin that I was afraid he would die before he was out of my sight, like the soldier who died under the shade of the elms.

I do not know that I shall ever understand the mind of a Chinese soldier. These farmers' sons, who are the wealth of China, are the salt of the earth; and like salt they cleanse the wounds, and burn out the tropical contagion of the air. They are men with little hope, except in victory; they live, I am told, even on the battlefields as though they obeyed the seasons. And in the middle of a battle, the soldier will stop and pause, looking at the deserted rice-field bordered with yews and say: "O God, why don't they begin the spring sowing?"

There is a long poem by Ai Ching, called "The Man Who Died A Second Time", which begins like this:

> *When he woke up*
> *He did not know he was still alive.*
> *He had been sleeping on a stretcher:*
> *Two soldiers carried him,*
> *And they did not speak.*

The weather was frozen in the cold wind,
The clouds sank low and moved swiftly.
Speechless, the wind shook the boughs.
Swiftly, swiftly they carried the stretcher
Through the winter forest.

He had passed through the flames of pain
And his heart was now in such tranquillity
That it resembled a battlefield after the fighting:
Tranquil like this.

But still the blood
Flowed from the wound in the soggy bandage,
Drip by drip,
Falling on the winter roads of China.

And on this same night
While the stretcher-bearers carried him,
A solemn procession, ten times larger than before,
Moved up to battle.
Thousand of feet
Rubbing away the remaining stains of his blood. . . .

February 10th . . . THE music of bugles, breaking out suddenly from a soldier's camp beyond the walls, set a thousand starlings in flight; and the eagles flashing gold in the heavens, and high above the eagles a small white cloud like a benediction. And then afterwards, the soldiers moving through the dust under the winter boughs. . . .

February 13th . . . I HAVE almost forgotten Bergery, and suddenly talking to a famous Chinese philosopher I thought I heard the exact intonation of his voice. He was talking about East and West—the one subject which seems paramount, and so important that all other subjects are dimmed beside it.

"But in China," he was saying, "we have no law imposed from above. We have no canon law; our jurisprudence is not codified as it is in the West. The West believes that man is sinful, and that in some sense all sins are religious sins—witness the survival of Deuteronomy on the laws of England. But we believe that men are good; we have never formulated a religious sanction for
554

our laws. We believe that men are good; the West believes that men are evil. We believe that when a child is born, he may be the mediator between Heaven and Earth, the great sage. But you believe that he may become a hero. . . ."

February 14th . . . THINKING of my childhood, and not understanding why so much that happened in my childhood is still so significant to me. My earliest memories are brief. Sitting at the foot of the stairs and reading that the war had ended, and not knowing why; a bombardment by Zeppelins on London—again, not knowing why; two deaf old women gazing into the reflecting windows of a cabinet of porcelain; a toy theatre, the knights and the dragons carved out delicately in blue and silver paper; endlessly writing English letters and inventing new letters—how much more majestic a g looked upside down!—and playing in hay-fields beside a great red brick wall the colour of a wound. And then the airships my father was building at Cardington, the unbelievable beauty of the lithe silver framework high in the heavens—all these, and always the dead soldier in the dust. I remember the dead soldier most, and though he must have died in peace-time and though he perhaps died of *delirium tremens,* all my horror of war is concentrated still on that slender figure lying in the dust.

These are memories of summer; there are memories of winter, but none from other seasons. I remember winters most of all, the cool snow, the frost patterns on the window-pane, the deep blue of heaven and the clean white of earth. That winter—I can hardly have been more than six—I spent every day tobogganing in the snow with Sophie. She wore a red woollen tam-o'-shanter and a red woollen dress, thick leather gaiters, and her little cream-coloured legs were frosted over with lumps of snow, and later they would turn bright red. There was a vast park with a lake, where black Australian swans preened themselves. There were peacocks nearly as tall as I was, and gate-keepers who were the image of God. We would go sliding down immense precipices, perhaps no more than twelve feet high; and I can still feel the stuff of the snow on my cheeks and hear the grating of the ice-crystals against the smooth hickory sleighs. All this was winter, a time of mounting excitement and capricious fortune, winters of content which have comforted me throughout my life. There would come days when the red roofs of houses would begin to show beneath the sodden crusts of damp snow, days when winter was visibly disappearing round the corners of the street. The trees were no longer white, nor were the windows covered with the miraculous patterns of frost; and no longer was the cold bed an inviting challenge each night—a bed whose ice-cold chastity had to be loved and tenderly placated each night, until sleep came to drowsy eyelids. In summer there was hay-fever, measles, whooping-cough, all the torments of the damned.

Children born in the country are conscious of the four seasons: their lives are at least twice as rich as the lives of the city-born. I think of Bedford now always under the snow, yet the place where we went tobogganing seems to have no connection with the park —it belongs to another world altogether. Though I remember perfectly the small pine-trees shrouded in frost and the crunch of the snow-crystals on the hickory sleighs, I remember little more. I was born in winter, and all the snows of the world are my accomplices in life. It seems that the world is timeless and spaceless in childhood; the eye is as innocent as the air we breathe; the touch of hands, the colours and the smells are more real and more enduring in childhood than at any other time. It is stupefying to realise that by the age of ten all the experiences of life have been accomplished. You have fallen in love, you have been deserted, you are alone and at the same time you belong to a community of children whose existence is absolute in your eyes; and nothing remains except the tedium of a later age. The crying of a child has always terrified me. I know, for I remember perfectly, that those things we cried about in childhood are as terrible as anything that brings tears in age. . . .

February 20th . . . He was a young student, like so many students, and he had just come from Pekin. He was not tall, and his eyes were very bright, not black but golden. He had the full face of the northern Chinese, and all the charm of youth.

"Prices have gone up in Pekin," he said. "Nothing is being sent there. Since last June we have eaten black bread and powdered meal. Our rice, our chickens, our pork, our cows are taken to Japan. There was a time when we still lived well, but that time is over—there is as much starvation in Pekin as there is in the unoccupied provinces. Now that the war is coming to an end, the Japanese are becoming more ruthless, and the traitors are becoming more afraid."

556

The Japanese soldiers he had met were afraid of the bombing. They spoke with great respect of the Allied aeroplanes, and their own large aerodrome on the south of Pekin and the great barracks to the west were heavily guarded with anti-aircraft guns. And still they were afraid. They would take you in a corner and whisper: "I have a great love for China, I have killed nobody—not even a dog. If the Allies come, will you protect me?" And all the time, with a ruthlessness which passed all description, they were murdering, murdering, murdering. . . .

"In the Japanese gendarmerie they have left the blood-stains on the wall. Students disappear. Only the schools where there are German professors are protected, and no one believes it will last long. We are taught Japanese ten hours a week; there are four hours of Chinese, and only two of English. And the Chinese professors teaching English are mortally afraid—they fear that just because they know English they will be arrested; so they deliberately teach badly."

He spoke of the journey south, along one of the great medieval trade-routes.

"We dare not carry anything, not even our school certificates. A typewriter may mean death—they will assume you are learned, smash the typewriter before your eyes and haul you off to prison. I came in winter. There had just been a terrific explosion inside the city—the *Pa lu chun*, the Eighth Route Army had sent in a detachment of dare-to-dies and blown up a magazine. The Japanese were restive. They made arrests everywhere, and not a single one of those whom they arrested was responsible for the explosion. We all suffered. They took more and more food off the market. They are devils, but they are afraid."

He talked of the journey through the wilderness of snow.

"I remembered a poem by Ai-ching. It was terribly real to me. I recited it all the way across the hills, and it used to move me to tears:

> *"Winter is lovely in no colour.*
> *Winter is lovely for no birds sing.*
> *In the winter forest a solitary walk is happiness;*
> *I will be like a hunter, lightly passing over,*
> *Nor do I think I will gain anything.*

"There were four of us, and at night we would sing ourselves to sleep. We brought with us an old teacher—a *lao shueh*, and we

557

attended him—it was exactly like the journeys of the T'ang Dynasty. I felt then for the first time how ancient China is. We were continually repeating events that happened thousands of years ago. Nothing changes in China, her youth least of all. And sometimes as we sat by the fire it was strange to pick up a piece of old newspaper and notice the date: we seemed to be thousands of years before our time."

February 25th, The Floods of Spring . . . THE children with bare legs were jumping in the great pools in the street. The sun shone; the pools were blue; the legs were golden. They were drenching one another in sheer joy of life, and as we passed T. whispered: "If only we could recapture their love for water and life."

February 27th . . . HE WAS squat and short, with an eagle nose and a terrific power of command. At first I thought he was Rewi Alley—a paler and younger Rewi Alley. He had come down from the north-west, where he was managing a cotton co-opera-tive, and he was full of his plans for the future; and I noticed that when he talked about Rewi, his voice was sweeter and he spoke with bated breath, as of a god.

He was full of his co-operatives.

"What was extraordinary was that Rewi had hit on something that was absolutely Chinese, and yet the Chinese had forgotten it. The co-operatives are as old as China—Rewi insists that the Shang and Chu bronzes are the products of co-operative craftsmen, and there is good evidence for it. In those days workmen were held in great respect. In the *I Li* it is related that the lesser members of a visiting court would be boarded with the families of crafts-men and merchants. And right through Chinese history, from the time when the Chinese lost their nomadic grazing economy and arrived at an agricultural irrigation culture, the same forces have been at work. Rewi knew a great deal about the overseas Chinese; he saw them creating their guilds, and becoming more powerful as the influence of the guilds increased, but when he came to Shanghai, though the guilds were still in evidence, the smaller craftsmen were working independently—they were shut out from the power of the guilds—and he saw all the terrible results of the closed door. He thought it would be best if all the Chinese, every single Chinese farmer or craftsman belonged
558

to a guild. The overseas Chinese gold-digging in New Zealand, the bakers of Suva in Fiji, the carpenters in Raboul, the store-keepers in the Rand, they were all members of the guilds. The whole wealth of China has risen from her guilds, and when the war came and China was impoverished, he looked to some sign that the guilds would revive their influence. It had happened before, and there was no reason why it should not happen again. In the days of the Sixth Emperor, the reformer Wang An-shih had attempted to imbue the Chinese with a sense of collective responsibility. There was, for example, the system of 'pao chia'— every ten families formed a 'chia' or a tithing, fifty families formed a great tithing, and ten great tithings formed a head tithing. The whole tithing was made responsible for the offences of any member, just as today in every street in China there is one man who is responsible for the offences of all the others. But in Wang An-shih's time, and in spite of the failure of his reforms, the principle of responsibility seems to have gone deeper than it has ever gone since—he smashed the pawn-shops, gave loans to farmers at two per cent interest, he tried to do away with the middle-man and he encouraged all those small groups of artisans. . . . What Rewi has been doing is nothing new. It is as old as China. . . ."

March 1st . . . BEHIND high walls, cut off from the rest of the world, lie the courtyards. Walking down the narrow lanes at night, listening to the *chink-chink* of mahjong tiles or watching a blue-quilted ricksha with rubber tyres and an immense silver lamp deposit a girl in silks at the small gate cut out of the walls, you are once more in the China of your dreams. It is impossible to know what is happening behind the walls. A sudden scream, the yelping of a dog, a light inexplicably waving among the green boughs of the trees—and at once your imagination is riding among legends. You imagine that the beautiful girl with the faintly overhanging lip is a concubine, the daughter of a peasant who sold her to a general or a merchant prince, and perhaps you will not be wrong. You try to imagine her whole life—the life of the slim creature in the white silk-embroidered dress—and always your imagination trembles, not knowing where to turn. In the lives of all these women there is mystery; and as you go down the dark street, blindly treading over dead dogs and black pools of refuse, you wonder interminably at the fate which has brought you to China.

March 2nd . . . R., who has been reading part of this diary, looked up suddenly so that the electric light shone on his long northern face.

"But you have made us much more idealistic than we are," he said.

"But you are idealistic," I replied. "I have never met such people. You are idealistic and practical, and that is why it is impossible to doubt the great future of China."

He talked about all the problems which sometimes make him cry out in despair—the underfed soldiers, the bribery, the hoarding and the corruption, all the sins of the bureaucracy and the still greater sins of the merchants.

"How can we have hope in the future when we see all this around us?" he said, and he seemed to be pleading against hope for still more hope to combat the invisible enemies. "Admit that we are good when we are young—it is true, for there is nothing quite so idealistic, so handsome, so capable and practical as a young Chinese. But when he gets older, what happens? He is caught in the net. He has to be a man of steel if he expects to escape."

He was worried. He could see the future, dark and menacing; and there was only this future. The youths from the Universities would go out and become merchants, spiritually bankrupt, hostile to change, utterly efficient in the tasks of bribery.

He stood up, and the light glowed on his high, noble forehead: "But it won't happen this time!" he exclaimed. "We are determined that it won't happen. And yet sometimes, walking in the street at night, watching the limousines crowded with the concubines of generals, I hope against hope."

March 3rd . . . THE geologist had been down to Indo-China before the war, and when we were talking of a possible invasion of Kunming—a last desperate effort by the Japanese to cut off the Burma Road at its source—we listened quietly, for we knew that he knew more than any of us.

"It's terrible country—all rocks, hills, sharp ravines. No tank could cross this country. The Imperial Army would have to go through the ravines along the river-beds, and there we could
560

bomb them mercilessly from the air. We could roll boulders on them." The idea of the boulders delighted him. "If they come along this way, I'm going to join the army. I know where the boulders are. A little stick of dynamite—just to set the boulder going—and four or five hundred Japanese soldiers riding on donkeys will be buried, and never be seen again." He was really delighted beyond words. The thought of *squashing* the Japanese was almost enough to make him forget the miseries of exile.

March 4th . . . T. is an authority on the rains. Whenever it is raining, he will tell me how long it will last, the direction of the winds, the nature of the clouds. Today, as we walked down the evil-smelling street which leads from the North Gate, a thunder-burst surprised us, and we took shelter in an arched doorway. "When it rains in summer, you will be astounded," he said. "So much rain, and such a little sky. It's extraordinary." He spoke of the nature of the monsoons, but his conversation was so technical that I have forgotten most of it. And then suddenly the rain ceased and a girl coming along the road shook off her wooden sandals and bathed her feet, and a moment later a hundred children, coming out of the side-streets, running helter-skelter, also began to bathe their feet, until the air was full of cries of laughter. . . .

March 7th . . . I HAVE been translating Chu Yuan again, partly because Bergery loved him, partly because it seems so extraordinary that the greatest of all Chinese poets should remain untranslated. There are good translations by a Japanese of Li P'o, but there are no good translations into English of Tu Fu or Chu Yuan. It is time that we got down to understanding the great wealth of Chinese culture, the tremendous treasures which are still unknown to the West.

Even now we half believe that at the beginning of Chinese civilisation there was little poetry; and all the hosts of the Yellow Race were barbarians fighting for their lives. We believe them to have been untutored; and vaguely we know that at some period in their existence they became suddenly civilised, producing exquisite pottery, fine paintings, delicate tiles, gossamer silks. We forget that these things grew slowly into their maturity, and from the beginning the Chinese possessed the arts of delicacy.

Here are three poems of Chu Yuan which were written over

two thousand years ago by the Chief Minister of a state in his exile:

THE GREAT UNITY, THE SOVEREIGN OF THE EAST

On this auspicious day, at the felicitous hour,
With long swords and jade guards in our hands,
With girdles of lapis lazuli tinkling ling-lang,
We offer jade gifts on mats of fairy grass,
Holding up fragrant grasses and jades.
We pour libations of pepper juice and cinnamon wine.
The drum-sticks are raised; we beat the drums.
Psalters and zithers unfold in a great harmony:
The ministrants dance in flowing silks and resplendent robes
A wafting fragrance fills the spaces of the hall,
And the five tones in crowded chorus sing:
Glory and gladness to the happy lord!

THE JUNIOR ARBITER OF FATE

... Whom are you waiting for among the clouds?
With you I wander the Nine Rivers.
The whirlwind and the waves arise.
With you I will bathe my hair in the pool of Hsien.
Let me dry your hair on the slopes of Yang.
Waiting for the beautiful one who has not yet come;
Facing the wind I sing my mad strains aloud.
With a roof of peacock feathers, pennons of kingfisher,
Ascending the Nine Heavens, weaving among comet-tails.
Grasping the long sword and protecting the heavenly virgins.
O you alone are fitted to be the leader of the people.

THE GOD OF THE RIVER

With you I wanaer the Nine Rivers.
The whirlwind and the waves arise.
Riding the water chariot with the roof of lotos leaves,
I am drawn by two dragons and the hornless serpent.
Climbing on K'ung Lung Mountains I look in the four
*   directions,*
My spirit wanders over the face of the deep.

The day is waning. Bemused, I forget my home,
Dreaming of the furthest reaches of the river.
In an abode of fish-scales, in a hall of dragons,
Under archways of purple-shell, in palaces of pearl,
O spirit, why do you dwell in the waters?
Riding the white tortoise and chasing the carp,
I wander with you among the small islets.
The swift-flowing freshet comes whirling down-river.
With a gentle bow you turn towards the East.
So I escort the beautiful one to the south anchorage.
Wave after wave comes to welcome me;
Multitudes of fishes bid me farewell.

March 13th, In Search of Wu San-kwei . . . I HAD gone up
the narrow staircase, where the steps were eaten by bole-weevils
and the wood was coloured with green fungus, expecting to find
the young scholar who is famous all over China for his researches
in the Ming Dynasty, but found only his children who were copy-
ing flower paintings from a book written in the age of the Mongol
Emperors. They were sitting at his desk, their lips and cheeks
coloured with faint lines of blue, green and red, the little pigtails with their brightly coloured ribbons sticking up vertically.

I did not know how long I should have to wait, and I felt
ashamed of being seen with his children in the room, for they
were so intent on their work. It was getting late. Through the
paper windows came the faint white light of the hidden sun. At
last the professor came in, very young, wearing thick spectacles,
a little stooped, and so gentle that it seemed impossible to believe
that the heavy steps on the stairway came from him.

"Ah, Wu San-kwei," he said. "You want to know all about Wu
San-kwei. Nothing could be easier." He took down a book from
his shelves, a long folio book printed on rice-paper and covered
with the yellow boards which indicate that the book was once in
the imperial collection at Pekin. And slowly, while the light
faded and the children continued to paint their flower paintings,
he read out the story of the prince who defied the Emperor, ruled
over a quarter of China, hating the Mings and the Ch'ings with
an equal hatred and dying at last reviled and almost forgotten by
the people of China.

". . . His palace was in Kunming, not far away from the
present Governor's yamen. He made the lake which you can see

563

now, and in the centre he erected a palace, of which nothing remains, called 'The Palace of the Crystal Wave'. And there he lived with the 'round-faced beauty' whose tomb you have seen and who died perhaps in the compound of the University. He was a short man, dark-faced, with a mole on the bridge of his nose; he was superstitious, cunning, eager for power. The Ming Emperors were wandering over the south of China, the Ch'ings were in power in the north and gradually extending their influence in the south. It was at this time that Yung Li, escaping from Foochow into Kwangsi, came under the influence of Wu San-kwei. Wu San-kwei pretended the most extreme loyalty and offered the young Emperor the protection of his own forces in Yunnan. The Emperor accepted this protection, but he was uncertain of Wu San-kwei's intentions, and when there came to his ears rumours of a plot against him—Wu San-kwei was known to be jealous of imperial power—Yung Li escaped over the border of Burma at Teng-yeh. Wu San-kwei determined to follow him. He sent embassies to Burma. He did everything possible to encourage the surrender of the Chinese Emperor. The Burmese, then as now, were treacherous. They captured the Emperor in an island. He was trussed up like a hen, and still trussed he was carried by sedan-chair to the frontier, where Wu San-kwei was waiting for him with a Manchu guard. The Emperor suspected the worst. He was not wrong, but for a long time he managed to hide his fears from himself, for now he was no longer bound and the Manchu guards whispered to him that he would soon be saved. And this was indeed the intention of the guards, who openly rebelled before the procession reached Kunming. The rebellion was short-lived. The Emperor, with his round face, protuberant forehead and long black silky beard had a face which we describe as 'trusting'. He trusted too much. The guards were killed, and among them there was an enormous giant over eight feet tall whose life lingered an unconscionable time in his body, so that they had to hack him to pieces before they were satisfied that he was dead. The Emperor continued his pilgrimage. The peasants offered fruits, which he dared not accept for fear they were poisoned. At this time Wu San-kwei found it profitable to pretend that he was a vassal of the Manchu Regent Ao Pai and sent emissaries to Pekin to enquire on the proper fate of an Emperor. Soon the answer came back that he was to be executed. There were signs and portents. The peasants were afraid. A shooting star fell on

564

the Serpent Mountain. The sky was overcast; the air thick with dust. This was the moment chosen for the execution. Wu San-kwei, who believed in oracles, was afraid, yet he dared not at this time seek to change the verdict of Pekin. The Emperor was strangled. . . ."

This was all that I wanted to know, but the quiet voice went on, describing the fate of the Emperor's wife and mother, who were sent on to Pekin. Tea was served in flowered cups. The children were no longer painting.

"We have this in common," the historian smiled. "We, too, have murdered our Emperors. . . ."

March 15th . . . THE children playing in the courtyard were acting a play. They had smeared their faces with white paint; the little boy held a paper sword and pretended to charge the invisible hosts of the enemy. Then it rained, and the paint fell away from their faces, but still they played. And all this might have happened anywhere else in the world except for one thing: they had all placed cardboard caps on their heads on which was written in great running Chinese characters: "American tank, American aeroplane."

March 16th . . . THE professor leaning over the test-tube in which a green sediment was boiling smiled happily. "This is an experiment of a particularly important nature," he smiled. "I am seeing whether cracked glass test-tubes can be riveted together. So far the experiment has been successful." The sediment turned brown, the silver cracks in the glass could be seen quite clearly now. He heaved a sigh of relief, and gazed with almost paternal affection at the small pile of tubes which had been cracked in their long journey from Pekin. "But of course only the most elementary experiments are possible. The matter which rivets them has to be taken into account."

In Paris I used to pass Mme Curie's old laboratory every day. Today in the campus of the greatest University of China, I see the same terrible dowdy buildings in which experiments of tremendous importance are being carried on. To these professors and students there is nothing so heart-breaking as the interminable lack of equipment. There was one test-tube which was cracked beyond repair. I took it home—it will be placed reverently in the same drawer as the papers I found on the battlefield of

Changsha and the grains of yellow earth which a friend brought me from Pekin.

March 20th . . . NEARLY every day the Governor's *mafu* leads a superb white horse down to the parade-ground outside the North Gate. There, in a green bowl of grass, surrounded by grave mounds and the low-lying purple hills, with rice-fields under water in the distance, the wild colts are playing with their manes streaming and their long silky tails stretched out like shining spears. I do not know any place so peaceful as the parade-green in the late afternoon. Usually there are a few thunder-bearing clouds on the horizon; a few idlers are gazing from under the shadow of trees; a coffin of unpainted white boards is being carefully removed through the white-washed gate at the end of the hospital wall, school-children are playing in the dust and a few bright aeroplanes are flying low overhead. But the colts are streaming like the wind in the green basin, and they alone have the air of *authenticity*. The rest is unreal, terrifying or irrelevant. And now I remember seeing a Chinese painting of some young colts playing in a field. It was a painting of the Yuan Dynasty, and there were such jade-green trees and lake-blue mountains in the distance. Everything was exactly the same, but the Chinese painter had improved on nature by making the horses ten times larger than life and the small boy sitting at the foot of the almond trees was ten times smaller than life. And yet you did not notice the incongruity. So it is now, while the rose-dappled colts jump invisible hurdles, rub their necks, trot eagerly and capriciously among the tall green grass. . . .

March 21st . . . OUR clothes are in rags. There is hardly a single professor and hardly a single student whose clothes are whole. And yet there is no complaint, even though it is beginning to rain continuously. "A man who pays attention to food and clothes can never be a Sage," said Confucius. So we wander with holes in our socks and at our elbows, and no one is ashamed.

T. showed me his shirt yesterday. With his coat on, he looked superbly well dressed in comparison with others. But with the coat off you saw a network of holes joined together with pieces of silk and string.

"But you should see me in my best gown," he murmured. "It smells of moth-balls, but once a week I take it out and look at it.

566

It is of pure silk, perhaps a hundred years old, for it belonged to my grandfather. No, I have refused to sell it—whatever happens I cling to my gown. When I go to Pekin, I shall wear the silk gown. . . ."

March 22nd . . . Matches cost twenty dollars a packet, and only a few of them strike fire. A bottle of ink costs three hundred dollars, and last week I gave the smallest of small dinners to three friends and found that even without wine it cost over two thousand. Only the millionaires and the very poor can afford to live here—"or the brave," added T., "for the brave have nothing to lose but their courage, and we are almost brave, for we live on hopes." A little while later he said: "It is a terrible fact, but we have learnt more about our countrymen from the inflation than from the war. Do you know, we started this war with the highest of all imaginable hopes; we are ending it with the same hopes, but we know now that we must learn to be rigorous against the enemies in our midst. Merchants must be taught. . . ." There was an extraordinary bitterness in his voice, and though I remembered that he came from a long generation of scholars, who had never taken part in business, I knew that he would fight against them with all his power.

March 24th . . . It has been raining all day. At night the rain comes through the roof and falls on my bed. I console myself this was the constant complaint of the great poet Tu Fu. But this afternoon I had my revenge. By pasting paper on the roof, it was possible to make the rain fall along the tiles outside, with the result that a perpetual waterfall falls outside my window, and I see the bare camellia trees and the great silver eucalyptuses through a curtain of silver rain. . . .

March 25th . . . "But where are we coming to?" T. exclaimed in alarm. He held in his hand a history of the world in two thousand pages in which China is mentioned on perhaps twenty pages. "This is extraordinary. Do you think it is possible that we don't belong to the world? All our arts, all our conquests. . . . And yet they write these things. . . . It is really most extraordinary!"

Sadness and pity glowed on his handsome northern face. "I shall write a book on the history of the world," he said, "and I

567

shall give exactly twenty-five pages to the West. And all those twenty-five pages will be devoted to Jesus Christ."

I am still wondering what he meant by this.

March 26th . . . MORE microfilms are coming in, but the photographs are so badly reproduced that they resemble black squares on the screen. This evening I watched P., a great physical chemist, gazing at a black square on the screen under which had been inscribed: "Schematic molecular structure of trinitrotoluene."

Microfilms are our only contact with the literature of the outside world. Without them we are lost, and for all that come we are desperately grateful. No books have arrived in my department of the University this year. Only a few propaganda magazines come by devious routes to these empty shelves.

"If there were books, if there were really enough microfilms," P. complained, "we would be able to bear our lot with greater equanimity. But the students are crying out for books, they want to plan the reconstruction of China, and this is the only thought in their heads—and so few books come, so few microfilms——"

He shook his head sadly and turned the projector slide. Another great square on the screen. "Schematic structure of the molecules of molybdenum."

March 27th . . . "BUT where do we go from here?" He was talking in a quiet voice with the faintest trace of an Oxford accent. "Bombs, torture, the killing of defenceless people. . . . Perhaps the war should last another ten years, for if it ends too soon we may not have learnt the lesson that the state exists for only one reason—to safeguard those who cannot guard themselves." And he went on a little later: "There is one thing that is still true, and we must write it up in letters of gold over all the village yamens of China, a statement—and it is the only statement which remains true of our time." We were silent before the words of the distinguished Chinese sociologist. Someone suggested the word "God"; someone else suggested "Heaven"; someone else suggested "Liberté, Egalité, Fraternité". He smiled: "I meant the opening sentence of the American Declaration of Independence."

March 29th . . . THE bird fluttering through the open window alighted on my desk. It was a golden-crested woodpecker with a long yellow beak. I have always hoped to be able to see
568

him at close hand, for he flies all day among the plum-trees far away in the garden. He was so close that I could see his heart beating and the faint silvery feathers under the breast. And this evening a huge moth, green and gold. . . . Is this an augury?

April 3rd . . . In an old letter-case I have found thirty or forty letters from Bergery written during the last seven years. They begin formally, almost roughly, for he could never write well to people he did not know. Afterwards they become more intimate, and they seem to disarm criticism with their smiles; but suddenly the thunder is aroused, they move with terrible speed, the handwriting becomes bolder and seems to leap from the page. It is then that he is at his best, for when he was wild he was still superbly controlled, and laughter flickers here and there through the strain of the coming war.

". . . and then I tell you with my heart's blood that we must build again—build, build out of children, out of innocence, out of the weight of a pear falling from a tree, out of the softness of rivers, out of learning, out of a starlit night the inhuman, because more than human, features of a future which we can love as we adore the sun. Oh, the urgency of it! Sometimes I feel that this war is only a storm breaking over the affairs of men, and we know from Lao Tzu that 'a storm cannot last a whole day, nor can the rain last for ever'. We see the flash of intermittent lightning, we do not see the sunlit peace. And yet it will come, not in my lifetime and perhaps not in yours, but we must work for it— every moment of our lives we must work for it. . . ."

"And then I ask myself how many of us have a sense of dedication. This above all. . . . Do you know, I felt at Geneva that not a single statesman was dedicated to peace. None had Amundsen's courage. They were fighting for place, for position, for the fruits of honour, and none knew that the greatest honour was the opportunity to serve the peace of the world. I have only met one ambassador who seemed to have been dedicated wholly and completely to peace. And this gaunt rugged Scotsman, with the courage of a lion and the manners of a courtier in Versailles, seemed to be like the Chinese Sages who by the power of their love for Heaven can walk unarmed and unarmoured among the lions, though he was himself a lion. This was real greatness, and since greatness is rare and hardly exists except among youths in

569

this war, it should be remembered that England produced at least one statesman who loved peace and hated war. . . ."

"The worst day of my life. Years ago. In an ambassador's garden in Pekin. The first secretary holding the hands of a Polish prostitute, and a foreign merchant entirely drunk shouting abuse at a Chinese scholar. 'You think you have got the measure of us. You haven't. You are still our slaves. We came out and conquered, and by God we are here to conquer and stay.' O God, God, God, have mercy, have mercy. . . ."

"With all my heart I know that we must make this world anew. We must find new laws, and we must obey them. And what laws are better than the laws of scholars and scientists—the silent unselfish application to truth? These shall be our models. We shall throw out all the damned hereditary aristocracy of money and position, and we shall put in their place mathematicians, Latinists, musicians, poets, writers and jurists. There will be no place for the diplomatic careerist in the world of the future. No longer shall we send ambassadors to Germany, who are well acquainted only with South American politics, and have no knowledge even of good German. We must begin anew. All our foreign relations must begin again. There must be embassies of peace among the youths; there must be constant interchange of scholars. Dante, Petrarch and Boccaccio were all scholars and ambassadors. We must do away once and for all with a system by which the representatives of countries are like the famous von Bülow, 'who pleased the Emperor but failed to please himself'. We must start again, and at this hour the beginnings of things are more important than their ends. We must learn again, from the very beginning, from the trees, from the laughter of children, from the strange shapes in rocks and from low-flying clouds that there is an art in love and all of us are ignorant of it. A great Chinese statesman of an earlier generation wrote a pamphlet with the significant title 'Learn'. So we must learn in all humility from the very beginning. . . ."

April 4th . . . On THE blue lake the soldiers were hanging out their washing beside the golden pagoda. All round the lake there is a kind of moat, covered with green duckweed, oily with the refuse of years, but the girls come down from their small houses and courtyards buried in dark streets and with their hands they clear a place in the moat and wash their clothes. After-
570

wards, kneeling in the sunlight, they scrub the blue cotton until
shines in the sun.

It was a heavenly day, the sun very high, the pagodas glitter
ing. Every day when I wander round this city I seem to find a
new lake. Yesterday, in the public gardens, I found an oval lake
among some fir-trees; soldiers lay in the long grass, horses were
rubbing their necks against the warm rocks, but what struck me
as more beautiful than any of these were the three misshapen
rocks in the centre of the lake. They were pure white and perhaps the height of a small boy. But they were carved so delicately, there were so many shadows, and they possessed so many
facets that I began to realise for the first time the terrible affection the Chinese possess for strange rocks. Through the firs a soldier wandered arm in arm with his girl, and it seemed suddenly
that this place was entirely removed from life, it was fairyland,
it was the Chinese earth. And even when a wounded soldier came
down the narrow lanes between the firs, it was still fairyland, because it was still China.

April 9th, Easter . . . The bells of the churches were ringing this morning. Over the broad sea of blue sky the white gulls
which have been hovering for days now made their way across
the lake to the low-lying blue mountains in the distance. The sun
danced, and you forgot even the coffins which the soldiers carry
on their backs, you forgot the heart-rending poverty amid plenty,
you forgot the inflation and the painted girls in the black limousines—you saw only this curious high sunlight which is more
delicate than anything else on the earth. Here, a mile above sea-
level, in a small town set beside a blue lake, protected by American aeroplanes, there is a freedom in the air which I have never
known anywhere else.

So we wandered in the afternoon around the blue lake, where
boys and girls were rowing in small canoes, past temples where
the goldfish abounded in pools, past the Hôtel du Lac, which has
been taken over by the Army, past the camel-back bridge and the
little kiosks which remind you of France. We must have been
wandering the whole afternoon, for when we came through the
white marble *pai-l'ou* archway, there were already thick clouds in
the sky. The famous poet was talking once again of Chou and
Han Dynasty bronzes.

"It was a time when men loved the earth," he said; "and there-

...ced bronze and iron, and made the objects of
...iful. But this time is going. Our temples are de-
...all-paintings by incompetent artists, our sense of
...ng destroyed by the inevitable collision with the

...not entirely gone," I objected, and spoke of the deli-
...rved wheel-barrows I had seen on the fields of Changsha,
...the peasants were returning to their shattered homes. "After
...war a new art will spring up, and a new literature. The Chi-
...e haven't lost their traditional virtues, and even if only a little
...the old culture remains it will flower up anew."

We had been walking through the Wen-lin Kai, and this street
of battered mud houses and rickety restaurants with the incongruous name of "The Forest of Learning" was smoking with
braziers and brilliant with electric lamps. The tea-shops were
open, crowded with students poring over their books; and sometimes a small cavalcade of cavalry would pass through the muddy
road, for it had rained during the previous night, and the mud lay
thick on the ground. At the end of the street lay the great West
Gate, and beyond it, now separated and alone, but once connected with the fifty-foot wall which surrounded the city, lay
another gate, smaller but more imposing in its suggestion of massive power.

The gates of China still seem to me to be more powerful than
the most splendid machines. They stand aloof, perfectly proportioned, with flaring roofs, buttresses, immense uncarved bricks
facing the walls of earth beneath. All over China the walls of
cities have been removed, but the gates remain. And now, in this
starlight, the unpainted but once yellow roof straining towards
the sky, the sheer slopes of the walls like plummets directed to
the heart of the earth, this gate seemed to be possessed with
supernatural powers. It was a gate through which no invaders
could pass. Solitary and alone, with its crumbling bricks gathering
on the slopes and stray horses eating the long grass which grew
among the stones, it still possessed the splendour of the ancient
dynasties. Black against the sky, towering among the stars, great
shoots of clouds winging their way past its flaring roofs, it was a
symbol of what China has been and always will be. And as
though he had overheard my thoughts, the poet was saying:
"China will last as long as her scholars and her arts endure. She
cannot fail. Like this gate, so massive, so broad, so tolerant. . . ."
572

And a little while later he said: "China will last forever. S
cannot fail, for her roots touch the earth and her spirit is contin
ally in the heavens. This gate, this tower."

I walked back alone, for he lived a little way outside the city,
in the "bad lands", where bandits sometimes come and hold professors to ransom; and sometimes I would turn round and look
up at this immense towering gate standing against the sky, and I
would hear the voice of the poet: "China forever."

THE END